FN Browning Pistols

Side-Arms that Shaped World History

Anthony Vanderlinden
Edited by Adam Firestone

Published and printed in the United States of America

Cover photography by Anthony Vanderlinden - Wet Dog Publications

Wet Dog Publications
5603-B West Friendly Avenue, Suite 166
Greensboro, North Carolina 27410
USA

ISBN: 0-9707997-4-8

Acknowledgments

Contributors to *The Belgian Browning Pistols*, whose contributions were carried over:

Leonardo Antaris, M.D.
Randy Bessler
James Blackburn
Merv Broten
Steven Fox
Henry Gaidis
Marcel Geurde
Joel Glovsky
Jean C. Kempf
Ryerson Knight
Ray Leslie
Joseph Lopez
Eugene Medlin
Toe Nomn
Alexander Stucki
Nico Van Gijn

Contributors to *FN Browning Pistols*:

Bob Adams
Harold Anderson
Ward Armstrong
John Bill
Christian Bogdan
Charles Bowles
Bob Burden
Robert Burgess
Allen Cayea
Robert Creamer
Stefan De Meyer
Lt. Col. Patrick Denamur
Leslie Field
Peter Free
Claude Gaier
Dean Gizzi
Freddy Greer
Tim Hawkins
Ned Heidenreich
Chip Hewlett
Glen Jensen
Leon Jones
Tom Knox
Eric Larson
Michèle Léonard
John Lindquist
Timo Martelius
Jim Mauloff
Rick McDonald
Chantal Mulkers
David Noll
Kevin Null
Wendell Patton
Dan Potter
Ron Pinkenburg
J.P. Reconnu
Reinolf Reisinger
Philip Rotmans
Wolf Roth
Robert Sauvage
Michael Shade
Peter Sheaf
Philip Schreier
Kevin Spaner
Blake Stevens
Jan Still
Claude Tait
Leroy Thompson
Michel Vandesteene
Mary Vanderlinden
Tony Vanderlinden
Jean-Louis Vanderstraeten
Dr. Bodo von Rhein
Dolf Voerman
Graham Waddingham
J. Weckx, B.V.V.W.
Doug Wicklund
Keri Wilde
Ralph Young
Ted Zajac

Browning Arms Co.
John M. Browning Firearms Museum, Ogden Union Station
Collector Grade Publications, Inc.
FN Herstal & Herstal Group
FN Manufacturing Inc.
Maanpuolustuskorkeakoulu Sotamuseo, Helsinki Finland
Musée d'Armes de Liège
National Automatic Pistol Collectors Association (NAPCA)
National Firearms Museum – National Rifle Association

Contributors to *FN Browning Pistols* who shared their expertise on specific topics:

John Bastin, Swedish matters
Bruce Buckner, Browning Arms Company pistols
Vincent Cozijn, Dutch matters
Carlos Davila, FN production practices
Andreas Giersch, postwar German police matters
Vic Glogovac, Yugoslav matters
Anders Jonasson, Swedish matters
Don Maus, Imperial German police matters
Janne Salopuro, Finnish matters
Marck Slootweg, Dutch matters

Special Recognition:

Adam Firestone, for his untiring effort in proofreading and editing
Jacques Maertens, for years of selfless commitment in assisting research and gathering documents and artifacts

Content

The History of Fabrique Nationale
1889-1896: A Heritage of Craftsmanship 6
1896-1914: Adversity Leads to Innovation 9
The 1914 Gala Evening and Presentation Pistols 17
The Sarajevo Affair 23
1914-1918: The Great War 27
1919-1929: From Recession to Recession 34
World War II: The Belgian Situation 44
World War II: Outside of FN's Gates 45
World War II: Inside of FN's Gates 49
1944-1950: Leaping into Production 60
1950-1960: Recovery through the Golden Sixties 65
1970-1980: Diversification in the Space Age 70
Modern Times 71

"Le Maitre" John Moses Browning 74
A Genius in the Shadows: Dieudonné Saive 82

Proofs and Markings
FN Manufacturing Markings 85
The Liège Proof-House and Proof Markings 88
World War II Occupation Markings 92
Acceptance Markings 93
Foreign Proofs 96

FN production Processes and Procedures 97
The John M. Browning Prototypes 103
FN's Sales Network 113

The FN Browning Model 1899 124

The FN Browning Model 1900 133
The Belgian Military FN 1900 143
The Austrian-Hungarian Purchases 148
The Mysterious Greek Contract 149
The FN 1900 in Imperial Russia 150
German Police use of the Model 1900 & 1905 152
The French and the FN Model 1900 154
Police Pistols in Denmark, Norway and Finland 156

The FN Browning Model 1903 158
The Swedish Acceptance 165
Imperial Russian Purchases 169
Ottoman Empire and Turkish Contracts 172
From Estonia to the Spanish Civil War 174
Paraguayan and Salvadoran Contracts 175
Service in the British Navy and German Police 176

The Husqvarna Model 1907 177

The FN Browning Model 1905 182
Imperial Russian General Staff Contracts 188
Imperial German Pistols 190
Shanghai Municipal Police Pistols 191
1940: Early German Occupation Production 193

The FN Browning Model 1910 194
- FN Browning 1910 in Belgian Service 201
- FN Browning 1910 in The Netherlands 204
- French & Syrian Police Orders 207
- The Model 1910 in Australia 208
- The Model 1910 in Finland 209
- FN 1910 in World War II: Germany and Japan 210
- Postwar Military Contracts 213

The Modèle 1910 Grand Browning 215

The FN Browning Model 1922 218
- The Many Yugoslav Orders 225
- The Many Dutch Variations 228
- The Mexican Contracts 235
- The FN 1922 for Greece 236
- The Turkish Contracts 236
- The French Orders 238
- The Romanian Contract 240
- The FN 1922 in Skandinavia: Denmark & Finland 241

World War II German Model 1922 Pistols 243
- WaA613 Accepted Pistols 244
- WaA103 Accepted Pistols 246
- WaA140 Accepted Pistols - Eagle N Pistols 247
- Postwar Belgian Government Contracts 252
- Postwar German Contracts 253

The FN Baby Browning 256

The Grand Rendement (High Efficiency) 261

The FN Browning Model 1935 GP (High Power) 269
- Belgian prewar Contracts 273
- Lithuanian High Powers 278
- Estonian Contracts 279
- The Paraguayan Order 280
- Argentine Contracts 280
- Chinese Orders 282
- The High Power in Finland 284
- Slotted Fixed-Sighted Pistols: The French GP 287

World War II German High Power Pistols 289
- Captured and Seized Pistols 290
- Pistols assembled prior to WaA613 292
- WaA613 Pistols 293
- WaA103 Pistols 296
- WaA140 Pistols - Eagle N Pistols 297
- Wartime Factory Reworks 302
- Post Liberation Pistols 303
- The Danish Orders 305
- Belgian Contracts: Regent and Royal 306
- Colonial Sales: The Congo 309
- The Netherlands adopts the High Power 311
- The High Power in West Germany and Austria 312
- The British L9A1 314
- The Alleged Oman Contract 315
- U.S. Law Enforcement Imports: Howco 316
- Mass Production of the High Power 317

The 100-Series Pistols 319

The Browning Arms Company Pistols 322

The History of Fabrique Nationale

1889-1896: A Heritage of Craftsmanship

For centuries, the Liège region has been a center for the manufacture of arms. Its artisans have a well deserved reputation for excellence based on the extraordinary high quality of the weapons they produced. Liège was an obvious and natural choice for industrial development. The Meuse valley, in which it lies, possesses an abundance of coal, iron and water; all the basic requirements for the manufacture of arms. Today, the Meuse valley is still referred to as "Le Pays Noir" (The Black Country), for its abundance of coal.

The Meuse river not only provided water for the industry, but was also a primary trade route for several centuries. The earliest known documents referring to Liège as an industrial center date to 1346 and note a number of guilds, including that of the arms makers. The evolution of European weaponry is closely linked with the history of Liège. As a result, Liège's history is no less tumultuous than that of Europe.

Through the centuries, Liège would arm many European states and principalities. Despite falling for many centuries into the French empire, Liège was an autonomous principality and enjoyed a large measure of independence. This freedom enabled the arms makers to trade their products across Europe. The superior finishing and engraving of Liège's high-grade firearms made the guns objects of desire to nobility, royalty, and the wealthy. The firearms guild relied upon and adhered to time honored principles of quality, craftsmanship and artistry. A journeyman arms maker undertook years of training under the supervision of a master before being considered worthy to practice his trade. As arms were made by hand, these standards and self-regulation were the only means by which the continued quality of Liège arms could be maintained. The craft was almost hereditary, being passed down through generations from father to son. As a result, production of arms in Liège was a cottage industry up to the industrial revolution.

A revolution in manufacturing processes began with the invention of the steam engine and continued with the dynamo, invented by the Liège craftsman Zénobe Gramme in 1869. The mechanization of the arms industry in Liège began in the 19th century with a number of small manufacturers including Ancion & Cie., Pirlot Bros., Renkin Bros., Dresse Laloux and Auguste Francotte, who were among the first to introduce modern manufacturing tools and techniques. Despite their relatively small size, these manufacturers were able to produce quality firearms in significant quantities. For example, during the Crimean War in 1854, these Liège arms makers supplied 20,000 Enfield pattern rifles to the British government.

The British order of 1854 may have been the catalyst for the creation of consortiums of arms manufacturers; the 20,000-rifle contract had been supplied by the combined efforts of the Ancion, Pirlot, Renkin and Francotte companies.

The large sizes of the contracts, the need for rapid delivery and growing competition forced manufacturers to formally unite their production efforts. The first formal arms making consortium in Liège was called "Le Petit Syndicat" (The Little Union/Association) of 1870. Le Petit Syndicat was formed to manufacture Comblain rifles for the Belgian government. Other associations followed, among whose undertakings was the manufacture of Chassepot rifles for the French government, Comblain muskets for the Greek government and Snider actions for the Ottoman Empire. The consortiums enabled small companies to win and fulfill large contracts, which would have been outside the capabilities of an individual manufacturer. Another significant consortium was "Les Fabricants d'Armes Réunis" (United Arms Manufacturers), which was set up in 1887 to convert 30,000 Beaumont rifles for the Dutch government. The association did not have much success with other contracts due to competition from German firms. Although "Les Fabricants d'Armes Réunis" did not receive many additional orders, it did have a significant impact on the development of a large contract for the Belgian government.

The Belgian government narrowly avoided involvement in the Franco-Prussian War of 1870. This spurred critical reviews of Belgium's military preparedness and eventually resulted in a general modernization of the Belgian military. This modernization included the re-equipment of Belgian forces with repeating rifles.

The quest for a Belgian repeating rifle began in 1880 when state arsenals attempted to convert single-shot Comblain rifles. The results were not satisfactory and existing repeating rifle designs were studied. Official military trials started in 1886 and included rifles from Kropatschek, Francotte, Remington-Lee and Nagant. The results of the trials were generally unsatisfactory, and the tests were extended through the end of 1888. Various designs were introduced and rejected through this period.

A contender from Mauser was introduced in November 1888. While promising, the Mauser rifle did not participate in the initial field tests of 1888. Instead, the board requested that certain modifications be made to the Mauser rifle prior to continued tests. The modifications were implemented, and the Mauser rifle was resubmitted for trials in 1889.

The May 1889 trials included designs from Mauser, Mannlicher, Nagant and Pieper. At the beginning of the trials, the government had established a close liaison with the Belgian arms industry, as there was significant political pressure to have the guns manufactured domestically in Liège.

Bids had been requested from local manufacturers including "Les Fabricants d'Armes Réunis" as early as 1887. No specific rifle design had been specified but a quantity of 150,000 rifles was indicated. 150,000 rifles represented a tremendous amount of work and the various manufacturers knew that this could only be achieved by creating a new corporation.

More than ten arms makers united, most of them members of "Les Fabricants d'Armes Réunis", and an agreement was reached on October 15, 1888. This agreement involved the creation of a new corporation with a value of three million Belgian francs. It took several months of negotiations before the company, Fabrique Nationale d'Armes de Guerre (FN - National War Weapons Factory), was incorporated on July 3, 1889. Disagreements as to the purpose of the company divided the investors even before the company was incorporated. H. Pieper, J. Jansen and A. Bormans for Dresse Laloux envisioned a long-term company. Louis Nagant, Auguste Francotte and other investors favored a short-term association, intended solely to fulfill the Belgian military rifle contract.

Management of the company was entrusted into the hands of the privileged shareholders. Ordinary shareholders did not enjoy financial dividends at first but their shares were turned into privileged shares over time.

FN shareholders in 1889	Privileged shares	Ordinary shares
Albert Simonis, Firearms Manufacturer	300	200
Jules Ancion & Co, Firearms Manufacturer	600	200
Dresse - Laloux & Co, Firearms Manufacturer	600	200
Manufacture Liègeoise d' Armes à Fue, Incorporated	600	200
The Brothers Dumoulin, Firearms Manufacturers	600	200
Joseph Jansen, Firearms Manufacturer	600	200
Henri Pieper, Firearms Manufacturer	1200	200
Pilot and Fresart, Firearms Manufacturers	600	200
Credit Général Liègeois	600	---
Nicolas Vivario, independent	300	---
Auguste Francotte, Firearms Manufacturer	---	200
Emile and Léon Nagant, Firearms Manufacturers	---	200
	6000	2000

FN was awarded the Belgian military contract despite the fact that no rifle had yet been accepted. Henry Pieper and Allard Bormans signed the contract with the Belgian government on July 12, 1889, nine days after the company was created. Fabrique Nationale d'Armes de Guerre was thus legally bound to provide the Belgian War Ministry with 150,000 repeating rifles of a type to be decided at later date. The price per rifle was set at 79 francs.

At the conclusion of comprehensive comparison and field-testing, the Mauser was selected as the new Belgian service rifle, along with the smokeless and rimless 7.65x53mm cartridge.

Upon selection of the Mauser rifle, a manufacturing license was obtained from Mauser Waffenwerke. Initially, FN contacted and negotiated with U.S. firms to supply the necessary machine tools. Problems with metric conversions made FN later turn to Ludwig Loewe in Germany for the required machinery and technical assistance.

The FN factory was under construction when the board of directors learned that the government was also seeking to buy three million 7.65x53mm cartridges. As a result, FN expanded into cartridge manufacturing. A contract was signed in May 1891 between FN, La Société d'Anderlecht (The corporation of Anderlecht), and the Deutche Metall-patronenfabrik of Karlsruhe. The corporation of Anderlecht was an older established munitions manufacturer in Belgium. The Deutche Metallenpatronen company was part of the Loewe group and supplied FN with all the necessary equipment on June 15, 1891. FN also signed an agreement with the German company for technical aid.

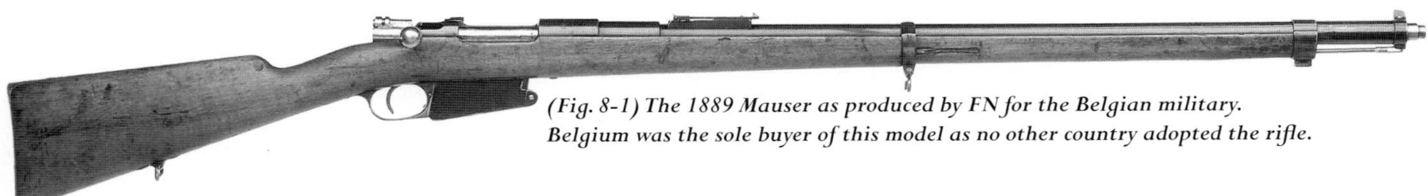

(Fig. 8-1) The 1889 Mauser as produced by FN for the Belgian military. Belgium was the sole buyer of this model as no other country adopted the rifle.

Factory construction continued throughout 1891. The first three Model 1889 Mauser rifles were assembled on December 31, 1891 and the official reception celebrating the first FN rifle was held two months later on February 6, 1892. By October 1892 the plant averaged daily production figures of 100 to 150 rifles, and ammunition production was higher than anticipated.

For the late 19th century, the FN factory was state of the art. In 1893 Scientific American wrote a lengthy article about the massive steam engine that generated electrical power and heat for the plant, in addition to driving production machinery. At the time it was one of the world's largest power generators.

The 150,000-rifle contract was completed by New Years Eve 1894. The Model 1889 was a five-shot, magazine fed bolt-action rifle, and was among the most advanced designs of the day. Indeed, this first order, and the high regard in which the Belgian Army held the FN Mausers helped to create FN's reputation for technical excellence. In short order, the company received orders from Brazil (June 1894), China (October 1894), Norway (January 1895) and Costa Rica (May 1895).

Success was not without a price. Auguste Francotte and Louis Nagant feared that FN's success was interfering with their own businesses and both decided to pull out of the company in July 1894. A dispute then arose between Mauser Waffenwerke and FN regarding a Chilean contract. Chile was planning to purchase 60,000 Spanish Mauser rifles from FN in December 1894. Mauser intervened, claiming that this contract was infringing on their Spanish Mauser patents. Chile envisioned a legal battle and cancelled the order with the Belgian company. FN fought a desperate legal battle and lost. This legal battle took a toll on the shareholders; five out of the eight primary shareholders sold out and left the company in February of 1896.

SCIENTIFIC AMERICAN

[Entered at the Post Office of New York, N. Y., as Second Class matter. Copyrighted, [illegible], by Munn & Co.]

A WEEKLY JOURNAL OF PRACTICAL INFORMATION, ART, SCIENCE, MECHANICS, CHEMISTRY, AND MANUFACTURES.

APRIL 1, 1893.] Scientific American. 201

Fig. 2.—THE GREAT DYNAMO, HERSTAL, BELGIUM.

(Fig. 8-2) An excerpt of the 1893 Scientific American article that outlined FN's magnificent power plant. This illustration only shows the dynamo, the complete steam power plant provided electricity, heat and energy to power the countless drive shafts that operated the manufacturing machines.

1896-1914: Adversity Leads to Innovation

As noted, the insecurity of the early FN investors led to a massive sale of their interests in the company. The German company Ludwig Loewe & Co. took this opportunity to acquire majority control of FN in 1896.

FN had become a successful competitor and this was not well tolerated by the German company. The Loewe group (who owned Mauser Waffenwerke) had been attempting to acquire a sizable share of FN for some time. The legal battle that precipitated the sell-off had plunged FN into debt. FN found itself in financial trouble and the new German majority ownership brought both advantages and disadvantages.

The greatest disadvantage was the harsh trade restrictions imposed on FN by Loewe. Military contracts were now rerouted to German and Austrian factories. Only Belgian military contracts would remain with FN. As a military supplier, FN's work was slowly grinding to a halt. The early Belgian bank loans were gradually transferred to German banks.

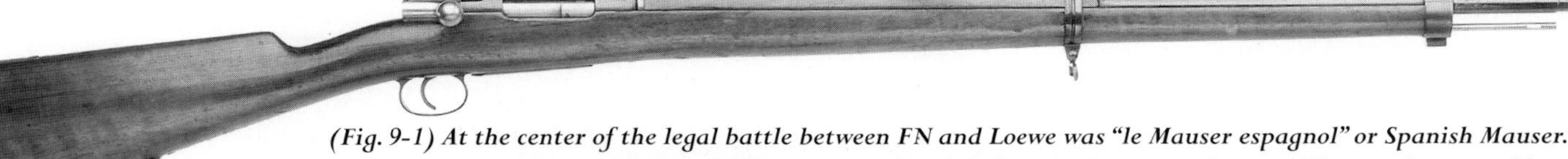

(Fig. 9-1) At the center of the legal battle between FN and Loewe was "le Mauser espagnol" or Spanish Mauser. This model was only manufactured for three years by FN before the German take-over. Thousands were sold to Brazil and Uruguay while FN actively sought more South American contracts.

FN's management soon realized that diversification and innovation were the keys to survival. The company explored the manufacture of various products that were not affected by the German restrictions. Among the earliest solutions was the production of bicycles and sporting arms.

In November 1896 FN plunged into the commercial firearms market and agreed to produce 50,000 .22 caliber sporting rifles. Soon afterwards, FN sealed contracts with other Liège gun makers to supply them with shotgun parts.

Military contracts were slim but still existent: 14,000 rifles and carbines were manufactured in 1896 for Uruguay in addition to 4.5 million rounds of ammunition(1).

The bicycle market was viewed as important for the survival of the company. In an effort to expand this market, FN sent their Director of External Affairs, Hart O. Berg on an exploratory trip to the United Stated in 1897 to analyze and study the latest U.S. bicycle innovations. Mr. Berg, was a native of Hartford Connecticut. While visiting his hometown, he had the good fortune to be introduced to John Moses Browning. Berg told FN's story to Browning, including the dire situation of the extensive and modern FN factory that had little to nothing to produce.

Hart O. Berg

Little is known about the life of Hart O. Berg, the man who brought John Browning to FN(2).

Hart O. Berg was a native of Hartford Connecticut. It is assumed that he was already residing in Belgium when he started working at FN on October 15, 1895. His job title was General Sales Agent and International Representative(3). Berg had immediate sales successes and positive interactions with FN customers. His 1895 and 1896 business dealings in Serbia and Spain were both deemed successful. He was promoted to Director of External Affairs(3) on June 6, 1896. In 1897 he traveled to Connecticut and met John Browning and returned with the legendary .32 caliber pistol. In January 1898 he traveled to Ogden, Utah in order to convince John Browning to supervise the pistol production at FN. It is known that Berg was unable to convince Browning to make that trip in 1898(4).

Berg submitted his resignation to FN on April 28, 1898, a few months after his return from Utah, leaving the company on July 1, 1898. On January 31, 1914 he returned to FN to meet once again with his old friend John Browning at the "Un Million" FN gala festivities (page 17). It is known that Hart O. Berg was still alive and living in Paris immediately following World War II.

(1) The orders from Uruguay may have been received prior to the German take-over.

(2) No photograph of Berg was located in time for this publication.

(3) Translation of his French language job title

(4) The idea that John Browning made his first trip in 1902 has widely been accepted by collectors and historians. In fact little is known of the events that took place between Berg's attempt in 1898 and 1902. There are some contradictions in period documents consequently we assume that 1902 was indeed John Browning's first trip to FN.

(Fig. 10-1) An early photograph of FN's entrance circa 1899, the famous rod iron gates had not yet been installed. The center of the factory entrance is pictured on this book's title page.

Berg and Browning struck up a friendship almost immediately. Browning left Berg with the prototype of a small .32 caliber automatic pistol, which later became the FN Browning Model 1899. Berg returned to FN filled with enthusiasm and introduced the little pistol on June 19, 1897. It did not take long for the FN staff[1] to share his views on the little pistol. The pistol fired 500 rounds without any malfunctions, something that was unheard of with any other automatic pistol at that time. Consequently, FN signed an agreement, less than a month later on July 17, 1897 with the Browning Brothers, for the production of the pistol. John Browning's pistol was to be a turning point for FN.

FN paid the Browning Brothers 2000 Belgian Francs for the initial production rights and a royalty payment of two Belgian francs per weapon. Additionally, the contract stipulated that a minimum of 10,000 Belgian francs were to be paid for the first two production years, even if the royalty sales did not achieve that amount. The Model 1899 pistol was sold at a price of about 30 Belgian francs, resulting in a seven percent royalty on each sale. Contrary to popular opinion, Browning had initiated a royalty relationship with FN prior to the introduction of the Auto-5 shotgun.

While FN was tooling up to produce the Browning pistol, other product development continued. That same year, FN explored automobile manufacturing and purchased a French quadricycle for research purposes. Attempts to purchase a manufacturing license from the French company failed but automobile manufacturing remained an option for the future.

Diversification progressed quickly; by 1898, FN had patented a revolutionary type of bicycle known as the FN Chainless (shaft-driven) Bicycle.

Pistol production started in January 1899, and FN displayed its first automobile prototype in March 1899. The company was growing fast and new technical, administrative, and commercial departments were created. By this time, the FN factory counted more than 3000 manufacturing machines.

By late 1900, FN had launched itself in automobile manufacturing, and was producing military Mauser rifles, shotguns, shotgun parts, ammunition, the small .32 caliber Browning pistols (model 1899 and 1900), and a line of bicycles. At the end of 1900, the first 100 FN automobiles were completed.

(Fig. 10-2) This early ad from FN's Paris agent illustrates the bicycle mechanisms. The ad is dated 1900 and predates FN's success at the Paris World Fair.

(1)This also included some German engineers from Berlin

(Fig. 11-1) The 1900 Paris World's Fair was a turning point for FN's new product lines. FN was awarded three prizes for innovative products for both the Chainless Bicycle as well as the new automobile. This ad, emphasizing the three prizes, was used on catalogs as well as large advertising posters between 1900 and 1905. In 1900 it only mentioned or depicted bicycles and automobiles. After 1902, the same ad was used but the word "motorcycles" was added. Note that it makes no mention of military arms.

(Fig. 11-2) FN's first automobile was technically advanced for its day and so recognized at the 1900 Paris World's Fair. It featured a round steering wheel at a time when many manufacturers were still using levers. Another great innovation was the multi-speed gearbox with a practical reverse gear. The body was suspended from its chassis making it comfortable to ride. Several body styles were available with various engine configurations.

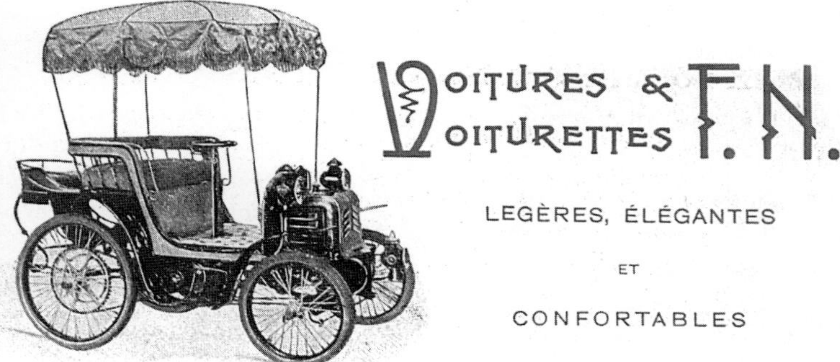

Although the FN Browning 1899 and 1900 pistols enjoyed tremendous sales, FN realized their limitations as military sidearms. Allegedly in 1901, FN asked John Browning to design a larger pistol in a more potent chambering.

The year 1902 brought further prosperity and larger product lines. The company had started a motorcycle division and the first single-cylinder motorcycle was produced in December 1901. John M. Browning brought his legendary Auto-5 shotgun to Herstal in February 1902 (see also page 9). The Auto-5 shotgun was the second Browning design to be introduced to the FN staff. As revolutionary as the first, FN did not hesitate to produce the gun and agree with John Browning's royalty payment request.

There is no doubt that the future relationship between John Browning and FN was discussed while John Browning was at FN. John Browning placed his first order with FN for Auto-5 shotguns. FN further discussed the need for a larger caliber automatic pistol, which became the third Browning design; the FN Browning Model 1903 pistol.

The automotive department also extended its line and partnered with the well-known French manufacturer, De Dion Bouton. It is not known how much of the car FN produced, but it is known that FN produced parts and or bodies for several De Dion automobiles. By the end of 1902 FN had introduced a prototype of its own 14HP car.

FN set up a research laboratory in 1904 and was one of the first Belgian companies to establish a research department. The lab's primary function was the testing of steel and other raw materials. By 1904 the company's daily production figures included 450 firearms, 250,000 cartridges, 150 bicycles and 40 motorcycles.

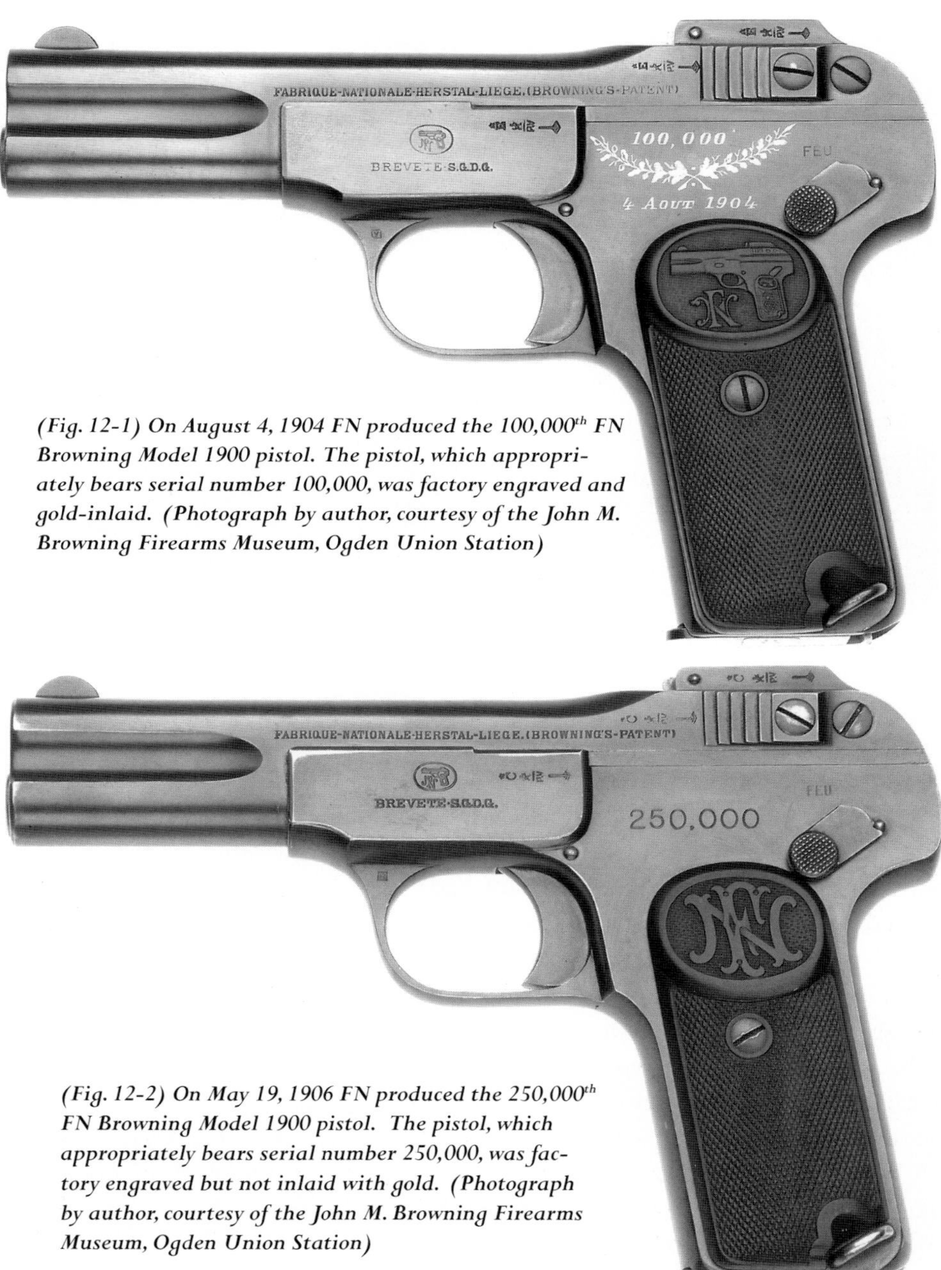

(Fig. 12-1) On August 4, 1904 FN produced the 100,000th FN Browning Model 1900 pistol. The pistol, which appropriately bears serial number 100,000, was factory engraved and gold-inlaid. (Photograph by author, courtesy of the John M. Browning Firearms Museum, Ogden Union Station)

(Fig. 12-2) On May 19, 1906 FN produced the 250,000th FN Browning Model 1900 pistol. The pistol, which appropriately bears serial number 250,000, was factory engraved but not inlaid with gold. (Photograph by author, courtesy of the John M. Browning Firearms Museum, Ogden Union Station)

The automotive division, which had enjoyed a prosperous beginning in 1900, was having difficulties after the main designer and engineer left FN to start his own company. Lack of space was also a problem and the automobile division halted production. The 14HP prototype, introduced in 1902, was never manufactured.

Expansion continued in 1905. New buildings were erected and an additional 4500 square meters (48,500 square feet) were added to the production facilities. Automobile production resumed after FN purchased a manufacturing license from the French company Rochet-Schneider, and the arms division was tooling up for the .25 caliber Browning 1905/06 Vest Pocket, which was first produced in 1906. On May 19, 1906 FN produced the 250,000th Model 1900 pistol.

The motorcycle division introduced a new model each year since its production began in 1902. In 1905 it introduced a revolutionary motorcycle, which would bring worldwide recognition for FN. The 1905 model was the first four-cylinder motorcycle; it was quiet and reliable. The four-cylinder design would influence other great marques like Henderson and Indian.

On May 24, 1907 FN reached an immense marketing agreement with John Browning. From that time forward the Browning name became a trademark for FN and could no longer be used by other manufacturers. The Browning name soon became a synonym for "automatic pistol" and is still recognized in the French and Russian languages as such.

Production capabilities reached daily figures of 150 Model 1900 pistols and 350 Model 1905 Vest Pocket pistols(1).

The FN automobile and motorcycle divisions further expanded their existing lines. Once again, FN introduced an automobile of its own design and this time it went into production as the Model 2000. The Model 2000 was available by 1907 as well as the line of Rochet-Schneider cars sold under the FN name. The automotive and motorcycle departments continued to release improved models. From 1908 forward, these departments released at least one model per year and in the case of the automotive department, as many as three different models.

In the summer of 1908, John Browning introduced FN to his new automatic pistol, which later became the Model 1910 (page 194). That same year FN produced the 500,000th Model 1900 pistol.

Meanwhile, FN continued to develop, produce and sell Browning firearm designs. The Browning firearm line increased in 1910, with the introduction of the .35 caliber Model 1900 rifle. This rifle was introduced by Browning in 1902 and had been earmarked for production in 1906. It is not known why FN opted to start production years later in 1910.

(Fig. 13-1) In 1908 FN produced the 500,000th FN Browning Model 1900 pistol. The pistol, which appropriately bears serial number 500,000, was factory engraved and gold-inlaid like the earlier 100,000th production milestone. (Photograph by author, courtesy of the John M. Browning Firearms Museum, Ogden Union Station)

(Fig. 13-2) A proud FN dealer, his staff and customers pose for a professional photograph circa 1908. From left to right we see the Model 1907 FN 4-cylinder motorcycle, rare FN Model 1907 1-cylinder motorcycle with variable transmission, Model 1908 FN 4-cylinder motorcycle, FN Model 1907 1-cylinder motorcycle with variable transmission (against wall), and a FN Chainless Bicycle.

(1) Although FN had such production abilities, it rarely made such quantities on a daily bases.

FABRIQUE NATIONALE D'ARMES DE GUERRE
~ HERSTAL ~
Bicicletta senza Catena
F. N.
MACCHINA IDEALE
MODELLI per UOMO e per SIGNORA
Scorrevole
Silenziosa
Rigida
SUCCURSALE PER L'ITALIA
A. FUSI & C. 16 PIAZZA CASTELLO: MILANO

(Fig. 14-1)

(Fig. 14-2)

(Fig. 14-3)

(Fig. 14-4)

(Fig. 15-1) The Model 1200 was introduced in 1910 as was the Model 1500 and 1560. FN averaged two to three new automobile models per year at the time. This specific car belonged to Mr. Andri, FN's general manager. (Photograph courtesy of FN Herstal)

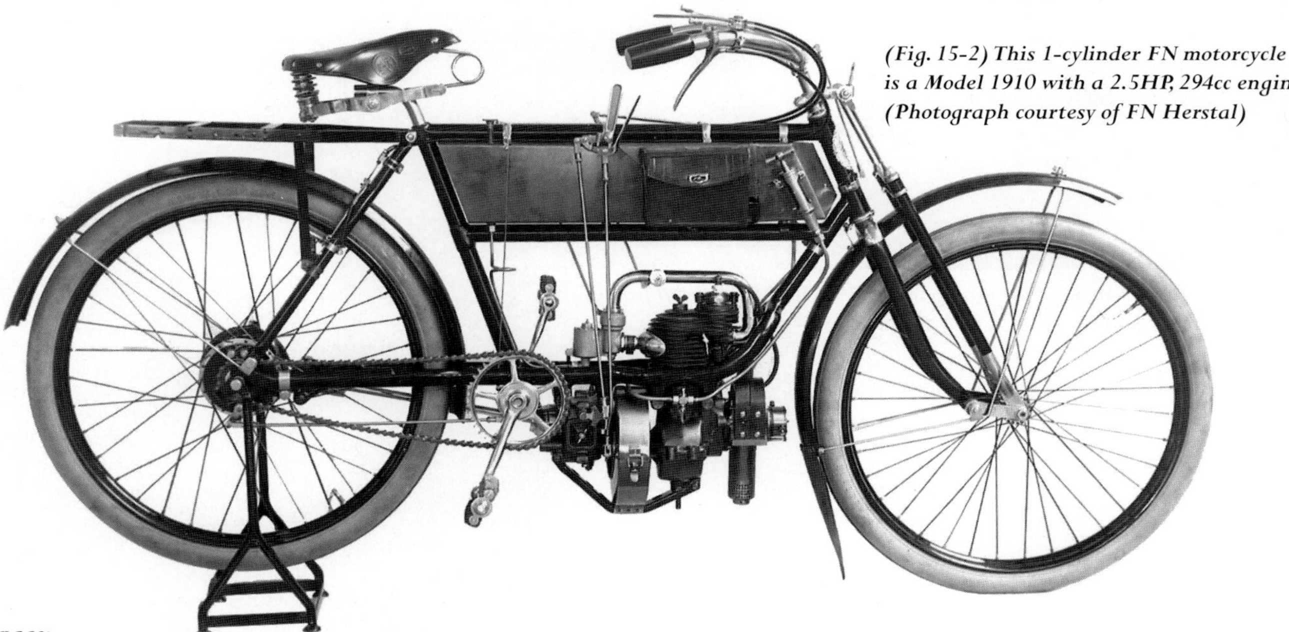

(Fig. 15-2) This 1-cylinder FN motorcycle is a Model 1910 with a 2.5HP, 294cc engine. (Photograph courtesy of FN Herstal)

Previous page:

(Fig. 14-1) An early Italian advertisement for the FN Chainless Bicycle, produced by FN's agent Fusi in Milan. The ad reads: "The FN Chainless Bicycle, the Ideal Machine – Models for Men and Women – Silent and Sturdy.

(Fig. 14-2) An FN Chainless Bicycle, produced for trade shows. FN's were always sold with quality Englebert tires. Note the advertisement thread on the tires. Englebert's quality was world renown. Years later Enzo Ferrari insisted on Englebert tires for his cars. (Photograph courtesy of FN Herstal)

(Fig. 14-3) FN actively pursued Belgian military contracts for the Chainless Bicycle. Multiple configurations were built to hold FN Mauser carbines and their bayonets. The Belgian military used plain chain driven bicycles and military sales were slim except for the Belgian Gendarmerie. (Photograph courtesy of FN Herstal)

(Fig. 14-4) The Belgian Gendarmerie commission inspects and approves their order of Chainless Bicycles early in the century. Note the unusual method of mounting the long bayonet, vertically from the handlebars. (Photograph courtesy of FN Herstal)

The year 1910 brought another great advantage for FN. John Browning signed an agreement with FN on June 24, 1910, giving FN first manufacturing rights to all of his inventions[1].

By 1914 there were seven Browning firearms being produced, the .22 caliber automatic takedown being the last to be put in production in 1914. Beside ammunition and the Browning designs, FN produced side-by-side shotguns, .22 caliber single-shot rifles, the original Model 1889 Mauser military rifle and a sporting version of the early Model 1893 Mauser[2].

There is little doubt that the catalyst to this progress with the chance meeting between John Browning and Hart O. Berg in 1897. The decisions and strategic moves that the company made after the German take-over made it possible for FN not only to survive but to flourish and establish itself as one of the world's preeminent arms makers.

(Fig. 16-1) Machining of FN Browning Model 1905 and 1910 pistol frames in the late 1910s and 1920s.

(Fig. 16-2) Machining of FN pistol barrels in the late 1910s and 1920s.

(1) The details of this agreement are not known to the author, the agreement may have expired by the time FN decided to produce the BAR and Browning Machine guns.

(2) As this model was for commercial sporting purposes, it did not fall under the German production restrictions, which primarily targeted the military Mauser rifles.

The 1914 Gala Evening and Presentation Pistols

On July 15, 1912 FN had produced its one millionth Browning pistol[(1)], and FN's management and staff wanted to demonstrate their tremendous appreciation and repay, in some small way, the debt of gratitude that the company owed John Browning. It took several months of preparation, but a celebratory gala was organized for January 31, 1914, providing enough time for FN's international sales agents to make their way back to Belgium from their globally dispersed offices. (Note: By the date of the gala, FN had produced an additional 300,000 Browning pistols since July 15, 1912.)

The gala celebration was held at FN's factory in Herstal. An ammunition hall was transformed into a large formal dining room and elaborately decorated. The awning was decorated in the Liège city colors (yellow and red); the carefully draped flags of all nations hung about the room's periphery. Tables were decorated with elaborate arrangements of red roses and other flowers. Large green plants were positioned all over the room. And floating in the air, framing the event in sound, was music provided by the FN orchestra, playing under the careful eye of FN's conductor, Mr. Nicolay.

(Fig. 17-1) January 31, 1914 the large gala celebration: The vertical white line next to the bust of King Albert I points out John Browning. Note that the walls were decorated with Browning products including Auto-5 shotguns and pistols. (Photograph courtesy of Browning)

While John Browning was the guest of honor, the other invitees were persons no less prominent. They included King Albert I of Belgium[(2)], prominent Belgian politicians, FN's worldwide agents and representatives of the Liège proof-house. Hart O. Berg, who had left the company years earlier (see page 9), returned to FN for the festivities. Current, former and retired FN employees rounded out the occasion.

Most of what is known today about the event comes from the extensive coverage by the Liège newspaper La Meuse. La Meuse reported details of John Browning's speech:

> *He was slow and selective in choosing his words. He was touched by the attention surrounding him and he apologized for not being able to communicate his feelings in a better way. His sincerity was felt throughout his speech, simple and yet touching.*

Although the article does not specifically state in what language John Browning spoke, it appears that Browning addressed the crowd in French, which he had learned at FN while talking to employees throughout the years.

Mr. Hubert, the Belgian Minister of Industry, presented John Browning with the medal of "la Croix du Chevalier de l'Ordre de Léopold" (the Knight's Cross of the Order of Leopold), one of Belgium's most prestigious medals (given both to civilians as well as military personnel). The same award was also given to FN's Inspector General Theol Boel, who was responsible for successfully organizing production and lowering production costs.

(1) It has often been reported that FN did not know exactly when the one-millionth Browning pistol was produced. Documents dating from 1912-1913 prove this to be incorrect.

(2) King Albert I was not present at the dinner, but a presentation pistol was accepted on his behalf by a Belgian official.

(Fig. 18-1) John Browning (tallest in center) poses with FN directors and FN's worldwide agents who traveled to Herstal for the festivities.

Mr. Andri, FN's general manager, also presented John Browning with a large winged sculpture[1] that had been commissioned specifically for the occasion, and created by the famed sculptor Victor Rousseau.

Engraved presentation pistols were given to John Browning, Val Browning, King Albert I and several of the honored guests. After the presentations, John Browning remained at the banquet, speaking with guests, providing autographs and even signing the event menu for several guests[1].

Photographs were taken that day and the following day with John Browning, the FN staff and FN agents.

(Fig. 18-2) A rare surviving program and menu from December 31, 1914. Note the cover with the sculpture that was presented to John Browning and the "Un Million" Vest Pocket illustration near the bottom. This program was autographed by John Browning and others, just as it was reported by the newspaper La Meuse.

(Fig. 18-3) The statue presented to John Browning by Mr. Andri remained in the Browning family for decades. This photograph circa 1970, shows the sculpture in the center of a flower bed at Val Brownings residence in Ogden Utah. (Photograph courtesy of Browning)

The 1914 Presentation Pistols

In 1964 a book was published claiming that there were only four 1914 "Un Million" gala presentation pistols. While this number has since acquired an air of legitimacy within the Browning collector community, there is no historical basis for this figure. FN factory information controverts this data and indicates that at least 20 pistols(2) were commissioned for the event. This number falls more in line with known FN practices. Specifically, with knowledge of the number of high ranking and important guests, FN would have prepared sufficient presentation pistols to prevent any real or perceived faux pas.

Of those 20, only five are confirmed and known to have survived(3). Two of these pistols are now on display at the John M. Browning Firearms Museum in Ogden, Utah. No record exists that conclusively identifies the pistol that was donated to John Browning.

The Val Browning Presentation Pistol

Val Browning attended the 1914 gala celebration. Records indicate that he received his pistol N° 456354 the morning after the event(4). Val Browning donated his pistol to the Browning museum in 1978. This pistol featured standard FN grips and was provided with a standard FN presentation case.

(Fig. 19-1) Val Browning's "Un Million" presentation pistol N° 456354 is on display at the John M. Browning Firearms Museum in Ogden, Utah. (Photograph by author, courtesy of the John M. Browning Firearms Museum, Ogden Union Station)

(Fig. 19-2) An older photograph showing the case of Val Browning's presentation pistol. Note the unusual and more decorative factory legend on the inside lid (compare with fig.185-2). This case is not currently on display at the John M. Browning Firearms Museum. (Photograph courtesy of Browning)

The MacFarlane Presentation Pistol

The second surviving pistol N° 456294 was either donated or sold to Mr. MacFarlane of Montreal, Canada in 1914. Mr. MacFarlane attended the gala evening(5) and was considered one of FN's most successful agents. Unlike any of the other pistols noted, this pistol has mother-of-pearl grips and has an elaborate silver FN embossed presentation case with small purse holster. The quality and nature of the craftsmanship confirms the case's originality. This pistol was not carried back by Mr. MacFarlane but was shipped to him after the event.

(1) La Meuse newspaper & Revue FN

(2) The author has opted not to divulge the serial numbers of these pistols in order to prevent the creation of forgeries.

(3) The author has received numerous reports of these pistols but upon serial number examination has found that some reports were duplicates. As such the author has often incorrectly reported that eight pistols survived.

(4) A period document states that Val Browning received the pistol the morning after the event as the young man looked bored during one of the meetings. Apparently the FN directors wanted to cheer up the young Val Browning.

(5) Mr. MacFarlane's name is specifically mentioned in the newspaper La Meuse.

The pistol, its presentation case and purse holster were in the private collection of Mr. Ryerson Knight for many years. Currently the pistol is held by the Canadian government and its fate is unknown[1].

(Fig. 20-1) Mr. MacFarlane's presentation pistol N° 456294 is the only one known to have the ornate silver embossed presentation case together with a leather purse holster (not shown). Note that the grips are factory mother-of-pearl grips. (Photographs courtesy of Ryerson Knight)

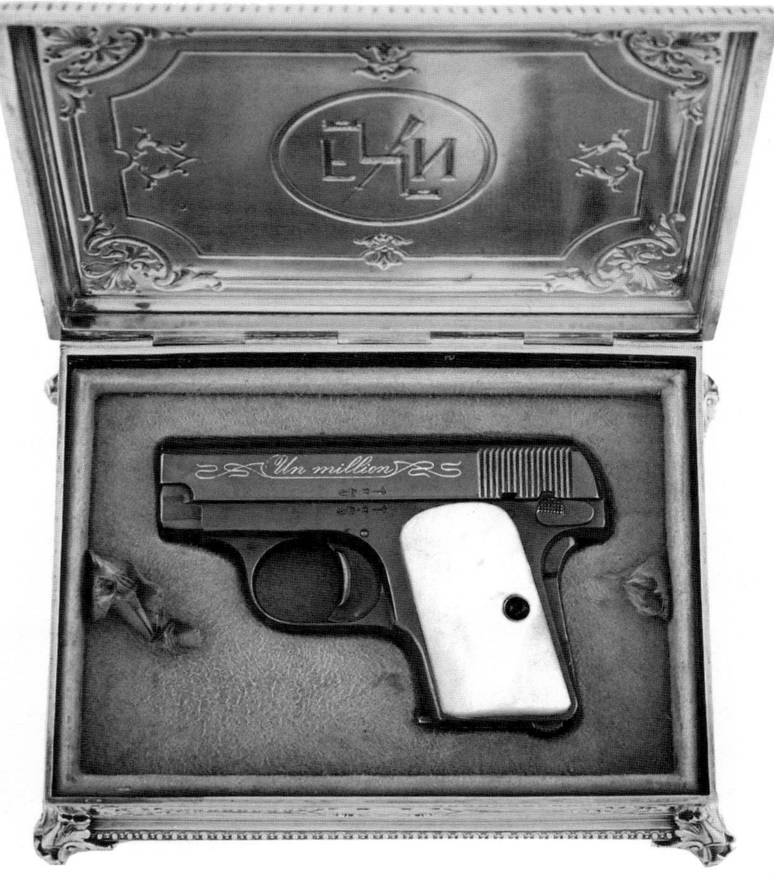

The Presentation Pistol from Mr. and Mrs. John Lindquist

The second pistol N° 456602 in the John M. Browning Firearms Museum was donated by Mr. and Mrs. John Lindquist of Ogden, Utah in 1982. Mr. Lindquist and Col. Reid Betz[2] learned that one of the "Un Million" pistols had been located and acquired it for the museum from Navy Arms Co., which had acquired the pistol in England. Mr. Lindquist purchased the pistol with the express purpose of donating it to the museum. In addition to this act of generosity, Mr. Lindquist donated an additional $4900 in unrestricted funds to the museum.

(Fig. 20-2) This "Un Million" pistol N° 456602 was purchased by Mr. John Lindquist for the John M. Browning Firearms Museum. The pistol was originally sold with a red velvet lined display case (see fig.21-1). The whereabouts of this case are currently unknown. (Photograph by author, courtesy of the John M. Browning Firearms Museum, Ogden Union Station)

(1) 2007: The author was involved in a series of efforts to preserve the pistol and avoid it from being destroyed by the Canadian government.

(2) Col. Reid Betz was the founder of the Browning Collectors Association and was active in preserving Browning's history.

(Fig. 21-1) Two excerpts of the provenance documents of the "Un Million" pistol (N° 456602). These documents are part of a series of correspondence between Col. Reid Betz, Mr. Lindquist and the president of Navy Arms Company. (Documents courtesy of John Lindquist)

RECEIVED OF John A. Lindquist, residing at Ogden, Utah
, the sum of Four Thousand dollars ($ 4,000.00) and
in trade in full payment of the following described firearm:

Maker's Name: Fabrique Nationale Herstal
Maker's Address: Liege
Country and Date of Manufacture: Belgium, January 1914
Model: 1905 Vest Pocket — Serial Number(s): 456 602
Condition (See other side for NRA Condition Standards): NRA Excellent
Ignition System: Center fire cartridge
Barrel(s): 1 — Barrel(s) Length: 2"
Caliber(s) or Gauge(s): .25 ACP
Over-all Length: 4-1/2" — Weight: 13 oz.
Accessories Included: Red velvet lined presentation case, poor condition
Markings, Engravings and Inscriptions (Describe): Inscribed "Un million" in gold inlay on left side of slide above Belgian proof marks

Navy Arms Company Inc.

689 BERGEN BLVD.
RIDGEFIELD, N.J. 07657
CABLE ADDRESS: SERARMAMENT, RIDGEFIELD, N.J.
TELEX: 134619 SER ARM RIDE
TELEPHONE: (201) 945-2500

March 24th, 1982

Col. W.R. Betz
Executive Director
BROWNING COLLECTORS ASSN.
1306 Walcott Drive
Ogden, Utah 84403

Dear Col. Betz:

I have owned the gun since 1957 or 1958. It was purchased from Parker-Hale, Birmingham, England. At that time, they had acquired it from an officer that took it from the Browning factory in World War II. The Serial No. which is 456602, speaks for itself.

When Parker-Hale acquired it, they contacted the Browning factory and they received a telegram to the effect that this was the Millionth Browning Pistol. Based upon this, the British Proof House agreed to give a proof exemption certificate when they proof tested it and turned it over to me, that means that on the records of the British Proof House, it was a historical piece and was not marked with the British proofmarks to alter its value. But, as you know, by law, every foreign gun must be proved before it leaves England.

Hiram Williams, the past president of Browning, has known the gun since the late 1950's, and one time he offered to trade a pair of Pigeon grade Brownings for it.

The gun is guaranteed in every way. The serial number can be checked from the Browning factory. The acquisition from Parker-Hale can be checked, and the records from the British Proof House will still be there. Enclosed is a picture of the gun. The price is $5,000.

Cordially yours,

NAVY ARMS CO.

Val J. Forgett
President

The Presentation Pistol from Sgt. Willis Burgess

The fourth pistol N° 456256 was found in Europe during World War II by Sgt. Willis Burgess. Sgt. Burgess was about 34 years old when he acquired the pistol. His son recalled the story of the pistol's discovery:

> *Dad and a buddy were riding in a jeep when they happened upon a party in progress. His friend was fluent in the language and they were invited to join in what I believe to be a celebration. There was a man there who ran an arms storage place. Conversation turned to guns and the man invited both Americans to look at them. Dad said there were guns of all descriptions; expensive looking rifles, shotguns and boxes of pistols. The man went into his office and returned with two handguns that he gave them as gifts. One was the "Un Million" pistol and the other was a pearl handle revolver. Both men wanted the revolver. They flipped a coin for choice and dad lost and accepted the "Un Million" pistol. From there he shipped the gun home and it remained in a closet until his death in 1998. On occasion he would get it out to look at or to show to one of us kids when we asked, along with other mementos including a Mauser pistol, several German medals, several German and European coins, some stamps and a small Nazi flag.*

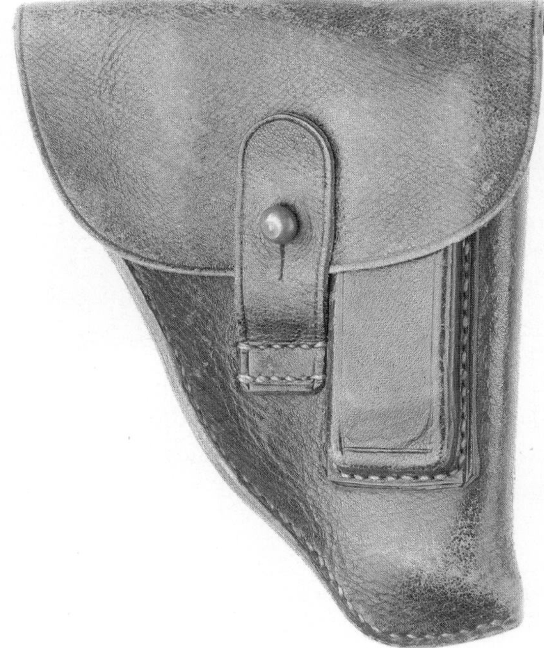

(Fig. 21-2) Sgt. Willis Burgess' pistol N° 456256 and the Sauer holster he carried the pistol in.

(Fig. 22-1) Sgt. Burgess during World War II in Europe. Note the small holster around his belt, close examination reveals that this is not the Sauer holster he used with the Un Million pistol. Although we do not know exactly where Sgt. Burgess obtained the pistol, he carried a one-dollar bill with him throughout the war. On this bill he marked places and dates where he served. From this we know that he was in the following places: Le Havre 12/27/44, Reims, Nancy, Paris, Brussels, Maestricht, Aachen 1/45, Siegfried line 1/6/45, Schmidt 3/45, Remagen 3/45, Fulda 5/45, Rotenberg 6/45, Furstenwald-Kassel, 7/45, Frankfort 8/26/45, Laufenselden 8/27/45. (Photograph courtesy of Robert Burgess)

The FN Factory Retained Presentation Pistol

The fifth pistol (N° 456,188) remained at FN.

The Mystery 1,000,000 FN Browning Model 1900 Pistol

We know that FN never reached production figures higher than 725.000 for the Model 1900 pistol. That fact makes this pistol most intriguing. The details of why it was engraved and gold inlaid are a mystery but two plausible explanations exist:

A- We know that Mr. Stassart had a few "Un Million" Model 1905 pistols made before the rest of the series, as such pistol N° 456256 was taken out of warehouse on December 27, 1913 before the others (January 27-30, 1914). Assuming that FN was looking at various designs and models, it is entirely possible that FN first considered marking FN Browning 1900 pistols for the gala celebration instead of the FN Browning 1905 pistols.

(Fig. 22-2) The mysterious 1,000,000 engraved and gold inlaid FN Browning 1900 pistol. Although details of its history may have been lost to time, it remains a significant historical piece. The lack of a serial number, the engraving style as well as the overall condition of this pistol, certify its authenticity. (Photograph courtesy of J. Weckx, B. V. V. W.)

B- The other possibility is that FN anticipated producing one million Model 1900 pistols and went ahead by having this specimen engraved ahead of time. Note that unlike all other production commemoratives (see pages 12-13), this model does not have a serial number. World War I impeded FN from achieving this production goal.

The Sarajevo Affair

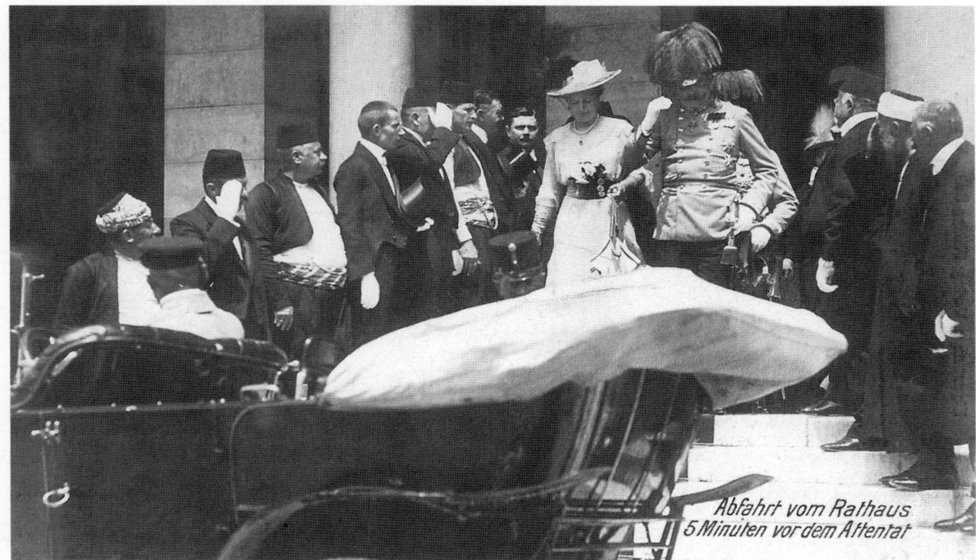

(Fig. 23-1) Archduke Franz Ferdinand and his wife, Duchess Sophie Chotek, as they left city hall on June 28, 1914, minutes before the assassination.

In 1875 the Bosnian Serbs began a revolt that ended in 1878 with the effective end of 500 years of Ottoman Turkish rule in the province of Bosnia-Herzegovina. While the Bosnian Serbs sought national unification with their compatriots in Serbia and Montenegro, their hopes were thwarted by the Great Powers of Europe. The Congress of Berlin, held from June 13 to July 13, 1878, declared that while Ottoman Turkey would retain sovereignty over Bosnia-Herzegovina, Bosnia-Herzegovina would be occupied and governed by the Austro-Hungarian Hapsburg Empire. The farce of Ottoman sovereignty over the province ended in 1908 when Austria-Hungary officially annexed Bosnia-Herzegovina. Resentment of the Austrian rule was strong, especially among young intellectuals and students. Many of these fervently desired a union with neighboring Serbia and Montenegro.

Seven patriotic students, part of a political group called Mlada Bosna (Young Bosnia), plotted to assassinate the heir to the Austrian throne, Archduke Franz Ferdinand. The plot was formed after the announcement of the Archduke's visit to Sarajevo, the Bosnian capital. The seven conspirators all had attended the Sarajevo Gymnazija (high school), their ages ranging from 16 to 27. All came from poor peasant backgrounds.

Ideologically fervent, but politically naïve, these students were perfect for exploitation by the radical elements of the Serbian government. They were recruited by a secret Serbian military society called "Unification or Death" (Ujedinjenje ili smrt), popularly known as the Black Hand. This secret society was founded in 1911 with the purpose of creating a greater Serbia and liberating Serbs under foreign rule. Serbian military officers were heavily represented among the Black Hand's members, with Colonel Dragutin Dimitrijević being one of the key leaders. Dimitrijević was the head of the Serbian intelligence department and was one of the primary organizers of the 1903 plot against King Alexander of Serbia. He was also allegedly involved in the assassination attempt of the Austrian emperor Franz Joseph in 1911 and again involved in an attempted plot to assassinate King Ferdinand of Bulgaria in February 1914.

Franz Ferdinand was determined to visit Sarajevo to review his troops and attend Austro-Hungarian military maneuvers. The trip's dangers were known; Franz Ferdinand had been warned about the risks by one of his ministers and had received a number of anonymous threats. To exacerbate the situation, the visit was considered extremely offensive by the Bosnian Serb population as it was planned for Kosovo Day, a national day of mourning for the Serbs that commemorates the fall of the Serbian Empire in 1389.

Major Vojislav Tankosić, Dimitrjevich's key lieutenant within the Black Hand, recruited Gavrilo Princip along with two other Bosnian Serb conspirators, Nedeljko Čabrinović, and Trifun Grabež. The three conspirators, Princip, Grabež and Čabrinović, practiced shooting a FN Browning Model 1910 pistol in a park near Belgrade (Serbia) under guidance of Milan Ciganović, who served as the Black Hand's intermediary for Tankosić. Princip proved to be the best (or worst, according to some sources) shooter. Marksmanship training was very limited as ammunition was both scarce and expensive. On May 27, 1914 Ciganović provided the conspirators with four FN Browning Model 1910 pistols, six bombs, cyanide capsules and money. The pistols were allegedly purchased and paid for by Dimitrijević personally, Tankosić providing the money. The assassins left Belgrade for Sarajevo, were spirited across the border by Serbian officials, and reached Sarajevo on June 3, 1914.

June 28, 1914

The Archduke's motorcade included four Austrian 1911 model Graf Und Stift[1] convertible automobiles. The Archduke and his wife, Duchess Sophie Chotek, were seated in the rear of the second car. The Archduke disliked the notion of personal protection and as a result, security was light. Few policemen had been posted on the route and the provincial military governor had refused to involve the military, being convinced that there were no assassination plots.

The seven conspirators took positions along the route, which ran from Sarajevo's railway station to city hall. They were spaced at wide intervals to provide for as many attempts on the Archduke's life as possible, and thus ensure operational redundancy.

(Fig. 24-1) A 1914 mourning card printed in Austria

At 10:15 a.m. the motorcade reached the first conspirator, Čabrinović. He armed his bomb and threw it at the Archduke's car. Franz Ferdinand saw the bomb being tossed. Čabrinović's aim was off, and the bomb bounced off the Archduke's car and exploded under the third car in the motorcade, injuring its passengers. Čabrinović fled but was quickly apprehended by the crowd[2] and arrested.

Franz Ferdinand took control of the situation and ordered the convoy to continue immediately after medical attention had been provided for the wounded.

The second conspirator, Vaso Čubrilović, was overwhelmed by fear and took no action.

The motorcade rapidly passed Princip and Grabež, and in the ensuing disorder both were unable to act amid the chaotic crowd. The convoy arrived safely at Sarajevo's city hall. In recognition of the apparent danger, the scheduled visit was greatly shortened. Despite this, the police chief and the military governor failed to take appropriate action. Indeed, the military governor refused to summon the Austrian troops, as they were not in dress uniform.

The motorcade was re-routed and departed city hall for the governor's palace, coincidentally passing in front of Grabež. In the event, Grabež failed to act. The plot seemed to have failed. Fate, however, was to intervene. The driver of the Archduke's car misunderstood the new directions and made a fatal error by turning into a narrow (dead end) street, placing the Archduke's car only five feet away from Gavrilo Princip. As the driver began to reverse direction, Princip pulled out his pistol and fired at the Archduke and Duchess. The Archduke was struck in the neck, the Duchess in the stomach. Both died before reaching the governor's palace. Princip was immediately apprehended.

Tracing the firearms used in the assassination indicated a link between the Serbian government, the Black Hand, and the conspirators: A Serbian official had purchased four FN Browning Model 1910 pistols in a Belgrade store[3]. Those same handguns were taken from the conspirators in Sarajevo. The Serbian Government was accused of fostering the assassination, and an ultimatum was sent to Serbia by the Austrian government. Diplomatic relations between Serbia and the Austro-Hungarian were severed and the Austrian-Hungarian army was mobilized.

The Pistols

Three of the conspirators trained with one FN Browning 1910 pistol in a park near Belgrade in May 1914 under Ciganović's guidance.

Ciganović gave the conspirators four FN Browning 1910 pistols on May 27, 1914, which they carried back to Sarajevo and used in the assassination plot.

The pistols' serial numbers were noted during the conspirators' trial, and discovered during research performed after the war.

The trial transcripts[4] indicate that pistols: 10126, 19074, 19.75 and 19120 were used in the assassination plot. Note the period in serial number "19.75". Upon examining a period keyboard, it is clear that the transcriber mistyped the key as lower case instead of upper case. As such the number is actually 19075.

Factory records further indicate that pistol 10126 was shipped to FN's Agent Kind in Berlin on January 11, 1913. Pistol 19126 on the other hand was shipped to the same FN agent in Belgrade as the other three pistols. It is therefore very likely that this exposes another error in the serial numbers.

Pistols N° 19074, 19075, 19120 and 19126 were all part of the same shipment to FN's Agent Charles Doucet in Belgrade[3]. This shipment left FN on December 3, 1913.

During the trials, two of the conspirators, Princip and Čabrinović, argued with the prosecutor over the origins of the Browning pistols[4]. They claimed that the pistols were French, and Čabrinović stated that the pistols were from a Parisian factory, which equipped the French army. It is obvious that the conspirators were aware that the slide-legend was in the French language, but their claims were totally unfounded.

Pistol N° 19075 was present as evidence during the trial[4].

SERBIE :

Ch. Doucet, 7, Condina, **Belgrade.**

SUÈDE & NORWÈGE :

P. Berghaus & C°, **Gothenbourg.**

SUISSE :

Amsler & C°, **Feuerthalen.**

TURQUIE :

Skon Sirakian, fournisseur de l'Etat, **Constantinople.**
J. Nikitis Erben, **Constantinople.**

(Fig. 25-1) An extract of a 1913 FN catalog outlining some of their most important agents and distributors. Charles Doucet is clearly listed as FN's agent for Serbia including his address in Belgrade and not Koksijde, Belgium as is often reported[3].

(1) Often incorrectly referred to as Benz convertible automobiles.

(2) One of the few period photographs shows police officers leading one of the conspirators into the police station. This famous photograph often is incorrectly credited as showing Princip. The photograph shows Cabrinovic and was correctly titled in 1914 "Bombenwerfer Cabrinovic" (Bomb thrower Cabrinovic).

(3) A 1980s French magazine article stated that the pistols were shipped to Doucet, a dealer in Koksijde, Belgium. This had led to confusion, with many consequent writings claiming that the pistols were purchased in Belgium. FN's period documents show Charles Doucet as FN's agent in Belgrade. It is unclear to the author why Koksijde Belgium was mentioned in the article as no link exists.

(4) Le Procès de Salonique, Juin 1917 by Boghitchevitch – Delpeuch Paris 1927

It was also noted that Čabrinović's pistol was not present as evidence. A period photograph taken at the trial shows only two pistols with magazines and ammunition.

After the assassination a Jesuit monk, Anton Puntigam, set up a memorial for the Archduke and his wife in Sarajevo[1]. The memorial was set up with the approval and support of the Imperial family. Part of the memorial showed the pistols and other artifacts including the shirt worn by the Archduke on the day of the assassination. The Jesuits moved the memorial when the war broke out to a Jesuit monastery in Vienna where it remained for decades[1]. It was well known among some collectors in Austria that the pistols were in a monastery[1]. This information proved to be correct as the Heeresgeschichtliches Museum (Austrian Museum of Military History) in Vienna acquired the pistols and placed them on permanent display in 2005.

The only remaining mystery is which of the four FN Browning 1910 pistols Gavrilo Princip used for the assassination of the Archduke and his wife.

For years the pistol that started World War I has been incorrectly identified as a FN Browning 1900 pistol. The origin of this misinformation is rather simple: Due to a lack of photographs many newspapers were left to draw illustrations of the event and subsequent trial. Some artists interpreted the handgun as a revolver (fig. 26-1) others, more sophisticated and better informed were aware that it was a Browning. The most common FN Browning at the time was the FN 1900 and artistic license quickly propelled a misconception that would last decades.

(Fig. 26-1) Artistic license in 1914 propelled the myth that a FN Browning 1900 pistol was used in the assassination. As no photographs of the assassination were available, period newspapers commissioned artists to render drawings of the assassination. Here a revolver is depicted, in many other papers a FN Browning Model 1900 was illustrated as it was the most common Browning model at the time. These depictions of the Model 1900 and the vague references to a Browning pistol started a myth which would last decades.

---

(1) Author's correspondence with Reinolf Reisinger
Le Procès de Salonique, Juin 1917 by Boghitchevitch – Delpeuch Paris 1927
The Sarajevo Trial by W.A. Dolph Owings
Compiled with assistance of Reinolf Reisinger, Vic Glogovac, Adam Firestone and Leslie Field.

1914-1918: The Great War

On June 28, 1914, Bosnian separatist Gavrilo Princip assassinated Archduke Franz Ferdinand, the heir to the Austro-Hungarian throne, with a FN Browning 1910 pistol. This event's repercussions rippled through Europe propelling the great powers into a chain of events that would result in the cataclysm of World War I. The Austro-Hungarian Empire demanded impossible concessions from Serbia. In a demonstration of Pan-Slavism, Russian diplomats offered promises of support to Serbia in the event of war. On July 5, 1914, Kaiser Wilhelm II countered the Russian guarantees with assurances of its own to the Austro-Hungarians. The German assurances were based on a belief that the Russians would not actually mobilize in support of Serbia.

The belief was mistaken. Like dominos, the European powers spiraled into a nightmare of mobilizations: Serbia mobilized its army against Austria. Austria mobilized against Serbia. Russia mobilized against Austria, Germany against Russia, and bound by treaties, France against Germany. Germany declared war on France and demanded the right to move troops through neutral Belgium. The Belgian government refused and the German invasion began on August 3, 1914. On August 4, 1914, the British government honored obligations to Belgium and declared war on Germany. World War I had begun.

The Siege of Liège

At the outbreak of war, the Belgian Army was in the midst of a general reorganization and modernization that had begun in 1913. As a result, the army was poorly prepared to meet the invasion. Despite this, the army was mobilized, and made ready to face the German assault. The Belgian Army of 1914 was not a force of maneuver as was the German Army, rather, the Belgians relied on the strength of their forts, which were emplaced and designed to protect important border crossings and major cities.

The average Belgian soldier was well armed with either a Belgian FN Model 1889 Mauser rifle or carbine. Personal weapons also included FN Browning Model 1900 pistols for officers, noncommissioned officers (NCO) and the gendarmerie. Machinegun formations were equipped with Hotchkiss and Maxim machine-guns. Uniforms however were totally inadequate for battle, some being reminiscent more of the Napoleonic era rather than modern warfare.

While the army was well supplied with modern small arms and ammunition, the artillery was generally obsolescent, and this shortcoming was to plague the Belgian Army throughout the way. The Belgians' defensive orientation resulted in the concentration of heavy guns in the forts, and comparatively few artillery pieces were available to engage the invaders in the field. The worst shortcoming, however, was the poor standard of training and discipline. Despite this, patriotism and King Albert's determination to resist inspired the troops to fight.

(Fig.27-1) An unhappy Belgian soldier poses in the early days of the war with his FN 4-cylinder motorcycle which had been hit by a mortar shell. FN equipped the Belgian army with numerous motorcycles before the war.

The Belgian forts resisted but ultimately did not stop the invasion. The Germans shelled the forts into submission, using massive artillery pieces that included 420mm railroad guns. Every Belgian fort would succumb to the same fate, a heroic resistance eventually shattered by German artillery.

Every six minutes a 420mm shell was fired at the Liège forts from a range that rendered Belgian counter-battery fire useless. The resistance of the Belgian soldiers in the Liège forts, especially the fort of Loncin under command of Colonel Naessens and General Leman became legendary throughout Belgium. Although the Loncin fort was entirely demolished, the officers and soldiers fought to the end, and became an inspiration for Belgian resistance.

(Fig.28-1) A 1918 photograph of the remnants of the central section of the fort of Loncin. This photograph was taken by Belgian soldiers after the armistice. It gives a representation of the size of the fort and the magnitude of the destruction.

(Fig.28-2) This medal was issued to commemorate General Leman and the Loncin fort battle.

Despite the unequal contest, the Belgians were delaying the German advance and wreaking havoc with the Schlieffen plan's critical timing, frustrating the German command.

The Germans feared the Belgian Francs Tireurs[1] during their advance through Belgium. As a result the shootings of the Francs Tireurs were heavily exaggerated; most German casualties were caused by Belgian military sharpshooters, and not civilian irregulars. German fear and frustration resulted in retaliation against the civilian population. Atrocities became commonplace and civilians were executed. Belgian units were often faced with German units who used civilian hostages as human shields. German burn squads walked through towns and burned house after house, many Belgian villages eventually suffered this fate[2]. Nowhere was this more tragic than in the city of Leuven / Louvain, where one of the world's oldest and largest libraries was deliberately burned to the ground a few weeks after the assault on Liège.

Captain Naessens and General Leman

August 6, 1914 Captain Naessens' famous speech as he addresses General Leman and the troops of the Loncin fort: *"General Leman has done us the honor to take refuge[3] in our fort. Shall we give up the General?" "No"* responded the fortress troops. *"Well than we have decided not to give up the general, we shall perish here. For either the fort will be blown up and I shall be blown up with you, or the German infantry will attack us. When they pass our last defenses, we shall form a last square. I shall keep seven rounds in my Browning[4], six for the enemy and the last one for myself and we will all go together to heaven[5]."*

General Leman and Captain Naessens commanded the fort till the bitter end, on August 15, when the fort finally succumbed to the German 280, 305 and 420mm artillery barrages. General Leman almost suffocated as he was trapped for hours under debris. Captain Naessens was seriously wounded but ultimately recovered. He was deported to Germany for the remainder of the war.

(Fig.28-3) General Leman, the defender of Liège, led the Belgian troops in the early stages of the German invasion, his determination to protect Liège made him famous and well respected.

While the Liège forts were being shelled, brutal street fighting took place in Liège and more notably in the suburb of Herstal where the FN plant was located. During the fighting, the Red Cross converted parts of the FN factory into hospital wards. Medical care was provided to Belgian and German soldiers as well as civilians. The FN factory was known in the Liège area and word got out quickly that FN had now taken on the role of a hospital.

The city of Liège fell on August 7, 1914; the forts surrounding the city resisted for a few more days until they were destroyed by German artillery barrages.

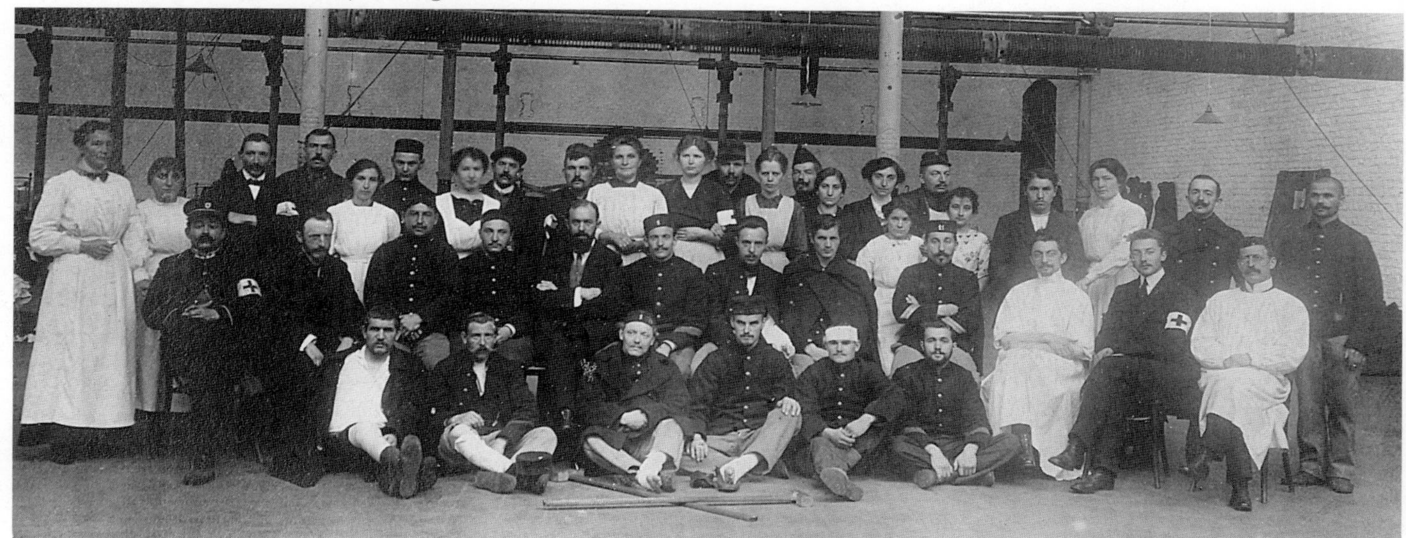

(Fig.29-1) The 1914 FN Red Cross staff and volunteers

(Fig.29-2) One of the improvised August 1914 Red Cross hospital wards at FN

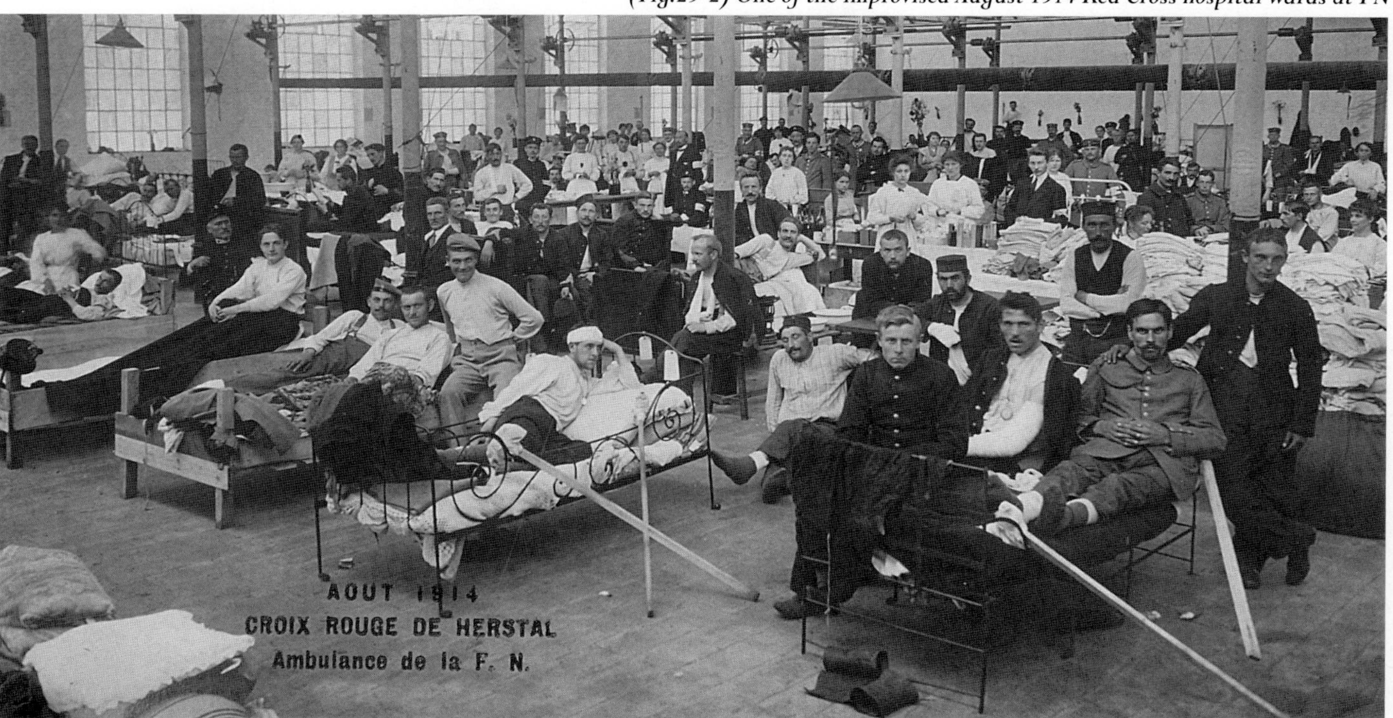

(1) An old French term dating back to the Franco-Prussian War of 1870. During the Franco Prussian War Francs Tireurs were French militia formations that operated unconventionally, waging guerilla war against the Germans. During World War I, the Germans used the term Francs Tireurs to refer to any Belgian shooters or sharp shooters who inflicted casualties on German forces. The Germans claimed that the Belgian Franc Tireurs were civilians involved in guerilla tactics while in fact these were Belgian military sharpshooters.
(2) In recent years the executions of civilians, burning of houses and villages have too often been attributed to wartime propaganda. Some claim that these acts were entirely made up in order to rally the Allies and gain support for the war. Period reports, testimonies, monuments and photographs attest to the truth of what was perpetrated on the population.
(3) General Leman had just avoided an assassination attempt
(4) Referring to his FN Browning Model 1900 pistol
(5) Translation of the French and Flemish text

(Fig.30-1) One of the improvised August 1914 Red Cross hospital wards at FN

BELGIAN REFUGEE.

About the 11th or 12th of August the Germans occupied Heure le Romain, which is near Oupeye. For two days they stayed there and behaved quite politely to the inhabitants. The Germans then discovered a building on the door of which had been placed some notices with reference to a cyclists' club. This notice was signed by the burgomaster of the place and a priest who was the honorary president of the club. It had been placed there before the war. On finding this notice they made all the inhabitants go into the church, among them even old men who had not been out of bed for over six years. They kept them there for 24 hours.

The Germans then sent for the burgomaster and the priest who had signed the notice and they demanded that 25 of the cyclists whose names had appeared on the notice at the school should be given up to them to be shot. The burgomaster and the priest refused to do this. It was not the burgomaster himself who was there, as he was ill, but it was the burgomaster's brother who came in his place. The priest said to the Germans that he was not going to give them any names, but if they wanted to shoot anybody they could shoot him.

The burgomaster's brother and the priest were then taken and placed against the wall of the church and bayoneted by the Germans. I did not see the actual killing myself. I understand the excuse for killing these people was that the notice about the cyclists' club was a military one. It was nothing of the sort, only a pleasure excursion.

I saw the people all put into the church by the Germans. I was hiding in the fields at the time. I then went back to my house at Oupeye. The next day I came back to Heure le Romain and saw that the whole village had been burnt.

On my return to Heure le Romain I saw a man and his wife and his infant son and his mother-in-law hiding in a garden. They were about 200 metres from where I was. The Germans approached and I heard shots. Subsequently I passed quite close to where the shots had been fired, and there I saw the bodies of the man and his wife and the baby. I heard afterwards that the baby was not killed but was taken charge of by the Red Cross people, whose hospital had been established in the Fabrique Nationale, which is at Herstal. The baby, so I was informed, eventually died at this hospital, but before he died photographs were taken of the injuries which had been done to him. These photographs are in the possession of the head of the Red Cross at Herstal.

(Fig.30-2 and 31-1) Extracts from "Evidence and Documents Laid Before the Committee on Alleged German Outrages". This report was compiled by the Committee On German Outrages upon request of the British government. Note the reference to the Fabrique Nationale hospital and National Factory in fig.31-1

(Fig.30-3) This allegorical World War I medal represents Lady Justice, commending the city of Liège by placing a ribbon over the Perron (see fig.91-1).

BELGIAN REFUGEE.

When the district of Herstal was occupied by the Germans, I was employed, together with many other inhabitants of the Commune, in picking up the wounded, Belgians and Germans alike, on the battlefield, so that they might be taken to the National Factory. The Germans were in occupation of the battlefield. I saw them fire on four civilians who were engaged in picking up the wounded. They were killed on the spot. Their names are unknown to me. They had done nothing to justify their being killed. Twenty civilians were killed in this way ; at least I am so informed. I saw killed only the four mentioned above. At this time, with the exception of wounded men, there were no Belgian soldiers in the Commune or the district.

(Fig.31-1) See fig 30-2

(Fig.31-2) A 1916 photograph shows a German officer aiming his FN Browning Model 1910 pistol at a birdcage. The photograph is marked: "German frightfulness: German soldier having taken part in the murder of all the occupants of a farm in Belgium turns his Browning upon a wee canary."

From Hospital to Kraftwagen Werkstatt

In the four years that followed, FN mirrored the country's resentment of the German occupation. The company ceased production and closed its doors in October 1914, ignoring the German requests to continue working.

The annual board meeting (February 20, 1915) resulted in a sharp argument while reviewing the records of the 1913-1914 fiscal year. The year had produced profits, and the board was undecided over dividend payments. The portion of the board representing German ownership interests in the company felt that dividends should be paid out to the shareholders, Belgian owners felt that this should not happen due to the circumstances of war. This fight drove owners further apart.

The board (despite the German majority ownership) opted to close the factory while continuing to pay the employees so long as they did not collaborate with the Germans. FN paper money was printed on October 1, 1914.

Later in October 1914, the German government demanded that the company restart production. The demand fell on deaf ears, and the German high command requisitioned FN machinery, tools and stocks of completed arms.

1915-1916

(Fig.31-2) FN employees are remanufacturing tools and parts in 1916. (Photograph courtesy of FN Herstal)

The board of directors convened again in January 1915, and determined to replace the factory equipment removed by the Germans. The plan was contingent upon obtaining guarantees from the German military government that the new tools would not be seized. These guarantees were obtained and a group of FN workers were active at the factory during parts of 1915 and 1916. Their primary function was to re-establish FN's manufacturing capabilities.

The board of directors continued to meet, but disagreements continued to divide the Belgian and German owners.

(Fig.32-1) FN employees pose in front of the factory in 1916. These workers were responsible for rebuilding some of the machinery and infrastructure that had been damaged by the Germans early in the war. Note that the workers are posed and that no women are present in the group. (Photograph courtesy of FN Herstal)

Meanwhile, the German government renewed pressure on FN to resume production. Mr. Alfred Andri, general manager, refused and was arrested and imprisoned in a camp in Gutesloh, Westphalia in May 1915. Georges Laloux, another FN director, was at same time caught smuggling documents to neutral Holland. He too was imprisoned.

1916-1918

As a result of this resistance, the Germans were unable to restart production. The factory was sequestered, and an automotive repair facility (Kraftwagen Werkstatt) was installed on the FN premises.

Anticipating a favorable outcome to the war, Belgian banks formed a corporation as early as the summer of 1918 to buy out the DWM (Loewe group) interests in the factory. The effort to reclaim the DWM shares took place from the German surrender in November 1918 until March 12, 1919[1] when DWM relinquished its interests of FN.

(Fig.32-2) The Germans were unable to restart production at FN. In 1917 they turned the factory into a vehicle repair facility or Kraftwagen Werkstatt. The signs at the gate indicate that they are hiring and looking for laborers.

Liège, a city of arms

In a 1972 newspaper article, a Liège building contractor reported that the "walls of Liège are filled with guns... few home renovations in Liège come up without hidden surprises." On many occasions, workmen discovered secret hiding places that had been used to hide members of the local population. During the First and Second World Wars, men were often hidden to prevent their deportation as forced laborers. The same shelters and hiding places were also used to hide Allied airmen and Belgian resistance members in World War II.

At the outbreak of the war, many of the arms makers' employees carried guns home from the factories to prevent them from being captured by the Germans. FN employees were no exception, and thousands of firearms were removed from the plant in August 1914. Some were hidden for the duration of the war and returned to the factory afterwards. Others, as circumstances changed, were never returned. Some were discovered years or decades later, others are certainly still hidden in Liège houses today, forming an unexpected source for mint, unfired and boxed pre-World War I FN Brownings. Some of these pistols are illustrated in this book, removed at the outbreak of the war, they surfaced years later as rare finds for the collector community (see fig.122-1 and fig.162-1).

As the the war progressed, the Germans imposed increasingly draconian laws to deal with the citizens of Liège and their arms. Following are some excerpts from edicts that were posted on bulletin boards around the city:

August 25, 1914 L'Union Des Fabricants d'Armes de Liège notice: All arms makers and their workers have to disable all firearms, either finished or unfinished by removing one critical piece (parts listed). As to parts in general, finished or unfinished, those may remain in the possession of the manufacturer or worker.

September 10, 1914 L'Union Des Fabricants d'Armes de Liège notice: Re-iterating to the arms manufacturers and workers that were recently arrested and detained after a German misunderstanding that it is allowed to keep guns and parts in house as long as they were rendered inoperable by the removal of one critical piece. In case the German military seizes property or arrests workers, please contact Mr. Ernest Neumann as soon as possible. New regulations will be distributed by and among the Germans in order to avoid future incidents.

January 10, 1915 Baron von Bissing, General Governor of Belgium, German notice: I have been made aware that there are still plenty of firearms in Belgium. Consequently I invite all individuals to turn in their firearms to their local city hall by January 15. Under the term firearm or arms, this is to include all military rifles, hunting shotguns, hunting rifles, cane rifles, pistols, revolvers and air (pellet) guns. Excluded are antique firearms. Also included are all (military) bayonets, hunting knives, knife canes. Also included is all military ammunition and sporting ammunition. Further all individuals that turn in a military rifle or bayonet by January 15, will be compensated with 1.50 Belgian franc per weapon. All hunting weapons, including rifle canes etc. will be registered with the name of the owner and returned after the war to their rightful owners. After January 15, it will be legal to perform searches to anyone deemed suspicious. Any weapons found will be confiscated and the owner will be persecuted according to the laws of war.

January 27, 1915 German Government notice: All arms workers are to bring all guns and gun parts (finished or unfinished) to the manufacturers. This transfer has to be performed by February 15. After this date, workers found in possession of gun parts will be punished.

February 17, 1915 Baron von Bissing, General Governor of Belgium, German notice: It is forbidden to export any metalworking machinery. All attempts of exporting such machinery will result in seizure of the equipment. Exception is made to the machinery that is exported to Germany under command of the (German) government.

Some of these notices were distributed by "l'Union Des Fabricants d'Armes de Liège" (Union of Liège Arms Manufacturers) in order to inform the arms makers and their employees of the German edicts. The increasingly restrictive nature of gun laws is apparent. Within a few months, the German government completely banned the private ownership of firearms in occupied Belgium. Interestingly, the last excerpt indicates a ban on exporting machinery. By 1915 this had become a problem for the Germans as Belgians were smuggling equipment to the free Belgian zone near the coast where Belgian arsenals and workshops had been established.

(1) A FN article indicates that DWM directors were forced to resign as early as January 2, 1919. Source: Revue FN

1919-1929: From Recession to Recession

The end of World War I brought a euphoric sense of optimism to industrialists who thought that they could return to the days of prewar prosperity. This optimism evaporated as the consequences of the war became only too evident. Rebuilding FN took more time than originally anticipated, and replacing lost machinery and manpower was not an easy task. Of even greater impact was the state of the world economy. The free market that existed in the prewar years had virtually vanished. FN, which had relied heavily on the export market, saw few sales due to protectionism and increased tariffs on its export products. The devaluation of the Belgian franc made the domestic market no better.

The Belgian franc was valued at only 14 percent of what it was before the outbreak of war. Automotive import taxes went from 10 to 45 percent in France, from 5 to 65 percent in Italy, and from 5 to 12 percent in the Netherlands. An era of protectionism began and markets around the globe saw similar increases in import taxes.

FN had realized a number of advantages from its prewar association with DWM. Financial resources for expansion were readily available. FN could call on the services of a highly trained engineering and design staff. Neither of these were available in the immediate postwar era, bringing new challenges for the FN management.

The period between 1918 and 1921 was very much marked by severe economic recession. Despite this, production resumed in most FN departments by June of 1919. The postwar market was glutted with World War I surplus, and there was no great demand for armaments. Emphasis was placed in the automobile and motorcycle departments, and new models were introduced in 1920. The automotive department had revived the popular prewar Model 1250 and was offering it as early as 1919. A new model, the 2150, was introduced in 1920. Unlike the prewar years, FN introduced only one new car and motorcycle model every year immediately after the war. Only a few sporting guns were introduced, with the .22 caliber Browning Trombone making its debut in 1921.

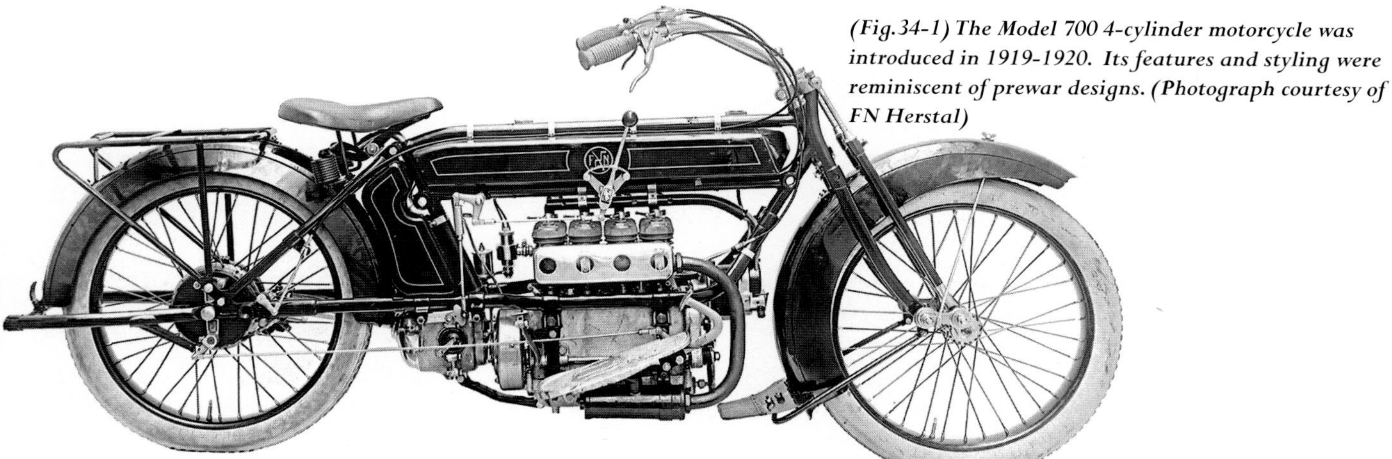

(Fig.34-1) The Model 700 4-cylinder motorcycle was introduced in 1919-1920. Its features and styling were reminiscent of prewar designs. (Photograph courtesy of FN Herstal)

In 1921 FN addressed labor problems by starting its own technical school. First called "école professionelle de perfectionnement des jeunes outilleurs" (professional school for the advancement of young tool workers), later it was simply called "école FN" (FN school). In the 40 years that followed, the FN school graduated 625 students of the 930 that attended.

In 1922 FN expanded this internal schooling system by adding the "centre de formation des auxiliaries de maîtrisse" (center for the development of supervisor assistants). Later school programs included the "centre de formation des régleurs de machines-outils" (center for the development of machine adjusters) and the "école de graveurs" (engraving school) in 1926.

The military market regained some momentum in 1922 with the introduction of the 1922 Mauser rifle and carbine. A modified 1910 pistol was also manufactured for Yugoslavia and was designated the Model 1922, and a sporting version of the Mauser rifle was also introduced.

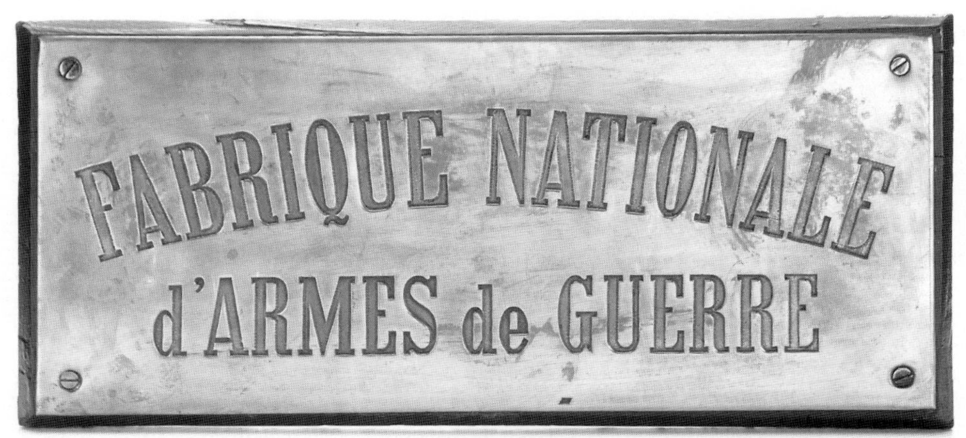

(Fig.35-1) This brass plaque stood at FN's entrance since the 1910s or early 1920s. It was removed when FN did away with the rod iron gates and fence in the 1970s.

By all accounts, another period of prosperity was setting in. 1924 saw the introduction of the modified 1922 Mauser rifle, known as the FN Model 1924, which quickly became a top seller throughout the world. The Yugoslav government, which had purchased military equipment from FN, contracted to have the company build and equip a state arsenal at Kragujevac. The famous Yugoslav Kragujevac arsenal was built and equipped with FN assistance (see also page 218). Automotive and motorcycle manufacturing equipment was modernized beginning in 1922. The automobile department was now introducing a number of new models each year; no less that five different models were available in 1924 (many more if one considers the many body style options). The M.50 and M.60 models introduced by the motorcycle department were very modern and were available with either a four or single cylinder engine.

The period that followed was marked by successes in the automobile and motorcycle departments. FN launched the FN 1300 car in 1924, and this model soon became FN's bestseller of all time. It was economical, sturdy, and reliable and was available in a wide variety of body types. The FN 1300 Sports model won several races including the 24-hour race at Francorchamps in 1925 and 1926.

In 1926 FN launched itself into the world of fast speed motorcycles and achieved a world speed record at Monza in 1926 with a modified M.67 motorcycle.

(Fig.35-2) The Model 1300 was introduced in 1923 and became FN's bestseller of all times. The car was available in a wide variety of bodies and amenities; from utilitarian models to Sport and luxurious custom coached versions including bodies made by famous coachbuilders like Dieteren, Vesters & Neirinck, Van den Plas and others. (Photograph courtesy of FN Herstal)

(Fig.35-3) A 1924-1925 advertisement best summarizes the features of the Model 1300: Simple, supple, silent, robust, rapid and resistant. The Model 1300 was known for its reliability and featured electric starter, four-wheel brakes and suspension. The model was popular as cars were taxed on their performance and the FN 1300 was rated at an affordable 10 HP.

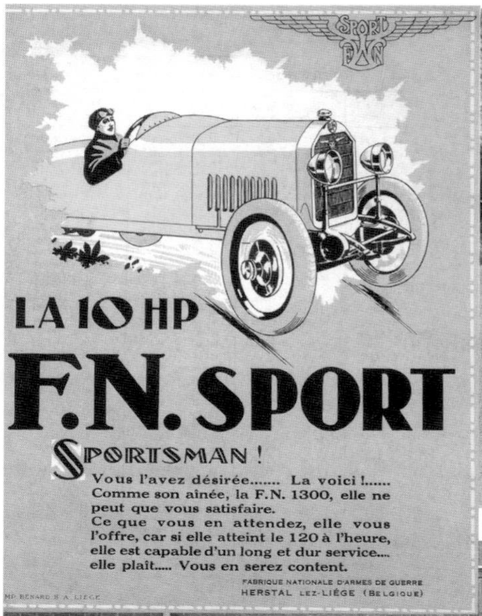
LA 10 HP
F.N. SPORT
SPORTSMAN !
Vous l'avez désirée....... La voici !......
Comme son ainée, la F.N. 1300, elle ne peut que vous satisfaire.
Ce que vous en attendez, elle vous l'offre, car si elle atteint le 120 à l'heure, elle est capable d'un long et dur service....
elle plait..... Vous en serez content.
FABRIQUE NATIONALE D'ARMES DE GUERRE
HERSTAL LEZ-LIÈGE (BELGIQUE)

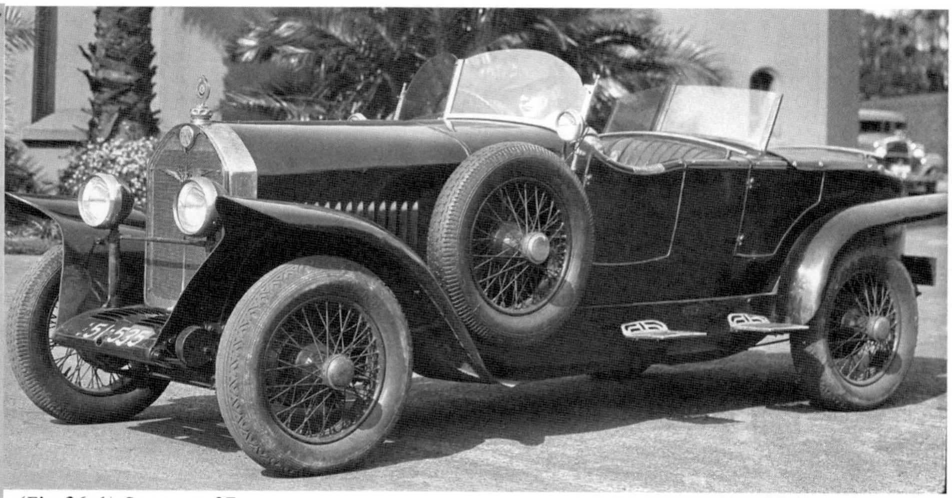

(Fig.36-1) See page 37

(Fig.36-2) See page 37

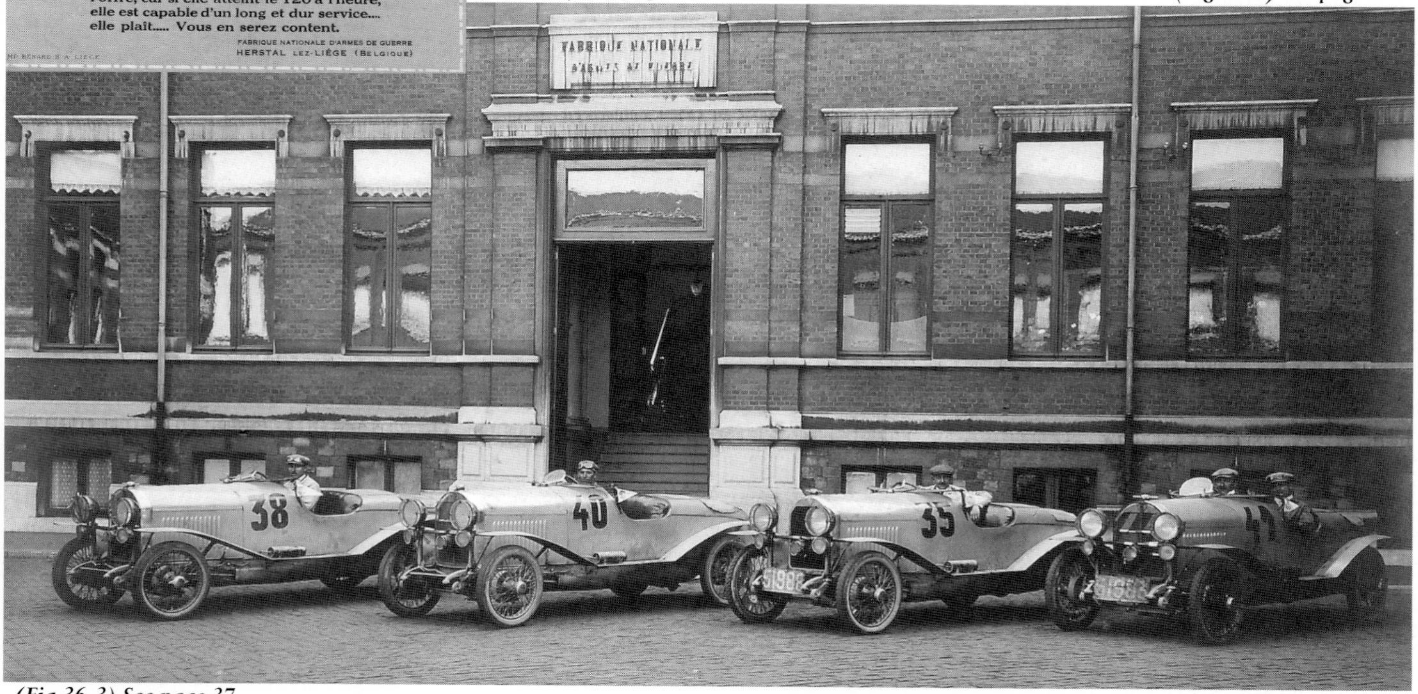
FABRIQUE NATIONALE
38
40
35

(Fig.36-3) See page 37

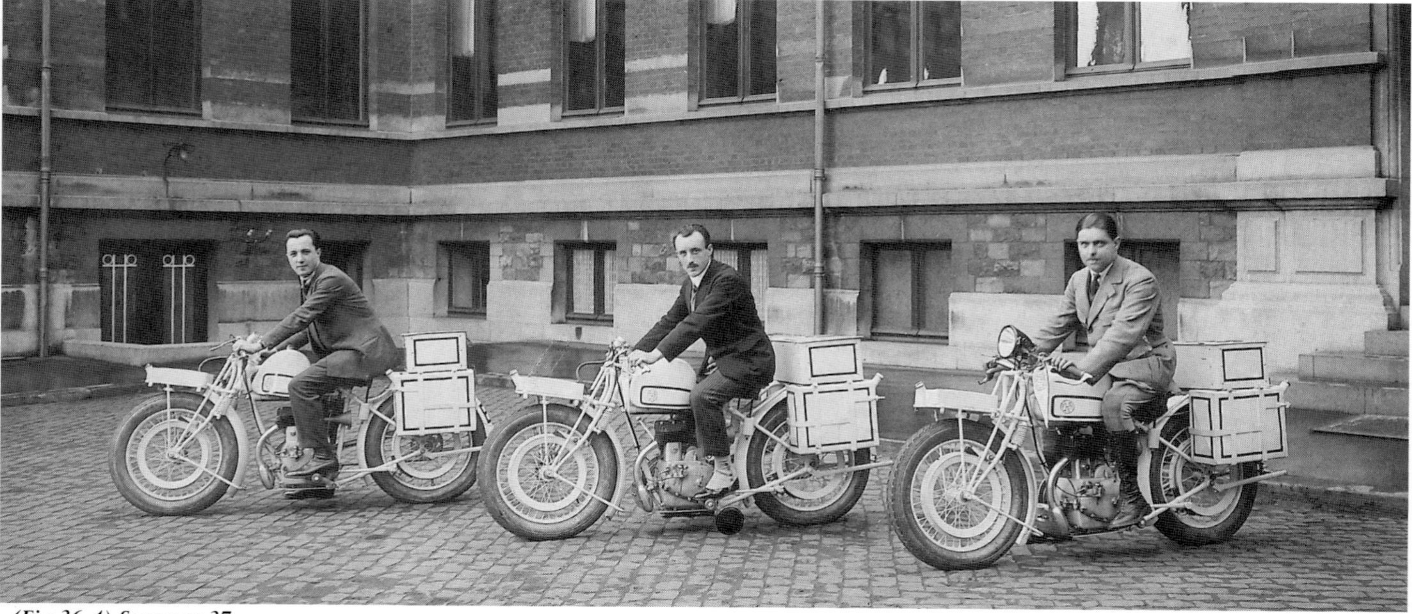

(Fig.36-4) See page 37

Three Belgian motorcyclists crossed the Sahara desert for the first time on motorcycles, riding FN M.70's in 1927. The event received coverage throughout the world, and the M.70 motorcycle became known as the "Sahara" model. The M.70 Sahara model broke many FN sales records. Another FN motorcycle, the M.67 speed model experienced a similarly high sales volume.

As a result of all this growth, firearms were no longer considered to be FN's main product group. While sales were good, there was no exponential growth in firearms revenues as there had been with automobiles and motorcycles. During this time of great prosperity there was also great sadness when John Browning died at FN in 1926.

(Fig.37-1) Produced between 1922 and 1924, the FN stenograph machine was built under license from the French company Grandjean.

(Fig.37-2) At least two variants of the FN MAP typewriter were produced during the 1920s and 1930s.This model was the more expensive variant with glass side windows.

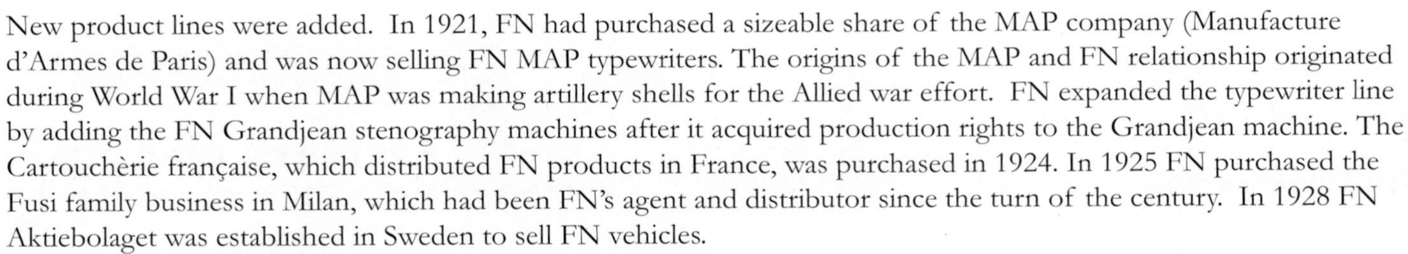

New product lines were added. In 1921, FN had purchased a sizeable share of the MAP company (Manufacture d'Armes de Paris) and was now selling FN MAP typewriters. The origins of the MAP and FN relationship originated during World War I when MAP was making artillery shells for the Allied war effort. FN expanded the typewriter line by adding the FN Grandjean stenography machines after it acquired production rights to the Grandjean machine. The Cartouchèrie française, which distributed FN products in France, was purchased in 1924. In 1925 FN purchased the Fusi family business in Milan, which had been FN's agent and distributor since the turn of the century. In 1928 FN Aktiebolaget was established in Sweden to sell FN vehicles.

1928 marked a major achievement for FN automobiles. Four adventurers had left Herstal in two specially prepared FN 1400 automobiles with the goal of driving from Herstal to Brussels and from there to Capetown, South Africa. While the journey itself had been previously made, it had been accomplished with tracked vehicles designed expressly for this purpose by Citroën.

In contrast, the FN team would attempt the trip with standard two-wheel drive production vehicles operating without any support vehicles. The trip was extensively prepared by the Ministry of Colonies in Brussels. The cars themselves were essentially basic production models painted white to reflect heat and equipped with numerous spare parts and spare tires. The rally ran from May through September 1928 and took the crews through terrain that included the Sahara desert as well as dense African jungle. One of the cars was lost when it caught fire but the crew managed to get to Cape Town with the second automobile.

The achievement was heavily publicized. Books and posters were sold and the surviving car was displayed in Brussels and in Liège.

(Fig.36-1, previous page) A 1920s advertisement for the FN 1300 Sports model with Torpedo coach

(Fig.36-2, previous page) A 4-door FN 1300 Sports model as delivered to Australia

(Fig.36-3, previous page) The FN racing team with their FN 1300 Sports automobiles posing on factory grounds. The team won first place in their category at the 24-hours of Francorchamps.

(Fig.36-4, previous page) April 1927, Mr. Bruneteau, Gimie and Weerens (l. to r.) pose with their M.70 motorcycles at FN before beginning their successful Sahara raid. Note the enlarged gas tanks.

FN benefits from Citroên's marketing ideas

French industrialist André Citroên's career began during World War I, when he established a factory to produce artillery shells for the Allies. Soon after the war, Citroên turned to automobile production. During the 1920s Citroên was building a French automotive empire in the same manner as Henry Ford had in the United States. While studying the Citroên history, one cannot but wonder about the marketing similarities of FN and Citroên. FN kept a careful eye on the competition, learning whenever possible, and incorporating the best technologies and concepts into its own production methods. American automaker Buick became the technical inspiration for FN's automotive engineering(1). Citroên, however was FN's primary competitor, as both companies catered to similar buyers.

In 1923, Citroên launched the "Raid Citroên, La Traversée du Sahara" (The Citroen raid, the Crossing of the Sahara) when its innovative and successful half-tracks crossed the Sahara desert for the first time. The half-tracks were built to military specifications, carrying large amounts of supplies and spare parts. Citroên was a consummate marketer, using the event to promote the company and later form the Citroên-Kégresse Company. One of the Citroên advertising slogans was "le chameau est mort, la Citroên le remplace" (the camel is dead, the Citroên replaces it).

In 1927, FN's motorcycle department sponsored the first Saharan motorcycle crossing without support vehicles. FN emphasized that the Model 70 motorcycles were standard production bikes fitted with enlarged gas tanks and supplied with a minimal number of spare parts.

In 1924/1925 Citroên launched La Croisière Noire (The Black Crusade) when its half-tracked vehicles drove successfully from Algeria to Capetown.

In response, FN launched the 1928 "Le raid au Cap" (The raid to the Cape), in which a pair of standard FN Model 1400 cars drove from Brussels to Capetown. The book and movies that followed the event were called "La Croisière Blanche" (The White Crusade).

Citroên's stunning accomplishments with their military style half-tracks were only of limited advertising value. The consumer market could not relate to buying or using a half-track vehicle. In contrast, FN's accomplishments were achieved with standard production vehicles, creating a sense that every man could be a Saharan adventurer if only he had an FN automobile. The marketing campaign was extremely effective.

In the mid-1920s Citroên published the automotive magazine "Bulletin Citroên". FN followed suit beginning in 1929 with the magazine "FN SPORTS". The magazine covers were richly illustrated by many famous artists of the time. Like the Citroên magazine, FN Sports covered various automotive, aeronautic and boating topics. Articles included reports on car shows, technical innovations and, of course, the occasional review of an FN product.

After FN ceased production of commercial automobiles, it purchased the manufacturing rights to the modernized Citroên-Kégresse halftrack to fill orders for the Belgian military (see fig.42-1).

(Fig.38-1) Top: The 1929 sales brochure for the FN 1400 automobile featured the surviving car of the Brussels-Capetown, South Africa, raid.

Books, posters and special edition magazines (below) were printed to capitalize on the achievement.

The Sahara motorcycle continued to sell extremely well. Demand outstripped production capacity, and to address this need the new Pré-Madame factory was established just north of the FN plant. The factory was set up with an assembly line in order to rapidly manufacture motorcycles.

The location of so many key industries in the region around Herstal caused concern in Belgian government circles due to the proximity of the German border. As a result of these concerns, an FN plant was established in Bruges, in western Belgium, in 1928. The facility's location was deliberately chosen so as to be as distant as possible from the German border in the event of a future invasion. FN Bruges was built as a munitions plant and was integrated into the Belgian rail system with a depot designed into the center of the plant. This led to Bruges being designated as the location to receive vital equipment from Herstal in the event of an invasion. This plan was formalized in the late 1930s.

(1) The general director of FN even owned a Buick after FN ceased automotive production in 1935. While the car was disabled during the 1940 German invasion, the Germans managed to get the car operable again.

FN was a leader in progressive social reform in the 1920s. By the late 19th century, FN was employing women and offering both retirement and medical benefit plans in association with the Red Cross. In the 1920s these programs were significantly enhanced. FN, which had a company doctor, now also built a surgical operating room at the Herstal plant, complete with a company ambulance that sped injured workers directly to the operating room, dramatically increasing the chances of recovery and survival.

FN established schools in the early 1920s for machinists and other skilled laborers. In 1926 an engraving school was established under Felix Funken. A journalist, covering FN in 1928 wrote, "People want to work at FN" and called the company "The Pearl of Belgian Industry".

(Fig.39-1) The Bruges ammunition facility and one of the manufacturing halls. The factory was entirely destroyed during World War II. (Photographs courtesy of Carlos Davila)

1929-1940: From Black Friday to World War II

The stock market crash of October 18, 1929 significantly impacted FN, most severely affecting the automobile department.

As in the period immediately following World War I, protectionist policies were enacted and import tariffs were increased. This, coupled with increasing competition from French and American companies severely hurt FN's automobile business. At the time, FN cars were primarily still built by hand, and could not compete with the high volume, low priced vehicles rolling off assembly lines in Detroit, Paris and Lyon.

FN's reaction to the crisis was the introduction of a large 8-cylinder model that resembled imported cars coming from Detroit. The model featured a large and powerful engine as well as a four-speed gearbox and several body type options including sporty two seaters, a large sedan and even a delivery truck. The FN-8, as the car was known, was a marvelous engineering feat (a standard production sedan beat the Grand Express train from Gibraltar to Brussels, and in 1932 three 8-cylinder roadsters won the 24-hour Francorchamps race), but it was the wrong car at the wrong time. It was expensive and simply not what the public needed or wanted during an economic depression.

FN's racing accomplishments were spectacular but the car did not sell. Only 371 (374 according to some sources) were produced. Other models, like the Prince Albert and Prince Baudouin, followed but even models named after the Belgian royal children did not revive sales figures. Production figured for both models totaled less than 2,000 cars. Ultimately it was the Belgian government that sealed the fate of the Belgian automobile industry. In 1935 the government announced that it would lower import taxes on automobiles. As a result, FN closed its automobile division. A smaller commercial and military division, specializing in commercial vehicles, trucks, buses and vans remained in operation.

(Fig.40-1) An entire collection of twelve advertising postcards was created to publicize the many different body styles available for the marvelous FN 8-Cylinder.

(Fig.40-2) A comparative view of automobile assembly at FN during the decades. Top: Hand assembly by one worker per automobile circa 1912. Bottom: Limited assembly line production towards the end of automobile production in the 1930s. (Photographs courtesy of FN Herstal)

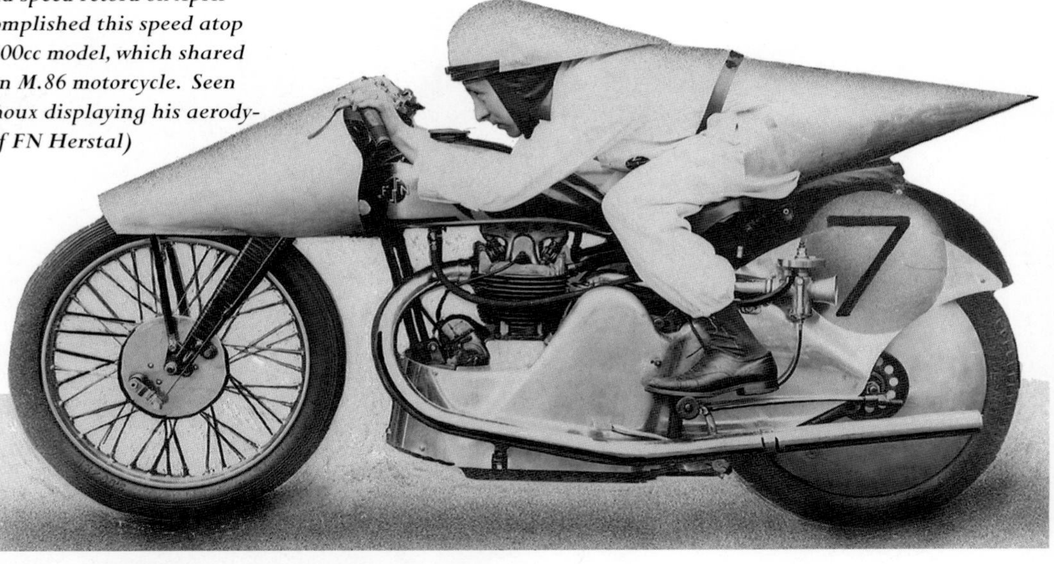

(Fig.41-1) René Milhoux set the world speed record on April 22, 1934 at 224.019 Km/h.[(1)] He accomplished this speed atop a specially built FN single cylinder, 500cc model, which shared many components with the production M.86 motorcycle. Seen here is a posed photograph with Milhoux displaying his aerodynamic outfit. (Photograph courtesy of FN Herstal)

(Fig.41-2) An accident on March 28, 1936, in the ammunition loading department, caused a massive explosion and claimed the life of eight employees[(2)].

The motorcycle division fared significantly better. Racing remained a priority and FN bikes won several world speed records (fig.41-1). The motorcycle division quickly adapted to the increasing military demands of the 1930s and introduced several military motorcycles; the M.12 model being the most prominent.

New commercial firearms were also unveiled. The Browning Superposed was placed into production in 1929 and the Baby Browning pistol (designed by Dieudonné Saive) in 1931. Still, initial sales were slow.

The depression is best summarized by FN's employment figures: In June 1929 FN employed 9,138 workers. By May 1934 this had shrunk to 2,580.

While FN's main growth areas in the 1920s had been in automobiles and motorcycles, the 1930s saw a return to FN's arms making roots. A new Mauser rifle was introduced in 1930 and named Model 1930. In 1931 the military Browning Automatic Rifle (BAR) was placed into production. Light and heavy Browning machine guns were available in various calibers starting in 1932. The Grand Rendement pistol was available in the early 1930s, but was supplanted by its derivative, the famous High Power pistol, in 1935. In 1936, Bofors licensed FN to produce the Swedish Bofors 40mm anti-aircraft gun. The Belgian Army bought a number (150) of these, as did France and Great Britain.

(1) Often incorrectly listed in some publications as 244.016 Km/h.

(2) The number of casualties varies depending on the various reports of news agencies.

(Fig.42-1) FN built Bofors anti-aircraft guns under Swedish license for the Belgian military starting in 1936. A 150 of these 40mm guns were supplied prior to the war. Years later (1953) FN built a larger and modernized 57mm version for the Belgian military.

(Fig.42-2) FN produced 140 artillery tractors for the Belgian Army under license of Citroên-Kegresse (see page 38). These half-track vehicles were outfitted with FN engines and manufactured between 1936 and 1940. Seen here is a FN 63T artillery tractor in action circa 1937.

(Fig.42-3) The Tricar was introduced in 1937 and was based on the M.12 motorcycle with 1000cc twin cylinder engine. Unlike most sidecars, traction was evenly provided to both rear wheels. Many configurations were manufactured including passenger models for officers, munitions supply vehicle (capable of transporting 10,000 rounds at once), fuel supply vehicle (500 liters) and anti-aircraft vehicle with .50 cal Browning machine gun as seen here. (Photograph courtesy of FN Herstal)

Beginning in 1935, FN made military four-wheel drive trucks, and in 1936 began to produce half-tracks.

Due to the depression, FN had not expanded its facilities between 1930 and 1937. In 1938 a large four-story building was erected at Herstal. The building housed administrative, human resources and ballistics departments, meeting rooms and a display room for FN products. An air raid shelter was also incorporated into the building[(1)].

In 1939 FN established facilities at Zutendaal, Belgium[(2)]. Zutendaal is a small settlement near the town of Genk[(2)] in the Flemish speaking province of Limburg[(3)], north of Liège. FN purchased over 1800 acres of land in the "les Campinnes" region[(4)]. Initially, the prewar operations at Zutendaal were small and limited to just a few workers loading specialized cartridges. FN had purchased this large tract of land as it provided a 5000 to 6000 meter ballistic range necessary to support planned expansion into large caliber munitions manufacture. The area had been specifically selected for its flat sandy land and sparse tree growth. It proved to be ideal for range operations, requiring little land clearing or leveling. Additionally, the Zutendaal facility was near the Belgian military base (and firing range) of Beverloo in Leopoldsburg[(5)]. The FN Zutendaal operation was officially set up in 1939 but FN had already been performing tests and limited functions in the area for many years. The area was used for many FN advertising and promotional photographs (fig.43-1).

The increasing threat posed by Nazi Germany created a climate of fear in Europe. Many European nations contracted with FN for their armament. The following nations purchased military equipment from FN between 1933 and 1940: Belgium, The Netherlands, Yugoslavia, Romania, Turkey, Denmark, Norway, Finland, Estonia, Lithuania, Greece, Ethiopia and China. The following nations were in the process of negotiating orders or special military projects before the German invasion: France, Great Britain, Sweden and Denmark.

(Fig.43-1) A 1933 FN publicity photograph: FN used the Zutendaal grounds to photograph their products in simulated use for advertising purposes. A whole series of FN weapons were photographed using the same actors. In later years, these photographs have been incorrectly attributed to Belgian army maneuvers. In this photograph we see an actor with soldier's overcoat (instead of officer's coat) holding a fixed sight Grand Rendement pistol with the officer's holster that was eventually adopted by the Belgian military in 1936. The actor in the center wears a non-regulation overcoat and trousers. The FN Model 1930 carbine on his back was never adopted by the Belgian military. The third actor holds a Model 30 Browning Automatic Rifle as used by the Belgian military. (Photograph courtesy of Collector Grade Publications, Inc.)

(1) This is another indicator that the FN planners were indeed anticipating war with Germany.

(2) The period spelling at the time was "Zutendael" and "Genck"

(3) Also "Limbourg" in French spelling

(4) "Les Campinnes" is de French name for what is now called "De Kempen" in Flemish

(5) At the time often referred to by its French name "Bourg Leopold"

1940-1944: World War II

The Belgian Situation

On Friday May 10, 1940 German forces invaded Belgium. The Franco-Belgian defense plan was unable to cope with the speed and shock of the attack, and in a matter of eighteen days the entire country was overrun. Reaction to initial engagements between the Franco-Belgian defenders and German forces were incoherent and inconclusive as the Blitzkreig had severely disrupted Allied command and control.

The Belgian military was ordered to surrender on May 28. Although the Belgian army was exhausted and depleted, it remained in the field, and continued fighting. King Leopold III's surrender was met with consternation by senior Belgian officers. By the 28th, the Belgian Army had been forced back to the western part of the country and was split between the northern armies, near Holland, and the southern armies in France, covering the Allied evacuation at Dunkirk (Operation Dynamo) from May 26 to June 4, 1940.

The treasonous monarch: Leopold III

King Albert of Belgium had gained global recognition for leading Belgian resistance against the Germans in World War I. His determination, patriotism and integrity made him the most beloved monarch of the Belgian dynasty. After Albert's untimely death in 1934, his son, Leopold III acceded to the Belgian throne Leopold married the Swedish princess Astrid and quickly gained popularity among the Belgian people. A year later, in 1935, Leopold III and Astrid were involved in an automobile accident in Küssnacht, Switzerland, which took Astrid's life. The circumstances of both accidents were suspicious. Some Belgians believed that their beloved King Albert had been the victim of an assassination plot. The automobile accident appeared to be part of a larger conspiracy to assassinate the Belgian royal family(1).

(Fig.44-1) King Leopold III in 1934

When the German Army invaded Belgium in 1940, Leopold III's reaction was far from the unbridled resistance his father had shown 26 years earlier. Belgian officials pleaded with him to follow the Belgian government into exile, but Leopold refused. On May 15, outraged Belgian ministers threatened to fight the king.

Eighteen days after the invasion began, Leopold signed the capitulation document. This outraged both the civilian population and the military. In a speech on French radio on May 28,1940, the Belgian prime-minister, Pierlot, condemned the king for violating the Belgian constitution.

Leopold's actions remain controversial to this day. In fairness it should be noted that Leopold was well informed of the desperate situation of the Belgian Army. He was aware that there was no escape for the army and that further retreat was impossible due to the fact that the few roads were clogged with refugees. The options were simply surrender or annihilation. Historically, the surrender overshadows the Belgian Army's heroic acts during the dark days of 1940. Were it not for the Belgians' screening of the British Expeditionary Force's (BEF) movements toward the Channel coast, the evacuation from Dunkirk would have been impossible.

Unlike his cabinet, Leopold III refused to take part in the Belgian government in exile in London. For the duration of the war, he was a comfortable prisoner of the Third Reich. On June 7, 1944 he was moved to a castle in Hirschstein in Saxony, where he remained until March 1945. Later he stayed in Strobl, Austria until the German capitulation. After the liberation of Belgium, Leopold remained in exile, and his brother, Prince Charles, assumed the throne as regent. In contrast to Leopold, Prince Charles spent the war as an active member of the resistance.

In a March 19,1950 referendum, 57 percent of Belgians voted in favor of Leopold resuming the throne. However, when he returned on July 22, Leopold was met with waves of violent demonstrations and strikes, in consequence of which he abdicated in 1951.

Both Prince Charles' years as regent and Leopold's brief postwar reign are reflected in markings on Belgian military arms. (see page 306)

(1) A number of modern historians believe that this conspiracy theory may have been well founded. The German command, seeking to avoid the mistakes of World War I, did not want the Belgian population to rally behind the same king or his son. By all indications, Albert would have fought the Germans with the same determination as he had during World War I. This conspiracy theory has remained a topic of debate for decades. Seventy years after Albert's death, the first analytical work on this topic was published in 2004. The book, "Le Roi Tué" (The Murdered King) reviews multiple theories about the death of Albert I.

(Fig.45-1) German fighter planes and dive-bombers relentlessly attacked retreating Belgian and French troops on overcrowded roads near the Franco-Belgian border. German pilots scrupulously targeted civilian refugees leaving behind devastation and carnage. Here German troops inspect some of the damage. The overcrowded roads played part in the reasons behind the Belgian capitulation.

Unlike the Netherlands or France, Belgium was placed under German military command in 1940. The military government was headed by Generals Alexander Von Falkenhausen and Eggert Reeder. Von Falkenhausen and Reeder believed in maintaining as much of the existing Belgian infrastructure as possible.

Having FN continue operations under the occupation posed particular difficulties for the German military government as Article 115 of the Belgian constitution prohibited Belgian arms and munitions manufacturers from accepting orders from an occupation force. The problem was resolved by having a German company purchase majority ownership of FN.

The German military command had its share of problems in Brussels as the war progressed. Von Falkenhausen's methods were considered too mild by the German high command and both van Falkenhausen and Reeder fell out of favor with Berlin.

The military command in Brussels had minimized forced labor deportations, recalling the stagnation of the Belgian economy during World War I when large numbers of Belgian workers were deported to Germany. Himmler and Göring grew more and more dissatisfied with their lack of control in Belgium. In response, the Sauckel policy, which deported skilled laborers to Germany was implemented in October 1942. In late 1944 the military government was replaced by a Nazi civilian administration, as in Holland and France. Fortunately for Belgium this change came late in the war; the civilian administrations in Holland and France were known to be far more brutal than the military administration in Belgium.

World War II Outside of FN's Gates

(Fig.45-2) A inside view of the Bruges facility, note the railroad tracks as part of the complex. (Photograph courtesy of Carlos Davila)

Prior to the war, the Belgian government had established an elaborate plan to move essential manufacturing assets to safe areas. This plan (known as the "Mobilization Service of the Nation") was drafted between 1937 and 1939 and included FN and its subsidiaries. A detailed evacuation plan was provided to FN to be implemented on military order or upon the opening of hostilities. Equipment was to be evacuated by train, and the train station in Bruges was upgraded to facilitate this movement. The Bruges ammunition plant had been built around rail tracks to facilitate unloading in the event of war. To further the implementation of this plan, FN acquired the French Mécanouty company in Courbevoie, a suburb of Paris in 1939. The plan was for FN Mécanouty to set up the Herstal equipment for the manufacture of weapons essential to the Belgian military.

Manufacture of Bofors anti-aircraft guns had been moved in early 1940 to a FN facility in Anzeghem (located in the western part of Belgium).

The evacuation order was given on May 10, immediately after German troops crossed the border. Machinery and tools were rushed onto trains according to plan. Unfortunately the planning and preparation was based on World War I conditions and technologies. Unknown to FN management or the Belgian government, German paratroopers had taken control of crucial railroad connections less then 30 hours after the FN evacuation order was issued. Railroad cars that had left FN for France and Bruges were intercepted and returned to Herstal. The Anzeghem facility benefited from its western location and was able to evacuate all its equipment towards Thouards in France. However, unlike Bruges no arrangements had been made in France to receive the huge amount of equipment and materiel. The equipment remained on railroad cars for over a year and was ultimately sold at auction in occupied Holland.

Three days after the evacuation, the equipment from the ammunition plant in Bruges was ordered onto four trains. The trains arrived at a French state arsenal near Toulouse.

The employees and management of the Bruges plant made it to Toulouse by automobile and immediately began setting up for production. However, France surrendered on June 22, only a few days after the Bruges equipment was readied for production. The Toulouse equipment was moved to Lubeck, near the North Sea in 1942.

On May 17 1940, the German command ordered the remaining FN managers, Mr. Pommerenke and Mr. Lecocq to restart production. They refused, with the consent of FN's board of directors. Unlike their World War I counterparts, the German authorities were not discouraged by this action.

On May 19, Lieutenant-General Stubb, in charge of the industrial equipment division of the German Army, informed Mr. Pommerenke and Mr. Lecocq of his decision to place the company under supervision of DWM (Deutsche Waffen und Munitionsfabriken of Berlin).

The German command sequestered the company on May 20, 1940. Three German officials spent approximately three weeks taking inventory, reviewing documents and inspecting the facilities. Finished guns and ammunition in FN warehouses were immediately moved to the Liège citadel (see fig.52-2 and fig.290-1).

At the conclusion of the inventory, a director from Mauser, Oberndorf arrived and immediately started recruiting a new work force (see also pages 243, 289, 290, 292).

On July, 1 Dr. Franz Sharpinet arrived from DWM Berlin and assumed duties overseeing the sequestration of FN.

LAISSER-PASSER

N°

Mr. Lecoq René

né

es… torisé à entrer dans l'usine

LIÉGE, le 1-7- 1940

Deutsche Waffen - u. Munitionsfabriken A.-G. Berlin für Fabrique Nationale d'Armes de Guerre Herstal-Liége

Signature :

(Fig.46-1) Mr. Lecocq's personal entry pass from July 1940. René Lecocq was one of two FN directors who stayed behind to take care of the company during the occupation.

Sharpinet was now instilled with the powers previously vested in FN's board of directors and management. FN's general manager Mr. Gustave Joassart, happened to be in England at the time of the invasion. England had invited FN to discuss plans to erect an arms facility for the production of .50 caliber Browning machine guns. Mr. Joassart returned to Belgium after a brief period in France. He met with Sharpinet and convinced him to allow 20 FN employees to set up an office in Liège. This office would deal with the company's prewar concerns, customers and contracts.

Two different offices were set up in Liège, free from the DWM sequestration, one office dealt with the prewar factory concerns including a contract for numerous FN buses for the city of Liège. The other planned for production of sporting goods and miscellaneous vehicles after the war.

(Fig.47-1) One of the trolleybuses for the city of Liège, completed by FN under German occupation. (Photograph courtesy of FN Herstal)

Mr. Joassart fled Belgium for England together with other key staff members (Mr. Laloux, Mr. Vogels, Mr. Dufrasne and Mr. Saive). All of them went to work for the British Ministry of Defense, except for Mr. Joassart. Mr. Joassart was named Under Secretary of State in the Department of Refugees, Employment and Social Welfare by the Belgian government in exile. His position was crucial in protecting FN's interests in conjunction with the production of the Inglis Browning High Power pistol in Canada.

FN became known as Werk Lüttich (Liège Works) and was grouped with the DWM plant in Karlsruhe and an occupied arsenal in Poznan, Poland. These plants were responsible for related products and were not relied upon for primary German war materiel.

The appointment of Albert Speer in Germany as armaments minister brought drastic changes to Belgium and FN. The most tangible of these was Sharpinet's May 19, 1942, replacement by Dr. Holl

Work conditions became significantly worse under Holl's supervision, deteriorating as materials grew increasingly scarce. Belgian raw materials were often exported to Germany. Skilled Belgian laborers were under constant danger of being deported to Germany. Slave labor and forced laborers from Eastern Europe arrived in the Liège area to replace Belgians that had been deported.

(Fig.47-2) FN issued this commemorative medal in 1953 in remembrance of Gustave Joassart and his long career at FN. Especially his ardent commitment to protect FN, and its production rights during World War II while working with the Britisch and Canadians with the establishment of the Inglis manufacture of the High Power, are remembered.

Holl did not honor Sharpinet's agreements. He had both FN offices in Liège closed and forced the employees to return to FN. Both FN managers, Mr. Lecocq and Mr. Pommerenke, were ordered to stay home.

After the Normandy landing of June 6, 1944, the Allied advance toward Belgium was rapid. In response, the Germans started evacuating FN machinery, parts and inventory on July 30, 1944.

The rail system in Western Europe was constantly under attack from Allied aircraft. The Germans transported FN parts and machinery down the river Meuse on barges. During the final days of the occupation the Germans took anything of importance that could be moved. Machines, FN automobiles, automotive engines and parts, gun parts and reams of documents were loaded onto the barges for transport to Germany.

Browning pistol parts were left behind as the Germans had not completed setting up production in other facilities and time ran out to evacuate the plant (see page 56). This situation helped FN restart production upon liberation.

The barges with FN equipment made it to Bremerhaven, but before they could be unloaded, they were sunk by Allied aircraft. For weeks following the sinking, the waters around Bremerhaven were awash with FN documents.

Holl turned the plant over to Lecocq and Pommerenke on September 1, 1944, departing Herstal on September 5 with the last of his staff. The last occupation troops left on September 7. Allied forces arrived the following day.

FN was in dire straits. In addition to the human losses, there was a tremendous shortage of machinery. Of the 8,113 manufacturing machines present before the war, 1,976 were either damaged beyond repair or had been stolen by the Germans. Most of the remaining tools and machinery were in desperate need of repair. The manufacturing halls were in shambles.

Compounding the problem, the whole Liège area was soon targeted by German V-1 and V-2 flying bombs and missiles. Three V-1 flying bombs hit the FN factory directly while two more exploded within 100 feet, inflicting serious damage. Many FN buildings were demolished by these German attacks, and it is worth noting that this devastation was not caused by Allied aircraft but by German flying bombs. The Allies had opted not to target occupied FN because of its location in a suburb.

(Fig.48-1 above and right) A German Christmas gift: V-1 bombs hit FN on Christmas day 1944 causing massive damage. (Photographs courtsey of FN Herstal).

World War II Inside of FN's Gates:
Forced labor, Shortages, Sabotage and Arms for the Resistance

After the Germans restarted production in 1940, available FN workers were approximately 10 percent of the prewar workforce. This was due to many factors including a desire not to aid the occupation in any way, the mobilization and war, and the incarceration of many men in German POW camps. Many civilians had also fled the area at the beginning of hostilities and were now scattered across Belgium and France. Others had left Liège and lodged with relatives in the countryside. World War I experiences had shown that during wartime, life in the countryside was far better than that in the urban centers.

While a small number of FN workers in 1940 and 1941 were collaborators, most worked to provide food and shelter for their families. Five members of the prewar managerial staff collaborated with the Germans: one doctor, one engineer and three department heads(1).

Production numbers in those years were low. This was due more to passive resistance measures such as work slowdowns and not to active measures such as widespread sabotage. However, by January 1942, production had been increased. About 5,200 workers were employed in three shifts, two complete and one partial. By March the number dropped to 4,900 but production continued to increase. Between 1942 and August 1944, the number of FN employees reached 13,000, reflecting the appointment of Albert Speer as the head of German war production and the introduction of the Sauckel policy.

A secret telegram delivered to Mr. Joassart in London in early 1942 indicated that there were frequent disruptions in production due to shortages of steel and other strategic metals. The same message indicated that 300 Model 1922s and 300 GPs (High Powers) were being produced dayly, in addition to 90,000 9mm rounds and 60,000 7.65mm and 6.35mm rounds(2). Tools were also scarce, many (hand) tools having been smuggled out of the factory by employees.

German letters indicate that the situation did not improve by 1943. A German report dated June 1943 complains about FN's workforce. It states:

> *"That the declaration of Total War and the consequent directive to put every able body at work did not work as it had in Germany. Strict orders and directives are issued from Brussels but not enforced, there is no agency, in Belgium that looks for individuals who skip work. Although (Belgian) individuals were ordered to work at FN, most work for a few days and then disappear. The rampant theft of ration stamps supports these activities. The White Army(3) and Radio London daily motivate the Belgians into these activities".*

The author of the report, Mergen, continues by stating that in his lifetime he has never seen such an organized enterprise and expresses his dislike that this takes place under German military command. He further complains about the scarcity of labor and lists several examples including: *"500 female workers were promised from Brussels and only 36 arrived. 400 were to come from Verviers and only 17 got to work".*

It is not known exactly how many slave laborers from Eastern Europe worked at FN. Once skilled Belgian laborers were deported to Germany, the Germans filled some of the labor gaps by transporting Eastern Europeans to the Liège area beginning in late 1942 or early 1943. Poles, Czechs and others are known to have been working under poor conditions in Belgium. The arrival of the Eastern Europeans coincided with increased resistance activity, raising the supposition that the Eastern Europeans put their experience with sabotage to use at FN. At least two eyewitnesses have detailed the numerous Eastern Europeans working at FN immediately after the liberation.

Some of the reports are almost clinical, dealing with production numbers, acts of sabotage, resistance activities, trials and verdicts. The day-to-day work was miserable for many. Conditions were unsanitary and food was scarce. As a result diseases such as dysentery were among the workers.

---

(1)The collaborating doctor was executed around the time of the liberation, the engineer vanished in South America after the war and the department heads were never allowed to return to FN after the war.

(2) Although these numbers are accurate, they cannot be used as guides to establish total production numbers as raw materials shortages stopped production on a regular basis. Surprisingly .25 caliber ammunition was produced at FN during the war.

(3) The White Army was one of many Belgian armed resistance groups

By war's end approximately 12,000 forced laborers had worked at FN. The Germans stopped production in early August 1944 to dismantle equipment for transport to Germany. Holl had received orders dated August 31, 1944 to remove and pack all production machinery and inventory so that the entire FN plant could be removed to Germany. Luckily for FN this order arrived too late and Holl abandoned this project just by removing what they previously had deemed important (various machinery, MK108 parts, P-38 parts and Mauser parts). The dismantling of FN equipment was not performed by FN workers. Instead, the Germans used 400 Polish POWs, all mechanics and engineers, to disassemble and pack the contents of the factory. During the disassembly process, machinery was sabotaged and key parts hidden After the liberation, one wartime FN supervisor showed Allied troops where the parts were hidden. The supervisor later found employment with the U.S. Army.

Standards of manufacture, fit and finish were progressively lowered during the course of the war as supplies of raw materials became more scarce and demand increased. This decreasing quality was in part due to conditions at the plant. Equipment was aging and in need of repair, and no new machines or replacement parts were acquired during the occupation. Repairs were all performed in house. Surprisingly, production figures increased even when raw materials grew scarce.

FN Production in 1942

Model 1922 pistol – complete pistol
High Power pistol– complete pistol
K98 Mauser stripped bolts
K98 Mauser stripped barrels
K98 Mauser miscellaneous parts
Various small and large caliber ammunition
Artillery shell primers
Airplane flaps (part only)
Axles for tracked armored vehicles
A series of revolver cylinders (part only) believed to be for a Swiss revolver
Miscellaneous steering wheel components
Engine blocks for military trucks
Small arms ammunition

FN Production in 1943

Items listed above plus:
MK 108 cannon receivers and parts
P-38 pistol frames, slides and possibly other small P-38 parts

(Fig.50-1) A wartime German P-38 assembled with a FN manufactured frame. Note the Eagle 140 proof marking which was applied to parts that passed initial quality control at FN. This marking is not to be confused with the WaA140 marking which is a military acceptance marking (page 92).

(Fig.50-2) Wartime FN ammunition: A standard 16-round 9mm Luger box, the label indicates that it was made in 1944 by "ch" the German code for the FN factory.

Organization of German inspection staff on August 1, 1944

Leiter (chief): Oberleutnant (W) Zorn.
Geschaftszimmer (secretaries): Fraulein Buttner, Fraulein Stahl.
Gruppenleiter Gerat (section leader, equipment): Technischer Inspektor Tennert.
Gruppenleiter Pistolen (section leader, pistols): Waffenmeister Porath.
Gruppenleiter Infanterie-Munition (section leader, small arms cartridges): Oberfeldwebel Pilz.
Lauf-Abnahme (barrel inspection): Feldwebel Hahn.
Gerat-Abnahme (equipment inspection): Wachtmeister Lehnen.
Karabiner-Teile-Abnahme (inspection of rifle parts): Unteroffizier Diekhofer.
Pistolen-Anschuss (test firing, pistols): Unteroffizier Pelzer.
Hulsen und Geschosse-Abnahme (inspection of cartridge cases and bullets): Unteroffizier Dreyer.
Hulsen-Beschuss (proof firing of cartridge cases): Unteroffizier Wittenstein.
Chemiker (chemical engineer): Feldwebel Opitz.

Note: Technischer Inspektor Tennert, a civil servant ranking as a Lieutenant, graduate of an engineering college, was the first Leiter (chief) of "Werk Lüttich", using inspector number 613. He was replaced by an unknown official with inspector number 103, who in turn handed over to Oberleutnant Zorn whose inspector code number was 140.

(Fig.52-2) An inside view of the Liège citadel: This photograph was taken immediately after the occupation. The citadel was a German arms depot for finished Liège guns immediately after the invasion of 1940. It quickly became a dreaded place as the Germans used it as a detainment, interrogation and torture facility (see also fig.290-1).

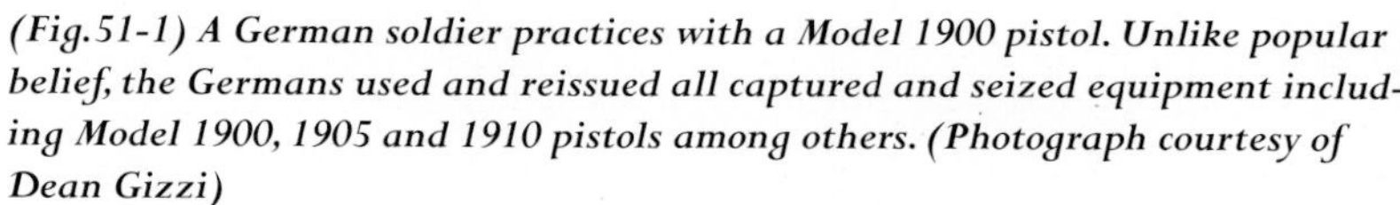

(Fig.51-1) A German soldier practices with a Model 1900 pistol. Unlike popular belief, the Germans used and reissued all captured and seized equipment including Model 1900, 1905 and 1910 pistols among others. (Photograph courtesy of Dean Gizzi)

World War II Inside of FN's Gates: Sabotage

Based on various reports and first hand accounts on wartime activities, it is evident that FN employees followed a deliberate logic as to where sabotage would most severely affect the German war effort. As such, critical weapons were most often targeted. These included the MK108 cannon and the K98 rifle, especially bolts. Pistols were less often targeted, but the same logic was applied; there is evidence of considerably more sabotage on High Power parts than on parts for the Model 1922 pistol.

A German report[2] on activities at FN from May 8 to May 23, 1943 gives an indication of the extent of sabotage activities: *From the daily production of 2000 K-98 bolts (body only), 500 to 600 bolts are rejected and repaired. Many repairs are performed in such a poor manner that the part will not last and the final part resembles the part before the repairs were performed in durability.*

By May 18, 1943, there were 17,000 rejected parts awaiting repair. By May 21, 1943, this number had grown to 30,000 rejected pieces. Upon examining 200 bolts, it was noticed that about 50 to 60 bolts were intentionally damaged. Some were damaged by hammer strikes or similar abuse[2].

In December 1942, the Germans forced Robert Collée back to work[2]. Prior to the war, he had been the head of FN's chemical laboratory, and he resumed this function. Unknown to the Germans, he was also an active resistance fighter with the Group Bayard and a member of A.L.[2] (Armée de la Libération / Army of Liberation). Towards the end of 1943, Collée had another resistance member, René Wéra, employed at FN as a forced laborer. Wéra became the supervisor of the heat treatment processes and was responsible for overheating many crucial parts produced by FN, including the receivers of the MK 108 canons for the new ME 262 fighter. Wéra consistently overheated the parts by about 20 percent. They passed FN inspections but were found useless and no FN MK 108 receivers were ever fielded as all were found defective. The faulty heat treatment made the parts strong enough to pass FN internal inspections, but brittle and readily breakable under regular use. This sabotage technique was applied on many FN parts including parts for the High Power pistol, specifically WaA140 and Eagle N marked High Powers.

Specifically the front sight often falls out of its dovetail slot or the front sight breaks in two while firing. The extractor breaks as the metal is brittle due to overheating in the heat treatment process. After 1942, the extractor was made to fit a specific pistol and was hand fitted in place. As a result of this practice, extractors were often sabotaged as they were no longer interchangeable without hand fitting, and a broken extractor would render a pistol useless.

(1) The Group Bayard and Armée de Liberation were two of many (armed) resistance groups operating in the Liège area.

(2) Une usine d'armement sous l'occupation ennemie by Philippe Questionne -Le Musée d'Armes, Liège Arms Museum.

(3) De Heldenstrijd der Maquis by Jos Hakker

- Hommage aux fusillés by Gilberte Maillard

World War II Inside of FN's Gates: Arms for the Resistance

The number of weapons stolen, smuggled or made for the resistance is unknown as is the extent of resistance operations. Only resistance activities that German forces interdicted became public knowledge. Mr. Philip Questienne, the recognized leader in research in this field, documents the following events[(1)]:

Early in 1941 a large number of High Power pistols disappeared. The Gestapo was able to recover a small number of these, and 20 people were arrested. Two of those arrested were sentenced to death while others were sentenced to slave labor.

In February 1942, 13 pistols disappeared from the assembly department. Three individuals were arrested and received light sentences ranging from one to two years in prison.

In June 1943, 12 FN employees were arrested and sentenced. They had been active smuggling out various arms for over two years. The leaders, Jacques Albert and Lambert Droixhe, were sentenced to death, together with five other participants Elisa Lambert, Jules Rigo, Jules Guelen, Céleste Stassen and Simon Vrancken.

On July 7, the Germans investigated a similar FN case involving 30 individuals. Three were arrested but did not reveal any names. All three were shot on August 3, 1943.

In February 1944, three other FN employees were sentenced for activities taking place in 1942. They were denounced by a coworker, who noticed that pistols were disappearing. Pistols were smuggled out in packs of 30 through a sewer line from FN to the outside streets. The FN employees were not sentenced to death but received sentences ranging from four to 10 years. The collaborator who denounced them was later sentenced after the liberation to forced labor.

On April 16, 1944 eight more FN employees were sentenced for arms smuggling and resistance activities. Two, Norbert Nizet and Vergetin were sentenced to death.

The accounts of the trials were publicized and therefore available. Lesser known are the operations that were successful.

One of the more successful resistance operations was the theft of a large batch of pistols by resistance members posing as members of the German Army. A German army truck arrived at FN, four soldiers in German uniforms presented the appropriate documents. The cargo of pistols was loaded and they left. Shortly afterwards, it was discovered that the soldiers, papers and truck were fake when the real truck arrived.

Not everybody at FN was involved in resistance work. Many appointed supervisors were Rexists and collaborated with the Germans. The resistance workers not only had to avoid the Germans but collaborators as well. Employees were randomly selected upon leaving the factory and were herded into a special room for inspection to ensure they were not smuggling arms.

One of the most feared supervisors was a collaborator named Massart[(2)]. He was sentenced after the liberation. Among the acts for which Massart was sentenced was the sexual abuse of female FN employees who were caught smuggling arms.

Wartime Belgium was a divided society. Belgium had a large number of collaborationist and indigenous Nazi groups. More than 20 of these groups operated throughout the occupation both in Wallonia and Flanders. Belgium had a higher percentage of collaborators than most occupied countries. At the same time, Belgium also accounted for a large number of resistance groups, many operating in various capacities such as intelligence gathering, and armed resistance. More than 600 clandestine resistance newspapers and periodicals were published in Belgium during the occupation, a number greater than in any other occupied country. Many of the armed resistance operations targeted both the Germans and the collaborators.

Finished pistols that were used by the resistance are today most often not identifiable as such, but there is a distinctive class of these guns that were assembled from parts smuggled out of the factory. These guns are referred to in the collector community as "Lunchbox Specials". They exhibit various degrees of finished parts. Due to their nature, most are unique specimens. Some lack specific markings and are complete including bluing, others have crude or handmade parts. These pistols exist from peacetime as well as wartime production and most often always lack proofmarks either Liège proofs (in peace time) or German proofs. A detailed analysis of each gun will most often reveal some details about when it was made.

Comparing Lunchbox Specials

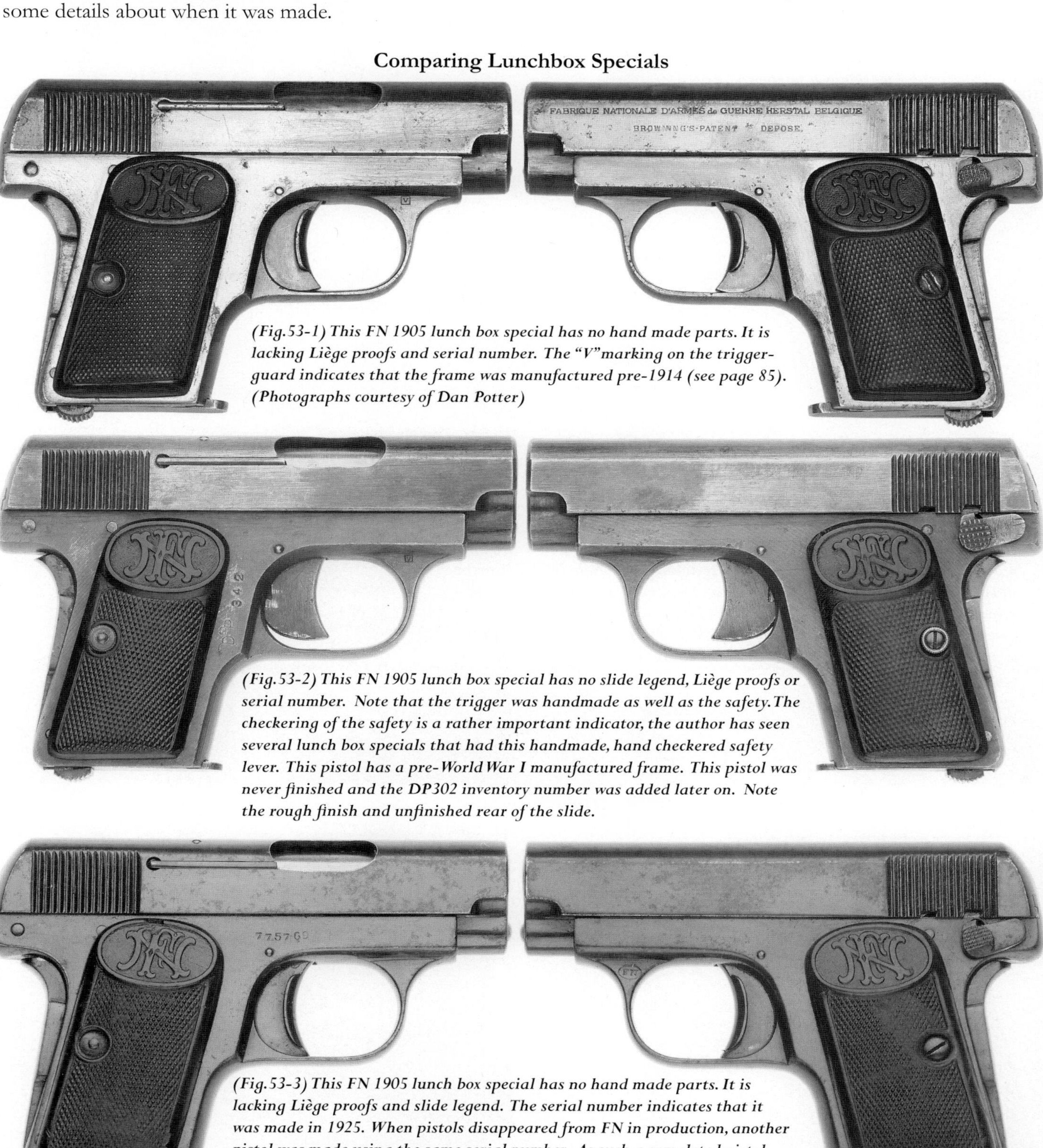

(Fig.53-1) This FN 1905 lunch box special has no hand made parts. It is lacking Liège proofs and serial number. The "V"marking on the trigger-guard indicates that the frame was manufactured pre-1914 (see page 85). (Photographs courtesy of Dan Potter)

(Fig.53-2) This FN 1905 lunch box special has no slide legend, Liège proofs or serial number. Note that the trigger was handmade as well as the safety. The checkering of the safety is a rather important indicator, the author has seen several lunch box specials that had this handmade, hand checkered safety lever. This pistol has a pre-World War I manufactured frame. This pistol was never finished and the DP302 inventory number was added later on. Note the rough finish and unfinished rear of the slide.

(Fig.53-3) This FN 1905 lunch box special has no hand made parts. It is lacking Liège proofs and slide legend. The serial number indicates that it was made in 1925. When pistols disappeared from FN in production, another pistol was made using the same serial number. As such a completed pistol with identical serial number was shipped from FN in December 1925.

(1) Une usine d'armement sous l'occupation ennemie by Philippe Questionne - Le Musée d'Armes, Liège Arms Museum.
(2) De Heldenstrijd der Maquis by Jos Hakker

(Fig.54-1) This World War I era lunchbox special Model 1910 pistol is devoid of proofs or serial number. There are three "B" markings on the slide, frame and barrel. The significance of these markings is unknown.

(Fig.54-2) This World War II lunchbox special Model 1922 pistol lacks German proofs, WaA140 acceptance markings and serial number. Note the late wartime slide-legend (fig.222-4). Note that this pistol was never completed, the hand grinding and polishing of frame and rear of slide was never performed. It is rare to encounter a pistol in this raw configuration. This pistol exhibits all the features of a resistance gun. (Photographs by author, courtesy of Ned Heidenreich)

(Fig.55-1) A French resistance fighter, with a FN Model 1922 pistol, arrests a collaborator. The photograph has the following caption: "Collaborationist seized at Rennes – A member of the French Forces of the Interior jabs his pistol into the back of an accused Nazi collaborator who walks toward captivity clutching a bunch of flowers in one hand. The arrest took place during a mass collaborationist roundup at Rennes soon after the Brittany capital was captured by U.S. troops, August 4, 1944. The police found it almost impossible to prevent angry civilians from revenging themselves on people who had collaborated with the Germans during their occupation of the town. "

(Fig.55-2) An occupation badge worn by a FN employee. In order to deter sabotage and theft, the Germans restricted movement for FN employees. Each employee was issued a colored badge with a German abbreviation of the department where he or she worked. The badges made it easy for the Germans and collaborators to see if an employee wondered out of their restricted work area. This specific badge stands for Geschaftfuhrung, an employee who worked on salaries and payroll. The abbreviations are not self evident and are difficult to identify. As such the meaning of many of these department abbreviations has been lost to time, including the MI and MR department abbreviations, often found on pistols.

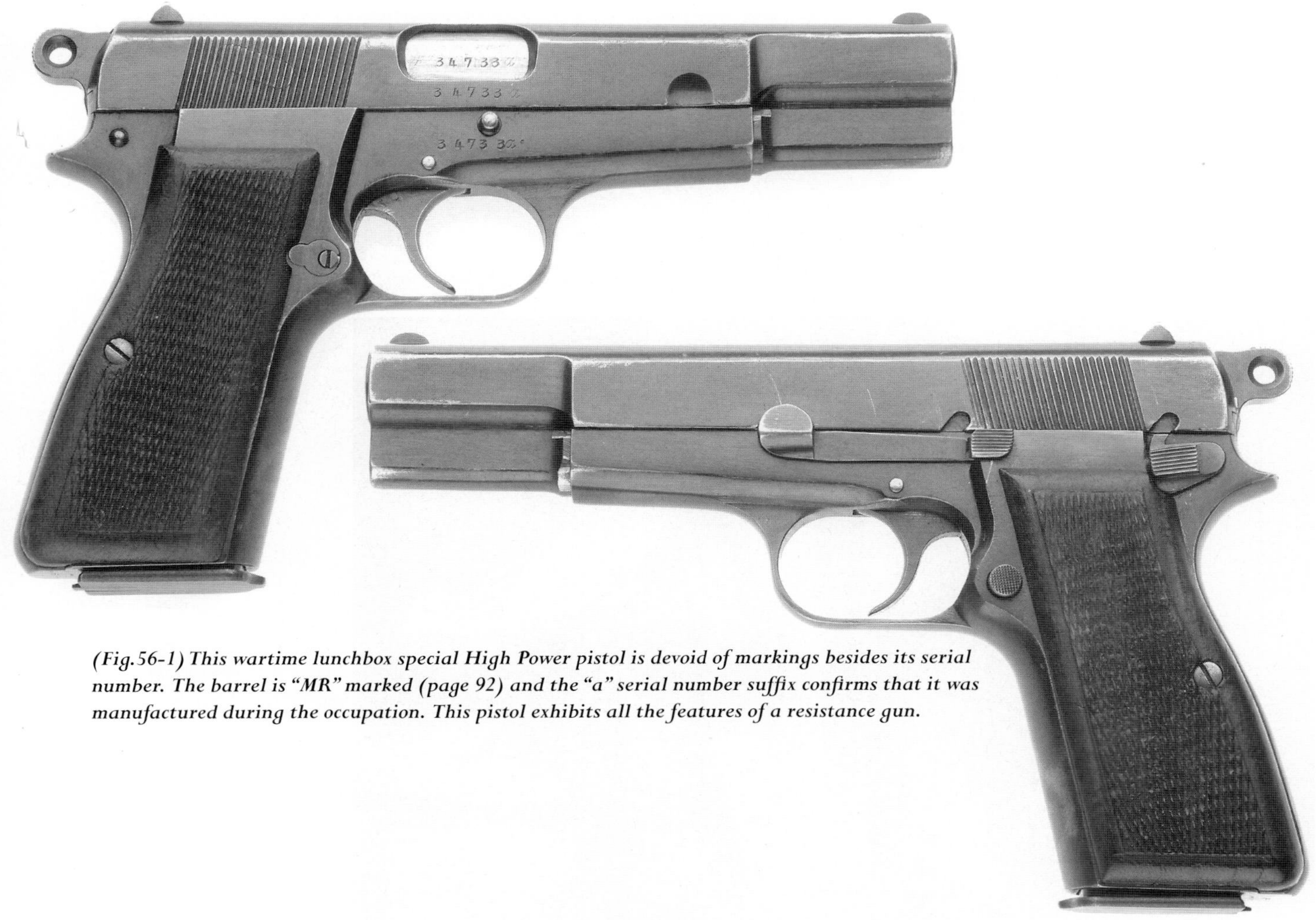

(Fig.56-1) This wartime lunchbox special High Power pistol is devoid of markings besides its serial number. The barrel is "MR" marked (page 92) and the "a" serial number suffix confirms that it was manufactured during the occupation. This pistol exhibits all the features of a resistance gun.

Moving the FN factory to Germany: The plans to build Browning pistols outside of FN

For years it has been assumed that the Germans just abandoned the Browning pistol parts and that no plans were ever made to produce Browning pistols outside of FN. Recently, evidence to the contrary has surfaced.

The Germans stopped production at FN in early August 1944, due to material shortages and the rapid Allied advance. They started disassembling machinery and packaging finished products for evacuation on July 30, 1944. By this time, the German staff had determined what equipment to remove and what inventory of parts had to be shipped. This first plan did not include moving the entire factory or moving the Browning pistol parts. The concept of manufacturing and assembling parts away from FN was not new, the rare DWM Model 1922 pistol (page 57) attests to the fact that assembly and manufacture at German factories was anticipated. Holl received orders on August 31, 1944 to remove and pack all production machinery and inventory so that the entire FN plant could be moved to Germany.

If the Allied advance had taken more time, it is likely that this order would have been executed. The problem of transportation to Germany may also have factored into the abandonment of this project. By mid-1944 there was no feasible way of shipping this volume of equipment; the Germans were retreating and the Allies had established air superiority over western Europe, attacking all German transports at will.

The DWM assembled Model 1922 pistol, is made from a FN slide, but was modified in production. The frame and wrap-around grips are DWM manufactured. The safety lever was upgraded and the grip safety was eliminated. This pistol displays serial number "2". If the Germans were working at starting production and assembly of the Model 1922 in Germany, it is safe to assume the same for the High Power pistol.

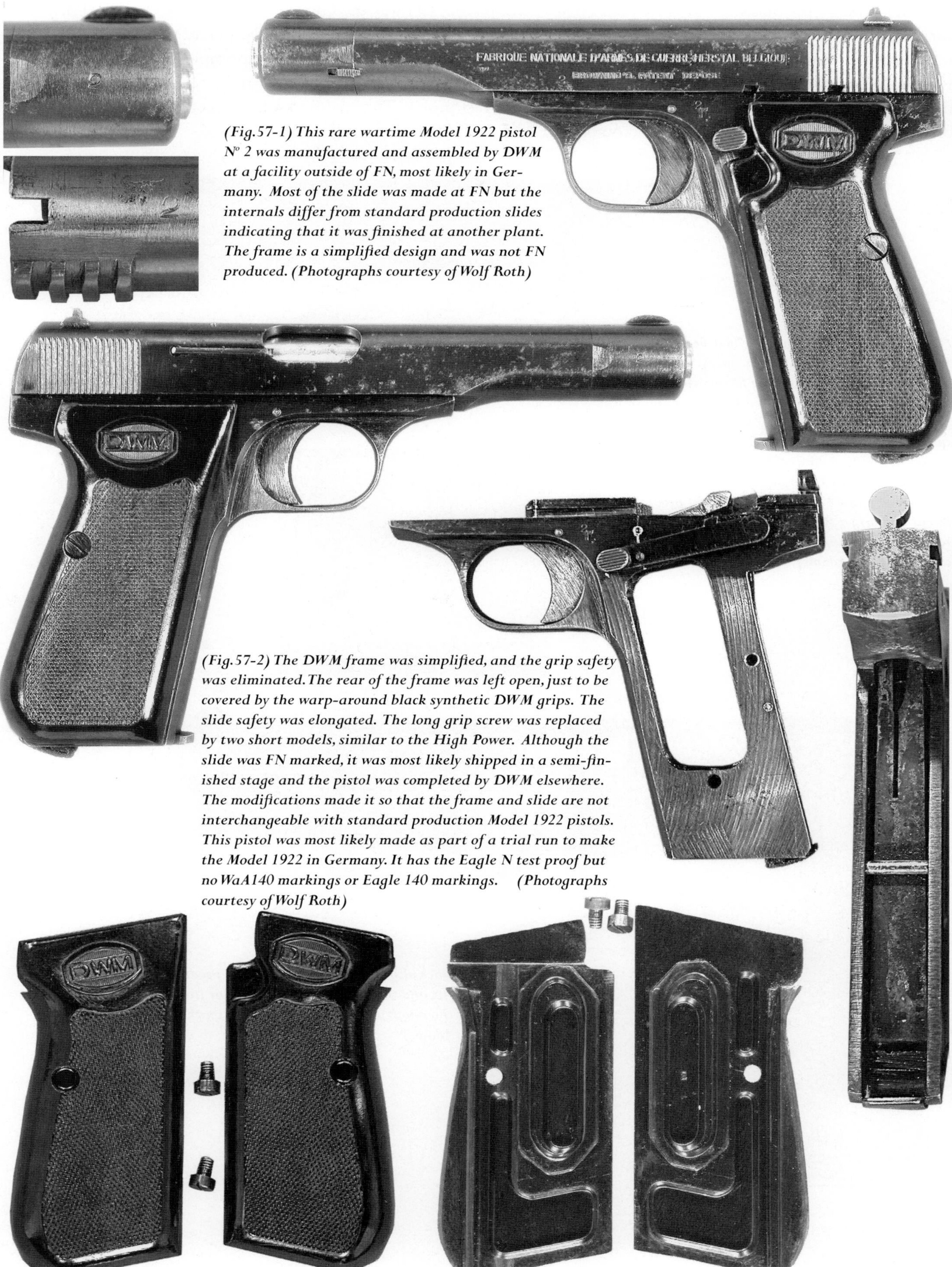

(Fig.57-1) This rare wartime Model 1922 pistol N° 2 was manufactured and assembled by DWM at a facility outside of FN, most likely in Germany. Most of the slide was made at FN but the internals differ from standard production slides indicating that it was finished at another plant. The frame is a simplified design and was not FN produced. (Photographs courtesy of Wolf Roth)

(Fig.57-2) The DWM frame was simplified, and the grip safety was eliminated. The rear of the frame was left open, just to be covered by the warp-around black synthetic DWM grips. The slide safety was elongated. The long grip screw was replaced by two short models, similar to the High Power. Although the slide was FN marked, it was most likely shipped in a semi-finished stage and the pistol was completed by DWM elsewhere. The modifications made it so that the frame and slide are not interchangeable with standard production Model 1922 pistols. This pistol was most likely made as part of a trial run to make the Model 1922 in Germany. It has the Eagle N test proof but no WaA140 markings or Eagle 140 markings. (Photographs courtesy of Wolf Roth)

Another mystery pistol is the CH44 marked High Power pistol. CH was the German factory code for FN. Early in the occupation, the Germans had opted for legal reasons to keep the FN and Browning's patent slide legend as Germany was not at war with the U.S. at that time. This was unique as most pistols in other occupied countries received German markings and designations. This pistol does not have the typical letter suffix in the serial number and also displays unusual machining markings. It has the German test proof. This pistol may have been assembled in a last ditch effort or may have been assembled outside of FN.

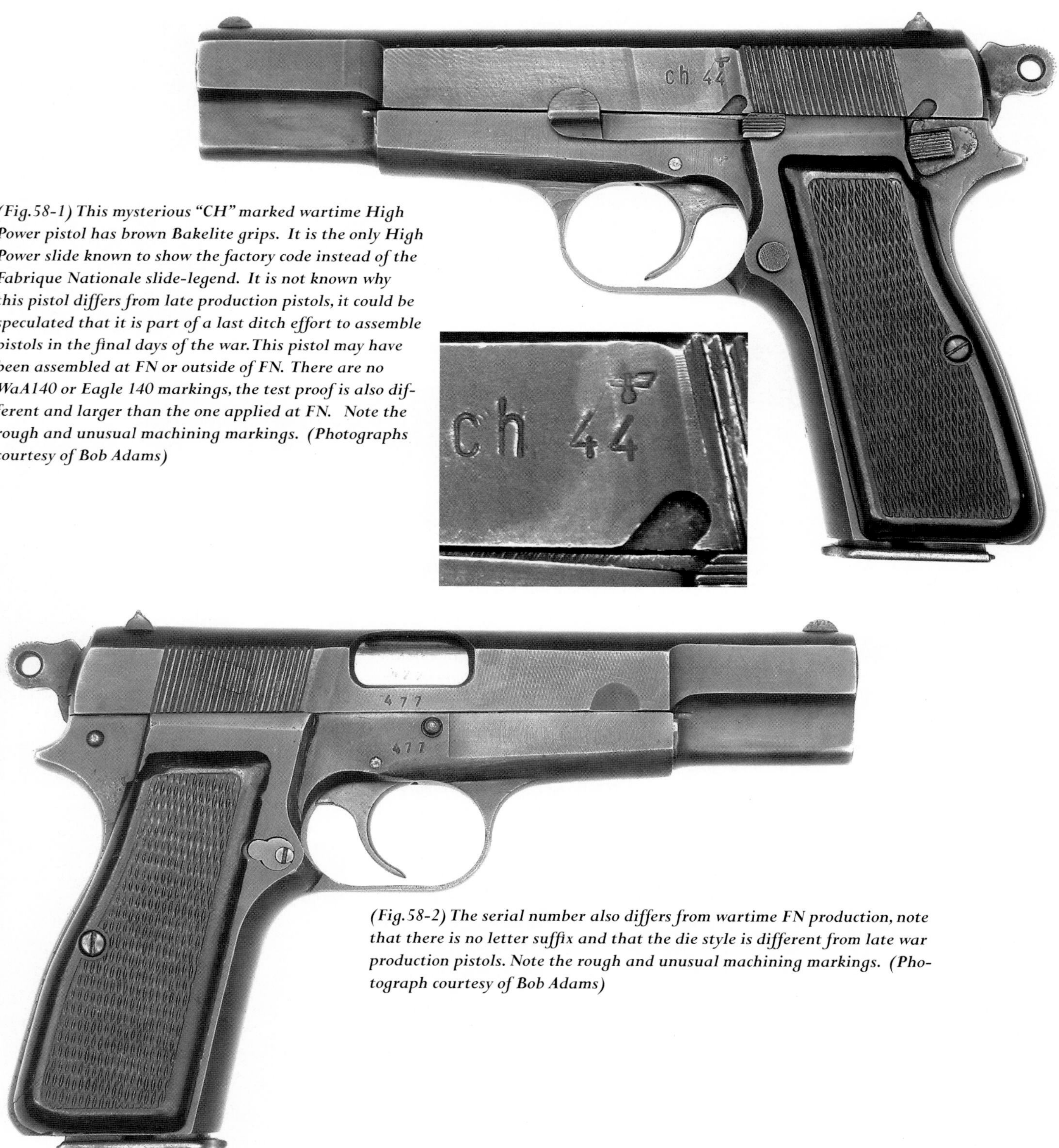

(Fig.58-1) This mysterious "CH" marked wartime High Power pistol has brown Bakelite grips. It is the only High Power slide known to show the factory code instead of the Fabrique Nationale slide-legend. It is not known why this pistol differs from late production pistols, it could be speculated that it is part of a last ditch effort to assemble pistols in the final days of the war. This pistol may have been assembled at FN or outside of FN. There are no WaA140 or Eagle 140 markings, the test proof is also different and larger than the one applied at FN. Note the rough and unusual machining markings. (Photographs courtesy of Bob Adams)

(Fig.58-2) The serial number also differs from wartime FN production, note that there is no letter suffix and that the die style is different from late war production pistols. Note the rough and unusual machining markings. (Photograph courtesy of Bob Adams)

Alexandre Galopin, an icon of FN history and Belgian industry, is assassinated on February 28, 1944.

Alexandre Galopin began his employment with FN in 1904. He had received a degree as a civil engineer in 1902 and completed apprenticeships in England, Germany and France. His last apprenticeship was with the noted chemist Henri Le Chatelier. While at FN he was quickly promoted to the design studio. His diverse abilities helped him to quickly ascend in the FN hierarchy. He was instrumental in the development of FN's research and technical labs and was considered a pioneer in Belgium for the development of such techniques and facilities. In 1913, he was promoted to director.

(Fig.59-1) Alexandre Galopin as photographed circa 1935

During World War I, Galopin worked for the Belgian government and the Allied cause. In 1915 the French minister Albert Thomas praised him for organizing the mass production of service rifles. The "Galopin Method" was so effective that the French government sought Galopin's aid in organizing the production of machine-guns and airplane engines.

After the war, he returned to Belgium and revived FN's production. In 1922 he was promoted to general manager(1). He represented Belgium at various international conferences. In 1923 he was asked to join the Belgian bank Société Générale and to reorganize its dealings with the Belgian mining industry. This work soon expanded to an overall modernization of the Belgian mining industry's business processes. He worked at rebuilding the coal mining industry after the Great Depression and remained a key figure in the Belgian coal industry. Galopin remained an important representative of the Société Générale banking complex, especially when it came to industry including the coal and steel industry. He remained a FN administrator until 1932 when he was elected as chairman of the board of directors, a role he kept until his death in 1944.

In addition to his work at FN, the Société Générale and the mining industry, he also served on the board of several important Belgian factories including the Cockerill steel corporation (1933-1944). Throughout the 1930s he became a recognized expert on the Belgian economy. In the early days of World War II, he led a group of core industrialists and bankers to find the most efficient ways to work under the occupation. The "Galopin Doctrine" was for laborers to return to work under the occupation in order to retain a semblance of an economy, yet at the same time deny the Germans the production of war material. This doctrine was considered a failure as the Germans did not supply the expected rations to Belgium without deliveries of industrial and military equipment. After this failed policy, Galopin focused on minimizing German damage to Belgian industry(2) and preparing plans for a Belgian recovery after the war. Galopin quickly learned about the German operational structure and the internal rivalry. He learned to exploit this rivalry and manipulated the German military administration in Brussels, the SS operating in Belgium and the command in Berlin (see page 45).

He remained independent in his belief as to of what was best for Belgium and its industry and did not always follow the recommendations of the Belgian government in London. At the same time, he used his ties in the Société Générale to fund the Belgian resistance. During the war, he was considered the master of the Belgian economy and his opposition to the German occupation had become apparent through the years. He was murdered in his home by members of the collaborationist group De Vlag(3) on February 28, 1944.

Definitions and parts of the wartime Galopin Doctrine were used after the liberation to determine guide lines for collaboration and to prosecute collaborators. Parts of his doctrine were voted into law on May 25, 1945.

(1) Some sources list his promotion as early as 1919

(2) This also included the Belgian coal mines which were severely exploited during the war. Mining was conducted with production as the sole emphasis, safety and engineering were ignored and mineshafts were excavated to such levels that collapses were imminent. It took years after the war to repair and control the damage inflicted due to reckless mining.

(3) De Vlag (The Flag): A Nazi collaborating group under control of the German SS. This group had its origins as a radical group in 1935.

(4) Congoposte.be - Charles Stockmans

September 1944-1950: Leaping into production

The frenzied German retreat was quickly turned into an advantage in the first days after the liberation. Large quantities of Browning pistol parts had been left behind. Assembly was pieced together and the first post liberation pistols went into warehouse on September 12, only four days after the liberation. FN was virtually the only arms manufacturer to be operational immediately after liberation.

Although FN was able to assemble guns, manufacturing was in total disarray. The Germans had looted all serviceable machinery, and what was left was in desperate need of repair and maintenance. The U.S. military posted several guards at the FN plant and it did not take long for GI's to go to FN and see what was being made. GI's and other servicemen came by the hundreds and purchased most of the assembled pistols and other guns that were left over from the occupation (see also page 250, 303). There are several accounts of American soldiers waiting for a specific pistol to be assembled and of others that insisted on purchasing a gun they just saw being put together. The servicemen brought optimism and hope to what else looked liked a grim situation. In those days there was no electricity and no heat. Working conditions were primitive. Many of the workers liberated after the Germans left had no other place to go. Lt. Chase, interviewed in 2002 stated that at night some displaced workers would sleep on the factory grounds in improvised sleeping conditions. The U.S. military quickly took note of FN's capabilities: The company was contracted to make mud-grips for U.S. Sherman tanks, and about 400,000 mud-grips were cast in FN's foundry.

The products made before the fall of Berlin were simplistic. The U.S. army placed an order with FN for the production of 5000 metal 5-gallon gas containers (often called jerry-cans).

After Germany's surrender, FN was contracted by the U.S. government to clean, refurbish, repair and pack most of the U.S. small arms used in the European theater.

Lt. Col. Chase visits FN after the liberation.

This write-up was compiled from two interviews with Lt.Col. Chase in 2002.

"Before the Battle of the Bulge I was in Liège, Belgium. I was enjoying some R&R in the city when some fellows showed up one day at a little café with several new pistols. They quickly convinced me to go over to this factory where I could buy anything I wanted including German pistols. At that time I had accumulated some money from several months of pay and was eager to buy something but not necessarily a pistol. I walked out by myself with some sketchy directions. All too soon I had left the city center and was walking around in what looked like residential areas or suburbs. On my way I encountered many civilians, who typically were very kind and usually smiled at me. I was enjoying my walk more than anything and was not sure I was going to find the factory. On the way, I did my best to ask for directions and always got help. A corporal on his way back from the factory finally put me on the right track and I found myself at the factory gate late in the afternoon. I asked the guard a few questions and he pointed out where I should go... The whole plant was open, it was like a large open house except there were few people. I walked around and saw some activity coming from one building where several GIs had gathered. There several women were working and building pistols. The guys were sweet talking the ladies and we had them all put a pistol together just for us. Some guys were buying many but I opted to buy only one. A man wrote up a ticket and explained in broken English where I had to pay for the pistol. An office with a white sign over the door was across the courtyard. On my way I crossed a group of poorly dressed and seemingly malnourished individuals. They were laughing and immediately approached me for some cigarettes, I realized that they were not locals but rather Eastern Europeans, although I am not sure from where. One fellow's English was surprisingly good. He was in bad shape and I can still remember his face and smile as if it happened yesterday. I handed out half a pack of cigarettes and all my matches and went on my way to the office. I must have wandered longer than what I expected because the office was closed by the time I got there. Instead of walking back to the workshop, I walked up to the guard at the gate as he was closer to me. I struck up a chat with him and learned that the factory was about to close for the night. There was no power in that region and everybody relied on daylight. The group of workers that I crossed in the courtyard were former slave laborers that had no place to go. While the locals were heading home at night, the others were setting up temporary quarters in the factory. They slept, ate and worked in the factory. I asked the guard if the pistol would still be there in the morning and so I returned the next morning with a friend. I showed him around, he bought a pistol and we both paid for it in the office. The cashier spoke very good English and his assistant wrote up a very detailed and elaborate receipt. With the receipt we walked back across the courtyard and showed it so that we could get our pistols. At the time I did not know what a High Power was, but that is what I bought and we knew the Germans used them. We were all convinced that the workers were putting the name "Browning" on the pistols as that was what we were familiar with. We thought that it was some sort of sales gimmick for us to buy the pistols. We had no idea that these were actual guns designed by Mr. Browning."

Author's note: Although Mr. Chase no longer owns the pistol and documents that he purchased in 1944, the meticulous FN records list him as buying pistol N° A151 on November 6, 1944.

(Fig.61-1) The FN foundry where the Sherman tank mud grips were cast. This photograph was most likely taken in the late 1940s. (Photograph courtesy of Browning)

(Fig.61-2) 1945: Refurbished U.S. M1 Carbines are treated with Cosmoline and crated. Note the wooden shoes on the workers. (Photograph courtesy of FN Herstal)

(Fig.62-1, next page) 1945: FN's boiserie (woodshop) workers shape new M1 Garand stocks and hand-guards by hand. (Photograph courtesy of FN Herstal)

(Fig.62-2, next page) 1945: U.S. M1 Garand rifles are stripped and worked on during refurbishing. (Photograph courtesy of FN Herstal)

(Fig.62-1, see page 61)

All small arms were to be reconditioned before shipment back to the U.S. Over 2.1 million U.S. military arms went through the FN "redeployment" program between June 1945 and June 1946.

Massive efforts were set up in 1945 to recover the stolen and missing manufacturing equipment. As a result, FN was able to recover 1,228 production machines between March 1945 and June 1946. Some 897 were found scattered through Belgium and 331 were recovered from Germany. Some of the machinery had been transferred to the arsenal in Poznan, Poland and FN management was unable to recover any of those from the occupying Soviet forces.

(Fig.62-2, see page 61)

Organization and restructuring was the primary objective for 1945. Complete production was reestablished at Herstal in 1946. Although guns and parts had been made since September 1944. It took until 1946 to restart complete production from raw materials and to acquire the desired quality and levels of fit and finish, that FN was famous for. Val Browning visited FN in 1945 and the Browning Arms Company was again buying Browning sporting guns from FN. At the same time FN was supplying firearms for law enforcement agencies throughout Europe, as most agencies' equipment had been seized by the Germans.

Sporting guns, which had been a secondary market in the prewar years, soon became FN's primary market.

The motorcycle division was also restarted and FN introduced the Model XIII in 1947. This motorcycle was a prewar design that was originally scheduled for production in late 1940. The M.XIII was a success; many individuals could not afford a car in the postwar economy and the motorcycle was a good alternative. The M.XIII was the last of the big FN bikes and remained in production until 1957.

FN struggled and was not very successful in getting some prewar military payments on outstanding invoices from Yugoslavia and Romania. Prewar military customers returned to FN. The Netherlands was one of the first to place large orders for military equipment after the war. This order was followed by several from the Nationalist Chinese Government, which was then engaged in a civil war with Chinese Communist forces. The newly independent nation of Egypt placed orders with FN as early as 1948 for military equipment. Central and South American customers were also lining up.

Herstal lez Liege, Belgium
November 29, 1945.

Mr. D. F. Carpenter,
Vice-President & Director of Manufacture,
Remington Arms Co., Inc.,
Bridgeport, Conn., U.S.A.-

Dear Don:

The Queen Mary, on which I took passage from New York to Southhampton, was delayed more than seventy two hours by storms, and then it was necessary to sit down in London and wait until transportation could be arranged for Belgium. I finally got on the job here November sixth.

The F.N. plant was badly damaged by V bombs. Several buildings were demolished and all of the glass blown out of the saw-tooth type structures, leaving machinery and tools exposed to the rainy, damp climate. Gradually, and courageously, they are reconstructing building (before they finish it will have required more than four acres of glass to replace the breakage) and reconditioning machinery, and are now producing 1922 model automatic pistols and Belgian military type 9 mm. pistols. They are re-tooling for the autoloading shotguns and expect to deliver enough guns to me next year to carry the Browning Arms Co. through - with the guns which we have ordered from Remington.

The price of living is terrific here, and the average wage (with resulting increase in materials) about 2.3 times 1940. The price of the autoloading shotgun is so high that there is no money in it, but I have managed to keep the American market situation well under control.

I have shown them my new model gun (as you remember it must be offered to them for the territory outside of the U.S.) but they want a gun which will not weigh more than 3 kgs. for the European market, and my gun, at present, certainly does not meet that requirement, since it weighs 7 lbs. 1 oz. I am, of course, bringing the model back with me.

I have been half promised passage on an American transport from Antwerp to New-York about December eighth. Such boats require from eight to twelve days for the crossing. Air crossings are simply unobtainable for civilians at present. Would like to get to Ogden for Christmas, and hope to get to New-York soon enough to have some talks with you before going West, but in any event, I can go from Ogden to Bridgeport or Ilion right after the first of the year to stay as long as necessary.

With best regards to all my friends at Remington's, I am

Very sincerely,

Val A. Browning

(Fig.63-1) A 1945 letter from Val Browning to Mr. Carpenter of Remington; note the references to the extensive V-1 damage and reconstruction effort. Note also the reference that only the Model 1922 and High Power pistols are being produced. Although correct, it should be noted that these are A-prefix pistols assembled from a combination of leftover German parts and newly manufactured parts.
As the letter suggests with the Auto-5 shotgun, all new manufacture from raw materials began later in 1946. (Document courtesy of Robert Creamer)

(Fig.64-1) In 1947 FN started production on the prewar designed FN M.XIII motorcycle. The first production models featured this elaborate front suspension made under Swiss patent. FN abandoned this after a year and introduced their own suspension built on multiple rubber bands. Shown here is a 1947 Luxury model FN M.XIII with 450cc engine. (Photograph courtesy of FN Herstal)

An agricultural department was set up in 1946. This department began to manufacture milking machines, and expanded its product line with the introduction of aluminum milk cans. Farm trailers were also built to accommodate the large milk cans. The agricultural department was established at the Pré-Madame facilities, which in the prewar years had housed only the motorcycle production.

The Belgian government approached FN in 1948 with a request for FN to produce jet engines. The Dutch and Belgian air forces were looking to buy Rolls Royce designed Derwent engines for their Meteor jet fighters. FN took on the task and launched itself into the design and manufacture of jet engines.

The recovery of FN appeared complete by 1950.

(Fig.64-2) 1940s portable FN milking machine and sales flyer

1950-1960: From recovery through the Golden Sixties

The 1950s once again brought prosperity to the company due to a number of events. NATO had formed in 1949 and FN was well positioned as it manufactured both ammunition and the High Power pistol, which was accepted by NATO as a standard weapon. Production of Dieudonné Saive's FN-49 rifle had by then started and the prospects of supplying a NATO standard military rifle to NATO countries appeared promising.

The motorcycle division still enjoyed strong sales of the M.XIII motorcycle and this was further aided when seven Belgian servicemen made an endurance trip with M.XIII's from Brussels to Kamina in the Belgian Congo (December 1950 through February 1951).

René Baeten also gained attention when he became national moto-cross champion on an FN motorcycle in 1950. He repeated this achievement in '51, '52, '53 and 1954

(Fig.65-1) FN's cross motorcycle was totally based on the M.XIII. It featured internal springs for the front suspension, introduced on all M.XIIIs in 1950. The engine was enlarged to 500cc with OHV. This model gained recognition as it won numerous European championships. (Photograph courtesy of FN Herstal)

(Fig.65-2) The 1953-1954 FN motorcycle sales brochure heavily emphasized all the period FN winnings including the European Cross Championships of Leloup and Mingels.

(Fig.66-1) Early 1951: Prince Baudouin, the future king of Belgium (center), inspects the M.XIII motorcycles from the raid Brussels-Kamina (former Belgian Congo). The raid of more than 8000 miles had successfully been completed by seven Belgian officers.

In 1953 the company produced parts for a larger 57mm Bofors anti-aircraft gun. Before the war the company had made complete 40mm guns.

Val Browning negotiated the production of the Double-Automatic shotgun with FN in 1950 and production started in 1954. That same year the legendary Fusil Automatique Léger (FAL – Light Automatic Rifle) was put into production. The FAL military rifle would gain worldwide recognition, and be adopted throughout the free world. It is often said that the FAL was to the free world what the AK-47 was to the Soviet Union.

Another advanced military product was the STRIM fire-through rifle grenade introduced in 1957 to complement the FAL rifle line.

The year 1958 saw the introduction of yet another great military gun; the Mitrailleuse d'Appui Général Modèle 1958 (MAG-58). This light belt fed infantry support weapon was the perfect squad companion to the FAL. Years later an updated version of the MAG-58 was adopted by the U.S. military and given the designation M240. To this day it remains the standard U.S. support weapon.

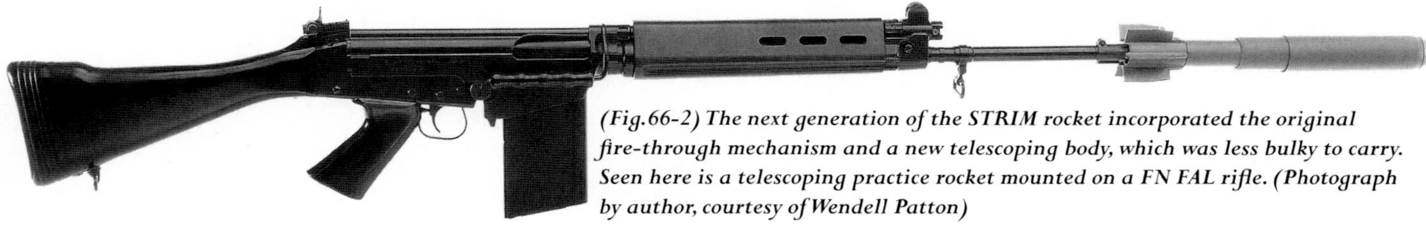

(Fig.66-2) The next generation of the STRIM rocket incorporated the original fire-through mechanism and a new telescoping body, which was less bulky to carry. Seen here is a telescoping practice rocket mounted on a FN FAL rifle. (Photograph by author, courtesy of Wendell Patton)

While military arms manufacture was back in full swing, FN expanded the jet engine line. The Derwent engine orders were filled and the company acquired other production licenses from Rolls Royce for the manufacture of other models. In addition to manufacturing it was expanding into repairing and overhauling jet engines. The Belgian and Dutch air forces were the main customers for FN jet engines. In 1958 FN partnered with BMW in Germany and Fiat in Italy for the production of the GE J.79 engine. This was the engine used by the F-104 fighter-bomber and was adopted by West Germany, Belgium, the Netherlands and Italy.

Motorcycle production declined in the 1950s. FN's last large motorcycle was the M.XIII. The market shrunk as motorcycles fell out of favor with the general public. Scooters and lighter motorcycles became the order of the day. The small M.22 model (option of 175 or 250cc engine) was introduced in 1953. A cross-country version was introduced a year later. In 1955 FN partnered with its old competitor Sarolea in order to produce the last model; the M.24 a 200cc motorcycle.

A military motorcycle vehicle, the AS-24 was introduced in 1960. The AS-24 was the worlds first ATV. Capable of being folded, it was air-droppable and could easily carry three men and equipment over rough terrain.

(Fig.67-1) Four Belgian paratroopers on an AS-24. Note the dedicated MAG-58 mount.The troopers are equipped with early FALs with wooden furniture. The AS-24 was purposely designed to ride low to the ground in order to minimize exposure to enemy fire.

FN remained in the spotlight of competitive sports when René Baeten obtained the world cross-country championship in 1958. Sales continued to dwindle and production of the small motorcycles stopped completely by 1961. FN continued to sell some mopeds but these too disappeared by 1964.

Although automobile construction had stopped in 1935, commercial and heavy vehicles were still made. FN took orders for over 4000 4-wheel drive trucks for the Belgian Army and delivered them by 1954. A year later FN manufactured the last of its electric trolley buses. These buses had been made in small quantities and on special order since 1932.

In 1958 FN produced the marvelous 4-wheel drive Ardennes military truck. This amazingly fast and small truck was available in different configurations and engine options including a waterproof engine as well as a multiple fuel type engine, which could run on a selection of various fuels. The artillery hauler configuration was capable of pulling a multi-ton load with a constant speed of 60 mph. Although technologically advanced, it was not a success and less than 250 were built in various configurations between 1958 and 1966. Heavy vehicle production ended in 1968.

(Fig.67-2) A 4-WD FN Ardennes truck, photographed at FN. (Photograph courtesy of FN Herstal)

(Fig.68-1) The FN Rocket (left) gave a sporty look to the scooter market and was a success in its day.

The FN Princess (below) tended to the more conventional moped buyer. This exotic looking advertising photograph was most likely taken at the royal gardens in Brussels. Although the photograph gives it an international flair, FN's target was really limited to the domestic market. (Photograph courtesy of FN Herstal)

FN continued to expand its product line but the company was now concentrating in highly technical and specialized industries. In 1958 FN partnered with the Société Générale Métalurgique and created the company Métallurgique et Mécanique Nucléaires. It was FN's first step into the nuclear field.

In 1959 the company went into the industrial knitting machine business after buying a division from OIP (Société d'Optique et d'Instruments de Précision - Optical and Precision Instruments Corporation). OIP also provided optics for FN arms including the FN-49 and FAL rifles.

The agricultural department expanded its product line and by 1960 included refrigeration systems, deep freezers and large milking stalls and installations.

The 1960s were known in Europe as the Golden Sixties. The economy was good and orders were pouring in. This period of prosperity also had its consequences. Labor unions had gained an increasing amount of power since the war. This power would manifest itself through the 1960s and continue up to the present day.

FN celebrated its 75th anniversary in 1964. Amidst the celebration there were the worries over increasing labor costs. By then, FN had more employees than ever before. More than 13,000 people were working for FN or FN's subsidiary companies. Thirty percent of the workforce was comprised of women.

Indeed, FN had been a leader and innovator at the turn of the century by employing women to work in the factory halls. In the sixties FN was accused of discriminating against its female workforce. Equality of wages and opportunity was sought, as the women had foundered while the company evolved. There were few women working in managerial or executive capacities. The manufacturing halls needed modernization in order to provide better working conditions.

By 1965 labor had become the main concern. Labor costs had risen over 50 percent in a mere three and a half years. FN caught international media attention when its female workforce went on a paralyzing strike. The strike lasted from February 9 until May 10, 1966. The demands for equal pay and opportunity were previously unknown on such a large scale.

Commercial guns were selling well in the early 1960s. FN had started producing a .22 caliber automatic pistol invented by Bruce Browning (Val Browning's son). Sales of commercial guns reached an all time high in 1965 and for the first time in history surpassed the sale of military firearms.

The .22 caliber T-bolt rifle was introduced in 1965 and the commercial BAR rifle was introduced two years later, in 1967. These were followed by the Model 130 pistol in 1970 (a modernized Model 1922 see page 321). Military sales decreased through the decade, but FN sought a new product line in the lighter 5.56x45mm military cartridge, which had been introduced in the U.S. with the M16 rifle. FN's response was the Carabine Automatique Légère (CAL) in 1968. It was a rifle that matched the FAL in quality but proved too complex and was later replaced by the simpler and easier to manufacture Fabrique Nationale Carabine (FNC) model.

FN's large scale diversification was gaining speed rapidly. In 1962 FN purchased three percent of Browning.

(Fig.69-1) A 1960s FN sales brochure advertising lightweight alloy components for the textile industry.

In 1964 FN partnered with Boeing and created FN Boeing Turbines. This company manufactured, sold and serviced small gas turbines. Four years later the company was dissolved.

The last of the F-104 J.79 jet engines was produced in 1968, after a production run of 10 years. FN's engine division had expanded and produced numerous engines and engine parts for various aircraft from 1964 well into the 1970s. Research and development kept increasing and FN started researching rocket fuel propellants in 1966.

The concept of manufacturing and assembling goods abroad and the need for automation in manufacturing were direct results of the ever increasing labor costs and encroaching labor unions. The latter part of the 1960s saw the introduction of more and more automated machinery including:

Barrel straightness measuring systems (1966)
An automated phosphating line (1967)
Automated fitting of barrels to receivers of over-under shotguns (1968)
Automated polishing (1969)
Heavy automation in ammunition production(1968)
Automated electrolyte bluing of components(1970)

(Fig.69-2) A 1960s FN foundry brochure advertising precision casting and the use of lightweight alloys

(Fig.70-1) The Belgian cyclist and five-time winner of the Tour de France, Eddy Merckx, visited FN in 1974. Here he is seen among elated FN workers, examining a Medalist and Renaissance High Power pistol.

1970-1980: Diversification in the space age

The economic boom of the 1960s came to a halt and FN found itself in financial trouble by 1971. Gun legislation and a rising global anti-gun sentiment made the company change its name from Fabrique Nationale d'Armes de Guerre (National War Weapons Factory) to Fabrique Nationale-Herstal (National Factory-Herstal)

The solution for the labor problem was continued investment in automation and expansion into other labor markets. The 1970s were marked by heavy investment in automated production means and an overall remodeling of the company. FN Viana, an assembly plant, was erected in Portugal in 1973.

Diversification continued on a massive scale throughout the 1970s. FN's independent centralized production of the prewar era was long gone. Partnership was the order of the day in the 1970s. Technological research and advances into new fields were FN's new goals. In 1970 FN partnered with a British company for the development of the ATLAS (Anti Tank Laser Assisted System) missile system.

Industrial hydraulics were manufactured in the early 1970s. The foundry was also remodeled and now included the capability of doing cost-efficient precision foundry work, which reduced the amount of polishing of parts and could even create ready to use parts. By 1977 FMP Aero was established, and this company took the concept of precision foundry to another level with investment casting. This production method virtually eliminated polishing and was of such precision that turbine blades were cast ready to use.

International cooperation in the jet engine industry expanded further. FN partnered with Pratt & Whitney in 1975 and was involved in the manufacture of F-16 jet fighter engine (F-100) components by 1976. For this, a new factory was built and the staff from the older Pré-Madame works was moved to the new facility. FN no longer bought manufacturing licenses as it did early on in the 1950s. Instead it co-produced specialty engine parts with other manufacturers. FN also produced engines for commercial airliners. Another important aspect of FN's diversification was its involvement and production of parts for the Viking engines, which powered the European Ariane space rockets.

FN's military division also expanded its horizons. The FNC rifle was introduced in 1978 as a successor to the CAL.

In 1978 FN introduced the POD; a modular, enclosed helicopter weapons platform. That same year a quick change barrel version of the .50 caliber Browning M2 heavy machinegun was introduced.

South America had always been a very important military market for FN and in 1978 the company expanded and created the FN Brazil (FN do Brasil) factory.

The commercial arms market continued to be very important and this was evidenced by the introduction of various models and market expansions. FN purchased a large share of Beretta in 1972. That same year the Law Enforcement division was established to tend to the specific needs of this market. The Liège over-under shotgun and B-2000 shotgun were introduced in 1972-1973. These models were designed to use more automated machinery in production. Production engineering reduced costs and made these models more competitive in price. FN's design departments received improved technology in 1975 and used CAD programs to develop new models. These included the .22 caliber International pistol, introduced in 1975, and the Challenger II, introduced in 1980.

As part of the French Arms conglomerate GIAT, FN purchased the French manufacturer Manuhrin and took over its line of quality revolvers. In 1976 the Barracuda revolver was introduced with interchangeable caliber options (9x19mm and .357 Magnum). The year 1977 was marked by FN's acquisition of Browning USA. The cooperation with Beretta created the FN Model 140 pistol (marketed and sold in the U.S. as the Browning BDA) in 1978 (see page 321).

FN Sports was set up in 1976 to deal with the sporting market. Sports wear, tennis rackets and golf clubs were soon introduced. Two years later the French company LERC was purchased. This company specialized in composites and allowed FN Sports to begin producing archery equipment and tennis rackets. By 1980 sailboards had been added to the line.

1980 - Modern Times: From recession and regrouping to success

In 1980, FN still employed 10,000 people. The '70s had been plagued with a constant increase in both labor costs and labor demands. It became obvious that the company was too diversified and that too many departments were unprofitable. By 1980 FN had more than 55 divisions, some which included extensive manufacturing plants and others were mere cooperations. The recession forced the company to question the profitability of many departments. A plan for recovery was established in 1986.

Under this plan, many divisions were closed or spun off, including the agricultural division, the electrical household appliance division and the industrial knitting machines division.

Prior to 1986, FN still continued to expand and enter markets, which were deemed profitable. The U.S. military had adopted the MAG as a coaxial machinegun on the M60 series of tanks as the M240 in 1976. In 1980 the U.S. military adopted the FN Minimi as the M249 Squad Automatic Weapon. NATO also accepted the intermediate 5.56x45mm round.

(Fig.71-1) FNMI Project Engineer Jonathan Derrick (l.) and Product Engineering Manager Olivier Coulombier load .45 caliber rounds in magazines prior to test firing FNP-45 pistols. Behind them are racks with M240 barrels that passed testing.

An American branch of the company, FN Manufacturing, Inc. (FNMI), was established in Columbia, South Carolina (1978) and its manufacturing capabilities were further ex-

Other fields were entered in the 1980s. FN manufactured escalators for the Brussels subway in 1981. Hydraulic platforms and industrial hydraulic booms were manufactured and FN went into robotics as well as plastic recycling. Robotics and other departments were short-lived and were closed or sold with the 1986 restructuring.
The engine division had suffered through the recession of the 1980s but was able to regain some ground in 1986 with the production of Airbus engine parts as well as parts for the GE110 engine which was sold to the U.S. military.

FN Sports adopted the Browning name in 1982. Browning abandoned sailboards and tennis rackets in 1988. That same year Browning acquired the USRAC company along with the Winchester trade name. By December 1988 FN owned 100 percent of Browning, all minority stockholders had sold their shares to FN.

Commercial arms continued to be profitable and new models were introduced in the latter part of the 1980s including several variations of over-under shotguns like the B-125, the GTI, the B-127, and the B-135. The automatic A-500 was introduced in 1988 as well as the BAR Mk. II rifle.

During the 1970s FN was absorbed into the French arms conglomerate GIAT, in 1998 this relationship came to an end and FN was purchased by the local Walloon government. From that moment FN became part of the Herstal Group. The Group mainly comprised of FN Herstal, Browning, FN Viana, Miroku, FN Manufacturing Inc. (FNMI) and Winchester. Continued restructuring in the new millennium forced the Group to seal off all financial drains and the decision was made to close Winchester in 2007. The road to recovery and success was complete.

The soon to be released book *Ars Mechanica, The Ultimate FN Book* covers the modern era in detail.

(Fig. 72-1) Standing in 2007 at FNMI in the board room are (from left to right): CEO and Chairman of the Board of the Herstal Group Mr. Philippe Tenneson, the author Anthony Vanderlinden, FNMI President Jean-Louis Vanderstraeten and FNMI Vice-President and former Winchester Vice-President Ralph Young. The boardroom was transformed into a museum display room in 2007 to include select guns from the Winchester factory collection.

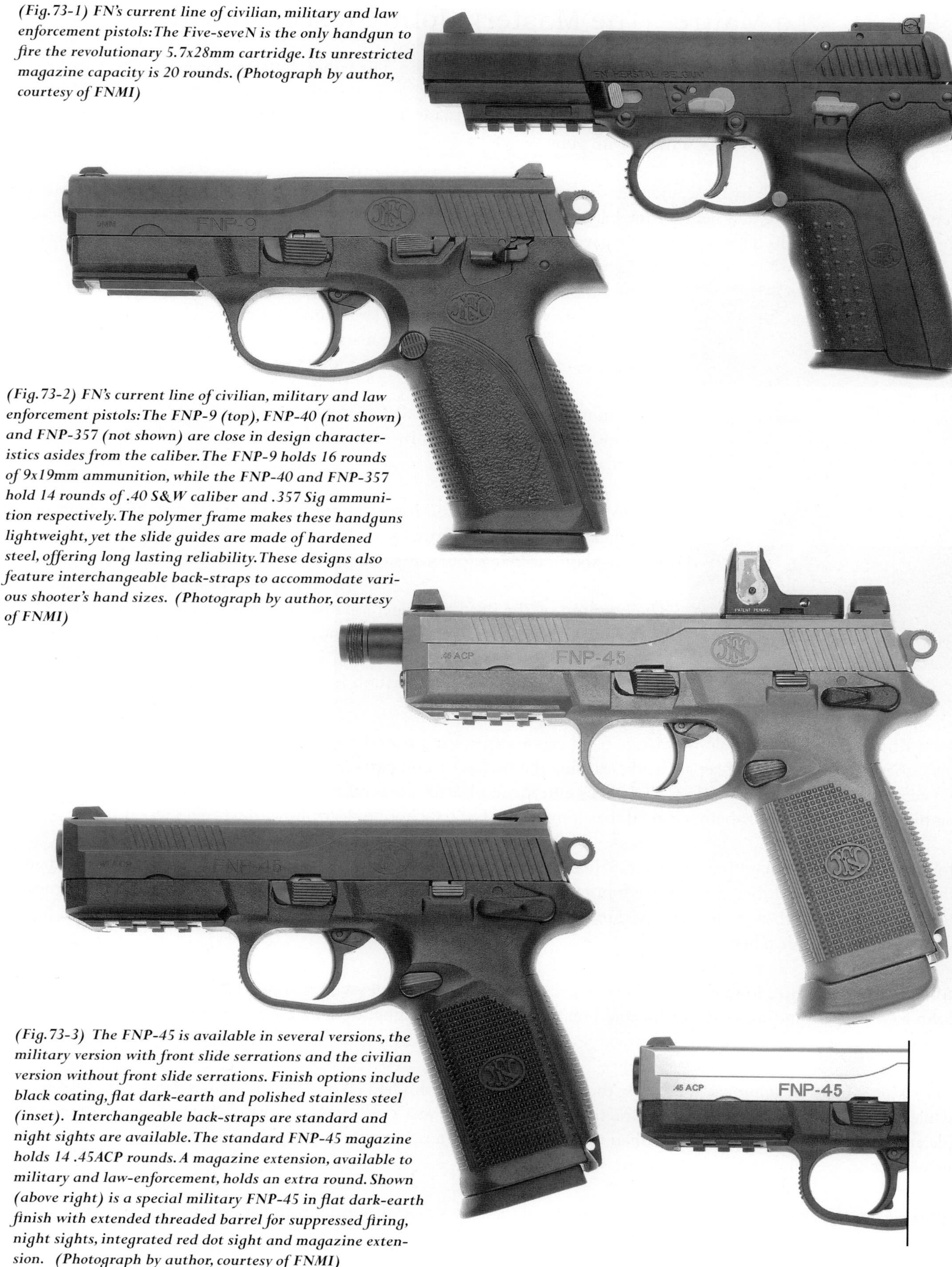

(Fig.73-1) FN's current line of civilian, military and law enforcement pistols: The Five-seveN is the only handgun to fire the revolutionary 5.7x28mm cartridge. Its unrestricted magazine capacity is 20 rounds. (Photograph by author, courtesy of FNMI)

(Fig.73-2) FN's current line of civilian, military and law enforcement pistols: The FNP-9 (top), FNP-40 (not shown) and FNP-357 (not shown) are close in design characteristics asides from the caliber. The FNP-9 holds 16 rounds of 9x19mm ammunition, while the FNP-40 and FNP-357 hold 14 rounds of .40 S&W caliber and .357 Sig ammunition respectively. The polymer frame makes these handguns lightweight, yet the slide guides are made of hardened steel, offering long lasting reliability. These designs also feature interchangeable back-straps to accommodate various shooter's hand sizes. (Photograph by author, courtesy of FNMI)

(Fig.73-3) The FNP-45 is available in several versions, the military version with front slide serrations and the civilian version without front slide serrations. Finish options include black coating, flat dark-earth and polished stainless steel (inset). Interchangeable back-straps are standard and night sights are available. The standard FNP-45 magazine holds 14 .45ACP rounds. A magazine extension, available to military and law-enforcement, holds an extra round. Shown (above right) is a special military FNP-45 in flat dark-earth finish with extended threaded barrel for suppressed firing, night sights, integrated red dot sight and magazine extension. (Photograph by author, courtesy of FNMI)

"Le Maitre" (The Master): John Moses Browning

John Moses Browning was born in Ogden, Utah on January 23, 1855. His father, Jonathan Browning, had settled in Ogden in 1852. Jonathan was originally from Illinois, but religious persecution forced him and many other Mormons on a western exodus. Jonathan left Nauvoo, Illinois in early 1846. The Mormon leader, Brigham Young, chose Jonathan to equip the Mormon wagon trains with guns.

Jonathan was a gunsmith by trade and spent most of his time repairing tools and firearms. He invented a couple of guns and improved several others for the harsh conditions of the western migration. He is best known for inventing the five-shot slider rifle. This repeater rifle gave pioneers a significant advantage, in a time when single-shot firearms were common.

(Fig.74-1) Jonathan Browning (Photograph courtesy of Browning)

The Mormon Church advocated polygamy and Jonathan was first married in Tennessee. He arrived in Ogden with a large family of eleven children. His second wife was Elizabeth Clark, whom he married two years after arriving in Ogden. She became the mother of John Moses and Matthew Sandifer Browning.

Jonathan married a third time in 1859, this time to Sarah Emmett who bore him seven more children. Jonathan Browning fathered a total of 22 children in the three marriages.

Due to age differences, John Moses did not have close ties with his siblings out of his father's first marriage. Growing up he was the oldest around the house, his brother Matthew being four years younger.

The boys out of the third marriage; Jonathan Edmund (Ed), William Wallace (Will), and George Emmett were close enough in age for close relationships to develop between them, John Moses and Matthew (Matt). These relationships were evidenced years later in the association John Moses had with his brothers in his first business venture.

John Browning's education did not derive from classroom study. From the age of six, John Moses spent his time in his father's shop doing basic repair work, learning the names of gun parts before knowing how to read or write. At seven he was working in several of his father's enterprises; learning a number of trades, including gunsmithing and tanning. His mother, Elizabeth, claimed that John only went to school to learn how to write up repair tags.

John made his first gun at the age of ten. He crudely assembled a piece of lumber, an old discarded barrel and an old flintlock mechanism. John and Matt went hunting with their flimsy rifle and with much luck, brought home a meal. Jonathan ate the catch over breakfast and took a look at the crude rifle. He was not impressed and questioned John why he had not made a better one.

About three years later John got an old broken shotgun from a customer who had purchased a reconditioned gun. John took it apart and realized that he could make all the parts. Jonathan watched him repair the gun and gave him a precious new piece of walnut for the stock.

John Moses finished school at age 15. By the age of 23 (1878) John had taken over the role of gunsmith. One day while John was repairing a rifle he remarked upon how badly it was made and how the design was unnecessarily complicated. He then commented to Jonathan that he could make a better rifle. Jonathan encouraged him and said that he would like to see John make his first gun.

John became absorbed by the project. He completed the new single-shot rifle from concept to finish in what is believed to be less than one year.

(Fig.75-1) John Moses Browning at the age of 18 (Photograph courtesy of Browning)

There were some difficulties in getting a patent for the new rifle. Nobody in Ogden knew how to obtain a patent. Matt and John decided to write a parts supplier. The company, Schoverling, Daly and Gales, replied and mailed them information on a patent attorney.

Just before he applied for this first patent, John married Rachel Teresa Child on April 10, 1879. The first years of their marriage were quite difficult. John was building a new shop, which strained his financial situation. That same year, his father, Jonathan, died at the age of 74. Jonathan claimed that one of the greatest pleasures of his life was when he first fired John Moses' single-shot rifle.

John Browning's patent for the single-shot was filed May 12, 1879. The patent gun was marked "J.M. Browning Ogden 1878". In 1878 John Browning invented a second variation of his single-shot rifle, but no production of that model ever took place.

John became head of the two families after his father's death, and he employed his brothers in the gun shop.

He was continually investigating new ways to earn money. He did not modernize his shop but made some arrangements with freighters to bring him guns for repair. As a result, his reputation penetrated to the most remote areas of the country. He turned out repairs as fast as he could.

(Fig.75-2) Rachel Teresa Child (Photograph courtesy of Browning)

Browning also placed a couple of signs around town to increase business. John Browning was fortunate to be a young entrepreneur at the right time and in the right place. The transcontinental railroad had joined near Ogden in 1869, making Ogden an important Union Pacific railroad connection between Omaha and California. The Browning Brothers' business boomed, but John was still not sure what to do with his patent. He felt uncomfortable selling the patent. Instead he started thinking about manufacturing the gun. John hired his half brother, Ed, and was thinking about building a small factory. The new facility was built literally debt free, using leftover bricks from one of Jonathan's business ventures. The land and tools were purchased from savings or from current income in the shop. A small damaged steam engine was purchased from the railroad freight yard, repaired and used to operate machinery for many years.

The factory was completed with the help of his brothers. John started training his brothers to manufacture the patented single-shot. The training proved educational for all concerned; shortcuts were discovered, and time and materials were saved in the process. John Moses always stayed proactive and anticipated the production needs. Barrels and forgings were ordered ahead of time.

A new sign was hung, with the announcement "New Browning Gun Shop". The fascination with the patent attracted a great deal of attention. The brothers were soon taking advance orders for the rifles. While the move to the new factory happened in only a couple of days, setting up the old and new machinery seemed to be a more difficult task. Fortuitously, Frank Rushton, an English gunsmith, happened to walk in that day. Frank Rushton had joined the Mormon Church in England and had recently moved to Ogden. He had walked in to offer assistance. After inspecting the machinery he concluded that the place would be set up and running in a few days. That evening Rushton was hired, his experience was quite valuable to the young enterprise.

John decided that an initial production goal of 25 single-shot rifles would be an impressive feat. Ed did the majority of the milling work, Matt made the stocks, and Sam and George worked on some of the smaller manufacturing tasks. John and Frank Rushton did the majority of the finishing and assembly. The production of the single-shot was going on concurrently with the repair work necessary to pay for salaries.

It took the crew only three months to manufacture the 25 rifles; the rifles were impressively displayed on the gun-rack. Matt slept in the shop at night, guarding the new rifles. Although John always appeared calm and confident, in reality he was often worried about his business. The new rifles meant either success or failure for the team. All rifles sold in a matter of a single week and John Browning had several hundred dollars in the bank. He gave his employees and his wife Rachel a five dollar gold piece as a reward. It is in these first years that a lifelong partnership developed between John and his brother Matt. In those years Matt established himself as the company's business manager while John evolved as the inventor.

(Fig.76-1) The Browning Brothers factory around 1882. From left to right: Sam Browning, George Browning, John M. Browning, Matthew S. Browning, Ed Browning and Frank Rushton. All members of the staff are holding a single-shot rifle, only two of these rifles were finished however, the others were pulled from production for this photograph. Note the spelling of the word "ammunition" also note the height of Frank Rushton compared to the Browning Brothers. This image includes the whole facade of the building, including the Browning Bros. sign depicting the single-shot. (Photograph courtesy of Browning)

Matt had longed for a sporting goods line but John had put it off while prioritizing the production of the rifle. Now that John had savings, he let Matt put in his first line of sporting goods. The shop was now a store and sales complemented the repair orders. John worried however that too much time was consumed in unprofitable sales talk.

There were enough materials left to make an additional 75 guns after the initial 25 were produced, and Matt placed a new order for 100 barrels. Matt's sporting goods dream was halted when the store was robbed and nothing was left on the shelves. John refused to replace the merchandise; he wanted everybody back at work as rifle orders were falling behind.

The shop never had more than a dozen finished rifles on the racks; days were filled with the manufacture of the single-shot and the incoming repair work. John Browning had little time for inventing but still managed to file for a patent on a new tubular magazine repeater rifle in 1882.

The application for this new patent was filed on March 20, 1882. By this time John had lost interest in the project and was busy inventing another design. The patent was filed on September 13, 1882. We must conclude that he designed and fabricated a completely new rifle in less than six months. This new model had a lever action and a tubular magazine. So few parts were involved that it may have been intended for manufacture in the shop.

John Browning eventually lost interest in the manufacturing part of the business. He was fascinated with inventing, but as soon as a model was designed, he lost interest and started working on an improved or total new design.

Early in 1883, the turning point came for the Browning Brothers. Andrew McAusland, a sales representative for Winchester, came across one of the Browning single-shot rifles (rifle N° 463). Mr. McAusland purchased the well-used rifle and mailed it to Winchester for evaluation, as it was a new and unseen design. The name and address on the rifle " Browning Bros. Ogden, Utah U.S.A." made it easy for Winchester to find the maker.

(Fig.77-1) The clear markings on the Single-Shot rifle made it easy for Winchester to find the inventor. (Photograph courtesy of Browning)

Mr. T.G. Bennett, vice-president and general manager of Winchester, left within a week for Ogden. He took with him the approval of Winchester's board of directors to buy the patent. Bennett was well aware of the sales potential this design had for Winchester. The Browning single-shot was adaptable to many calibers, including cartridge sizes Winchester was lacking in its product line. Mr. Bennett was quite surprised when he walked in the Browning shop. He was even more surprised when he met the young Browning brothers who made the best single-shot he had ever seen. The negotiations were easy, Bennett wanted the rifle and John Browning wanted out of manufacturing. John Browning preferred inventing and envisioned his brothers working on new designs instead of manufacturing old ones.

Without much thought, John asked Bennett for 10,000 dollars while telling him about a new design he had in mind. They settled on eight thousand. The alliance between John Browning and the Winchester Company would last nineteen years and revolutionize firearm manufacturing. No contract was ever set up by an attorney between the two parties. T.G. Bennett left Ogden that same day for New Haven. The brothers were happy, the store would be partially transformed into a sporting goods store, and repairs would still be performed.

There were plenty of materials left to make single-shots, and back-orders were accumulating. Winchester's payment arrived on time, but the brothers kept making rifles until Bennett intervened. John admitted later on in life, to his embarrassment, that he did not realize that they had to cease production after selling the patent.

John went back to inventing and continued working on the tubular magazine repeater. His new design was made for large cartridges and he filed the patent application in May 1884. The patent was issued by October, John and Matt were now ready for their first trip east to Winchester. The model John carried would become the successful Winchester model 1886. This was the first of many trips for John Browning and his brother. The world was opening up for the inventor.

As John Browning grew older he designed gun after gun. His revolutionary designs began to conquer the world of firearms. The idea of an automatic firearm came to John Browning at the Ogden gun club in 1889 as he was watching a friend shoot. He noticed that gasses from the muzzle were moving clover ten feet ahead. Harvesting this energy could mean a totally self-functioning gun. A simple experiment with an old Model 1873 rifle back at the shop proved John's theory. At that time John told his brother Matt that they were maybe ten years away from making a machine gun. The idea was immediately conceptualized, improved and John Browning patented his first gas operated mechanism on January 6, 1890. Several additional patents were filed in the following five years. From the concept of a machine gun he evolved to the idea of an automatic pistol. The first automatic pistol patent was filed on September 14, 1895. Three more patents followed on October 31, 1896, all three revealing revolutionary mechanisms.

Matt had written the Colt's Patent Firearms Manufacturing Company as early as 1890. He informed Colt about their invention and also inquired about their interests in an automatic machine gun. John was not happy with the fact that the letter insinuated that they had a finished gun. He called the device they had at the time "a crude first step." John soon concluded that this gun could only have a military purpose. He soon lost interest in his machine gun designs and went back to his favorite; sporting arms. John worked on a repeating shotgun for Winchester and was soon to bring it to Bennett.

Before the trip John asked Matt to write Colt inquiring if they were interested in a demonstration of their machine gun. Colt manufactured the Gatling gun and had experience with government contracts. John and Matt were still not sure if Colt knew who they were. A cordial response came from Colt indicating that they were only acquainted with the Gatling gun and that the Gatling sales left a lot to be desired; most being sold abroad. The letter complemented the inventor on the Winchester model 1886 and invited them over on their next business trip. John believed the invitation to be only a formality as the shop was selling quite a few Colt revolvers. He was enthusiastic however about learning more about machine guns, little suspecting that he would teach Colt. The Brownings arrived at Colt early in 1891 and John was somewhat uncomfortable with his unfinished gun. Colt's staff witnessed the gun firing 200 rounds without mishaps and soon looked beyond the crude finish of the gun. The brothers were invited to stay a couple of days for further talks. In their discussions they agreed that the machine gun market had to be cultivated and that this would take time. The staff at Colt was surprised that the brothers had never seen a Gatling gun.

A letter from Colt arrived several months later; it described the interest of some naval officers in an unofficial demonstration. The requirement was set that the gun had to fire for three minutes continuously, it had to fire 1800 rounds without the barrel melting down. John had the ammunition belts made by a tent-maker under his supervision. Ed and Matt inserted the cartridges into the canvas belts. John Browning made the trip by himself. He wanted to minimize the attendance just in case anything went wrong. The whole preparation and the actual firing of the gun filled John Browning with uncertainty; no firearm had ever taken such a pounding. The demonstration ended with a red barrel and 1800 rounds fired without stoppage.

No contract was signed between John Browning and Colt at that time, both knew that sales of machine guns were years ahead. John promised Colt first chance at an improved model of his machine gun. and he had the model ready within a year while still inventing guns for Winchester.

The machine gun later became the Colt 1895 Automatic Machine gun. John insisted that Colt put its name on the gun, as this would look better with the military. John however conducted the trials himself. The Navy first tested the machine gun in 1893, and all tests were finalized by January 1896. The final trials included[1] an improved Gatling model firing a 6mm smokeless cartridge, the 1895 Colt Machine Gun, the Maxim machine gun and a French Hotchkiss. The Colt 1895 was selected and an initial order of 50 was placed in 1896[2], making this the first automatic machine gun to be accepted by the U.S. military. The 1895 model saw action in the Boxer uprising and in the Spanish American War, where it was nicknamed the "Peacemaker". This model was the first of many Browning models to be used by the U.S. military. From that moment, to the end of the Korean War, all machine guns used by the U.S. military were Browning designs.

In 1894 John began working on his first automatic pistol. He completed the .38 caliber gas operated pistol in 1895. Later, John introduced the pistol to Colt and the pistol was test-fired in Hartford on July 3, 1895. A contract was signed a year later (July 24, 1896). The contract gave Colt the rights to manufacture four of the Browning pistol patents. John Browning had invented three of these prior to the contract's signing.

Colt deferred from producing any of the pistols in the first years, probably to continue their strong revolver sales. In 1897 John Browning made another trip to Hartford Connecticut and met Hart Berg.

Mr. Berg was a director of Fabrique Nationale d'Armes de Guerre. He was originally from Hartford but living in Belgium at the time. Mr. Berg was in Connecticut to learn more about advances in the manufacture of bicycles, which was a new product line for FN (see page 9).

Hart Berg and John Browning got along immediately. John had brought his latest invention; a small .32 caliber pistol that he personally favored. After hearing about the struggles of the FN company, John decided to hand Berg the pistol to take back to Belgium. It is not clear if Colt ever saw the pistol or if Colt had refused to buy it, but the pistol left for Belgium. The pistol shot 500 rounds without any failures.

(Fig.79-1) The Browning Brothers sold the Browning designs extensively in their stores. Shown left is a turn of the century ad for the Colt Model 1900 pistol. John Browning fancied his small .32 caliber pistol and illustrated the FN Model 1899 in the Browning Brothers catalog (seen right is an extract of the 1904 inside cover). Although excluded from distribution in the U.S. by agreement, FN shipping records indicate that several Model 1900 pistols were shipped to the Browning Brothers. It appears that the Browning Brothers would indeed give these or sell these to persistent customers.

The Fabrique Nationale engineers were as enthusiastic about the pistol as Colt had been a few years earlier about the machine gun. A contract for production was signed at FN on July 17, 1897 and was sent to the Browning Brothers. They acknowledged receipt and payment on July 26, 1897[(3)]. In January Hart Berg was sent to Ogden to convince John Browning to supervise production of the new pistol. He failed to convince John Browning to go to Belgium but left Ogden with many manufacturing tips and details.

During the ensuing year FN geared up for production and produced prototypes. The first production pistols appeared in January 1899. FN's success with the first Browning pistol forced Colt to produce the Colt 1900 pistol.

John Browning left for his first European voyage in 1902[(4)]. It was the end of almost 20 years of cooperation between the Browning Brothers and Winchester. Winchester had turned down his automatic shotgun offer and by mere coincidence Marcellus Hartly of Remington died while John was waiting to meet him.

John was not acquainted with world travel. On his first trip to Belgium he decided to visit Paris first, where he visited a tailor and got more acquainted with European customs. He arrived in Liège on a rainy day in February. His visit was unannounced. This time he carried with him his famous automatic shotgun and his customary uncertainty.

John was not quite ready for the reception he got at FN. Somewhat shy; he was surprised at the enthusiastic welcome he received. Most likely he was unaware what the pistol had done for the company and the Liège region. John saw for the first time FN's manufacturing halls filled with workers and machines turning out his pistol. The shotgun was received with much enthusiasm.

---

(1) John M. Browning, American Gunmaker by John Browning, Curt Gentry
(2) The Browning Machine Gun, Volume I by Dolf Goldsmith
(3) Note the short transit duration from Herstal Belgium to Ogden Utah in 1897. It took only nine days for the actual documents to travel this typical route: From Liège to Brussels by rail, from Brussels to the Belgian coast or Calais by rail, from the coastline to Dover by steamer, from Dover to Liverpool by rail, from Liverpool to New York by transcontinental liner. From New York to St. Louis on to Omaha and finally Utah.
(4) It is generally accepted that John Browning made his first trip to Belgium in 1902 with his Auto-5 shotgun design, although it should be noted that there are indications that his first trip may have been earlier.

(Fig.80-1) Left: Matthew S. Browning in later life
Right: John M. Browning at the age of 65
Center: The Order of Leopold bestowed on John M. Browning at FN in 1914 (see page 17).
(Photographs courtesy of Browning)

John had an interpreter assigned to him while at FN, the difficulty of translating technical language soon forced him to learn French. By the time he left FN, he knew every part of his shotgun and pistol in French.

John had no problem getting along with the FN employees and the workmen; after all he was a gunsmith among gunsmiths.

During his three-month stay in Liège John Browning became well known by the local residents, his height and appearance stood out and the American drew a great deal of attention.

In 1907 John Browning granted FN the exclusive right to use his name as a trademark (see page 12).

Travel became so regular that from 1902 on, John Browning spent a year and a half of his remaining life on ocean liners, traveling back and forth to Belgium. He made a total of 61 trips to FN. From the turn of the century to his death, John Browning worked on at least two designs simultaneously. From 1900 on he primarily worked with FN and Colt. John Browning was the father of most small arms in use today; either the operating systems or the guns themselves are still in widespread use. He invented the pistol slide and pioneered many automatic firing systems. He introduced countless different mechanisms, many of which got lost in time with some of his handmade prototypes. Besides the guns and the countless mechanisms, John Browning helped design the 6.35mm (.25ACP), 7.65mm (.32ACP), 9mm (.380ACP) and .45ACP cartridges.(1)

In 1926 John embarked on his 61st trip to Belgium. This time his wife Rachel accompanied him for the first time. John and Rachel spent Thanksgiving in Liège in the company of their son Val and his family. The following day John and Val went to the factory. John joined Val in his office, he complained of chest pains. John M. Browning died of heart failure soon after the company physician was summoned.

(Fig.80-2) This bronze plaque was erected by FN in remembrance of John Browning. Note the inclusion of FN's first pistol and the Auto-5 shotgun.

(1) The ACP designation stands for "Automatic Colt Pistol". This designation became common in the U.S. after Colt introduced the Browning pistols.
Auhor's note: This chapter provides a brief overview of the life of John Moses Browning and some of his dealings with FN. For a complete and detailed biography, please see the book "John M. Browning, American Gunmaker" by John Browning and Curt Gentry.

(Fig.81-1) The new Browning Brothers store, the first floor was the sales floor while the second floor (below) was John Browning's workshop. This building still stands today on Wall Avenue in Ogden, Utah. The workshop flooring still shows markings of where John Browning's workbench was located. Currently the façade still shows where the Browning Brothers letters once stood. (Photographs courtesy of Browning)

A Genius in the Shadows; Dieudonné Saive

Dieudonné Saive's work is often overlooked as a result of FN's use of the Browning trademark. Mr. Saive was a skilled engineer who worked relentlessly at both improving existing FN firearms and his own, original designs.

(Fig.82-1) Mr. Dieudonné Saive (Photograph courtesy of Collector Grade Publications Inc.)

Dieudonné Joseph Saive was born in Wandre, Belgium on May 23, 1888. After graduating from Liège's Higher Education Industrial School and Professional School of Mechanics in 1906, Saive began working as a toolmaker in FN's mechanical workshops. During World War I, Saive escaped the occupying German forces and left for England. There he worked as a machinist at the Vickers machine-gun company, calibrating machinery.

Saive returned to Belgium in 1919 and resumed his employment with FN, working in the Cartoucherie (munitions department). In 1920 he moved to the Firearms Technical Office, where he was responsible for designing tools and small gun parts. In 1922 Saive was transferred to the gun manufacturing department, where, by 1924, he was entrusted with supervising assembly and factory proofing. Less than two years later, Saive became John Browning's assistant and manager of FN's small arms production.

The project that was to immortalize Dieudonné Saive began when Saive modified a Model 1903 pistol to accept a 15-round staggered magazine. The effort resulted from a French request for a high capacity service pistol.

The pistol and magazine were shipped to John Browning and two prototypes were returned; known as the Model of 1922 (see page 261). Simplification and numerous modifications of these prototypes would result in the creation of first the Grand Rendement (High Efficiency) and ultimately the Grande Puissance (High Power) pistols. The famous High Power pistol should be more accurately recognized as a Saive, rather than a Browning, design.

After the death of John Browning in 1926, Dieudonné Saive was promoted to chief arms designer. Around 1927, he designed a new pocket pistol in 6.35 caliber, later known as the Baby Browning. In 1928 he traveled to Yugoslavia(1) and helped to establish the Kragujevac arsenal. In 1929 he was again promoted, and made responsible for the production of the new FN Browning Automatic Rifle (BAR). In 1930 he became FN's general production manager for military firearms. In 1932 he left the production floor to focus on new product development. Among his accomplishments in this role were the introduction and beginning of mass production in 1935 of the High Power pistol and improvements in the Browning Automatic Rifle including a rate reducer and modifications to allow for interchangeable barrels.

Mr. Saive refused to cooperate with the Germans during World War II and briefly worked on FN commercial projects away from the German presence. He escaped to England in 1941 together with Messrs. Joassart, Laloux, Vogels and Dufrasne. This time, Saive was no longer a simple machinist but carried with him the secret plans for an advanced self-loading rifle(2).

The self-loading project had been hidden from the Germans. Once in England, Mr. Saive worked under the British Armament Design Establishment (ADE). During this time, Saive constructed no fewer than 50 different prototypes of the self-loading rifle, which, at the time was of great interest to the British.

In England, Saive worked on a number of projects, including the development of his self-loading rifle, the Oerlikon Automatic 20mm cannon and on plans for the production of the High Power pistol. The self-loading rifle would become the EXP-1, the forerunner of the SAFN (FN-49) rifle.

As the war progressed the need for armament continued, the Canadian request for the High Power pistol, opened the opportunity to direct the future of the High Power production away from England. The British had shown little interest in honoring FN's ownership and manufacturing rights of the pistol.

The Canadian contract and manufacturing rights for the High Power pistol were negotiated by Mr. Joassart. This contract protected FN's ownership rights while permitting the Allies to manufacture necessary weapons.

Mr. Joassart made arrangements for Mr. Saive to travel to Toronto and assist in the preparations for High Power production. The British reluctantly released Mr. Saive for two months while parts were being manufactured for the EXP-1 rifle. The British were reluctant to release Mr. Saive as they had discovered the high quality of his work. Mr. Saive arrived in Toronto on December 27, 1943.

After FN was liberated, Mr. Saive became one of the first Allied weapons designers to inspect and examine the new German intermediate round (7.92mm Kurz). Immediately after the war, Mr. Saive developed an automatic rifle chambered for this round. The self-loading rifle itself was reworked to work with several calibers. The SAFN became the inspiration for the famous Fusil Automatique Léger (FAL).

The High Power pistol continued to evolve under Saive's supervision and both double action and lightweight versions were developed. The double action model of 1952 never went into production, but the lightweight, alloy framed, High Power was marketed several years later.

Dieudonne Saive retired from FN on November 30, 1954, passing away on October 12, 1970.

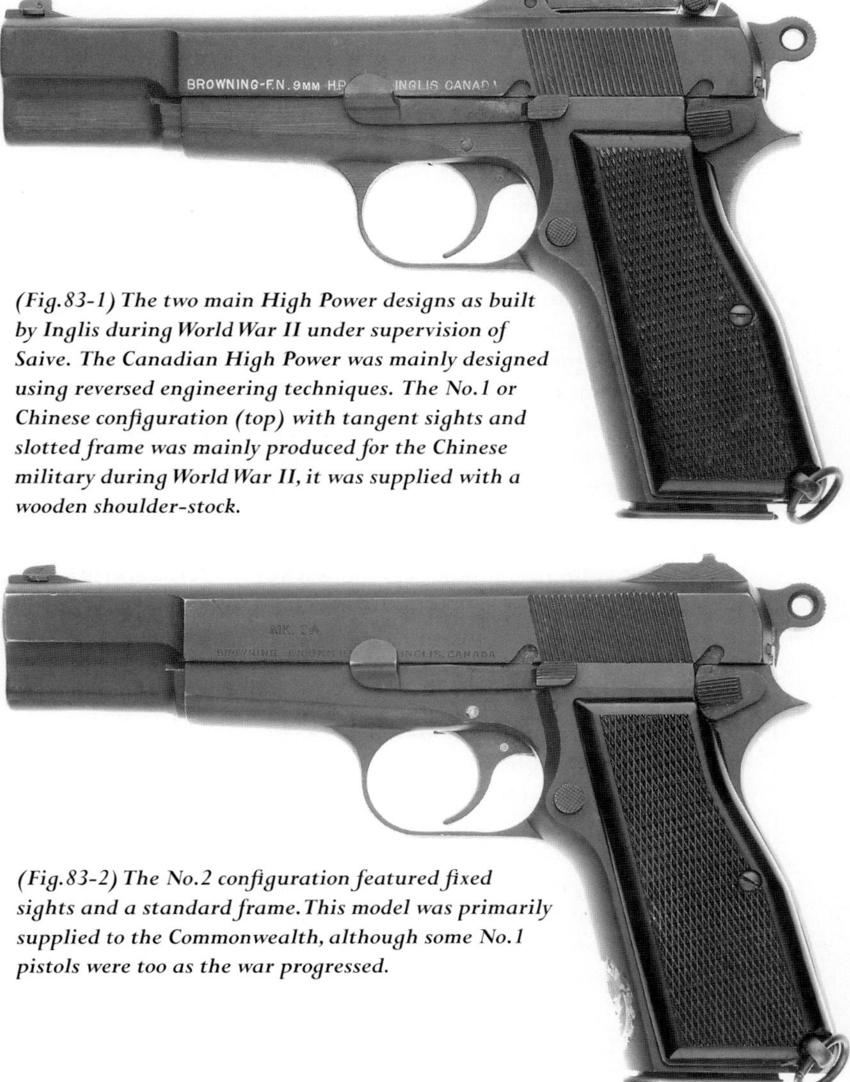

(Fig.83-1) The two main High Power designs as built by Inglis during World War II under supervision of Saive. The Canadian High Power was mainly designed using reversed engineering techniques. The No.1 or Chinese configuration (top) with tangent sights and slotted frame was mainly produced for the Chinese military during World War II, it was supplied with a wooden shoulder-stock.

(Fig.83-2) The No.2 configuration featured fixed sights and a standard frame.This model was primarily supplied to the Commonwealth, although some No.1 pistols were too as the war progressed.

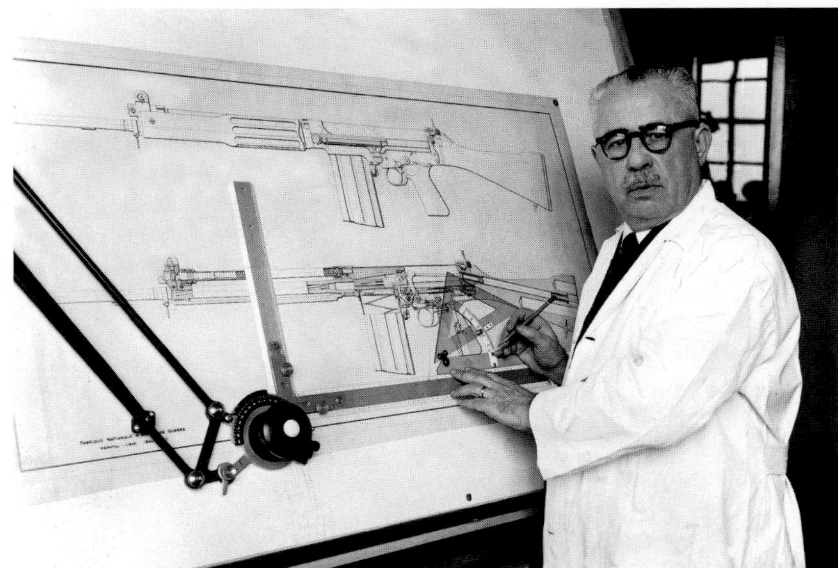

(Fig.83-3) Mr. Dieudonné Saive in front of his drawings of the world famous FAL rifle. (Photograph courtesy of FN Herstal)

(1) Then known as the Kingdom of Serbs, Croats and Slovenes

(2) FN-49 The Last Elegant Old World Military Rifle by Wayne Johnson

Some of Dieudonné Saive's Accomplishments

Following is a chronological list of some of Mr. Saive's accomplishments

1920: Modification and improvement on Mordant style ejectors.
1921: Half block FN barrels
1922: Modification of the FN Browning 1903 pistol magazine to a staggered, double stacked configuration. Shipped to John Browning in order to develop a new military pistol on French request.
1927: Early development of the Baby Browning pistol (production started in 1931).
1927-1933: Development of the Grand Rendement (High Efficiency) pistol.
1929: Modification to the Browning BAR automatic rifle to accept a firing rate reducer.
1930: Development of mounting systems for Belgian military machine guns.
1932-1934: Development of three military semi-automatic infantry rifles (short recoil).
1932: Development of an automatic firing rate reducer for Browning machine guns (various calibers for fighter planes).
1934: Development of a 9mm sub-machine gun for the Belgian military (see fig.84-1).
1934: Development of 7.65mm Long pistols for French trials.
1934/1936: Development of synchronized firing device for machine guns on fighter planes.
1935: Development of an automatic firing rate reducer for Browning machine guns (12.7 mm) for fighter planes.
1935: Modification to the Browning BAR automatic rifle to accept interchangeable barrels. The production model was known as the BAR-D ("D" for "Démontable" or removable).
1935: Development of interchangeable barrels for heavy machine guns.
1935-1936: Development of mounting systems for the Dutch East Indies .50 Cal. Browning machine guns.
1936: Development of a military semi-automatic infantry rifle (gas operated).
1936: Development of mounting systems for the Belgian military Browning machine guns.
1939: Development of a geared mounting system for the Belgian military .50 Cal. Browning machine guns.
1941: Development of the Browning Double Automatic shotgun.
1943: Development of a triple mounting system for the Oerlikon automatic cannon.
1943: Further Development of continuous feed system for the 20mm Oerlikon cannon.
1945-1948: Final development of the gas-operated infantry rifle (FN-49).
1947-1954: Development of the Light Automatic Rifle (FAL).
1950: Development of two 9mm sub-machine gun models.
1951: Development of new mounting systems for the Belgian military machine guns.
1952: Development of double-action and lightweight versions of the High Power pistol.

(Fig.84-1) The quest of the Belgian military to adopt a sub-machine gun led Saive to develop this 9mm design in 1934. It was made available with 20 and 30-round magazines. The FN model was never produced as the Belgian military purchased Pieper machineguns instead. Built under license, the Pieper guns were based on the German MP.28.

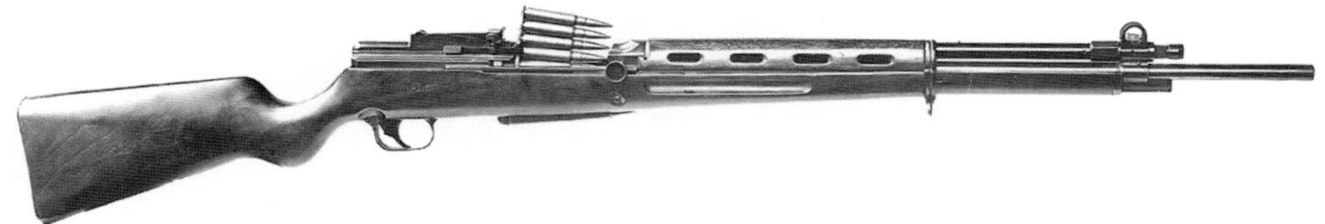

(Fig.84-2) Saive's 1937 gas operated self-loading rifle prototype shares a lot of similarities with the later production FN-49 rifles. (Photograph courtesy of FN Herstal)

Proofs and Markings

A) FN Factory Manufacturing Markings

It is important for a collector to distinguish the five types of markings found on a pistol.
This section deals with part A

A: FN applied manufacturing markings
B: Liège proofs
C: World War II applied markings (when applicable)
D: Government or Military acceptance markings (when applicable)
E: Foreign proofs applied as import markings (when applicable)

As mentioned in section B, parts and finished pistols were submitted to the Liège proof-house. The factory was invoiced for all proofing. Manufacturers immediately instilled their own quality checks in order to avoid paying for firearms that would fail to meet proof-house standards.

FN applied a number of small markings as part of their own quality control. These markings (can) indicate the following:
- Which operator manufactured the part
- Which inspector inspected the part
- If a part was rejected
- When a part was made
- FN final inspection

FN's Pre-World War II Final Inspection Markings

Most of pre-World War II FN firearms were stamped with FN's final inspection stamp. This is the stamp of the head of FN's quality control. This stamp is important to collectors as it helps date a pistol.

V (square) 1899-1914: This is FN's second[1] final quality control stamp and is a valuable aid at identifying pre-World War I production pieces.

V (round) 1919 - early 1930s: This is FN's third final quality control stamp and denotes manufacture in the interbellum years. It should be noted that this marking was introduced in 1912 and also appears on firearms made between 1912 and 1914, during those years however the marking was accompanied by the V square marking listed above.

A (square) early 1930s – 1940: This is FN's fourth and final prewar quality control stamp.

FN's Post World War II Production Date Markings

FN did not adhere to any final inspection markings or date codes during the 1944 and 1945 assembly of wartime parts. Those pistols are identifiable by the "A" prefix in their serial number. Once FN started producing entire guns from raw materials in 1946, the company was able to control quality throughout. Instead of reverting to a final inspection marking as was customary in the prewar era. FN introduced a final date code. These code markings were applied to most major parts once they passed quality control. Collectors should use these markings to identify when a part was produced and not necessarily a pistol. Pistols were often assembled from a mixture of completed parts and display several date codes on their parts. As a guide the later date codes on select parts are usually an indicator of when a pistol was assembled. As production was still gearing up, 1946 was the only year where the same code marking was used throughout the entire year (a square box with the digit "6"). Starting in 1947, FN changed the code marking by altering the shape around the digit. Each variation indicates the quarter (trimester) of the year in which a part was manufactured. Collectors have often assumed that the marking was just struck lightly on one side, instead these slight variations were intentionally made to identify the year and quarter of production.

---

(1) The first marking is not illustrated as it predates pistol manufacturing

Tableau des différentes empreintes trimestrielles, telles qu'elles doivent être visibles sur les pièces d'armes depuis 1946.

Année	1er trim.	2e trim.	3e trim.	4e trim.	
1946	[6]	[6]	[6]	[6]	
1947	[7]	7	7	7	
1948	8	8	8	8	
1949	9	9	9	9	1er et 2e trim. la queue du 9 se termine par une virgule renversée le 2e trim. le cadre est spécial.
1950	0	0.	0	0	le zéro est accompagné d'un point dans le coin intérieur gauche ou 4e trim. la barrette droite enlevée.
1951	1	1	1	1	
1952	2	2	2	2	
1953	3	3	3	3	
1954	4	4	4	4	
1955	5	5	5	5	
1956	6	6	6	6	
1957	7	7	7	7	Sans barette sur la queue du 7.
1958	8	8	8	8	L'anneau supérieur > que l'inférieur.
1959	9	9	9	9	Pour le 3e et 4e trim. les chiffres sont cubique.
1960	0	0	0	0	1er et 2e trim. le zéro est rectangulaire avec petits rayons de coins. 3e et 4e trim. le zéro est de forme trapézoïdale avec petits rayons de [illegible]
1961	I	I	I	I	1e et 2e trim. barette inférieure double de la barette supérieure. 3e et 4e trim. le bout du chiffre vient en contact avec le cadre
1962	S	S	2	2	chiffre renversé latéralement 1e et 2e trimestre.
1963	ε	ε	ε	ε	" "
1964	4	4	4	4	" " "
1965	2	2 2	2	2	" " (voir note 1904)
1966	a	a	a	a	" "
1967	5	5	5	5	" "

Prévisions pour la prochaine décade 1968-1977

Année	1er trim.	2e trim.	3e trim.	4e trim.	
1968	◇8	◇8	<8	/8	
1969	◇9	◇9	<9	/9	
1970	◇0	◇0	<0	/0	"0" ovalisé au maxi.
1971	◇1	◇1	<1	/1	
1972	◇2	◇2	<2	/2	
1973	◇3	◇3	<3	/3	
1974	◇4	◇4	<4	/4	
1975	◇5	◇5	<5	/5	
1976	◇6	◇6	<6	/6	
1977	◇7	◇7	<7	/7	

(Fig.86-1) FN document[1] showing date codes as applied to parts. Notes:
1949: First and second trimester, the leg of the letter nine resembles a comma
1958: The digit "8" is upside down
1959: Third and fourth trimester: The digit "9" is square
1962: First and second trimester: The digit "2" is in mirror image

(1)The author has opted not to divulge the code markings for the last 30 years as those are modern and have little collector interest.

The complexity of FN's internal factory proofing

Any advanced collector or connoisseur of FN firearms will agree that FN products are the best built in the world. This quality reputation not only comes from the vigorous Liège proof-house testing but originates with FN's strict standards and quality control.

The elaborate system employed at FN to test and proof a part at the factory is overly complex and elaborate. The author has therefore opted to only highlight some of the main quality control aspects. Each department has its own internal quality control and checks.

This overlook only reviews the proofing and checks of pistol parts manufacture:

Each machine operator is responsible to do some simple cursory inspections of the parts they manufacture. These basic machinists' inspections are to take place during manufacturing as well as during any down time when the machine is not operating.

Each department and manufacturing hall has their réviseurs and réviseuses (male and female revisors or inspectors). The inspectors work at the manufacturing machines as well as at inspection tables.

Typically only a few samples are reviewed at the manufacturing machine to check that the machine and machine operator are working within the set tolerances.

Each machined part is moved to an inspection table where inspectors perform two types of checks. A visual inspection of the part followed by a tolerance inspection using gauges.

If a part fails inspection, it is classified under one of three types of rejects:

1) Part with critical fault: This part can cause danger or malfunction and will be discarded.
2) Part with serious fault: This part will shorten the lifespan of the weapon but the problem can be corrected in assembly or by further work on the part.
3) Part with minor fault: The part's critical areas are in spec but a non-critical aspect of the part falls out of specifications. The defect will not hinder or impact the operation of the gun. As an example, the hammer of a pistol falls in the set dimensional specifications but the hammer itself is too wide. The width of the hammer will not affect the gun's operation or service life.

The inspectors at the inspection tables are under the careful supervision of a "chef de table" or table master. The table master of each table and all the inspectors of a department fall under the management of a "réviseur principal" or the department's principal inspector. Department principal inspectors in their turn report to the "contremaitre de révision" or general inspection overseer. This general overseer or inspector is the person responsible for communication between manufacturing, technical labs and assembly lines.

(Fig.87-1) A High Power frame is checked to see if it falls within acceptable production tolerances. (Photograph FN Revue)

B: The Liège Proof-House and its Proof Markings

It is important for a collector to distinguish the five types of markings found on a pistol.
This section deals with part B

- A: FN applied manufacturing markings
- B: Liège proofs
- C: WWII applied markings (when applicable)
- D: Government or Military acceptance markings (when applicable)
- E: Foreign proofs applied as import markings (when applicable)

Belgian firearms have been proofed since the 15th century. The legislative basis for the Belgian proof house is the May 10, 1672 decree of Prince-Bishop Maximilian of Bavaria. Under this decree, all barrels were to be tested, and once approved, would be marked indicating that the barrel met or exceeded the established standards.

Complaints about a batch of low quality barrels prompted requests for official testing and proofing. There was a concern in the gun trade that Liège would acquire a poor reputation regarding the quality of its firearms. To maintain the Liège reputation, manufacturers agreed with proofing in order to eliminate any substandard barrels from getting into the stream of commerce. Over time Belgian proofs became assets for dealers and manufacturers as the proofs indicated quality and safety.

The definitive or final proof mark used in the 16th and 17th century is called "Le Perron" or the Perron. The Perron is a monument in Liège that originated in the 14th century. It is the symbol of the city of Liège and is found on the city coat of arms. During the Middle Ages, Liège was a self-governing and independent city. As a result, the Perron symbolized both freedom and the free city of Liège.

On December 14, 1810 Napoleon I decreed a specific inspection process as well as the nomination of the director of all proof-houses of the (French) Empire. Because Belgium was part of France at the time, it was under the same requirement. Although the same requirements were honored throughout the empire, each proof-house had its own unique markings.

After Napoleon's defeat, the Congress of Vienna (1814-1815) decided to erect a buffer against France and unite the Northern and Southern Netherlands including the Princedom of Liège under the rule of King Willem I of the Netherlands.

Frictions soon arose between the southern nobility and the northern government. In 1830, some of the southern provinces united and declared independence. This declaration resulted in the Belgian war of independence and the formation of a new independent state (1830-1831).

In 1836 a Belgian Royal Decree reaffirmed the need for the proof-house.

On May 24, 1888, a law was enacted that prohibited the sale, or display, of unproofed firearms. This law also required that guns made outside of Belgium be tested prior to sale in Belgium. The law had other requirements that form the basis of the current proofing process employed today.

The Belgian Royal Decree of March 1, 1891 introduced testing requirements for smokeless powder.

In 1893 the final or definitive proof was changed to the "Epreuve de Liège" (ELG or Proof of Liège). It is still used today as the official mark of acceptance referred to as the definitive or final proof mark.

In 1878 the proofing facilities were expanded and a pyrotechnics lab was installed. This lab marked the introduction of ballistic testing and also elevated the proofing to a far more scientific and measured process.

(Fig.89-1) The Liège proof-house as photographed circa 1965 (Photograph courtesy of Browning)

In 1910 the Liège proof-house was moved to a new and expanded facility. The original proof-house in the Rue Navette was closed and the building sold. The new facility was only 750 meters from the old proof-house but included a capacity many times over the original facility.

Firearms were proofed to ensure uniformly high standards of quality and safety. Parts that passed testing were stamped with the appropriate proof mark. Certain proof marks are an indication that the arm/barrel in question has withstood one or more firings with a specified overcharge or "proof" load.

Because of the large number of firearms produced by FN, the Belgian government established a satellite department of the Liège proof house within FN's manufacturing facilities. This "in-house" system eliminated the need to ship parts or completed guns for testing and delivery of completed firearms.

Over time, the number of proof marks applied to the guns varied. However, appropriate parts were stamped accordingly and unless all the marks were present, the gun could not be sold.

Over the years, there were changes in proofing requirements. Although fewer proofs are used on current production guns, the laws that govern proofing and the proof-house remain similar to earlier versions. All guns manufactured or modified in Belgium or imported into Belgium, must be submitted to the proof-house for testing. The Belgian government does not accept foreign proofs. The Belgian proofing system represents the most stringent government testing applied to any firearm.

Summery of some of the most important decrees from 1672 to 1910 affecting firearm proofing and the Liège proof-house

1672:	Mandatory proofing of all barrels
1810, Dec. 14:	All firearms destined for trade are to be proofed (Imperial French Decree)
1818, August 18:	Guidelines set for provincial enforcement by police of previous decree (Royal Dutch Decree)
1836, March 29:	First Belgian Royal Decree affirming the proof-house and its functions
1862, March 10:	Matters relating to firearm proofing are transferred from the Department of Foreign Affairs to the Ministry of the Interior.
1864, June 20:	All modified firearms have to be re-proofed
1885, Nov. 24:	Authorizing the expenditure of a minimum of 5000 Belgian francs for the Liège Firearms Museum
1888, May 24:	A Belgian law was enacted that prohibited the sale or display, of unproofed firearms
1891, March 2:	Establishment of smokeless powder testing and guidelines
1892, January 17:	New guidelines were set for proofing small caliber military arms.
1903, Nov. 18:	Change of guidelines for proofing revolvers, carbines and pistols that useless smokeless ammunition
1907, August 31:	Authorization for moving the Liège proof-house to the rue Fond des Tawnes in Liège
1908, April 27:	Authorization for the sale of the building at Rue Navette where the old proof-house was situated

The proof-house process (as listed in 1910)

A general director, who relies on four department heads, supervises the proof house.
The proof house has four departments:
*Service of ballistics
*Service of workshops and storehouses
*Service of proofing
*Service of administration and accounting

This example follows the proofing process of a new barrel:
An armorer or manufacturer brings the barrel to the proof-house and deals directly with the "service des ateliers et magasins" (service of workshops and storehouses). The item is received and logged in. From receiving, the item goes immediately to an inspector. The inspector visually inspects the part (visité par un inspecteur - visited by an inspector).

If the item fails visual inspection, it is immediately returned to the customer. If the item passes visual inspection it goes to "la salle de calibre" or caliber room. There the barrel is measured and stamped with its caliber. The caliber on the barrel is the first stamping applied. After measurement it is moved to "la salle de charge" or loading room. In the loading room, the end of the barrel is plugged. This plug consists of an insert that has a center hole for loading propellant and a standardized (lead) projectile is loaded from the muzzle. The barrel is then moved to "la salle d'amorce" or primer room where a propellant is loaded through the hole in the plug. At this point the barrel is taken over by the proofing service. The barrel is now located in the "hall des tirs aux canons" or barrel shooting hall. This hall consists of 12 chambers, six for unfinished barrels and six chambers for mounted barrels and actions. Each chamber can handle 60 unfinished barrels at one time or 40 assembled barrels. These chambers are made out of armored steel and the unfinished barrels are placed in heavy steel securing blocks. They are fired with the muzzle pointing towards a sandy area located in the rear of the facility. The sand is purposely kept moist in order to offer more resistance. Fired projectiles are frequently recovered from the sand and send to the foundry where these are melted back into projectiles.

After firing, the barrels are moved to "la salle de lavage" or washing room where the barrels are cleaned through submersion in a mixture of soap water and salt. Steaming is also used in order to get the barrels clean. From there they are moved to "le service de controle après le tir" (proofing service after firing). The barrels are first visually inspected for damage or cracks. Further the barrels are mounted on a pressure machine. These are subjected to compressed water up to 60 ATM of pressure. The inspector carefully checks for any water seepage that may come through a cracked barrel wall. The cracks are usually so thin that it is not visible with the naked eye. This process was upgraded in later years to more modern technologies such as UV light inspection. If the barrel passed inspection it was stamped, weighed and measured. The relevant information was entered on the certificate, which was to remain with the barrel.

This process only highlights the first stage of the proofing of a barrel. In all, there are four stages:
*1 proofing after the barrel is manufactured
*2 After it is mounted to the receiver (if applicable) or installed
*3 After installation and the firing mechanism, cycling and loading has been properly adjusted
*4 Final or definitive proof

Mounted barrels are fired again in the "halls des tirs des canons", this time however they are mounted in chambers for mounted barrels and the complete action or assembled pistol is mounted in a securing rack or mount (chevalet). The controller fires the gun remotely with the aid of a pull cord.

(Fig.90-1) The receiving hall (above) where customers dropped off their arms for proofing. A firing hall (right) where pistols as well as shotguns were tested. Photographs taken in 1910 shortly after the opening of the new facilities. (Courtesy of Robert Creamer)

Liège Proofs

This proof is found on pistol barrels that passed a black powder test with 30 percent excess pressure. Before 1903 this proof was usually the first proof to be applied to a pistol barrel, the proof virtually disappeared from pistols after 1924. This proof is found on all pistol barrels made prior to 1924.

This proof was established in 1903, this provisional proof was voluntarily used until 1924 at which time it became a mandatory proof. The lion represents the Belgian state symbol, the letters "P.V." stand for "Poudre Vive" (smokeless powder).

Before 1924: The proof is found on a pistol barrel indicating that it past the smokeless powder test. This proof is also found on essential parts like frames and slides, indicating that the parts passed the fitting requirement.

After 1924: The proof maintains the same functions as before 1924 but also replaces the barrel proof (above) and the Perron proof on frames and slides. This proof is found on pistols manufactured after 1903.

The "Perron" proof was used on pistols until 1924.
On barrels it indicates that the barrel locking mechanism was not weakened during manufacturing.
On frames and slides it indicates that the fitting and functioning are accepted. On frames and slides the Perron proof complements and finalizes the "PV" proof. This proof was used between 1903 and 1924.
The proof mark is found on all pistols manufactured before 1924. The Perron is the city symbol of Liège.

Epreuve de Liège (Proof of Liège) or final proof.
This proof mark is found on barrels which successfully passed final testing (barrel mounted and test fired on the gun). These tests were conducted with both black powder and smokeless powder. This proof is found on all FN pistols.

Belgian guns are marked with inspectors' markings, these markings are usually the same for all parts but a variation can be observed in a correct matching gun. The inspector not only performs the test but visually inspects the part. Like the craftsmen who make the guns, the inspectors are trained to detect the smallest flaw in manufacturing. Each inspector has an identifying letter, this letter is assigned to them and has no relationship to their name. A few combination letters have been noted especially early on in the century, this was most likely done to differentiate inspectors with similar letters. Note that inspectors letters were not applied on guns between 1968 and 1973[(1)].

A few inspectors, their letter codes and employment years:[(1)]

A - Nicholas Woit 1911-1940
A- Louis Cominoto 1951-1954
A- Antoine Loncin 1960-1960
B- Charles Roland 1927-1959
C- Louis Brenu 1924-1948
C- Dieudonné Francard 1959-1968
D- René Marechal 1951-1968
E- Auguste Jamart 1924-1959
F- Lambert Alexandre 1927-1953
G- Josef Charlier 1928-1959
H- Christophe Woit 1938-1968
J- Pierre Neuprez 1930-1968
K- Walthere Delsaux 1929-1968
L- Antoine Salmon 1937-1968
M- Louis Couchant 1923-1952
M- Maurice Scorpion 1959-1968
N- Henri Florkin 1927-1958
O- Charles Watrin 1928-1965
P- Adolphe Delcommune 1952-1960
Q- Gaspard Dewilde 1952-1968
R- Sylvain Wagemans 1951-1965
S- Charles Daenen 1952-1968
T- Clement Laenen 1952-1968
U- Hubert Charlier 1923-1953
U- Jacques Fuchs 1960-1968
V- Isidor Maçon 1929-1953
W- Nicolas Wolfs 1952-1968
X- Alfred Regnier 1937-1964
Y- Léon Chesnoy 1927-1955
Y- François Delsaux 1959-1968
Z- Théodore Degobort 1924-1949
Z- Martin Luyten 1952-1968

(Fig.91-1) The Perron of Liège as it stands on the Place du Marché (Market Place). (Photograph courtesy of Andre Vanderlinden)

(1) Trade & Hallmarks on Firearms in Belgium by Bruno Joos De Ter Beerst

C: World War II Occupation Applied Markings

The Liège proof-house closed its doors after the German invasion in May 1940. Proof-house inspectors went home and usually took their dies with them. FN factory inspectors ceased their work as well and no prewar factory markings were applied during the wartime production. The Germans did honor the Liège proof system and completed guns did not require German acceptance.

German markings indicate who made the part, the proofing of the part and finally acceptance by the German military.

Test proof: Applied to all guns as a final proof indicating proper operation. Pistols with only the test proof are non-military (commercial) pistols.

WaA613 (Waffenamt 613): First Waffenamt (German military acceptance marking) used at FN. The WaA613 marking is the marking of Chief Inspector Tennert. The WaA numbers were assigned to an individual and remained their assigned marking wherever they supervised inspection. Chief inspectors supervised no less than 10 departments at FN, each department had its own head inspector but only the Waffenamt number of the chief inspector was used throughout the factory. The Waffenamt marking was not personally applied by the chief inspector but by his staff. WaA613 was used at FN from September 1940 through April 1941. The WaA613 marking was only used at FN while Tennert was the chief inspector. Tennert was demoted or was assigned to other duties in April 1941 (see page 50 for Tennert's functions in 1944). Transition parts can be observed with WaA613 markings as well as WaA103 markings. Pistols displaying all three acceptance markings; WaA613, WaA103 and WaA140 can be factory repairs or transition pieces. The WaA613 marking does not appear at any other plant during the war.

WaA103 (Waffenamt 103): Second Waffenamt (German military acceptance marking), used at FN from May 1941 to December 1941. The name of the chief inspector is unknown. Like Tennert, he remained at FN with various duties (see above) and the WaA103 marking does not appear at any other plant during the war.

WaA140 (Waffenamt 140): Third and final Waffenamt (German military acceptance marking). Used at FN from January 1942 to the end of manufacturing under the occupation in 1944. This acceptance code was assigned to Chief Inspector Zorn. The functions of the chief inspector remained similar as before under WaA613 and WaA103 (see above). See page 50 for the structure of the staff in 1944. The Waffenamt marking does not appear at any other plant during the war.

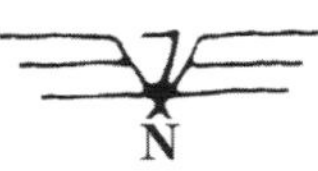

Eagle N: Used at FN from January 1942 to the end of manufacturing under the occupation in 1944. This code was used on non-military (commercial) pistols. It was only used at the same time the WaA140 acceptance code was in effect.

Eagle 140: Used at FN from January 1942 to the end of manufacturing under the occupation in 1944. This marking was not a German military acceptance marking, but rather an indication that the part passed specific German military proofs or tests. The part was most likely complete or in an advance stage of completion. This code was only used on parts shipped from FN to other plants. The marking was used at the same time the WaA140 accepting code was in effect.

MR

Departmental marking[1], indicating that the part is completed and ready for assembly. MR marked parts were assembled and completed at FN, while MI or Eagle 140 parts were shipped to other factories. All departments at FN were coded with two or three letters, the meaning of these department abbreviations has been lost to time (see fig. 55-2).

MI

Departmental marking[1], indicating that the machining of the part is not complete and that the part is not ready for assembly. MI marked parts were shipped to other factories for finishing, proofing and assembly. All departments at FN were coded with two or three letters, the meaning of these department abbreviations has been lost to time (see fig. 55-2). The use of the MI marking was not unique to FN.

---

(1) All departments at FN were coded during the war. These codes were two or three letter abbreviations of the German department's name. It should be noted that these department names were in German and not in French. It is not clear of the marking was applied at the MR or MI department or if the marking signifies its destination. As such the MR department could indicate the assembly department.

D: Acceptance Markings

Acceptance markings are often confused with proof marks. Often marks are incorrectly referred to as commercial proofs or military proofs. This terminology is incorrect and implies that only commercial guns received proof marks.

All (FN) firearms received Liège proofing (as outlined previously). The proofing process is mandatory regardless of what the purchasing agent's function was; commercial, law enforcement or military.

The difference is summarized as follows: Liège proof marks are applied to all manufactured guns and certify that the firearm was manufactured according to set quality standards; that the firearm retains its integrity while firing and that the firearm meets or exceeds safety standards. In short it certifies that the materials and manufacturing methods used result in a firearm that is safe for use with its designated ammunition.

Military acceptance markings on the other hand can be applied either during assembly processes or after a firearm has been received by the purchasing agent. Many purchasing countries opted to accept and mark firearms (and / or parts) in order to guarantee or document any or all of the following:

That the firearm was accepted and logged into a government warehouse
That the firearm was property of the government
That the stamped part(s) did conform to the requirements of the purchaser
That the gun functions properly

The practice of accepting firearms was a practical and administrative function. Stamped and accepted guns were considered state property and were documented in property logs. Records were maintained as to whom the pistols were issued. The markings were also a theft deterrent as they indicated state property. The process of accepting and test firing guns was also a way of eliminating any potential manufacturing defects and returns. This was considered important by many governments as freight costs could be significant. It was more economical to ensure proper functioning prior to the guns being shipped, issued or distributed. As such collectors should understand that acceptance markings do not merely indicate that a gun functions properly.

FN customers had several acceptance options including:

A) Sending an acceptance commission to FN to accept individual parts and completed guns. FN was often held responsible for giving these commissions access to manufacturing blueprints and supplying them with testing tools, testing facilities and warehouse facilities. Characteristically these commissions ranged in size from one to seven men who spent weeks or months at the factory. Some commissions set up small offices (in Liège) from where administrative work was handled while others worked at the FN plant.

B) Appointing a FN employee to accept the guns. This FN employee became a temporary representative of the buyer and was held responsible for the work by both the buyer as well as FN.

C) Hiring accepting officers from the Belgian Ministry of Defense. Although Belgian state arsenals did not produce any guns for foreign nations, the Belgian government did have a paid service where Belgian accepting officers worked for foreign buyers. This service was regarded as another method to promote domestic and private manufacturing while avoiding a conflict of interest with the manufacturing plant. The Belgian accepting officers and accepting service was always kept in high regard and their integrity was crucial.

Many accepting officers or agents marked the entire gun after it was accepted, other would go further and accept parts before assembly. As such many contract guns have distinct acceptance markings on many of their parts. It should be noted that many accepting agents and officers were quite diligent and accepted many parts beyond those required by the contract. These parts were ultimately assembled into other contracts or commercial guns, resulting that acceptance markings can be found on parts not proper to the specific pistol contract.

Some governments opted to go through the acceptance process although not all decided to accept guns at FN or in Belgium. Many guns were accepted in their country after the guns were received.

Belgian Military Acceptance Markings

The Belgian military not only accepted guns but also accepted specific parts. As such Belgian officers were present at FN marking parts before assembly. Finished guns were typically shipped to "La Manufacture d'Armes de l'Etat de Liège" (MAE or State Arms Manufacturer) a prominent state arsenal. The MAE was also commonly known as "Manufacture d'Armes de l'Etat". At FN it was often referred to as "Manufacture d'Armes de Liège". Although different, these names all refer to the same arsenal.

Evidence indicates that parts were stamped at FN but that the final guns were accepted and stamped at the MAE.

The MAE had for long manufactured and repaired firearms for the Belgian military. This role slightly changed in the 1890s when FN became the sole supplier of the Model 1889 Mauser rifle. At the time the MAE changed its function to repairing equipment. Manufacturing was limited to spare parts only.

During World War I, the MAE re-established itself as a manufacturer. After the war, it was in charge of repairing and refinishing guns. As such the MAE, never manufactured complete pistols but did refinish and repair pistols some with arsenal replacement parts.

La Manufacture d'Armes de l'Etat de Liège (MAE) Timeline

1830-1890:	Primary supplier and repair facility for Belgian military small arms.
1891-1914:	Small arms manufacturing was yielded to FN. The MAE was responsible for manufacturing spare parts, repairing and refurbishing arms.
1900:	First FN Browning 1900 pistol is supplied to MAE.
June 1914:	MAE receives last shipment of FN Browning 1900 pistols.
August 1914:	Successfully evacuates manufacturing machinery and spare parts inventory during the German invasion. The MAE staff and equipment follow the Belgian retreat to Antwerp and ultimately to the Belgian coast.
1915:	The MAE sets up repair facilities in Calais and smaller satellite repair facilities in unoccupied Belgium. Many FN employees escape the German occupation and start working for the MAE. The MAE is renamed "Ateliers de Réparation du Materiel des Armes Portatives" (Small arms repair workshops). No less than 95,000 Belgian Mausers were repaired. Thousands of antiquated French bayonets are modified for use with the Model 1889 Mausers.
December 1915:	The Belgian government in exile purchases manufacturing facilities in England. The MAE sends staff including previous FN employees and engineers to start production of the Model 1889 Mauser rifle and carbine.
1915:	The Belgian government in exile seeks to limit its dependency on French supplies and purchases Colt 1903 pistols in order to replace the losses of FN Model 1900 pistols. The first Colt 1903 pistols are supplied to the MAE in Calais in June 1915.
1916:	The Belgian government in exile supplements the British manufacturing of the Model 1889 Mauser rifle and carbine by contracting with Hopkins and Allen of Norwich Connecticut to supply Model 1889 Mausers.
April 1916:	The Model 1889 Mauser is rushed into production in Birmingham, England.
1919:	The MAE resumes functions in Liège and starts refurbishing wartime equipment including Colt 1903 pistols and surviving FN Browning 1900 pistols.
1919:	First FN Browning 1910 pistol delivered to the MAE. These were accepted by the Belgian military as the Model 1900 was no longer being produced.
1919-1929:	MAE duties are limited to repairing existing equipment; in 1927 the MAE starts updating and converting machine guns.
1930:	MAE receives first shipment of FN BAR machine guns.
1933:	MAE receives 1000 High Efficiency pistols for field trials.
1934:	MAE receives last significant order of FN Browning 1910 pistols.
1935:	MAE receives first shipment of High Power pistols.
1935:	MAE modifies existing rifles and carbines for the assembly of the Belgian Model 1935 Mauser rifle.
1936-1940:	MAE modifies existing Model 1889 rifles and carbines into the Belgian Model 1889/36 Mauser rifle.
September 1944:	MAE staff starts recovering (captured) war material.
October 1944:	The U.S. military uses the MAE facilities and the MAE staff relocates.
November 1944:	MAE operates under the new name "Atelier Central d'Armement" (Central Armament Workshop).
1948:	The MAE name is changed to "Arsenal d'Armement" (Armament Arsenal).
1952:	Manufacturing is discontinued, functions are limited to repairs only.
1958:	The MAE in Liège is closed, all functions are transferred to the arsenal of Rocourt (page 308).

MAE markings applied at FN

Inspector Acceptance: The following markings were applied by arsenal inspectors on parts that were destined for Belgian military contract guns. These markings were applied at FN and indicate which inspector performed the inspection.

Inspector's Part Acceptance: Typically found early in the century, most often on Model 1900 pistols. Note that many more variations exist, these have been observed on Belgian military Model 1900 and early Model 1910 pistols. These markings are small and may require a magnifying glass for proper identification[1].

Inspector's Part Acceptance: Typically found on Belgian military Model 1900 or 1910 pistols.

Inspector's Part Acceptance: Typically found on Belgian military High Power pistols. This inspector was active circa 1931- early 1940.

Inspector's Part Acceptance: Typically found on Belgian military High Power pistols. These inspectors were active in the Spring of 1940 until May 10, 1940.

Epreuve du Gouvernement Belge (Belgian government proof):
This marking was applied to assembled parts to indicate that the parts passed inspection and were property of the Belgian state. The marking was only applied once per gun or applied to major components. This marking was applied at FN at the same time as the inspector marking (see above).

MAE markings applied at the Belgian state arsenal

MAE arsenal acceptance marking: These markings indicate that the gun was accepted and passed testing at the state arsenal. It can be considered redundant as FN pistols had already passed the Liège proof-house proofing. Guns received in arsenals were tested without exception; whether they were proofed at Liège or not was immaterial. This testing procedure was used as the arsenal repaired, modified and manufactured parts as well. As they supplied only the Belgian military, they were exempt from Liège proofing but were required to conduct their own testing.

Found on Belgian military Model 1900 and 1910 pistols[1].

Introduced in the mid 1920s and found on Belgian military Model 1910 pistols as well as High Powers (1935 to 1940). Also found on Belgian military Model 1922 pistols acquired in the first year after World War II.

Found on postwar Belgian military pistols[1]. The marking does not denote the year of acceptance but rather the year the marking was introduced (1946, 1947 and 1952).

MAE: Manufacture d'Armes de l'Etat
This marking indicates the location where the pistol was received. It is found primarily on High Power pistols and was not always applied. This marking was applied at the state arsenal.

(1) Other similar variations can exist and are not illustrated

E: Foreign Proofs

Some countries like Great Britain, Czechoslovakia and the Austrian-Hungarian Empire required foreign made pistols to undergo their own proofing. This system was not only instilled to check quality standards but also to inventory imported firearms, mark these as legally imported and for collecting import tariffs on foreign made pistols.

Great Britain

British proofs are not frequently encountered on FN firearms. It is possible that Lepersonne (see page 116) made special arrangements with the British government in order not to have the FN pistols marked. Numerous pistols that went to Lepersonne do not have British proofs. As Lepersonne distributed and forwarded firearms throughout the British Empire, the firearms may have been exempt. Firearms sold outside of England did not require proofing. Privately imported firearms were proofed as well as firearms used for official purposes (see fig.176-1).

(Fig.96-1) A privately imported Model 1899 pistol N° 2592 with British proofs (see fig.128-1).

The Austrian-Hungarian Empire

All firearms imported into the empire were proofed in either the Vienna, Prague, Weipert, Ferlach or Budapest proofhouse. Each firearm was marked with an inventory number followed by the two-digit proofing year.

(Fig.96-2) A 1913 imported Model 1900 pistol (see page 148). This pistol was proofed at the Vienna proof house, this can be determined by the small letter next to the NP marking. The small letter designates the first letter of the proof house.

Czechoslovakia

The Czechs retained the proofing practices from the Austrian-Hungarian empire. The Czechs used the Bohemian double tailed lion from the early 1920s through 1926. In 1927 the lion was replaced by a bow and arrow marking surrounded by a circle for the Prague proof-house or surrounded by a hexagon for the Weipert proof-house. The two digit year abbreviation remained in effect.

(Fig.96-3) (l. to r.) 1925 Czech lion proof on Model 1905 N° 726411, 1927 Prague proof on Model 1922 N° 202864, 1938 Weipert proof on Model 1905 N° 1074545. (Photographs courtesy of Kevin Null)

(Fig.96-4) Prior to 1927, the proof-house number was applied on the slide with the Bohemian lion and date as seen on this 1925 proofed Model 1905 pistol N° 726411. After 1926 the proof-house number was moved to the front grip-strap (fig. 96-5).

(Fig.96-5) Note the front grip strap proofing number 7168 on this 1930 Prague proofed Model 1905 pistol N° 987554. (Photograph by author, courtesy of Wendell Patton)

FN Production Processes and Procedures

Production

It is important for a collector to understand some of FN's processes and procedures. An in depth understanding will help avoid common misconceptions.

Slide Legends

Slide legends can be a guide for identifying a production period, but more often than not, these lead to confusion as FN employed a system that operated on demand and volume and not on any chronological method of operation.

Each roll engraving that was used for marking the slides was purposely made different. As such, several slide legends were used through time, many concurrently.

Roll engraving machine 1 usually performed the majority of the work.
Roll engraving machine 2 was only operated when machine one was backlogged.
Roll engraving machine 3 was only operated when demand exceeded the combined capacities of 1 and 2.

As a result, it is common to see pistols manufactured on the same day with two different slide legends. On occasions, a particular roll-engraving machine was selected to run a complete contract in order to create a uniform look on all contract pistols.

Early Production Serial Numbers

Collectors often seek pistols produced at early part of the production run with low serial numbers. Single, double and triple digit serial numbered guns are considered more desirable and often demand a price premium.

Seeking out serial number "1" with FN produced pistols can be a futile ambition. FN typically streamlined machinery and production as the first pistols were produced. In most cases the first pistols failed in house proofing and were never completed. This is the case for the Model 1900, 1905, Baby and High Power pistols. The exceptions are the pistols that were first produced for contracts like the Model 1903 and 1922.

Serial Numbers by Model

FN Browning Model 1899: Ascend from number 1. After number 9999 had been reached, the serialization was restarted with an "A" prefix (e.g., A1, A2, etc.). This serial number practice was identical to the old Mauser numbering system that had been used with the FN Model 1889 and 1893 Mauser rifles. The Model 1899 was the only pistol to use this numbering practice.

FN Browning Model 1900, 1903, 1905, Baby: Ascend from number 1. Serial numbers were not restarted after the First or Second World Wars.

FN Browning Model 1922: Ascend from number 200,000. Serial numbers started at 200,000 in an unusual effort to work around the Yugoslav contract requirement. This was FN's first attempt at separating contract numbers from serial numbers. This practice was never introduced on any other model. Serial numbers were restarted in 1946[(1)]. Consequently, Model 1922 pistols with numbers above 200,000 are typically prewar. Prewar guns with serial numbers below 100.000 are contract guns while guns in the 100,000 range are automatically postwar guns (see also page 222).

FN Browning High Power: Ascend from number 1. Pistol serial numbers were restarted in 1946[(1)]. Prewar production did not ascend logically. As a military pistol, FN produced the pistols in blocks of serial numbers, as such some prewar pistol ranges were never manufactured. (example: The prewar Finish contract in the 21.000 range was produced in 1940 while at the same time FN was producing Belgian military contract pistols both in the 21.000 range as well as in the 40.000 range (see also page 271))

(1) Excludes wartime or post liberation 'A' prefix numbering practices

Contract Numbers

From 1899 through 1922, FN followed a policy not to mark a pistol with only a contract number. Contract numbers were always added and were in a different location from the pistol's serial number. The location of the contract number was specified by the customer and was most often marked near the customer's crest or contract marking. The Yugoslav order of the Model 1922 changed this policy. After 1922 pistols are found that do not have any serial numbering but only a contract number. Post 1922 pistols with contract numbers do not always have a crest, making it difficult to differentiate a standard serial number from a contract number.

FN contract numbers usually ascend from number 1 and follow an upward consecutive trend. Note that prewar contract guns always start with 1 while postwar pistols can have a 0 in front of the digit, e.g., 01. The addition of the 0 is an indication of postwar numbering. It is not customary for a contract to start at any other number but 1 (01, 001) unless specifically specified by the customer to complement pistols already on order or already in inventory.

Finishes

Blue: The FN rust blue was standard on all prewar guns. This type of rust blue has a medium gloss finish and appears gray / blue in color.

Rust bluing remained in use by FN from the 1890s until 1962 when it was replaced by salt bluing. The appearance of the rust blue finish was consistent throughout the decades. Factory original pistols will therefore always show the same color of blue but with different wear patterns.

FN used fire blue on triggers of the early pistols. As a result, the Model 1899 pistols had fire blue triggers. Early production Model 1900 pistols also had fire blue triggers and it is known that FN put fire blue triggers on first year production commercial guns like the Model 1900, 1905 and 1910. This was most likely done to increase the appeal of a new model.

After World War I (circa 1922) FN implemented a high gloss deep blue finish on the their luxury line (Modèles de Luxe). This finish was similar to Colt's early charcoal finish. This finish was always applied to engraved guns. All guns noted by the author with this finish date from before 1930 and it is the author's opinion that FN abandoned this practice in the early 1930s.

In 1962 FN replaced rust bluing with salt bluing. Salt bluing was faster and easier to apply. This bluing is black-blue in color compared to the gray-blue of the earlier rust blue. Salt bluing wears differently than rust blue and wear is often considered less attractive than on rust blue. In 1970 FN automated polishing and bluing, diminishing much of the personal attention to detail and bluing craftsmanship of earlier years.

Blue turning plum in color: Plum bluing can be attributed to various factors including, too strong of a bluing solution, incorrect bluing solution and rebluing over existing bluing. The plum color can be visible immediately after the bluing has been applied or bluing can degrade over time to where it turns plum in color.

A Liège proofed FN pistol will never turn plum in color unless it was refinished after it left the factory. No factory plum pistols have ever been noted by the author. Plum finished pistols are almost always wartime production or refinished.

Black Enamel: Black enamel was introduced at FN upon a request of the French Navy in the late 1920s or early 1930s. FN sprayed the black enamel paint over a phosphate primer in order to make the paint more resilient to wear. The black enamel finish was only sold twice in the prewar era, both for navy use (see page 205 and 238).

After World War II and especially after 1950 black enamel guns gained popularity for their ability to resist rust and wear. A few pistols have been observed that did not have the phosphate primer under the black. These pistols were all from the 1970s era or later. It is possible that FN abandoned the phosphate primer finish or that these pistols were repainted without proper primer application.

Phosphate: No FN pistols ever left the factory in the prewar era with a phosphate[(1)] finish. Phosphate was at that time only used as a primer for enamel paint covering. Only the magazine tubes of the High Power pistol were finished in a green phosphate in the prewar era (see page 271).

Phosphate finishes as a final application never gained popularity at FN. These finishes were ultimately applied as a final finish upon requests of customers or as an option in the postwar era. Through the 1950s and 1960s phosphate became more accepted and FN started to offer it in their line of military finishes. A 1957 FN test indicated that an oil soaked/treated phosphate finish was five to 20 times more resistant than just a phosphate finish without oil treatment. The black enamel paint over a phosphate finish was 70 times more resistant than plain phosphate, so FN recommended and favored their enamel finish.

Nickel: FN has always offered a nickel finish on its pistols prior to 1930 but rarely advertised the finish. Only agents and retailers advertised the finish on occasion as an option. Prewar factory nickel pistols are rare. A 1920s internal FN memo explains the reason for the scarcity of nickel pistols: Nickel plating was not performed in the arms manufacturing halls but rather was outsourced to the motorcycle division. The motorcycle department prioritized their own production needs and pistol plating was performed only when time would permit. This also explains why nickel pistols always seem to appear in batches of serial numbers.

Factory nickel work can always be identified by the blue-black finish on the trigger and safety. FN discovered early on that the thickness of the nickel plating interfered with the operation of some parts. As such FN only applied the base primer to these parts and no plating was applied. The finish on the trigger and safety is not bluing but rather a plating catalyst that is almost black in color and shows some dullness.

Chrome: Nickel plating was fragile and FN opted to replace nickel plating in the early 1950s with harder and more resilient chrome plating. Chrome plating was offered in satin finish in order to mimic nickel plating, as such much 1950s literature still refers to nickel while in fact the factory used chrome plating. Metal preparation and application differences offered different finishes including satin chrome and bright chrome. Chrome pistols were often accentuated with gold plated triggers.

Grips

Vulcanite or Hard Rubber: Vulcanite was the first material used by FN for pistol grips. All FN 1899 and 1900 pistol grips were made out of Vulcanite. Vulcanite grips were abandoned after 1914.

Horn: The introduction of the Auto-5 shotgun brought horn to FN. Butt plates were fabricated by pressing animal horn under high pressure into a mold. Animal horn was a byproduct of local slaughterhouses and was available at no or little cost. The Model 1903, 1905, 1910 and 1922 all had animal horn grips in the prewar era. Production of horn grips was abandoned during World War II (see also fig.100-1).

Wood: Wood was introduced with military pistols. FN's first use of wood dates to the early large Model 1899 and the Grand Browning. The High Efficiency and High Power all had wood grips in the prewar era. Prewar High Power grips had red paint applied to the back of the grips. This practice started with the High Efficiency. Grips so painted are often referred to in the U.S. collector community as "red backed" grips. The purpose for this special paint was to create a moisture barrier that would prevent moisture from getting trapped between the wood and the metal of the frame. The practice was suspended during World War II and reintroduced in 1945-1946. It was entirely abandoned in the 1960s.

The Germans introduced wooden grips to the Model 1922 in 1942. Throughout the war, the Model 1922 grips were early plastic, wood or Bakelite. Wood or plastic was used after the war for the Model 1922. In 1946 FN introduced wooden grips for the Model 1910. Wood or plastic was used for the remainder of Model 1910 production.

(1) The author refers to phosphating instead of Parkerizing. Both systems are similar and provide identical results. Parkerizing was a name associated with the U.S. Parker company who perfected phosphating. There is no indication that FN was associated with the Parker company and so the author opted not to use this terminology.

(Fig.100-1) Grips can easily be identified by checking the back. Horn grips always have a solid backing (l.) while wartime synthetics and postwar plastics have visible molding patterns (r.)

Bakelite: Bakelite, an early form of synthetic material, was brittle. It was easy to mold and was very detailed but did not resist shock well and was prone to breaking. FN never used Bakelite in the prewar era; the Germans introduced it during World War II when they suffered shortages of wood and other synthetic materials. Bakelite grips were also used by FN in the immediate post liberation era but abandoned once production restarted in 1946.

Plastic early: The first black synthetic grips date from the early days of the occupation in 1940, these are found on the Model 1905, Model 1910 and 1922 pistols. As all cattle was requisitioned by the German military, FN no longer had access to the horn byproducts of the meat industry. The Germans ingeniously modified the horn press operation to a molding operation. This early form of synthetic is more coarse than modern plastics, and has less detail than later synthetics.

Plastic modern: Used after World War II, modern black synthetic grips were used on the complete pistol line including the Model 1905, 1910 and variants, 1922 and variants, Baby and High Power.

Production Economics

When thinking about FN production, collectors should remember that the company was running a production line and was not in the business of building a line of collectibles with clean temporal breaks between the introduction of new features and the discontinuance of old ones As a result, very little was wasted at FN; old parts were used up concurrently with the introduction of new and improved parts.

Wicker baskets: For decades FN worked with wicker baskets for holding and moving parts around in the factory. Consequently, parts with older design features may have been on the bottom of a basket while newer designed parts lay on top. Different parts required more or less time to produce, so there were rarely the same quantities of parts on hand. As an example, safeties required little machining and there may have been thousands of safeties on hand at any given time while slides required extensive machining and would have been in shorter supply. If a change was brought to the safety, it could take months or years before the new safety was standardized into the production as a mix of old and new parts were used.

Recalls: The concept of recalling a product is totally American. Often collectors refer to the round barrel cam on early High Powers and how these were recalled and replaced by square cam barrels (page 270). This is incorrect. Although FN did introduce a change in the production, no parts were recalled or discarded; rather, all were used up.

Warehousing

Some warehouses rotate inventory; this practice being intended to move the old stock first. This was not the case at FN. Often it appears that FN employed a 'first in, first out' policy although that is not entirely correct either.

Contracts: Pistols destined for particular contracts were earmarked and were usually stored in a warehouse, just to be shipped days later when the contract quantity had been reached.

Most contracts with special markings were usually made and not pulled from warehouse inventory. The warehouse inventory was usually used to supply commercial orders or even small contract orders that did not have special markings or numbers. As such we see that most, if not all, of the High Power contract pistols were built after receiving the order and not pulled from warehouse as is often believed by U.S. collectors(1).

Exit date: Finished guns could spend one day in warehouse or could remain there for decades. As an example, some post liberation Model 1922 pistols, serial numbers A4415, A4418, A4424, A4425, A4428, A4444, A4448 were all entered in warehouse on September 14, 1944 just days after the liberation, yet these pistols remained in inventory until December 29, 1986 when they were issued to FN's internal security personnel. This is an extreme example but it was not unusual for a pistol to remain in inventory for years.

In and Out: Some pistols have multiple entry dates as well as multiple exit dates in the records. These pistols were sales samples either showing a new feature, model or engraving style. Some pistols show two entry dates with only one exit date. These pistols usually were manufactured prior to the war, hidden during the occupation and returned after the liberation. While they were hidden they were not logged out, but were logged back in upon their return just to be sold and logged out at later time. Because of the detailed system and the meticulous record keeping habits of the FN warehouse employees, it is clearly possible to identify the course an item took.

Entry date: The entry date is a very good indicator when a pistol was built. Finished pistols were typically entered on the day of completion.

Language

Business conducted at the factory was always in French; this is reflected in all internal factory documents. FN did communicate with its agents and customers in predominately French, English and German but also Spanish, Dutch and Italian. Imperial Russian dealings were handled in French so were Polish and most African dealings, Scandinavian customers were dealt with in German.

Pistols and parts were often given French names by the workers. Workers in the past also conversed in a language called "Wallon"[(2)]. This language was more than just a regional dialect or slang, it is comprised of a vocabulary almost independent from French.

Workers therefore often mixed French and Wallon and had their own language when it came to specific models as well as parts or activities relating to manufacturing.

Wallon was a source of frustration for the Germans in both world wars. Some of the German officers had a good understanding of French but were dumbfounded when it came to Wallon. During the occupations, the official language was German and not French.

FN's agents, who relied on telegrams, and later Telex, used a secret written language to communicate with the factory. Everything was communicated in code, including model designations, quantities, country names, prices, commissions, etc. These codes were not used in conjunction with an actual language; entire messages were coded including nouns and verbs. Each FN agent, factory representative or man in the field was issued a bound codebook with translation for them to use but never to share. The codebooks were considered top secret and FN employees that received them had to sign strict confidentiality agreements.

Terminology

Prototype or tool room prototype: A prototype usually denotes a hand made or tool room sample. Prototypes are made for design innovations and were typically for internal use only. Prototypes have usually no serial number and no Liège proofs.

Pre-production run: A small amount of pistols, fully functional for trials, evaluations or sales samples. Pre-production runs usually amount to a handful of pistols and have Liège proofs and a serial number. Pre-production samples were made on FN manufacturing machinery with relatively little hand finishing or fitting in comparison to a prototype. Pre-production samples were most notably made on the FN Browning 1903, the Grand Browning and High Efficiency pistol variants.

Trials gun: A trial gun can be either a standard FN production gun submitted for trials, a standard production gun with customized features or an entire new design made specifically for the purpose of the trials.

---

(1) Examples of such are the Chinese and Finish contracts see page 282 and 284

(2) Wallon as referred to above is a language, it is not to be confused with Walloon which denotes the southern French speaking part of Belgium.

Accessories: Spare Parts, Magazines, Cleaning Rods and Manuals

Accessories like cleaning rods, spare magazines and spare parts were all charged at extra cost and were requested by the customer. Today we often assume that the typical FN box was supplied but that was not the case. The cardboard box, instruction manual, spare magazine and cleaning rod were a typical package made up for retailers and agents. Government buyers determined what quantities of accessories they wanted.

Manuals or booklets were also optional, and FN made these available in many languages. A purchasing nation could order a specific manual from FN in its native language. These included the information and the designations that the customer wanted. See page 173 for a rare FN produced Turkish manual for the FN Browning 1903 pistol.

Many governments purchased a few manuals and later printed their own. A typical example is the manual for the Dutch contract Model 1922 pistols. The Netherlands bought one manual for every 500 pistols before printing them domestically.

Armorer Kits: FN's ability to sell to armies worldwide was often the result of their armorer's program. The author does not know when this was instituted but armorer kits were available for decades especially after World War II. FN trained and supplied foreign military armorers by sending FN representatives to the customer's facilities. Special tools and parts kits or armorers kit were provided if the customer participated in the program (see examples fig.224-4 and fig.272-5). As a result, each pistol model had a dedicated quantity of spare parts with which the armorers worked. The quantities of parts varied from model to model.

Supplied spare parts by FN were always unnumbered.

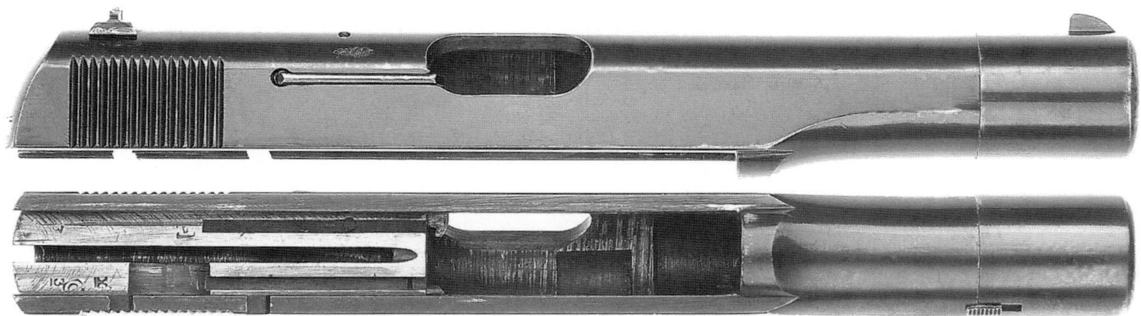

(Fig.102-1) A late 1930s Model 1922 replacement slide and barrel lug, note that no serial numbers are present. The front sight was factory cut, although rarely encountered FN did modify the front sights on Model 1903 and Model 1922 pistols if requested by the customer.

Pricing and Shipping

Government contracts were usually priced without any accessories, box or shipping container. Contracts were priced for customer pick up at the factory. If this was not suitable, the customer could select from an array of shipping options, including crates, crate lining, etc. Crates were often custom made according to customer demands and specifications outlined in the contract. Customers selected the quantity of pistols per crate and the way these were to be packaged. The customer could arrange for shipping or have FN handle it directly. Many foreign governments opted to have the merchandise shipped to a Belgian warehouse so that they could combine the shipping with other supplies from other European vendors. It is therefore not unusual that shipments were forwarded to Liège or Antwerp. Some purchasing governments opted to have their merchandise delivered to the port of Antwerp where they could select their own freighters.

The John M. Browning Prototypes

The John M. Browning Firearms Museum features the largest collection of surviving prototypes made by John Browning. The museum is open to the public and is located approximately 30 minutes north of Salt Lake City, in Ogden Utah. The collection features John Browning's hand made prototypes, and was assembled years after the passing of John Browning. The firearms were mainly bought or donated by the various manufacturers with whom the Browning Brothers dealt.

Rare and significant factory commemorative pieces like the 100,000th, 250,000th and 500,000th FN Browning 1900 pistols are also on display (see pages 12-13), as are two of the 1914 "Un Million" commemorative Browning pistols (see page 19).

Many of John Browning's handmade arms are present, including pistols, sporting arms and military arms. More than 100 Browning prototypes are shown including some designed by Val Browning, John M. Browning's son.

Although the collection boasts most of the known John Browning prototypes, many prototypes were reused and modified by the inventor. It is therefore unknown exactly how many different designs and models the inventor made. Signs of alterations and works in progress can be seen on many of the prototypes.

All of John Browning's center-fire pistol prototypes are featured in this chapter, not only those that were important or used by FN. A design evolution is clearly visible in these pieces, and the pistols are therefore presented in chronological order. Further, it is interesting to note how FN maintained many of the original inventor's designs while Colt often opted for modifications.

Both Colt and FN's production pistols were made to strict tolerances and are known for their high quality. John Browning's pistols were never polished or finished. However, the reader should not be mistaken about the functioning quality of these prototypes. The tolerances on the prototypes are generally tighter than those of the production pistols. The operation and cycling of some of these prototypes were significantly smoother than the later production pistols. Once again this displays Browning's genius and his ability to hand make guns that function better than those the world's best manufacturers could fabricate.

Browning 1894 Prototype in .38 Caliber

Gas operated, toggle mechanism – design inspired from the early Browning machine gun.
U.S. Patent applied on September 14, 1895 - Patent 580,923 was granted on July 3, 1895.
Shown to Colt on July 3, 1895. The manufacturing and sales rights were sold to Colt on July 24, 1896 among other pistol designs. This model was never produced.

(Fig.103-1) The 1894 toggle mechanism prototype. (Photographs by author, courtesy of the John M. Browning Firearms Museum, Ogden Union Station)

Browning 1895 Prototype in .32 Caliber

Blowback design.
U.S. Patent applied on October 31, 1896 - Patent 580,926 was granted on April 20, 1897.
The manufacturing and sales rights were sold to Colt on July 24, 1896 among other pistol designs.
This model was never produced.

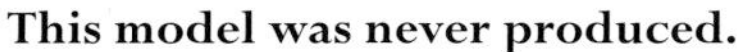

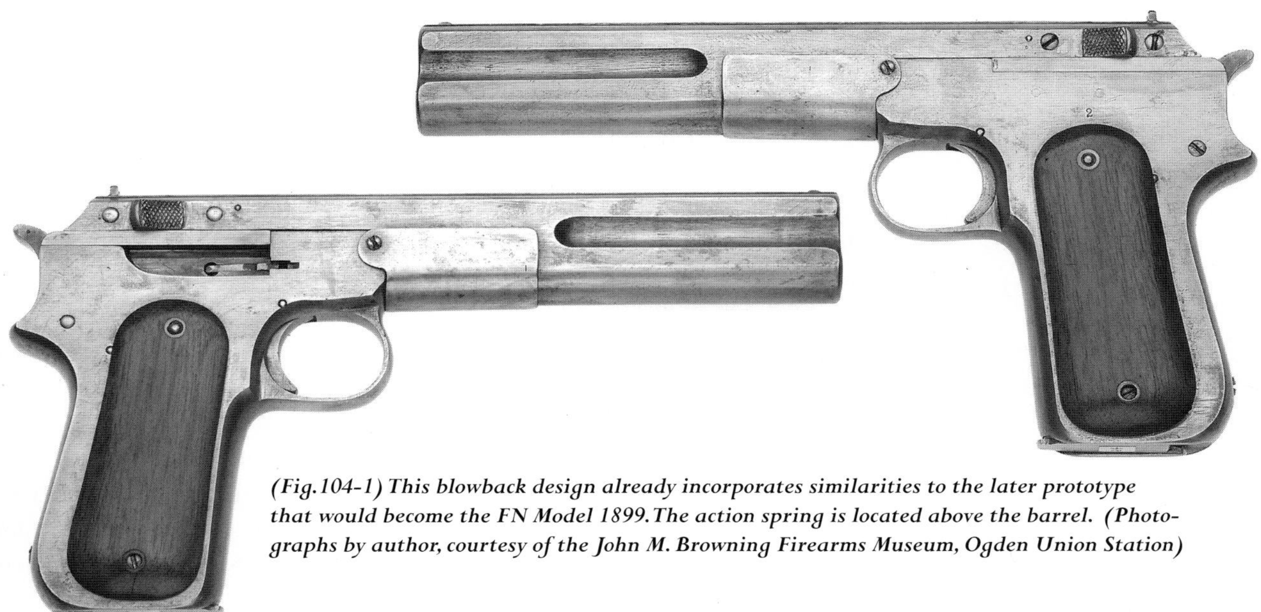

(Fig.104-1) This blowback design already incorporates similarities to the later prototype that would become the FN Model 1899. The action spring is located above the barrel. (Photographs by author, courtesy of the John M. Browning Firearms Museum, Ogden Union Station)

Browning 1896 Prototype in .38 Caliber (I)

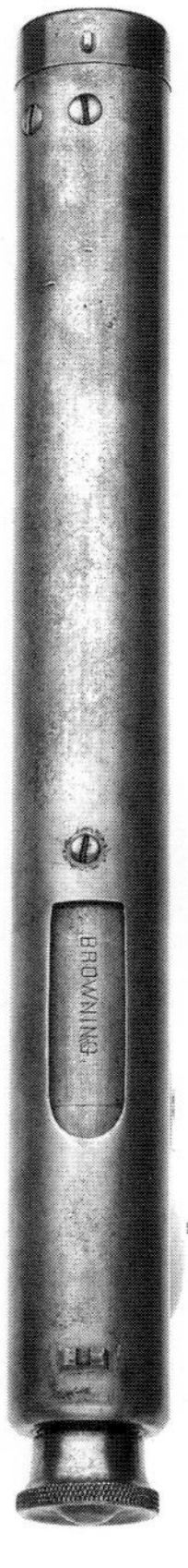

Short recoil operated. Rotating barrel locks to the slide. The recoil spring encloses / surrounds the barrel.
U.S. Patent applied on October 31, 1896 - Patent 580,925 was granted on April 20, 1897.
The manufacturing and sales rights were sold to Colt on July 24, 1896 among other pistol designs. This model was never produced.

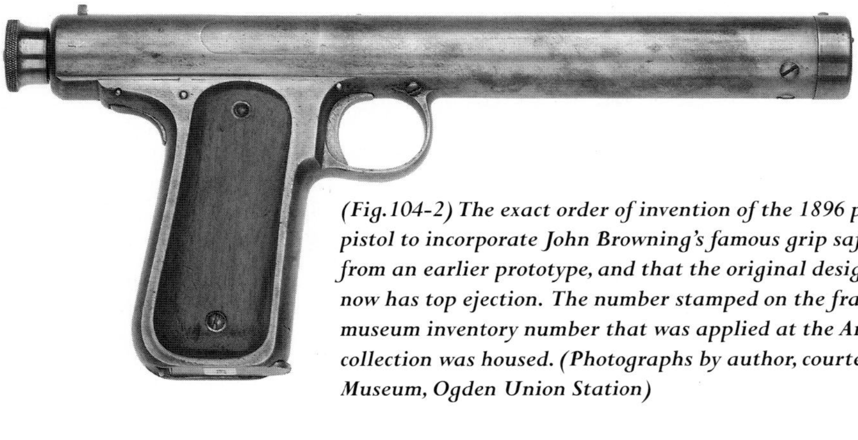

(Fig.104-2) The exact order of invention of the 1896 prototypes is not known. This is the first pistol to incorporate John Browning's famous grip safety. Note that it has been reworked from an earlier prototype, and that the original design had side ejection, while this model now has top ejection. The number stamped on the frame is not a period number but rather a museum inventory number that was applied at the Armory decades later where the Browning collection was housed. (Photographs by author, courtesy of the John M. Browning Firearms Museum, Ogden Union Station)

Browning 1896 Prototype in .38 Caliber (II)

Short recoil operated. Barrel positively locks to the slide. Locked breech at firing. Barrel and slide recoil.
U.S. patent applied on October 31, 1896 - Patent 580,924 was granted on April 20, 1897.
The manufacturing and sales rights were sold to Colt on July 24, 1896 among other pistol designs.
This model was never produced.

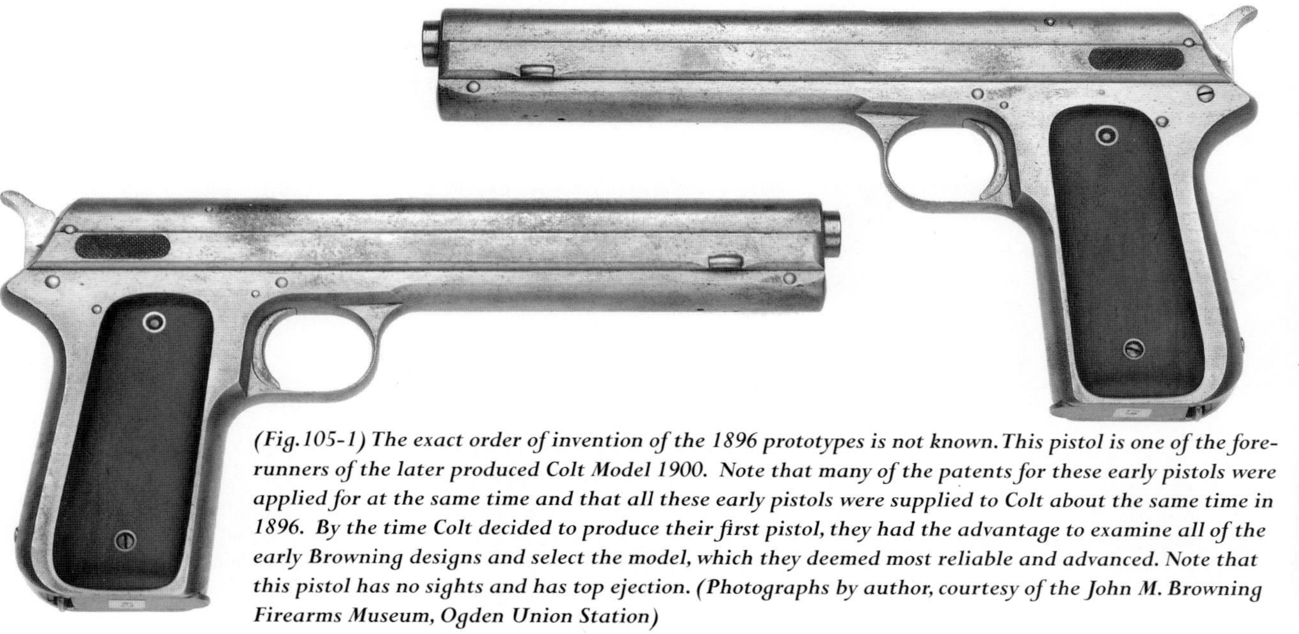

(Fig.105-1) The exact order of invention of the 1896 prototypes is not known. This pistol is one of the fore-runners of the later produced Colt Model 1900. Note that many of the patents for these early pistols were applied for at the same time and that all these early pistols were supplied to Colt about the same time in 1896. By the time Colt decided to produce their first pistol, they had the advantage to examine all of the early Browning designs and select the model, which they deemed most reliable and advanced. Note that this pistol has no sights and has top ejection. (Photographs by author, courtesy of the John M. Browning Firearms Museum, Ogden Union Station)

Browning 1896 Prototype in .38 Caliber (III)

Short recoil operated. Barrel positively locks to the slide. Locked breech at firing. Barrel and slide recoil.
U.S. patent applied on November 7, 1901 - Patent 708,794 was granted on September 9, 1902.
The manufacturing and sales rights were sold to Colt on July 24, 1896 among other pistol designs.
This model was never produced.

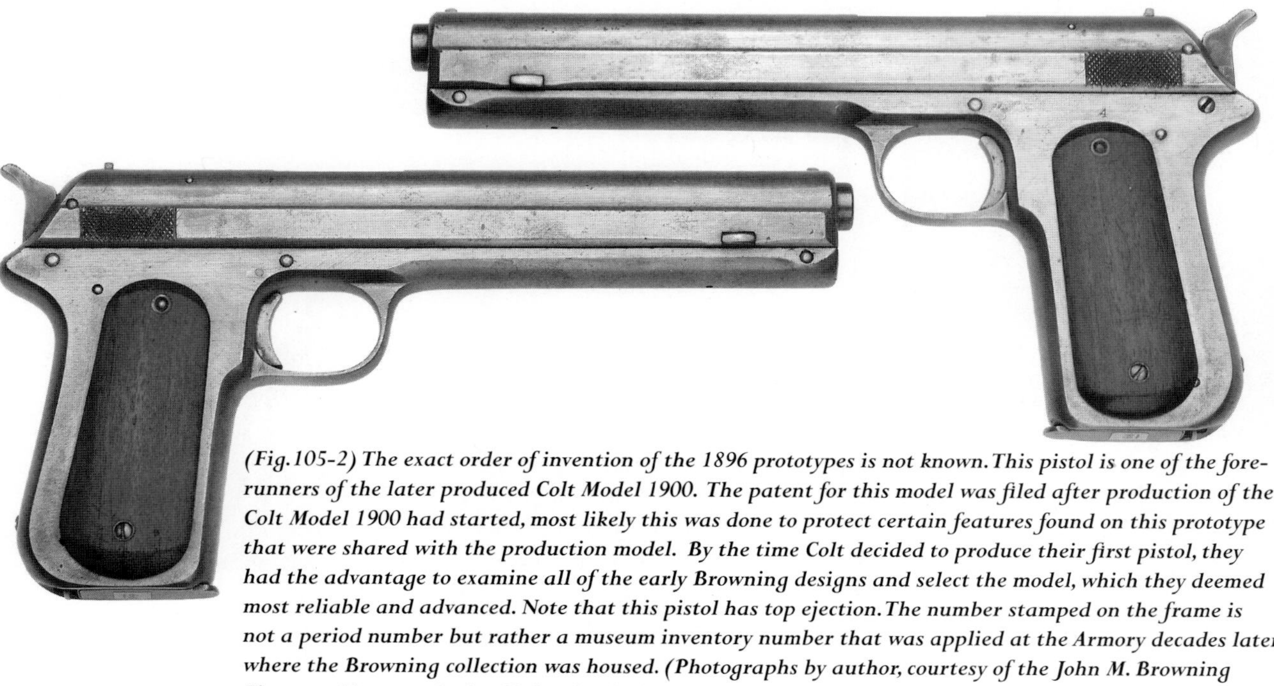

(Fig.105-2) The exact order of invention of the 1896 prototypes is not known. This pistol is one of the fore-runners of the later produced Colt Model 1900. The patent for this model was filed after production of the Colt Model 1900 had started, most likely this was done to protect certain features found on this prototype that were shared with the production model. By the time Colt decided to produce their first pistol, they had the advantage to examine all of the early Browning designs and select the model, which they deemed most reliable and advanced. Note that this pistol has top ejection. The number stamped on the frame is not a period number but rather a museum inventory number that was applied at the Armory decades later where the Browning collection was housed. (Photographs by author, courtesy of the John M. Browning Firearms Museum, Ogden Union Station)

Browning 1896 Prototype in .38 Caliber - Produced as Colt Model 1900 & 1902

Short recoil operated. Locked breech.
U.S. Patent applied on October 31, 1896 - Patent 580,924 was granted on April 20, 1897.
Evaluated by Colt on June 29, 1896.
The manufacturing and sales rights were sold to Colt on July 24, 1896 among other pistol designs.
This model was produced as the Colt Model 1900, Model 1902 Sporting, Military and Pocket Model.

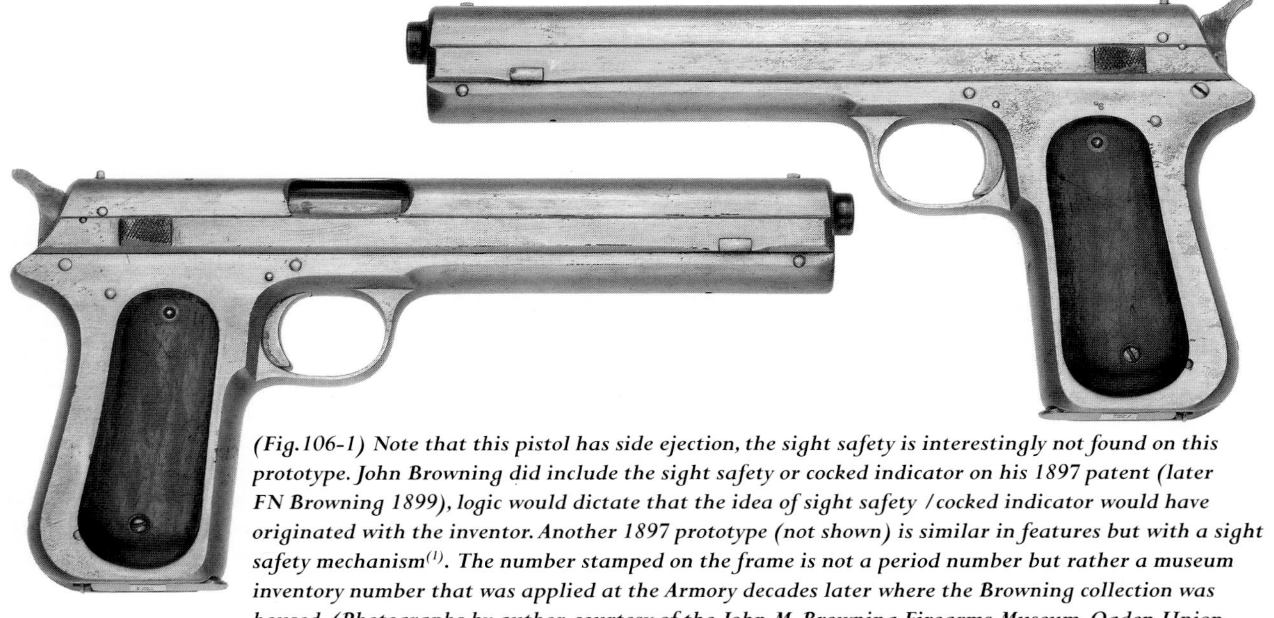

(Fig.106-1) Note that this pistol has side ejection, the sight safety is interestingly not found on this prototype. John Browning did include the sight safety or cocked indicator on his 1897 patent (later FN Browning 1899), logic would dictate that the idea of sight safety / cocked indicator would have originated with the inventor. Another 1897 prototype (not shown) is similar in features but with a sight safety mechanism[1]. The number stamped on the frame is not a period number but rather a museum inventory number that was applied at the Armory decades later where the Browning collection was housed. (Photographs by author, courtesy of the John M. Browning Firearms Museum, Ogden Union Station)

Browning 1897 Prototype in .32 caliber - Produced as FN Browning Model 1899 & 1900

Blowback design.
U.S. Patent applied on December 28, 1897 - Patent 621,747 was granted on March 21, 1899.
Unknown if seen by Colt but brought by Hart Berg to FN in 1897 (see page 9, 124).
The manufacturing and sales contract were finalized on July 26, 1897.
This model was produced as the FN Browning Model 1899 and Model 1900.

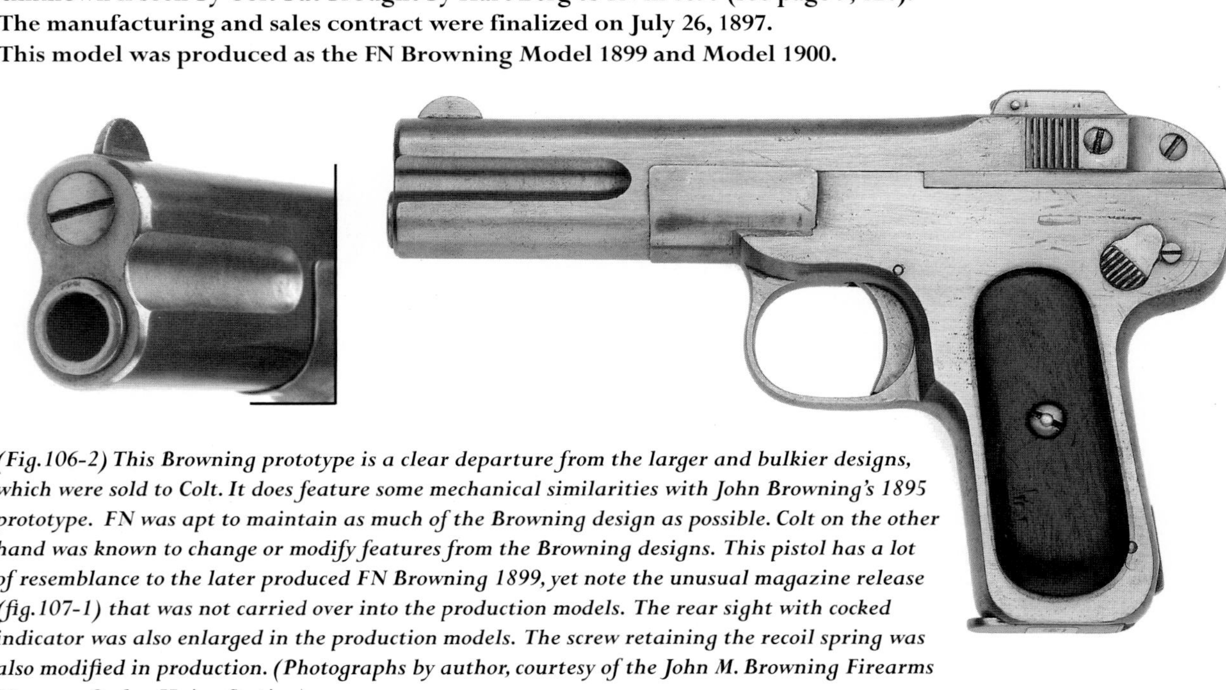

(Fig.106-2) This Browning prototype is a clear departure from the larger and bulkier designs, which were sold to Colt. It does feature some mechanical similarities with John Browning's 1895 prototype. FN was apt to maintain as much of the Browning design as possible. Colt on the other hand was known to change or modify features from the Browning designs. This pistol has a lot of resemblance to the later produced FN Browning 1899, yet note the unusual magazine release (fig.107-1) that was not carried over into the production models. The rear sight with cocked indicator was also enlarged in the production models. The screw retaining the recoil spring was also modified in production. (Photographs by author, courtesy of the John M. Browning Firearms Museum, Ogden Union Station)

(1) This pistol is in a private collection and was not inspected by the author

(Fig.107-1) John Browning's prototype magazines featured one view-hole. FN increased this to three view-holes in 1899, later production featured six view holes (see fig.127-1). (Photographs by author, courtesy of the John M. Browning Firearms Museum, Ogden Union Station)

Browning 1901 Prototype in 9x20mm Caliber
Produced as FN Browning Model 1903 & Husqvarna Model 1907

Blowback design.
This prototype was made upon request from FN for a large military style pistol.
The design is similar to the 1901 patent as later produced by Colt (page 108).
This model was produced as the FN Browning Model 1903 and Husqvarna Model 1907.

(Fig.107-2) The prototype pistol is very similar to the later FN and Husqvarna production models. Interestingly enough, John Browning's slide release lever is far superior in functionality than the production models. It is entirely possible that the original trials pistols had a similar slide release lever but that this was modified during the Swedish trials (see page 158, 165). Note the inventor's preference for small sights. The open magazine design was produced with almost no changes (see fig.163-1). Note that the barrel lock bushing design was not transferred into production, instead the model found on the .32 caliber 1901 prototype was adopted for FN production (page 108). This indicates that FN inspected both prototypes. (Photographs by author, courtesy of the John M. Browning Firearms Museum, Ogden Union Station)

Browning 1901 Prototype in .32 caliber - Produced as Colt Model 1903 & 1908 (Model M)

Blowback design.
U.S. patent applied on April 3, 1902 - Patent 747,585 was granted on December 22, 1903.
This prototype was shown to Colt on July 16, 1901.
This model was produced as the Colt Model 1903, 1908 (Model M).

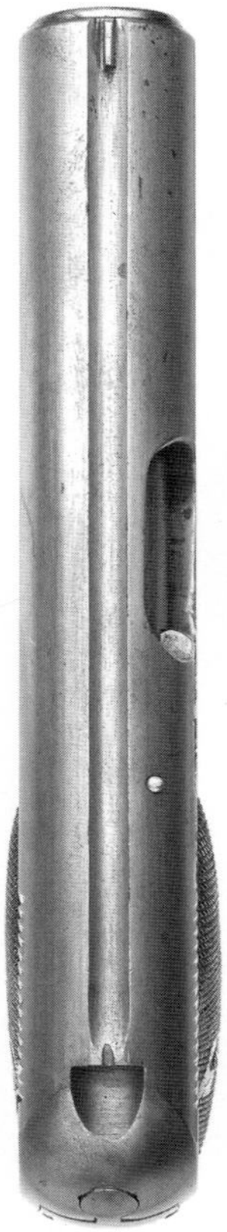

(Fig.108-1) Colt produced this prototype as their Model M and was marketed as Model 1903 or 1908. Unlike FN, Colt did introduce an array of changes to the design. Although Colt was looking for a compact pistol, they enlarged the overall size of the design. The slide and barrel were lengthened. The safety lever was modified and the sights were changed. An untrained eye could easily confuse this prototype with the prototype for the later FN Browning Model 1910 (page 110). These two prototypes share similar sizes and features. Note the sights on this prototype, which were kept on the 1910 prototype and so introduced on the FN Browning Model 1910. (Photographs by author, courtesy of the Browning Museum - Union Station)

Browning 1905 Prototype in .25 Caliber
Produced as FN Browning Model 1905/06 and as Colt Pocket Model 1908.

Blowback design.
Belgian patent 184656 filed on May 9, 1905.
U.S. patent applied on June 21, 1909 - Patent 947,478 was granted on January 25, 1910.
First produced by FN in 1906, introduced by Colt in 1908.

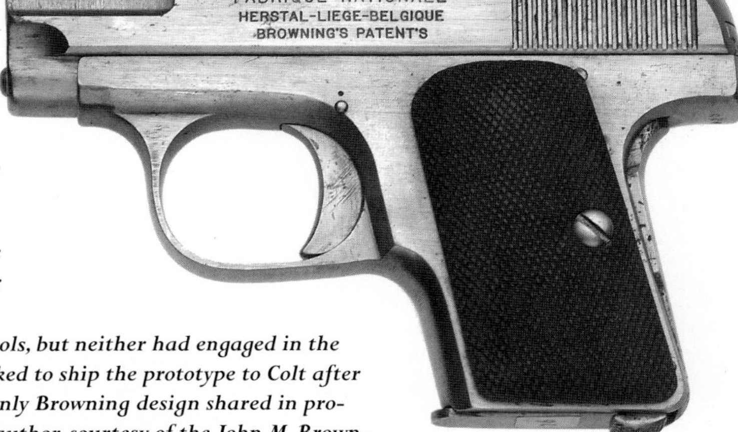

(Fig.108-2) This prototype was created in 1905 and soon made it into the hands of FN engineers. Production on this commercial pistol started immediately after a short tooling-up period (page 182). It was patented in the U.S. only after Colt decided to produce the pistol as well. Belgian patents were filed in 1905 and FN production had started before the patents had been granted. This prototype shows a Fabrique Nationale slide-legend with address and Browning patents marking. This English language slide legend was most likely added by Fabrique Nationale in order to claim ownership on the production rights.
Up to 1908, Colt and FN produced Browning pistols, but neither had engaged in the production of exactly the same pistol. FN was asked to ship the prototype to Colt after production had started. This prototype was the only Browning design shared in production by both Colt and FN. (Photographs by author, courtesy of the John M. Browning Firearms Museum, Ogden Union Station)

(Fig.109-1) FN's early production pistols are almost identical to the inventor's prototype. Colt on the other hand added the safety lever from the Browning 1901 prototype (page 108). The concept of the added slide safety was included in FN's post 1908 production (fig.183-1). Note the magazine with one view-hole. (Photographs by author, courtesy of the John M. Browning Firearms Museum, Ogden Union Station)

Browning 1908-1909 Prototype in .45 Caliber

Short recoil operated. Locked breech.
This prototype was built for U.S. trials, it is a variant with internal hammer. This model was not accepted and never produced. It is part of the evolution process that led to the adoption of the 1910 Browning design commonly known as the Colt Model 1911.

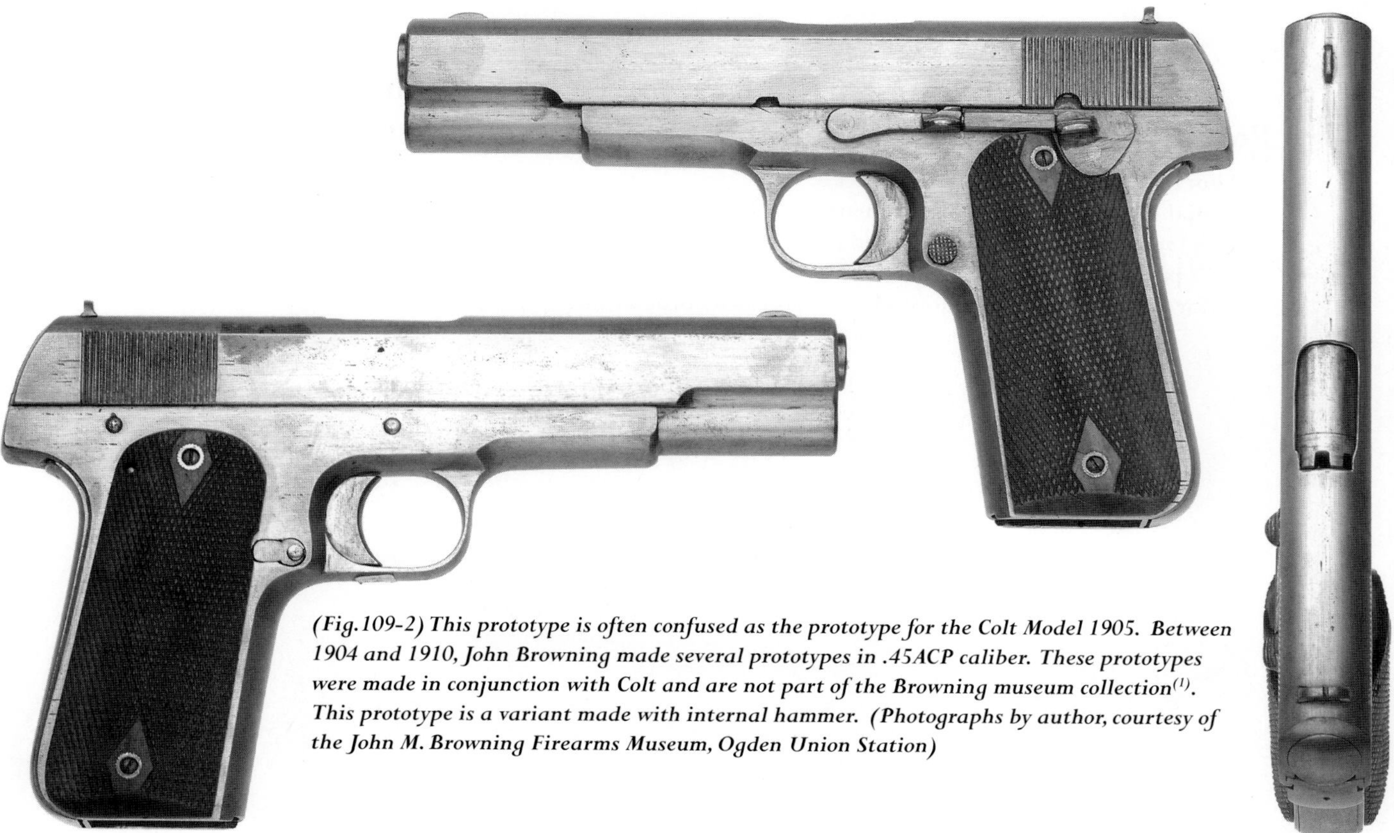

(Fig.109-2) This prototype is often confused as the prototype for the Colt Model 1905. Between 1904 and 1910, John Browning made several prototypes in .45ACP caliber. These prototypes were made in conjunction with Colt and are not part of the Browning museum collection[(1)]. This prototype is a variant made with internal hammer. (Photographs by author, courtesy of the John M. Browning Firearms Museum, Ogden Union Station)

(1) At least four prototypes are shown in the book *The Government Models* that are not part of the Browning Museum. These pistols were made and assembled by John Browning in conjunction with Colt.
The Government Models by William H.D. Goddard

Browning 1908-1910 Prototype in .32 caliber – Produced as FN Browning Model 1910

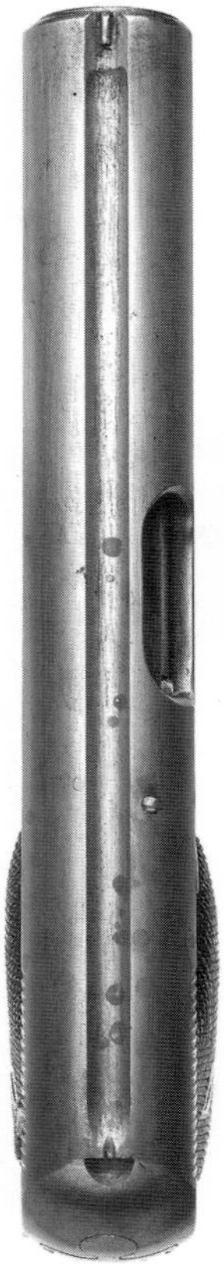

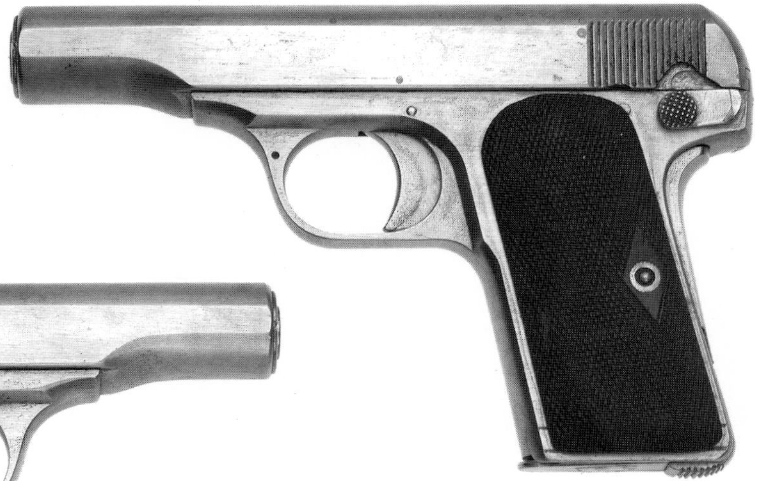

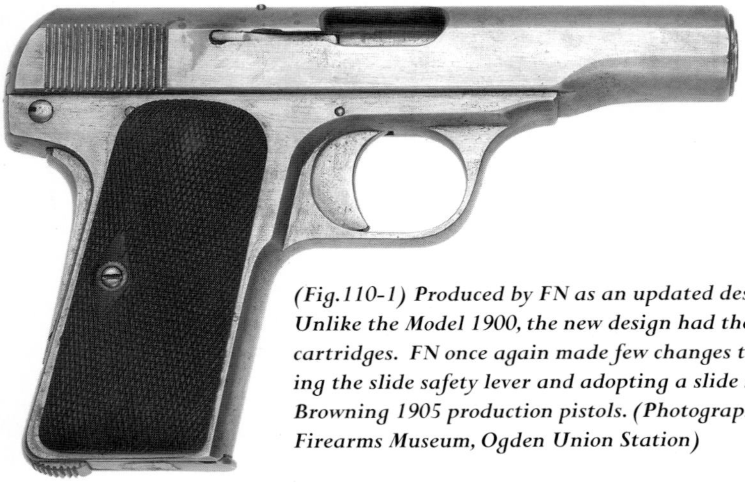

(Fig.110-1) Produced by FN as an updated design to the older FN Browning Model 1900. Unlike the Model 1900, the new design had the ability to fire .32 as well as .380 caliber cartridges. FN once again made few changes to the inventor's prototype except for modifying the slide safety lever and adopting a slide safety lever similar to the one in use on the FN Browning 1905 production pistols. (Photographs by author, courtesy of the John M. Browning Firearms Museum, Ogden Union Station)

Browning 1909-1910 Prototype in .45 Caliber
Produced as Colt Model 1911, FN Browning Grand Browning and others.

Short recoil operated. Locked breech.
Initial U.S. patent applied on February 17, 1910 - Patent 984,519 was granted on February 4, 1911.
Belgian patent 229828 was granted on October 19, 1910.
This prototype was built for U.S. trials, it is one of the last if not the last prototype in a string of evolutions before the U.S. military adopted the pistol as its official sidearm.

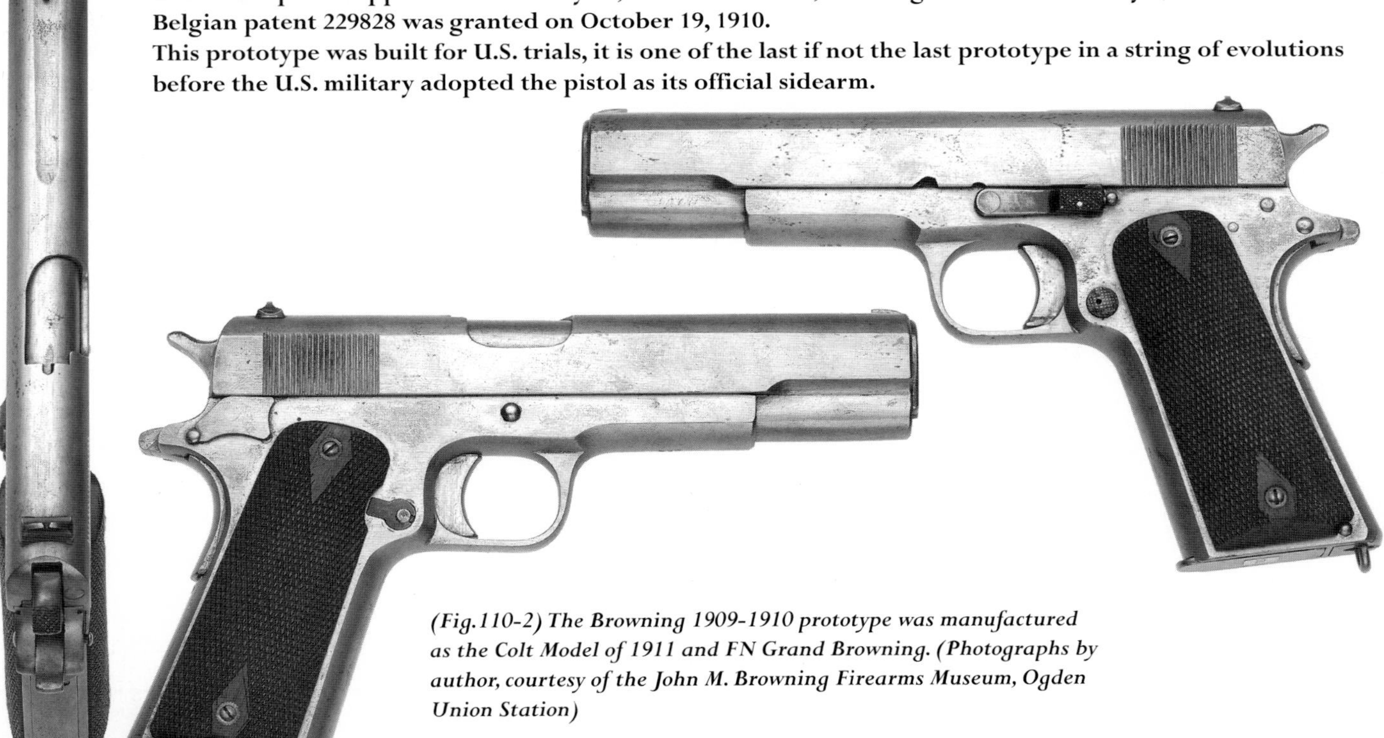

(Fig.110-2) The Browning 1909-1910 prototype was manufactured as the Colt Model of 1911 and FN Grand Browning. (Photographs by author, courtesy of the John M. Browning Firearms Museum, Ogden Union Station)

Browning 1921-1922 Prototype in 9x19mm Caliber

Blowback design with concealed hammer.
This model was never produced.

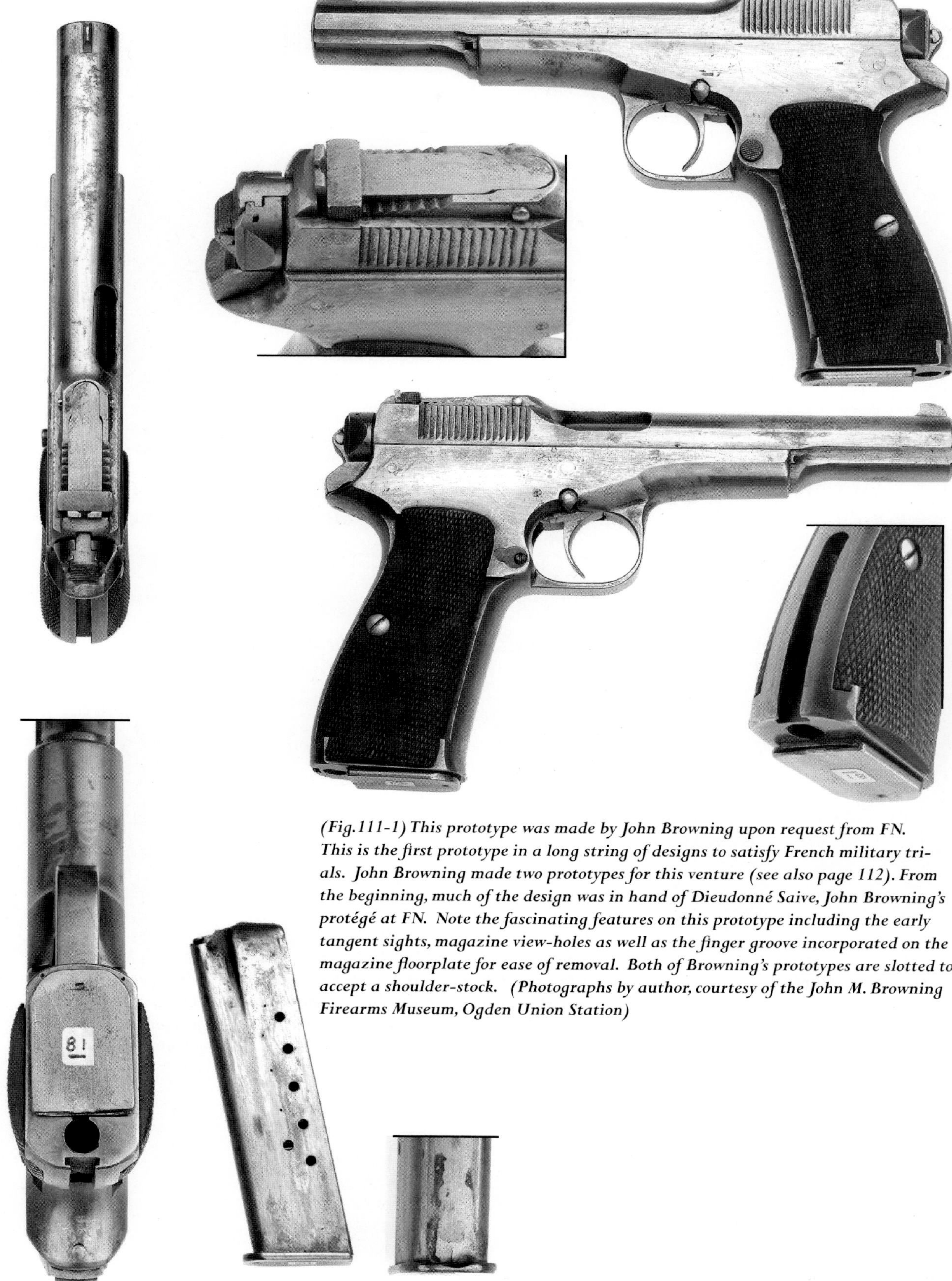

(Fig.111-1) This prototype was made by John Browning upon request from FN. This is the first prototype in a long string of designs to satisfy French military trials. John Browning made two prototypes for this venture (see also page 112). From the beginning, much of the design was in hand of Dieudonné Saive, John Browning's protégé at FN. Note the fascinating features on this prototype including the early tangent sights, magazine view-holes as well as the finger groove incorporated on the magazine floorplate for ease of removal. Both of Browning's prototypes are slotted to accept a shoulder-stock. (Photographs by author, courtesy of the John M. Browning Firearms Museum, Ogden Union Station)

Browning 1921-1922 Prototype in 9x19mm Caliber

Short recoil operated. Locked breech.
U.S. Patent applied on June 28, 1923 - Patent 1,618,510 was granted on February 22, 1927.
This model was never produced.

(Fig.112-1) This prototype was John Browning's last pistol design. It was made for French trials upon request of FN together with the preceding blowback design. This design would eventually evolve under direction of Dieudonné Saive and became the Grand Rendement and later High Power pistol.The original magazine and tangent sights for this pistol are missing. (Photographs by author, courtesy of the John M. Browning Firearms Museum, Ogden Union Station)

FN's Sales Network

World's Fairs: FN Exhibits Worldwide

In their day, the World's Fair expositions were a gateway to international markets. While the expositions attracted significant numbers of retail customers, they also fostered name recognition and impressed both the public and government officials with FN's latest innovations. FN capitalized heavily on the expositions after having great success at the Paris World's Fair in 1900.

Prior to World War II, the fairs were as much trade shows as they were public spectacle. Unlike modern trade shows, which are specific to a given marketing or manufacturing sector, the World's Fairs displayed innovations across a broad spectrum of industries. The larger fairs were divided into country specific pavilions. Exhibitors could participate in their own country pavilion or could set up their own lavish exhibition building. These buildings were typically built specifically for the fair and were most often demolished after the event. Judging committees were established to award various prizes to the exhibitors. These prizes became marketing tools for the manufacturers, often reflecting high quality and innovation.

FN started exhibiting soon after the completion of the factory. In the 1890s, the factory was one of the most modern arm producers in the world and the company proudly showed their line of Mauser rifles.

FN's success gained momentum after the introduction of the chainless bicycle (1897), the first FN automobile (1900), the four-cylinder motorcycle (1905) and, of course, the introduction of the Browning pistol (1899). FN enjoyed an overwhelming amount of publicity and name recognition with its Browning pistol and Browning line of firearms.

(Fig.113-1) A rare view of a FN display in France circa 1905. The photograph features FN bicycles, single-cylinder motorcycles and the 1905 four-cylinder motorcycle. On the right we can distinguish a FN 1900 automobile. Note the Parisian agent's information.

It became apparent in Paris in 1900 that the automotive and motorcycle departments would benefit from the fairs more than the arms department. FN's marketing efforts in the early years set the tone for company advertising prior to World War II. The motorcycle and automobile departments advertised their product lines heavily while the arms department was lower key and capitalized on Browning's reputation and name recognition.

As they were magnets for international customers, FN used the fairs to introduce its products to various markets. The fairs were also an avenue to establish dealerships and representation in new markets. It often became the responsibility of FN's agent or representative in a city or country to coordinate and run the exhibit. As such, there were different exhibits set through the years, varying in size and splendor. The factory backed the agents but usually left them in charge of the event. If an event was determined to be of particular importance, the factory would handle everything directly with the agent in support.

There is a clear correlation between the strategies FN followed before World War II and the overall success of the company.

As the era of the world's fairs came to an end after World War II, FN's worldwide representation began to diminish. FN's market share steadily declined through the decades after World War II. The last great market dominated by FN was that of the post-war infantry weapons, which saw huge numbers of sales, and large numbers of licensing agreements for the FAL rifle and MAG58 machine gun. The lessons learned in the early years were no longer valued and as a result, FN's world influence and market share steadily declined.

Little is known of FN's representation at the 1893 Chicago and 1894 Antwerp fairs. Following is a list of FN's participation in prewar World Fairs:

1893 Chicago
1894 Anvers (Antwerp)
1897 Bruxelles (Brussels)
1900 Paris
1905 Liège
1906 Milan
1910 Bruxelles (Brussels)
1910 Buenos Aires
1913 Gand (Ghent / Gent)
1922-1923 Rio de Janeiro
1929 Barcelona
1930 Liège
1930 Anvers (Antwerp)
1931 Paris
1935 Bruxelles (Brussels)
1939 Liège (Exposition de l'Eau / Water Exhibit)

(Fig.114-1) The massive and lavish FN building at the 1910 Brussels World's Fair was one of the focal points of the whole fair. The building was located next to the Pavilion of Uruguay. FN always had a large presence at fairs but went all out in 1910 with their own palatial exhibit building.

(Fig.114-2) The 1913 fair was largely organized by FN's agent Houard in Ghent. Note the array of FN Mauser variants as well as the many different bayonet configurations. The FN Browning 1900 pistols are mounted above the Auto-5 sporting guns. This photograph only shows the firearms, a whole floor was dedicated to FN and displayed automobiles, bicycles and motorcycles. (Photograph courtesy of FN Herstal)

(Fig.114-3) FN exhibited in the "Arms and Cycles" pavilion at the 1930 Liège fair. FN was not only an exhibitor at the fair but also sponsored the event and provided logistical support motorcycles for the event.

(Fig.115-1) The 1928 Brussels Automotive Show displayed the M.70 Sahara motorcycle on a massive scale. The wall of 105 completed M.70 motorcycles represented FN's production capability in an eight-hour workday. The motorcycle up front is one of the Sahara endurance motorcycles (see page 25-26). The display stand was a map that showed the route of the Sahara endurance rally. The whole display capitalized on the success of FN's Sahara rally and FN's production capability.

The FN Agents

There is a perception that economic globalization, multinational corporations and the network of international trade are thoroughly modern concepts, and that the late 19th and early 20th centuries were periods of isolation and limited trade. In fact, nothing could be further from the truth.

One example of the fallacious nature of this perception is the speed at which the Browning Brothers and FN communicated with each other. This is evidenced by the first contract - signed and mailed from Herstal, Belgium on July 17, 1897 and received by the Browning Brothers in Ogden, Utah on July 26, 1897; a mere nine days later.

Although travel was slow in comparison to today's standards, this should not be confused with a limitation of trade. From the early days of the 20th century to the outbreak of World War II, FN had a presence and representation throughout all of Europe, most major Asian cities, a great deal of the African continent (or at least that portion comprising European colonies) and established representatives in the Americas. Most of the representatives were knowledgeable and respected businessmen native to the territories in which they worked. Several however were working for FN directly and dispatched from Belgium. In many cases these individuals moved together with their families to distant lands in order to establish FN's market. The little that is known today of these representatives indicates that these families usually did not return to Europe but remained in their adopted countries. Examples include the Van der Ghote family, representatives for Argentina and the Verlinden family in the Philippines.

A FN representative was called an "Agent". Agents had the responsibility to represent the company, deal and negotiate government contracts and sell FN merchandise in a wholesale as well as retail capacity. Many agents set up storefronts in order to sell directly to the public.

Agents had the ability to act as distributors and sell wholesale to dealerships. Dealers could sell retail and wholesale but were restricted from dealing with government officials. Retailers were usually local stores or department stores that dealt only in the retail trade.

In most cases, governments and retailers placed their orders with the FN agent in their country. The agent would then forward the orders to FN. In turn, FN shipped the merchandise directly to the agent who would forward it to the ordering party. Large government orders were shipped directly to the buyer in order to save time and freight expenses. Small government orders were shipped to the agent. Shipping often depended on logistics and economics; there was no comprehensive set of shipping guidelines as this often was stipulated in contracts or agreements with individual agents.

Following is a reconstructed list of agents, dealers and retailers from the early 20th century up to the World War II period. Through the years, some dealers became agents, which adds to the confusion of who had what function at what time. Not all operated through the entire period. Outlets listed as department stores could also have been sporting goods chains.

Australia:	**Agent – Alcock & Pierce, Melbourne**
	Dealer – Stewart & Allwood, Sydney
	Retailer – Evans & Balfour, Melbourne
Austria:	**Agent – Zissu, Vienna**
	Dealer – Zultner, Vienna
	Department stores – Genshow, Vienna
Argentina:	**Agent – Tombeur, Buenos Aires**
	Agent – Van der Ghote, Buenos Aires
Belgium:	**Agent – Schroeder, Liège**
	Agent – Houard, Gand
	Dealer – Van Cauwenberghe, Antwerp
	Retailer – Pire, Antwerp
	Dealer – Laloux, Liège
	Dealer – Stassart, Liège
	Dealer – Janssen, Liège
Belgian Congo:	**Dealer – Windfohr Armes**
Brazil:	**Agent – Laport, Rio de Janeiro**
Canada:	**Agent – MacFarlane, Montreal**
Colombia	**Agent - Leocadio Arango**
Czechoslovakia:	**Agent – Nowotny, Prague**
Denmark:	**Agent – Simonsen & Nielsen, Copenhagen**
Estonia:	**Agent – Freybach, Tallinn**
France:	**Agent – Parent & Leroy, Paris**
	Agent – Cartoucherie française, Paris
	Dealer – Manufacture française d'Armes et Cycles
	Retailer – Eaton & Co., Paris
	Retailer – Faure LePage, Paris
Germany:	**Agent – Wagener, Hamburg**
	Agent – Deutscher
	Agent / Department stores – Genshow, Berlin
	Department stores – Genshow, Hamburg
	Department stores – Genshow, Köenigsberg
	Department stores – Genshow, Koln
	Department stores – Genshow, Nurnberg
	Agent / Department stores – Kind, Berlin
	Department stores – Kind, Hamburg
	Department stores – Kind, Hunstig
	Department stores – Kind, Nurenberg

(Fig.116-1) Two exquisite presentation gifts commissioned by FN staff and their agents in order to sway heads of state into buying FN products. (l.) 1938 High Power custom work for King Farouk of Egypt. (r.) 1938 High Power custom work for President Benavides of Peru. (Photographs courtesy of Collector Grade Publications, Inc.)

Great Britain:	Agent – Louis Lepersonne, London[1]
Hungary:	Agent – Skaba, Budapest
India (British Empire):	Retail – Lyon & Lyon, Calcutta
	Retail – Walter Locke & Co, Calcutta
	Retail – Walter Locke & Co, Simla
	Retail – Walter Locke & Co, Lahore
Italy:	Agent – Achille Fusi, Milan
Netherlands:	Agent – Allard, Maastricht
New Zealand:	Agent – McCarthy, Dunedin
	Agent – William Hazard, Auckland
	Department stores – Tisdall, Christchurch
	Department stores – Tisdall, Oakland
	Department stores – Tisdall, Wellington
Peru:	Agent – Laport, Lima
Philippines:	Agent – Verlinden, Manilla
Portugal:	Agent – Empis, Lisbon
Romania:	Agent – Zissu, Bucharest
Russia, pre-1917:	Agent – Vetter & Hinkel, Moscow
Serbia:	Agent – Charles Doucet, Belgrade
Singapore:	Dealer – Robinson
Spain:	Agent – Manuel Pardo, Madrid
	Dealer – Quintana Hermanos
Sweden:	Agent – Berghaus, Gothembourg
	Dealer – Bastmann, Stockholm
Switserland:	Agent – Deletra
	Agent – Glaser
	Agent – Amsler, Feuerthalen
Turkey:	Agent – Nikitis[2], Istanboul
	Dealer – Fuad Baban, Ankara

(Fig.117-1) Most Agents and some dealers printed their own sales catalogs and sales literature. This allowed them to concentrate on the products they cared to sell and also promote the FN products in their language of choice. The most elaborate of these catalogs were made by Schroeder, Lepersonne, Fusi, Alcock & Pierce and McCarthy.

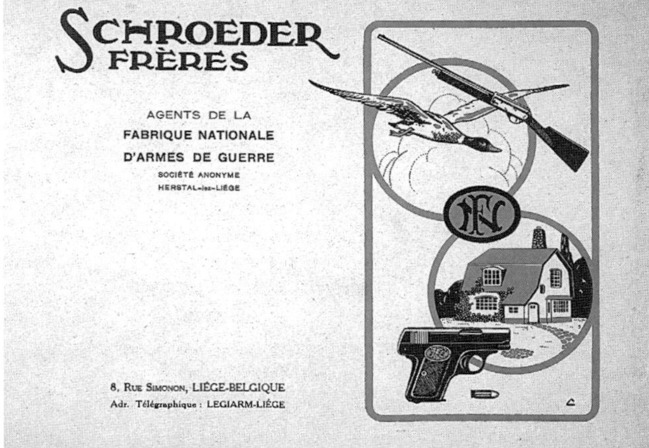

(Fig.117-2) Note the deception warning on the special notice. This extract is out of the Australian Alcock & Pierce catalog.

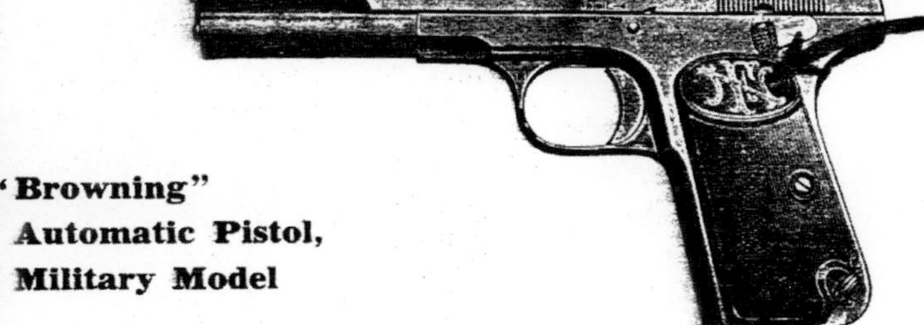

SPECIAL NOTICE,

Unless the Pistol is marked FN (as shown here), it is not a genuine "Browning." Any person telling you that a Pistol without this Brand "is as good" or "the same as a 'Browning,'" is deliberately trying to deceive you.

(Fig.117-3) FN sponsored the printing of some of the agents' catalogs. Fusi's catalog (l.) in Italian was sponsored by FN but printed in Italy. Others were printed in Belgium on request of the agent and shipped from FN. McCarthy in New Zealand ordered most of his literature through FN and had his company information included on all his promotional FN literature.

(1) Louis Antoine Georges LePersonne was a naturalized British citizen of Belgian origin

(2) Also spelled Nikitits

(Fig.118-1) Mr.Van der Ghote immigrated from Belgium to Argentina as FN's sales agent in the early 20th century (Seen on the left next to his FN 1300 car). He set up a lasting legacy in Argentina, dealing primarily in FN automotive products, he founded a FN motoring club. What started with casual Sunday outings and picnics, evolved over the years into competitive racing.Van der Ghote became famous for organizing endurance races and can be traced back as the founder of the Rallye of the Andes, although named differently at the time, the race still takes place every year and draws professional drivers from all over the world. As Van der Ghote grew older, his sons took over the business. The family was heavily involved with FN and kept the FN name alive during both world wars. After World War II, the sons concentrated on Italian motorcycles and other products as FN closed its automotive departments.

(Fig.118-2) The Fusi family of Milan got involved with FN prior to the turn of the 20th century with Achille Fusi as the original agent. A true family business it brought FN market share to Italy, which was dominated by domestic brands like Beretta. The Milan based company was ultimately purchased by FN in 1925 but the family continued to manage the business. Seen here are the Fusi family members at the FN stand of the 1930 Liège World Fair (see fig.114-3). (Photograph courtesy of FN Herstal)

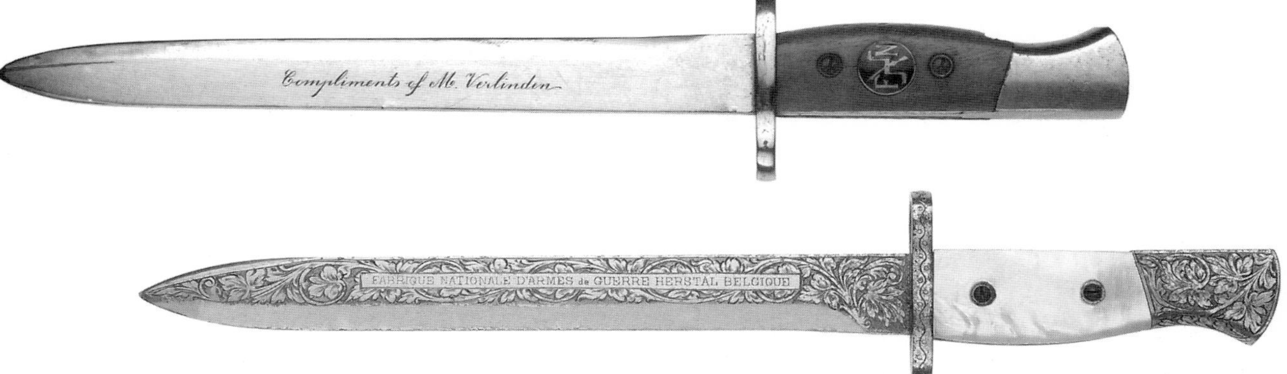

(Fig.118-3) FN agents had at their disposal factory gifts and mementos to donate to significant customers. Often these gifts were given in order to sway buyers into doing business with FN. Depending on the buyer, gifts extended from presentation bayonets / letter openers to fully engraved guns. Pictured here is a basic presentation bayonet as given by Mr. Verlinden from Manila. Three styles of presentation bayonets were available, seen here is also one of the two engraved styles with mother-of-pearl grips. The rare factory nickel presentation cartridges (above) would have been given to buyers of ammunition or Mauser rifles. Factory presentation gifts were usually given to large government buyers and are rare in the collector community.

FN Agent and Dealer Markings

From the earliest days of pistol manufacturing in 1899, FN promoted the Browning name. In addition, FN provided mechanisms for dealers, agents and retailers to promote themselves. FN provided imprinted catalogs containing the agents' contact information. Factory cases were available with the agent's or dealer's name imprinted on the inside (see fig.128-1 and 185-1) and the pistols could also be roll-engraved with the agent's, dealer's or retailer's information.

However, these services were not free, and while some dealers and agents opted for imprinted cases, the practice gradually disappeared in the early twentieth century. Engraved pistols on the other hand were ordered by some of the most dedicated dealers and agents. Others quickly got into the practice of marking or engraving their sales pistols themselves or outsourcing the work locally at reduced costs.

As a result, pistols exist today with both FN applied dealer markings as well as aftermarket markings. FN dealer markings are typically roll or hand engraved. The practice of marking pistols was popular prior to World War II, with its heyday in the early twentieth century. Still, only a small percentage of the pistols were marked, making these interesting collector pieces. After World War II, some pistols were stamped with importer - dealer stamps. These stamps were applied more for identification purposes than for marketing or name recognition.

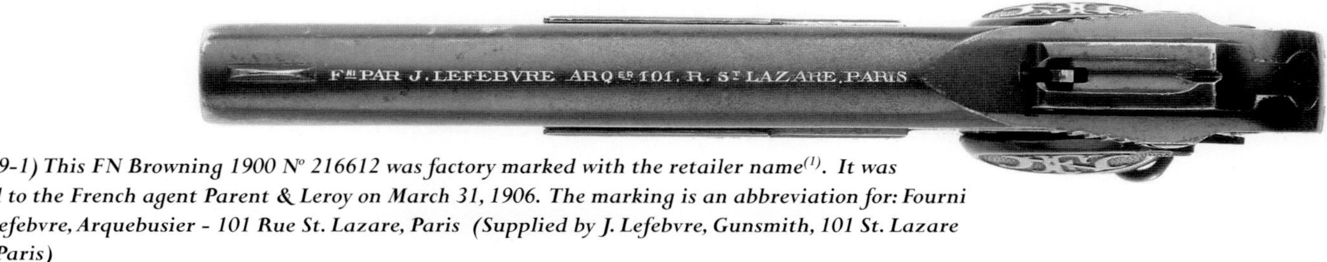

(Fig.119-1) This FN Browning 1900 N° 216612 was factory marked with the retailer name(1). It was shipped to the French agent Parent & Leroy on March 31, 1906. The marking is an abbreviation for: Fourni par J. Lefebvre, Arquebusier - 101 Rue St. Lazare, Paris (Supplied by J. Lefebvre, Gunsmith, 101 St. Lazare Street, Paris)

(Fig.119-2) This early FN Browning 1900 N° 69570 was factory marked with the Colombian agent's name. It was shipped from FN on November 4, 1903.

(1) Retailers and dealers could order special factory markings from their FN agent. Although the markings were factory applied, the shipment was most often sent to the FN agent.

(Fig.120-1) This FN Browning 1900 N° 664456 was retailer marked by Robinson Singapore after it left the factory. Orders for Singapore and India were handled and forwarded by Louis Lepersonne in London. This pistol was shipped from FN to Lepersonne on November 7, 1913.

(Fig.120-2) This FN Browning 1910 N° 398701 was marked with the retailer's name Evans & Balfour in Melbourne Australia. (Photograph by author, courtesy of Kevin Null)

(Fig.120-3) The typical small "Manufacture française d'Armes et Cycles de Saint Etienne" marking was applied after it left the factory. This Model 1910 pistol N° 56824 was scheduled for shipping to Zissu in Vienna on July 27, 1914 but was rerouted to France after the Sarajevo affair and ensuing military escalation. (Photograph by author, courtesy of Wendell Patton)

(Fig.120-4) The small "Manufacture française d'Armes et Cycles de Saint Etienne" marking was applied after it left the factory. The Model 1900 pistol N° 614832 has the marking applied on top of the slide. This pistol was shipped from FN on September 14, 1912 (see also page 154).

(Fig.120-5) Although listed as a FN customer, Mestre & Blatge was not a FN agent or dealer. Mestre & Blatge was an automobile manufacturer in the 1910s, later the company focused on making automobile and motorcycle parts. Facilities were located in Paris, France, Rio de Janeiro, Brazil and Vancouver, Canada among others. This specific pistol was shipped to FN's agent in Canada, Mac Farlane, on July 28, 1913. Pistols shipped to Rio de Janeiro were shipped directly from FN to Mestre & Blatge and not to an agent. The reason behind this is unknown. The letters on the slide M.B. of C. stand for Mestre Blatge of Canada, these were applied after the pistol left the factory. These pistols were most likely used as side-arms for security personnel.

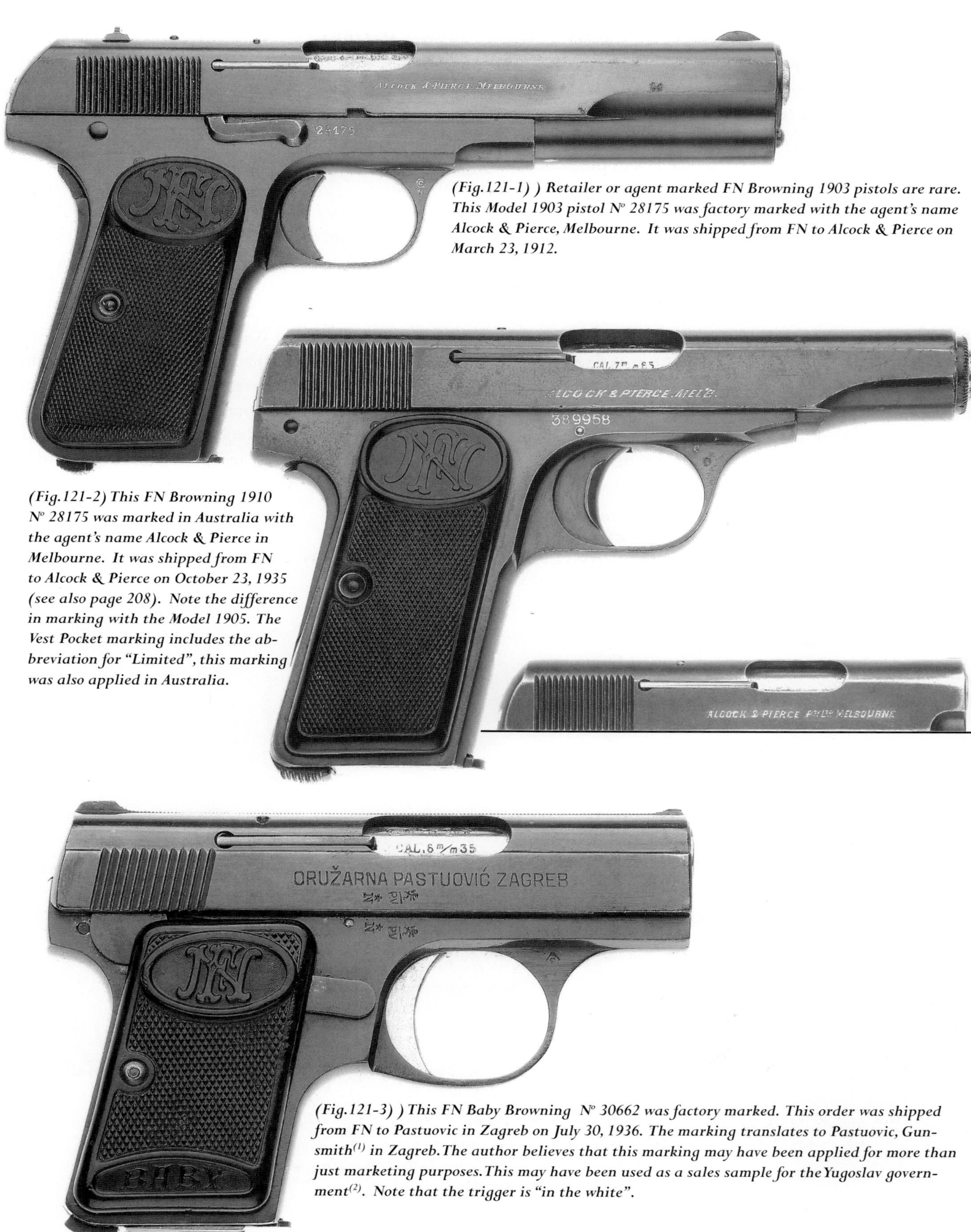

(Fig.121-1)) Retailer or agent marked FN Browning 1903 pistols are rare. This Model 1903 pistol Nº 28175 was factory marked with the agent's name Alcock & Pierce, Melbourne. It was shipped from FN to Alcock & Pierce on March 23, 1912.

(Fig.121-2) This FN Browning 1910 Nº 28175 was marked in Australia with the agent's name Alcock & Pierce in Melbourne. It was shipped from FN to Alcock & Pierce on October 23, 1935 (see also page 208). Note the difference in marking with the Model 1905. The Vest Pocket marking includes the abbreviation for "Limited", this marking was also applied in Australia.

(Fig.121-3)) This FN Baby Browning Nº 30662 was factory marked. This order was shipped from FN to Pastuovic in Zagreb on July 30, 1936. The marking translates to Pastuovic, Gunsmith[1] in Zagreb. The author believes that this marking may have been applied for more than just marketing purposes. This may have been used as a sales sample for the Yugoslav government[2]. Note that the trigger is "in the white".

(1) Can also be translated as "Arms Dealer"

(2) Several Model 1905 and 1910 pistols were shipped to Pastuovic with this marking. The author entertains the possibility that these markings were ordered for source recognition as Pastuovic was trying to secure contracts with local officials. Pastuovic may have tried to establish himself as a FN agent in Zagreb.

FN Agents Request Extended Barrel Pistols

FN agents were also responsible for ensuring compliance with local gun laws, facilitating importation and proofing in their respected countries. Pistols imported into the Austrian-Hungarian Empire, Czechoslovakia and others had to be proofed domestically (see page 96).

Requests from a small number of dealers in the Austro-Hungarian Empire and Czechoslovakia prompted FN to produce long-barreled versions of the Model 1900, 1905 and 1910 pistols. Concealed firearms laws in those markets restricted the sale of pistols with an overall length of less than 15cm (5.9 inches or 150mm) from magazine well to muzzle. Such pistols were not banned but required a permit. Pistols with a (magazine well to muzzle) length greater than 15 cm (5.9 inches) did not require a permit. Agents quickly requested that FN produce longer barrels to facilitate commercial sales.

Most of the extended barrel pistols found today date from the period prior to World War I as these laws were more prevalent in that era. Some however date as late as the 1930s. There is no indication that FN supplied more extended barrel pistols in those markets than regular pistols, in fact it appears that the extended barrel models were more the exception than the rule. Because of the limited distribution, these pistols are rarely encountered today. Unlike standard barrels, FN always blued the extended barrels. This is the only instance where FN blued barrels prior to World War II. Obviously this was done for aesthetic reasons. Extended barrels are numbered and proofed like standard barrels. These were shipped from FN assembled into the pistols and were not replaced or installed by the FN agents.

Observed or reported pistols with extended barrels
FN Model 1900 N°: 629661, 633635, 633871, 671278
FN Model 1905 N°: 23578, 944954, 958270, 971952, 1038324, 1069639
FN Model 1910 N°: 20607, 20642, 20702, 52512, 63121

(Fig.122-1) This FN Browning 1900 N° 629661 was manufactured in 1912 but never shipped. This pistol disappeared during World War I. Its condition implies that it was most likely hidden during the war (see page 33).

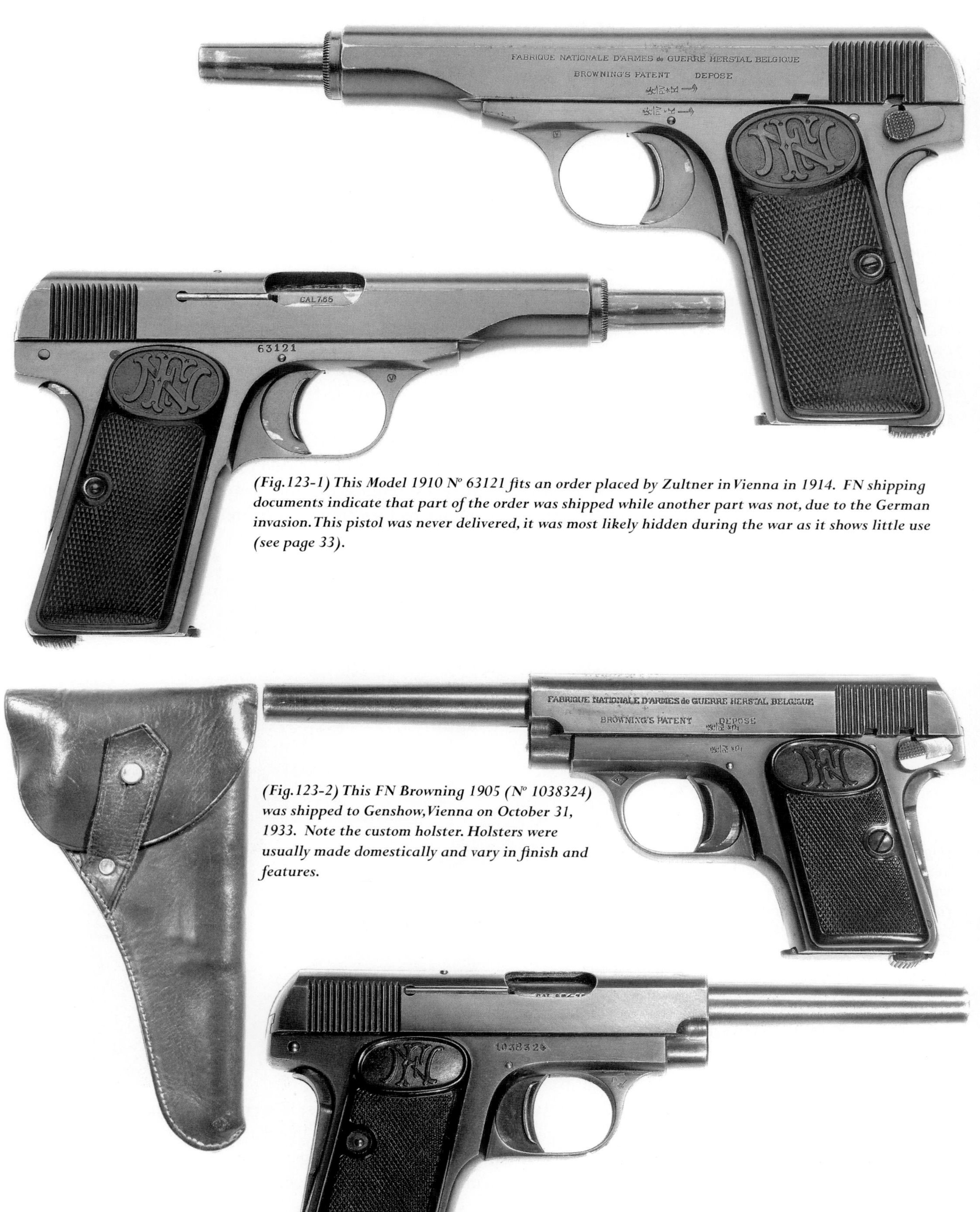

(Fig.123-1) This Model 1910 N° 63121 fits an order placed by Zultner in Vienna in 1914. FN shipping documents indicate that part of the order was shipped while another part was not, due to the German invasion. This pistol was never delivered, it was most likely hidden during the war as it shows little use (see page 33).

(Fig.123-2) This FN Browning 1905 (N° 1038324) was shipped to Genshow, Vienna on October 31, 1933. Note the custom holster. Holsters were usually made domestically and vary in finish and features.

The FN Browning Model 1899

Development History

The Model 1899 was the first handgun produced by FN. The manufacturing rights were purchased from the Browning Brothers on July 17, 1897, less than a month after Hart O' Berg brought it back from the U.S. (June 19, 1897). It took FN only a few months to tool up for production, the first prototypes were made in July 1898 and the first production pistols were manufactured and sold in January 1899. FN's total tooling and startup costs were a mere 12,000 Belgian francs (see contract details on page 10).

During the first Belgian Army trials in 1899, the FN Browning Model 1899 pistols competed against the Mauser, the Bergmann, the Roth, Mannlicher, Borchardt and Borchardt-Luger pistols. At the trials' conclusion, the Belgian War Department decided to retain the Browning(s), the Borchardt-Luger and Mannlicher pistols for further trials.

Sometime after the introduction of the Model 1899 pistol, FN introduced a larger version designed specifically for military customers. For clarity's sake, these variations will be referred to as the large Model 1899 and compact Model 1899. These are not factory designations; it is unknown if there was a separate factory designation for the large Model 1899.

It appears that the large Model 1899 was first entered in one of the subsequent Belgian military trials during the middle of 1899. In October 1900 the large Model 1899 pistol was submitted together with the new Model 1900 pistol for British trials. By December the British Small Arms Committee had rejected the 7.65 mm cartridge due to its poor penetration characteristics.

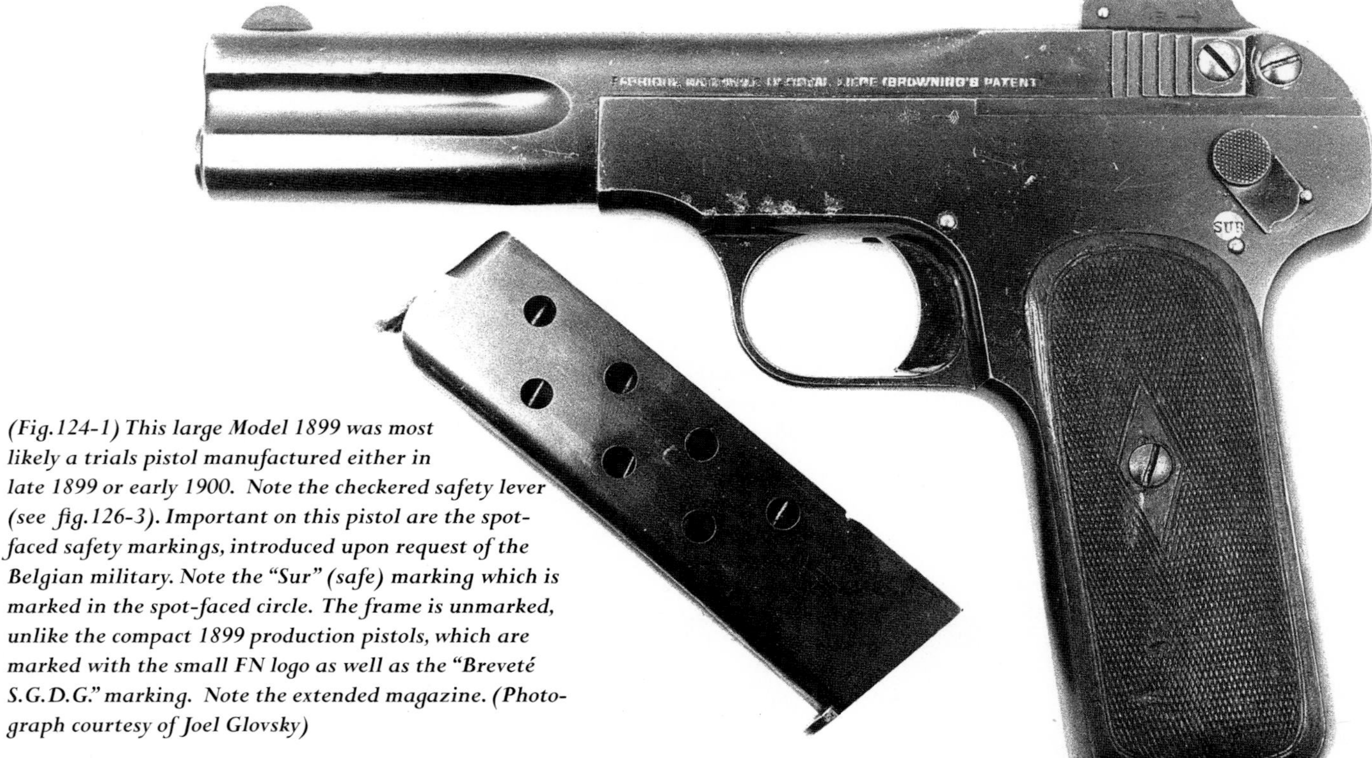

(Fig.124-1) This large Model 1899 was most likely a trials pistol manufactured either in late 1899 or early 1900. Note the checkered safety lever (see fig.126-3). Important on this pistol are the spot-faced safety markings, introduced upon request of the Belgian military. Note the "Sur" (safe) marking which is marked in the spot-faced circle. The frame is unmarked, unlike the compact 1899 production pistols, which are marked with the small FN logo as well as the "Breveté S.G.D.G." marking. Note the extended magazine. (Photograph courtesy of Joel Glovsky)

Because of its unpopularity in the military market, very few large Model 1899 pistols were manufactured. Only a handful of these trials and sales pistols are known to exist. The few that are still in existence today all appear to have the spot-faced safety markings (see fig.144-1). The spot-faced safety markings were requested during the first or second Belgian trials. This indicates that the pistols were manufactured after production of the compact models had started.

The main difference between the large and compact model is the extension of the frame and slide. Like all Model 1899 pistols, the large model has the sight safety (cocked) indicator[(1)].

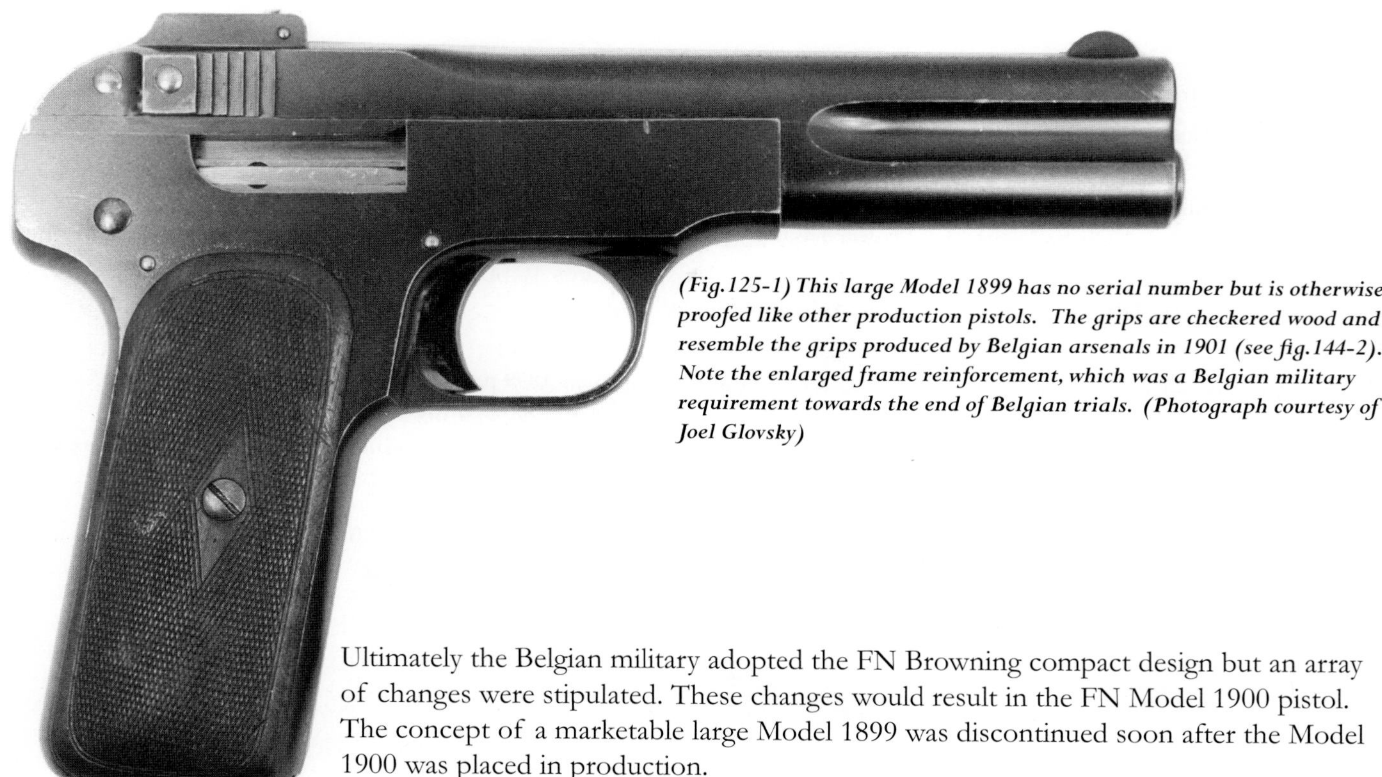

(Fig.125-1) This large Model 1899 has no serial number but is otherwise proofed like other production pistols. The grips are checkered wood and resemble the grips produced by Belgian arsenals in 1901 (see fig.144-2). Note the enlarged frame reinforcement, which was a Belgian military requirement towards the end of Belgian trials. (Photograph courtesy of Joel Glovsky)

Ultimately the Belgian military adopted the FN Browning compact design but an array of changes were stipulated. These changes would result in the FN Model 1900 pistol. The concept of a marketable large Model 1899 was discontinued soon after the Model 1900 was placed in production.

The compact Model 1899 evolved into a commercial success. FN kept the Model 1899 in production while it was filling the first Belgian Army order for 10,000 Model 1900 pistols. The initial idea was to produce the Model 1899 for commercial sales and manufacture the Model 1900 for the Belgian military.

This initial idea of manufacturing two similar pistols proved to be unpractical and expensive. The Model 1899 was phased out in 1901. Parts were used up and Model 1899 pistols were sold together with the newer Model 1900. In some instances, it is possible to see a Model 1899 pistol with some newer Model 1900 parts(2).

When introduced in January 1899, the Model 1899 retailed for about 30 Belgian francs. 1000 rounds of FN 7.65mm ammunition sold for 55 Belgian francs. FN reached in 1899 a production capacity of 100 pistols a day(3).

The Model 1899 was sold primarily on the commercial market. A few pistols were used in military trails but no country adopted the pistol for military use. FN made presentation cases available for the pistol. A factory nickel version was available but the model preceded the introduction of standardized factory commissioned engraving in 1903. One such exception is the pistol donated to President Teddy Roosevelt (page 132).

The Model 1899 was simply called "Pistolet Browning". At the time, FN did not know that many more Browning models would follow. The relationship with the Browning Brothers was still in its infancy and FN had no reason to specify a model year or further designation.

Later after the introduction of the Model 1900, the Model 1899 pistol was often referred to as "modèle de pré-série" (pre-series model).

(1) An oriental copy of the large Model 1899 exists with almost identical markings and features. This copy can immediately be identified by the magazine release. This magazine release on the copy resembles the one found on FN Model 1903 pistols (see fig 163-1).

(2) The pistols are easy to identify as all are part of the "A" prefix production range. Several variations have been noted as these were assembled with miscellaneous parts; some have occurred with lanyard rings, others have Model 1900 grips. Most often, the later checkered safety lever was used instead of the early variant with concentric grooves.

(3) Although FN had such production capabilities, it rarely made such quantities on a daily bases.

FN Model 1899: Features & Specifications

Serial Numbers

According to a 1914 "La Meuse" newspaper article, about 3900 pistols were manufactured during the period 1899-1900. Approximately 10,000 pistols were manufactured in 1900.

The pistols manufactured in 1899 and 1900 have consecutive serial numbers from 1 to 9999. FN maintained the same serialization practices as it had with the Model 1889 and 1894 Mauser rifles. Once the four digits were used up, they introduced a letter prefix. Characteristically each letter prefix indicates 10,000 units but no letter prefixes beyond "A" exist on the Model 1899 as it was discontinued during the "A" prefix run.

Production and serial number data for the Model 1899 are as follows: **1899 production: N° 1-3900**
1900 production: N° 3901-9999
1900-1901 production: N° A1- A4500+ approximately

Reported serial numbers on pistols manufactured in 1899:
19 (Belgian Army trials pistol), 21, 36, 156, 205, 703A, 841A, 952, 2692, 3131.
Reported serial numbers on pistols manufactured after 1899: 5071, 7929, 9152, 9580 (nickel finish), 9649 (nickel finish), 9979
A61, A181, A345, A861, A923, A1468, A1584, A1670, A2075, A2544, A3086, A4012, A4558

Slide Legends and Safeties

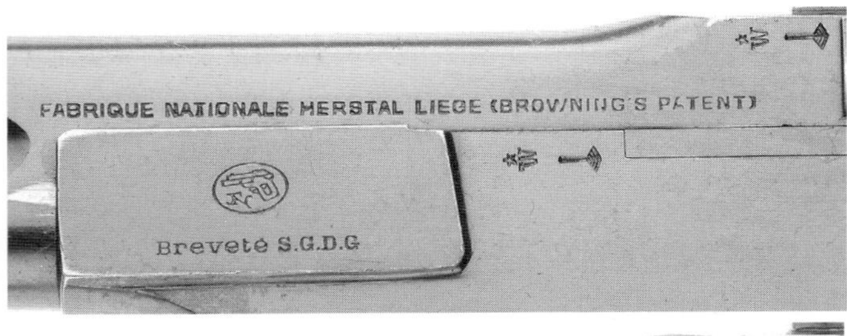

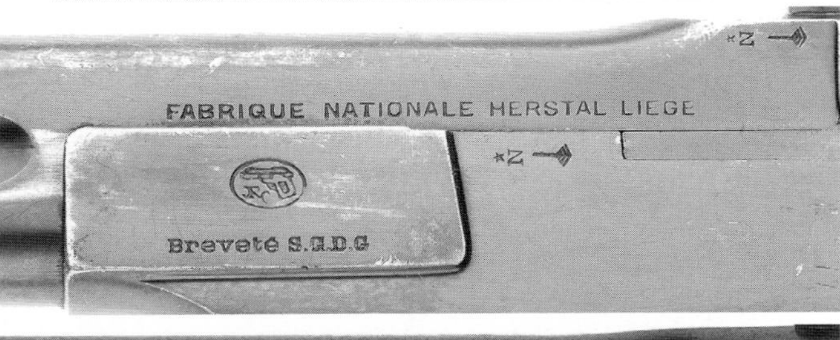

(Fig.126-1) Both slide legends (top and center) with and without "Browning's Patent" marking were used throughout the production of the Model 1899. There is no indication that one slide legend superseded the other one.

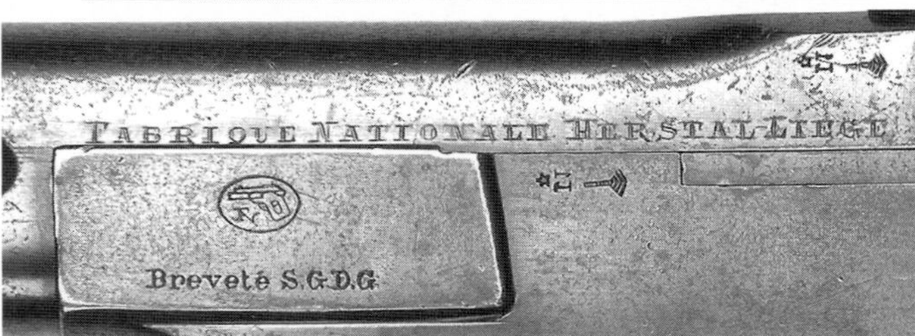

(Fig.126-2) A few slide legends were hand engraved on early guns. The reason behind the hand engraving is unknown as earlier pistols have been noted with roll engraved legends. This pistol is N°156. (Photograph courtesy of Bob Adams)

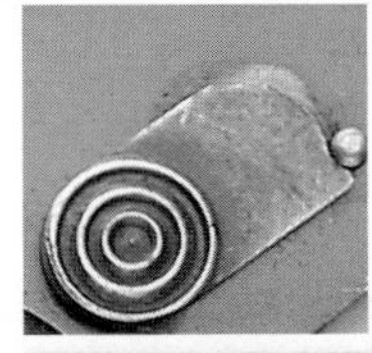

(Fig.126-3) Production safety levers had concentric grooves. Checkered safety levers (below) were introduced during the Belgian trials. Although most of the Model 1899 pistols had safety levers with concentric grooves, some early 1899 trials pistols had checkered variants. Late production pistols can also have checkered safety levers, which are actually Model 1900 levers used in late Model 1899 assembly.

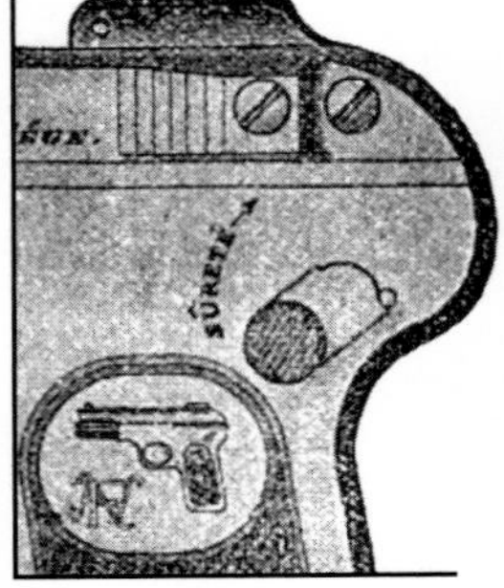

(Fig.126-4) Drawing (l.) out of the 1911 Dutch Edouard de Beaumont retailer catalog. The drawing is often encountered in early instruction books and catalogs. This type of safety marking was applied to a few of the early Belgian trials pistols. A Belgian army trials pistol (N° 19) was equipped with this safety marking. (Illustration courtesy of Nico Van Gijn).

Pistol N° 36 still shows the faint "Sureté" marking (left), most likely this was also a Belgian trials pistol. Note the checkered safety lever. (Photograph courtesy of Janne Salopuro)

Specifications Summary

FN Browning Model 1899 compact
Manufacturer: Fabrique Nationale d'Armes de Guerre
U.S. patent: 621747
Filing date: 12/27/1897 **Issue date:** 3/21/1899
Period offered: January 1899-late 1901
Caliber: 7.65x17mm (.32 ACP)
Operating system: Blowback
Length: 158mm
Barrel length: 100mm
Weight: 595 grams
Grips: Vulcanite (hard-rubber)
Magazine capacity: Seven
Sights: Fixed with sight-safety incorporated
Options: None
Finish offered: Blue (1899-1901), nickel (1900-1901)
Engraving patterns: None
Production quantity: 3900 produced in 1899, estimated over 10,500 produced 1900-1901

FN Browning Model 1899 large
Manufacturer: Fabrique Nationale d'Armes de Guerre
Period offered: Mid 1899-late 1900
Caliber: 7.65x17mm (.32 ACP)
Operating system: Blowback
Length: 184mm
Barrel length: 122mm
Weight: 764 grams
Grips: Checkered wood
Magazine capacity: Eight
Sights: Fixed with sight-safety incorporated
Finish offered: Blue
Engraving patterns: None
Production quantity: Unknown, no mass production

FN Model 1899: Accessories

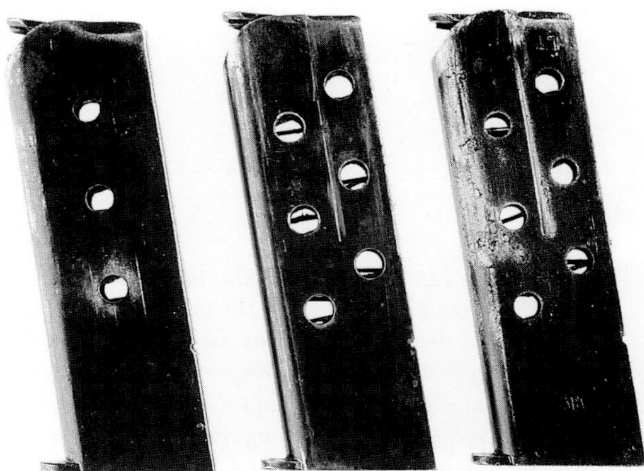

(Fig.127-1) Magazines for the Model 1899 and 1900 are interchangeable. The earliest 1899 magazines were manufactured with only three view-holes (left). These magazines are rare today and were soon replaced in manufacturing with the six view-hole version. Two types of six view-hole magazines were issued with the Model 1899 and Model 1900 pistols. Both are similar except the size of the view holes, 5mm (center) and 4mm (right). The FN logo was introduced in the mid 1900s after several competitors started introducing copies resembling the Model 1900.

PISTOLET
AUTOMATIQUE
A RÉPÉTITION
BROWNING (A 7 COUPS)
BREVETÉ DANS TOUS LES PAYS
FABRIQUE NATIONALE
D'ARMES DE GUERRE
HERSTAL-LIEGE (Belgique)

(Fig.127-2) A rare French language instruction book for the FN Model 1899. This type of large manual was most likely sold as an accessory and was not part of the pistol sale. This booklet includes instructions on shooting, maintenance and operation of the pistol including large foldout diagrams of the pistol.

(Fig.127-3) A turn of the century FN 7.65mm cartridge box. The box shows the Model 1899 compact pistol. (Photograph courtesy of Alexander Stucki)

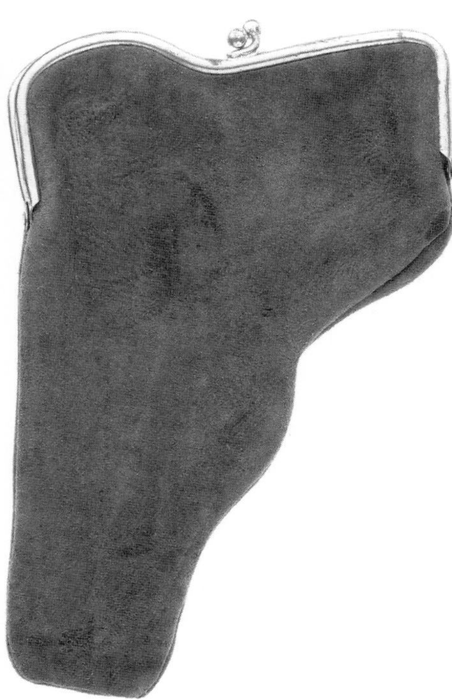

(Fig.128-1) Although not manufactured by FN, FN offered suede pistol purses as accessories for the Model 1899, 1900, 1905 and 1910.

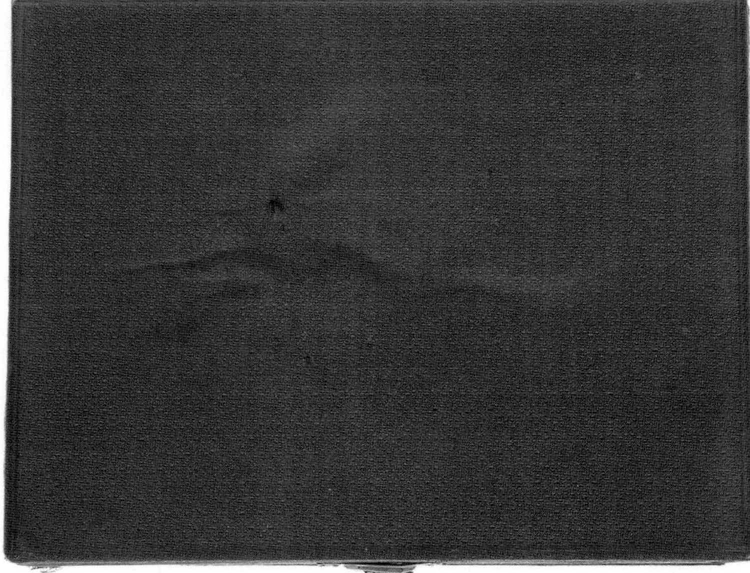

(Fig.128-2) The rectangular black leather case for the FN Model 1899: The interior lid is covered with green satin and was not printed with a dealer name. The base is French fitted for the Model 1899 and will not seat the larger Model 1900. The flat screwdriver and cleaning rod are correct period accessories. This case belongs to pistol N° 21 (see also Model 1900 cases on page 138).

(Fig.128-3) The black leather covering consists of only the top layers of the hide, making the leather very thin. A fine pattern is embossed into the leather, which is mounted over a wooden shell. Note the decorated single closure latch, most cases had two simple closure latches. FN did not manufacture these cases and purchased them from vendors, as such variants do exist.

(Fig.129-1) The black canvas case with rounded corners for the FN Model 1899 is larger in size than the square leather model. The interior lid is covered with green satin and was printed with FN's Spanish agent name and address (below). The base is French fitted for the Model 1899 and will not seat the larger Model 1900. The round screwdriver (fig 139-1) is often missing in these cases as the screwdrivers were often removed and used for other tasks. This case belongs to pistol N° 2592.

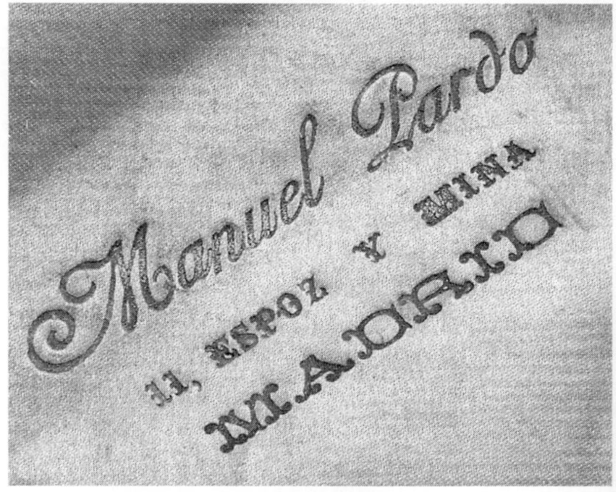

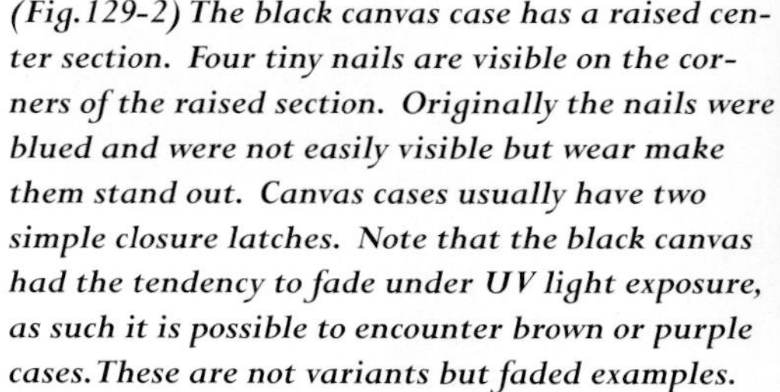

(Fig.129-2) The black canvas case has a raised center section. Four tiny nails are visible on the corners of the raised section. Originally the nails were blued and were not easily visible but wear make them stand out. Canvas cases usually have two simple closure latches. Note that the black canvas had the tendency to fade under UV light exposure, as such it is possible to encounter brown or purple cases. These are not variants but faded examples.

FN Model 1899: Production Pistols

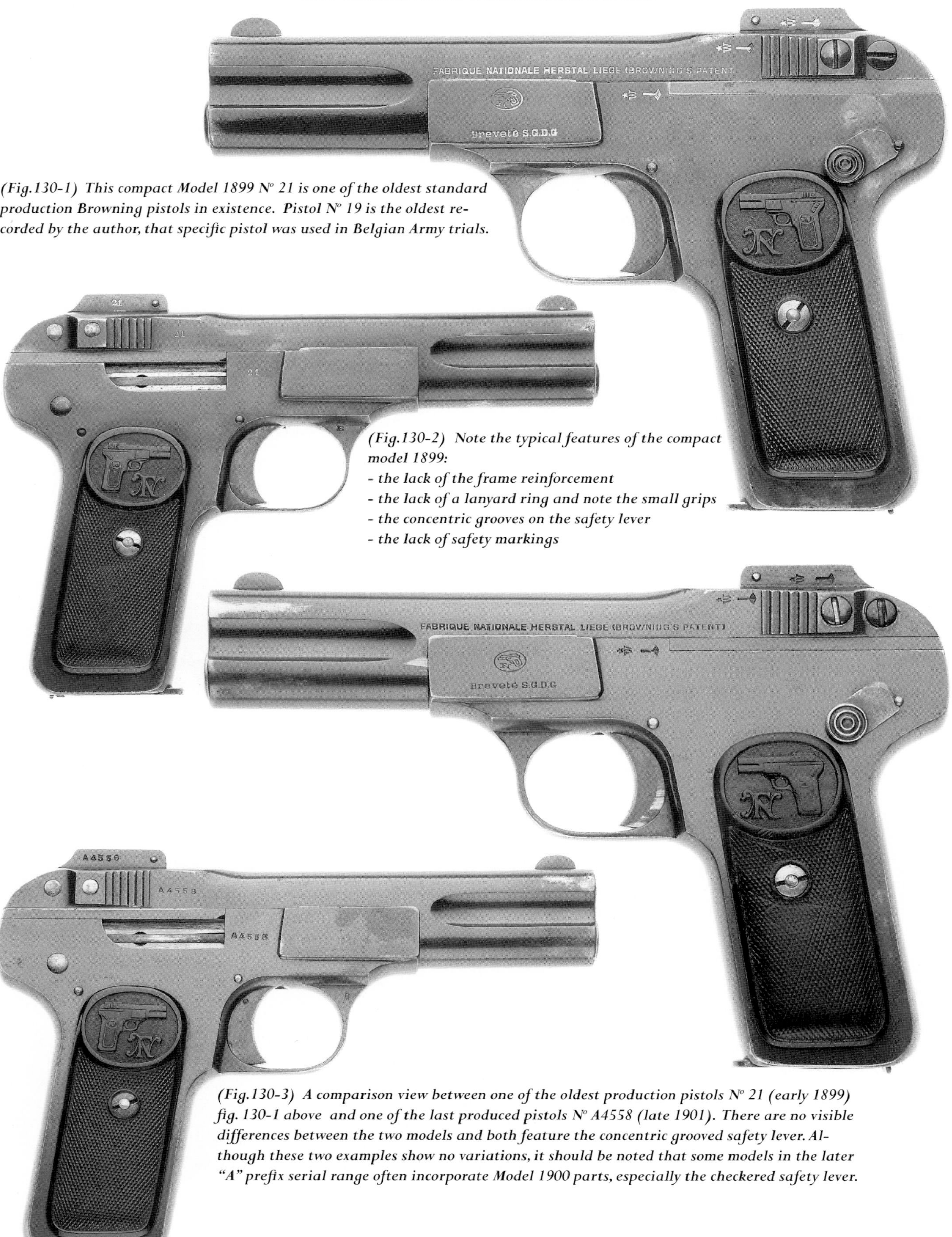

(Fig.130-1) This compact Model 1899 N° 21 is one of the oldest standard production Browning pistols in existence. Pistol N° 19 is the oldest recorded by the author, that specific pistol was used in Belgian Army trials.

(Fig.130-2) Note the typical features of the compact model 1899:
- the lack of the frame reinforcement
- the lack of a lanyard ring and note the small grips
- the concentric grooves on the safety lever
- the lack of safety markings

(Fig.130-3) A comparison view between one of the oldest production pistols N° 21 (early 1899) fig. 130-1 above and one of the last produced pistols N° A4558 (late 1901). There are no visible differences between the two models and both feature the concentric grooved safety lever. Although these two examples show no variations, it should be noted that some models in the later "A" prefix serial range often incorporate Model 1900 parts, especially the checkered safety lever.

(Fig.131-1) Polishing of the muzzle area became standard on the Model 1899 and remained a standard feature on the Model 1900. This area is always a good indicator to see if a pistol has been refinished. Note that this does not apply to nickel plated pistols.

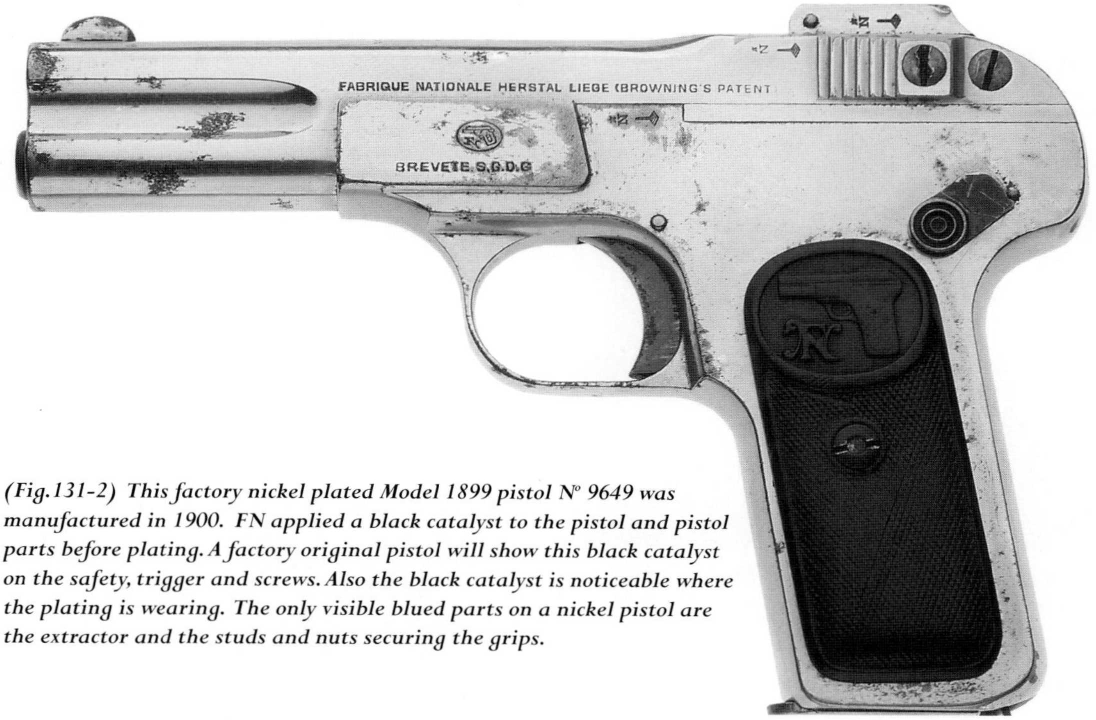

(Fig.131-2) This factory nickel plated Model 1899 pistol N° 9649 was manufactured in 1900. FN applied a black catalyst to the pistol and pistol parts before plating. A factory original pistol will show this black catalyst on the safety, trigger and screws. Also the black catalyst is noticeable where the plating is wearing. The only visible blued parts on a nickel pistol are the extractor and the studs and nuts securing the grips.

(Fig.131-2) Each factory original nickel pistol came with a nickel plated magazine. Original nickel plated magazines feature standard blue followers in order to guarantee the proper movement as nickel plating added to the dimension of the follower. This practice started at the turn of the century and remained in effect for most models including the Model 1900, 1903, 1905 and 1910. Refinished magazines usually lack a blue follower.

President Teddy Roosevelt's FN Browning Model 1899

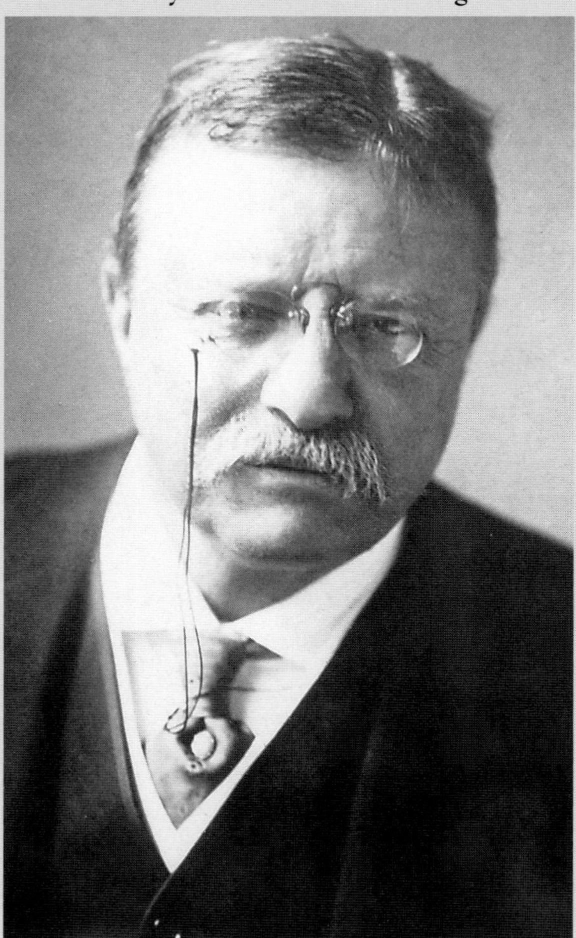

(Fig.132-1) President Theodore Roosevelt (Portrait photograph courtesy of Philip Schreier, National Firearms Museum)

President Theodore Roosevelt's Model 1899 pistol was manufactured in 1900. According to Phil Schreier, with the National Firearms Museum, a wooden box arrived at the White House in 1902. The outside was marked "Theodore Roosevelt, The Executive Mansion". The pistol is finally engraved and gold inlaid and features factory mother-of-pearl grips. The pistol came in a FN presentation case. President Roosevelt kept the pistol in a bedside drawer in the White House. After he left office, he retained the pistol in his bedroom until his death in January 1919. His oldest son, Theodore Jr. inherited the pistol. Theodore Roosevelt Jr. served the country with distinction in the Great War. As brigadier general, he was the only general officer to hit the beaches of Normandy with the first wave on June 6, 1944. For his actions in Operation Overlord he was awarded the Medal of Honor. His son, Cornelius Van S. Roosevelt, donated the pistol to the National Firearms Museum in 1987 where it has been on exhibit since.

The engraving style and workmanship are of outstanding quality. The author has not been able to establish any link between this engraving and consequent engraving styles done by the factory starting in 1903 (see page 140). The engraving was most likely commissioned by the factory in the Liège area. It is possible that John M. Browning asked FN to ship a pistol to the president. President Roosevelt and John M. Browning were personal friends, although the author has not been able to determine when exactly their friendship started. President Theodore Roosevelt is known to have visited Ogden and spent summers with the Browning Brothers.

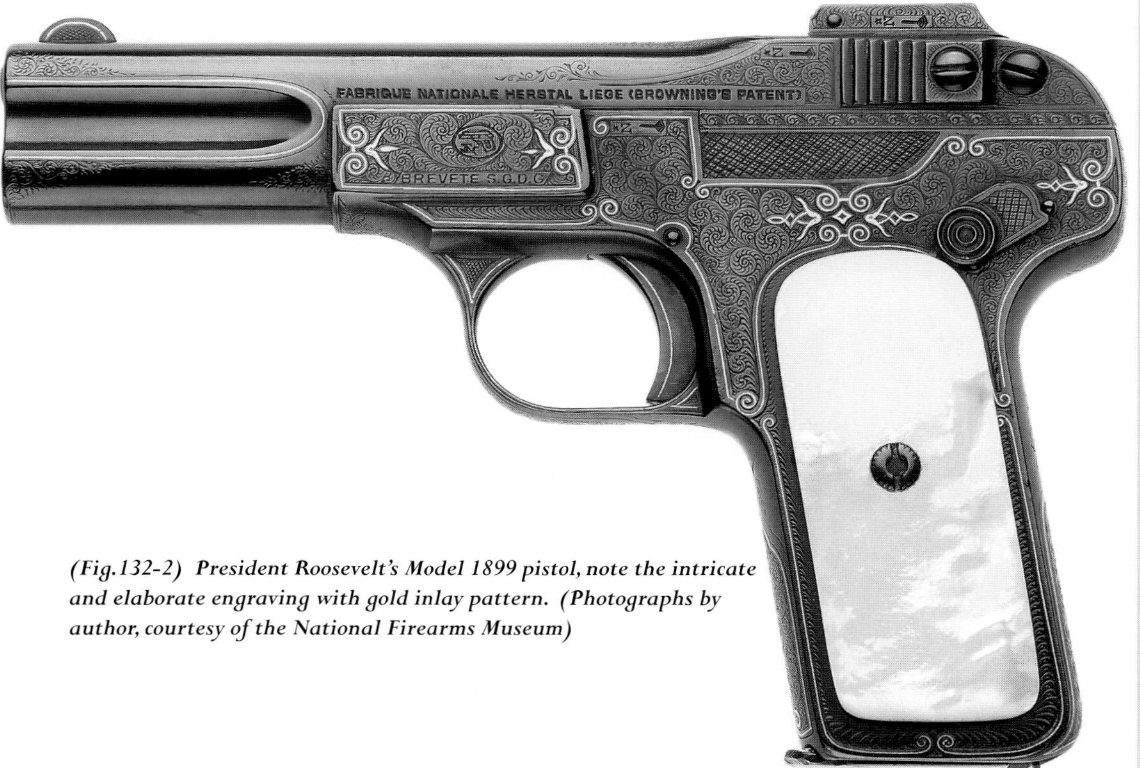

(Fig.132-2) President Roosevelt's Model 1899 pistol, note the intricate and elaborate engraving with gold inlay pattern. (Photographs by author, courtesy of the National Firearms Museum)

The FN Browning Model 1900

Development History: The Belgian Military Dictates Changes

During Belgian military trials in 1899, the FN Browning 1899 pistols faced stiff competition from Mauser, Bergmann, Roth, Mannlicher, Borchardt and Borchardt-Luger pistols (see page 124).

Ultimately the trials commission selected the compact version of the FN Browning Model 1899. With the notification that their submission had been the trials' successful candidate, FN received a list of design modifications that would have to be incorporated into the pistol to render it suitable for military use. The Belgian War Department's requirements dictated that both the frame and grip panels be enlarged and reinforced, a lanyard ring be installed and that safety markings be stamped on spot-faced circles on the frame. The resulting pistol was to become the FN Browning Model 1900.

The FN Browning Model 1900 was the first practical and reliable automatic handgun to be adopted by any army. While the Swiss adopted the Luger pistol that same year, the FN Browning Model 1900 was much easier to manufacture, and significantly more reliable.

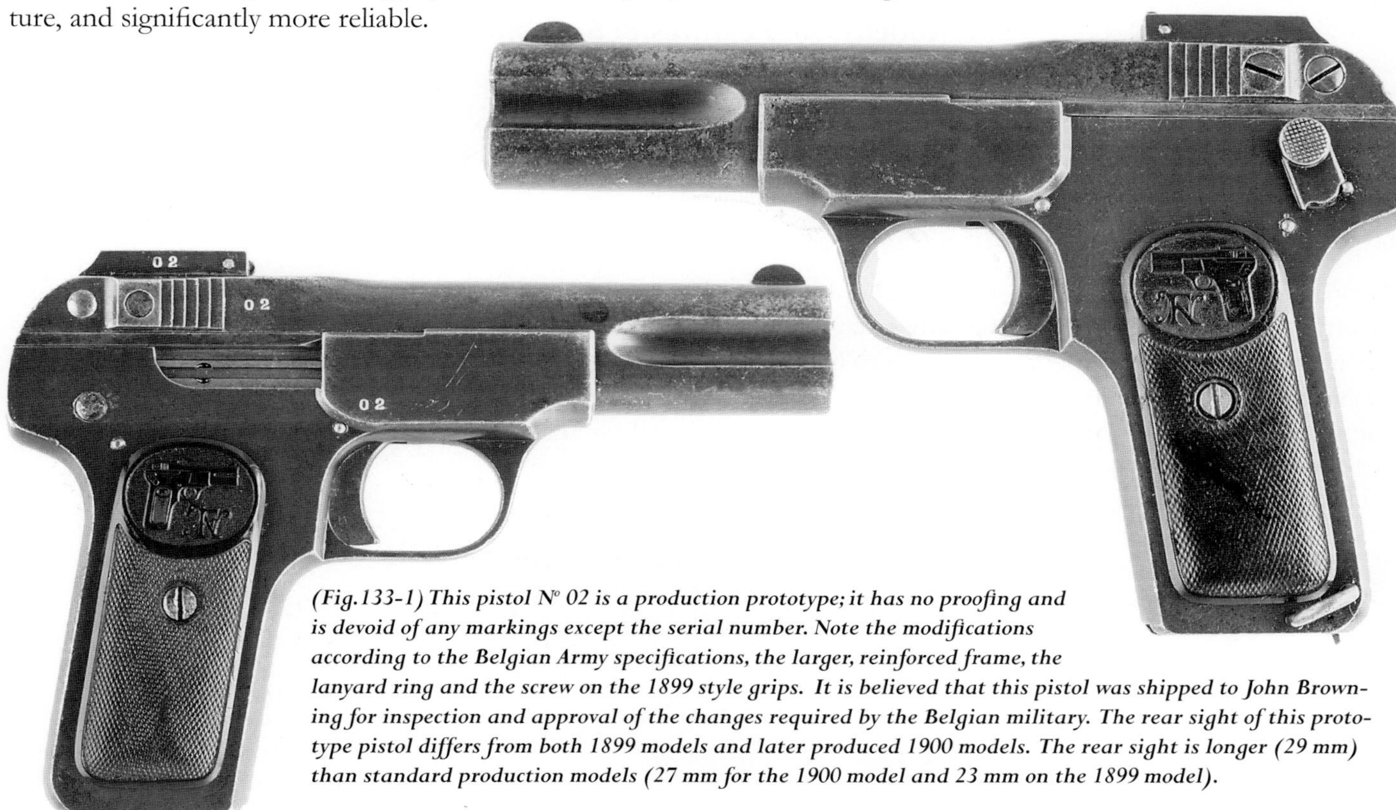

(Fig.133-1) This pistol N° 02 is a production prototype; it has no proofing and is devoid of any markings except the serial number. Note the modifications according to the Belgian Army specifications, the larger, reinforced frame, the lanyard ring and the screw on the 1899 style grips. It is believed that this pistol was shipped to John Browning for inspection and approval of the changes required by the Belgian military. The rear sight of this prototype pistol differs from both 1899 models and later produced 1900 models. The rear sight is longer (29 mm) than standard production models (27 mm for the 1900 model and 23 mm on the 1899 model).

FN submitted the Model 1900, along with an enlarged Model 1899, to English military trials in December 1900. The pistols were dropped from the army trials based on the inadequate performance of the 7.65mm cartridge. In 1901 the British Navy arrived at the same conclusion. The Model 1900 was evaluated by Denmark in 1902, Sweden and France in 1903 and Russia in 1904. A small order of six pistols was also shipped to Katanga in the Congo Free State (known as the Belgian Congo after 1908) in March 1901. None of these countries adopted the pistol as a standard military sidearm, but all would eventually recognize its advantages for law enforcement and special departmental use in their armed forces. Indeed, while the pistol's small size and reliability had resulted in adoption by the Belgian military, the same characteristics were to make it a favorite of both police organizations and civilians alike. The Model 1900's greatest sales successes throughout its production span were on the commercial market.

FN began production in 1900 pursuant to the Royal decree designating the Model 1900 as the new Belgian military pistol. The majority of Model 1900 production in 1900 was dedicated to fulfilling Belgian military orders.

As a result, the Model 1899 was kept in production for the commercial market. Commercial sales of the Model 1900 began in January 1901. The Model 1900 remained in production until the German invasion of August 1914. By that time, sales had dwindled due to the popularity of the newer Model 1910 pistol. Despite this, FN kept the pistol in production to meet Belgian military orders.

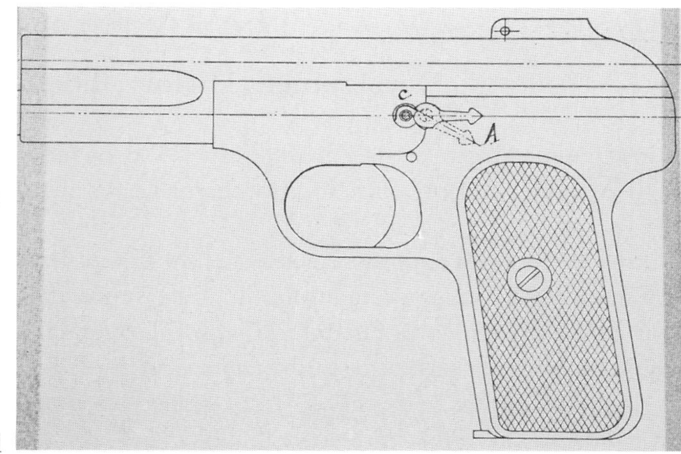

(Fig.134-1) A loaded chamber indicator was patented for the Model 1900 on May 9, 1909 but was never introduced in production.

The pistol was initially known as "Le Pistolet Browning" (the same nomenclature as the earlier Model 1899). FN began to use the "Modèle 1900" designation only after the company began producing other Browning pistol models. The first indication of the Model 1900 designation appeared in 1902[1]. Later, after the introduction of the Model 1910, the 1900 Model was most often referred to as "Le Vieux Modèle" (The Old Model).

FN Model 1900: Features & Specifications

Serial Numbers

The total production quantity for the Model 1900 was approximately 724,550. One of the last Model 1900's shipped was pistol N° 721116, on October 11, 1920. This was most likely one of the many pistols returned to FN after World War I (see page 33). Three more pistols were located in warehouse (see warehouse practices on page 100) in the 1980s and those were sold, new in the box, in Australia.

FN Browning Model 1900 pistols were produced between 1900 and 1914. Production of the first commercial pistols was erratic and large gaps exist in the early serial number ranges. As is typical of early FN production, the first pistols were never completed. Pistol N° 11 appears to be the first commercial pistol built and was removed from warehouse by FN's manager, Mr. Andri, on May 11, 1901. Only 13 pistols were produced in the 1-200 serial number range. Large scale serial production commenced around serial number 200 and significant shipments to dealers began in February 1901. An estimation of the 1900 production quantities is as follows:

-1900-1901:	**10,000 FN 1900 pistols**
-1901-1902:	**21,700 FN 1900 pistols**
-1902-1903:	**40,000 FN 1900 pistols**
-1903-1907:	**328,300 FN 1900 pistols**
-1907-1910:	**275,000 FN 1900 pistols**
-1910-1914:	**49,550 FN 1900 pistols**

Slide Legends

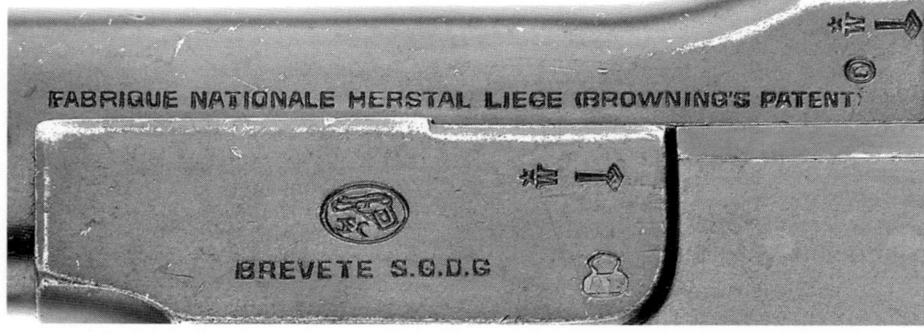

(Fig.134-1) Pre-1907 slide legend variant. This specific legend was applied to a first year production pistol.

(Fig.134-2) Pre-1907 slide legend variant. This specific legend was applied to a 1905 production pistol.

(Fig.135-1) Post May 1907 slide legend variant with "Browning's Patent" nomenclature on the frame. This specific legend was applied to a 1908 production pistol.

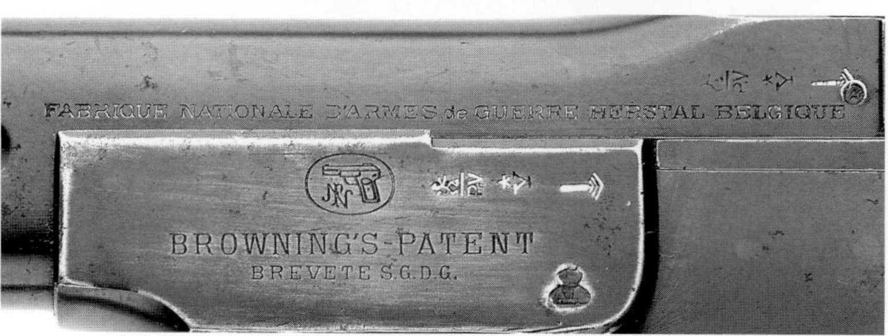

(Fig.135-2) Post May 1907 slide legend variant with "Browning's Patent" nomenclature on the frame. This specific legend was applied to a last year (1914) production pistol.

Slide and frame variants through production years

It is easy to observe many variations of the rounding of the rear of the Model 1900's frame and slide. While many collectors have attributed these as production variants, these differences are not design modifications but rather a result of the manual grinding of the pistols' frames by machinists. Through the years many workers finished these pistols and the rear of the pistol was ground and polished once assembled (like the Model 1910 and 1922, compare with fig.54-2). Different machinists ground differing curves on the pistol. Production of the main component parts remained virtually unchanged throughout its production span.

Grips, Magazines & Safety Markings

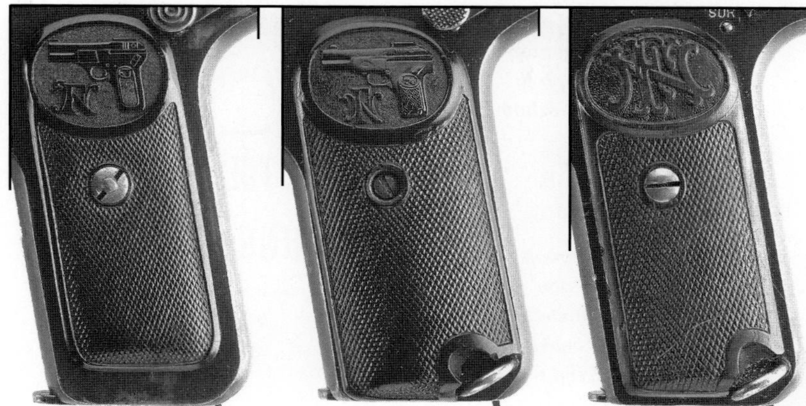

(Fig.135-4) The small thin grip-plates of the model 1899 (left) were replaced with the early Model 1900 grips (center). The early 1900 pistol logo grips (center) were replaced with the larger FN monogram (right). This change occurred somewhere in 1905 around serial number 200,000[2].

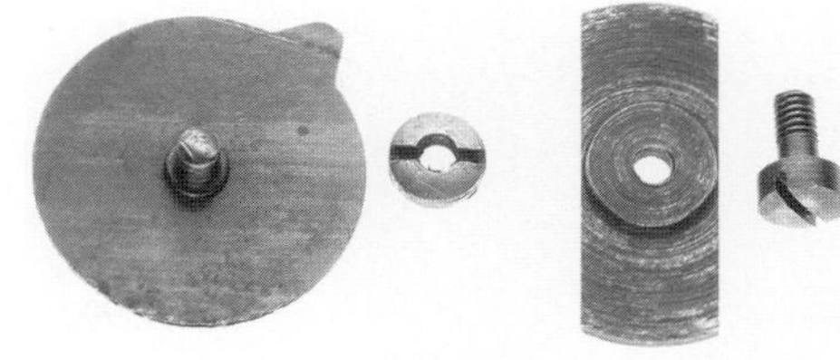

(Fig.135-3) The stud and nut of the Model 1899 (left) was replaced by a screw with threaded rectangular back-plate on the Model 1900.

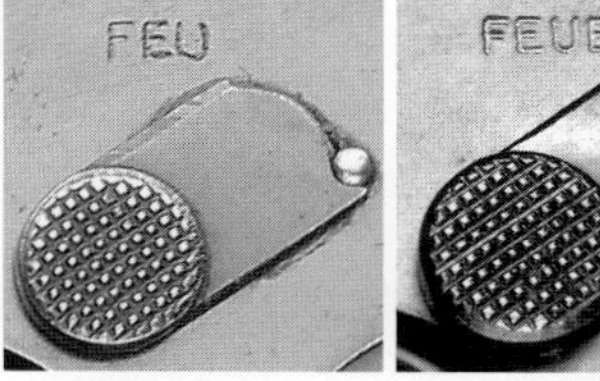

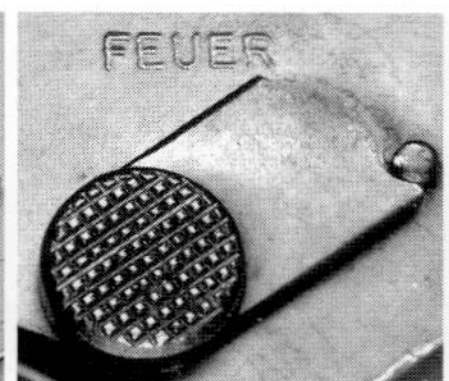

(Fig.135-5) Standard production safety markings were always marked in French (Feu, Sur). Customers had options to order the safety markings in German (Feuer, Sicher) or English (Fire, Safe). The English variant is the rarest. (Photograph courtesy of Christian Bogdan)

(Fig.135-6) Model 1900 magazines can easily be distinguished from Model 1910 magazines by the notch in the spine. Early magazines were unmarked; the FN logo was introduced circa 1904. Unlike the Model 1910 magazines, the model 1900 magazines do not feature a caliber designation.

(1) The Model 1900 designation may have appeared earlier; the 1902 date is based on period literature.

(2) Due to FN's production and assembly practices (see page 100) some pistols in the 190,000 range appear with the new grips while others beyond the 200,000 range still retain the earlier pistol logo grip models.

Specifications Summary

FN Browning Model 1900
Manufacturer: Fabrique Nationale d'Armes de Guerre
Model known as: "Pistolet Browning" (early in production), Modèle 1900 (starting circa 1902), "Le Vieux Modèle" (The Old Model - internal designation used after the Model 1910 was introduced in 1912)
Period offered: 1900-1914
Caliber: 7.65x17mm (.32 ACP)
Operating system: Blowback
Length: 164mm
Barrel length: 102mm
Weight: 625 grams
Grips: Vulcanite (hard-rubber)
Magazine capacity: Seven
Sights: Fixed with sight-safety incorporated
Options: None
Finish offered: Blue, nickel
Engraving patterns: Six types
Production quantity: 724,550

FN Model 1900: Accessories

Standard Model 1900 commercial pistols were sold with a cardboard box, cleaning rod, instruction manual and three dummy rounds. It is not known which instruction manual was supplied with the pistols. The surviving instruction manuals are larger and do not fit in the cardboard box. In concert with FN practices at the time, these larger instruction manuals appear to have been an extra accessory. It is likely that the enclosed instruction manual was printed on onionskin colored paper like those of the later Model 1905 and 1910 pistols.

(Fig.136-1) A combination wood and cardboard factory box for a Model 1900 pistol. Note the small serial number label. (Photograph by author, courtesy of Graham Waddingham)

(Fig.136-2) A German language instruction booklet for the Model 1900 pistol. The booklet features a gray, light green cover with multiple foldout views of the pistol. Note the "1900" reference on the cover.

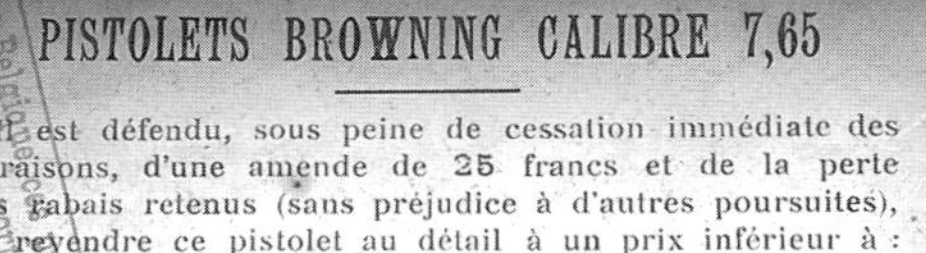

PISTOLETS BROWNING CALIBRE 7,65

Il est défendu, sous peine de cessation immédiate des livraisons, d'une amende de 25 francs et de la perte des rabais retenus (sans préjudice à d'autres poursuites), de revendre ce pistolet au détail à un prix inférieur à :

Francs 45,00 pour le pistolet bronzé ;
Francs 46,50 pour le pistolet nickelé.

Sera considérée comme infraction à cette prescription, la remise gratuite avec le pistolet d'un objet quelconque autre que ceux donnés par la Fabrique Nationale avec chaque pistolet.

FABRIQUE NATIONALE D'ARMES DE GUERRE, S. A.
HERSTAL-LEZ-LIÈGE.

(Fig.136-3) Price control label affixed to the interior of the box. This French language label warned retailers from selling the pistol below the set retail price and states: "It is forbidden to sell this pistol under the set retail price of 45 francs for blue guns and 46.50 francs for nickeled pistols under penalty of 25 francs, suspension of dealer rebates and suspension of (future) deliveries. Any item, except those included by FN with the pistol, given free of charge at the time of the sale will also constitute as an infraction to this rule." (Photograph by author, courtesy of Graham Waddingham)

(Fig.137-1) A combination wood and cardboard factory box for the Model 1900 pistol. Note the wrap-around serial number label. (Photograph courtesy of John Bastin)

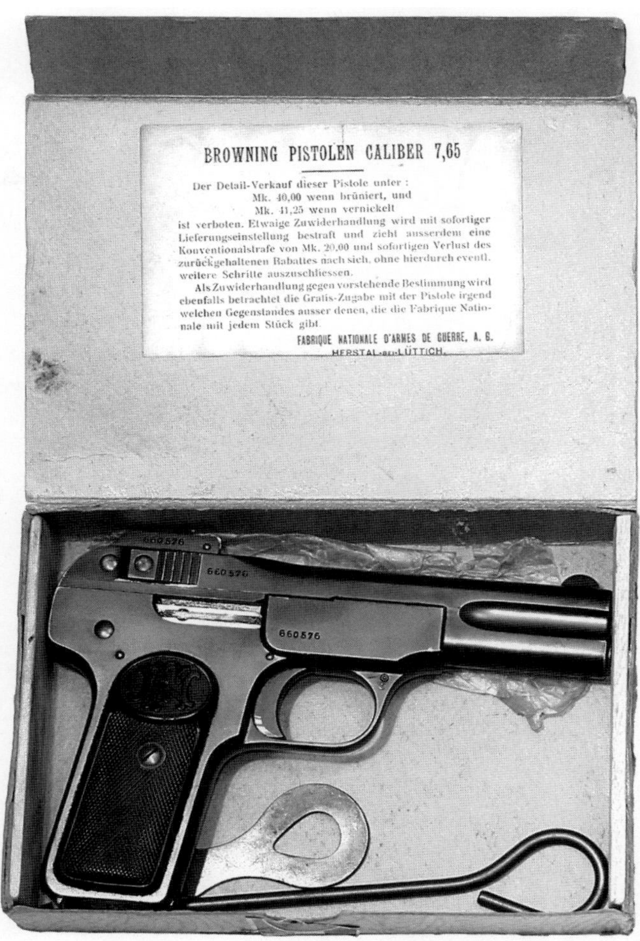

(Fig.137-2) An open view of the factory box with pistol, cleaning rod, screwdriver and wax paper. Note the German language price control label. (Photograph courtesy of John Bastin)

Factory presentation cases were available starting with the Model 1899 and were carried over with the Model 1900. Although similar in appearance, the interior of the Model 1899 and 1900 cases differ dimensionally as the Model 1900 pistol is slightly larger. As such Model 1899 and 1900 cases are not interchangeable.

Catalogs indicate that presentation cases were available as an enhancing accessory and engraved pistols were most often delivered in presentation cases.

The interior of the cases were lined with green satin(1) and the exterior was either black canvas(2) or fine black leather. Leather cases were more expensive. Early Model 1899 presentation boxes usually did not have the factory name and logo marked on the inside of the box. FN distributors had the option to have their name and address printed on the inside. The practice of printing the dealer name and address on the case's interior fell out of favor after the introduction of the Model 1900. The Fabrique Nationale name and address was printed instead but custom printed cases remained available as an option.

(Fig.137-3) Front view of a canvas covered presentation case with center closure clasp

---

(1) The interior satin of the cases may appear light or sometimes of an entire different color, this is primarily due to fading.

(2) The exterior of the canvas case may appear brown or purple, this is a reaction to UV light exposure, originally these cases were black in color.

(Fig.138-1) FN presentation cases were not manufactured by FN but purchased from various specialty suppliers like Fonson and Vandenhove in Brussels. Characteristically FN presentation cases were black on the exterior and green on the interior. The exterior consisted of canvas, fine leather was a more expensive option. Most case designs have been observed in either black dyed canvas or fine black leather. The interior lid is always covered with green satin, usually with FN's corporate name and factory location imprinted in gold. The interior of the case is French fitted to the pistol, close examination will reveal if the case was made for the Model 1899 or 1900, the latter being slightly larger. Cases exposed over long periods of time to UV light have deteriorated. The black leather often appears to be gray or dark brown, the black canvas has turned brown or purple. Interior colors exposed to UV light have shifted from dark green to yellow.

This square edged presentation case is the largest variant made, it measures about 150x190mm. The closure hardware consists of a single latch. Note the satin bands that hold the screwdriver and cleaning rod. There is ample space for the accessories.

(Fig.138-2) A proportional view of the large canvas presentation case (150x190mm) with square corners and the small leather presentation case (135x180mm) with rounded corners.

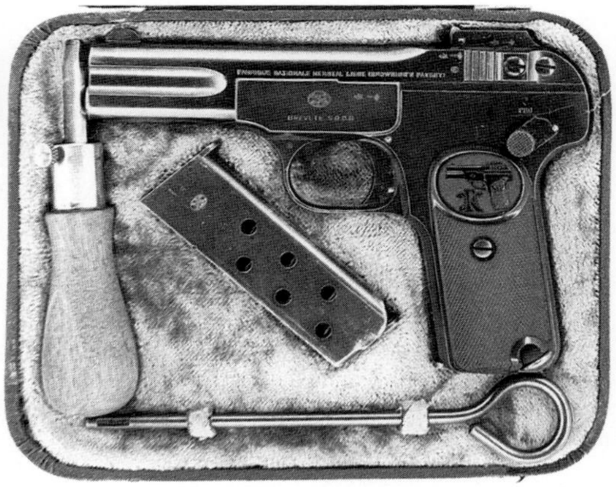

(Fig.139-1) These presentation cases with round edges appear identical but are different in dimensions, note the layout of the tools and use of different screwdrivers.
Top: This case features FN's rare wooden handle screwdriver, the cleaning rod lays flat in the case and the spare magazine lays diagonally. The closure hardware consists of double latches.
Left: The flat screwdriver is partially hidden through a slot in the case. The cleaning rod stands vertically. The closure hardware consists of double latches. (Top photograph courtesy of J.C. Kempf)

Luxury Models: Nickel Plating and Factory Engraving

Once FN realized the sales potential of the Model 1899 and 1900, the factory began to produce highly finished or engraved pistols for commercial sales. Nickel plating was an option with both the Model 1899 and Model 1900. Interestingly, FN's literature rarely shows nickel finish pistols. Retailer catalogs on the other hand often represent nickel models as an affordable upgrade to the basic blue model (see manufacturing practices page 99).

Observed or reported commercial nickel finish Model 1900 pistols: 150079, 168896, 199232, 191907, 353690, 584362, 644025, 647743, 649139, 694931

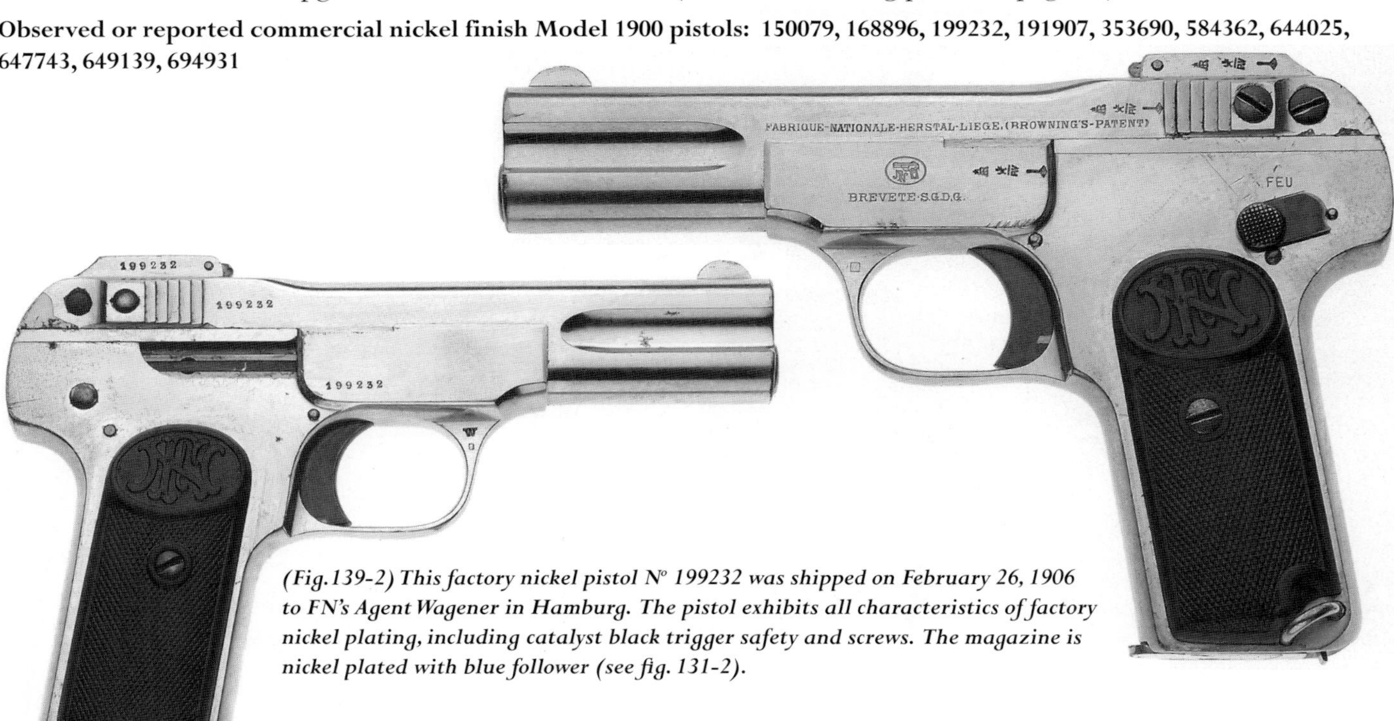

(Fig.139-2) This factory nickel pistol N° 199232 was shipped on February 26, 1906 to FN's Agent Wagener in Hamburg. The pistol exhibits all characteristics of factory nickel plating, including catalyst black trigger safety and screws. The magazine is nickel plated with blue follower (see fig. 131-2).

Factory engraving began in 1903-1904 when FN launched a line of "Modèles de Luxe" or luxury models. It is not known how many styles were initially available, nor is it known if these pistols were engraved at the FN factory or sent out to artisans in the Liège area. FN's creation of an engraving school in 1926 has often created the false impression that FN did not engrave in-house prior to 1926. Engraving at FN started in 1903 and was first seen on Model 1900 pistols and Auto-5 shotguns. At some point in the early 1900s, FN standardized the engraving styles and offered a line of six engraving styles. Although the patterns were standardized, there are many differences in detail and workmanship resulting from the skill level of the engraver.

Engraved pistols were available either in blue or nickel finish with standard black vulcanite, ivory or mother-of-pearl grips. Most buyers willing to pay extra for grips opted for the expensive mother-of-pearl grips making the ivory grips the most rarely encountered option.

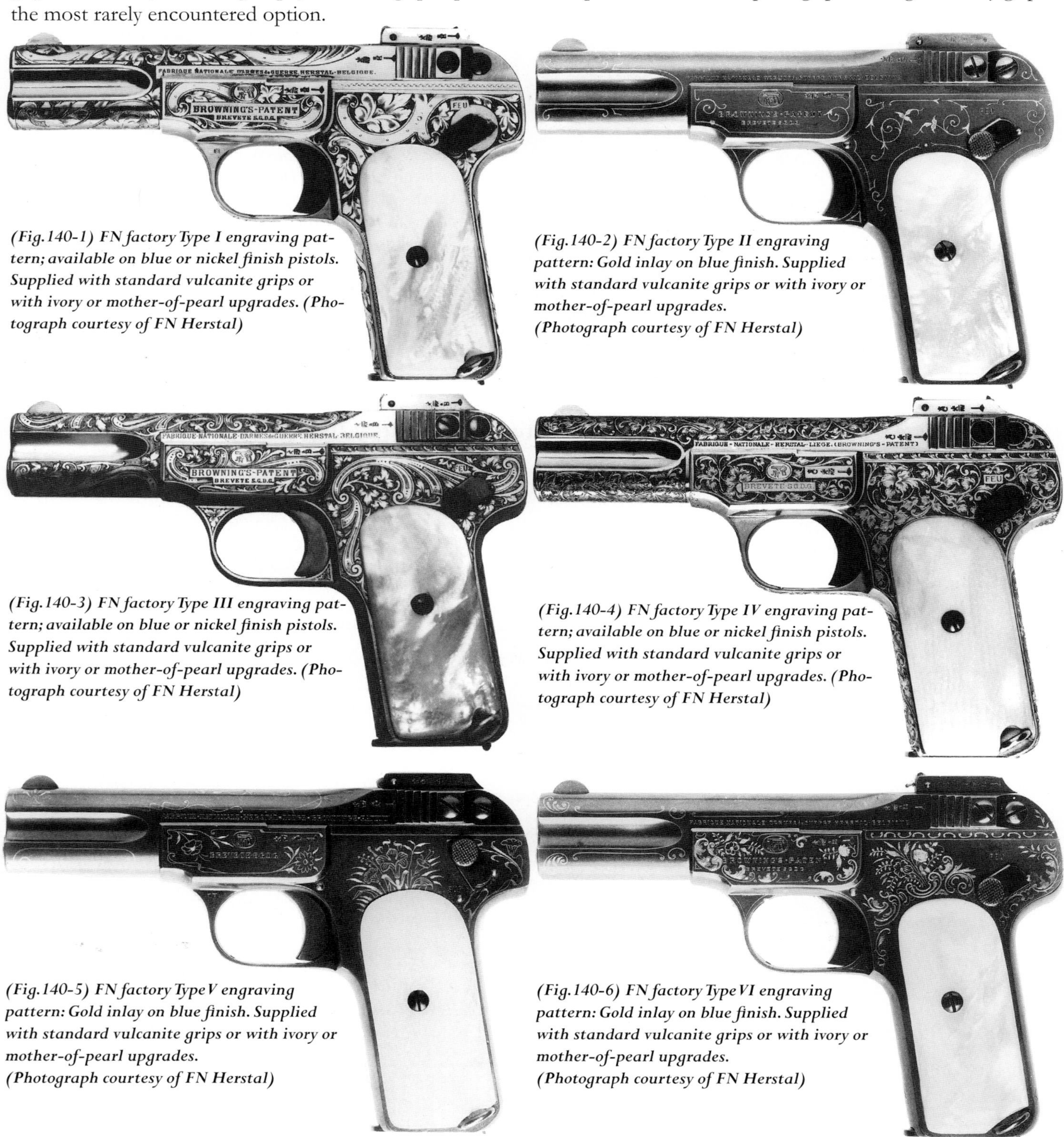

(Fig.140-1) FN factory Type I engraving pattern; available on blue or nickel finish pistols. Supplied with standard vulcanite grips or with ivory or mother-of-pearl upgrades. (Photograph courtesy of FN Herstal)

(Fig.140-2) FN factory Type II engraving pattern: Gold inlay on blue finish. Supplied with standard vulcanite grips or with ivory or mother-of-pearl upgrades. (Photograph courtesy of FN Herstal)

(Fig.140-3) FN factory Type III engraving pattern; available on blue or nickel finish pistols. Supplied with standard vulcanite grips or with ivory or mother-of-pearl upgrades. (Photograph courtesy of FN Herstal)

(Fig.140-4) FN factory Type IV engraving pattern; available on blue or nickel finish pistols. Supplied with standard vulcanite grips or with ivory or mother-of-pearl upgrades. (Photograph courtesy of FN Herstal)

(Fig.140-5) FN factory Type V engraving pattern: Gold inlay on blue finish. Supplied with standard vulcanite grips or with ivory or mother-of-pearl upgrades. (Photograph courtesy of FN Herstal)

(Fig.140-6) FN factory Type VI engraving pattern: Gold inlay on blue finish. Supplied with standard vulcanite grips or with ivory or mother-of-pearl upgrades. (Photograph courtesy of FN Herstal)

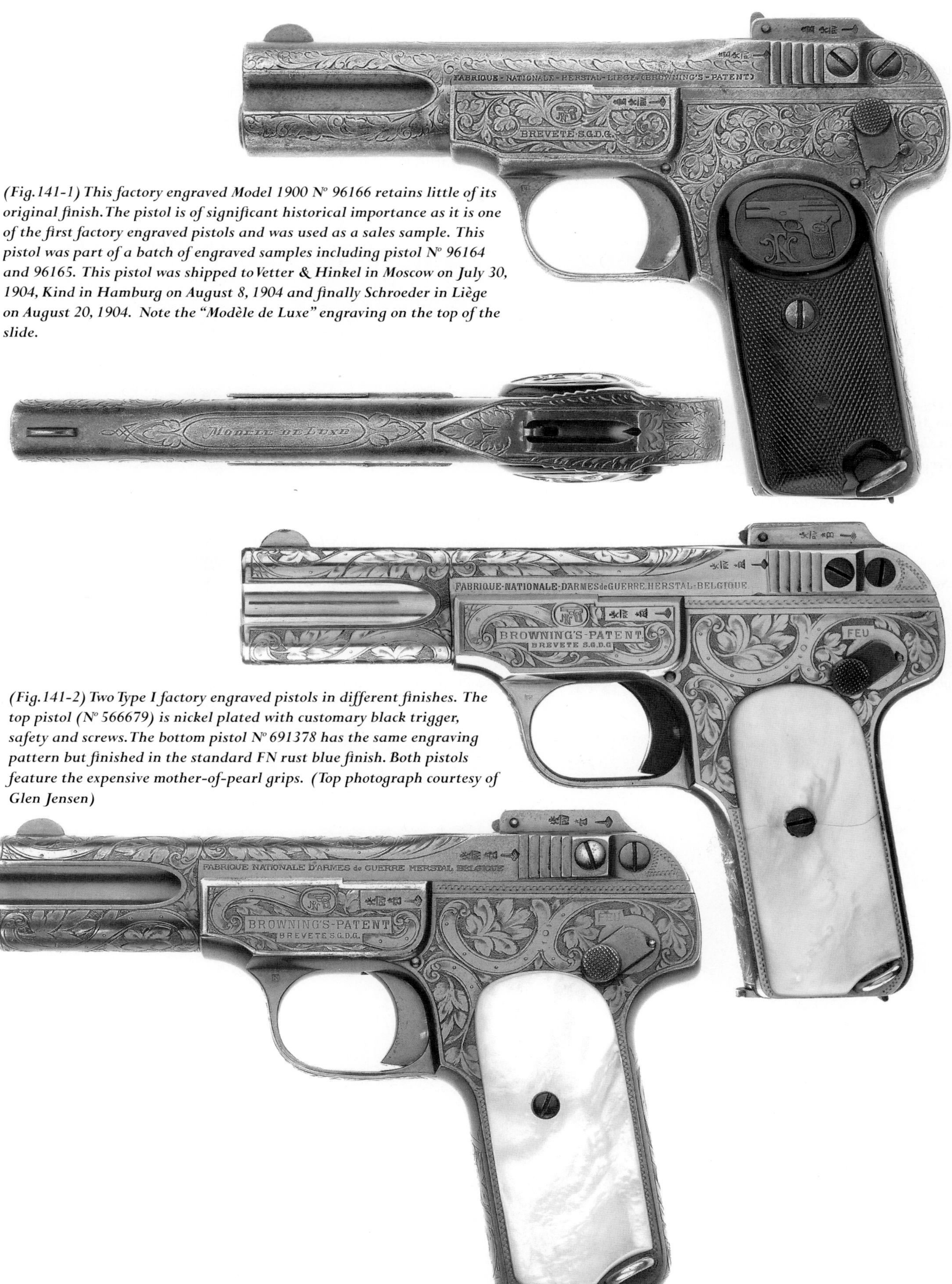

(Fig.141-1) This factory engraved Model 1900 N° 96166 retains little of its original finish. The pistol is of significant historical importance as it is one of the first factory engraved pistols and was used as a sales sample. This pistol was part of a batch of engraved samples including pistol N° 96164 and 96165. This pistol was shipped to Vetter & Hinkel in Moscow on July 30, 1904, Kind in Hamburg on August 8, 1904 and finally Schroeder in Liège on August 20, 1904. Note the "Modèle de Luxe" engraving on the top of the slide.

(Fig.141-2) Two Type I factory engraved pistols in different finishes. The top pistol (N° 566679) is nickel plated with customary black trigger, safety and screws. The bottom pistol N° 691378 has the same engraving pattern but finished in the standard FN rust blue finish. Both pistols feature the expensive mother-of-pearl grips. (Top photograph courtesy of Glen Jensen)

Because of the Model 1900's popularity, pistols were often engraved as presentation pieces or as gifts. Many variations of presentation pistols have been noted. These pistols are usually engraved with both the recipients' names and meritorious actions. Most of these pistols were engraved after leaving the factory, and are beautiful examples of period craftsmanship. Retailers and distributors like "La Manufacture Francaise d'Armes et Cycles de St. Etienne" were able to increase their profit margins by commissioning their own engraving. Many retailers offered engraving patterns or accepted requests and custom designs from their customers. Distinguishing FN factory engraving from post factory work can be a challenge. The six engraving patterns on page 140 provide a good starting point.

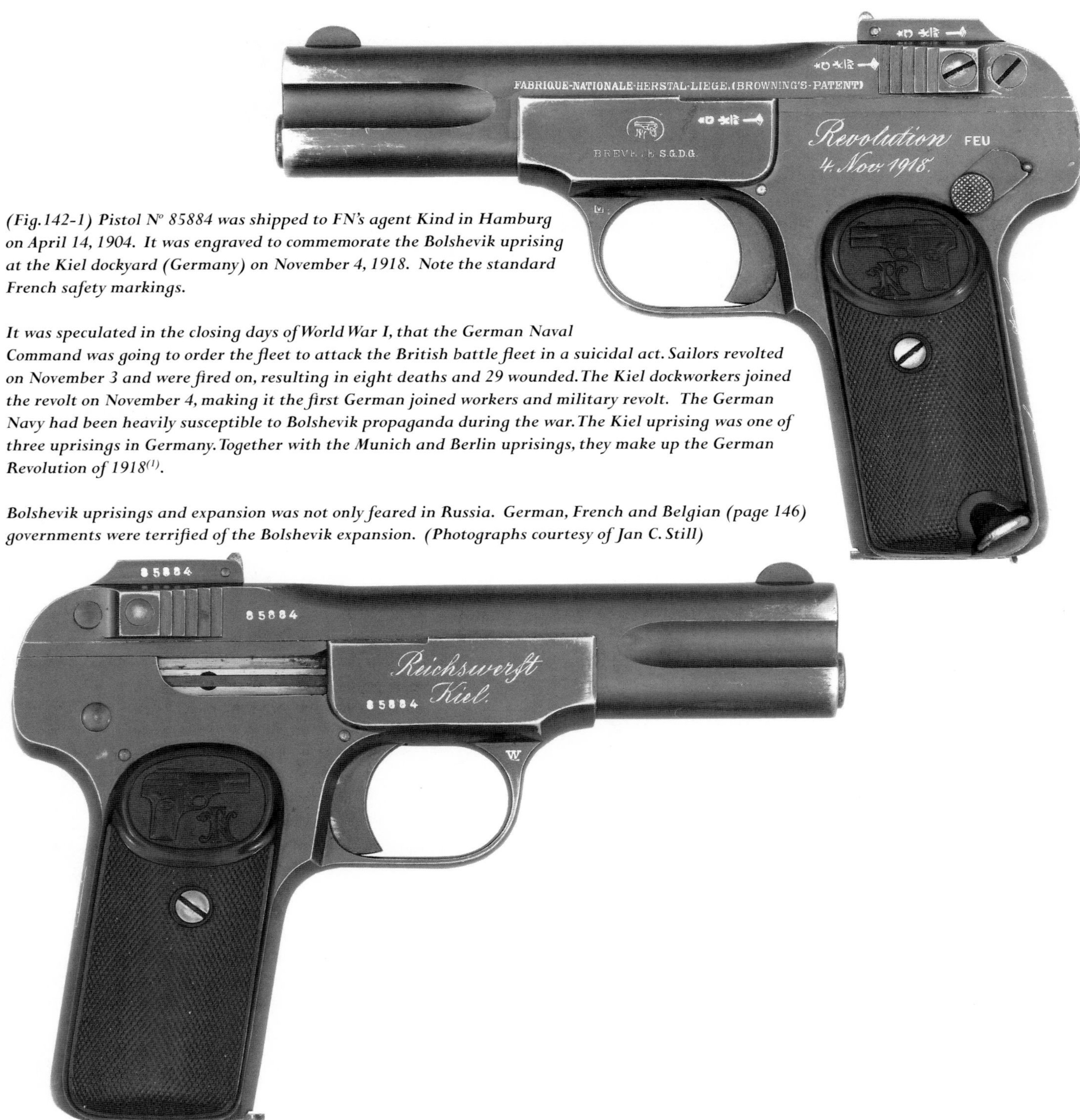

(Fig.142-1) Pistol N° 85884 was shipped to FN's agent Kind in Hamburg on April 14, 1904. It was engraved to commemorate the Bolshevik uprising at the Kiel dockyard (Germany) on November 4, 1918. Note the standard French safety markings.

It was speculated in the closing days of World War I, that the German Naval Command was going to order the fleet to attack the British battle fleet in a suicidal act. Sailors revolted on November 3 and were fired on, resulting in eight deaths and 29 wounded. The Kiel dockworkers joined the revolt on November 4, making it the first German joined workers and military revolt. The German Navy had been heavily susceptible to Bolshevik propaganda during the war. The Kiel uprising was one of three uprisings in Germany. Together with the Munich and Berlin uprisings, they make up the German Revolution of 1918[1].

Bolshevik uprisings and expansion was not only feared in Russia. German, French and Belgian (page 146) governments were terrified of the Bolshevik expansion. (Photographs courtesy of Jan C. Still)

(1) The German Revolution of 1918 - mars.wnec.edu
- Central Powers Pistols by Jan Still

The Belgian Military FN 1900

(Fig.143-1) Belgian officers practice with their FN Browning 1900 pistols circa 1908.

The Belgian War Ministry placed an initial order for 10,000 pistols[1] in 1900. The pistols were ordered with special plain black grips without the FN monogram. These grips had screws instead of the earlier Model 1899 nuts and studs. The safety markings were roll marked on spot-faced circles on the frame ("FEU" for fire and "SUR" for safe). The special black grip-plates proved to be brittle and broke easily. Some of these broken grips were often replaced early on with checkered wooden grips made in Belgian arsenals.

The black grips and spot-faced circles were dropped from production around 1901. From 1901, the Belgian military purchased standard production pistols.

The first order had its own serial range due to the non-standard production features[2], and was intended for issue to army officers. By October 1901 the gendarmerie and mounted artillerymen were equipped with the pistol. On May 6, 1905 the decision was made to standardize and update the side-arms of non-commissioned cavalry officers. By 1910 virtually all Nagant revolvers in the active duty Belgian forces had been replaced by the Model 1900. The National Guard was equipped with the pistol by October 1912. The FN 1900 pistol was the standard sidearm of the Belgian forces during World War I. Accepted Belgian Military pistols can be identified by the military acceptance markings (see page 95).

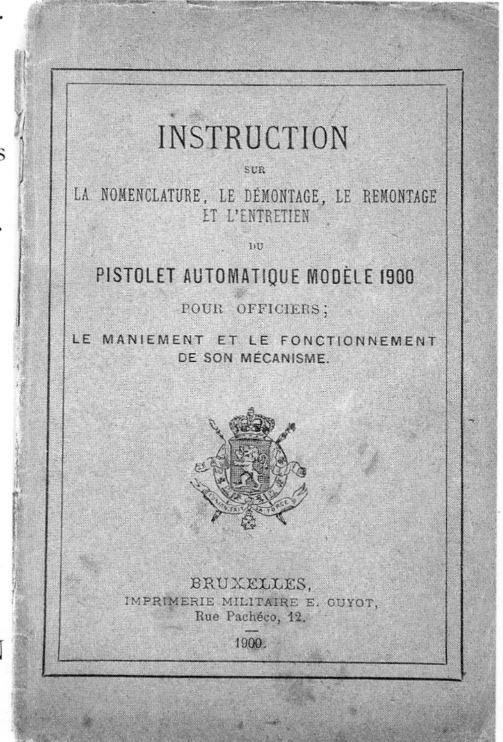

INSTRUCTION

SUR

LA NOMENCLATURE, LE DÉMONTAGE, LE REMONTAGE ET L'ENTRETIEN

DU

PISTOLET AUTOMATIQUE MODÈLE 1900

POUR OFFICIERS;

LE MANIEMENT ET LE FONCTIONNEMENT DE SON MÉCANISME.

BRUXELLES,
IMPRIMERIE MILITAIRE E. GUYOT,
Rue Pachéco, 12.

1900.

(Fig.143-2) A rare first edition Belgian military instruction booklet for the Model 1900

Three Belgian military variants exist:
A: Early pistols featuring Belgian acceptance markings with spot-faced safety markings and plain black synthetic grips
B: Early pistols featuring Belgian acceptance markings with wooden arsenal made replacement grips
C: Standard FN production pistols featuring Belgian acceptance markings

Observed or reported serial numbers: 511, 676, 1201, 1863, 2915, 3034, 3942, 6440, 7736, 10641, 10681, 10686, 11107, 11231, 11956, 12345, 12752, 694998, 698887, 704720, 704763, 719209, 719622, 720927, 725153

(1) There are contradicting figures relating to the first order. Some indicate 10,000 while other indicate 20,000. It is possible that the initial order of 10.000 was increased to 20.000, a common practice at the time.

(2) This was incorrectly denied in the book The Belgian Browning Pistols (Wet Dog Publications, 2001). New information has surfaced since the publication of the earlier volume to confirm the separate serial range.

(Fig.144-1) This early Belgian military pistol N° 511 was manufactured in 1900. This pistol still retains the original fragile black synthetic grips. Undamaged grips are rarely encountered today. This pistol has the spot-faced circles around the safety markings. This pistol has the arsenal acceptance marking "JR".

(Fig.144-2) This Belgian military pistol N° 6440 was manufactured in 1900. This pistol was issued to the Belgian gendarmerie, as indicated by the large "W" stamped next to the serial number. This pistol has the wooden replacement grips and has the circles around the safety markings but these are no longer brightly polished. This pistol has the arsenal acceptance marking "AF".

(Fig.145-1) This Belgian Army pistol N° 719209 was part of the last order of 1914. This pistol has the arsenal acceptance marking "AA". This pistol exhibits standard FN production features.

(Fig.145-2) A rare photograph of Belgian machine-gunners and their assistants during World War I. The gunner's assistant on the left is holding a Spanish Ruby pistol, one of few supplied by the French early in the war. The assistant in the center holds a Belgian military Colt 1903 and the assistant on the right holds a FN Browning 1900.

King Albert's Presentation Pistol

The assassination of Franz Ferdinand of Austria propelled the world into a global war. Belgium was drawn into the conflict on August 4, 1914 when Germany invaded.

The Belgians resisted gallantly but were overmatched by the enormous German invasion force. Often the troops were outnumbered five-to-one during the first month of the war.

By November, King Albert had retreated with the remnants of the Belgian army behind the Yser river in the western part of the country. He refused to be pushed into France and the army stood its ground. King Albert remained with his troops and took residence with the queen in La Panne in a summerhouse on the beach near the trenches.

By the end of October, 1914,the front stabilized and the stalemate of trench warfare had begun. King Albert's priorities shifted from resisting the German invasion to supplying his troops.

King Albert routinely spent time in the trenches. Most often he would wear a military overcoat without any insignia so that he would not be recognized. The subterfuge was often too effective; there are numerous accounts of Belgian officers, assuming the king was just another soldier, ordering him to fatigue duty, and of private soldiers accepting and treating him as one of their own.

(Fig.146-1) A surrealist portrait of King Albert in 1915. His face and hair are intertwined with battle-scenes. The portrait is marked "l'Ame de la Belgique" (the Soul of Belgium).

Later in life, Queen Elisabeth recalled that there was always somebody at the door of the summerhouse wishing to extend their apologies for their inadvertent disrespect. King Albert's incognito excursions in the trenches gave him a keen awareness of his soldiers' living conditions and needs

The Presentation Pistol

Albert's willingness to live with his soldiers made him one of the most respected men of the day. It is believed that Belgian officers made arrangements to have one new FN Browning 1900 pistol engraved as a gift to the king for his birthday. This gift may have had a practical function; Belgian officers often tried to convince Albert to carry a weapon, as he was known to walk through the trenches unarmed.

The scarcity of materials made finding a new pistol a difficult task. How the pistol made it from the occupied zone to Belgian lines remains a mystery. The same is true for the engraving; it is not known where the work was performed but it is believed that the engraving was done behind enemy lines as many artisans were in the trenches. The pistol is engraved and inlaid in 24-karat gold: "La Panne 1915" and "Vaincre ou Mourir" (Victory or Death). The left side of the pistol is engraved with King Albert's royal crest.

Mr. Woodbury

By the end of 1915 King Albert had Belgian, British, French as well as Senegalese soldiers under his command. Mr. E. Woodbury, an Australian officer, was placed under command of King Albert in 1916. Mr. Woodbury worked as a liaison between King Albert and Commonwealth troops. He visited the king and queen often for tea, discussing military matters but also as a social guest of the house. It did not take long for Mr. Woodbury to befriend the royal couple. He spent many hours talking to King Albert in his study. Apparently Mr. Woodbury always marveled at the FN Browning 1900 pistol that was in its case just to the left of King Albert's desk. The sleek and compact design of the pistol must have been appealing to Mr. Woodbury who carried a bulky British Webley service revolver. Albert did not carry the pistol as the Belgian officers had hoped; the pistol remained in its case in Albert's small study in the beach house in La Panne for the duration of the war.

After the armistice was signed on November 11, 1918, many leaders feared the new world order. The Russian army had dissolved and Russia was in the throes of a civil war between Bolshevik and White Russian forces. Reports of vandalism and looting soon followed as the German armies returned home. Rumors of a Belgian proletarian revolution were rife. A socialist official in the Belgian government managed to convince Albert that a revolt had started in the capitol of Brussels.

The news was false, but Albert and Elisabeth took action immediately nonetheless. The Belgian cavalry was summoned and Albert decided to ride out immediately towards Brussels to restore order. Queen Elisabeth opted to accompany Albert to Brussels, ahead of the cavalry force. The royal couple left La Panne at once. As there was no time to secure all their belongings, they decided to give them away to their friends rather than run the risk of their being looted. Nurses were summoned to the house at La Panne and Queen Elisabeth gave away all the available linens among many of her personal possessions. Mr. Woodbury came to say farewell and was surprised to receive the pistol he had admired for years.

Albert and Elisabeth rode out with the cavalry and saw for the first time the devastation that the war had brought upon the country. The Belgian population cheered them along the entire route. Some of the photographs today show Albert and Elisabeth on horseback entering the city of Ghent, the same city where a hundred years earlier, the treaty ending the War of 1812 had been signed. Eventually King Albert and Queen Elisabeth arrived in Brussels. There they found no revolution, only cheers from a joyous population.

After the war

Mr. Woodbury returned to Australia after the war with his prized possession. In 1919 he traveled to California after learning that King Albert was traveling through the United States. King Albert and Queen Elisabeth made this trip in order to meet and thank all those who were involved with helping Belgium and the war effort. As the royal couple traveled through the United States they met Herbert Hoover, who later became the president of the United States. Herbert Hoover had managed the Belgian relief organization and had without doubt managed to keep the country of Belgium from starving during the war.

The Royals also met with the Browning family in Utah, in appreciation of John Browning's designs and how they helped Belgium before and during the war. Mr. Woodbury was able to meet King Albert in California. It is said that they spent half an hour walking near the beach, in a setting much like La Panne. It is not known what the men discussed, but Mr. Woodbury remained in touch with the royal family for the remainder of his life. Every holiday season he sent Christmas wishes to the king and queen. The pistol remained a cherished souvenir of his friendship with Albert and Elisabeth.

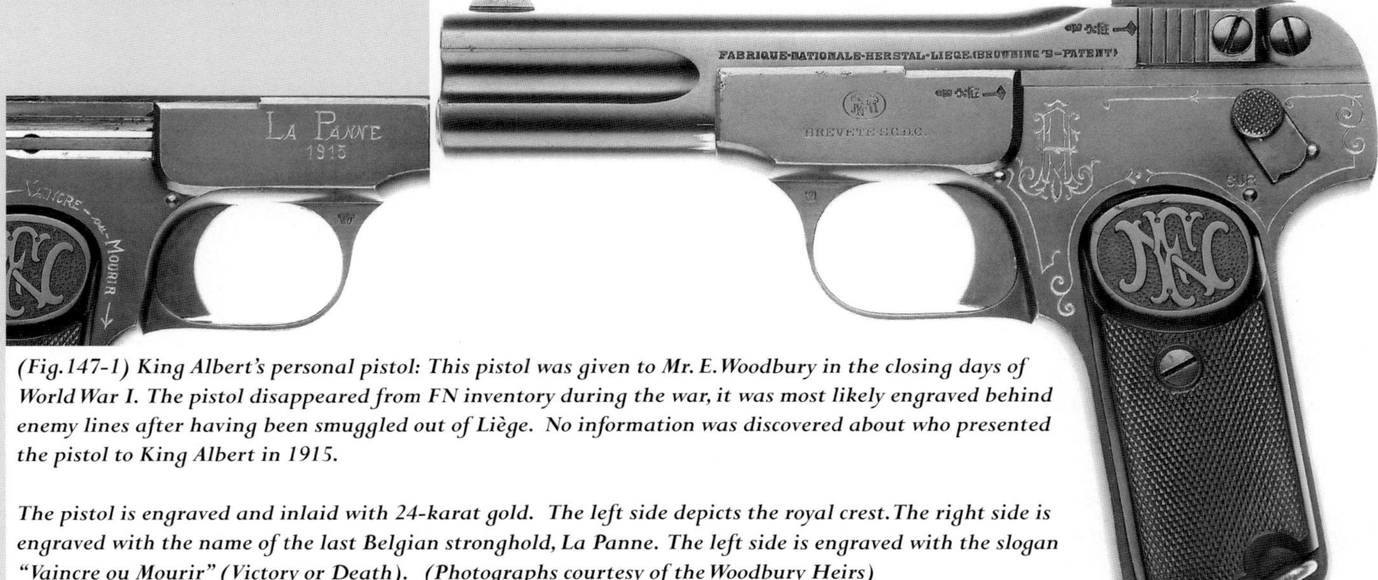

(Fig.147-1) King Albert's personal pistol: This pistol was given to Mr. E. Woodbury in the closing days of World War I. The pistol disappeared from FN inventory during the war, it was most likely engraved behind enemy lines after having been smuggled out of Liège. No information was discovered about who presented the pistol to King Albert in 1915.

The pistol is engraved and inlaid with 24-karat gold. The left side depicts the royal crest. The right side is engraved with the name of the last Belgian stronghold, La Panne. The left side is engraved with the slogan "Vaincre ou Mourir" (Victory or Death). (Photographs courtesy of the Woodbury Heirs)

(Fig.147-2) According to Mr. Woodbury's testimonial; King Albert did not use or carry the pistol. It was always present in its presentation case in his study in La Panne. This wartime photograph, dated December 17, 1917, shows King Albert at his desk in La Panne, it is believed that the presentation case is visible in this photograph.

The Austrian-Hungarian Purchases

A number of Model 1900, 1903 and 1905 pistols have been noted with Austrian proofs on the left side of the frame. All pistols sold in the Austrian-Hungarian empire were proofed with Austrian proofs after leaving Belgium (see page 96). The Austrian proofs easily identify where the pistols were sold but do not reveal their use. It is known that the empire purchased at least one order of pistols in 1913 for their military. Several officers carried FN Browning 1900's acquired on the commercial market. At least 770 pistols were in military inventory[1] in 1914.

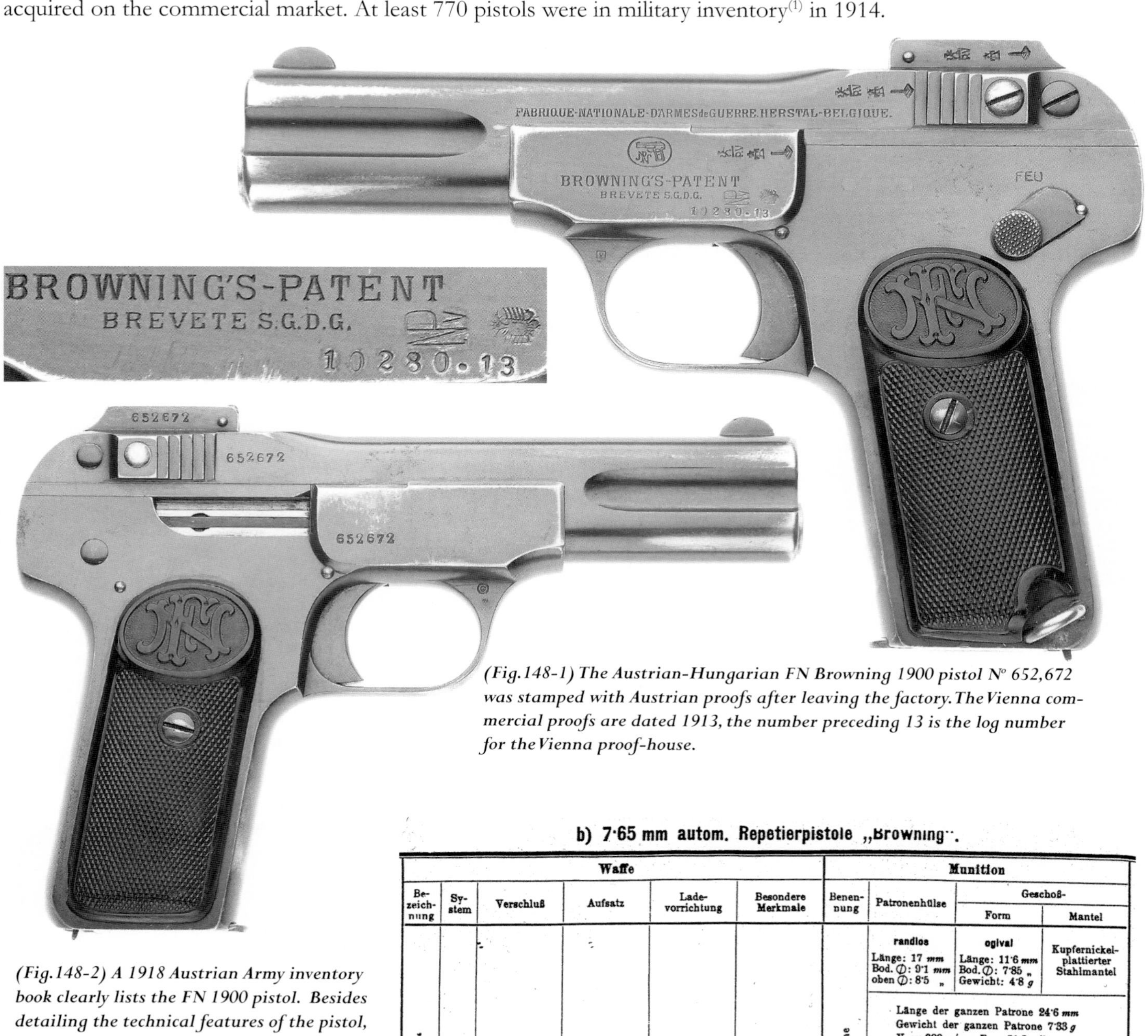

(Fig.148-1) The Austrian-Hungarian FN Browning 1900 pistol N° 652,672 was stamped with Austrian proofs after leaving the factory. The Vienna commercial proofs are dated 1913, the number preceding 13 is the log number for the Vienna proof-house.

(Fig.148-2) A 1918 Austrian Army inventory book clearly lists the FN 1900 pistol. Besides detailing the technical features of the pistol, it lists details about the ammunition: "Cartridges are packed 25 per box and have either a German or French label." This indicates that Austria-Hungary was also purchasing ammunition from Belgium or France before the war. (Document courtesy of Merv Broten)

b) 7·65 mm autom. Repetierpistole „Browning".

Waffe						Munition			
Bezeichnung	System	Verschluß	Aufsatz	Ladevorrichtung	Besondere Merkmale	Benennung	Patronenhülse	Geschoß- Form	Geschoß- Mantel
aut. Repetierpistole „Browning"	Browning	Feststehender Lauf, unverriegelter Kolbenverschluß, der beim Schusse nach rückwärts bewegt wird	Korn und Grinsel am Verschlußstück	Auswechselbares Magazin für 7 Patronen, das von unten in den Pistolengriff eingedrückt wird	Sicherung an der linken Seite; Griffschalen mit dem Monogramm	7·65 mm M. 14 scharfe Pistolenpatrone	randlos Länge: 17 mm Bod. Ø: 9·1 mm oben Ø: 8·5 „	ogival Länge: 11·6 mm Bod. Ø: 7·85 „ Gewicht: 4·8 g	Kupfernickelplattierter Stahlmantel
							Länge der ganzen Patrone 24·6 mm Gewicht der ganzen Patrone 7·33 g $V_0 = 300$ m/s; $E_0 = 21·8$ m/kg		
							Art der Verpackung der Patronen: 25 Stück Patronen in einer Schachtel mit französischer und deutscher Aufschrift: 25 Patronen Kal. 7·65 für automatische Pistolen System Browning und System Steyr. In M. 88 Gewehrpatronenverschlägen nach Bedarf eine Anzahl Schachteln verpackt. Etikette am Verschlagdeckel: „... St. 7·65 mm für Steyr- oder Browning-Repetierpistolen schf. Patronen".		

(1) A noted Austrian collector states that the military FN 1900 pistols were not proofed like the commercial pistols. The author has not found any information to confirm or deny this statement

The Mysterious Greek Contract

Little is known about the Greek contract Model 1900 pistols. Only one example has surfaced. A period Greek ordinance manual shows the pistol but does not give any details about its use or inventory quantities. It is fair to assume that the contract was small. The examined pistol indicates an issue number of 298. This does not necessarily confirm that all pistols were FN 1900 models. Factory records indicate shipment in 1912. The nickel finish and marking was applied at FN similar in style to the Imperial Russian pistols.

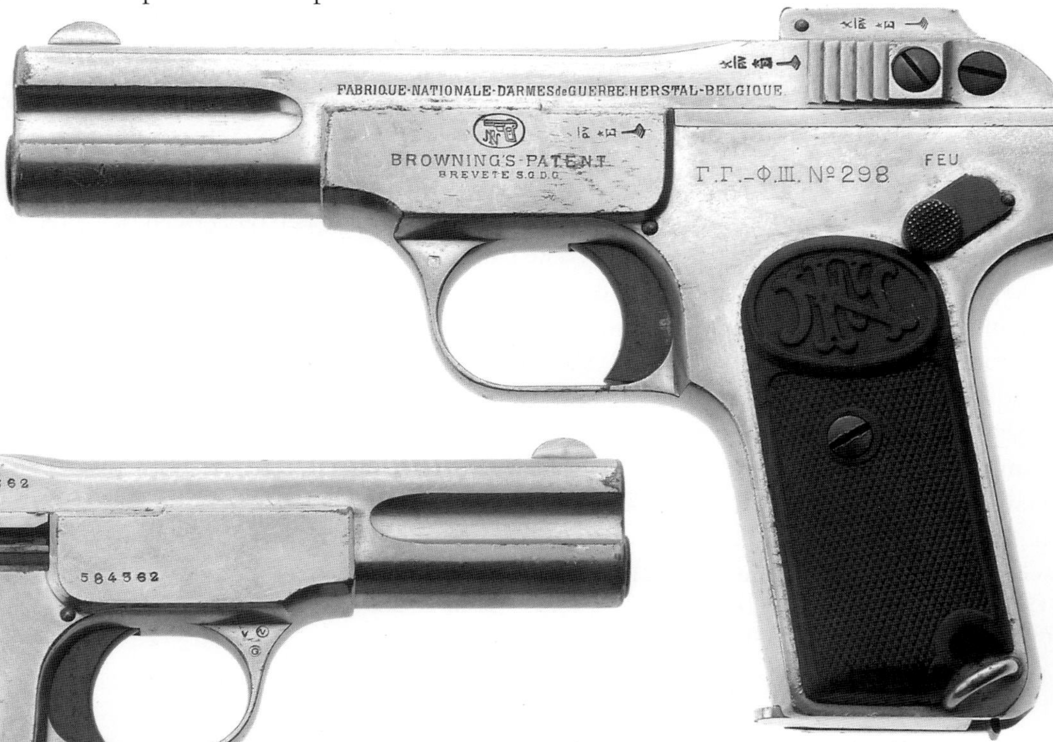

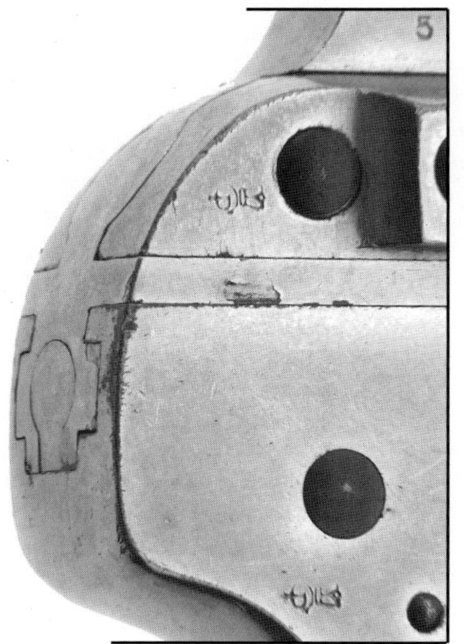

(Fig.149-1) Greek officers' pistols resemble those supplied to the Russian Imperial School. The pistols were factory marked with Greek letters and issue number before nickel plating. This Greek pistol N° 584362 was shipped from FN on June 15, 1912. The pistol exhibits all characteristics of factory nickel plating, including catalyst black trigger, safety and screws (page 139). The magazine is nickel plated with blue follower (see fig. 131-2). The issue numbers suggests that there may have been at least 298 pistols shipped to Greece. No information has been located, only a period manual and this pistol confirm the existence of the contract. Note the small proof marks on the frame and slide. (Photographs by author, courtesy of Ted Zajac)

The FN 1900 in Imperial Russia

The Imperial Russian government purchased Model 1900, 1903 and 1905 pistols for its Imperial General Staff academy graduates (see also page 188). These guns can be identified by the crossed Mosin-Nagant rifles marking on the frame. Two finishes have been noted on these Russian contract guns; blue and nickel.

It is often believed that the nickel finish, as well as the Mosin-Nagant markings were added in Russia. This is incorrect. Close examination of the Russian pistols indicates that the bluing as well as the nickel finish was applied after the marking had been engraved. The nickel and blue finish on these pistols are identical to standard FN finishes. Additionally, the nickel finish guns have unplated triggers and safeties. This was standard FN plating procedure to ensure correct tolerances for fit and operation of these parts (see page 99).

It is believed that the nickel finish guns were issued only to outstanding graduates. The exact amount of contract orders for this pistol is not known, most guns were documented as having been delivered by FN to the Imperial School between December 1907 and 1914. The shipments sometimes coincided with deliveries of Model 1905 Vest Pocket pistols (page 188). Additionally, some rare examples of the Model 1903 exist with the crossed Mosin-Nagant engraving. The majority of these Russian contract pistols were ordered and delivered between 1905 and 1910 with fewer contracts between 1910 and 1914. FN was one of many suppliers to the Imperial Russian military, as such the crossed Mosin-Nagant Rifle markings appear on various pieces of equipment including binoculars, walking sticks, compasses, and watches. Close examination of these items indicates variations in the style of the crossed Mosin-Nagant marking. These differences are attributable to variations in the manufacturers' interpretations of the marking and engraving capabilities. These subtle differenes lend further credence to the idea that the markings were applied by manufacturers and not Russian acceptance authorities.

Observed or reported serial numbers: 333938 (issue N° 2177), 349865 (issue N° 3905), 352250, 353096, 353690 (issue N° 4395), 354153 (issue N° 4316), 383260 (issue N° 5205), 407099 (issue N° 5864), 549629 (issue N° 6773), 673523 (issue N° 2177), 676385 (issue N° 7802), 700604 (issue N° 7986), 700770 (issue N° 7916)

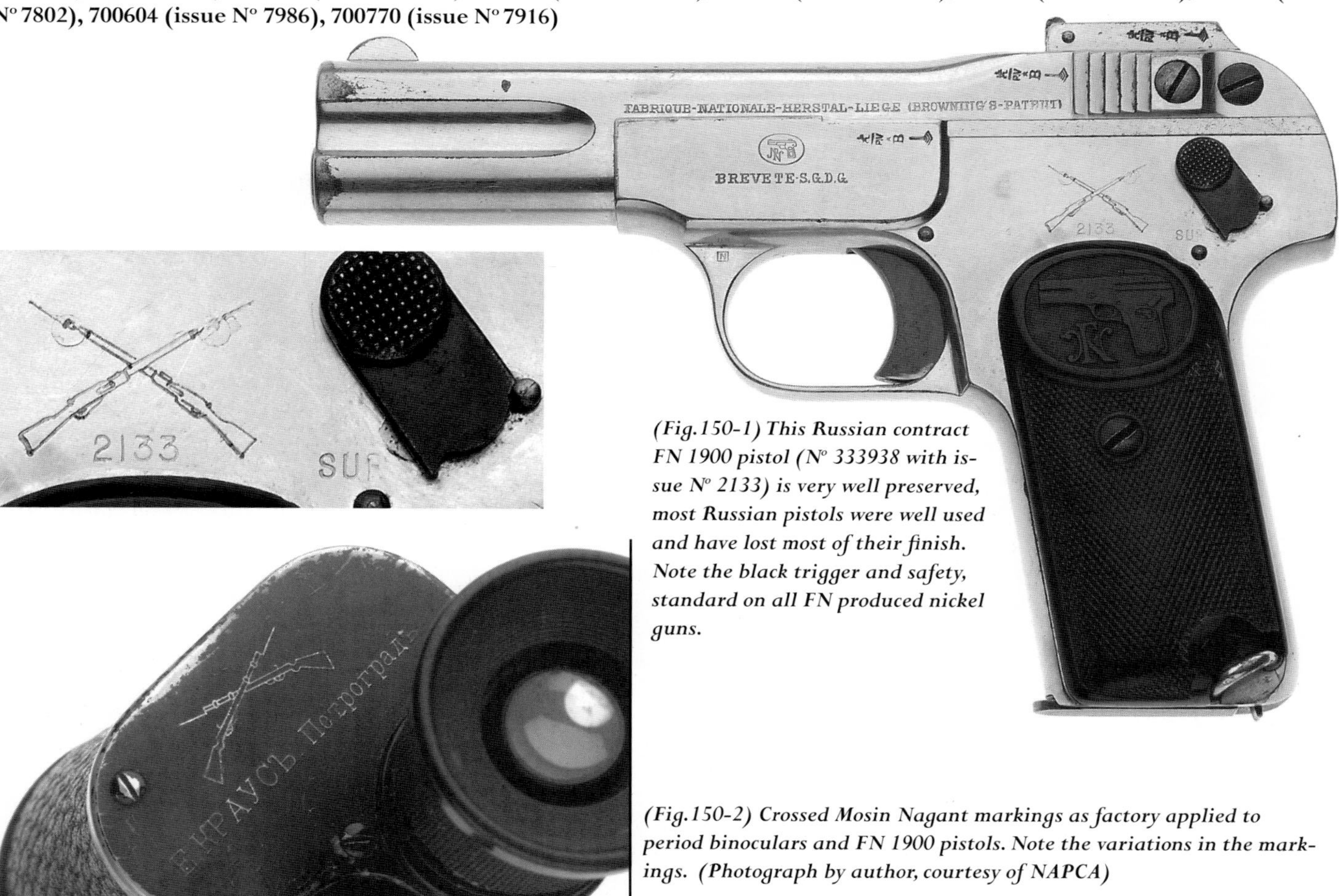

(Fig.150-1) This Russian contract FN 1900 pistol (N° 333938 with issue N° 2133) is very well preserved, most Russian pistols were well used and have lost most of their finish. Note the black trigger and safety, standard on all FN produced nickel guns.

(Fig.150-2) Crossed Mosin Nagant markings as factory applied to period binoculars and FN 1900 pistols. Note the variations in the markings. (Photograph by author, courtesy of NAPCA)

(Fig.151-1) Another variation in the crossed Mosin-Nagant markings, this time as applied to a wrist compass. (Photograph by author, courtesy of NAPCA)

(Fig.151-2) A Russian FN 1900 N° 475930 with unknown Russian property markings (Photograph courtesy of Janne Salopuro)

The assassination attempt on Vladimir Lenin

In 1918 a FN Browning 1900 pistol was used in an assassination attempt on Vladimir Lenin. During the early days of the Russian Revolution, many parties and factions competed for power. The Bolsheviks were at the time a minority party. To rally support, Lenin gave speeches at a large number of meetings and demonstrations. Late in 1918 he gave a speech in the Mikhelsen factory. As he left the stage he was shot twice by Fannie Efimovna Kaplan. Kaplan was a young woman who had been part of a radical anarchist movement. She claimed to have operated alone and never revealed how she acquired the pistol. Years later it became obvious that she had been part of a larger and more organized group.

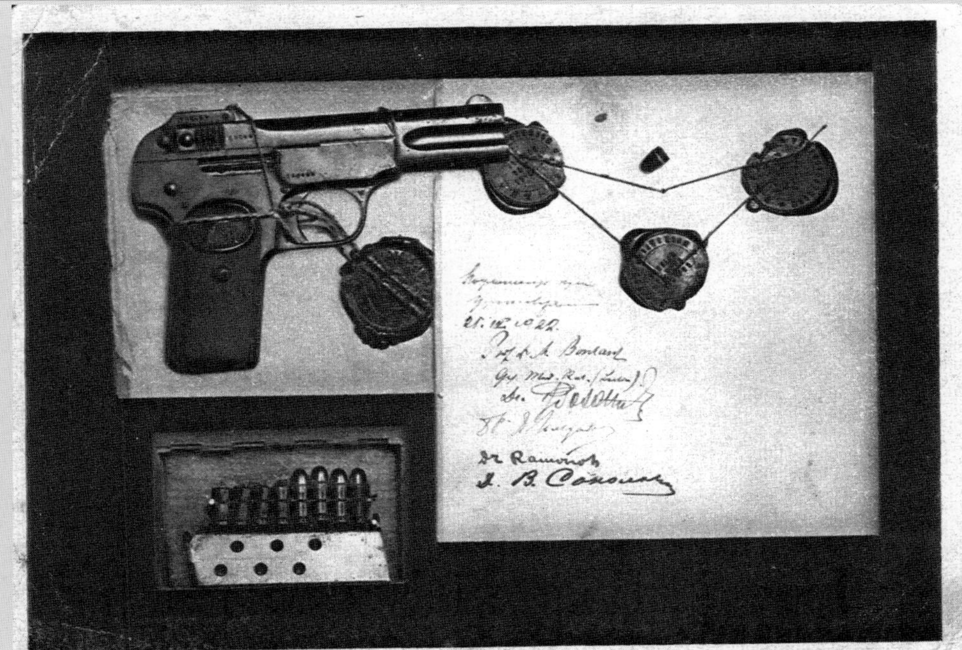

(Photograph courtesy of Janne Salopuro)

Lenin was struck twice; one bullet hit him in the shoulder, another, life threatening, struck him in the neck. A third bullet hit a bystander. Lenin hovered between life and death but ultimately recovered. The round that hit him in the shoulder remained in his body until his death in 1922. Fannie Kaplan was executed a few days later.

Shown here is the pistol used by Fannie Kaplan. The pistol and cartridges were kept in Soviet archives. The bullet shown near the muzzle is the one recovered from Lenin's body.

German Police Use of Model 1900 and 1905 FN Browning Pistols

by Don Maus

Model 1900 Brownings were adopted by the Prussian police at a very early date and were purchased for a period of about ten years. They may also have been purchased by other German states but there are no known pistols that can be identified as belonging to organizations other than the Prussian police. Beginning about 1910, the Prussian police began purchasing the Model 1907 Dreyse pistols in lieu of the FN pistols. However, many of the FN pistols remained in police service until at least into the 1930s.

In a letter dated May 27, 1910 to the Prussian Minister of the Interior, the Polizeipräsident (Police Commissioner) of Berlin requested permission to begin purchasing Dreyses in lieu of the FN pistols. He noted that there were 940 FN pistols in the Berlin police inventory at that time. Given the inertia of a bureaucratic purchasing organization, it is likely that more FN pistols were added prior to the switch. German police pistols were marked with property markings and numbers, these markings were either applied at FN as part of the contract requirements or were marked in Germany. The highest observed Berlin police property number on a Model 1900 is 1415. Recorded serial numbers on pistols with Prussian police markings range from 15239 to 388166 (1902-1908).

Prussian police pistols are identified by markings in the form K.P.P.X.N°123 or K.P.D.X.N°123. The first three letters in these markings stand for Königliches Polizei-Präsidium (Royal Police Presidium) and Königliche Polizei-Direktion (Royal Police Directorate), respectively. The X is an abbreviation for the location of the police unit. These markings are found on the left side of the frame above the grip on Model 1900s and on the right side of the slide on Model 1905s. A few variations have been observed, such as the use of the abbreviation "Pr." instead of "P." for Präsidium and the marking K.G.SG.N°1 which is unidentified.

The Imperial Prussian police were (and the German police still are) organized within Presidiums and subordinate Directorates. The Presidiums were located in major cities and were headed by a Polizeipräsident. The Polizeipräsident was responsible for police matters for that city as well as the Directorates in neighboring cities within his jurisdiction.

There is no known period documentation specifying the location abbreviations to be used in Imperial police markings. It is often assumed that the abbreviations specified for the Weimar Schutzpolizei (Schupo), in an April 1922 Prussian Ministry of the Interior order, also apply to Imperial-era markings. While this works for Berlin (B.) and a few other locations, it is generally inapplicable.

The Schupo abbreviations represented the names of Prussian governmental districts (Regierungsbezirke), not specific cities. As an example, the abbreviation "F". was specified for the governmental district of Frankfurt/Oder in Schupo markings but represented the city of Frankfurt/Main in Imperial police markings. The meanings of only a few of the Imperial police abbreviations are known with certainty. The German contract pistols are easily identified by the safety markings in German (FEUER, SICHER) instead of the traditional French markings (FEU, SUR).

The "1920" Weimar marking signifies that the gun complied with the Treaty of Versailles for use after World War I. After being stamped with the "1920" marking these were only used as police guns. Some pistols do occasionally surface with just the German safety markings and no police markings. These pistols were either special order commercial guns or military pistols. It should be noted that FN shipped standard commercial pistols with French safety markings to German dealers. German safety markings were shipped only on special order.

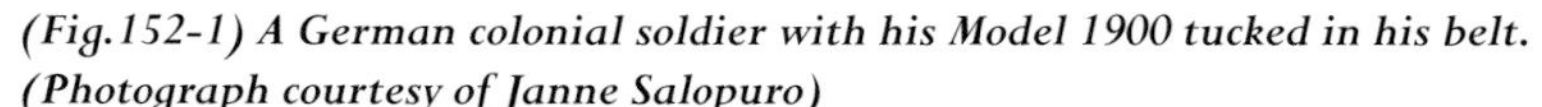

(Fig.152-1) A German colonial soldier with his Model 1900 tucked in his belt. (Photograph courtesy of Janne Salopuro)

(1) Detlef Völkel, Die geschichtliche Entwicklung der Faustfuerwaffen der deutschen Polizei von 1893 – 1945 (The Historical Development of Handguns of the German Police from 1893 to 1945), in Deutsche Waffen Journal, Dec. 1983 & Jan. 1984

Observed and reported German police pistols:

15239	K.P.D.DR N°39	Königliche Polizei-Direktion Dortmund? (French safety markings)
39819	K.P.D.M. N°44	Königliche Polizei-Direktion Münster?
42389	K.P.D.M. N°458	Königliche Polizei-Direktion Münster?
42750	K.P.D.M. N°561	Königliche Polizei-Direktion Münster?
52240	K.P.P.B. N°392	Königliches Polizei-Präsidium Berlin
52938	K.P.Pr.B. N°347	Königliches Polizei-Präsidium Berlin
68265	K.P.P.F. N°80	Königliches Polizei-Präsidium Frankfurt/M
	(1920 marked, also marked S.W.I170 on front gripstrap for Schutzpolizei Frankfurt/M (W.I.))	
171006	K.P.P.B. N°58	Königliches Polizei-Präsidium Berlin
	(Also marked S.Ar.II.C.5.on front gripstrap for Schutzpolizei Arnsberg Kommando II)	
175588	K.P.P.M. N°26	Königliche Polizei-Präsidium Münster?
194943	K.P.P.B N°133	Königliches Polizei-Präsidium Berlin
	(Also marked K.Br.56 on front gripstrap for Kriminalpolizei Breslau)	
249330	K.P.P.F. N°197	Königliches Polizei-Präsidium Frankfurt/M
	(1920 mkd, also marked S.W.I.72 on front gripstrap for Schutzpolizei Frankfurt/M (W.I.))	
275339	K.P.P.B. N°1415	Königliches Polizei-Präsidium Berlin
332624	K.P.D.A. N°91	Königliche Polizei-Direktion Aachen?
338778	K.P.D.G. N°17	Königliche Polizei-Direktion Gleiwitz
347439	K.P.D.C. N°81	Königliche Polizei-Direktion Cassel (Kassel)?
374968	K.P.P.F. N°304	Königliches Polizei-Präsidium Frankfurt/M
378067	K.G.SG. N°1	Unidentified
388166	K.P.P.B N°336	Kriminalpolizei Breslau (marked on front gripstrap)

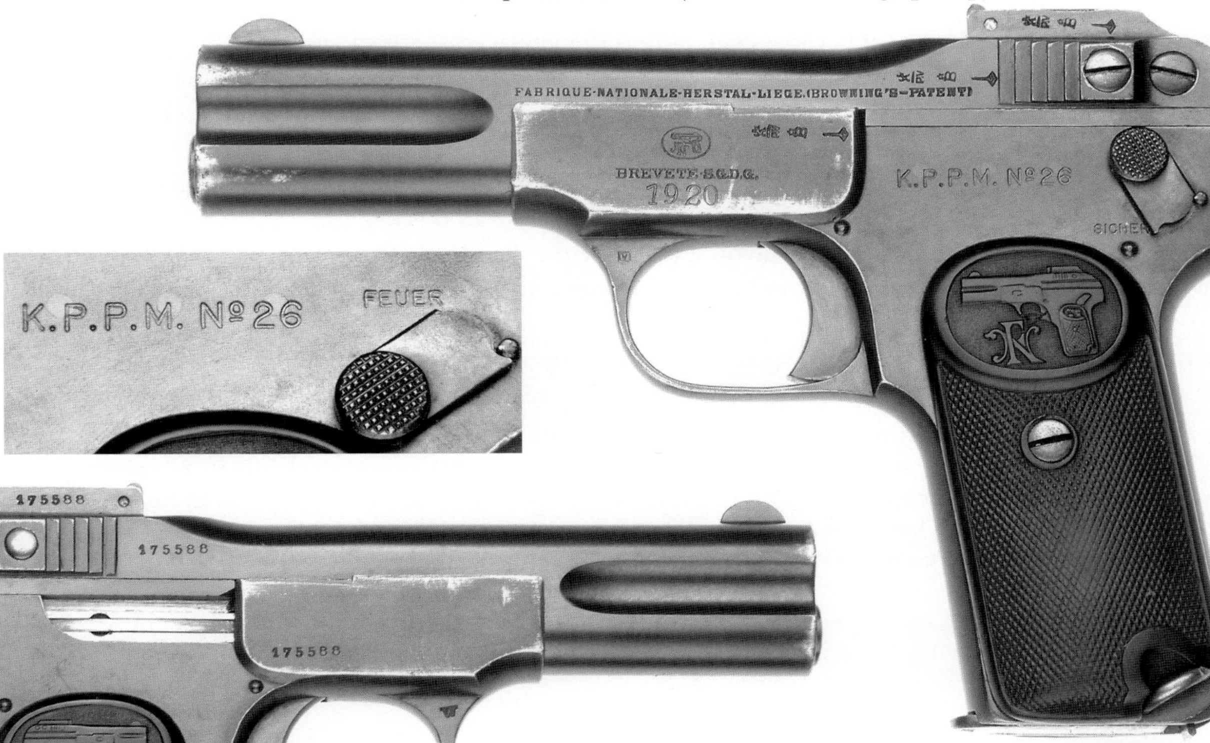

(Fig.153-1) German police pistol N° 175588 was shipped from FN on May 11, 1903. Note the German safety markings, K.P.P.M (Königliche Polizei-Präsidium Münster) marking and the "1920" Weimar marking. This pistol has a matching magazine (N° 26).

The French and the FN Model 1900 pistol

Although France did not accept the FN Browning Model 1900 as a military firearm in the 1903 trials, the pistol surfaces throughout France's early 20th century history

La Bande a Bonnot (Bonnot's Gang)

Jules Bonnot is famous in French history as a cold blooded murderer and gangster. He led a gang of robbers in 1912. The gang was known for its senseless killing and introduced France to a new kind of crime involving fast getaway cars and automatic pistols. The French authorities caught up with the gang and began to arrest the members one by one. The unarmed French police attempt to arrest Bonnot was disastrous. He escaped, killing and wounding officers. Gang members were reputed to carry two Model 1900 pistols - one in each hand. So as not to be outgunned, the French police abandoned their standard revolvers and adopted Model 1900 pistols when attempting to arrest Jules Bonnot for the second time. This time they took no chances and even used dynamite. Jules Bonnot died from wounds suffered during a spectacular gunfight with the police in April 1912.

Although Bonnot's gang only existed for a short period, it left a lasting impression in France. The Bonnot incidents erased all skepticsm when it came to the adoption of automatic pistols. As a result, beginning in 1912, the French police organizations began to re-equip with the Model 1910 pistol.

Les Nettoyeurs de Tranchée (Trench Sweepers)

At the beginning of World War I it became evident that France faced serious logistical and supply problems. Nowhere was this more acute than in the supply of military pistols. The many variations of Spanish pistols imported satisfied some of the demand, but the quality of the Spanish subcontracted pistols often left much to be desired.

Although no more were available from occupied Belgium, all Model 1900 pistols on the retail market were pressed into service. Some officers had purchased their Model 1900's prior to the war and it became a favorite with the French military. Beginning in 1915, it became the favorite pistol of the Trench Sweepers. The Trench Sweepers were special units whose function was to ensure that no Germans remained after terrain had been captured.

Identifying French World War I FN 1900 pistols is almost impossible. Some of the pistols have prewar retailer markings and inventory numbers while others just show inventory numbers.

The meaning of these inventory numbers is often disputed. Three explanations exist:

A: The inventory number was applied prewar by La Manufacture d'Armes et Cycles de St. Etienne[1].

B: The inventory number was applied at the outbreak of World War I and was applied to all firearms available, even those that had no military function.

C: The number is strictly a World War I French military inventory number.

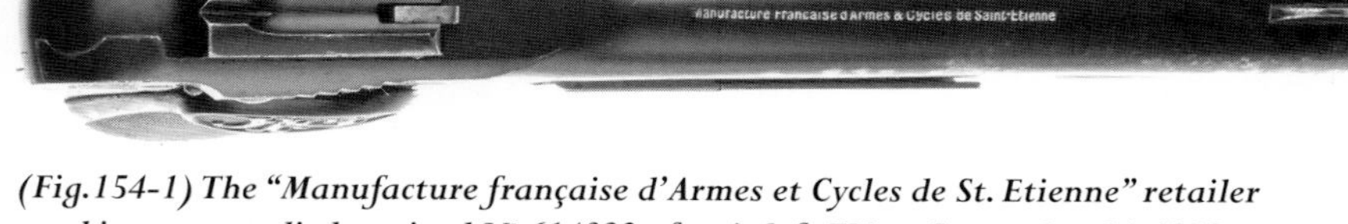

(Fig.154-1) The "Manufacture française d'Armes et Cycles de St. Etienne" retailer marking was applied to pistol N° 614832 after it left FN on September 14, 1912. This pistol was marked with the inventory number 6803. See fig 120-4 for a detail of the retailer marking.

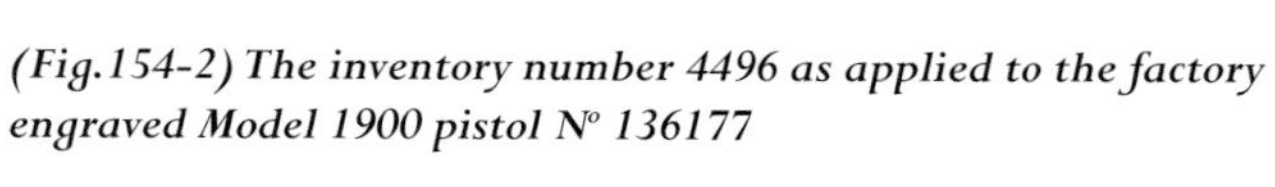

(Fig.154-2) The inventory number 4496 as applied to the factory engraved Model 1900 pistol N° 136177

(Fig.155-1) French World War I pistols are almost unidentifiable. All were acquired from the French commercial market. Pistols distributed by "La Manufacture d'Armes et Cycles de St. Etienne" were marked by the distributor. Pistol N° 614832 has both the "Manufacture" commercial marking as well as an inventory number at the magazine well, most likely indicating World War I use.

(Fig.155-2) This Type I factory engraved Model 1900 pistol N°136177 was shipped to Parent & Leroy in Paris on July 23, 1905. It is not retailer marked by La Manufacture d'Armes et Cycles de St. Etienne as it was not sold by them, but it does have the inventory number on the magazine well. The pistol was arsenal refinished at some point.

(Fig.155-3) A large 1915 illustration out of the French magazine L'Illustration shows trench sweepers at work with FN 1900 pistols.

(1) Although most Manufacture marked guns have the crudely stamped inventory number, the author has encountered two pistols, which were not sold by La Manufacture but featured the inventory number. The exact meaning of the inventory number remains unknown.

Police pistols in Denmark, Norway and Finland

Denmark

Most of the Danish Model 1900 pistols were initially issued to the Danish RPLT (Rigspolitiet- Federal Police) and later reissued to the local police. The Danish police remained unarmed for a long period of time. In 1906 the official police magazine "Politivennen" printed letters from officers requesting to be armed with pistols. In 1908 the "Dansk Politiforenging" (Danish Police Officers Association) put in an official request for sidearms with the Minister of Justice. Politicians feared that armed officers could participate in a coup d'etat, and officers remained unarmed until 1920. In that year officers were issued pistols on the condition that the firearms remained locked at the police station when the officers were off duty. Many of the guns were transferred from the Rigspolitiet, which had been established in 1911. In 1920 four pistol models were accepted for Danish police use: The FN Model 1905, the Mauser Model 1910, The Walther Model 4, and the Dreyse Model 1907. In 1921 this was extended to include; the Bayard M1908 (7.65mm), the FN Model 1900, the FN Model 1910 (7.65mm, for use by detectives), the Walter Model 5 (for use while on body guard duty) and the Walther Model 9. The FN pistols used by the Danish police were not purchased new from FN. Instead these were purchased used on the military surplus market after World War I. It is not known how the Danes marked their pistols, if they marked them at all. Later Danish police pistols (see page 241) were clearly marked.

Norway

The Norwegian police pistols were acquired in similar fashion as the Danish pistols. Most were first purchased from the World War I surplus market. As such it is possible to encounter prewar contract pistols and especially prewar German police pistols with Norwegian police markings. Law enforcement equipment and practices were almost identical between Denmark and Norway.

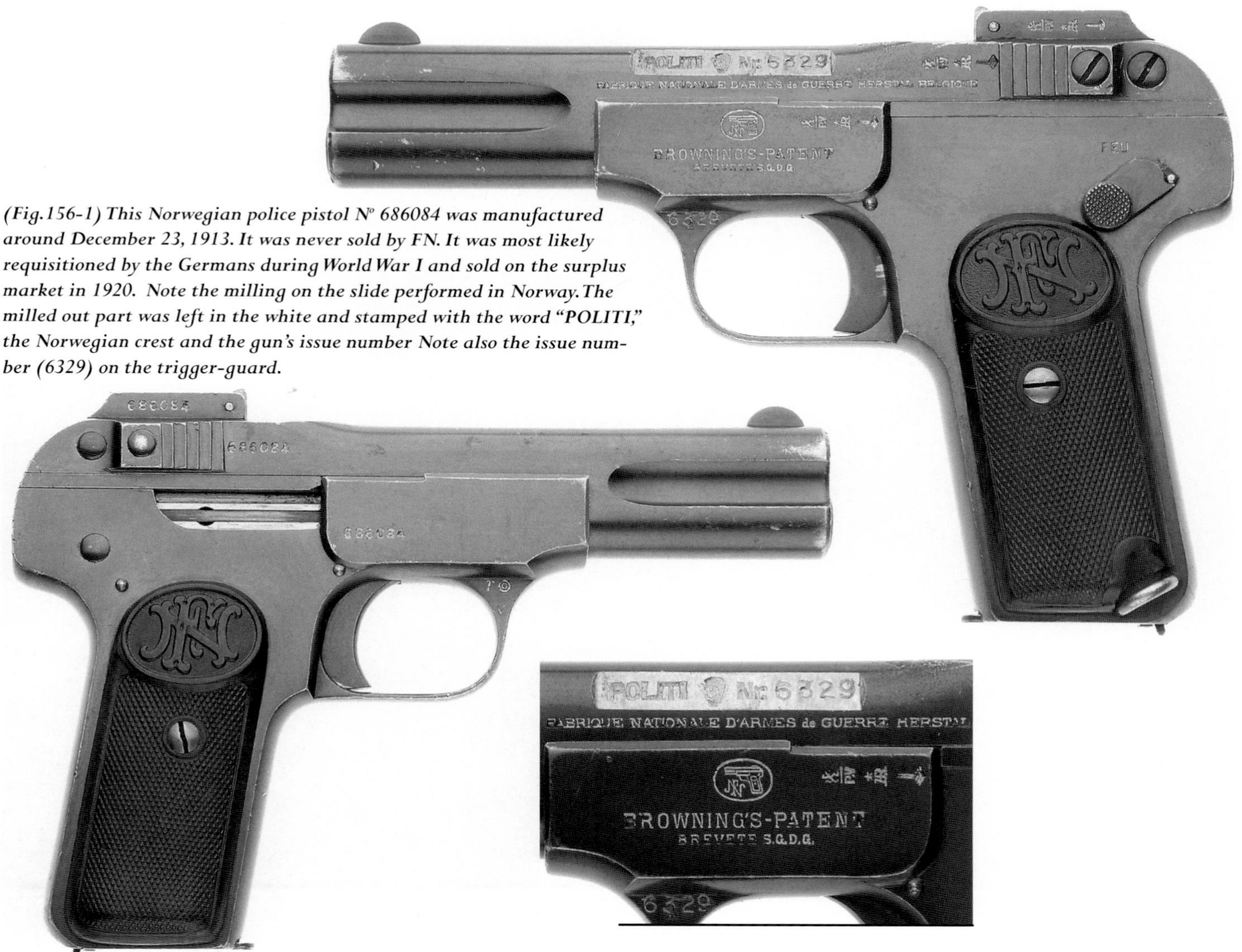

(Fig.156-1) This Norwegian police pistol N° 686084 was manufactured around December 23, 1913. It was never sold by FN. It was most likely requisitioned by the Germans during World War I and sold on the surplus market in 1920. Note the milling on the slide performed in Norway. The milled out part was left in the white and stamped with the word "POLITI," the Norwegian crest and the gun's issue number Note also the issue number (6329) on the trigger-guard.

Finland

The Model 1900 was first used in Finland as early as 1904 during the struggle for independence and was later used in the Finnish Civil War. Many commercial pistols and captured Russian gendarmerie pistols were used. After Finland gained its independence, more Model 1900 pistols were acquired for police duty. These were to be used also in the 1939-1940 Winter War, the 1941-1944 Continuation War, and again during the Lapland War, 1944-1945.

The Finnish police pistols are difficult to recognize as they do not carry any specific markings. These pistols remained in police inventory as late as the 1980s. The pistols can only be identified by the replacement grips. The grips were manufactured in Finland of black Bakelite or black plastic and illustrate the Finnish police emblem. One thousand grip pairs were manufactured by Ahlstrom Inc. between 1947 and 1949. This emblem illustrates a police logo with sword, while the original grip-plates illustrated the standard FN logo.

(Fig.157-1) A Finnish FN Model 1900 police pistol with Ahlstrom manufactured replacement grips. (Photograph courtesy of Timo Martelius, Maanpuolustuskorkeakoulu Sotamuseo / Military Museum of Finland)

The struggle for independence

This photographic portrayal of a young woman in Finland tells a story of a thousand words. Verna Erikson smuggled machine gun belts to the White Guards in Helsinki in 1918. With the collapse of the Imperial Russian empire, Finland struggled for independence. Ideological young women were smuggling guns and supplies for the White Guards. Erikson was a student at the University of Technics in Helsinki. At the time this photograph was taken she carried three machine gun belts, a total of 1350 rounds. The FN Browning 1900 pistol was most likely for her protection.

A FN Model 1900 pistol marks a turning point in Finland's history once again in 1904. Finland was at the time part of the Russian Empire, although in the form of a semi-autonomous grand duchy. Since 1898 Finland had gone through a Russification program overseen by the Russian Governor-General Nikolai Ivanovich Bobrikov.

Appointed by Tsar Nicholas II, Bobrikov attacked and dismantled any entities that promoted a distinct Finnish identity. Bobrikov was determined to annihilate Finnish identity in schools, universities, media, the army, postal services, language, monuments and courts. Virtually every aspect of Finnish life and language were under attack. The Russification program ended with the assassination of Bobrikov in 1904.

Bobrikov was murdered on the steps of the senate by the Finnish nationalist Eugen Waldemar Schauman. Schauman was an accountant, who had been seeking an opportunity to assassinate Bobrikov. He purchased his FN Model 1900 pistol around New Years Day 1904. Prior to the actual assassination he had his pistol checked at a local gun store. He fired three rounds at Bobrikov and turned the pistol against himself by firing two rounds in his own chest. Bobrikov died the following night from his injuries.

The FN Browning Model 1903

Development History: Le Grand Modèle - Modèle de Guerre

Soon after the introduction of the Model 1899 pistol, FN came to the conclusion that military selection boards showed a preference for larger caliber pistols with perceived improvements in accuracy. The introduction of the large Model 1899 had not satisfied the military requirements for a larger caliber. In 1901 FN turned to John Browning for a large military pistol. The results were two prototype pistols that both Colt and FN would produce.

Browning and Colt collectors have often debated which firm initiated the design request first. John Browning simply modified his designs to both suit Colt and FN. Both Colt and FN produced the pistol as their Model 1903[(1)]. It is likely that both Colt as well as FN got to see and inspect both Browning prototypes as the FN 1903 incorporates features found on both pistols (page 107-108).

Interestingly enough, the same Browning designs were made to appeal opposite markets. The existing Colt pistols (Model 1900 and 1902) were bulky and were not popular as pocket pistols. Colt had witnessed the success of the FN Model 1899 and 1900 and wanted to capture the consumer market by introducing a smaller and practical pocket model.

At the same time, FN was seeking to appeal to military buyers by introducing a larger pistol in a heavier caliber as well as a longer barrel and slide for increased accuracy.

Unlike with the Model 1899, FN was wise not to rush production on this model. At that time, FN enjoyed only about three years experience in the pistol market. Despite this limited experience, FN realized immediately that the physical size of the large Model 1903 pistol would generate little commercial interest. With the Model 1903, FN adopted a production strategy that would be repeated with every military pistol they would introduce including the Grand Browning in 1914 and the Grand Rendement in 1929-1930. This strategy included the production of a small lot of pistols that would be used as sales samples for evaluation as well as trials. FN was not interested in repeating the manufacturing changes that they had to implement when the Belgian Army requested changes to the Model 1899 pistol.

In 1902, when FN made their first Model 1903 prototypes, they had completed the transition of manufacturing and distributing the Model 1899 for the Model 1900. This transition was considered inefficient and wasteful. FN was now more interested in securing a large military contract and incorporating any requested changes into the initial manufacturing.

It is not known exactly how many pistols were manufactured in the pre-production run. Surviving documents indicate that these pistols were in high demand by several FN agents. The same pistols were shipped back and forth to FN and were even used in trials. Letters dated January 1904 and September 1904 (see fig.159-1) show the lack of trials and evaluation pistols and indicate the interest of the Norwegian military's artillery branch in acquiring 100 to 500 pistols for field trials. There is little doubt that the production of the pistol can largely be credited to the efforts of FN's Swedish Agent Paul Berghaus. Mr. Berghaus had created great interest within Norway and Sweden. Although Mr. Berghaus requested on numerous occasions to buy quantities of trials pistols, none were made available for Norwegian field trials. It is not known today why FN chose to ignore the Norwegian interest. The quantities the Norwegian government wanted to purchase were most likely not large enough for FN to justify production start-up costs.

The FN Browning 1903 went into production at FN in 1907 after the Swedish contract was received (see page 165).

FN produced a shoulder-stock for the pistol in combination with an extended 10-round magazine. The addition was a FN concept and did not originate with John Browning. This accessory was introduced to compete in the military market with Mauser and Luger. The pistol with shoulder-stock was often marketed as an 11-round carbine transformation.

(1) The FN Browning 1903 is often incorrectly referred to as a copy of the Colt 1903.

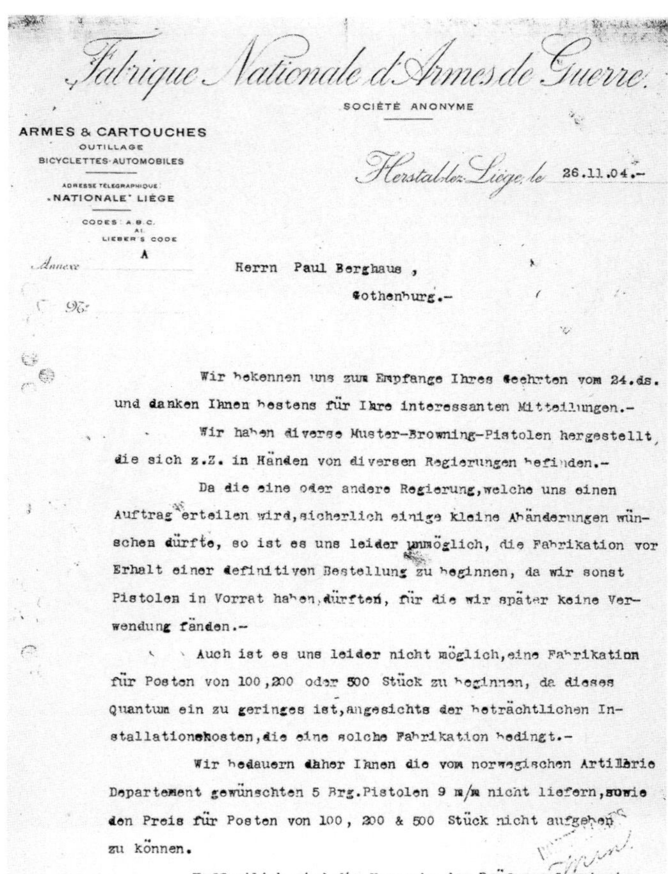

Fabrique Nationale d'Armes de Guerre.

SOCIÉTÉ ANONYME

ARMES & CARTOUCHES
OUTILLAGE
BICYCLETTES-AUTOMOBILES

ADRESSE TÉLÉGRAPHIQUE:
"NATIONALE" LIÉGE

CODES: A.B.C.
AI
LIEBER'S CODE

Herstal-lez-Liége, le 26.11.04.-

Annexe

Herrn Paul Berghaus ,
Gothenburg.-

Wir bekennen uns zum Empfange Ihres Geehrten vom 24.ds. und danken Ihnen bestens für Ihre interessanten Mitteilungen.-

Wir haben diverse Muster-Browning-Pistolen hergestellt, die sich z.Z. in Händen von diversen Regierungen befinden.-

Da die eine oder andere Regierung,welche uns einen Auftrag erteilen wird,sicherlich einige kleine Abänderungen wünschen dürfte, so ist es uns leider unmöglich, die Fabrikation vor Erhalt einer definitiven Bestellung zu beginnen, da wir sonst Pistolen in Vorrat haben dürften, für die wir später keine Verwendung fänden.-

Auch ist es uns leider nicht möglich,eine Fabrikation für Posten von 100,200 oder 500 Stück zu beginnen, da dieses Quantum ein zu geringes ist,angesichts der beträchtlichen Installationskosten,die eine solche Fabrikation bedingt.-

Wir bedauern daher Ihnen die vom norwegischen Artillerie Departement gewünschten 5 Brg.Pistolen 9 m/m nicht liefern,sowie den Preis für Posten von 100, 200 & 500 Stück nicht aufgeben zu können.

Hoffentlich sind die Versuche der Prüfungs-Commission

A select few factory cut-away pistols were produced. These cut-away pistols have only surfaced in Sweden and it is believed that the cut-away pistols were made on special request by Sweden. FN also made available the option of tangent sights to military buyers. Tangents sights were restricted to orders of 500 pistols or more. No orders of tangents sights are known to exist and no samples are known to have survived.

As was often the case with FN Browning pistols, the model designation went through several iterations. It was introduced as "Le Modèle de Guerre" (The War Model), at the same time it was also advertised and referred to as "Le Grand Modèle" (The Large Model). FN workers often had the tendency to name the models and it became internally known as "Le Modèle Suédois" (The Swedish Model). The "Model 1903" designation was introduced years later when FN tried to clarify its model designations.

FN's early insight on their market proved indeed to be correct as the pistol found only a small commercial market. It was considered a military gun, its size and weight never gained interest with the European commercial market. FN agents carried the pistol but many retailers did not.

(Fig.159-1) This November 26, 1904 letter from FN to their agent Paul Berghaus in Sweden states that FN had loaned several trials pistols to various governments. The letter confirms that FN would not start production for orders of 100, 200 or 500 pistols as this would be cost prohibitive. The letter also makes mention that FN will not be able to provide the Norwegian Artillery with five FN 1903 pistols nor wil they be able to provide pricing for 100, 200 or 500 pistols. (Document courtesy of Anders Jonasson)

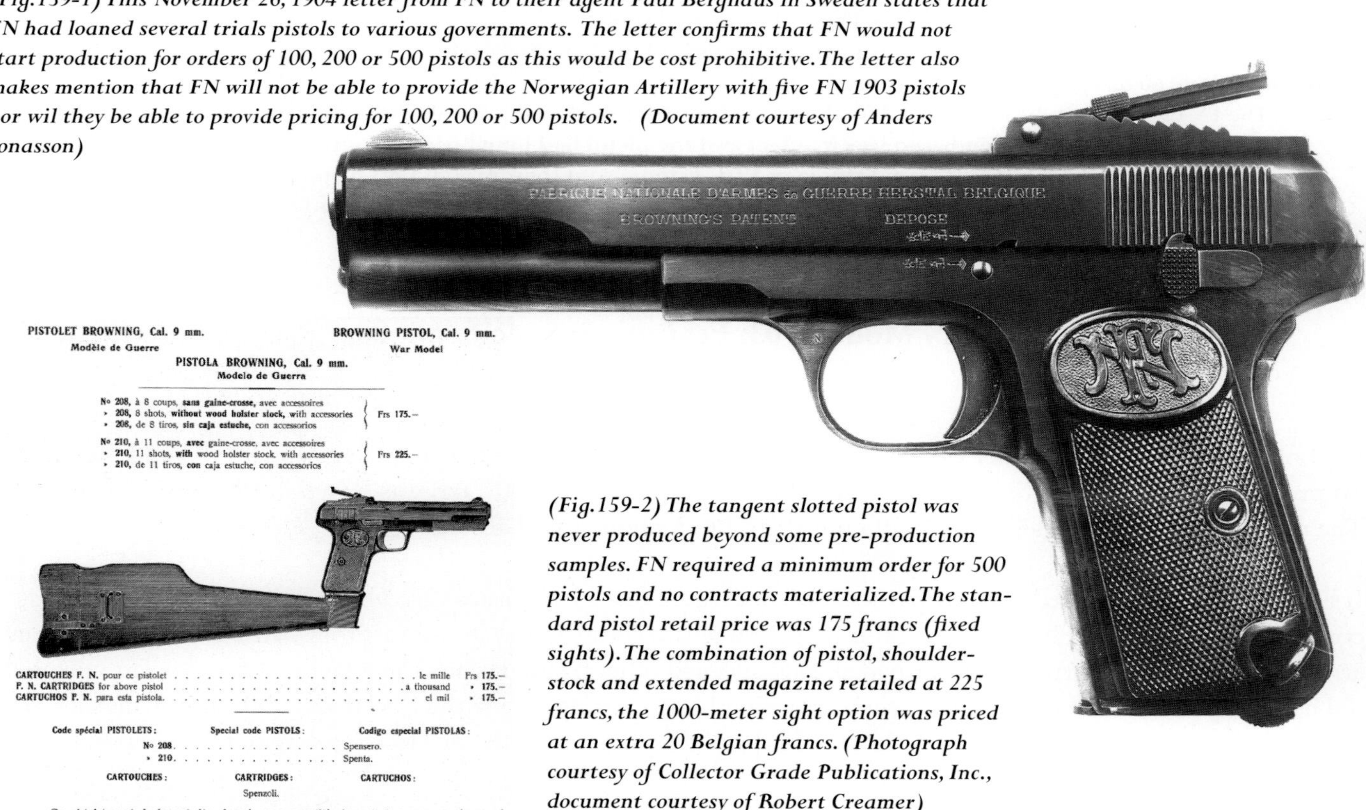

PISTOLET BROWNING, Cal. 9 mm.
Modèle de Guerre

BROWNING PISTOL, Cal. 9 mm.
War Model

PISTOLA BROWNING, Cal. 9 mm.
Modelo de Guerra

No **208,** à 8 coups, **sans gaine-crosse,** avec accessoires
» **208,** 8 shots, **without wood holster stock,** with accessories
» **208,** de 8 tiros, **sin caja estuche,** con accessorios
} Frs **175.**–

No **210,** à 11 coups, **avec** gaine-crosse, avec accessoires
» **210,** 11 shots, **with** wood holster stock, with accessories
» **210,** de 11 tiros, **con** caja estuche, con accessorios
} Frs **225.**–

CARTOUCHES F. N. pour ce pistolet . . . . . le mille Frs **175.**–
F. N. CARTRIDGES for above pistol . . . . . a thousand » **175.**–
CARTUCHOS F. N. para esta pistola. . . . . el mil » **175.**–

Code spécial PISTOLETS: **Special code PISTOLS:** **Codigo especial PISTOLAS:**

No **208**. . . . . Spensero.
» **210**. . . . . Spenta.

CARTOUCHES: **CARTRIDGES:** **CARTUCHOS:**
Spenzoli.

Ce pistolet peut également être fourni, pour quantités importantes, **avec une hausse à 1000 mètres,** moyennant supplément de **20** francs net.

That pistol can furthermore be supplied, as far as large quantities are ordered, **with sight up to 1000 metres,** in which case a supplement of **20** francs, nett, will be charged.

La misma pistola puede tambien suministrarse, cuando se trata de cantidades importantes, **con alza hasta 1000 metros;** el suplemento seria de **20** francos, neto.

(Fig.159-2) The tangent slotted pistol was never produced beyond some pre-production samples. FN required a minimum order for 500 pistols and no contracts materialized. The standard pistol retail price was 175 francs (fixed sights). The combination of pistol, shoulder-stock and extended magazine retailed at 225 francs, the 1000-meter sight option was priced at an extra 20 Belgian francs. (Photograph courtesy of Collector Grade Publications, Inc., document courtesy of Robert Creamer)

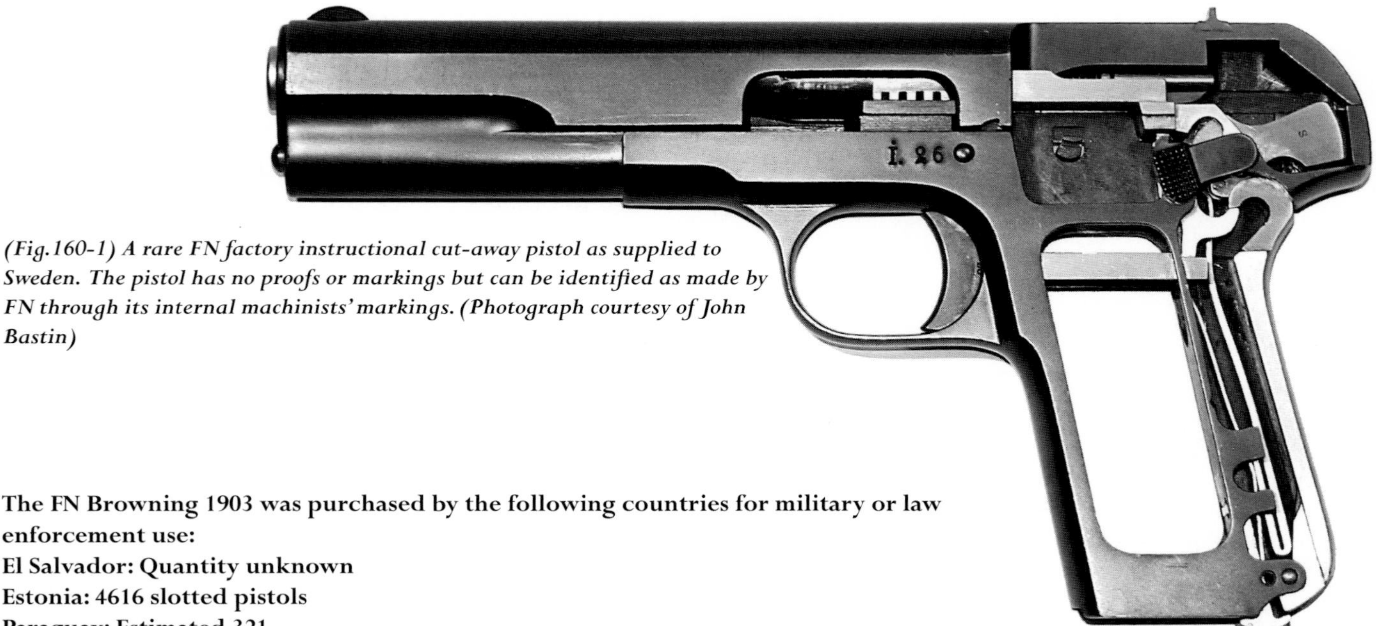

(Fig.160-1) A rare FN factory instructional cut-away pistol as supplied to Sweden. The pistol has no proofs or markings but can be identified as made by FN through its internal machinists' markings. (Photograph courtesy of John Bastin)

The FN Browning 1903 was purchased by the following countries for military or law enforcement use:
El Salvador: Quantity unknown
Estonia: 4616 slotted pistols
Paraguay: Estimated 321
The Netherlands: 80 (non-slotted) pistols for the Dutch Navy[1], designated as "Automatisch Pistool No.2 (Browning)"
Imperial Russia:
- **OKX: Estimated 5500**
- **Moscow Police: As many as 3113**
- **Imperial Officers' School: Unknown, estimated at less than 100**
- **Railway Police: Estimated at less than 500**

Sweden: 10,000 (non-slotted) purchased by the Swedish government
- **Several thousands shipped to Berghaus, FN's agent in Sweden, for sale as commercial pistols to military personnel.**

Ottoman Empire and Turkey:
- **First police variant during Ottoman Empire: Estimated 8000**
- **Subsequent Turkish variations: Unknown, estimated at less than 1000 each**

United Kingdom: 60 or 100 pistols for Navy use
Spain: The FN Browning 1903 pistols used by the Spanish Republicans in the Spanish Civil War were not purchased from FN as an international arms embargo was in effect and the pistol had long been discontinued. These pistols were purchased as surplus equipment from Estonia in 1936. Estonia sold their Model 1903 pistols among tons of other equip ment to the Spanish in order to raise funds for the purchase of High Power pistols and other equipment.

FN Model 1903: Features & Specifications

Serial Numbers

FN only produced 58,442 model 1903 pistols, all in caliber 9mm Browning Long[2]. The Model 1903 had the smallest production run of any FN Browning pistol. Production started in 1907 and was halted in 1914 with World War I. The model was available again from 1919 until 1927. Production ceased around 1927[3].

It has often been speculated that the poor sales figures were due to the pistol's blowback design. In actuality it was a combination of factors. FN introduced this model quite late compared to its competitors. Most of the modernizing armies had already performed trials or had already adopted other pistol designs. The fact that the Belgian military[4] did not accept the model nor the new 9mm Browning Long cartridge made the FN Model 1903 a difficult sale. Several trial documents show no reference to the blowback design or any reference to shortcomings of blowback designs in general.

Serial numbers ascended in logical order starting with number 1. Production seized in 1914 around number 37,000. Numbering continued uninterrupted after World War I. It appears that the first 10,000 Swedish contract pistols had their own serial range and were produced before commercial production began.

The earliest commercial pistol shipment appears to be pistol number 35 which was shipped for evaluation to Lepersonne in London on April 10, 1908, it was later returned to FN. Production seized around 1928 and the last pistol, number 54494, was shipped from FN warehouses on June 17, 1935(3).

FN tried to appeal to the military market by numbering most of the pistol parts. The full or abbreviated serial number is found on the frame, slide, barrel, barrel-bushing, hammer, trigger, magazine and grips. No other FN production pistol has as many numbered parts as the Model 1903 pistol

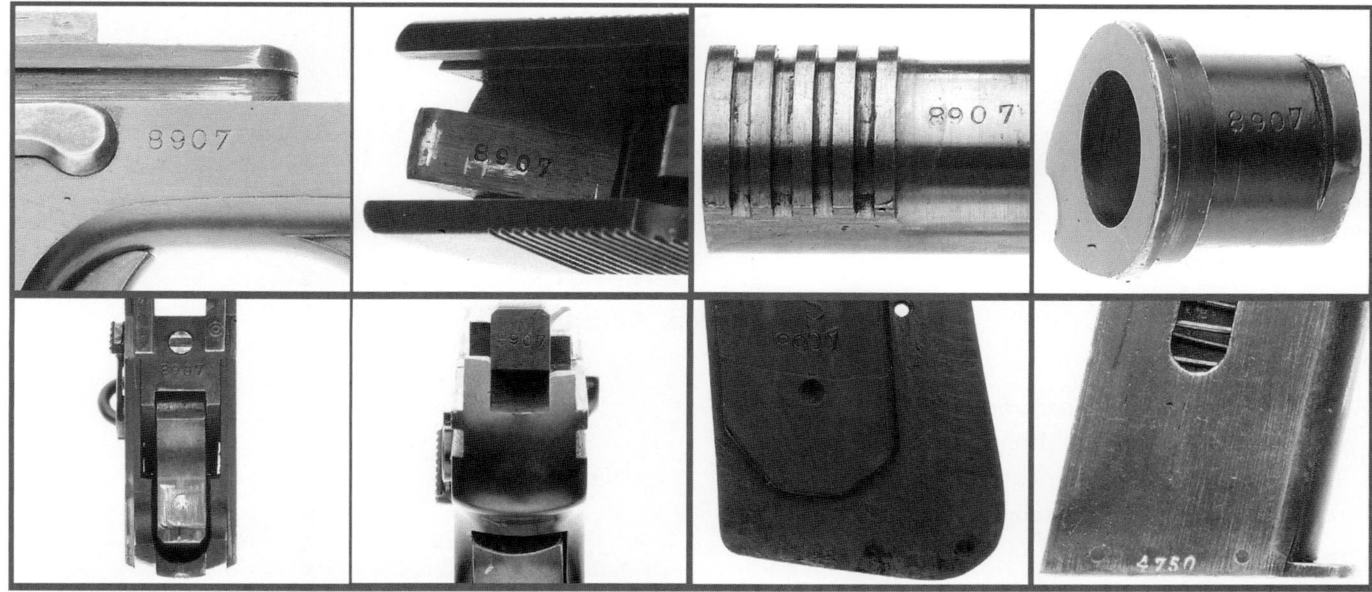

Slide Legend Variants

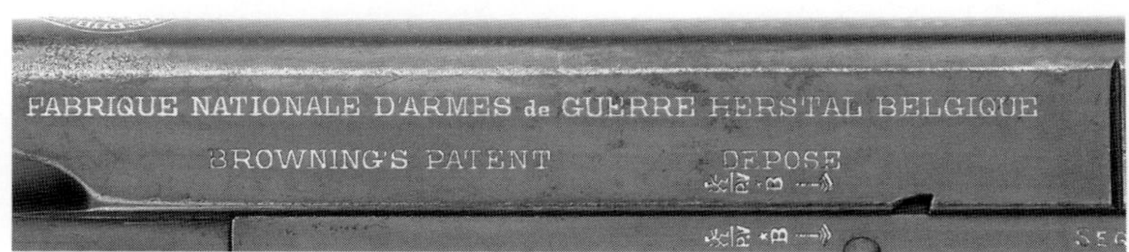

(Fig.161-1) Slide-legend variant with large lettering: One of only three slide legend variants used on the Model 1903. This variant is often encountered with slotted pistols. This variant is the least encountered and was used throughout the production span.

(Fig.161-2) Slide-legend variant with small lettering: One of only three slide legend variants used on the Model 1903. This variant is most often encountered on pistols that are not slotted for shoulder-stock. This variant was used throughout the production span but is most often encountered on early production pistols.

(Fig.161-3) Slide-legend variant with small lettering: One of only three slide legend variants used on the Model 1903. This variant is most often encountered on pistols that are not slotted for shoulder-stock. This variant was used throughout the production span.

(1) The Model 1903 was supplied in very small quantities to the Dutch government for trials in 1904 but ultimately the Luger was preferred. However in 1922 the Dutch Navy purchased 80 pistols (not slotted for shoulder-stocks) for their air crews (see also page 205 on Dutch acquisitions).

(2) No Model 1903 pistols were produced in .380 caliber. Such conversions were performed decades later in the U.S. on pistols imported from Sweden. No pistols were ever produced during World War I. German World War I use of the FN Browning 1903 was limited to prewar manufactured guns.

(3) Production seized with the announcement of the Grand Rendement in 1928. The FN Browning 1903 was not in production until 1930 or 1935 and superceded by the High Power as listed in some publications.

(4) There is some indication from a pre-World War I Belgian military publication that some Belgian officers might have personally bought a FN Model 1903 but no examples have been found by the author. Officially the pistol was never adopted by the Belgian military.

Specifications Summary

Manufacturer: Fabrique Nationale d'Armes de Guerre, Herstal Belgique**.** Also manufactured in Sweden under license by Husqvarna
U.S. patent: 747585 **Filing date:** 4/3/1902 **Issue date:** 12/22/1903
Model known as: "Modèle de Guerre" (War Model) / "Le Grand Modèle" (Large Model) / Later: "Modèle 1903"
Period offered: 1903-1914/1919-1927. Actual mass production started in 1907.
Caliber: 9mm Browning Long / 9x20mm
Operating system: Blowback
Length: 205mm
Barrel length: 128mm
Weight: 980 grams
Grips: Animal horn
Magazine capacity: Seven, optional 10-round extended magazine available for use with shoulder-stock
Sights: Fixed, optional tangent sights offered but never produced
Options: Slotted frame to accept shoulder-stock
Finish offered: Blue, nickel
Engraving patterns: Three factory types
Production quantity: 58442

FN Model 1903: Accessories

Guns were sold in a cardboard box with a spare magazine, cleaning rod and three dummy cartridges. The optional shoulder-stock held the extended 10-round magazine and cleaning rod.

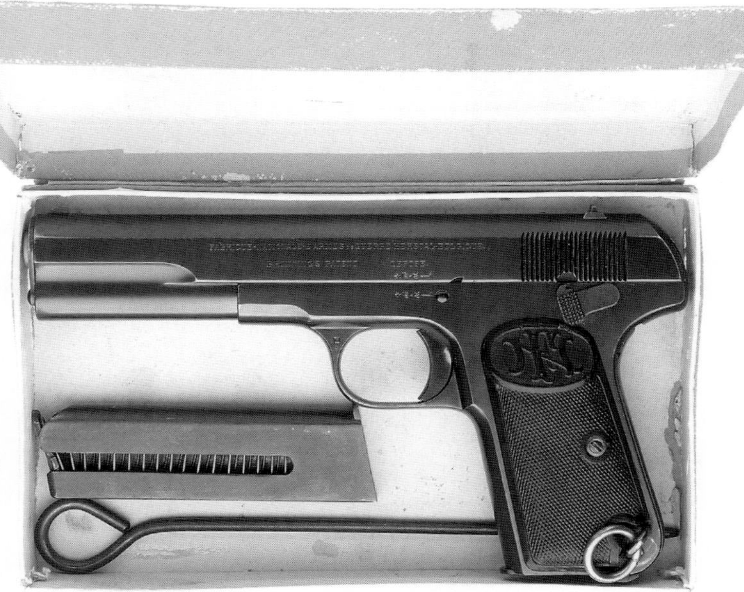

(Fig.162-1) This FN 1903 N° 13889 disappeared from the FN warehouses during World War I (see page 33). This specific gun is new in its original mustard colored box. The box has the typical embossed FN logo.

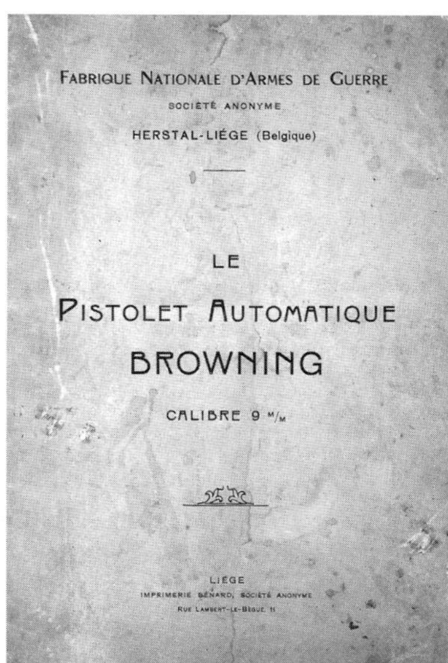

FABRIQUE NATIONALE D'ARMES DE GUERRE
SOCIÉTÉ ANONYME
HERSTAL-LIÉGE (Belgique)

LE
PISTOLET AUTOMATIQUE
BROWNING
CALIBRE 9 m/m

LIÉGE
IMPRIMERIE BÉNARD, SOCIÉTÉ ANONYME
RUE LAMBERT-LE-BÈGUE, 11

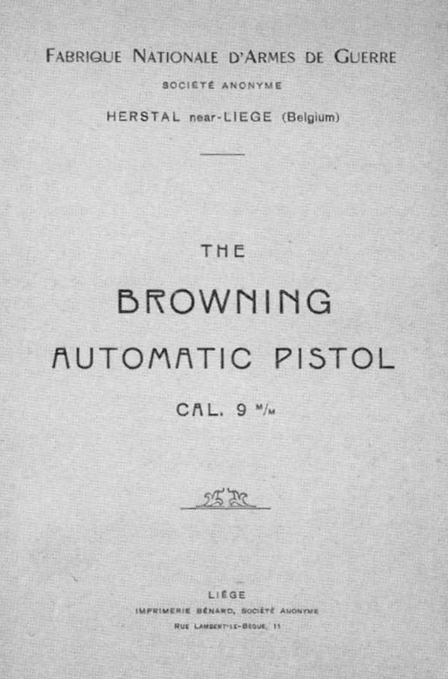

FABRIQUE NATIONALE D'ARMES DE GUERRE
SOCIÉTÉ ANONYME
HERSTAL near-LIEGE (Belgium)

THE
BROWNING
AUTOMATIC PISTOL
CAL. 9 m/m

LIÉGE
IMPRIMERIE BÉNARD, SOCIÉTÉ ANONYME
RUE LAMBERT-LE-BÈGUE, 11

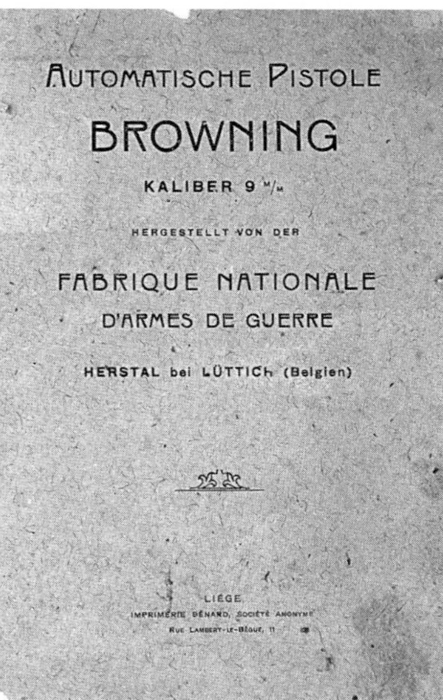

AUTOMATISCHE PISTOLE
BROWNING
KALIBER 9 m/m
HERGESTELLT VON DER
FABRIQUE NATIONALE
D'ARMES DE GUERRE
HERSTAL bei LÜTTICH (Belgien)

LIÉGE
IMPRIMERIE BÉNARD, SOCIÉTÉ ANONYME
RUE LAMBERT-LE-BÈGUE, 11

(Fig.162-2) Brown (English and French language) and purple (German language) cover instruction books. These oversized manuals were sold as an accessory.

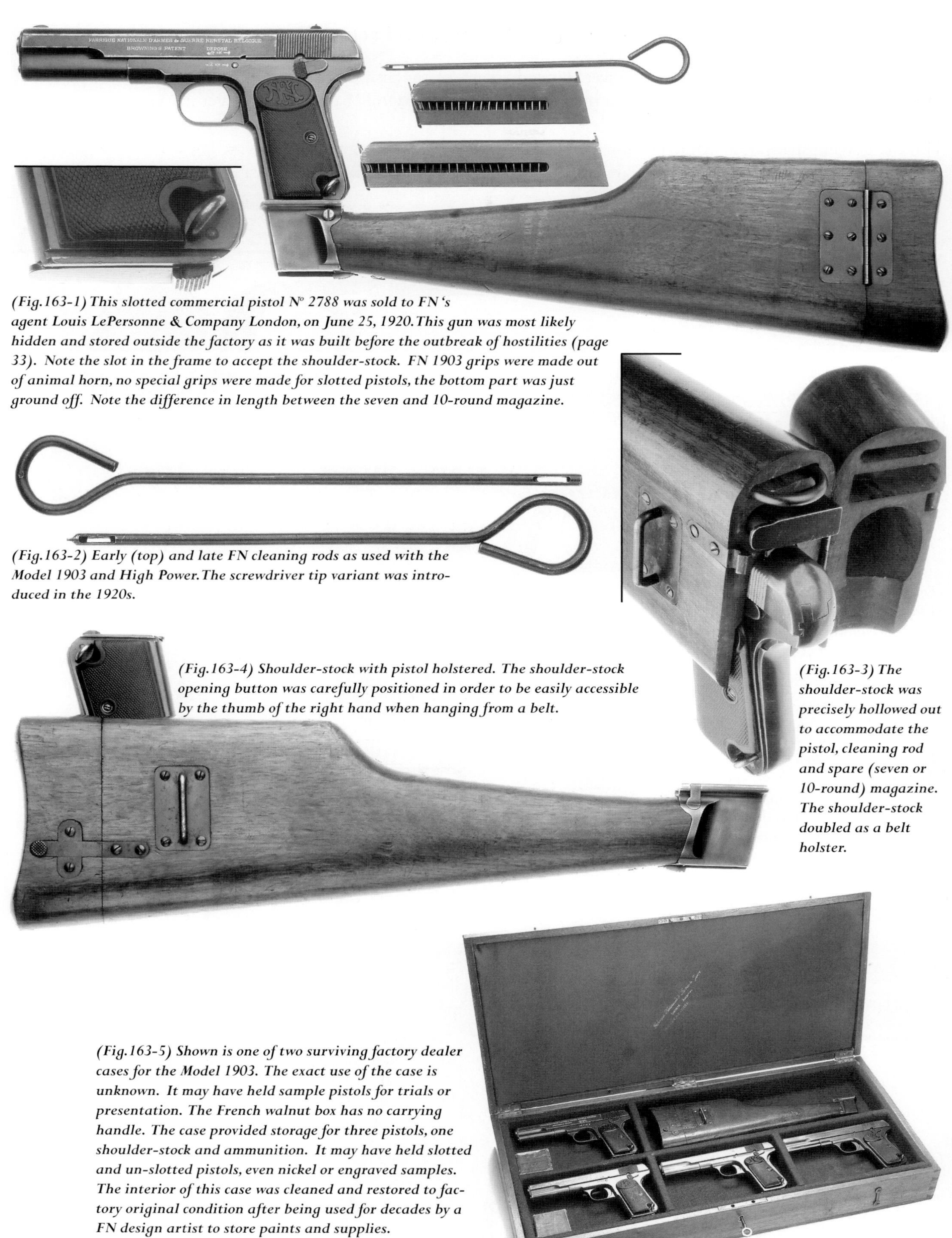

(Fig.163-1) This slotted commercial pistol Nº 2788 was sold to FN's agent Louis LePersonne & Company London, on June 25, 1920. This gun was most likely hidden and stored outside the factory as it was built before the outbreak of hostilities (page 33). Note the slot in the frame to accept the shoulder-stock. FN 1903 grips were made out of animal horn, no special grips were made for slotted pistols, the bottom part was just ground off. Note the difference in length between the seven and 10-round magazine.

(Fig.163-2) Early (top) and late FN cleaning rods as used with the Model 1903 and High Power. The screwdriver tip variant was introduced in the 1920s.

(Fig.163-3) The shoulder-stock was precisely hollowed out to accommodate the pistol, cleaning rod and spare (seven or 10-round) magazine. The shoulder-stock doubled as a belt holster.

(Fig.163-4) Shoulder-stock with pistol holstered. The shoulder-stock opening button was carefully positioned in order to be easily accessible by the thumb of the right hand when hanging from a belt.

(Fig.163-5) Shown is one of two surviving factory dealer cases for the Model 1903. The exact use of the case is unknown. It may have held sample pistols for trials or presentation. The French walnut box has no carrying handle. The case provided storage for three pistols, one shoulder-stock and ammunition. It may have held slotted and un-slotted pistols, even nickel or engraved samples. The interior of this case was cleaned and restored to factory original condition after being used for decades by a FN design artist to store paints and supplies.

Luxury Models: Nickel Plating and Factory Engraving

Commercial sales of the FN Model 1903 were limited. Many of the pistols sold on the commercial market did not have a slotted frame and most were sold to military personnel (see page 121 for applied dealer markings).

Three engraving styles were offered by the company, only three factory engraved pistols are known to have survived worldwide. Nickel pistols are equally scarce. No factory nickel pistols are known to exist in the U.S.

(Fig.164-1) A rare factory nickel pistol N° 44332. Note the traditional black trigger and safety. This pistol is shown without magazine. (Photograph courtesy of John Bastin)

(Fig.164-2) FN factory engraving Type I, reproduced from a FN Luxury catalog. This engraving pattern was available on blue as well as on nickel finish guns. This engraved pistol was available with standard grips, ivory grips or mother-of-pearl grips.

(Fig.164-3) FN factory engraving Type II, reproduced from a FN Luxury catalog. This engraving pattern was available on blue pistols, the engraving was inlaid in gold. The engraved pistols were available with standard grips, ivory grips or mother-of-pearl grips.

(Fig.164-4) FN factory engraving Type III, reproduced from a FN Luxury catalog. This engraving pattern was available on blue pistols, the engraving was inlaid in gold. The engraving style was referred to in the catalog as "Modern Style." This engraved pistol was available with standard grips, ivory grips or mother-of-pearl grips.

The Swedish Acceptance

(Fig.165-1) Swedish officers practice with their FN 1903 pistols in 1909. (Photograph courtesy of Anders Jonasson)

The Swedish government pursued the adoption of a pistol and conducted its initial trails in the 1903-1904 period. They following pistols were purchased for trials; two Luger Parabellum 7.65mm pistols, two FN Browning 1900 pistols, two Colt Browning 9.5mm pistols, two 7.65mm Mannlicher pistols, four Mannlicher carbine-pistols, one Hamilton pistol in 6.5mm, two FN Browning 1903 pistols and two 8mm Frommer pistols.

Although the Luger outperformed competitors in accuracy, the FN Browning 1903 pistol was selected for its reliability in extreme conditions. It was considered sturdy, reliable and suitable for the local climatic conditions. Minor modifications were requested as a result of the trials, including improved sights and a stronger safety mechanism. Paul Berghaus, FN's agent in Sweden, handled all trials and contract negotiations.

Sweden accepted the gun as its official sidearm and gave it the military designation "m/07", the navy designation was "M/07" (M capitalized). The m/07 refers to "Model of 1907", the year the pistol was officially adopted. Sweden placed their initial order for 10,000 FN Browning 1903 pistols. No sizeable additional orders were placed after this order. Many additional pistols were however shipped to Berghaus directly for sale to military personnel and for commercial sales.

A June 11, 1907 FN document places the original Swedish contract at 9000 pistols. It is known however that 10,000 un-slotted pistols were supplied without shoulder-stocks. It was common practice for a purchaser to place additional orders, during or after their initial contract was being filled. A small number of slotted pistols were used with factory shoulder-stocks and were also accepted by the Swedish military, these pistols were most likely special orders from military personnel handled by Berghaus directly. A small amount of cut-away pistols were ordered from FN. It is believed that this order was placed at the same time of the 10,000 pistols. These pistols were made for instructional purposes and bear no Liège proofs and have no FN slide legend. Less than a handful of these cut-away pistols survive today in Sweden (see fig. 160-1).

(Fig.165-2) Swedish officers practice with their FN 1903 pistols in 1909. (Photograph courtesy of Anders Jonasson)

Officers in the Swedish military purchased their own guns either from the government, the commercial market (retailers) or from Berghaus.

All Swedish military accepted guns have the inspector's initials stamped on the rear, military guns have the Swedish crown stamped above the inspector's initials. Guns were inspected and accepted at the Carl Gustaf facility, the state arsenal at Eskilstuna. Refer to page 178 for a list of Swedish inspector markings.

(Fig.166-1) A Swedish officer practices with his FN 1903 in 1913. (Photograph courtesy of Anders Jonasson)

It is not known for certain if World War I was the catalyst for domestic production in Sweden or when Sweden purchased the manufacturing license from FN. The Swedish government may have purchased the license either before or after the war. It is also possible that Paul Berghaus negotiated the manufacturing license during the war while Belgium was occupied. The Husqvarna company started production in 1917 (see page 177).

Although the Swedes had requested some design changes prior to the adoption of the pistol, the improvement of the front sight came as an afterthought. At some time, the Swedes decided to cut the half-moon shaped front sight into a quarter size shape, exposed sharp edges were left in the white to improve visibility. There are conflicting reports on when this modification occurred. Some Swedish sources claim that originally all pistols had half-moon shaped front sights and that the transformation occurred in Sweden during the 1930s or even during World War II. The author believes that this alteration was communicated with FN just prior to World War I and that FN modified some pistols for shipment to Sweden. This is concluded from the fact that numerous pistols exist that include the modified sight but were never shipped to Sweden(1).

After World War I, Paul Berghaus continued to sell and distribute the FN Model 1903. Although the Husqvarna was in production, FN Model 1903 pistols remained on the commercial market. Husqvarna pistols were not in constant production and were not always available. As such a small military contract was shipped from FN in 1926 to Berghaus. These FN Model 1903 pistols had been made around 1925 and were remaining inventory at FN. They can be identified by the "ST" marking followed by the issue number on the receiver. This marking is applied in the same fashion as the military regimental markings but the guns bear no military acceptance markings. The "ST" marking was identified as "Stockholms Tygstation"(2), a military repair and storage facility. In 1934 there were eight such stations throughout the country. Sweden placed the first and one of the last contracts for the FN Model 1903, observed "ST" pistols are in the 53,000 range.

(Fig.166-2) Swedish officers practice with their FN 1903 pistols in 1913. (Photograph courtesy of Anders Jonasson)

The Swedish government placed a request with FN in the latter 1930s for assistance with converting the FN 1903 / Husqvarna design to 9mm Parabellum (9x19mm). It is not known if FN took on the challenge as the model had been discontinued years earlier.

Some Swedish FN 1903 pistols as well as Husqvarna made pistols have been found with the Finnish "SA" acceptance mark, these guns found their way into Finland with Swedish volunteers during the Finnish Winter-War in 1939-1940.

Lowest observed or reported Swedish contract pistol: N° 113
Highest reported pre-World War I Swedish contract pistol: N° 11593
Observed or reported "ST" marked contract pistols: N° 49887 (ST 388), N° 50344 (ST 522), N° 53383 (ST 498), N° 53805 (ST 176)

(1) Several FN 1903 pistols were shipped from FN with modified front sights to dealers like Kind in Berlin as well as Alcock &Pierce in Melbourne. Pistol N° 13889 shown on fig 162-1 also shows the modified front sight.
(2) Author's correspondence with John Bastin

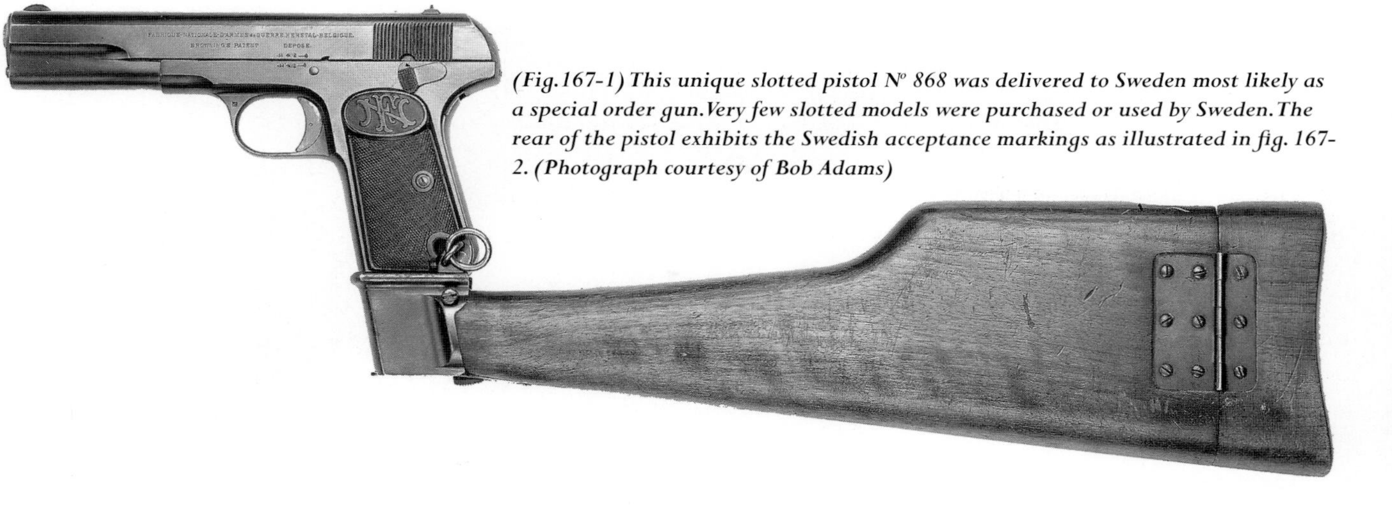

(Fig.167-1) This unique slotted pistol N° 868 was delivered to Sweden most likely as a special order gun. Very few slotted models were purchased or used by Sweden. The rear of the pistol exhibits the Swedish acceptance markings as illustrated in fig. 167-2. (Photograph courtesy of Bob Adams)

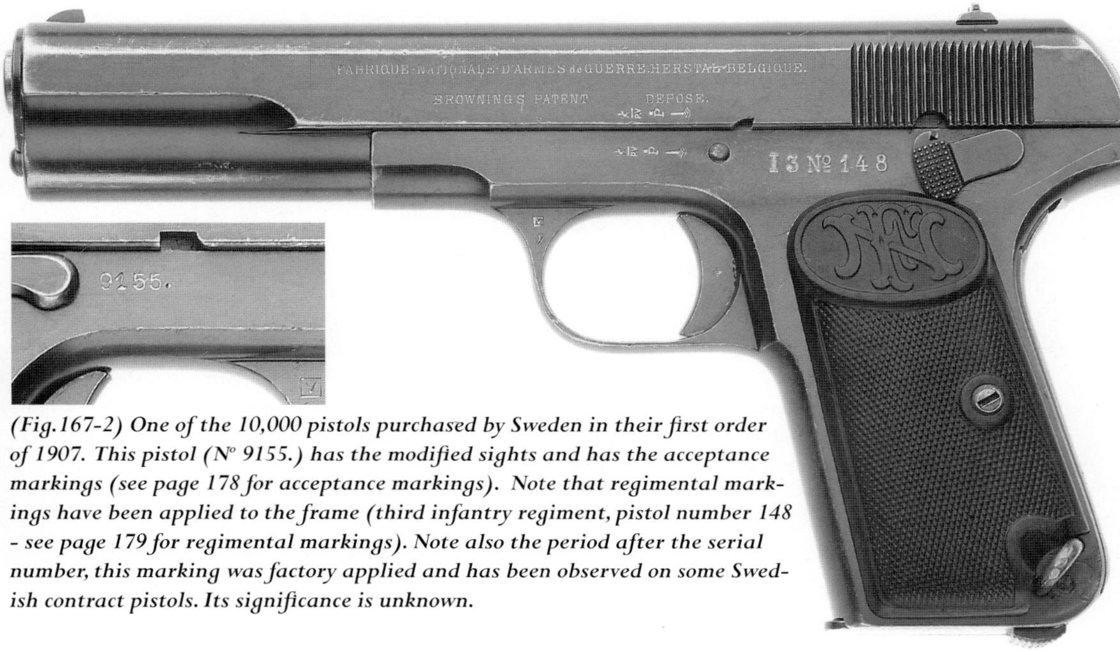

(Fig.167-2) One of the 10,000 pistols purchased by Sweden in their first order of 1907. This pistol (N° 9155.) has the modified sights and has the acceptance markings (see page 178 for acceptance markings). Note that regimental markings have been applied to the frame (third infantry regiment, pistol number 148 - see page 179 for regimental markings). Note also the period after the serial number, this marking was factory applied and has been observed on some Swedish contract pistols. Its significance is unknown.

(Fig.167-3) Dummy pistols were used in training. These dummy pistols were made in Sweden out of cast iron and painted black, the official designation for the dummy pistol is "Pistolattrapp m/28" (dummy pistol model 28). There was only a provision for a lanyard. Officers in training or on maneuvers wore the dummy pistol in holster with the lanyard properly attached. The lanyard used was the model m/1899. Introduced in 1899, this lanyard was used with the m/1887 revolver as well as with the m/07 pistol and dummy pistol. Early lanyards were made out of leather while later models were made out of fabric.

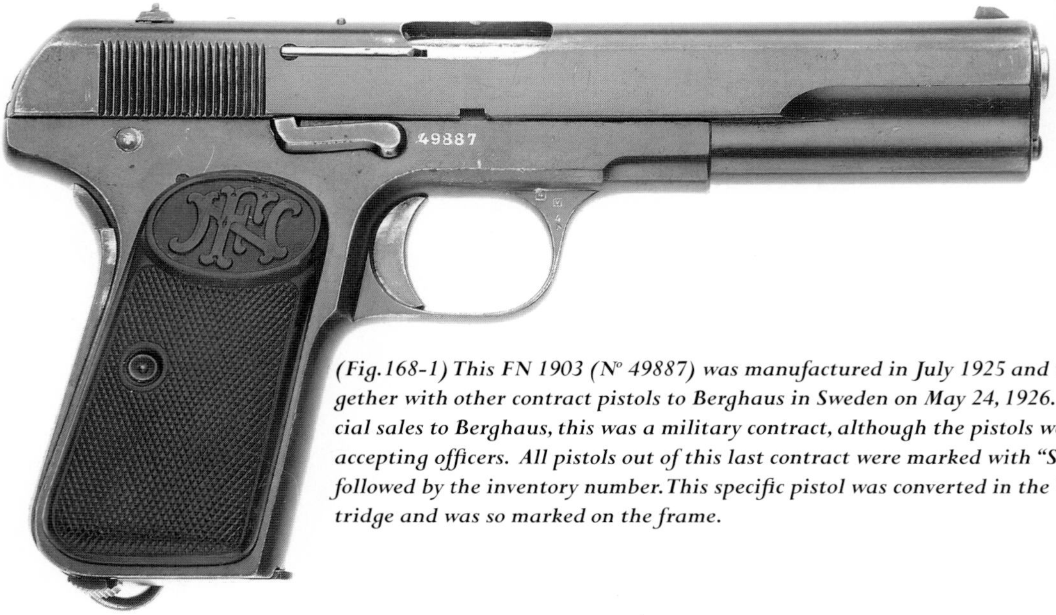

(Fig.168-1) This FN 1903 (N° 49887) was manufactured in July 1925 and was shipped from FN together with other contract pistols to Berghaus in Sweden on May 24, 1926. Unlike previous commercial sales to Berghaus, this was a military contract, although the pistols were not marked by the usual accepting officers. All pistols out of this last contract were marked with "ST" (Stockholms Tygstation) followed by the inventory number.This specific pistol was converted in the USA to fire the .380 cartridge and was so marked on the frame.

(Fig.168-3) A Swedish officer practices with his FN 1903 in 1913. (Photograph courtesy of Anders Jonasson)

(Fig.168-2) Swedish m/07 accessories were often transferred from older Swedish revolvers. The "Oljefoder" (oil container, top right) was introduced in 1864. It was used with the m/1887 revolver and still used with the m/07 pistol. These containers were hand-made by inmates in Swedish prisons and all have different characteristics as no two are alike. The oil container in the center was introduced in the 1930s at the end of the m/07 service. Cleaning rods are sometimes marked with the pistol serial number or the Swedish crown.

The Imperial Russian Purchases

FN supplied the Imperial Russian government with the FN Browning Model 1903 pistol right after the Russo-Japanese war. Four Russian contract variations are known to exist. Characteristically the Russian FN Browning Model 1903 pistols are factory marked with Cyrillic letters. Most Russian contract pistols were slotted to accept shoulder-stocks. Shoulder-stocks were supplied to Russia from FN with most of the orders.

The majority of pistols were marked with three Cyrillic letters. The О.К.Ж. letters stand for Области Жандармский Корпус (Oblasti Zandarmeriiski Korpus - District Gendarmerie Corps). This contract has often been confused as being a Serbian contract. Pistols used in Serbia were purchased on the commercial market and have no special markings. The Russian Gendarmerie pistols (estimated at 7000) were extensively used throughout the Russian empire, several pistols were left behind in Finland after World War I and consequently used by the Finns.

The Moscow Metropolitan Police pistols, factory marked Mock. Stol. Policija, were purchased after the initial gendarmerie acquisitions. These pistols were purchased in limited quantities, archive documents hint that as many as 3113 may have been purchased, however the highest observed issue number is 1180.

The rarest of the Russian 1903 pistols are the presentation pistols given to the graduates of the Russian Imperial General Staff Academy. These pistols are marked with the crossed Mosin-Nagant rifles and issue number, these were similar to the Model 1900 and 1905 presentation pistols (page 150, 188). Some of the guns delivered to the Imperial General Staff Academy were factory nickel guns.

The transit police or railroad police pistols were marked северо зона железных дорог (Severo-Zapdnykh Zheleznykh Dorog - Northwest Railway Administration). These were used by the Northwest Railway Gendarme-Police Administration. This agency was one of 24 railway administrations in Imperial Russia. These administrations were operating on specific lines and most bear the name of the line they served (e.g. Moscow-Archangel Railway Administration). It is not known how many railway administrations used FN's or specifically the Model 1903. The Northwest Railway Administration pistols were shipped to FN's agent Schiffer in St. Petersburg on August 28, 1911. Unlike other Russian contracts, these were shipped to the agent. The agent may have handled this contract due to its small size. The quantity of pistols shipped is estimated at less than 100 pistols.

There is a difference in the shoulder-stocks used among the Russian contracts. The Moscow Police pistols and the presentation pistols both had standard FN shoulder-stocks. The first 4000 gendarmerie pistols were ordered with a special shoulder-stock and slot, often referred to as a short slot / stock. The shoulder-stock connecting lug had no securing lock for the pistol, the shoulder-stock hinge has only two rows of screws as well as a small lanyard stud. Only Russian gendarmerie pistols in the 15,000 to 22,000 serial number range have the short slot and were issued with the special short stock. The slot on the frame of these pistols only extends to 90 percent of the frame's length. It is believed that the short stock was specially ordered for mounted gendarmerie who could only use one hand to connect or disconnect the shoulder-stock.

Observed or reported Imperial Russian contract pistols:
O.K.Z. Gendarmerie pistols: 15207, 15348, 15569, 15745, 15763, 15849, 16280, 17252, 17421, 17450, 17875, 18326, 20223, 27867, 28103
Mock. Stol. Policija - Moscow Metropolitan Police pistols: 30777 (issue N° 103), 30917 (issue N° 282), 32497 (issue N° 1180)
S.Z.Zh.D. Northwest Railway Administration pistols: 23940 (issue N° 50), 24050 (issue N° 46 or 47)

(Fig.169-1) Factory applied Russian contract markings are always found on the right side of the slide, just forward of the ejection port. From left to right: Gendarmerie contract, Moscow Metropolitan Police contract and railroad police contract. Note that all Russian contract markings show the issue number of the pistol. These pistols were numbered during production and issue numbers do not ascend simultaneously with pistol serialization.

(Fig.170-1) *Russian gendarmerie pistols were made with the short slot. Note that this pistol Nº 20223 has the short slot on the left side and regular slot on the right side. Note how the slot only extends up to 90 percent of the pistol frame (see inset of pistol Nº 17252). The O.K.Z. marking with issue number was also marked on seven and 10-round magazines as well as on shoulder-stocks. (Photographs by author, courtesy of Steven Fox and NAPCA)*

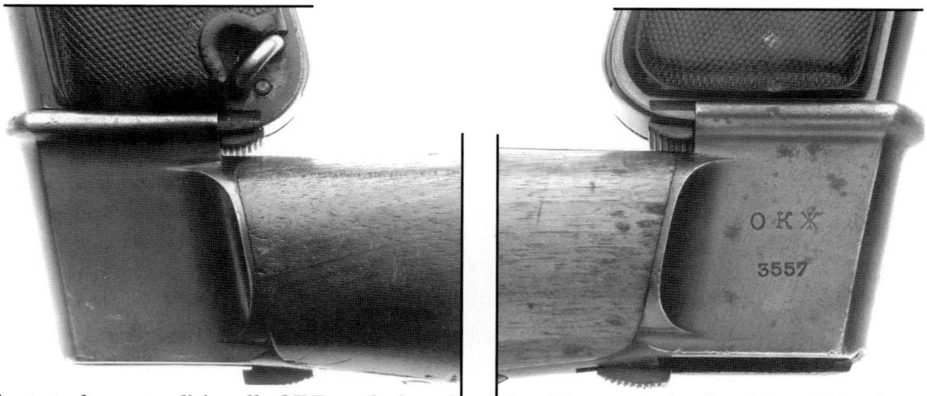

(Fig.170-2) *Russian short stocks are traditionally OKZ marked on the right of the connecting lug (above). Russian short stock Nº 21756 below is an exception and shows the pistol's serial number instead. The connecting lug of the short stock slides over the groves of the pistol frame and remain on the frame without being locked into place like on conventional stocks. Note the lack of a securing button and mechanism (compare with fig.163-1), in this case, the stock is locked into place by the use of the 10-round magazine. The belt hanging hardware is small and round and the hinge on the stock only has two rows of screws instead of the standard three. (Photographs by author, courtesy of Steven Fox and NAPCA)*

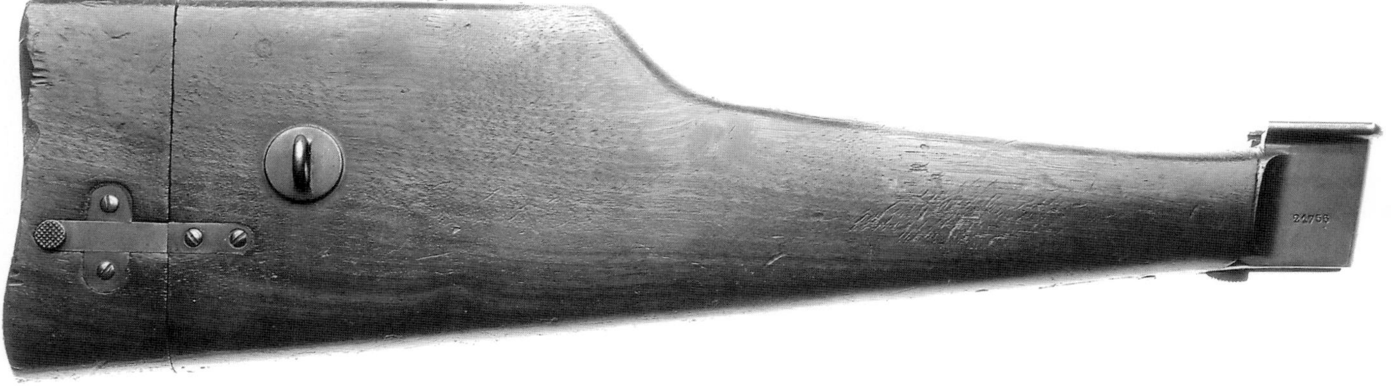

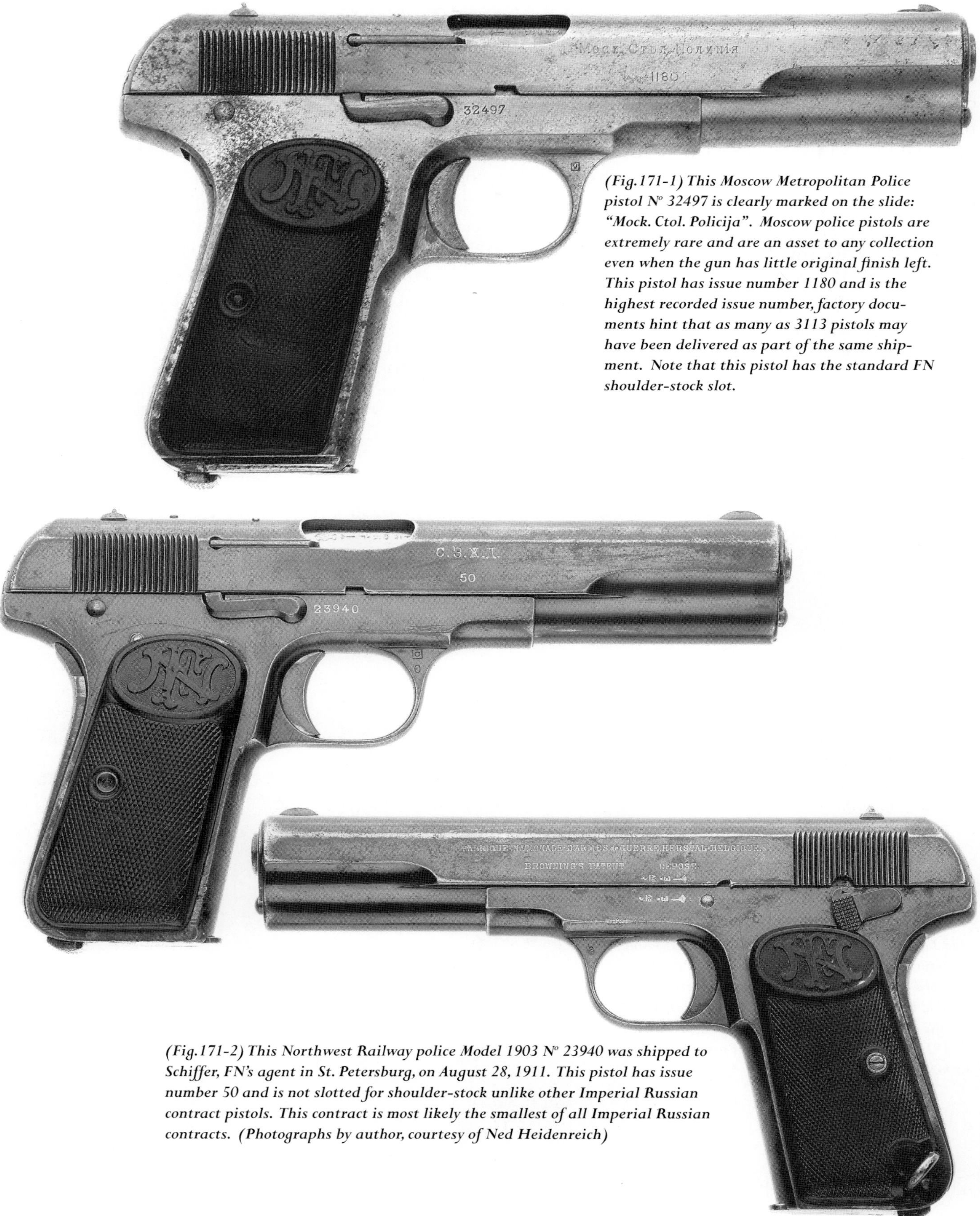

(Fig.171-1) This Moscow Metropolitan Police pistol N° 32497 is clearly marked on the slide: "Mock. Ctol. Policija". Moscow police pistols are extremely rare and are an asset to any collection even when the gun has little original finish left. This pistol has issue number 1180 and is the highest recorded issue number, factory documents hint that as many as 3113 pistols may have been delivered as part of the same shipment. Note that this pistol has the standard FN shoulder-stock slot.

(Fig.171-2) This Northwest Railway police Model 1903 N° 23940 was shipped to Schiffer, FN's agent in St. Petersburg, on August 28, 1911. This pistol has issue number 50 and is not slotted for shoulder-stock unlike other Imperial Russian contract pistols. This contract is most likely the smallest of all Imperial Russian contracts. (Photographs by author, courtesy of Ned Heidenreich)

The Ottoman Empire and Turkish Contracts

An estimated 8000 pistols were purchased by the Ottoman Empire. The initial order dates from around 1908, additional orders were filled on scheduled contract dates. Pistols were often shipped around February 15, and prewar orders are known for 1910, 1911 and 1914. All contract guns were distinctly marked at FN, the top of the slide was roll engraved with the crest of Sultan[1] Abdul Hamid II. The slide was engraved with the word "Authority" in Turkish and the gun's issue number. This issue number does not correspond with the gun's serial number nor do Turkish issue numbers ascend in numerical order with the serial numbers. This is due to the FN production habits of the time, contract guns were taken from standard production for roll engraving. None of the Ottoman pistols were slotted for stocks. These pistols were widely issued throughout the empire by police or gendarmerie. In 1923 the Ottoman Empire became Turkey, and small additional orders were placed with FN after 1923. Pistols were no longer roll engraved with the "tughra" or sultan's crest. Some were marked "Police" on the top of the slide with the issue number. Later versions showed the Turkish republic marking as a crest. This official state symbol was introduced in Turkey in 1926 and was used until approximately 1929.

Observed or reported Ottoman Empire - Turkish contract pistols: 10650, 11180, 11616, 11859 (issue N° 467), 12399 (issue N° 2463), 12633, 13764, 26067, 26124, 26694, 27044 (issue N° 4934), 27186, 27403 (issue N° 5307), 27424, 27587 (issue N° 5456), 27638 (issue N° 5549), 33718 (issue N° 5955), 33909(issue N° 6071),34406, 34413, 34544 (issue N° 6744), 34634 (issue N° 6777), 35513, 36898, 36323 (issue N° 6860), 37027, 37089 (issue N° 7550), 27208 (issue N° 7682),37240, 37244 (issue N° 7698), 37398, 37429 (issue N° 7931),38084, 44278, 48740

(Fig.172-1)) This Turkish police pistol N° 27587 has the issue number 5456 on the slide next to the Turkish word for "Authority". The markings were factory applied including the crest (see fig 173-3). This specific pistol was shipped from FN on September 20, 1911. Note the star and crescent proof found on Turkish contract pistols.

(1) The tughra, shown as the main body of the design, was used by the Ottoman Empire since the early 1800s. The flower (smaller design to the right) denotes this crest variant as belonging to Sultan Abdul Hamid II.

(Fig.173-1)) A rare 1908 Turkish instruction manual for the Model 1903. These were printed in Liège in Turkish complete with foldout diagrams of the pistol.

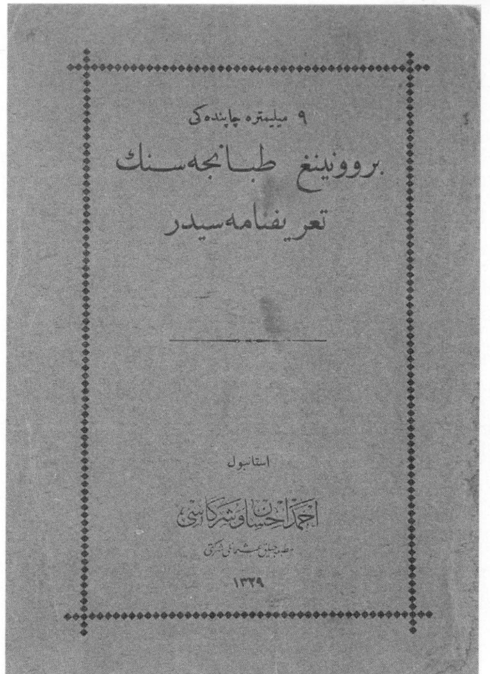
۹ میلیمتره چاپنده کی
بروونینغ طبانجه سنك
تعریفنامه سیدر

استانبول
احمد احسان وشرکاسی
۱۳۲۹

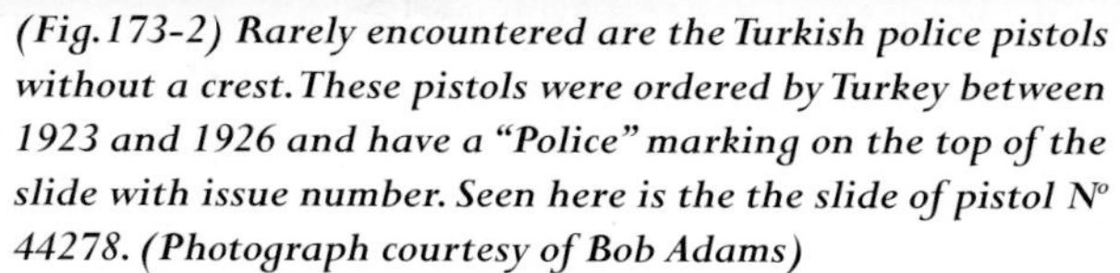

(Fig.173-2) Rarely encountered are the Turkish police pistols without a crest. These pistols were ordered by Turkey between 1923 and 1926 and have a "Police" marking on the top of the slide with issue number. Seen here is the the slide of pistol N° 44278. (Photograph courtesy of Bob Adams)

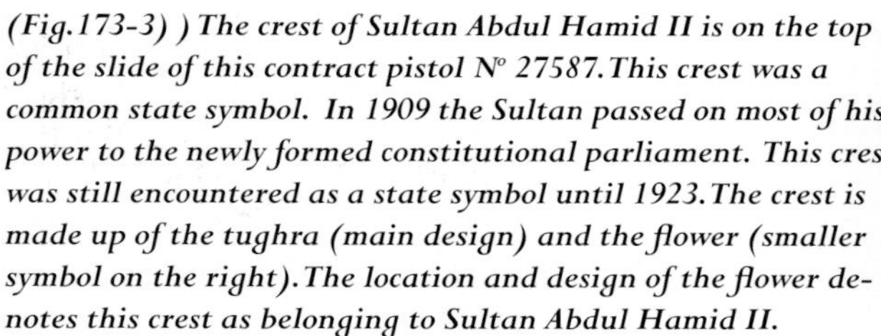

(Fig.173-3)) The crest of Sultan Abdul Hamid II is on the top of the slide of this contract pistol N° 27587. This crest was a common state symbol. In 1909 the Sultan passed on most of his power to the newly formed constitutional parliament. This crest was still encountered as a state symbol until 1923. The crest is made up of the tughra (main design) and the flower (smaller symbol on the right). The location and design of the flower denotes this crest as belonging to Sultan Abdul Hamid II.

(Fig.173-4)) This 1926 Turkish police pistol N° 48740 was most likely part of the last of the Turkish orders. This specific pistol was shipped from FN on February 11, 1926 to Nikitits in Istanbul, FN's agent in Turkey. Note that the crest differs from the Ottoman Empire pistols, the tughra is no longer present and has been replaced by the Turkish republic marking which was a widely used state symbol between 1926 and 1929. The 1922 date is part of the crest and most likely refers to the year of the abolishment of the sultanate.
(Photographs by author, courtesy of John Bill)

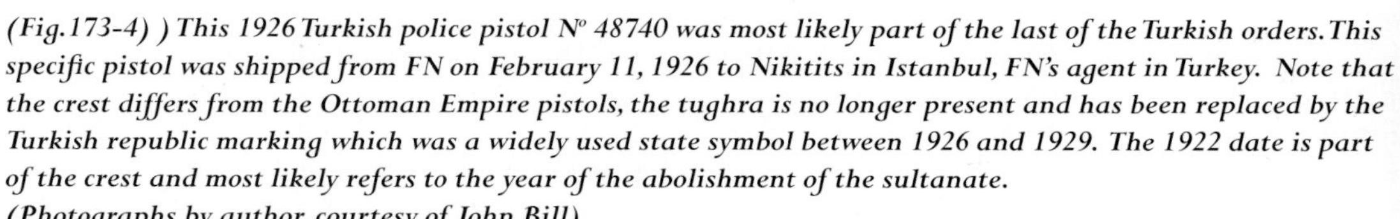

From the Estonian Military to the Spanish Civil War

The Estonian contract pistols were purchased starting in 1922 after the Estonian independence. Approximately 4616 Model 1903 pistols were purchased throughout the years. The rear of the pistols was stamped in Estonia with the letters "SOM" for Sojaministeerium (War Ministry). The pistols are often mistaken for Swedish contract pistols because of the location of the SOM marking (compare with fig.167-2).

The Ministry of Interior Affairs purchased 2000 FN Browning Model 1910 pistols. As such the Model 1910 pistol was the standard police pistol until 1940.

All pistols were maintained at the state arsenal in Tallinn. The arsenal manufactured replacement parts for the pistols and also made some .22 caliber conversion barrels for training. Parts as well as accessories were produced in Tallinn.

The 9mm Browning Long cartridge was considered obsolete in 1936. Estonia sold 4400 pistols and the majority of their shoulder-stocks to the Spanish Republicans in 1936. The pistols were sold along with 9mm Browning Long Suomi machine guns as surplus material. Although there was an international arms embargo in effect, many countries took advantage of the Spanish Civil War and the Spanish Republican armament problem and sold their outdated equipment in order to raise funds. The pistols were shipped in the first quarter of 1937 and were only a small part of the arms trade. Aircraft, ammunition and all sorts of small arms were sold by a variety of nations. Estonia's shipments were limited to two or three cargo ships[1].

Most of the surviving FN 1903 shoulder-stocks found in the world today come from Spain and originated with the Estonian orders. The shoulder-stocks survived but the pistols' whereabouts are unknown.

Estonia's purchases:

Order of acquisition December 24, 1921: 2000 pistols, 2000 shoulder-stocks, 500 holsters, 4000 extended 10-round magazines and 2000 standard seven round magazines, 500,000 cartridges. The order arrived in Tallinn in April 1922. At this time the FN Browning 1903 pistol became the standard Estonian military pistol.

Order of acquisition December 8, 1922:	**390 pistols and 40,000 cartridges. The order arrived in Tallinn in January 1923.**
Order of acquisition March, 1923:	**100 shoulder-stocks.**
Order of acquisition July, 1923:	**30,000 cartridges.**
Order of acquisition 1925/1926:	**1460 pistols with shoulder-stocks and unknown amount of magazines and ammunition. This order was entirely destined for the Estonian Kaitselit (Home Guard). The Kaitselit was issued the pistol for the first time in 1926.**
Order of acquisition March, 1928:	**720,000 cartridges.**
Order of acquisition 1931:	**136 new barrels and other unknown accessories.**
Miscellaneous purchases:	**Approximately 22 pistols were purchased for the military on the commercial market in Estonia. Approximately 72 pistols were purchased for the Kaitselit (Home Guard) on the commercial market in Estonia.**

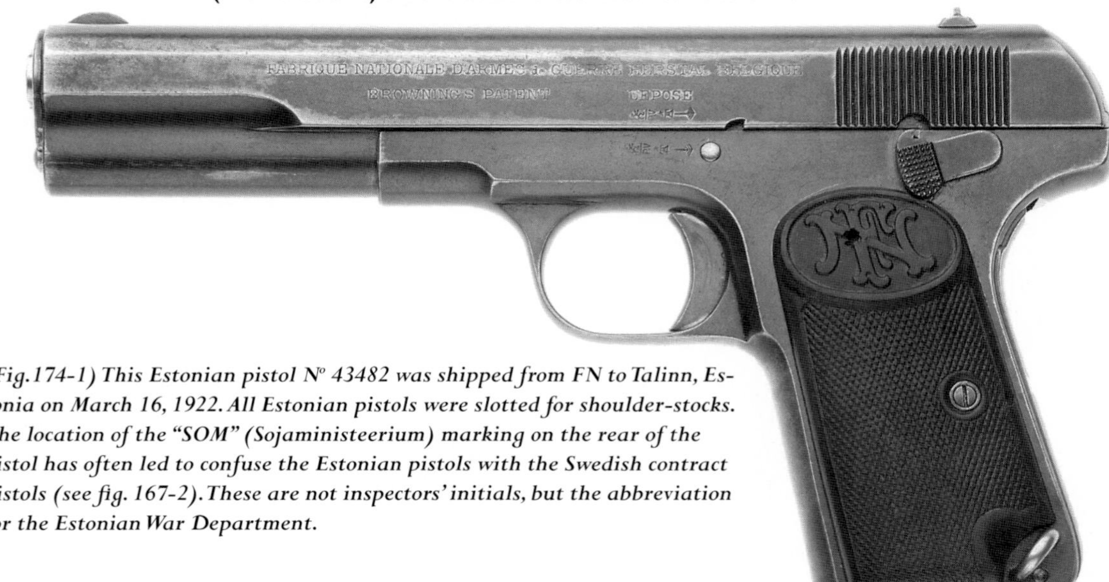

(Fig.174-1) This Estonian pistol N° 43482 was shipped from FN to Talinn, Estonia on March 16, 1922. All Estonian pistols were slotted for shoulder-stocks. The location of the "SOM" (Sojaministeerium) marking on the rear of the pistol has often led to confuse the Estonian pistols with the Swedish contract pistols (see fig. 167-2). These are not inspectors' initials, but the abbreviation for the Estonian War Department.

(1) Arms For Spain by Gerald Howson

The Paraguayan and Salvadoran Contracts

Little is known about the Paraguayan and Salvadoran contracts. Serial numbers indicate that both contracts were delivered around 1927. The Paraguayan contract was dated "1927" and marked "Modelo Paraguayo B" followed by the contract number. These pistols were part of the last contracts of the FN Browning Model 1903. In 1927 the pistol was discontinued and replaced in 1929 by the Grand Rendement. It appears that all pistols delivered in the last year were already manufactured and pulled from existing stock piles before being marked.

Only a few examples have been noted from the Paraguayan contract. Allegedly 324 pistols were purchased by Paraguay in 1927, together with 5000 rounds of 9mm Browning Long ammunition. There have been reports that there was an original 1907 Paraguayan contract. The author has not found any evidence of such a contract, only pistol N° 31 was reported with 1907 Paraguayan contract markings.

Observed or reported Paraguayan and Salvadoran contract pistols
Paraguay: 47873 (contract N° 101), 48978 (contract N° 223), 49741 (contract N° 301)
El Salvador: 46616, 46816

(Fig.175-1) This Paraguayan pistol N° 49741 is factory marked on the slide "Modelo Paraguayo 1927 B. 301". The Paraguayan crest is engraved on top of the slide. Another unique characteristic of this contract are the safety markings in Spanish. This is the only variation of the Model 1903 pistol that has safety-markings. These pistols are not slotted to accept shoulder-stocks.

(Fig.175-2) As customary at the time, the Salvadoran crest is located between the front sight and ejection port on the top of the slide. Like the Paraguayan contract, the Salvadoran pistols were not slotted to accept a shoulder-stock. The size of the contract is unknown, seen here is the crest of pistol N° 46816. (Photograph courtesy of Bob Adams)

Service in the British Navy and German Police

A mysterious order was placed in late 1913 by FN's agent Louis Lepersonne in London. The order for 100 slotted pistols was shipped from FN on January 9, 1914. It is not known if the original destination for the order was the British Navy, it was however too large an order for Lepersonne's commercial clientele. British documents indicate that 60 pistols with ammunition were obtained by the British Navy in December 1914[(1)]. The pistols were designated "Browning Automatic .38" and were intended for Chilean warships taken over by British Admiralty[(2)]. Chile had placed orders for battleships in England in 1910, these were scheduled for delivery in 1914 and 1915. Upon the outbreak of World War I, the British purchased these ships from the Chilean government. The Chilean battleship, Almirante Lattore, was in its final stages of completion and was renamed "Canada". The other battle ship, Almirante Cochrane, was converted into an aircraft carrier but production was postponed and it was only completed after the war. Ultimately the ships were sold back to Chile.

British pistols were most likely inspected at Royal Small Arms Factory Enfield and are so marked. Interestingly the pistols are not broad arrow proofed, it is not clear why the Model 1903 pistols were not marked with the traditional British military acceptance markings. Lepersonne's imported pistols did not follow traditional British proofing protocol (see page 96). It is not known if all 100 pistols out of Lepersonne's order were issued to the British Navy.

Reported serial numbers: 35782, 36098, 36117

(Fig.176-1) The Royal Small Arms Factory Enfield inspection marking as found on British navy pistol N° 35782 (Photograph courtesy of Peter Sheaf).

The Model 1903 was not the preferred choice of Imperial German Police forces. Only one example of German police use has been documented. This unusual selection may be contributed to its use in a province of Alsace-Lorraine. Although part of the German Empire and administered out of Berlin, the region did benefit from much autonomy. Unlike other police departments in the German Empire, which preferred the Model 1900, this department selected the relatively new Model 1903. The only known surviving pistol was shipped from FN to its agent Genshow in Berlin on August 5, 1908. It was part of a small order for 12 Model 1903 pistols.

(Fig.176-2) This Model 1903 N° 8907 was shipped from FN on August 5, 1908 to FN's agent Genshow in Berlin. The pistol was stamped on the slide after it left the factory. FN's hard steel made the stamping difficult to apply, the marking reads: "ORTSPOLIZEIBEHORDEN N° 4" (local police department) followed by the French name of the town. The digit "4" was struck in a separate operation. Considered that the name of the town is listed, the digit refers to a precinct or most likely the pistol issue number as Alsace-Lorraine towns were usually small with only one police department office. The name of the town is French but not entirely legible.

(1) Correspondence with Peter Sheaf

(2) The Technical History and Index. -A serial history of technical problems dealt with by Admiralty Departments. Gunnery Training during the War, Small Arms and Machine Guns, Aircraft Armaments. -- Technical History Section -- Admiralty May 1920

The Husqvarna Model 1907

Development History

The Model 1907 was not the first Belgian pistol to be manufactured at the Husqvarna plant. Francotte Lefaucheux m/1871 revolvers had been made in Sweden between 1872 and 1874. Some years later, in 1893, the Husqvarna plant manufactured Nagant revolvers for both the Swedish army and navy (m/1887), as well as for Norway.

The Husqvarna Model 1907 closely resembles the FN Browning 1903 in all aspects including manufacturing quality and finish. The first Husqvarna Model 1907's were made in 1917, the decision to manufacture the pistols owing to Sweden's inability to acquire pistols from FN during World War I. Records are unclear as to whether the manufacturing license was purchased before, or just after the war.

The Husqvarna pistols bore the same military designation as those purchased from FN: Svensk Automatisk Pistol m/1907 (Swedish Automatic Pistol model 1907).

The m/07 designation does not refer to a Swedish manufacturing year but to the year in which the Swedish army accepted this pistol model. As a result, the m/07 designation includes both the FN Browning 1903 pistols as well as the Swedish manufactured Husqvarna pistols. Civilian or commercial pistols were designated "Automatpistol No.500" in the Husqvarna catalogs.

Early Husqvarna pistols were all in blue finish and were marked with two different slide legends, which included the Browning name (see page 179). After the war FN intervened as only FN had the rights to the Browning trade name.

Though Husqvarna manufactured pistols for military as well as commercial sales, there were no military exports until FN stopped manufacturing the FN Browning 1903. In the mid-1930s FN was approached by a Colombian agent seeking to purchase the FN Browning Model 1903 for the Colombian government. As FN's production of the pistol had ceased in 1928 FN deferred the sale to Husqvarna. The Colombian contract was the only significant export of Husqvarna manufactured pistols, likely due to the export restrictions within the licensing agreement between Husqvarna and FN.

No Swedish Brownings made at the Husqvarna plant were slotted for shoulder-stocks and like the Belgian FN Browning 1903, all pistols were chambered for the 9mm Browning Long (9x20mm) cartridge.

Many pistols were converted in the U.S. by the importer, Golden State Arms, to .380 ACP (9x17mm) as a marketing technique (the original cartridge was deemed too difficult to obtain). Golden State Arms stamped the converted pistols "Cal .380" on the slide. This configuration is not an original Belgian or Swedish variant as sometimes reported. While most Husqvarna pistols left the factory with a high polish blue finish, this is rarely seen today. The Swedish military engaged in regular repair and refitting of its pistols and refinished most of the m/1907 inventory throughout the years. Refinished pistols show either a phosphate or dull blue finish over sandblasted metal.

The serialization on the 1907 Husqvarna pistols is not necessarily sequential; specific serial ranges were requested by various branches of the military.

Prior to the adoption of the m/40 Lahti pistol, a few m/07 pistols were chambered for the 9x19mm cartridge. Today, only serial numbers 1 and 5 of this order still exist. These pistols were manufactured by Husqvarna, although it is believed that the Carl Gustav factory was involved in the trials. Magazines were modified to work properly with the 9x19mm cartridge.

According to some Swedish sources, 15 Husqvarna pistols left the factory with 9x19mm barrels and 10 FN made pistols were modified to 9x19mm in 1941. It is reported that these 9x19mm Husqvarna pistols are in the serial number range of 80931-80945.

The m/07 pistol was replaced by the m/39 (Walther HP). Germany however halted deliveries when the war broke out and Sweden was forced to look for a replacement. The Lahti (m/40) was selected as it was believed to be easier to manufacture than the m/39.

As the m/40 became the primary pistol in the Swedish military, the m/07 was kept in reserve. In 1986 the m/40 pistol was retired after an accident where the slide cracked and the parts hit the shooter in the forehead. Forty-five years after the adoption of the m/40, the old m/07 was pressed back into service until a new pistol was adopted. Less than two years later, in 1988, the m/88 (Glock 17) and m/88B (Glock 19) were adopted.

Husqvarna Model 1907: Features

Serial Numbers & Production Numbers

The erratic serialization of pistols is broken down by approximate years :

1917:	1-300	Commercial sales
1917-1918:	301-1550	Supplied to the military
1917-1918:	1550-5500?	Supplied to the military
1918:	90211-96000	
1918:	100,001-100,577	Commercial sales
1918:	100,578-100,661	Artillery contract
1919:	12051-16050	
1921:	100,976-101,006	Artillery Contract
1926-1927	102,077-102,733	Artillery contract
?-1933	46351-47350	
1934-1938	43000-86213	
1937:	104,000-105,000	771 exported to Antioquia, Columbia
1939-1942	105,000-107,000	
1942-(1944)	107,000-107,516	Last pistols assembled from existing parts; all were sold on the commercial market

Husqvarna production numbers according to year:

Year	Swedish military	Commercial
1917	2854	209
1918	9361	827
1919	9000	93
1920	6000	140
1921	10303	59
1922	2750	48
1923	4250	40
1924	3000	38
1925	-	38
1926	800	21

Year	Swedish military	Commercial
1927-1932	631	-
1933	1000	53
1934-1937	-	564
1938	900	112
1939	2025	95
1940	25653	2021
1941	10290	210
1942	400	171
1943-1944	13	-

Inspector Markings

The following inspector markings have been noted (see fig167-2 and 180-2):

H.C. C.J	For the inspecting officer Hyltén-Cavallius and armorer Carl Edward Johansson. Found on Husqvarna and Belgian made FN 1903 pistols.
J.V. C.R	For the inspecting officer Captain Jacques Virgin, supervisor Carl Rundlöf. Found on Husqvarna and Belgian made FN 1903 pistols.
G.W. C.R	For the inspecting officer Captain Julius Weibull, supervisor Carl Rundlöf. Found on Husqvarna and Belgian made FN 1903 pistols.
H.S. C.J.	Armorer H. Segerdahl, supervisor Carl Edvard Johansson. Found on Husqvarna and Belgian FN 1903 pistols.
H.S. C.R.	Armorer H. Segerdahl, supervisor Carl Rundlöf. Found on Husqvarna and Belgian FN 1903 pistols.
T.T. H.K.	Armorer Tor Thorsson - inspecting officer Captain Helge Kolthoff. Found only on Husqvarna pistols.
G.B.	For the inspecting officer Captain Gustav Björkenstam. Found on Husqvarna pistols.
T.T. B.F.	Armorer Tor Thorsson - inspecting officer Captain Birger Friedlander. Found only on Husqvarna pistols.
T.T. H.A.	Armorer Tor Thorsson - inspecting officer Captain Hugo Abramsson. Found only on Husqvarna pistols.

Other official markings found on m/07 pistols include the Swedish crown. This is an acceptance marking found on all military pistols. It should not be confused with a crown stamped over the letter "H" indicating a commercial gun that was proofed at Husqvarna. Some guns have additional markings found on the frame, often referred to as regimental or unit markings. These are; I for Infantry regiment, A for Artillery regiment, K.FL for Royal Navy, F for Air Force, K1 for first cavalry regiment, K2 for second cavalry regiment and K3 for third cavalry regiment.

Some Navy guns have also a symbol stamped that resembles a cat's paw. This symbol was phased out in the early 20th century. Unofficial markings often include the individual owner's initials.

Slide variants through production years

HUSQVARNA VAPENFABRIKS AKTIEBOLAG
BROWNING'S-PATENT

This first slide legend was used only in 1917 -1918, including the first 300 commercial guns. Approximate serial range 1-5500. The use of the Browning trade name was abolished once FN complained after World War I.

HUSQVARNA VAPENFABRIKS AKTIEBOLAG
SYSTEM BROWNING

This second slide legend was introduced either at the same time or right after the first variation. This is found on pistols manufactured around the same time frame in 1917-1919 and again in 1926-1927 with artillery contract purchases.

This slide legend is more often encountered than the first variation; it has been noted in a serial range intersecting with the first variation (1300-1400) as well as in the 12000, 35000 and 100,000-102,000 range. It is most likely that this slide legend was applied to specific military contracts after 1918 to remain consistent with previous shipments, such as the artillery purchases. Most guns seen with this slide legend are blued or have been refinished with a military style phosphate finish over sandblasted metal.

HUSQVARNA VAPENFABRIKS AKTIEBOLAG

Early guns with this slide legend were blued, later guns were phosphated. This legend, considered the third variation, is often encountered on guns with serial numbers that would suggest early production. This is due to the erratic serialization of pistols during production years. This is the most commonly encountered slide legend.

HUSQVARNA VAPENFABRIKS AB

This legend is found sporadically on late production pistols. The slide legend is characteristically marked in italics. This type is noted on pistols in the 104,000 serial range, mainly produced in 1938 and later.

Husqvarna Model 1907: Accessories

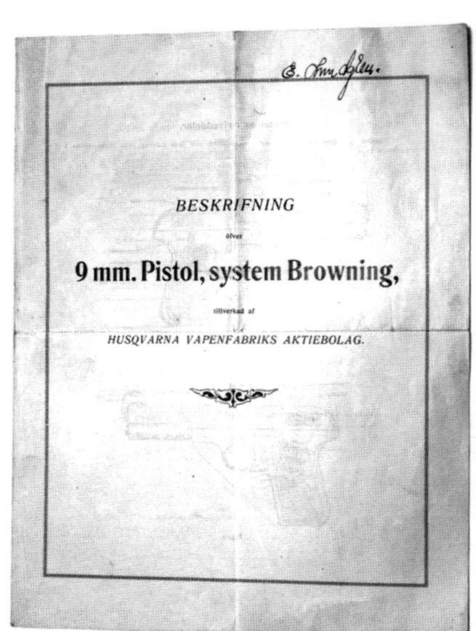

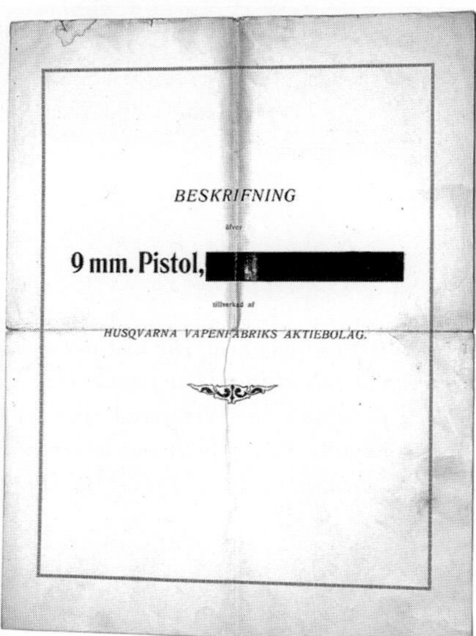

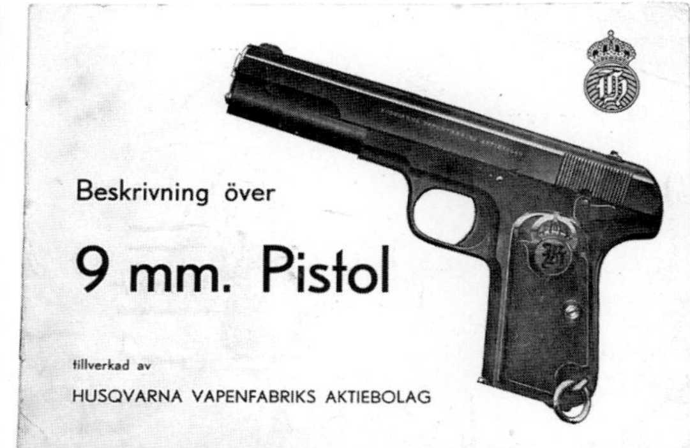

(Fig.107-1) Rare factory manuals for the Model 1907 Husqvarna. Note how the Browning trade name was obscured after FN objected to its use. (Photographs courtesy of John Bastin)

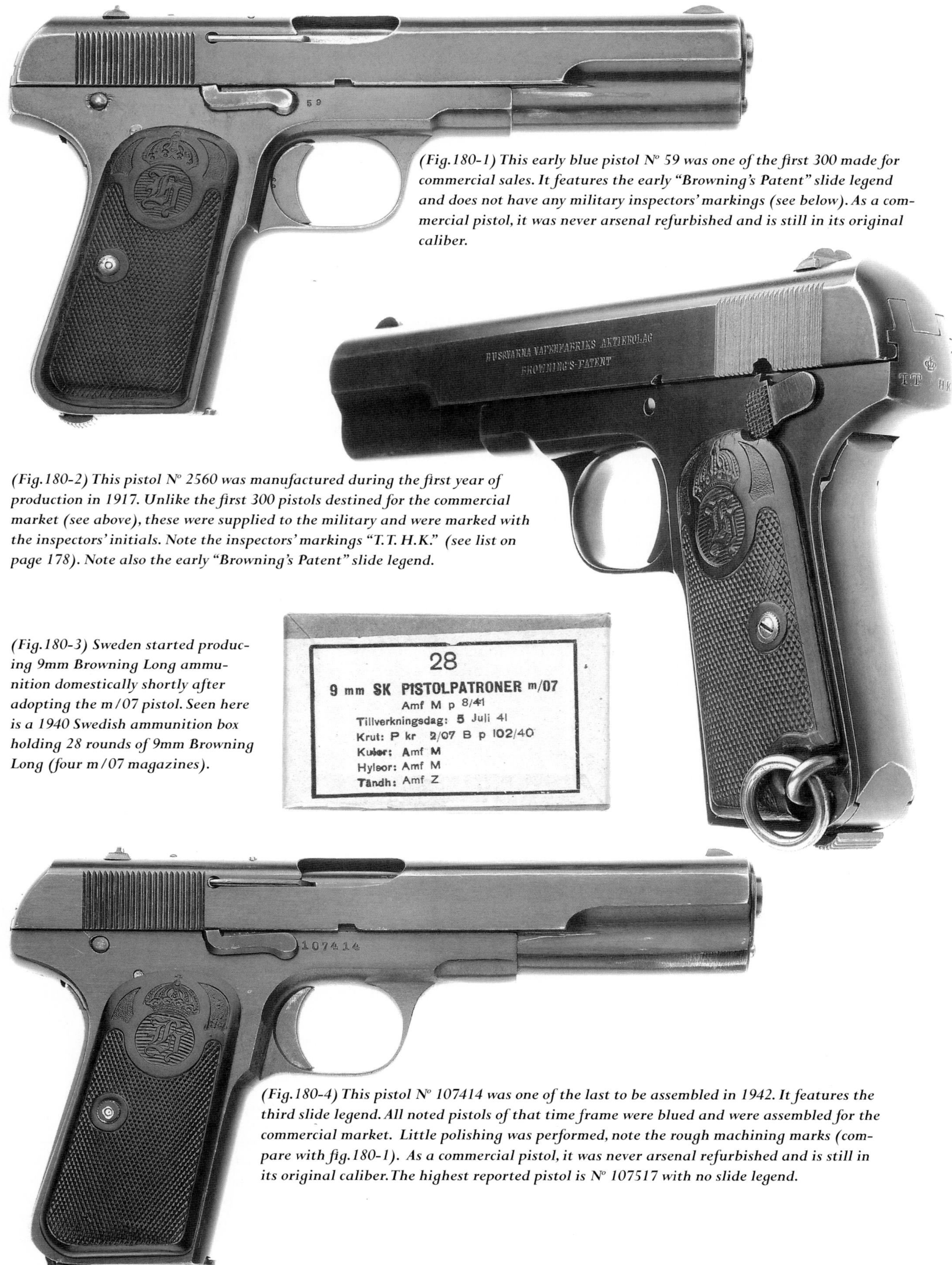

(Fig.180-1) This early blue pistol N° 59 was one of the first 300 made for commercial sales. It features the early "Browning's Patent" slide legend and does not have any military inspectors' markings (see below). As a commercial pistol, it was never arsenal refurbished and is still in its original caliber.

(Fig.180-2) This pistol N° 2560 was manufactured during the first year of production in 1917. Unlike the first 300 pistols destined for the commercial market (see above), these were supplied to the military and were marked with the inspectors' initials. Note the inspectors' markings "T. T. H.K." (see list on page 178). Note also the early "Browning's Patent" slide legend.

(Fig.180-3) Sweden started producing 9mm Browning Long ammunition domestically shortly after adopting the m/07 pistol. Seen here is a 1940 Swedish ammunition box holding 28 rounds of 9mm Browning Long (four m/07 magazines).

(Fig.180-4) This pistol N° 107414 was one of the last to be assembled in 1942. It features the third slide legend. All noted pistols of that time frame were blued and were assembled for the commercial market. Little polishing was performed, note the rough machining marks (compare with fig.180-1). As a commercial pistol, it was never arsenal refurbished and is still in its original caliber. The highest reported pistol is N° 107517 with no slide legend.

(Fig.181-1) Arsenal reworked in Sweden, this pistol N° 24690 was sandblasted and phosphated. The phosphate finish is the most common finish encountered. Note the regimental markings and early "System Browning" slide legend. The .380 marking was applied in the U.S. at the time of conversion. (Photograph by author, courtesy of Michael Shade)

The U.S. 380 caliber conversion

Due to a lack of 9mm Browning Long ammunition, importers like Golden State Arms opted to convert the Husqvarna and some Swedish contract FN 1903 pistols to the more common .380 caliber. Consequently some dealers have propelled the myth that the pistols were converted in Swedish arsenals or that the .380 FN pistols were built by the Germans during World War I.

The pistols were converted in the U.S and marked "CAL 380".

Golden State Arms sold the pistols with the accompanying spec sheet.

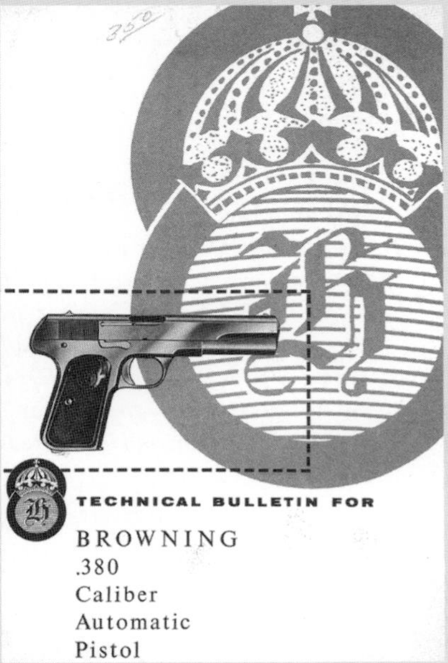

TECHNICAL BULLETIN FOR
BROWNING
.380
Caliber
Automatic
Pistol

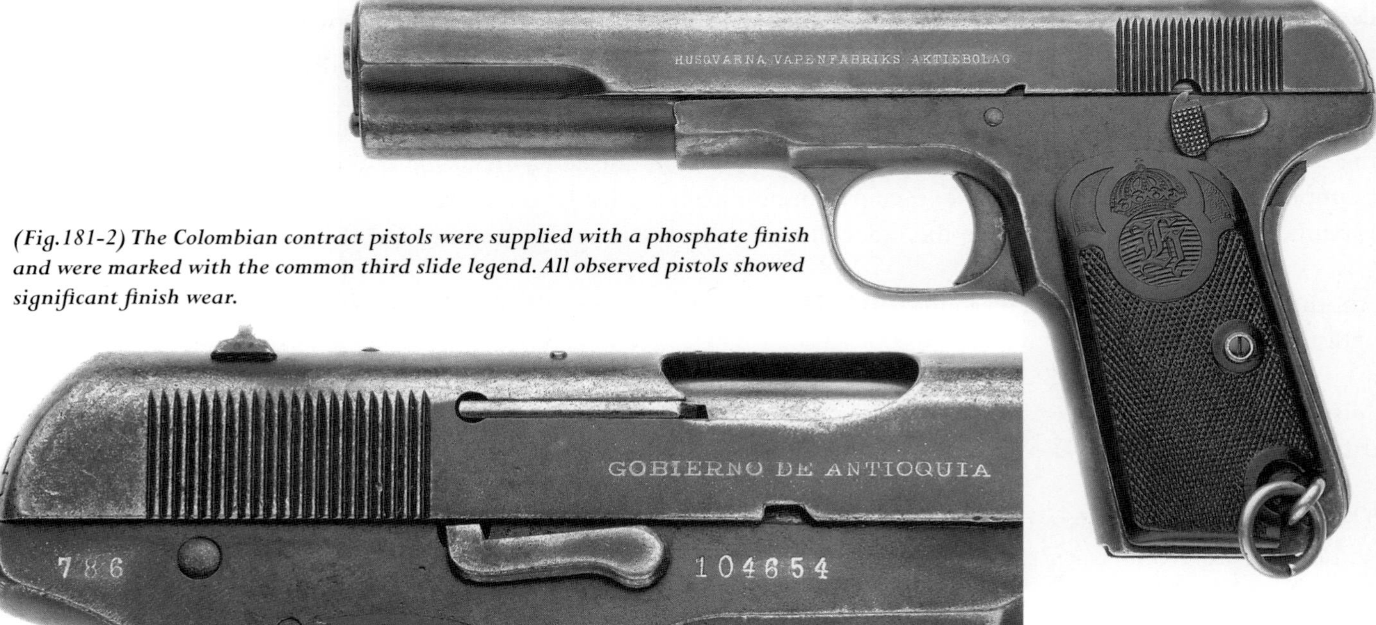

(Fig.181-2) The Colombian contract pistols were supplied with a phosphate finish and were marked with the common third slide legend. All observed pistols showed significant finish wear.

(Fig.181-3) This little known and rare contract variation was manufactured in 1937. This pistol N° 104654 was marked and supplied to Antioquia, a district in Colombia. About 771 of these pistols were sold to Columbia with FN approval after FN had discontinued production. Most likely these pistols were used in law enforcement. Note the gun's issue number (N° 786) stamped near the rear of the pistol. This small contract was the only foreign contract for the Husqvarna 1907, due to licensing restrictions with FN. Observed serial numbers: N° 104340, 104654, 104880.

The FN Browning Model 1905 (1906)

Development History

The Model 1905 was the third handgun to go into mass production at FN. The prototype was received at FN in 1905 and in less than a year the first pistols were manufactured and sold in July 1906. Several patents were filed and it took months before the Belgian government granted all patents. As a result, early Model 1905 pistols are found without the "deposé" marking in the slide-legend (fig.182-1).

Like the preceding Model 1899 and 1900 pistols, the Model 1905 was intended for the commercial market (unlike the military Model 1903, see page 158) and FN had no reservations about beginning production as quickly as possible.

(Fig.182-1) An early FN Browning 1905 pistol N° 1459. Note that the word "DEPOSE" (registered) was stamped after the pistol was manufactured. FN production started before the Belgian government granted the patent to FN. Early pistols were marked only with Browning's Patent. The word "deposé" refers to the fact that the patent was issued by the Belgian government. (Photograph by author, courtesy of Ted Zajac)

The model was an immediate success. Like most of FN's early pistol models, the Model 1905 had many designations. It was first known as Pistolet Browning 6.35mm. Subsequently it became the Vest Pocket Model (Modèle de Poche) and was later referred to by FN as the Model 1906 (for the first year it was produced).

Compounding the confusion, in the U.S. the pistol was alternately known as either the Model 1905 (for the year John Browning designed it). Some dealers also sometimes called it the Baby Browning during the 1920s. The Baby Browning became a model of its own in 1931 (see page 256).

The production pistol was almost identical to John Browning's prototype (see page 108). In 1908 Colt started production of its version of the Vest Pocket Model, making it the only time FN and Colt produced the same Browning design. The slide safety, which often has been attributed to Colt, was actually patented by FN in 1906, and introduced into FN production around the same time Colt started production of their Vest Pocket pistol.

Initially, an estimated 130,000 pistols were made without the slide-safety, the change gradually taking effect in 1909. As the supply of stockpiled parts was used up, some pistols were finished with a slide safety while others were not. As an example, pistol N° 178881 had no slide safety but nominally earlier pistol N° 133193 did as well as N° 183626. These variants are commonly identified in the U.S. collector community as First and Second Variation.

Another change was introduced around 1911: The smooth trigger was replaced by a more ergonomic grooved model with flanges (see fig.183-2).

Although the Model 1905 was made primarily for the civilian market, it did have a strong following among military officers of many nations, and was used by police detectives in a number of countries.

The most prominent contract sales for the model were to the Imperial Russian Military Academy (see page 188). A number of pre-World War I pistols have been reported with factory applied Arabic or Farsi markings, but the specific contract and markings remain unknown.

The use of the Model 1905 pistol remained popular throughout the 1920s and 1930s, and as late as World War II, they were frequently carried by German officers, as can be attested to by the numerous accounts documenting the capture of FN Model 1905 pistols by Allied soldiers.

Surprisingly those pistols date often from the pre-World War I era. The model was never produced during World War I, although captured pistols were used extensively in both conflicts.

A few pistols were assembled during the first months of the German occupation in World War II. A few pistols were manufactured between 1946 and 1950 before production seized in favor of the Baby model.

FN Model 1905: Features & Specifications

Serial Numbers

The following is a rough guide to approximate production serial numbers. Serial numbers were not restarted on this model, so the serial number also indicates quantities produced by the end year.

August 1906- 1909:	**Appriximately 130,000 (first variation without slide safety)**
1914:	**Appriximately 550,000**
1919-1940:	**Appriximately 1,008,000**
1946-1950:	**Limited production with large serial number gaps, highest recorded number is 1,311,256**

As was customary at FN, most of the lowest serial numbered pistols were never completed or sold (see page 97). The fist pistol shipped from FN was serial number 2, shipped to the Browning Brothers on July 31, 1906. Gaps in serial numbers remain until about serial number 80 when production was perfected.

Slide and frame variants through production years

FABRIQUE NATIONALE D'ARMES de GUERRE HERSTAL BELGIQUE
BROWNING'S PATENT

First year production slide legend without "Deposé" marking. Pistols that were still in warehouse by the time FN received the Belgian patent, were stamped by hand as in fig.182-1.

FABRIQUE NATIONALE D'ARMES de GUERRE HERSTAL BELGIQUE
BROWNING'S PATENT DEPOSE

Slide legend as used from 1907 through the 1930s. Subtle variants exist

FABRIQUE NATIONALE D'ARMES DE GUERRE HERSTAL-BELGIQUE
BROWNING'S PATENT DEPOSE

Slide legend as used through the 1930s, in 1940 as well as in 1946-1947

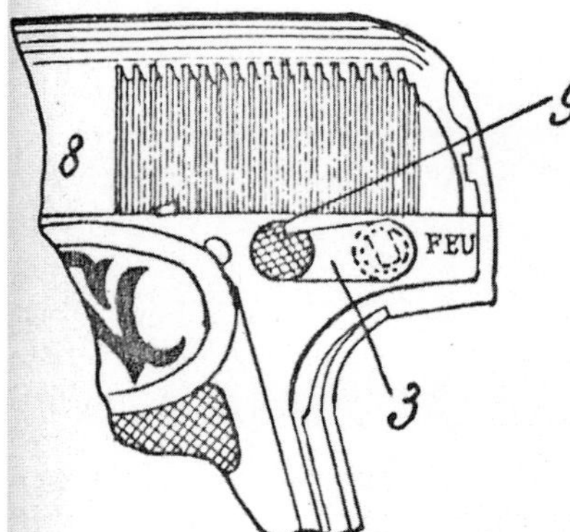

(Fig.183-1) The slide safety was patented By FN on November 10, 1906.The initial safety lever traveled 180°, an improved design without safety markings was introduced in 1909.

(Fig.183-2) Early production pistols did not have trigger flanges.Trigger flanges were introduced into production circa 1911, around serial number 220,000.These were introduced after the slide safety.

Specifications Summary

Manufacturer: Fabrique Nationale d'Armes de Guerre, Herstal Belgique
Belgian patent: 184656 **Filing date:** May 9, 1905
Period offered: 1906-1947 (none produced during World War I), limited production during and after World War II
Caliber: 6.35x15.5mm (.25 ACP)
Operating system: Blowback
Length: 114mm
Barrel length: 54mm
Weight: 340 grams
Grips: Animal horn (ivory or mother-of-pearl optional), black plastic during 1940 assembly and postwar production
Magazine capacity: Six
Sights: Fixed sights incorporated in the slide
Options: None
Finish offered: Blue, nickel **Engraving patterns:** Six

FN Model 1905: Accessories

(Fig.184-1) A 1920s instruction book for the Model 1905. These books were available in several languages, including French, English, German and Spanish. The covers were updated through time to reflect accomplished sales figures. Covers vary in colors (green, red, burgundy, brown) with numbers indicating the 300,000, 600,000 and 1,000,000 sales milestones.

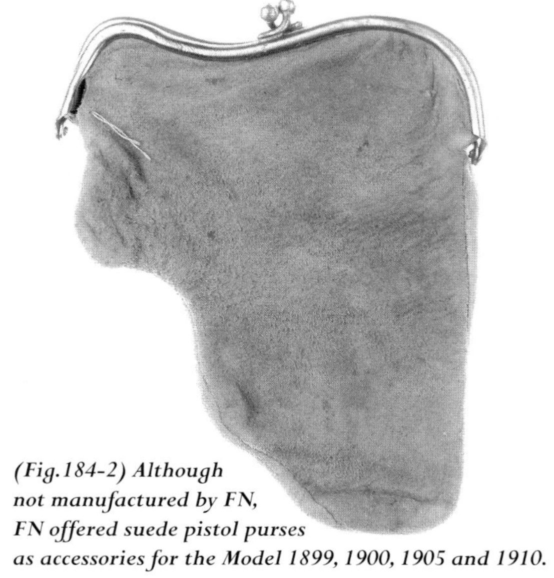

(Fig.184-2) Although not manufactured by FN, FN offered suede pistol purses as accessories for the Model 1899, 1900, 1905 and 1910.

(Fig.184-3) FN Browning 1905 N° 183626 in its original box: This pistol was shipped on July 22, 1909 to FN's agent Wagener in Hamburg, Germany. Note that this pistol is already equipped with the slide safety. The early green box is the standard FN pattern with embossed FN logo. The box end label is an unusual feature for FN and was not retained over time. The pistol serial number is written in pencil on the bottom as was customary.

FABRIQUE NATIONALE D'ARMES DE GUERRE

HERSTAL-LIÈGE (BELGIQUE)

INSTRUCTIONS

POUR LA

MANŒUVRE DU PISTOLET AUTOMATIQUE BROWNING

CAL. 6,35 ‰ à triple sûreté.

1) **Pour enlever le chargeur.** – Tenir le pistolet de la main droite, incliné à droite, déclancher l'arrêt du chargeur au bas de la poignée à l'aide de la main gauche et retirer le chargeur avec l'index.

2) **Pour remplir le chargeur.** – Tenir le chargeur dans la main gauche ; saisir une cartouche de la main droite, le culot vers le haut, l'engager entre les lèvres du chargeur en repoussant le transporteur et la pousser, le culot contre la tranche plane.

(Fig.184-4) Pre-World War II commercial pistols were shipped in the box with a folded instruction sheet. Seen here is a partially folded 1920 instruction sheet in French. Prewar sheets were printed on plain onionskin colored paper, postwar folding instructions were printed on oil resistant glassine paper starting in the 1947/1948 era (see fig.214-3).

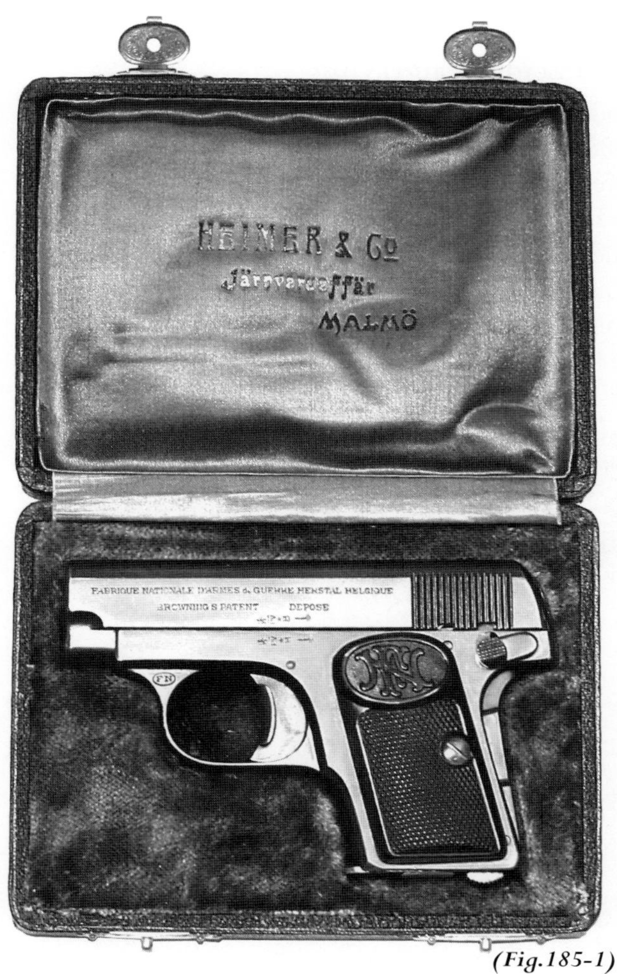

(Fig.185-1)

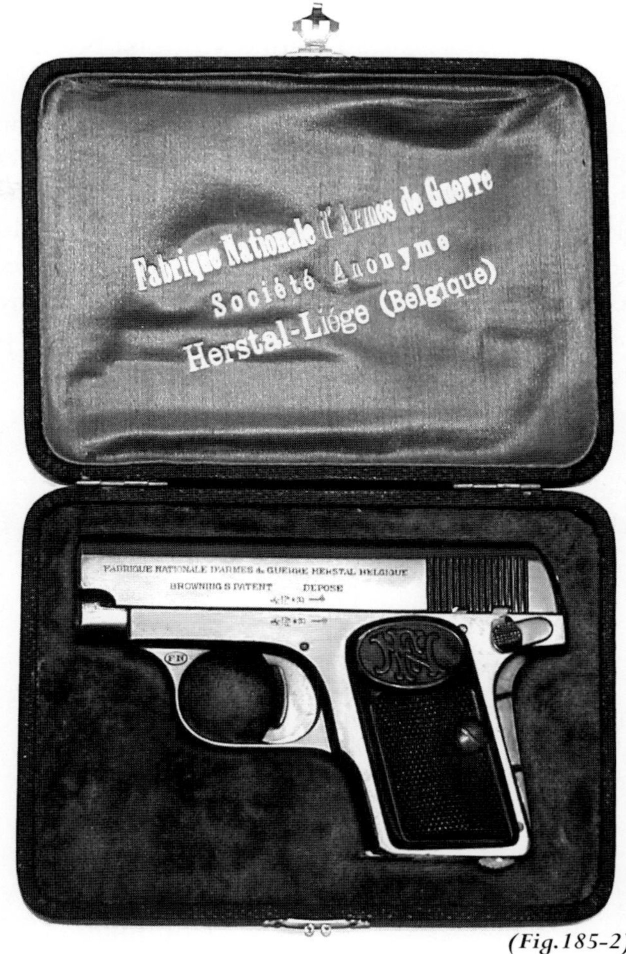

(Fig.185-2)

(Fig.185-1) An early FN presentation case (pre-1910). Note the more square corners of this early case. The interior is imprinted with the Swedish retailer information "Heimer & Co. Jarnvaruaffar Malmo (Heimer & Co. Hardware Store, Malmo). Malmo is the third largest city in Sweden. Case imprinting was optional and was popular in the early 1900s. The case is lined with a vivid green satin unlike later cases, which are more subdued in color. This color can be compared to forest green unlike the later cases, which resemble dark sea green. (Photograph by Daniel Bergman, courtesy of John Bastin)

(Fig.185-2) A pre-1914 presentation case with FN factory name imprinted. This case is larger than the post World War I cases (fig. 185-3). The case is lined with the traditional green satin and gold lettering. Note the single closure clasp. (Photograph by Daniel Bergman, courtesy of John Bastin)

(Fig.185-3) A 1920s-1930s FN black canvas presentation case. Note that the external features are identical to the prewar FN Baby case (see fig.260-1), the inside is French fitted specifically for the Model 1905. This case has the traditional green satin interior with gold lettering. Note the two closure clasps.

(Fig.185-3)

Luxury Models: Nickel Plating and Factory Engraving

Upgraded variants of the Model 1905 were offered shortly after production began. Buyers could purchase presentation cases in either black canvas or leather. A nickel finish (see fig.188-1) was available as well as six different engraving patterns. The patterns were known as types. Standard grips were black horn, but ivory and mother-of-pearl were also available, the latter being the most expensive. After World War I, FN used the special engraving patterns to boost sales in a depressed market. A special high polish finish was introduced circa 1922 and was used on all high-grade commercial guns throughout the 1920s. This finish required additional polishing, it featured a more attractive high gloss look but was also more fragile than FN's standard rust blue finish. The high polish finish features a deep blue color while FN's standard rust blue finish has a more prevalent gray look. FN discontinued the high polish finish in the early 1930s (see also page 98, 199).

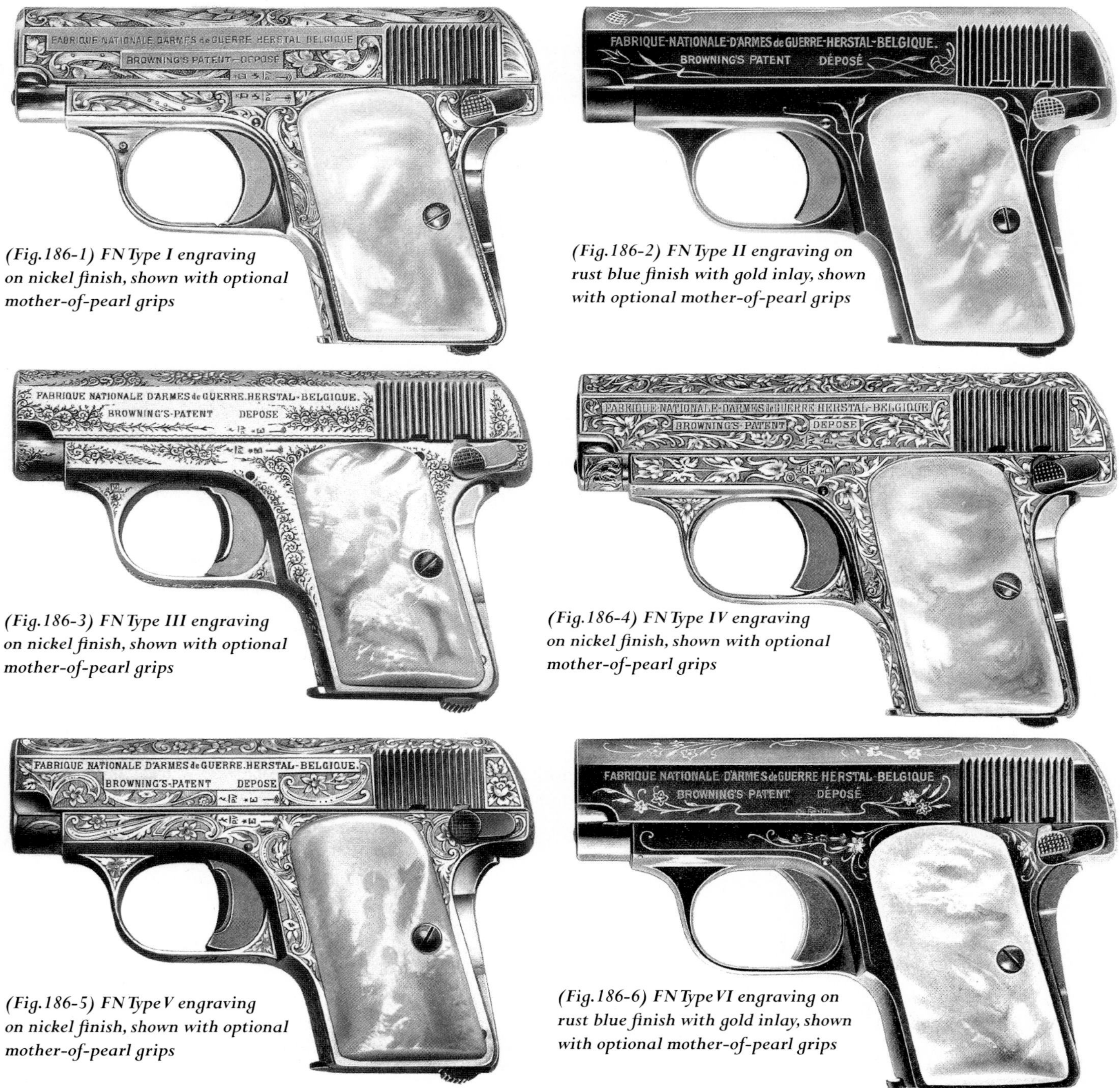

(Fig.186-1) FN Type I engraving on nickel finish, shown with optional mother-of-pearl grips

(Fig.186-2) FN Type II engraving on rust blue finish with gold inlay, shown with optional mother-of-pearl grips

(Fig.186-3) FN Type III engraving on nickel finish, shown with optional mother-of-pearl grips

(Fig.186-4) FN Type IV engraving on nickel finish, shown with optional mother-of-pearl grips

(Fig.186-5) FN Type V engraving on nickel finish, shown with optional mother-of-pearl grips

(Fig.186-6) FN Type VI engraving on rust blue finish with gold inlay, shown with optional mother-of-pearl grips

(Fig.187-1) Pistol Nº 196875 has full coverage engraving. Although the quality of engraving is consistent with FN engraving, the pattern is not a known FN Type. The rust blue is consistent with FN bluing. It is not possible to authenticate the work as factory engraving, many period pistols were engraved after leaving the factory. Dealers and agents often commissioned local engravers in order to save costs. This pistol was shipped to Genshow in Berlin on June 1, 1910. Note that it has the slide safety but does not have the trigger with finger flanges (fig.183-2).

(Fig.187-4) "The best insurance against theft and death is still a FN Browning pistol"; 1920s advertisement from FN's Agent Leon Houard in Ghent.

(Fig.187-2) This factory engraved Type II Model 1905 Nº 735441 was completed on March 3, 1925 and shipped to FN's agent Kind in Hunstig, Germany on November 5, 1926. This pistol was engraved at the time when FN employed a high polish blue finish instead of the traditional rust blue on their high-grade guns. The high polish blue finish was discontinued in the early 1930s.

(Fig.187-2) This Type III factory engraved FN Browning 1905 Nº 555251 was shipped to FN's agent Franck in Germany on September 14, 1912. The pistol is finished with the traditional FN rust blue finish and features rare factory ivory grips. A GI captured the pistol from a Japanese officer on Wake Island in 1945. (Photograph by author, courtesy of Eric Larson)

Imperial Russian General Staff Academy Contracts

The Imperial Russian government purchased FN Model 1900, 1903[(1)] and 1905 pistols for its Imperial General Staff Academy graduates. The Imperial Nicholas Military Academy[(2)] (Imperatorskaya Nikolaevskaya Voennaya Akademiya) in St. Petersburg was one of two top elite officers' schools in Russia. These guns can be identified by the two crossed Mosin-Nagant rifles and issue number roll engraved on the frame. Numbers ascend in logical order, yet are not model specific[(3)]. Both blue and nickel finishes have been noted on these Russian Model 1900 and 1905 contract guns. Sales of the Model 1905 pistols were concurrent with sales for the Model 1900 pistols, with both models often being included in the same order (see also page 150).

It is often believed that the nickel finish, as well as the Mosin-Nagant markings were added in Russia, but this is incorrect. Close examination reveals that the bluing, as well as the nickel finish, was applied after the marking had been engraved. The nickel and blue finish on these pistols are identical to standard FN finishes. Additionally the nickel finish guns have a black trigger, magazine release (and safety). This was standard FN procedure to assure correct spacing and operation of these parts (see finishes on page 99). It is not known why some pistols were ordered in blue finish while the majority was ordered in nickel finish. The orders usually date from 1908 and on. Most of the Imperial Russian contract pistols did not have the slide safety.

A small number of these Russian contract Model 1905s are found in the U.S. These pistols were traded and brought back by U.S. servicemen who served in Russia (Archangel and Murmansk) during the Allied intervention after World War I. Accounts of one such trade from family members of the serviceman indicate that the pistol was traded for a ham![(4)]

Reported or observed serial numbers:
17881 Nickel finish, shipped May 3, 1909
36883 Blue finish, issue number 2022
43379 Nickel finish
72227 Nickel finish, issue number 5746, shipped July 1, 1908
76046 Nickel finish, issue number 5977
76699 Nickel finish, issue number 6030
80435 Blue finish, issue number 6635, shipped Feb. 4, 1908
86896 Nickel finish, issue number 7191, shipped Feb. 22, 1908
96276 Blue finish, issue number 7938
103389 Shipped on April 15, 1908
104473 Nickel finish, issue number 9506
178881 Blue finish, issue number 5746, shipped May 3, 1909
370314 Blue finish, issue number 12893

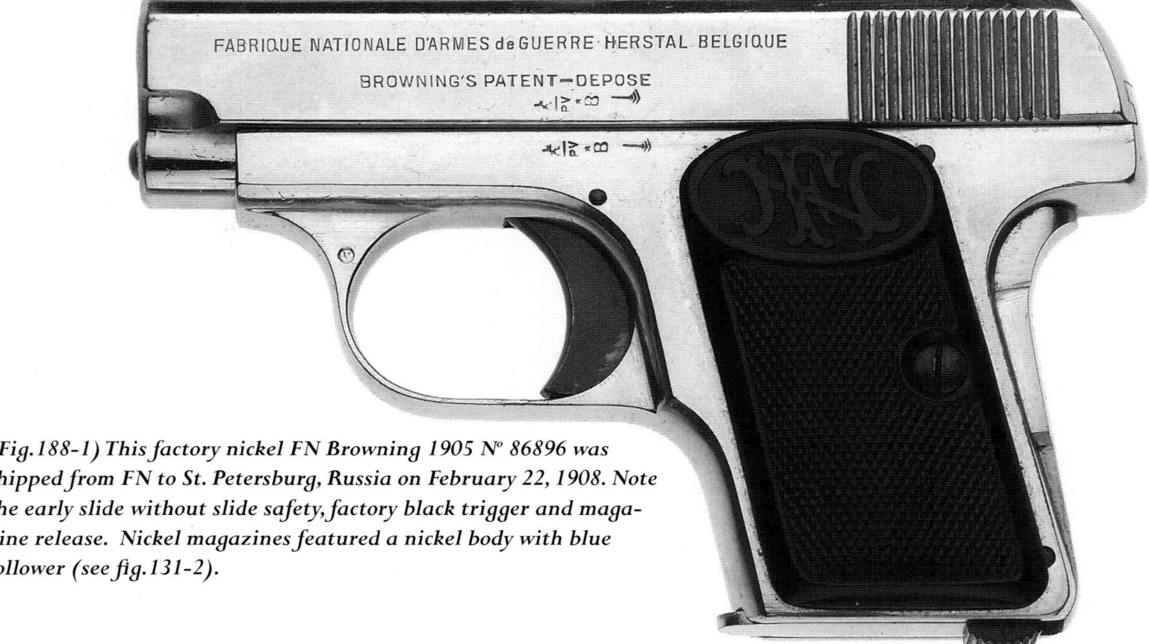

(Fig.188-1) This factory nickel FN Browning 1905 N° 86896 was shipped from FN to St. Petersburg, Russia on February 22, 1908. Note the early slide without slide safety, factory black trigger and magazine release. Nickel magazines featured a nickel body with blue follower (see fig.131-2).

(1) Only one Model 1903 with Mosin-Nagant markings is known to survive in a European museum collection.
(2) Although shipped to the Imperial Nicholas Military Academy, it is not known if the pistols were destined solely for this academy or distributed among other St. Petersburg military academies.
(3) The Mosin-Nagant number ascends through the years and contracts, but numbers are not specific to a model, so it is theoritically possible to encounter a Model 1900 and a Model 1905 with sequential Mosin-Nagant numbers.
(4) The U.S. serviceman traded the pistol and holster with a (White) Russian officer. Graduates of the elite officers' schools often remained loyal to the Czar and endured miserable conditions including famine.

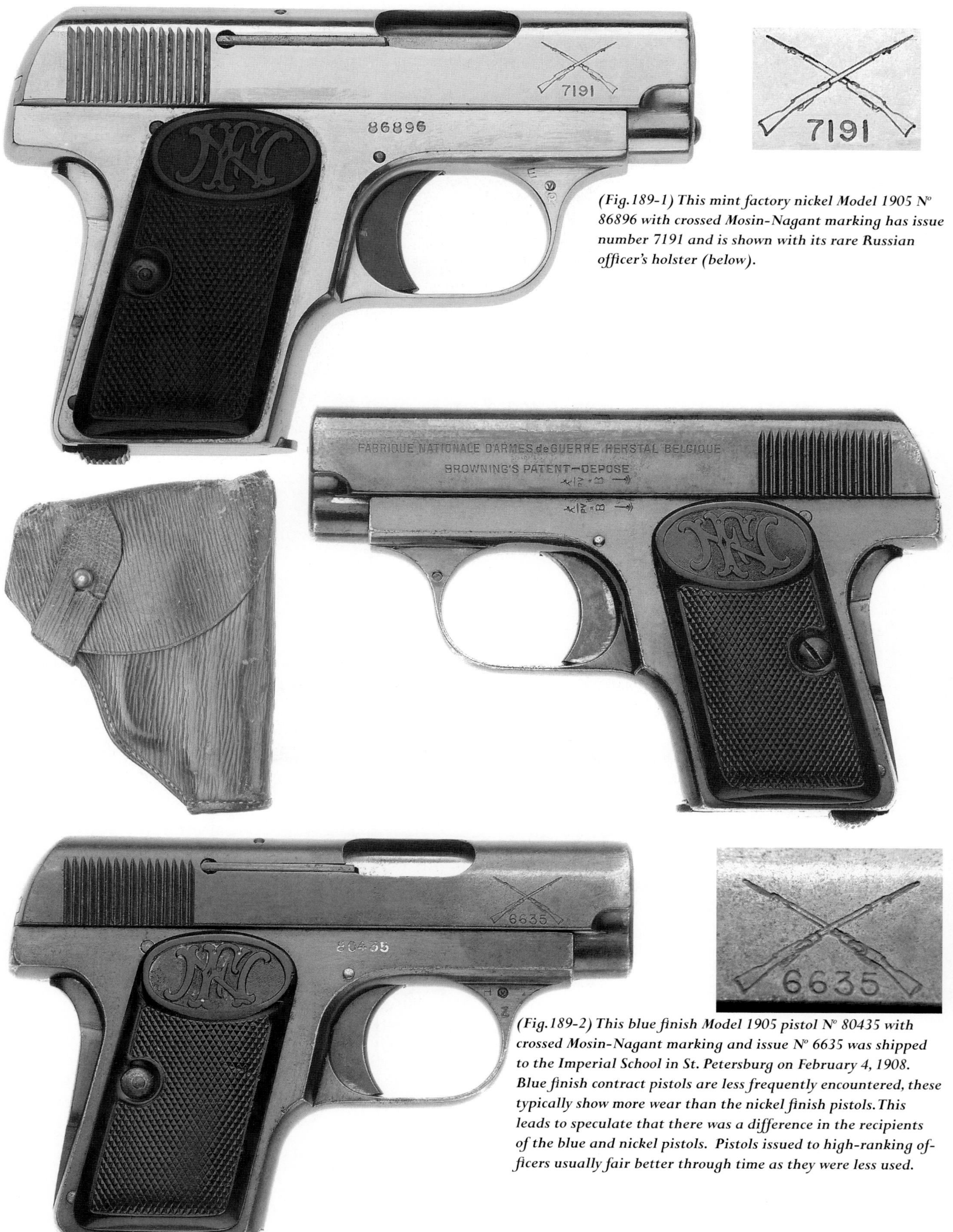

(Fig.189-1) This mint factory nickel Model 1905 N° 86896 with crossed Mosin-Nagant marking has issue number 7191 and is shown with its rare Russian officer's holster (below).

(Fig.189-2) This blue finish Model 1905 pistol N° 80435 with crossed Mosin-Nagant marking and issue N° 6635 was shipped to the Imperial School in St. Petersburg on February 4, 1908. Blue finish contract pistols are less frequently encountered, these typically show more wear than the nickel finish pistols. This leads to speculate that there was a difference in the recipients of the blue and nickel pistols. Pistols issued to high-ranking officers usually fair better through time as they were less used.

Imperial German Detectives' Pistols

Prussian police forces used the FN Browning 1900 extensively (see page 152 for structure and details on Imperial German use). FN Vest Pocket pistols are however rarely encountered with Prussian police markings. It is believed that these smaller pistols were used by plain clothes detectives instead of uniformed policemen. These Model 1905's were not widely distributed and have only surfaced with one identifying marking for what is believed to be the Presidium of Munster (see page 153 for details on markings).

Reported serial numbers:
316309 K.P.D.M. N° 85: Königl. Pol.-Direktion Münster
316348 K.P.D.M. N° 66: Königl. Pol.-Direktion Münster
506085 K.P.D.M. N° 156: Königl. Pol.-Direktion Münster

(Fig.186-1) This Model 1905 N° 506085 with German Police marking was manufactured on July 29, 1914. It was part of an order, marked at the factory but not shipped before the German invasion.

Shanghai Municipal Police Pistols

The Treaty of Nanking of 1842 opened China to international trade, and subsequent exploitation. The treaty dictated the cession of Hong Kong to Great Britain, and the opening of five Chinese seaports, including Shanghai, to foreign trade. French and American agreements with the Chinese followed quickly upon the heels of the British treaty, taking advantage of the weak and appeasing Chinese emperor. The French Concession was declared in 1862, and in 1863, the British and Americans formed the International Settlement by merging the British and American concessions.

The foreign residents of Shanghai maintained their western ways. Few learned Chinese and trade was made possible by pidgin English; a mixture of English, Chinese, Indian and Portuguese. The foreigners referred to themselves as Shanghailanders.

Business in Shanghai proved extremely profitable and the city grew at a rapid rate. The population doubled between 1895 and 1910 and nearly tripled in the next 20 years to a staggering three million inhabitants. This growth was also spurred in the 1920s and early 1930s by the warlords who controlled the countryside, turning Shanghai into a refugee destination. In addition to the growing numbers of Chinese who made Shanghai their home, a large number of White Russians arrived in Shanghai in the years after the Bolshevik Revolution of 1917.

In 1853-1854 the British created the Shanghai Municipal Council, and with it the Shanghai Municipal Police or SMP. Up until the first decade of the twentieth century, the SMP was typically staffed by Chinese or Sikh (Indian) policemen under supervision of British officers. After 1917, White Russian officers joined the ranks of the SMP.

Other White Russians joined the Shanghai Volunteers; a uniformed military battalion, 150 men strong. The Shanghai Volunteers became an auxiliary unit to the SMP.

As Shanghai grew so did organized crime. Racketeering, prostitution, opium distribution and arms trading[(1)] were the stock in trade of organizations like the Green Gang Society and the Big Eight Mob. Corruption was widespread, touching city officials, police departments and the SMP. However, Europeans typically overlooked the corruption as long as crimes against Europeans were investigated and solved. Criminal enterprises were fueled by the fact that the concessions did not have any centralized law enforcement. Criminals committed crimes in one enclave, and avoided prosecution by walking across the street into another enclave.

Shanghai's law enforcement extended to the SMP, the French Sureté (French Concession police) and the Chinese police[(2)].

During the 1920s and 1930s, the head of the Sureté's detective force was not only known for his ties to organized crime, but also for being the head of one of the city's largest gangs! Many of the Chinese detectives hired by the Sureté had criminal records or were directly involved in the Green Gang Society.

In the late 1920s and 1930s about 70,000 foreigners called Shanghai home. The SMP was at that time about 5000 men strong.

Pistols used by the SMP varied widely. Colt supplied the SMP in excess of 3600 Colt 1908 pistols in .380 caliber starting in 1925[(3)]. Many more however ended up in the hands of the SMP although not directly shipped to the SMP and were marked accordingly in China. Only 12 Colt Vest Pocket pistols were shipped to the SMP in 1929. Colt 1911 pistols were also shipped to the SMP but found to be too large for the smaller Asian hands. SMP pistols were marked extensively, cartridges were also marked as were the bullets. The bullets were marked for identification after a shootout, the cases to deter theft. All ammunition was marked by the manufacturer.

---

(1) Starting in 1919 German, French, Belgian, Italian, American and Swiss arms dealers descended on Shanghai peddling surplus World War I materiel. Many operated independently, while others associated themselves with local organized crime.

(2) Later in the 1930s, the Japanese gendarmerie took much control over the Chinese police. In the 1930s the SMP appeased the Japanese. Before World War II there was cooperation between the Japanese gendarmerie and the SMP.

(3) The Colt Pocket Hammerless Automatic Pistols by John W. Brunner

Colt pistols were either ordered with special features or were converted later on to include special features. Most notable is the lanyard ring and magazines with viewing holes. The latter was done to discourage police officers from selling their cartridges and loading their magazines with spent practice cases.

It is not known how extensively FN supplied the SMP. No Model 1910 or 1922 pistols have surfaced with SMP markings. It is known however that the SMP ordered an unknown number of FN vest pocket pistols. These were shipped in the 1930s and were not subject to special modifications (e.g., lanyard rings or magazine viewing holes).

A FN 1900 (N° 608619) did exist with SMP markings[(1)]. The same source also listed that 56 Belgian pistols were in SMP inventory by 1915[(2)].

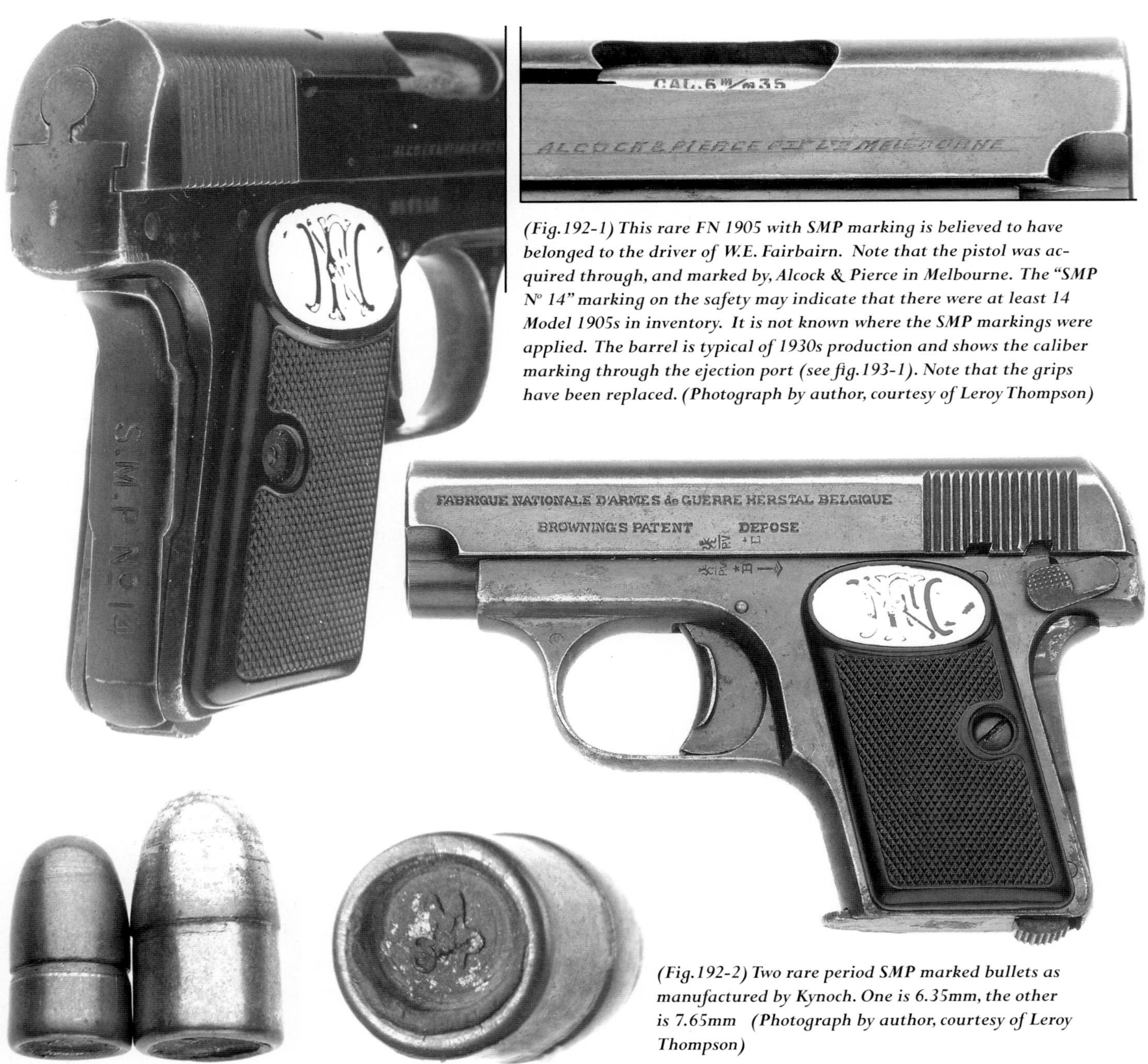

(Fig.192-1) This rare FN 1905 with SMP marking is believed to have belonged to the driver of W.E. Fairbairn. Note that the pistol was acquired through, and marked by, Alcock & Pierce in Melbourne. The "SMP N° 14" marking on the safety may indicate that there were at least 14 Model 1905s in inventory. It is not known where the SMP markings were applied. The barrel is typical of 1930s production and shows the caliber marking through the ejection port (see fig.193-1). Note that the grips have been replaced. (Photograph by author, courtesy of Leroy Thompson)

(Fig.192-2) Two rare period SMP marked bullets as manufactured by Kynoch. One is 6.35mm, the other is 7.65mm (Photograph by author, courtesy of Leroy Thompson)

(1) Author's correspondence with Leroy Thompson

(2) The Legend of W.E. Fairbairn, Gentleman and Warrior: The Shanghai Years by Peter Robbins

1940: Early German Occupation Production

A Small amount of Model 1905 pistols were completed at the factory in 1940 early on in the German occupation (see also Model 1910 on page 211 and High Power on page 292). This work was performed from July to August 1940 before the arrival of the first weapons inspector (WaA613 code). These pistols usually were in the final stages of assembly and have pre-invasion applied Belgian proofs. One characteristic of these pistols is that they feature synthetic grips instead of the prewar horn grips. This is due to the fact that horn was unavailable during the war. Unlike other wartime assembled and produced pistols, the wartime assembled Model 1905 pistols were logged in warehouse logs. All pistols were shipped to FN's prewar agent Fusi in Milan, ultimately these pistols were shipped to Japan and used by Japanese officers. It is not known if Fusi had an outstanding order from Japan. It is the only known FN agent to place an order and receive merchandise during the occupation.

The pistols feature prewar characteristics, the use of black synthetic grips alone is not a positive indicator of wartime assembly.

The following Model 1905 pistols were shipped from FN to Fusi during the occupation. This list only reflects a cross section of the occupation shipments to Fusi on September 16, 1940.
1083849, 1083951, 1083982, 1083985, 1083986, 1083988, 1083989, 1084007, 1084009, 1084038, 1084059, among others

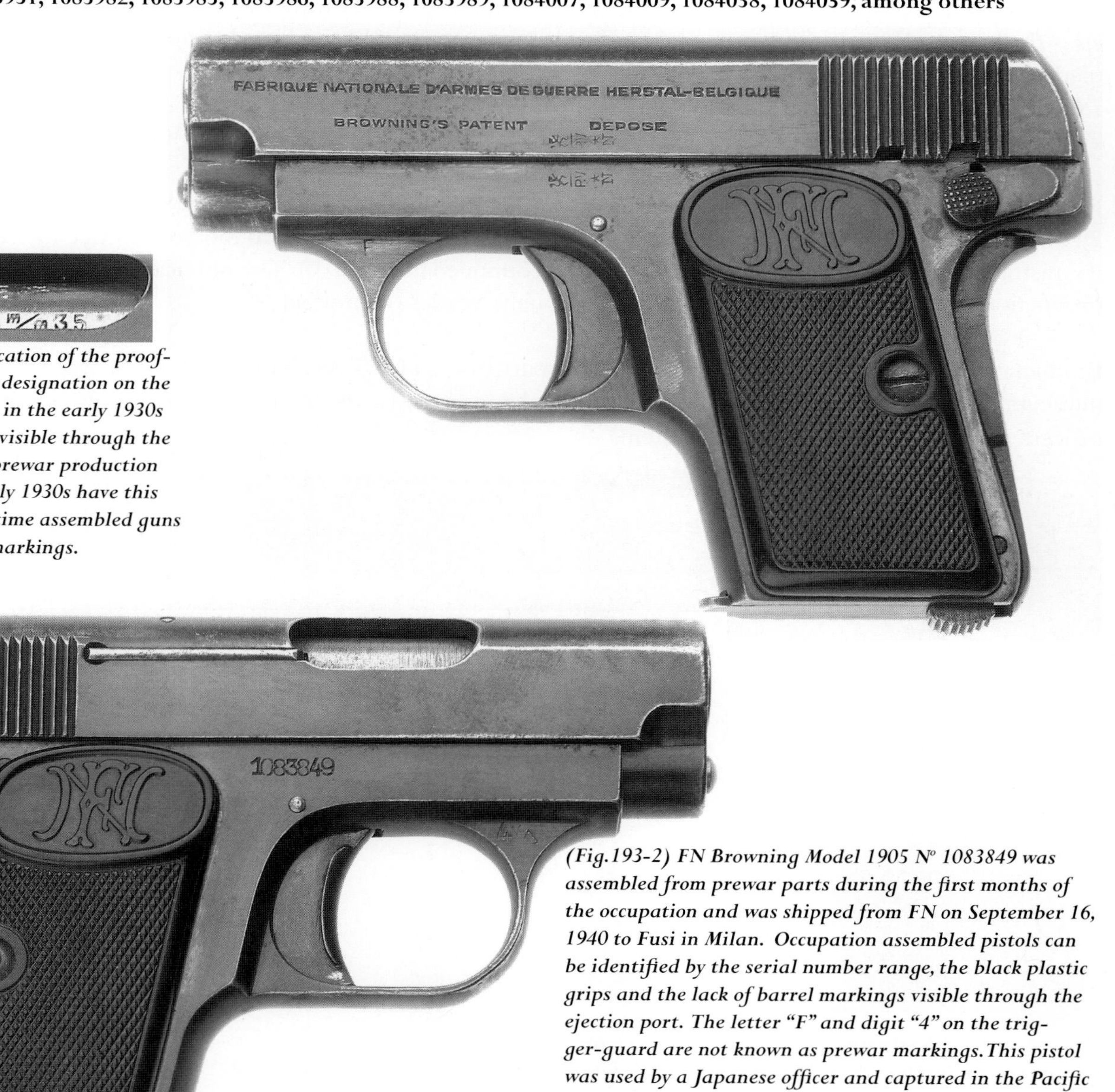

(Fig.193-1) The location of the proofmarks and caliber designation on the barrel were moved in the early 1930s so that these were visible through the ejection port. All prewar production starting in the early 1930s have this feature. Some wartime assembled guns lack these barrel markings.

(Fig.193-2) FN Browning Model 1905 N° 1083849 was assembled from prewar parts during the first months of the occupation and was shipped from FN on September 16, 1940 to Fusi in Milan. Occupation assembled pistols can be identified by the serial number range, the black plastic grips and the lack of barrel markings visible through the ejection port. The letter "F" and digit "4" on the trigger-guard are not known as prewar markings. This pistol was used by a Japanese officer and captured in the Pacific Theatre. (Photographs by author, courtesy of Harold Anderson)

The FN Browning Model 1910

Development History

The FN Browning 1910 pistol was based on John Browning's design of 1908 and was patented in Belgium on February 20, 1909. Production started in 1912.

Model 1910 sales mirrored those of the 1900 model. Its compact size resulted in broad appeal throughout FN's sales market. Originally known as "Le Nouveau Modèle" (The New Model), it was renamed the "Model 1910" following World War I.

To promote the new pistol, FN's advertising quickly changed its focus from the Model 1900 to the Model 1910. As a result of this abrupt change, many collectors are under the misconception that Model 1900 production ceased in 1912. This is incorrect; the Model 1900 remained in production until World War I as a result of Belgian military orders and was renamed "Le Vieux Modèle" (The Old Model).

The Model 1910 had a sleek, modern design that lent itself to multi-caliber production (7.65x17mm /.32 ACP and 9x17mm /.380 ACP) without manufacturing modifications. The only difference between 7.65mm and 9mm models is the barrel. A quick change of the barrel will convert a pistol from one caliber to the other. Magazines were marked with a specific caliber, but any magazine will function in either caliber pistol as the only difference between 7.65mm and 9mm magazines is the number and placement of cartridge view holes. Although it was common knowledge that all parts were interchangeable, FN never offered the pistol as a kit with both barrels.

Pistols manufactured during the first months of production were assembled with FN 1910 pistol logo grips (fig.196-2). For the first year of production the slide had a distinguishing long curve at the bottom (see fig.194-2). Both the pistol logo grips and early slide variant were discontinued in late 1913. The physical characteristics of the 1914 production pistol remained almost unchanged through decades of production.

Production was halted due to the German invasion in 1914, and as a result the Model 1910 was used in limited numbers in World War I. Some stocks of completed guns were confiscated by German forces in 1914 and sold to officers through the German arsenal system.

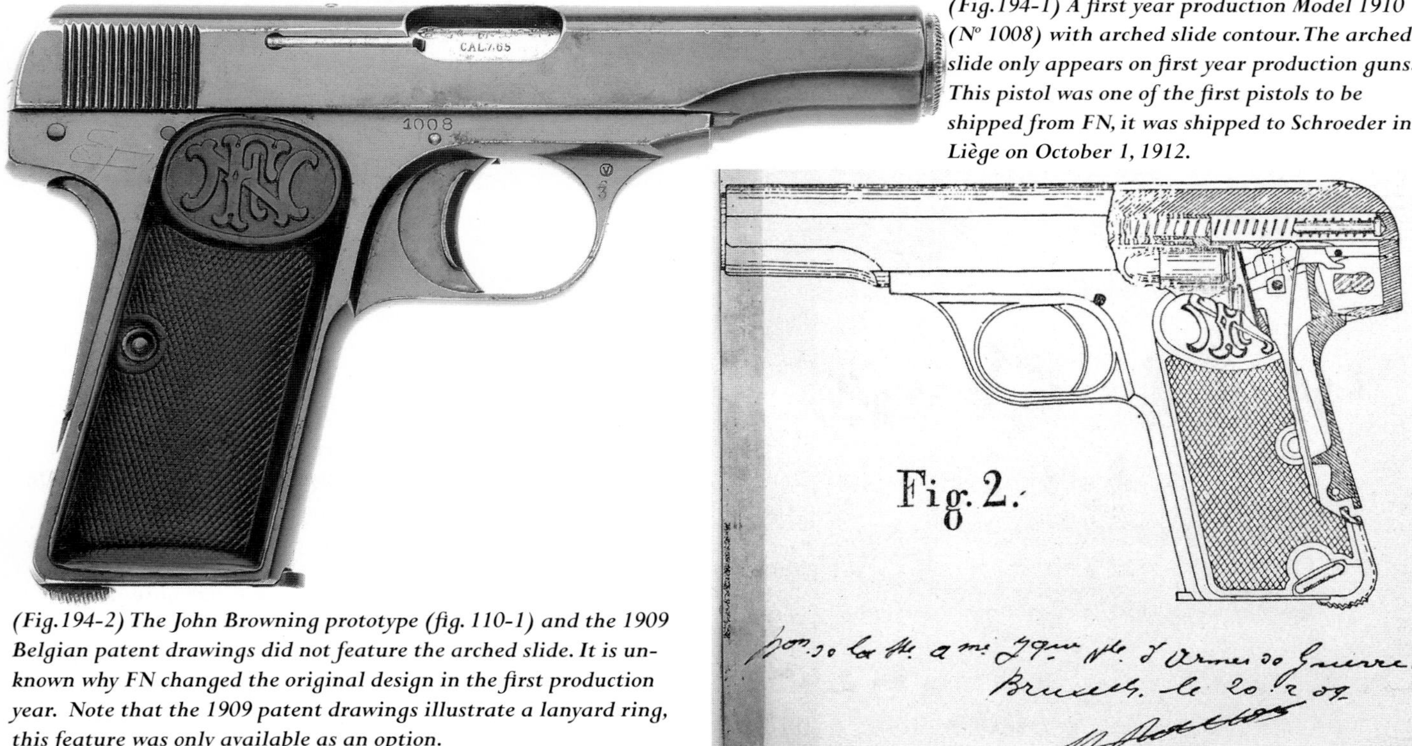

(Fig.194-1) A first year production Model 1910 (N° 1008) with arched slide contour. The arched slide only appears on first year production guns. This pistol was one of the first pistols to be shipped from FN, it was shipped to Schroeder in Liège on October 1, 1912.

(Fig.194-2) The John Browning prototype (fig. 110-1) and the 1909 Belgian patent drawings did not feature the arched slide. It is unknown why FN changed the original design in the first production year. Note that the 1909 patent drawings illustrate a lanyard ring, this feature was only available as an option.

Production was resumed after the war, in 1919. Assigned serial numbers followed prewar numbers sequentially. FN ceased manufacturing the Model 1900. As a result, the Belgian military adopted the FN Browning 1910 as its standard sidearm.

Export military sales of the Model 1910 declined in the 1920s with the introduction of the Model 1922. Model 1910 sales in the 1920s and 1930s focused on the commercial market, police organizations, and the Belgian military.

Model 1910 production halted during the Nazi occupation. While some small quantity assembly took place during the first months of the occupation in 1940. Production resumed after the liberation of the plant. The first post-liberation Model 1910 pistols were assembled with leftover wartime Model 1922 parts. By 1946, some 30,000 pistols had been sold to French police agencies and several hundred pistols had been sold to American soldiers. Those post-liberation pistols featured an "A" prefix serial number like the Model 1922 (see page 250).

After World War II, FN shipped the Model 1910 with plastic or wood grips instead of the prewar horn grips. The magazines were marked differently (see fig.196-2).

The Netherlands became the main customer for the Model 1910 after World War II. In the late 1940s the designation was changed to "Model 10." The Model 10 was discontinued in the early 1970s and replaced by the "Model 110" (see page 319).

FN Model 1910: Features & Specifications

Serial Numbers

Production started in late 1912 and the earliest shipping records date from early October 1912[1].

Between 63,000 and 70,000 pistols were made prior to the German invasion in 1914[2]. No production took place during World War I and pistol serial numbers continued sequentially in 1919, at approximately serial number 70,000. Serial numbers ascended in logical order throughout the interwar era.

By the time the Germans invaded in May of 1940, FN serial numbers had reached 460,000. This number did not include special contract pistols made after 1922[3]. After World War II, FN continued the prewar serial number sequence. Collectors should note that large contract orders were filled after World War II, each with its own contract number range. Postwar pistols with numbers from 1 to approximately 30,000 are contract guns. The last Model 1910 pistol (N° 684653) was shipped from FN in November 1975, at the time it was referred to as a Model 10.

Slide Legends

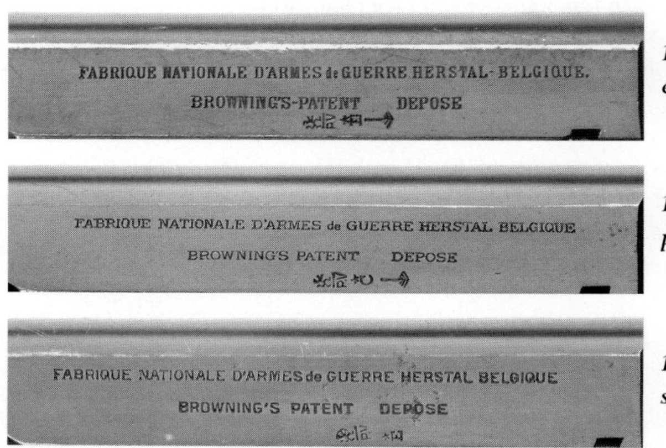

Pre-World War I slide-legend variant with Serif fonts: This variant is observed on early production pistols (1912-1913). Note the lower case "de".

Pre-World War I slide-legend variant with Serif fonts: This variant is observed on pistols produced predominately in the 1913-1914 period. Note the lower case "de".

Post-World War I slide-legend variant with Sans-Serif fonts: This variant is observed on pistols produced in the 1919-1930 period. Note the lower case "de".

(1) Here again we see FN's practice of shipping random numbers: Pistol N° 1008 was shipped on October 1, 1912 while pistols N° 56, 94, 138 were shipped to Fusi on October 22, 1912. Earlier serial numbers like N° 1 were shipped later. Pistols N° 2, 44, 48, 60, 66, 80, 93 were never completed.

(2) There are gaps in the 1914 production serial ranges.

(3) FN started contract numbering circa 1922 after the introduction of the Model 1922 (see also page 220).

1920s slide-legend variant with Serif fonts: This variant is observed on pistols produced predominately in the 1925-1929 period. Note the lower case "de".

1930s slide-legend variant with Sans-Serif fonts: This variant is observed on pistols produced throughout the 1930s. Note the uppercase "DE".

1930s slide-legend variant with Sans-Serif fonts: This variant is observed on pistols produced predominately in the 1935-1940 period. Note the uppercase "DE" and "S.A." (Société Anonyme – Incorporated) nomenclature.

1930s-1950s slide-legend variant with Sans-Serif fonts: This variant is observed on pistols produced predominately in the 1934-1940 and 1946-1950s period. Note the uppercase "DE".

Modern slide-legend variant: This variant is observed on pistols starting in the 1950s. Note the lighter (less deep) markings of the postwar engraving machines.

Grips and Magazines

(Fig.196-2) Grips (see pre/postwar identification aid on page 99-100) - From left to right:
1-Pre-World War II horn grips (many variants exist). These can be identified by their backing (see fig.100-1). 2-Post-World War II plastic - thin mold. Plastic grips can be identified by the backing (see fig.100-1) and by the rim and detail of the FN logo. The rim around the FN logo is usually thinner and more detailed than horn grips. Thick mold plastic grips are less detailed and used in the immediate postwar era (see Model 1922 example on fig.223-1). 3- Post-WWII wood grips exist in either basic style or with fancy checkering (see page 201).

Inset left: A detail view of the rare and early production FN 1910 pistol logo grip, only used in the first months of production. (Photograph courtesy of Ryerson Knight)

(Fig.196-3) Magazine markings (center): 1- The FN logo in oval (top) is characteristic of pre-World War II manufacture. The caliber designation is usually marked under the logo. Some early magazines do not have a logo and caliber marking, others only show the oval logo. 2- Introduced by the Germans during World War II on Model 1922 production, the "-F.N.-" marking became standard on postwar production. The 9mm magazine has five view-holes while the 7.65mm magazine features six view-holes (top right).

Barrel Bushings

(Fig.196-4) A selection of flat as well as rounded barrel bushing variants, both with and without key holes. See fig.203-4 and fig.206-1 for barrel bushing keys.

Specifications Summary

Manufacturer: Fabrique Nationale d'Armes de Guerre
Model known as: Pre-World War I: "Le Nouveau Modèle" (new model) - Post World War I: "Modèle 1910" - Late 1940s: "Model 10"
Period offered: 1910-1914 / 1919-1940 / Few assembled in 1940 during World War II under German occupation / 1945-1975
Caliber: .32 ACP / 7.65x17mm or .380 ACP / 9x17mm
Operating system: Blowback
Length: 153mm (depending on barrel bushing style)
Barrel length: 88mm
Weight: 580 grams (7.65mm) / 570 grams (9mm)
Grips: Animal horn in prewar years / wood or plastic after 1945
Magazine capacity: 7.65mm: seven rounds / 9mm: six rounds
Sights: Fixed, raised sights available on customer request (see fig.206-2)
Options: Lanyard ring
Finish offered: Blue, nickel
Engraving patterns: Six factory types
Production quantity: Total estimated production 704,247 (est. 69,000 total pre-World War I / est. 467,760 total pre-World War II)

FN Model 1910: Accessories

(Fig.197-1) A horizontal 1920s instruction book. Most often encountered in red, this beige example was printed in Liège for FN with the agent's name and address. Many variants in cover details exist. Instruction books were printed in French, Dutch, German, Italian and English.

(Fig.197-2) A 1930s instruction book with red cover. These were printed in a multitude of languages.

(Fig.197-3) A 1930s instruction book with brown cover. These were printed in a multitude of languages.

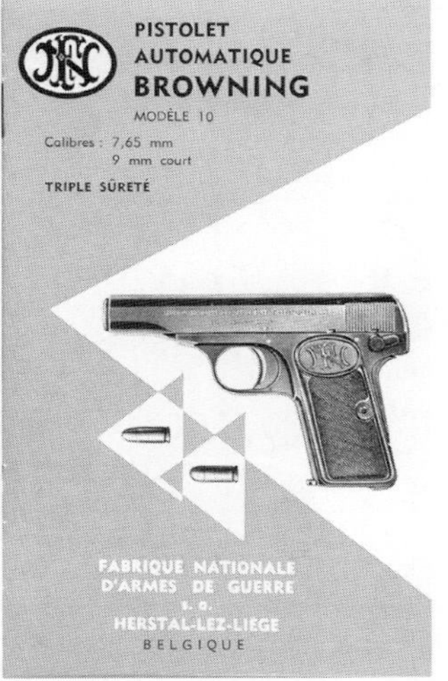

(Fig.197-4) Yellow and white 1950s instruction booklet for the Model 10.

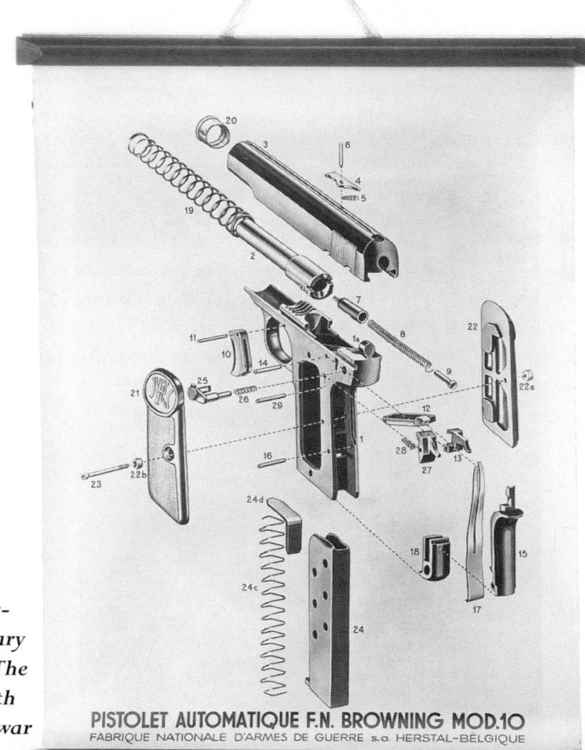

(Fig.197-5) FN offered large class-room instruction posters for military and law-enforcement customers. The posters were made out of linen with wooden slats. Illustrated is a postwar variant.

(1)

(Fig.198-1) clockwise:
1-An early pre-1914 FN hinged cardboard box for the Model 1910 pistol. Note the reference on the added label for "Le Nouveau Modèle". 2- A typical inter-bellum hinged FN logo embossed box, these were made out of dark green cardboard or purple cardboard (rare). Postwar cardboard boxes are light green in color. 3- Postwar two-piece plastic boxes were made out of black, brown, burgundy or white plastic.
4- German aftermarket 4mm conversion kits were an affordable way of practice shooting. These kits were made for a multitude of pistols. Note the Model 1912 nomenclature.

(2)

(4)

(3)

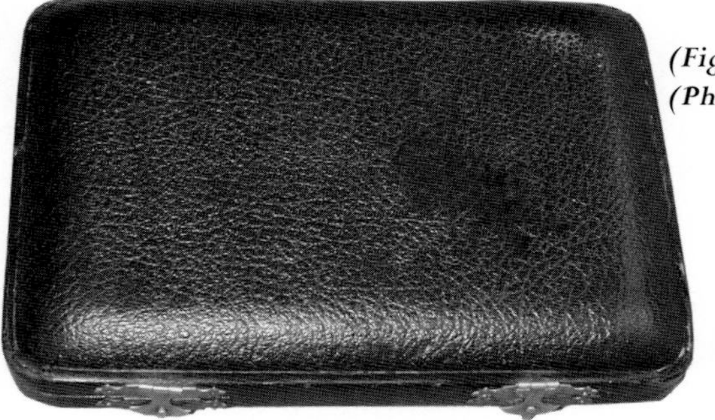

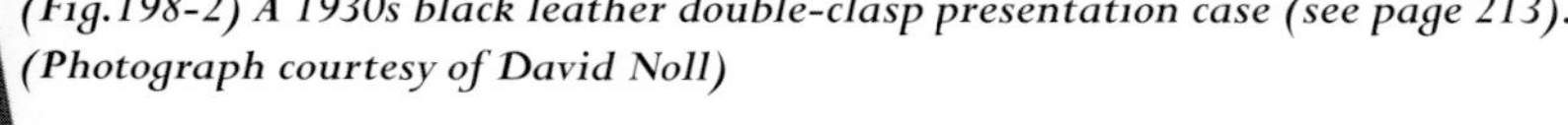

(Fig.198-2) A 1930s black leather double-clasp presentation case (see page 213). (Photograph courtesy of David Noll)

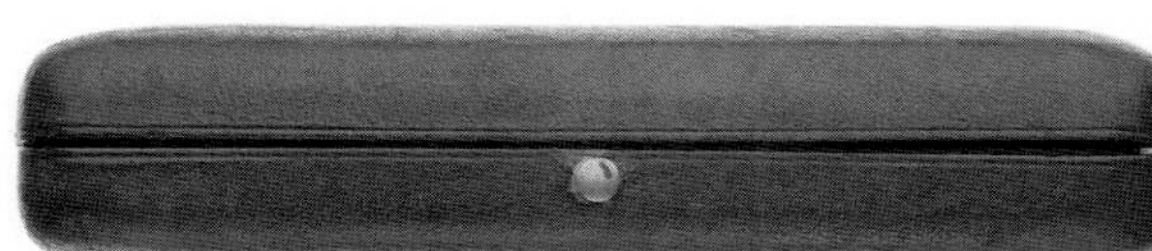

(Fig.198-3) This rare brown leather presentation case is lined with blue satin. The Belgian royal supplier, Edouard Vandenhove in Brussels, made it for FN. Vandenhove made this style case in the 1910s and early 1920s. The case and pistol were donated to John M. Browning (see fig.200-2). Note the push-button closure hardware.

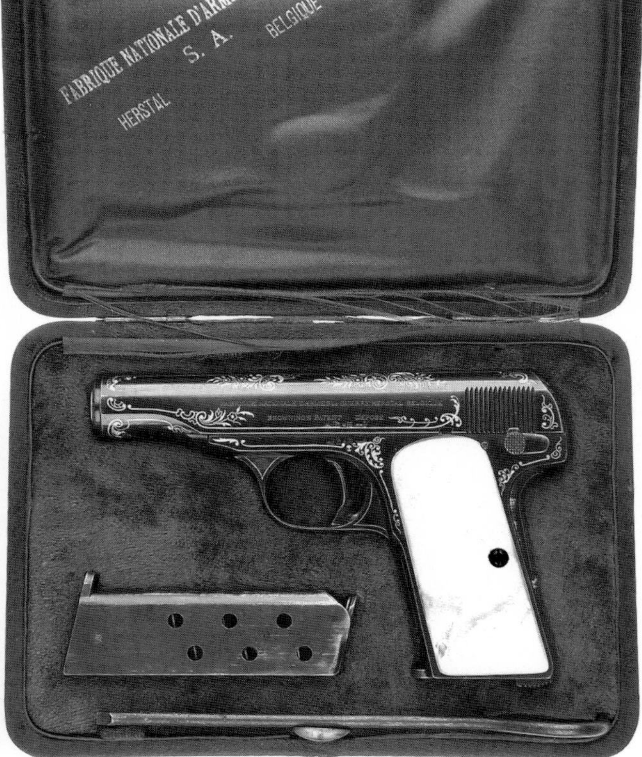

Luxury Models: Nickel Plating and Factory Engraving

The Model 1910 was primarily made for the commercial market (see page 119 for applied dealer markings). Special finishes were introduced almost immediately after 1912. FN offered the pistol in engraved styles as well as a nickel finish prior to 1914[1]. After World War I, FN used the engraving patterns to boost sales in a depressed market. A special high polish finish was introduced circa 1922 and was used on all high-grade commercial guns throughout the 1920s. This finish, which required additional polishing, featured a more attractive high gloss look but was more fragile than FN's standard rust blue finish. The high polish finish features a deep blue color while FN's standard rust bluing has a predominately grayish cast.

Retail catalogs frequently mention the nickel finish but this is rarely discussed in factory literature (see page 99). Factory nickel plating can always be identified by the blue/black finish on the trigger and safety. This reflects the nickel plating's interference with the operation of some close tolerance parts. FN applied only a base primer to these parts and no plating. The blue/black finish on the trigger and safety is not bluing but rather a plating catalyst that is almost black in color and shows some dullness.

Six engraving patterns were offered in the 1920s. It is likely that these were identical to the pre-World War I patterns. Only the bluing differed in the 1920s. FN discontinued the high polish finish in the early 1930s. This change coincides with an increase in military contracts. The engraving patterns remained unchanged, but FN reverted back to its standard rust blue finish.

It is unclear when FN restarted engraving the Model 1910 after World War II. Too few factory engraved pistols are known to exist in order to establish a trend.

Collectors should be cautious when purchasing an engraved pistol. Very few of the pistols in circulation were factory engraved. Many engravers reproduce these old patterns[2] and often these pistols are sold as originals. Buyers should compare the factory blue finish to other original pistols. Although the engraving can be reproduced, most reproductions feature incorrect bluing colors. All patterns presented by the factory were guidelines for the engraver. Each pistol will feature small differences and interpretations of the engraving pattern. Minor pattern deviations should therefore not be used as guidelines to evaluate the originality of an engraving. Factory engraving cannot usually be authenticated through photographic study. The execution of the engraving has to be felt by hand.

Engraved pistols were offered with a variety of grips and upgrades. The basic black horn grips were standard on engraved guns in the pre-World War II era.

Upgrades included ivory and mother-of-pearl. Factory ivory grips are rarely encountered on pistols today as it was an abundant material in the prewar era. Most customers willing to pay for upgrades opted for mother-of-pearl grips. Original ivory or mother-of-pearl factory grips can easily be identified as these are made out of one piece and do not have a separate backing material that fits in the frame (see fig.200-3).

The engraving styles were available on blue guns or optionally on nickel plated guns.

In the postwar era, grips were usually limited to fancy checkered wooden grips or later synthetics resembling mother-of-pearl.

(Fig.198-3) This early factory nickel pistol N° 53509 was shipped to Genshow, Berlin on February 12, 1914. Note the typical black safety and trigger.

(1) FN continued to market the engraved FN 1900 models in their Luxury catalog in 1913-1914. Examples of the pre-1914 engraving types for the Model 1910 are rare.

(2) The author opts not to illustrate complete patterns in order to discourage reproductions.

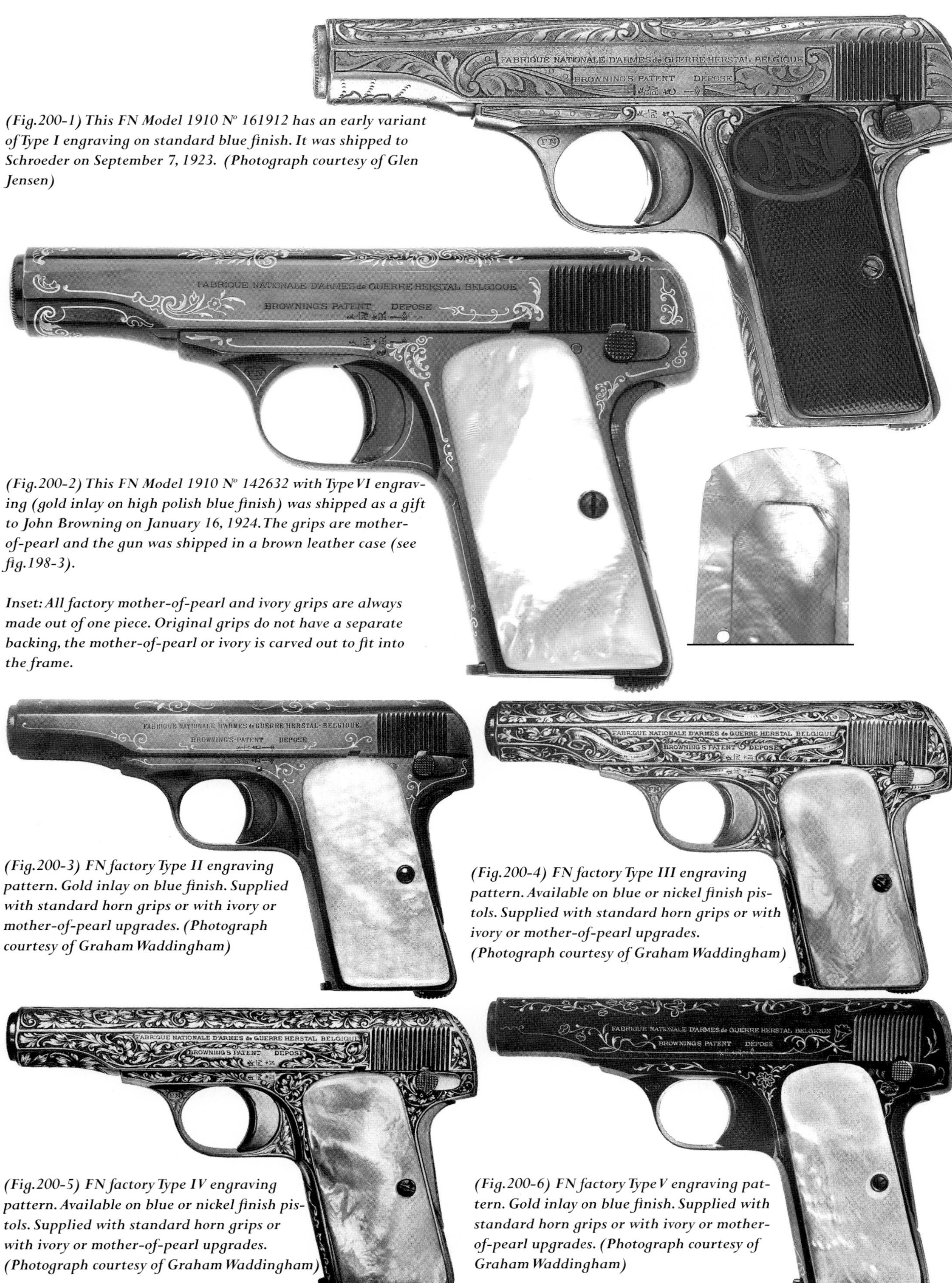

(Fig.200-1) This FN Model 1910 N° 161912 has an early variant of Type I engraving on standard blue finish. It was shipped to Schroeder on September 7, 1923. (Photograph courtesy of Glen Jensen)

(Fig.200-2) This FN Model 1910 N° 142632 with Type VI engraving (gold inlay on high polish blue finish) was shipped as a gift to John Browning on January 16, 1924. The grips are mother-of-pearl and the gun was shipped in a brown leather case (see fig.198-3).

Inset: All factory mother-of-pearl and ivory grips are always made out of one piece. Original grips do not have a separate backing, the mother-of-pearl or ivory is carved out to fit into the frame.

(Fig.200-3) FN factory Type II engraving pattern. Gold inlay on blue finish. Supplied with standard horn grips or with ivory or mother-of-pearl upgrades. (Photograph courtesy of Graham Waddingham)

(Fig.200-4) FN factory Type III engraving pattern. Available on blue or nickel finish pistols. Supplied with standard horn grips or with ivory or mother-of-pearl upgrades. (Photograph courtesy of Graham Waddingham)

(Fig.200-5) FN factory Type IV engraving pattern. Available on blue or nickel finish pistols. Supplied with standard horn grips or with ivory or mother-of-pearl upgrades. (Photograph courtesy of Graham Waddingham)

(Fig.200-6) FN factory Type V engraving pattern. Gold inlay on blue finish. Supplied with standard horn grips or with ivory or mother-of-pearl upgrades. (Photograph courtesy of Graham Waddingham)

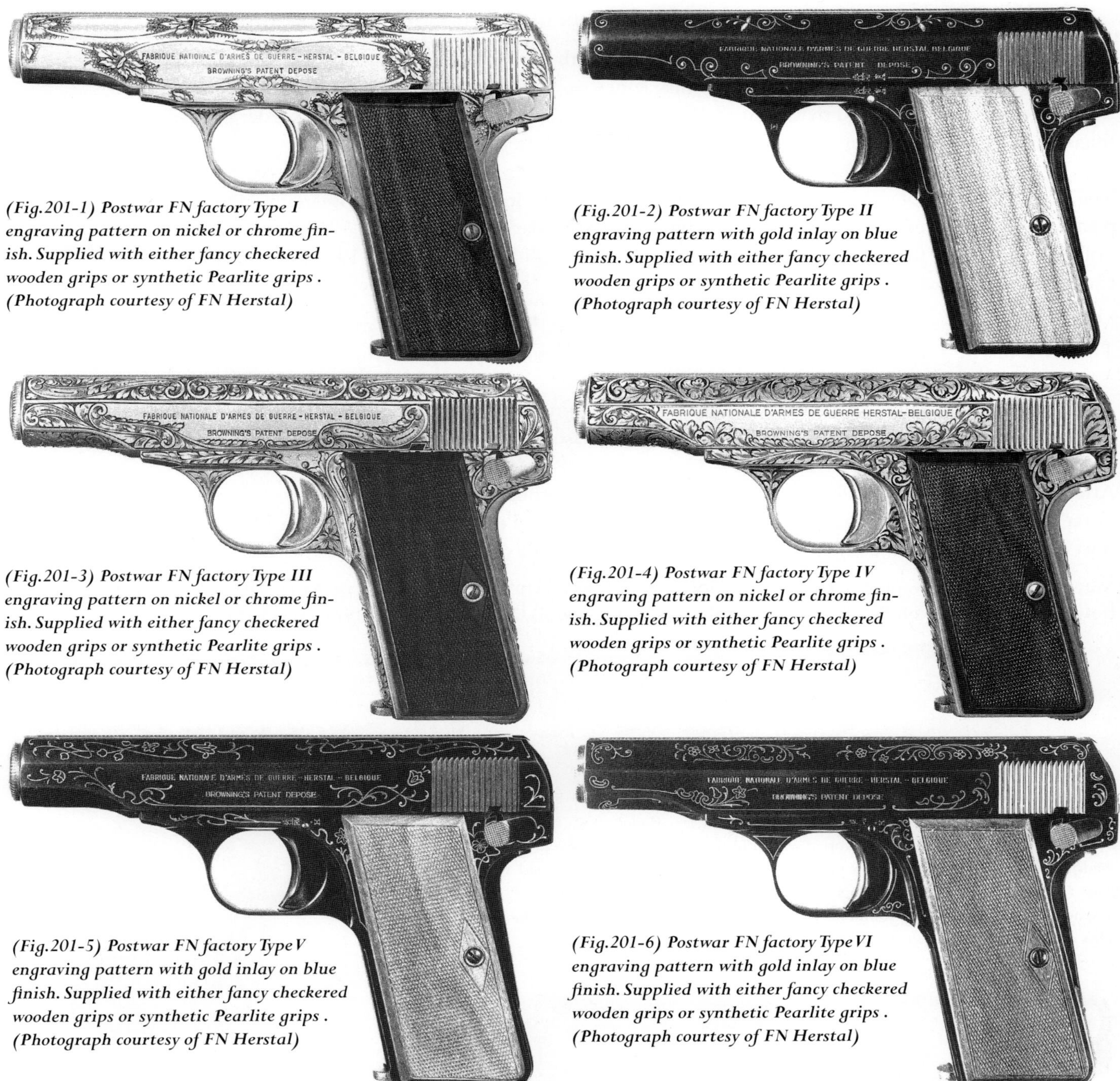

(Fig.201-1) Postwar FN factory Type I engraving pattern on nickel or chrome finish. Supplied with either fancy checkered wooden grips or synthetic Pearlite grips . (Photograph courtesy of FN Herstal)

(Fig.201-2) Postwar FN factory Type II engraving pattern with gold inlay on blue finish. Supplied with either fancy checkered wooden grips or synthetic Pearlite grips . (Photograph courtesy of FN Herstal)

(Fig.201-3) Postwar FN factory Type III engraving pattern on nickel or chrome finish. Supplied with either fancy checkered wooden grips or synthetic Pearlite grips . (Photograph courtesy of FN Herstal)

(Fig.201-4) Postwar FN factory Type IV engraving pattern on nickel or chrome finish. Supplied with either fancy checkered wooden grips or synthetic Pearlite grips . (Photograph courtesy of FN Herstal)

(Fig.201-5) Postwar FN factory Type V engraving pattern with gold inlay on blue finish. Supplied with either fancy checkered wooden grips or synthetic Pearlite grips . (Photograph courtesy of FN Herstal)

(Fig.201-6) Postwar FN factory Type VI engraving pattern with gold inlay on blue finish. Supplied with either fancy checkered wooden grips or synthetic Pearlite grips . (Photograph courtesy of FN Herstal)

The FN Browning 1910 Pistols in Belgian Service

After World War I, FN did not resume Model 1900 pistol production. This decision forced the Belgian military to adopt the newer Model 1910, which was accepted for service without any modifications. The first Belgian military order for the Model 1910 pistol was shipped in 1919, the year FN resumed production.

The new Model 1910 pistols replaced Model 1900 pistols that had been lost during the war. The surviving Model 1900 pistols remained in service and were used concurrently with the Model 1910 through the 1930s. The last sizeable order of Model 1910's for the Belgian military was shipped in 1933. By the mid-1930s, plans were in place to supersede all FN Browning 1900, 1910 and Colt 1903 pistols with the FN High Power. Select soldiers and NCOs who used pistols in the Belgian military were the first to receive the High Power. This exchange program was still in progress at the time of the German invasion in May 1940. Many officers went to war in 1940 still equipped with the FN Browning 1900, 1910 and Colt 1903. The Belgian military did not accept the Model 1922 until after the Allied liberation of Belgium in 1944 (see page 252).

The FN Browning 1910 Pistols in Belgian Service (continued)

Most of the accessories for the Model 1900 were used with the Model 1910. Holsters, cleaning kits and ammunition were common. As Model 1910 magazines were not compatible with those of the Model 1900, the Belgian military requested that all Model 1910 magazines be marked with "1910" in order to easily distinguish them from the older Model 1900 magazines.

The Model 1910 pistol was also purchased by municipal police forces throughout Belgium. Many of these pistols were purchased in small quantities and many were unmarked. The Model 1910 pistol remained in police service up to the German occupation in 1940. No High Power or Model 1922 pistols were purchased for municipal police use in the prewar era.

Many of the Belgian military pistols were refurbished in the 1930s. As a result, many encountered today are refinished. The work was performed to factory standards, and it is difficult to distinguish the refinished pistols from originals.

Model 1910 pistols were used by Belgian military advisors in Abyssinia before the Italian invasion in 1935. Belgian officers training Ethiopian troops recommended the purchase of FN equipment to the Ethiopian government.

After World War I, the Model 1910 was also used by white officers in the Belgian Congo's military organization, the Force Publique. After November 1940, Belgian officers of the Force Publique used their Model 1910 pistols in support of British troops in combat in Ethiopia (1941) and Nigeria (1942-1943)

Noted serial numbers on Belgian military pistols: 72921, 73688, 74197, 74271,77203, 77848, 79011, 82691, 294147, 294378, 430651
Noted serial numbers on Belgian police pistols: 144152 (Courtrai), 228281 (Mons), 291978 (Verviers)

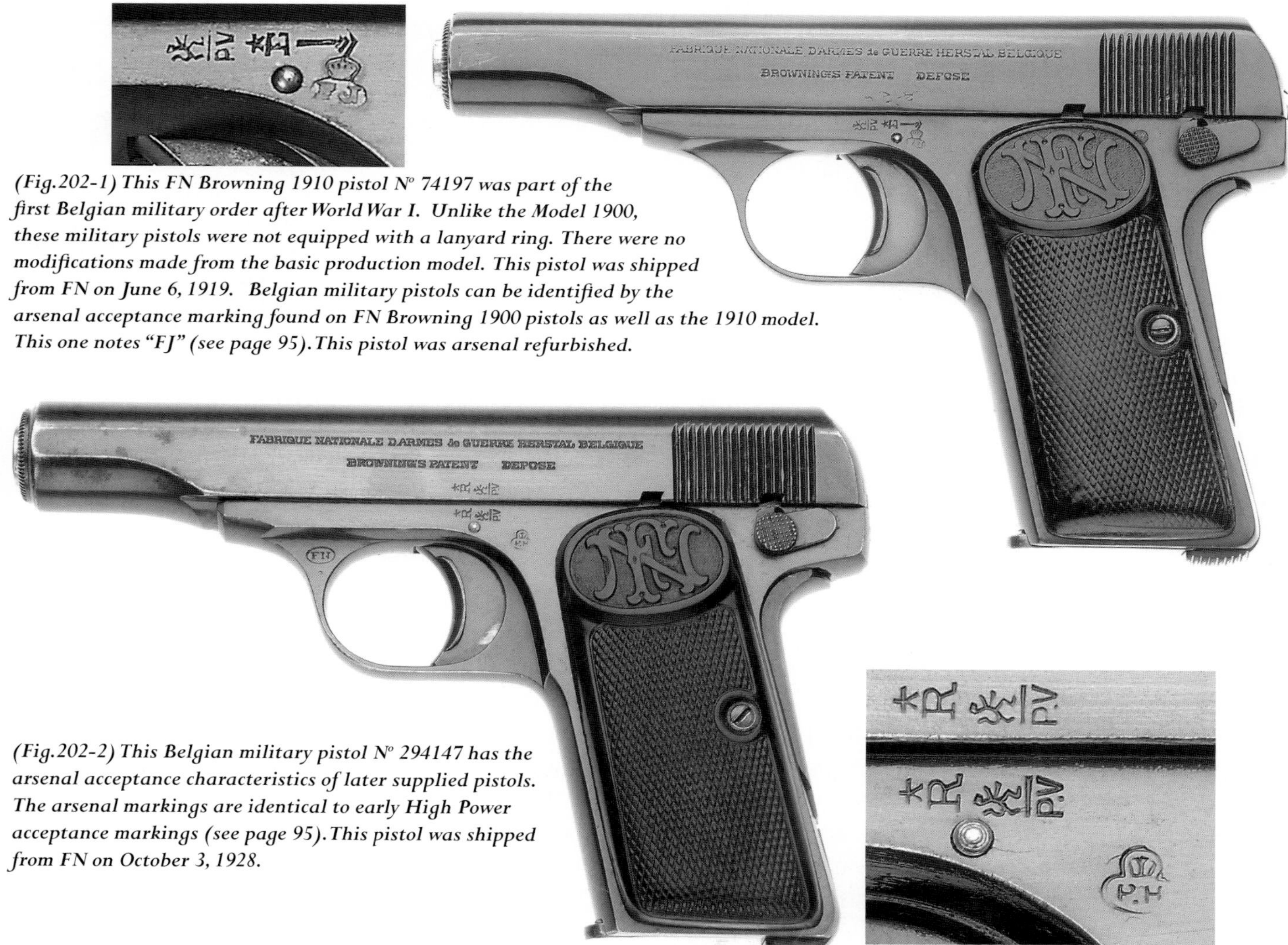

(Fig.202-1) This FN Browning 1910 pistol N° 74197 was part of the first Belgian military order after World War I. Unlike the Model 1900, these military pistols were not equipped with a lanyard ring. There were no modifications made from the basic production model. This pistol was shipped from FN on June 6, 1919. Belgian military pistols can be identified by the arsenal acceptance marking found on FN Browning 1900 pistols as well as the 1910 model. This one notes "FJ" (see page 95). This pistol was arsenal refurbished.

(Fig.202-2) This Belgian military pistol N° 294147 has the arsenal acceptance characteristics of later supplied pistols. The arsenal markings are identical to early High Power acceptance markings (see page 95). This pistol was shipped from FN on October 3, 1928.

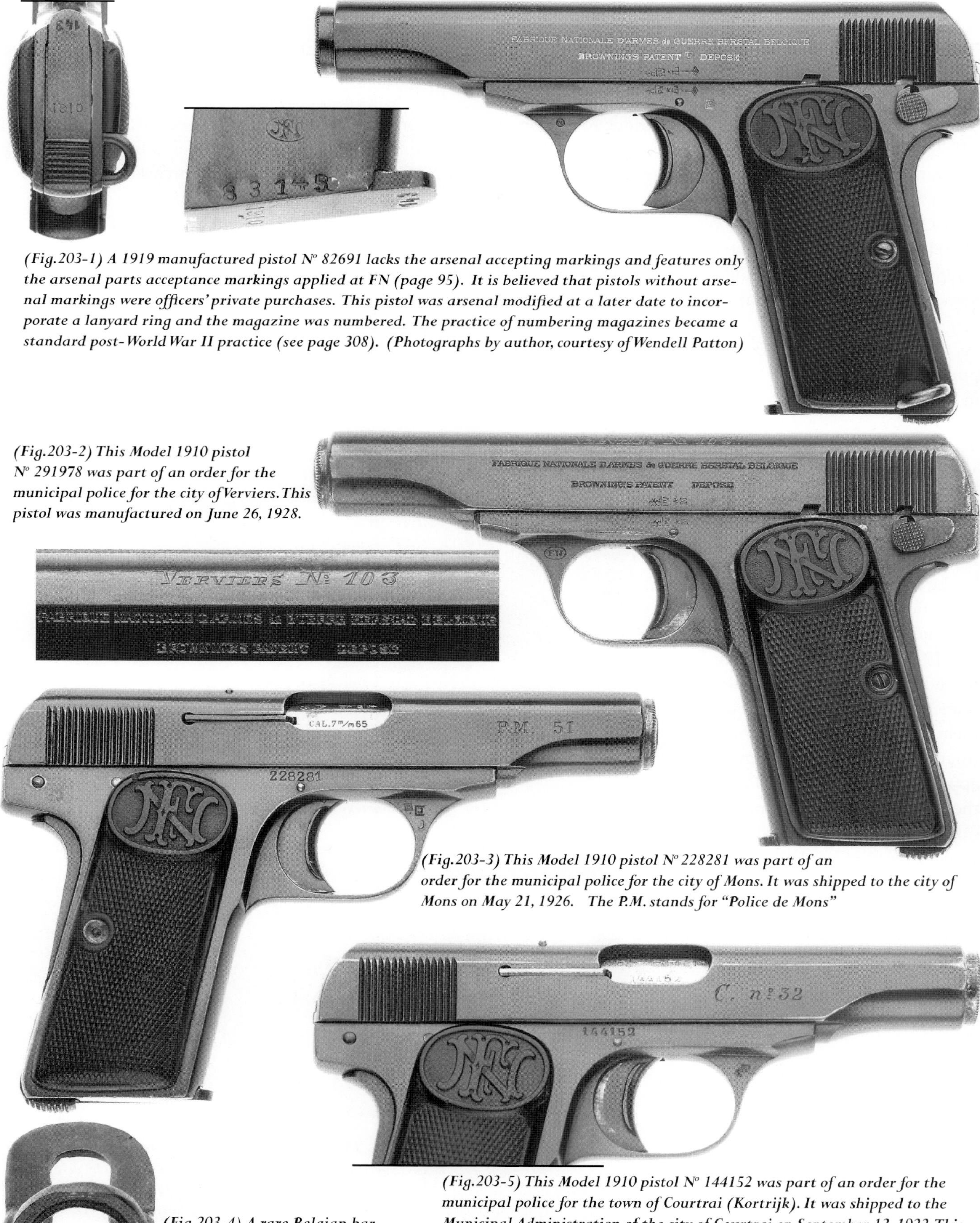

(Fig.203-1) A 1919 manufactured pistol N° 82691 lacks the arsenal accepting markings and features only the arsenal parts acceptance markings applied at FN (page 95). It is believed that pistols without arsenal markings were officers' private purchases. This pistol was arsenal modified at a later date to incorporate a lanyard ring and the magazine was numbered. The practice of numbering magazines became a standard post-World War II practice (see page 308). (Photographs by author, courtesy of Wendell Patton)

(Fig.203-2) This Model 1910 pistol N° 291978 was part of an order for the municipal police for the city of Verviers. This pistol was manufactured on June 26, 1928.

(Fig.203-3) This Model 1910 pistol N° 228281 was part of an order for the municipal police for the city of Mons. It was shipped to the city of Mons on May 21, 1926. The P.M. stands for "Police de Mons"

(Fig.203-4) A rare Belgian barrel-bushing key. The construction suggests arsenal manufacture.

(Fig.203-5) This Model 1910 pistol N° 144152 was part of an order for the municipal police for the town of Courtrai (Kortrijk). It was shipped to the Municipal Administration of the city of Courtrai on September 13, 1922. This order consisted of an estimated 40 pistols. The pistols were factory engraved with the "C" for Courtrai and the pistol issue number.

The FN Browning 1910 in The Netherlands and Dutch Colonies

The Dutch initially inquired about the Model 1910 pistol in 1914 as part of a plan to replace the revolvers used by the "Koninklijke Marechaussee" (Royal Military Constabulary).

The Dutch determined the 7.65mm cartridge to be underpowered for "Koninklijke Marechaussee" use (compare with M25 No.1 pistol on page 228-229). As a result, the Model 1910 pistol in .380 caliber was tested and found suitable. A quote for 950 to 1000 pistols was requested, but the outbreak of World War I put a halt to all purchases.

By 1925, the Dutch decided to purchase the Model 1922 for law enforcement and later for the military. The Model 1910 became an affordable alternative for smaller government agencies, like the "Departement van Financien" (Department of Finances) and the "Nederlandsche Bank" (Dutch National Bank). The Model 1910 was also used in some cities by the "Gemeente Politie" (municipal police).

As tensions rose in the 1930s more Model 1910 pistols were purchased by these smaller agencies. The National Bank purchased both Model 1910 and 1922 pistols. One hundred Model 1910 pistols were purchased by the National Bank in November 1934.

The "Departement van Financien" purchased 600 Model 1910 pistols in 1936. The Dutch Navy also adopted the Model 1910 in 1937.

Model 1905 and 1910 pistols were purchased by the government of the Dutch Antilles. These pistols were used by the municipal police, the Department of Justice as well as the Department of Colonies. Pistols shipped between 1946 and 1947 display the Wilhelmina crest on the side of the slide. The Dutch ordered numerous pistols for various departments including the Gemeente Politie (municipal police), various ministries and approved factory security. Pistols show the Wilhelmina crest, but markings do not necessarily reveal the department where they were used.

(Fig.204-1) This 1946-1948 era supplied pistol with issue number 0000 is believed to be a factory sample to illustrate the Wilhelmina marking, the pistol has no serial / contract number or barrel proofs. Pistols ordered by Holland were marked like this sample gun. (Photograph courtesy of Vincent Cozijn)

Model 1910 pistols exhibiting the Juliana crest were most often refurbished Wilhelmina pistols, either a new slide with Juliana crest was fitted over an existing frame or the Wilhelmina crest was removed and the Juliana crest was applied.

(Fig.204-2) A post 1948 reworked Model 1910 pistol. This specific pistol was turned into a Model 110 by using an older 1910 frame with a modern Juliana marked 110 slide. (Photograph courtesy of Vincent Cozijn)

In service of the Dutch Navy: "Pistool Automatisch No.4 & No.5"

One of the more interesting of the Dutch purchases was the acquisition of the Model 1910 by the Dutch Navy. The Dutch military was run by several departments, each making their own purchases and giving specific designations to small arms. This has led to much confusion among collectors. The Dutch Navy used about 40 Luger pistols (Pistool Automatisch No.1) after 1918. Twelve pistols were confiscated from a stranded German Submarine (UC-8). Twenty-eight Luger pistols were purchased, and consequently all 40 pistols were issued to naval aircrews.

In 1922, the Luger pistols were replaced by 80 FN Model 1903 pistols. This pistol was designated "Pistool Automatisch No.2" (Automatic Pistol No.2). In 1928 the Luger (Automatisch Pistool No.1) was adopted as the standard navy sidearm. This time the pistol was issued to commissioned, non-commissioned officers and members of the Naval Air Service. The Model 1903 remained in service but only with pilots and observers. In 1933 a third pistol, the Sauer Model 1930, was adopted. The Sauer was to be used by officers only as a self-defense weapon while on ship, Lugers and other small arms were locked on ship. The Sauer received the designation "Pistool Automatisch No.3.'

The Dutch Navy decided to purchase the FN Browning 1910 in 1937 because it was unable to acquire additional Sauers. The Navy purchased the "Pistool Automatisch No.4" (Automatic Pistol No.4, in 7.65mm) between 1937 and 1940. The FN 1910 pistol was acquired in 7.65mm to compliment the existing 870 Sauer pistols in that same caliber. After the war the navy adopted the same Model 1910 pistol in 9mm and designated it "Pistool Automatisch No.5."

The quantities of pistols purchased were limited. Commissioned officers were the only armed men on ship out of for fear of mutiny. Model 1910 pistols were initially purchased for those officers. However, in October 1939, policy changes were implemented and non-commissioned officers were also issued pistols for shipboard use.

The FN 1910 contract numbers started with number 1 in 1937 and ascended through the orders.
Orders for the Dutch Navy Model 1910 pistol included:

1937:	**60 pistols**
1938:	**150 pistols**
1939:	**100 pistols**
1940:	**100 pistols (January 16, 1940 order: Most likely this small order was delivered before the German invasion.)**

Observed pistol numbers:
61, 93, 166, 287

(Fig.205-1) The Dutch and French Navy purchases of the 1930s were the first to be factory finished with black enamel. The Dutch Navy property mark is found on the rear of the pistol. Characteristically this is the place for the accepting inspector marking. In this case, it is marked with the anchor and crown, designating naval issue. The "J" marking on the trigger-guard is the acceptance marking of the Dutch accepting officer; Lt. Janssen (see fig.232-3). This is not a reference to Queen Juliana. The contract number "166" is marked on the frame, slide and on the barrel.

The Dutch Ministry of Finance Contract

The "Departement van Financien" (Department of Finances) placed an order in January 1936 for 600 7.65mm pistols. The pistols were marked with the year of issue, FN slide-markings, serial number and contract number. Unlike standard production, these pistols were built with a lanyard ring and raised sights. The contract serialization began with 501, to complement pistols already in inventory. A subsequent order for 400 pistols followed in November 1937. The contract numbers continued at 1101 and the pistols were marked "1938" for their delivery date. The Dutch requested the elimination of the FN production serial number with the second contract. The contract number was now marked on the frame and slide. This was not the case with the first contract, which had standard FN production serial numbers with a separate contract number. These pistols were used by plain-clothes duty inspectors as well as Dutch customs.

After the first order was received, the D.v.F. ordered 625 barrel bushing keys in August 1936. Additionally 400 keys were ordered simultaneously with the second pistol order in 1937. In total 1025 keys were supplied to the D.v.F.

After the war, the D.v.F. adopted the Model 1922. These pistols were accepted like all military pistols.

Prewar Model 1910 pistols reported or observed:
393435 D.v.F. 1936 N° 635
393512 D.v.F. 1936 N° 712
393660 D.v.F. 1936 N° 860
393808 D.v.F. 1936 N° 1009
393852 D.v.F. 1936 N° 1052
1368 D.v.F. 1938 N° 1368

Postwar Model 1922 pistols reported:
A85561 D.v.F. N° 85561 slide is marked with Wilhelmina crest
A85724 D.v.F. N° 85724 slide is marked with Wilhelmina crest
A85994 D.v.F. N° 85994 slide is marked with Wilhelmina crest
A86065 D.v.F. N° 86065 slide is marked with Wilhelmina crest
A108854 D.v.F. N° 108854
A111430 D.v.F. N° 111430
A111436 D.v.F. N° 111436

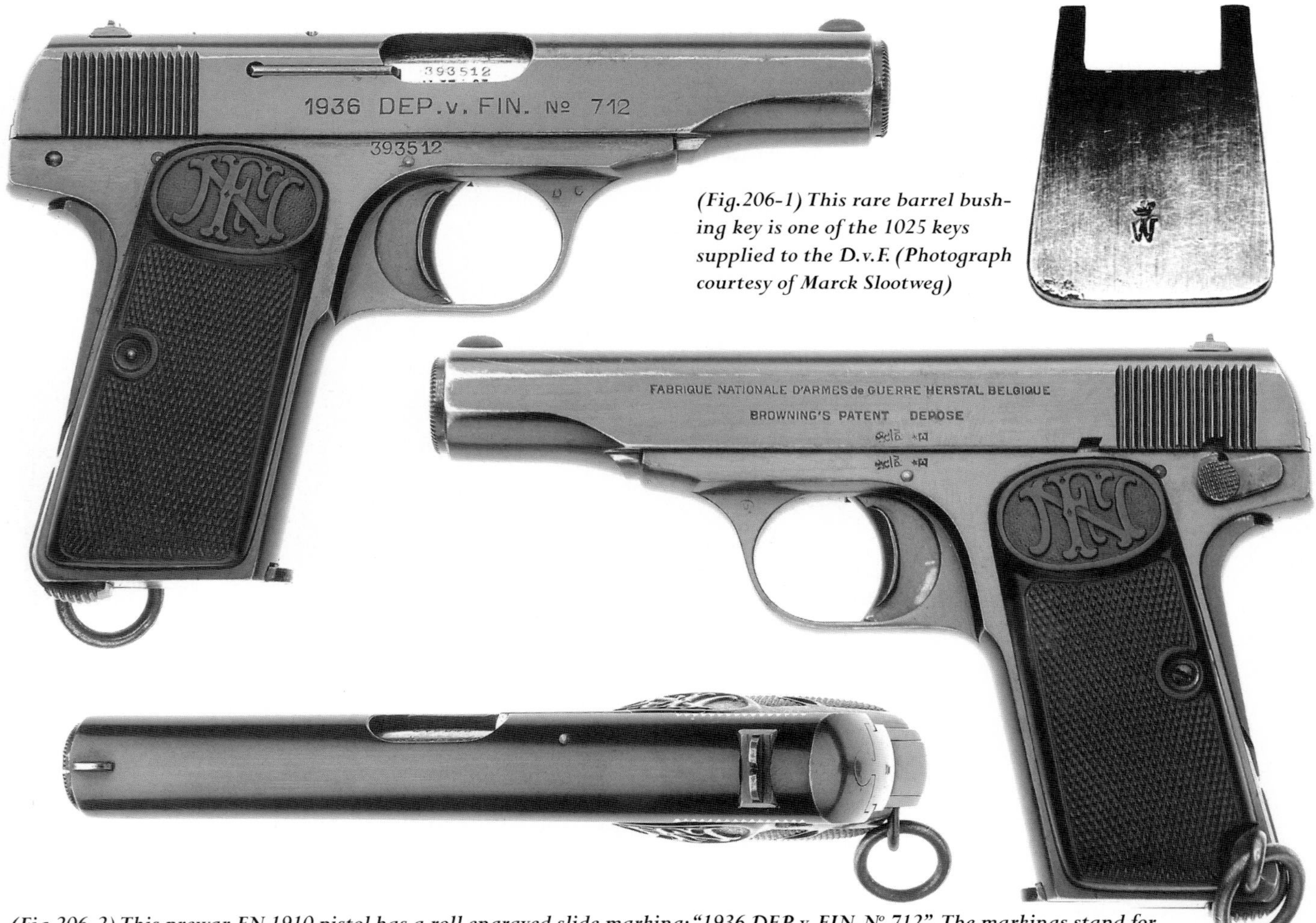

(Fig.206-1) This rare barrel bushing key is one of the 1025 keys supplied to the D.v.F. (Photograph courtesy of Marck Slootweg)

(Fig.206-2) This prewar FN 1910 pistol has a roll engraved slide marking: "1936 DEP. v. FIN. N° 712". The markings stand for the year of issue followed by Departement van Financien (Department- Ministry of Finances) and the contract number. The serial number 393512 is visibly marked on the barrel. This model is in 7.65mm and was manufactured in the same year as marked. Note the specific raised sights requested by the Dutch for this contract. Note also the lanyard ring.

French & Syrian Police Orders

The Parisian Police was exposed to FN Browning pistols early in the 20th century. Police officers, not equipped with FN pistols, were often confronted with criminals who used them. A firefight between police and gangs (page 154) made the Parisian police painfully aware of their tactical disadvantage. The French Model 1892 revolver was outdated, and over the course of several years, the police finally adopted an automatic handgun. The Model 1910 was purchased in relatively large quantity during both the interwar and immediate post-war periods. Some 30,000 Model 1910 pistols were ordered in 1945 in an effort to rearm police forces after the Nazi occupation. Some of these guns were marked at the factory, while others received post-manufacturing markings. The majority of these pistols were never marked at all. All French police Model 1910 pistols are in 7.65 caliber.

(Fig.207-1) Although pistol N° 316486 has no special markings, the added special lanyard is an indication of French use. This pistol was shipped from FN on November 4, 1929 to la Cartoucherie française in Paris (page 116). (Photograph by author, courtesy of Michael Shade)

(Fig.207-2) Pistol N° 358455 was factory marked with the Parisian police marking P. de P. (Préfecture de Police). This pistol was shipped on January 13, 1932 to la Cartoucherie française in Paris and was not equipped with a lanyard ring. (Photograph by author, courtesy of Tom Knox)

Part of the Ottoman Empire prior to World War I, Syria fell under French rule after the war. As in France, the Model 1910 pistol was selected for the Syrian police. Orders were placed for Model 1910 pistols marked "Syrian Police" in both French and Arabic. Quantities of this order(s) are unknown. Syrian police pistols were delivered to "La Cartoucherie française" in Paris.

In 1946 Syria gained its independence and purchased High Power pistols for its military prior to 1950. The Model 1922 pistol was selected as a law enforcement pistol. These orders were discontinued when Syria became aligned with and a client state of the Soviet Union.

(Fig.207-3) This Syrian police pistol N° 362360 was marked in French and in Arabic, it has the issue number 20. This pistol was delivered to "La Cartoucherie française" in Paris on March 21, 1932. (Photograph courtesy of Bob Adams)

The Model 1910 in Australia

The distribution of the Model 1910 in Australia is linked to the zealous sales ambitions of FN's Agents Alcock & Pierce.

Several variants have been observed included commercial pistols that were pressed into service. After the British retreat at Dunkirk in 1940, a worldwide call was made for arms throughout the British Empire. Various arms, including FN Model 1900 and 1910 pistols, were donated by civilians to be shipped to England for military use or for domestic use in Australia. These pistols were marked with a military district number and inventory number(1).

An unknown quantity was purchased for the postal service around 1935, these pistols were marked "C of A P.M.G" for Commonwealth of Australia – Postmaster General(2).

Later some of these pistols were marked with an "S" in between arrows indicating that the pistol was marked for disposal.

The private security firm of Mayne Nickless was founded in 1886 by John Mayne and Enoch Nickless. The company started as a parcel delivery company in Melbourne and soon expanded into security services including secure transports of valuables and armored transports. The May Nickless company purchased an unknown quantity of Model 1910 pistols in 1965(2).

(Fig.208-1) This Alcock & Pierce marked FN 1910 N° 389958 was shipped to Australia on October 23, 1935. It was turned in for the war effort during World War II and was marked 3th Military District (Victoria), pistol number 66. This marking is usually not found on the frame of Model 1910 pistols but rather on the right side of the slide.

(Fig.208-2) Pistol N° 343014 was marked during World War II, 3th Military District (Victoria), pistol number 1935. The letter "S" surrounded by arrows indicates that the pistol was later marked for disposal. (Photograph courtesy of Janne Salopuro)

MAYNE
NICKLESS

(Fig.208-3) A drawing of the May Nickless property marking as it was applied to the Model 1910. This marking was stamped on the right side of the slide under the extractor.

(1) Author's correspondence with Graham Waddingham

(2) The Hayes Handgun Omnibus

The Model 1910 in Finland

Finland acquired relatively small quantities of Model 1910 pistols throughout the 1930s for law-enforcement agencies. Orders were increased in 1939 before the outbreak of the Winter War with pistols being used by the military, police and the prison department. FN further supplied Finland with 2500 Model 1910 pistols when shipping the High Power order in February 1940. Known in Finland as the "FN-10" or "m/1910", the majority of pistols in use during the 1930s did not have lanyard rings. The 1940 order was delivered with lanyard rings.

Finnish pistols can be identified by any of the following characteristics:

- -The military "SA" ("Suomen Armeija" - Finnish Army) marking
- -The Finnish police dagger etched marking or the black plastic replacement grips with police logo
- -The Vankeinhoitolaitos stamped or etched marking indicating use by the Finnish prison service
- -The Tampella factory property marking. Tampella was a producer of various heavy industries including steel. Some of the products manufactured were locomotives, artillery and heavy guns, boilers, turbines, mining drills and machinery. Tampella was founded in 1861, located in Tampere, Finland, the corporation went bankrupt in 1990. The pistols were carried by security guards in the various plants.

(Fig.209-1) This 1940 delivered pistol N° 458539 was first used by the military and later used by the Finnish police. Note the SA marking and Finnish police replacement grips. The lanyard ring may have been removed once the replacement grips were fitted. This pistol does not have the etched police logo on the slide. (Photograph courtesy of Timo Martelius, Maanpuolustuskorkeakoulu Sotamuseo / Military Museum of Finland)

(Fig.209-2) This Finnish police pistol N° 366133 was shipped from FN on October 26, 1932. Note the etched police dagger emblem on the slide. This pistol is equipped with Finnish police logo replacement grips. (Photograph courtesy of Janne Salopuro)

(Fig.209-3) Pistol N° 421761 has the Tampella factory property marking engraved on the slide. This pistol was shipped from FN on November 27, 1937.

(Fig.209-4) This Finnish prison service pistol N° 399385 was shipped from FN on November 30, 1936. It has both stamped as well as etched property markings. The logo on the slide represents a key fitting a key hole. (Photographs courtesy of Janne Salopuro)

FN 1910 Pistols in World War II: Japanese Orders and German Occupation Assembly

Japan: The Nationalist Chinese government of Chiang Kai-shek was an important FN customer throughout the 1930s. The Chinese purchased FN Mausers, FN M86 motorcycles, machine guns, High Power pistols and ammunition over several years. The Chinese government was considered one of the largest customers of the 1930s. After Japan invaded China, FN discontinued commercial interaction with the Imperial Japanese government.

A sizeable quantity of FN Browning 1910 pistols were used by Japanese officers during World War II. Small quantities of these pistols were shipped in 1937 with a growing escalation in 1938, 1939 and 1940. The largest order of 3000 pistols was shipped by FN's main agent in Liège, Schroeder(1) on March 2, 1940. It is not known if the Japanese approached FN directly or completed the transaction through Schroeder. Like most FN agents, Schroeder pursued various government orders. It is not known if the pistols were ordered directly by the Japanese military or by a Japanese retailer who in turn supplied the Japanese military.

A sizeable quantity of FN Browning 1910 pistols were used by Japanese officers during World War II. Small quantities of these pistols were shipped in 1937 with a growing escalation in 1938, 1939 and 1940. The largest order of 3000 pistols was shipped on March 2, 1940. Schroeder dealt with many government and commercial customers. As a result, not all Model 1910 pistols shipped to Schroeder were destined for Japan. It is difficult to assign a serial number range to the Japanese orders due to FN's warehousing policies. Pistols for these orders were pulled from FN inventory and were not built on contract.

Assessing the number of Model 1910 pistols purchased by Japan is made more difficult by the fact that the Japanese used captured pistols during the war. These included pistols captured in Manila and Shanghai, both of which had active FN agents and dealers.

The pistols shipped from Schroeder went to "Matsuhara." FN's shipping logs most often list the name of the dealer or agent. This has been interpreted that Schroeder sent the pistols to a Mr. Matsuhara. While this is a plausible explanation, Schroeder records did not necessarily list the name of dealers but often locations. Matsuhara is also a port city in Japan. One of the entries indicates shipment to "Matsuhara - Osaka." The combination of Osaka's status as a major commercial center and Matsuhara being a common Japanese name, lends credence to the conclusion that Matsuhara may have been the dealer's name or a corporate name.

The Japanese Model 1910 pistols can most often be identified by the kanji character Dai stamped on the barrel or frame. The significance of this character is reported as being Dai Nippon or Great Japan(2).

(Fig.210-1) Pistol N° 457045 was shipped from Schroeder in Liège to Matsuhara, Osaka on March 2, 1940. It was part of a batch of 3000 pistols shipped from Schroeder. The pistol has the typical kanji marking near the serial number and is the pistol with highest recorded serial number.

The fact that the Japanese used pistols which originated as commercial guns has created much confusion among collectors. Pistols were pulled from standard FN production and the kanji character on the frame has often been reproduced. Japanese pistols without kanji character can be identified through their provenance and accompanying holsters, but the only true method of authenticating a Japanese pistol is through the shipping records. During the course of researching this volume, the author has identified at least ten pistols that had counterfeit kanji markings. Shipping records for those pistols varied largely from Germany, to France to Sweden, among other countries. The range of pistols used by Japanese officers varies extensively but it should be noted that most frauds in the U.S. have been concentrated in the 1920s- early 1930s production era rather than the later 1930s or 1940 pistols. This may be due to a larger availability of unmarked earlier pistols.

Reported Japanese pistols:
369049, 387184, 409714, 416111, 416739, 435379, 442834, 446309, 449525, 453341, 454291, 454653, 456419

Authenticated Japanese pistols:
409475: Shipped from FN on July 7, 1937
423497: Shipped from FN on Jan. 11, 1938
453326: Shipped from FN on December 13, 1939
454143: Entered in FN warehouse on September 30, 1939 – Shipped on December 31, 1939
457045: Shipped from Schroeder on March 2, 1940

(Fig.211-1) Pistol N° 226754 was shipped from FN to Lepersonne in London on April 17, 1926. It was most likely forwarded to a retailer in the British Empire. This pistol was captured during World War II and marked with a Japanese character and inventory number.These markings are unusual and rare. (Photograph by author, courtesy of Bob Burden)

Germany: An estimated 6064 pistols were completed at FN in July and August 1940 during the first months of the occupation. This work was performed before the arrival of the first German weapons inspector (WaA613 code). Occupation assembled pistols were usually in the final stages of assembly, have Belgian proofs and feature synthetic grips instead of the prewar horn grips. This is due to the fact that horn was unavailable during the war (see page 100). The wartime assembled pistols were not entered in warehouse logs and do not show up in FN archives. Most feature prewar characteristics, some pistols were engraved as presentation pieces for prominent Nazi party members.

The use of black synthetic grips alone is not a positive indicator of wartime assembly. An undated wartime memo indicates that a FN employee discarded finished triggers in the sewers. Although undated, this reference can be placed early in the occupation. Although the Germans were not able to resume production of entire pistols immediately, they assembled pistols and made certain parts including grips and triggers. A positive indicator of early occupation pistols is the combination of crudely made triggers without finger flanges as well as the use of the black synthetic grips (see also page 292). Wartime 7.65mm Model 1910 magazines have eight view-holes instead of the traditional six.

Like the Model 1910, the Model 1905 pistols assembled during the war also feature synthetic grips. Most pistols used during World War II were of prewar manufacture. The Germans used Model 1910 pistols captured from the Belgian and Dutch military, among others. The Model 1910 was used by the Germans as officers' pistols, along with Model 1905 Vest Pocket and Model 1900 pistols.

Reported or observed model 1910 pistols assembled in 1940 during the occupation(3): 467217, 468562, 470329, 470690, 471366

---

(1) Schroeder's company was not affiliated with Genshow in Germany as is referred to in some publications.

(2) Japanese Military Cartridge Handguns 1893-1945

(3) There is no clear indicator of when prewar production stopped at FN. Pistols were logged by serial numbers and huge gaps exist in the 1940 production (considerable gaps start at circa 458,000, the highest observed wartime assembled pistols fall in the 470,000 range).

(Fig.212-1) Pistol N° 470690 was assembled in the first months of the occupation (July-August 1940) prior to the introduction of the WaA613 acceptance code. These pistols can easily be identified by the wartime manufactured trigger without finger flanges. These triggers show crude machining marks, which stand out from the prewar machined parts. The synthetic grips were wartime made due to the unavailability of animal horn. This pistol has a wartime magazine with eight view-holes.

(Fig.212-3) A few of the July-August 1940 assembled Model 1910 pistols were engraved as presentation pieces for Nazi party officials and prominent Germans. It is not known who engraved the pistols, the pattern is not a FN prewar pattern but the bluing and polishing methods applied to the pistols are identical to prewar FN work. Pistols were engraved for specific individuals and their initials or monogram were engraved on the pistol, only the location and style of monogram varies among the presentation pistols. Pistol N° 471366 has all the typical wartime features including trigger without finger flanges, plastic grips and a magazine with eight view-holes. The initials of the recipient are either "SG" or "GS".

(Fig.212-2) An early 1920s manufactured pistol N° 90536 was captured and reissued by the Germans. The Germans used just about all captured FN pistols including pre-World War I models like the Model 1900 and 1905 (see fig.51-1). The name of the German user was engraved on the slide, this is another example of German markings being engraved and not stamped. Special service markings (fig.249-2), names and property markings (fig.291-1) were engraved and not stamped with dies[1]. (Photograph courtesy of Allen Cayea)

(Fig.212-4) All wartime 7.65mm Model 1910 magazines have eight view-holes. The magazine is marked with the oversized and stretched FN logo (see fig.244-2).

(1) Wartime applied usage markings are always (roll) engraved. Observed pistols with die stamps alleging use by elite troops, SA or SS units have always proven to be frauds.

(Fig.213-1) A German soldier enjoys target shooting with a Model 1910 on a snowy day.

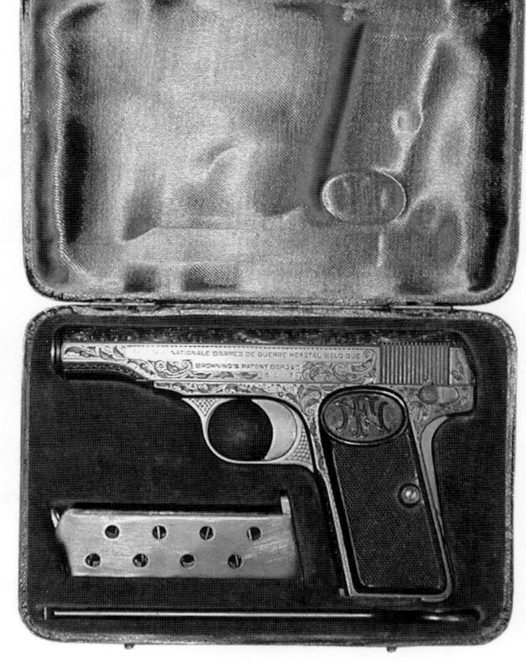

(Fig.213-2) Pistol N° 470329 was assembled from prewar parts during the first months of the occupation, the pistol features the typical wartime made trigger and synthetic grips, note the spare magazine with eight view-holes. The pistol was made into a presentation gift for Franz Hofer. Hofer was a long-term member of the Nazi party, having joined in Austria 1931. In 1932 he was appointed Gauleiter of Tyrol but arrested by the Austrian government for his involvement in the illegal Nazi party. Later in the 1930s he worked in Berlin and was re-appointed Gauleiter of Tyrol and Voralberg after the Austrian Anschluss. In 1940 he was promoted to governor of Tyrol-Voralberg. Through the war, he continued to rise in ranks. The circumstances of the event where the pistol was presented have been lost to time. It is not known who engraved the pistols, the pattern is not a FN prewar pattern but the bluing and polishing methods applied to the pistol are identical to prewar FN work. The case is a typical prewar FN presentation case. (Photographs courtesy of David Noll)

Post War Military Contracts

After World War II, the High Power became FNs primary military pistol. A few countries like Belgium, France and The Netherlands continued their tradition of using the Model 1910. In Belgium and France (page 207) this was limited to police use, and only when the Model 1922 was not favored. The Model 1910 was used by Belgian plain-clothes officers.

The Netherlands used the Model 1910 for law-enforcement and military use (page 204).

New customers for the Model 1910 included Canada, Burundi, Nigeria (intelligence service), Rwanda, Venezuela, and Peru among others.

Although used as a military side-arm, the Model 1910 was often sold in conjunction with the High Power. In many cases, the Model 1910 was issued as a self-defense weapon for officers.

Peru purchased the Baby Browning and Model 1910 in the mid 1950s for use by air force and army officers. The High Power was purchased for general military use.

Post War Military Contracts (continued)

At the same time Venezuela also purchased the Model 1910. This acquisition is most likely due to Venezuelan president Marcos Pérez Jiménez, a military officer who after graduating from military school in Venezuela, studied further in Peru and retained close connections with the Peruvian military. President Jiménez most likely chose the Model 1910 as an officers' weapon after learning of the Peruvian acquisition.

Canada purchased 192 7.65mm Model 1910 pistols in 1974 for senior officers stationed in Europe(1).

Pistols shipped to African nations were used for both military and law-enforcement functions. In most cases, these pistols are still in use.

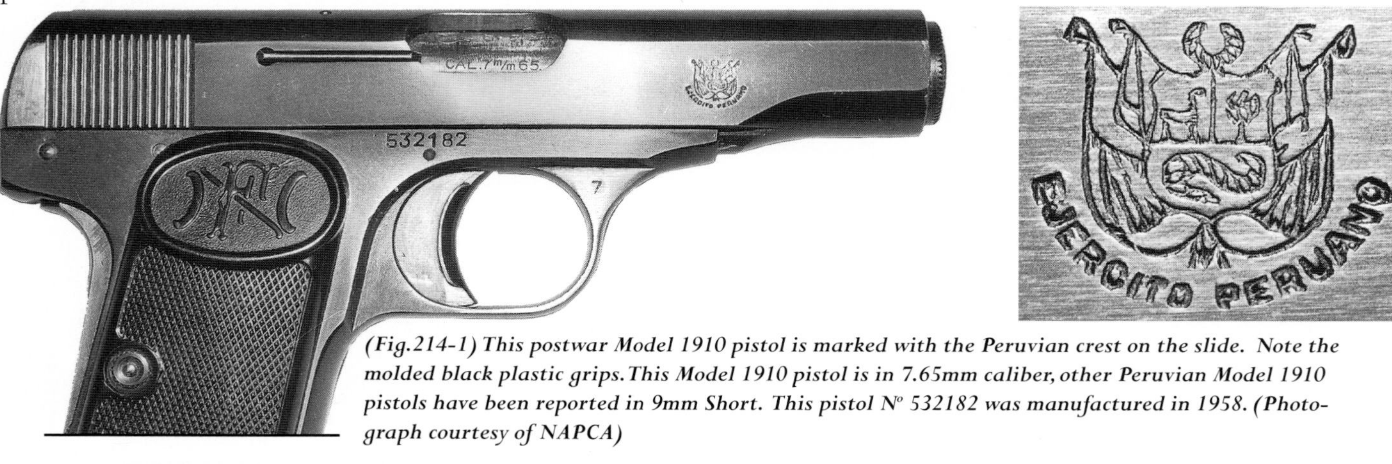

(Fig.214-1) This postwar Model 1910 pistol is marked with the Peruvian crest on the slide. Note the molded black plastic grips. This Model 1910 pistol is in 7.65mm caliber, other Peruvian Model 1910 pistols have been reported in 9mm Short. This pistol N° 532182 was manufactured in 1958. (Photograph courtesy of NAPCA)

(Fig.214-2) Venezuela was a long-standing customer of FN, purchasing large quantities of long arms and ammunition both prewar and postwar. In the postwar era, Venezuela purchased FN Mauser rifles, FN-49s and FALs. Pistol acquisitions were limited to the High Power and Model 1910. This Model 1910 has contract N° 02239. The contract markings "Fuerzas Armadas de Venezuela" (Armed Forces of Venezuela) with crest were factory applied. Both the crest and contract markings of the Peruvian and Venezuelan contracts were applied using FN's postwar engraving techniques, which resulted in lighter (less deep) markings.

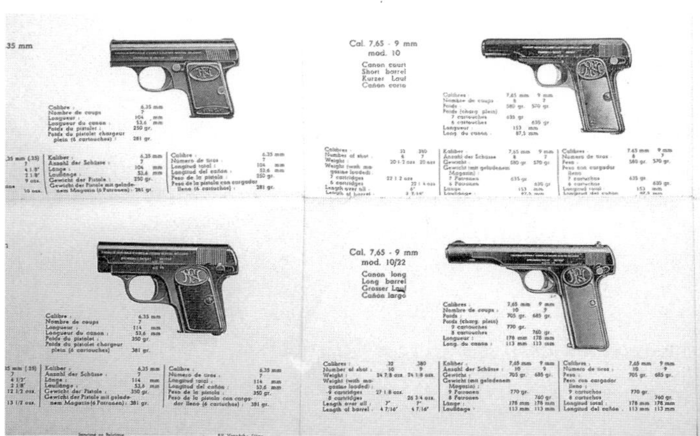

FABRIQUE NATIONALE D'ARMES DE GUERRE, S. A. - HERSTAL-lez-LIÈGE (BELGIQUE)

PISTOLETS AUTOMATIQUES BROWNING
BROWNING AUTOMATIC PISTOLS
AUTOMATISCHE BROWNING PISTOLEN
PISTOLAS AUTOMATICAS BROWNING

CAL. : 9 mm
GRANDE PUISSANCE — HIGH POWER
HOCHLEISTUNG — GRAN POTENCIA

Cal. 7,65 - 9 mm mod. 10

Cal. 7,65 - 9 mm mod. 10/22

(Fig.214-3) FN replaced the typical onion-skin colored paper instruction sheets with an oil-resistant glassine type paper in the late 1940s. Both instruction sheets as well as spec sheets were included in the shipping boxes. This 1950 oil resistant glassine spec sheet still features the Model 1905.

(1) Canadian Military Handguns 1855-1985 by Clive M. Law

The "Modèle 1910 Grand Browning"

Development History

FN's decision to develop the Grand Browning was a direct response to the advent of Colt's Model 1909 and Model 1910 pistols. These pistols represented a dangerous encroachment on FN's market share due to the interest in the powerful new cartridge for which they were chambered. This cartridge, developed by Winchester for Colt, was called the 9.8mm Auto.

The development of Colt's new pistol was no surprise to FN. Under the FN Colt market agreement, FN had been offered the same design by John Browning. FN had patented the .45 caliber Browning design that was manufactured by Colt as the Model 1905. This Belgian patent was filed by FN and granted as patent 184667 on May 19, 1905.

The Belgian publication Revue de l'Armée Belge indicates in their March-April 1909 issue, that FN already had a 11mm pistol, this may indicate that FN had received John Browning's 1908 prototype and may have been working towards a production pistol.

John Browning's prototype of 1910, a direct forerunner of the Colt .45 Model of 1911, was patented by FN on October 19, 1910 under patent 229828. Both Colt and FN had access to the Browning prototypes, therefore FN did not copy the Colt Model of 1911 as is often reported. Rather FN developed the Modèle 1910 Grand Browning from the Browning prototype as it had done with all previous Browning models.

The General Manager of FN, Mr. Andri, ordered the production of three Modèle 1910 Grand Browning pistols in .45 ACP caliber (11.43 x23mm) on August 16, 1910. Exactly three months later Mr. Andri, ordered production of 20 more pistols.

The Colt 1910 pistol in 9.8mm Auto was demonstrated in the Balkans in 1911, and was popular due to the new cartridge's increased stopping power. The Balkans were not covered by any sales territory agreements between FN and Colt, and FN faced the prospect of being shut out of a lucrative new market.

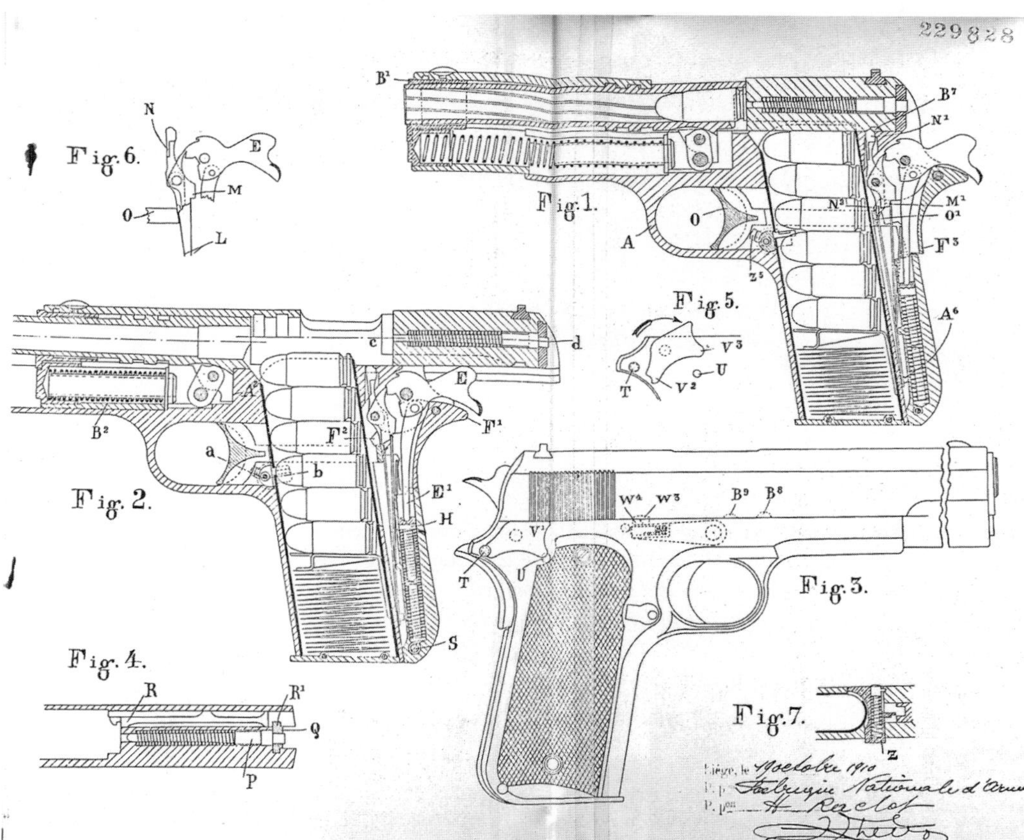

(Fig.215-1) ***Belgian patent 229828 was granted to FN on October 19, 1910. This patent related to Browning's original prototype of 1910. The prototype of 1910 had the handle at a 75 degree angle versus the straight handle of Browning's 1909 prototype, it also featured an improved ejector design. The U.S. patent for this design was actually granted on February 14, 1911. Both FN and Colt inspected the prototype in 1910 and filed for the patents. The Belgian patent was issued prior to the American patent, indicating that the FN Grand Browning was developed from John Browning's prototype and not a copy of the U.S. Model 1911 as is often reported.***

In mean time, Colt had continued the development of the Model 1910 pistol chambered for the .45 ACP, the United States government adopted the pistol as the Automatic Pistol, Caliber .45, Model of 1911. In light of this success, Colt dropped its pursuit of both the Balkan market and the 9.8mm Auto cartridge.

FN was, like Colt a year earlier, interested in the improved ballistic characteristics of the Colt - Winchester 9.8 mm Auto cartridge. In the following years FN invested in the development of a proprietary version of the round, which was called the 9.65x23mm Browning. By 1914 both the pistol and the new cartridge were ready for production, and a small quantity was manufactured prior to the German invasion. Based on the marketing model used with the FN Model 1903, it is likely that FN would have secured a large military contract prior to mass production of the Modèle 1910 Grand Browning. While FN was ready for production at the time of the invasion, it is not known if any contracts had been secured.

After the war, with the surplus market flooded with Colt 1911 pistols, it was not economically viable for FN to offer a similar, competing design. Instead of trailing Colt in the market with a similar pistol chambered for a different cartridge, FN abandoned the project. The Modèle 1910 Grand Browning was briefly reintroduced for the French Army trials in 1922.

Rumors circulated in 2004 and 2005 that FN was considering re-introducing the Grand Browning, but no additional information was obtained by the time of printing.

(Fig.216-1) Archive photographs of pistol N° 107 show several differences with N° 127. The slide safety and the slide stop have serrations instead of checkering. The grips are made out of a synthetic material instead of wood. The inspector marking is different which may indicate that these were built at different times. The caliber of N° 107 is not known, it is not known if this pistol has survived through time. (Photographs courtesy of FN Herstal)

(Fig.217-1) This 9.65 mm Grand Browning N° 127 is one of the few manufactured prior to World War I. Note the checkering on the slide safety and the slide stop. This pistol differs from pistol N° 107, which has serrations on these parts instead of checkering. All major and some minor parts of this pistol are marked with the last digit of the serial number, "7". Parts numbering was done similarly to the Model 1903 in order to cater to the military market. Numbered parts include the magazine, grip-panels, barrel, barrel-bushing, recoil spring cap, recoil spring guide, barrel-link, link retaining pin, slide stop and safety. Note the wooden grips and the pin / locking system securing the grip-panels. The two-tone magazine holds eight rounds. (Photographs courtesy of Leonardo Antaris, MD)

(Fig.217-2) Note the magazine floor-plate split-tail locking system, similar to the later High Power magazine. (Photograph courtesy of Leonardo Antaris, MD)

The FN Model 1922

Development History: Early Transition Pistols

The Kingdom of Serbs, Croats, and Slovenes (later to become Yugoslavia) was formed after World War I. This new nation found itself depleted of armament after the Balkan Wars and World War I. The Serbs[(1)], which were a majority in this newly formed government, were FN customers since the 1890s. Their quest for a new handgun would lead to the development of the Model 1922.

The Model 1903 and Model 1910 were early contenders. The Model 1903 was considered too expensive. The Model 1910 drew attention because of its price and chambering for the 9mm Short (9x17mm or .380 ACP) cartridge. Chambering was an important consideration important as the Serbs had stockpiles of 9mm Short cartridges.

The Model 1910 pistol did well, but was considered to be lacking in accuracy. A request was placed for a pistol with the Model 1910's characteristics with a longer barrel and greater accuracy. FN, still recovering from the World War, was eager to accommodate its customers.

FN's Bureau d' Etudes (research office) came up with some cost saving solutions. Knowing that this new customer could not afford the development and production of a new pistol, FN modified the 1910 to save tooling and production start-up costs.

A forged metal cap[(2)] with a raised front sight was added to the 1910 slide so that it could accommodate the longer barrel. The slide was fitted with a modified Model 1903 rear sight.

A series of prototypes and trials pistols were completed between 1921-1922. This series included the following configurations[(3)]: **Model 1910 frame with modified 1910 slide, assembled with long barrel, barrel lug and raised sights.**

Modified 1910 frame (elongated with one extra round capacity) with modified 1910 slide, assembled with long barrel, long barrel lug and raised sights.

Modified 1910 frame (elongated with two extra rounds capacity) with modified 1910 slide, assembled with long barrel, long barrel lug and raised sights.

Modified 1910 frame (elongated with two extra rounds capacity) with elongated 1910 slide, assembled with long barrel, short barrel lug and raised sights.

The frame of the Model 1922 was not immediately lengthened to its present size. Experiments were made retaining the frame of the 1910 pistol and tests were also performed with a frame that accommodated only seven instead of eight rounds.These transitional guns were produced for a brief period and the early features were soon dropped. It is not known how many transition pieces were made or how many variants existed.

Eventually the Serbs settled on a version with an extended frame, elongated slide and small barrel lug. This version became the definitive Model 1922. The Model 1922 pistol was the first large contract between FN and Yugoslavia after World War I. It was followed by the development of the FN Model 1924 Mauser, and FN's assistance in the construction of the state arsenal at Kragujevac and the establishment of Mauser rifle production in Yugoslavia.

(Fig.218-1) Plans for the arsenal at Kragujevac were drafted by the architects Polak and Hoch in Brussels. This February 1924 rendering shows the layout of the arsenal facilities. It only took about two years to erect the principal facilities. (Photograph courtesy of Carlos Davila)

(Fig.219-1) A rare transition pistol N° 140777 with standard Model 1910 frame but with extended slide and short barrel lug. The serial number is part of the Model 1910 production. The serial number is repeated on all standard parts and the barrel lug is numbered "77". Although the overall length of the pistol is identical to later standardized production pistols, the slide is shorter and the barrel lug is longer. Note the location of the barrel lug release lever, this early location is in fact superior to the later Yugoslav adopted side location. Note that the barrel lug is proofed. (Photograph by author, courtesy of John Bill)

(Fig.219-2) The ambidextrous safety lever was a great innovation that was not carried over to the standardized production model. (Photographs by author, courtesy of John Bill)

(Fig.219-3) A comparative view of the transition barrel lug with a standardized production barrel lug: Note the shorter slide and longer barrel lug on the transition gun. Note that the external dimension of the transition barrel lug is longer but the bayonet locking mechanism is considerably shorter than later production pistols. The overall size of the transition barrel lug (body and bayonet locking mechanism) is smaller than later production pieces. (Photographs by author, courtesy of John Bill)

(1) Although the Kingdom was formed from a coalition, the Serbs headed the armaments programs with FN.

(2) Also referred to as barrel lug. The cap was forged not stamped as is often reported

(3) Most likely there were more than four configurations presented

Development History: Production Pistols

Once specifications of the Model 1922 were finalized, the Kingdom of Serbs, Croats, and Slovenes placed an order for 60,000 pistols on February 28, 1923.

FN considered this model a military pistol and mass production started only after the contract was executed (see Model 1903 page 158).

The Serbs required that the pistols be marked only with consecutive contract numbers. Prior to 1923 FN never marked pistols solely with the contract number. Pistols were externally marked with serial numbers and showed a separate contract number if the customer so desired. The contract number was not without controversy. FN proceeded by adding an internal serial number to the contract pistols (see also page 225).

Production of the Model 1922 started at serial number 200,000[1]. The reason for this apparently arbitrary number has been lost to time. It is likely that FN decided to continue Model 1910 serialization with the Model 1922. FN Model 1910 production reached almost 200,000 by the time the Model 1922 went into production. The internal numbering system was abandoned with the first Dutch orders in 1925.

External serial numbering continued in the 200,000 range for commercial pistols. The marking of contract pistols with only the contract number was an option available for an additional fee. Contract numbering was not always purchased. As a result, there are many military and law enforcement pistols that have factory contract markings in addition to standard FN serial numbers in lieu of contract numbers.

Like the Model 1910, the Model 1922 was available in both 7.65 and 9mm Short calibers. Calibers were interchangeable by replacing the barrel. Magazines were marked with either 7.65 or 9mm and drilled with the number of view holes appropriate to the marked caliber. All magazines functioned with either caliber. Magazines were marked like the Model 1910 (fig.196-2).

The Model 1922 remained unchanged throughout the 1920s and 1930s. Available options included contract markings, contract numbering and the addition of a lanyard ring. Most orders were supplied with beveled barrel lugs but there were exceptions, like the French order (page 238).

Replacement parts for the Model 1922 were unnumbered. Countries like Holland purchased extensive amounts of replacement parts. These parts were numbered by the customer. Differences in numbering styles can be an indicator of post factory numbering. FN did not offer a luxury line of engraved Model 1922 pistols. The Model 1910 targeted the commercial market while the Model 1922 was intended for military and law enforcement sales.

The only engraved guns made by the factory were commissioned on special order or specially made for exhibits. Collectors should exercise caution when purchasing an engraved pistol. Only one of the pistols encountered by the author (fig. 221-2) is known to be factory original work. A number of prewar and early postwar Model 1922 pistols have been observed featuring simple gold line engraving. These pistols are almost always represented as factory originals but are in fact modern creations.

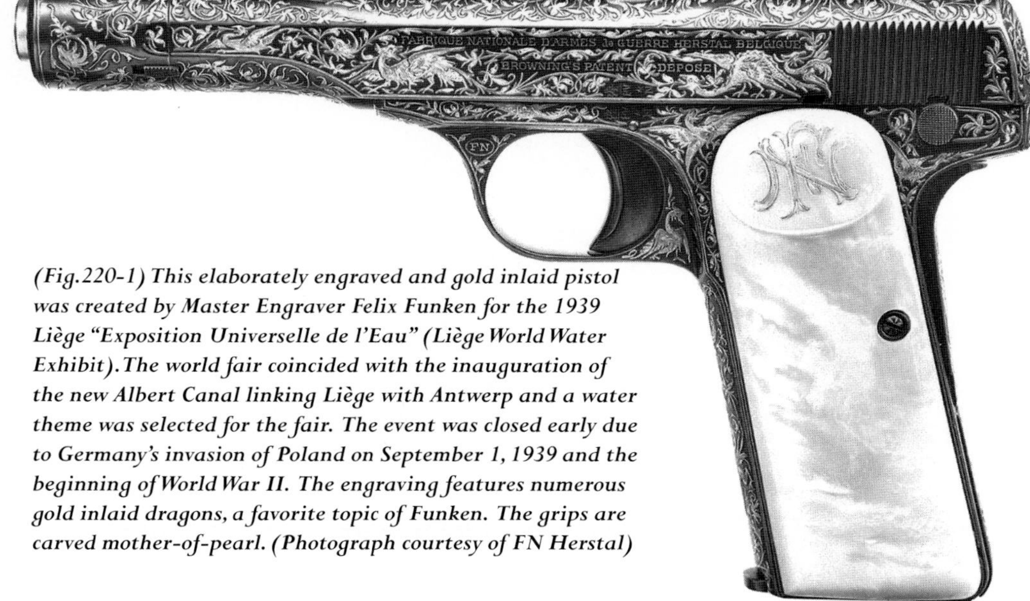

(Fig.220-1) This elaborately engraved and gold inlaid pistol was created by Master Engraver Felix Funken for the 1939 Liège "Exposition Universelle de l'Eau" (Liège World Water Exhibit). The world fair coincided with the inauguration of the new Albert Canal linking Liège with Antwerp and a water theme was selected for the fair. The event was closed early due to Germany's invasion of Poland on September 1, 1939 and the beginning of World War II. The engraving features numerous gold inlaid dragons, a favorite topic of Funken. The grips are carved mother-of-pearl. (Photograph courtesy of FN Herstal)

(Fig.221-1) This elaborately engraved and gold inlaid pistol was created by Master Engraver Felix Funken for the 1939 Liège "Exposition Universelle de l'Eau" (Liège World Water Exhibit). This world fair coincided with the inauguration of the new Albert Canal linking Liège with Antwerp and a water theme was selected for the fair. The event was closed early due to Germany's invasion of Poland on September 1, 1939 and the beginning of World War II. The engraving features an Egyptian theme, a popular subject at the time. The grips are carved mother-of-pearl. (Photograph courtesy of FN Herstal)

General Martinez' FN Browning 1922

Few factory engraved Model 1922's are known to exist. One was a presentation pistol given to El Salvador's General Martinez. The pistol was ordered and supplied to Schroeder in Liège on January 7, 1929 and shipped on to Brussels for forwarding on January 10. At the time General Martinez held important positions in the Salvadoran army. It is likely that Schroeder's intent was to influence Martinez toward purchasing FN products. At the time El Salvador was not a significant FN customer.

On March 1, 1931 a military coup deposed El Salvador's President Arturo Araujo, and the vice president and minister of war, General Maximiliano Hernandez Martinez was installed as president. An ardent anti-communist, Martinez was not without controversy. Communist peasant and worker factions were repressed and civil liberties dwindled as the years went by. Repressive and dictatorial, Martinez was also a patriot, seeking to elevate his country out of poverty. He centralized the banking system and the printing and issuance of currency, set up a mortgage bank and created funding mechanisms for farmers and artisans. He adopted economic protectionism, banning importation of finished goods and machinery deemed harmful to the local economy. Many factories, roads and bridges were constructed. The Salvadoran constitution prohibited Martinez from running again after 1939, so he amended the constitution and remained president until May 9, 1944. Relations with the U.S. were troubled, and the U.S. did not recognize the Salvadoran government for over two years.

President Martinez cherished his engraved Model 1922. Reliable accounts including testimonies from his daughter and eye witnesses, recall how he carried the pistol in his belt without a holster. The pistol was more than ceremonial. One day, after learning of a coup d'etat in progress, he used his Model 1922 to shoot a guard who refused him entrance to a building. Armed with the Model 1922 he confronted his officers, who were gathered around a conference table.

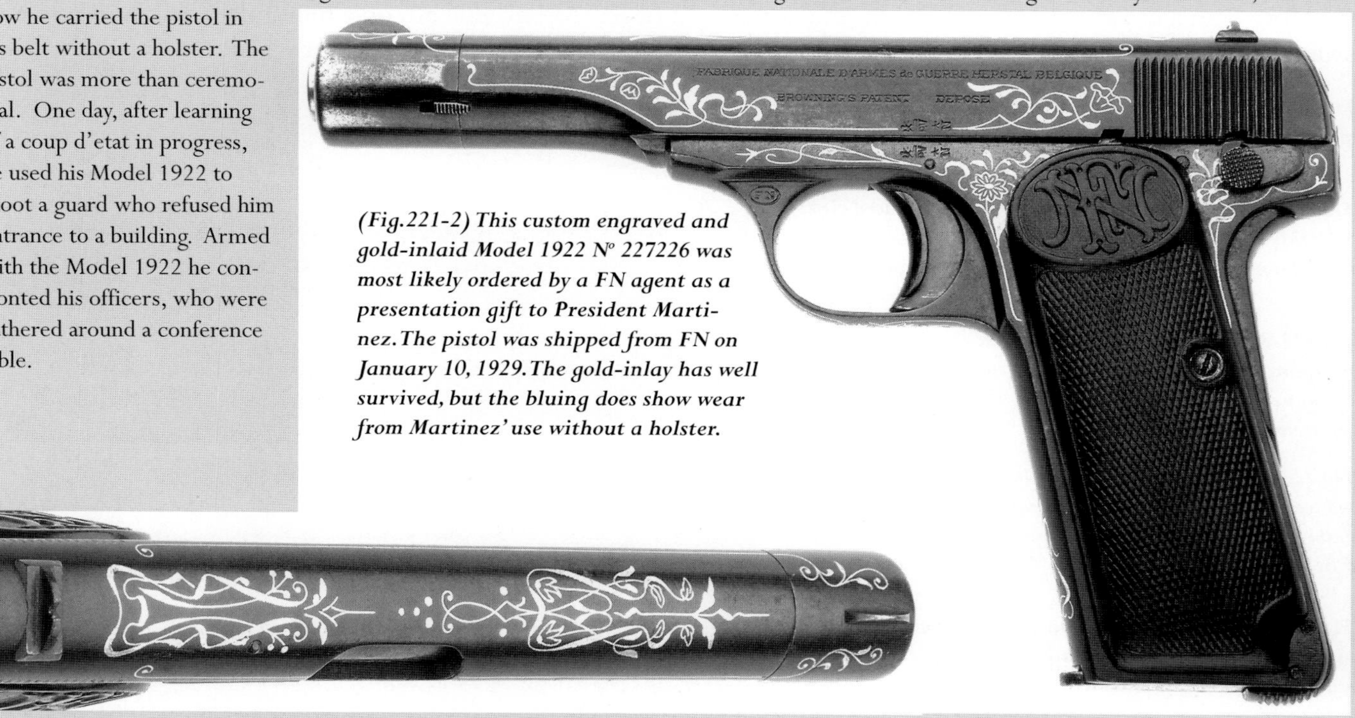

(Fig.221-2) This custom engraved and gold-inlaid Model 1922 N° 227226 was most likely ordered by a FN agent as a presentation gift to President Martinez. The pistol was shipped from FN on January 10, 1929. The gold-inlay has well survived, but the bluing does show wear from Martinez' use without a holster.

FN Model 1922: Features & Specifications

Serial or Contract Numbers

N° 200,000 – approximately 285,000: Standard prewar production serial numbers, all pistols have Liège proofs.

N° 1- 69,000: Prewar contract production: Pistols most often display prewar contract markings (crest) and Liège proofs.

N° 01 or 0001 to 9,999: Postwar contract numbers, note that the addition of a "0" prefix is a postwar habit. The "0" prefix indicates a contract. Pistols show Liège proofs with or without special markings.

N° 1- approximately 180,000: Standard postwar production serial numbers. Pistol has Liège proofs but does not show any special contract markings. Large serial number gaps exists in the postwar ranges, not all serial numbers were manufactured.

"A" prefix: Found on the Model 1910, 1922 and High Power pistol. Immediate post-liberation production. Few Model 1910 pistols are marked with this prefix as the slide and parts originated from wartime Model 1922 parts. Note that FN had large stockpiles of "A" prefix parts and many were assembled and sold for years after the war.

Overview on Model 1922 Numbers and Production Years

- **Standard serial numbers start at 200,000 around 1925 ending in the 285,000 range in May 1940**
- **Contract numbers: 1-69,000 range from 1923 until May 1940**
  Note that these numbers are duplicated among the contracts. Both the Yugoslav and Dutch orders reached contract numbers above 60,000.
- **A prefix serial numbers: September 1944 through 1945 and often assembled later**
  - **A1-?: Numbers not recorded by FN**
  - **A001-?: Unknown contract numbers not recorded by FN**
  - **A4001-A5251: Sold primarily as commercial pistols, sold to American soldiers, servicemen and factories**
  - **A75001-A86100: Sold primarily to Holland as a military contract**
  - **A90001-A97700: Sold primarily to Belgium as a military contract**
- **Standard serial numbers 1-180,000 from 1946 up to 1975**
- **Few postwar contracts had contract numbering. Contract numbers started with 01, 001 or 0001 depending on the size or digits used e.g. a contract for 1000 pistols started with number 0001.**

Slide Legends and Slide Serrations

Slide serrations cannot determine pre or postwar manufacture. The same variants appear on both pre and postwar pistols. Slide legends can help determine manufacturing eras but not manufacturing dates (see manufacturing on page 97). More than a dozen variants of slide legends have been observed, several with only minor differences. The following highlight the major differences:

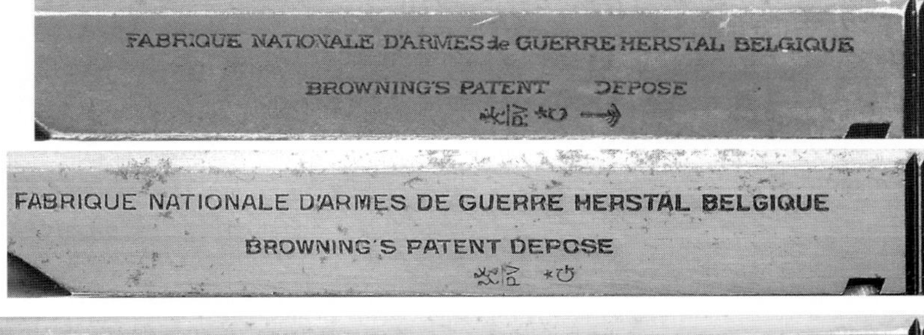

(Fig.222-1) Early legend with lower case "de" used from 1922 up to circa 1934.

(Fig.222-2) Most common style of legend, introduced circa 1932; this style of lettering with minor variants was used throughout the 1930s, World War II, the 1940s, and 1950s.

(Fig.222-3) FN legend with "S.A" (Société Anonyme – Incorporated) inclusion. Introduced in the mid 1930s, this legend was sporadically used up to 1940 when production requirements were high (page 97).

(Fig.222-4) Wartime replacement legend introduced in 1943 and used through the war including the post-liberation assembly. Note that the legend is misspelled (Belcique instead of Belgique)

(Fig.222-5) Fine postwar legend introduced early in the 1950s and used through the end of production. Lettering is finer and lighter than previous variants.

Grips

A glance at the grips of a Model 1922 can reveal if the gun was manufactured in the prewar, wartime, or postwar eras. Checking the back of the grips (fig.100-1), the FN logo and the border around the logo helps in identifying the material and manufacturing era.

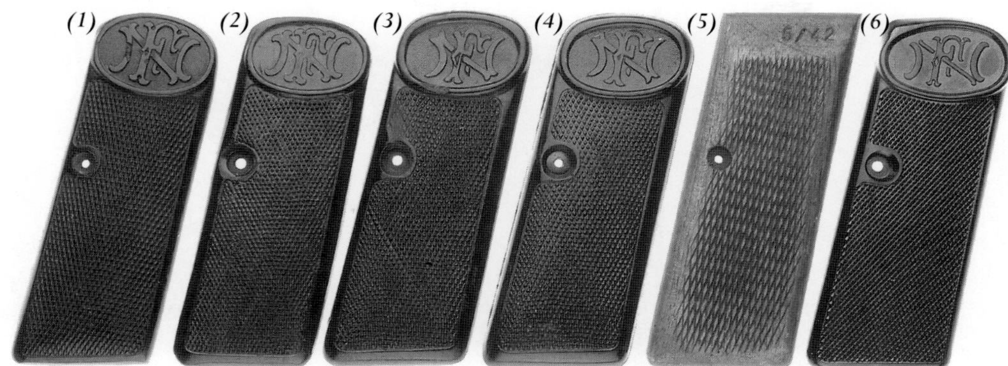

(Fig.223-1) 1- Pressed horn, dyed black. Several minor variants exist. This is the standard pattern used in the prewar era. The backside shows no molding patterns rather a flat pressed surface (fig.100-1).
2- Black molded synthetic, introduced during the occupation in 1940 as no horn was available. The back shows a molding pattern (fig.100-1).
3- Black molded synthetic with wide rim around logo. Introduced during the war and used throughout the war and 1940s.
4- Chocolate brown Bakelite grips, same pattern as previous model, introduced late in 1943 and used through the occupation as a substitute material. Also used in early 1944 post-liberation assembly.
5- Checkered wooden grips, introduced in 1942 as a substitute material and used throughout the war. Some commercial wartime pistols have been noted with manufacturing dates stamped on the grips. FN used checkered wooden grips in their postwar manufacturing but those were finely checkered and finished.
6- Postwar molded black plastic grips with fine FN logo. The fine FN logo is an indicative of postwar manufacture. Variants of postwar plastic grips have either the top corner extension at the logo (shown) or do not have the extension.

Barrel Lugs

There is no apparent logic in the differences in prewar finished lugs. They are not an evolution of the manufacturing process. Un-beveled and beveled lugs have appeared throughout the 1930s. Prewar un-beveled lugs are less common; the French contract guns were manufactured with un-beveled lugs. FN did make an effort to supply the same lug to the same customer, even when purchases were made over a length of time. The differences in barrel lugs have no relation to weight or point of impact when shooting, all observed lugs with or without bevel weight in at 37 grams.

FN streamlined production in the 1940s and eliminated the use of beveled barrel lugs. An un-beveled lug can indicate postwar manufacture.

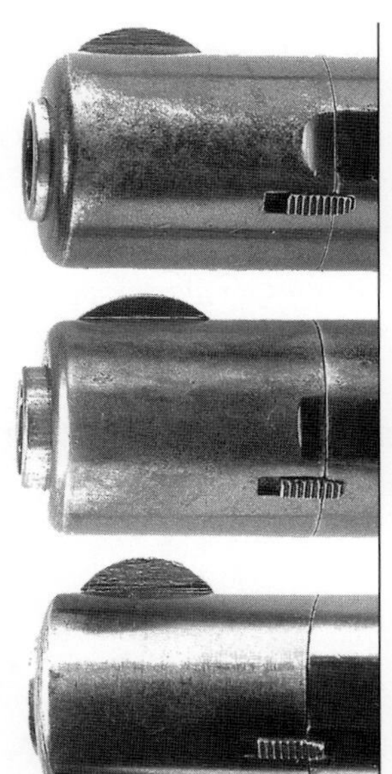

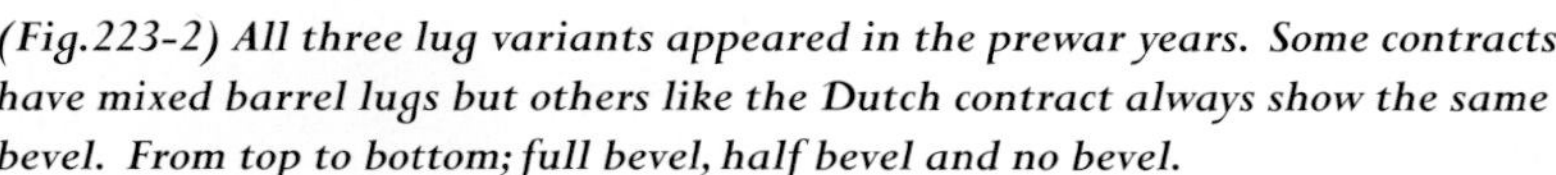

(Fig.223-2) All three lug variants appeared in the prewar years. Some contracts have mixed barrel lugs but others like the Dutch contract always show the same bevel. From top to bottom; full bevel, half bevel and no bevel.

Specifications Summary

Model known as: Early: "Modèle 10/22" / Late: "Modèle 1922"
Period offered: 1923-1940 / Mass produced during World War II under German occupation / 1944-1975
Caliber: .32 ACP / 7.65x17mm or .380 ACP / 9x17mm
Operating system: Blowback
Length: 178mm
Barrel length: 113mm
Weight: 705 grams (7.65mm) / 685 grams (9mm)
Grips: Animal horn in prewar years / wood, synthetic or Bakelite during World War II / wood or plastic after 1945
Magazine capacity: 7.65mm: nine rounds / 9mm: eight rounds
Sights: Fixed
Options: Lanyard ring
Finish offered: Blue, black enamel
Engraving patterns: Special order only pre-1940 / some patterns introduced after World War II

FN Model 1922: Accessories

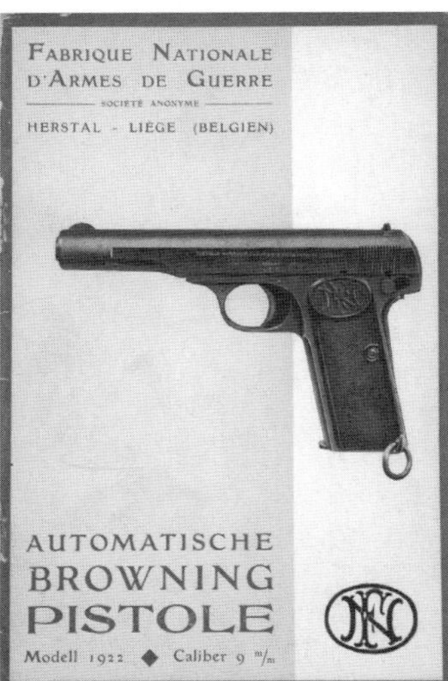

(Fig.224-1) (l. to r.) Brown and beige 1936-1937 instruction book, late 1920s beige and white instruction book, light and dark green 1933 instruction book. Typical multi-color postwar instruction booklet. All instruction books were available in a multitude of languages including, French German, Spanish, English and select in Dutch and Italian.

(Fig.224-2) Prewar and postwar cardboard boxes consisted of a dark-green hinged box (125 x 185mm) with embossed FN logo. A printed box was also used in the postwar era. Unlike the embossed box, the printed box opened on the sides. A less common plastic two-piece box was also used in the postwar era (see Model 1910 example on page 198). Depending on the order, a foldout instruction booklet with blue cover could be included in the box, most often however the oil-resistant glassine paper instructions were used (see fig.318-3).

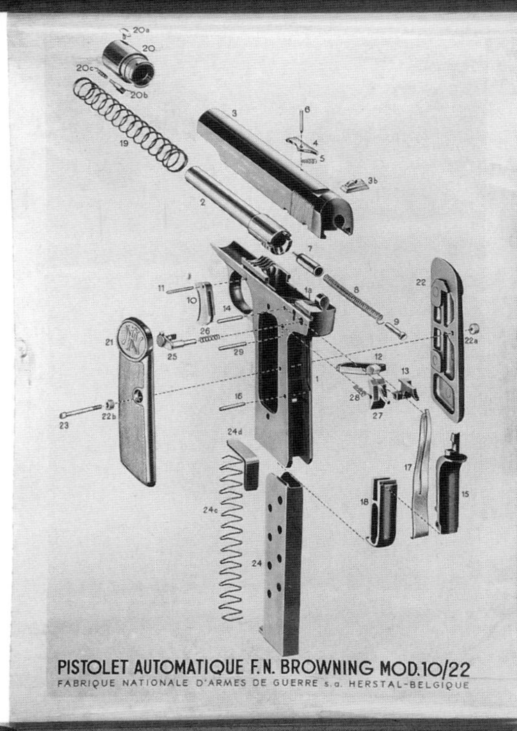

(Fig.224-3) FN offered large classroom instruction posters for military and law-enforcement customers. The posters were made out of linen with wooden slats. Illustrated is a postwar variant.

(Fig.224-4) Sight adjustment tools were part of armorers' kits supplied by FN. It is believed that these sight adjustment tools were also made during the war. It is unknown when this specific tool was manufactured.

The Many Yugoslav Orders

Many small nations obtained their independence when the Austro-Hungarian Empire dissolved in 1919. The Kingdom of the Serbs, Croats and Slovenes was a newly independent state, formed from a coalition of different areas, cultures and religions. This broad cultural and political background created a significant armaments problem. The unification had brought together a collection of diverse weaponry with different calibers and systems. In addition World War I and the Balkan Wars had left most of the nation's small arms in a poor state of repair. Handguns in use by the Yugoslav armed forces at the time included: the 1891 Belgian 7.5mm Nagant revolver, 7.65mm Spanish manufactured Ruby pistols, the Austrian 9x21mm 1912 Steyr pistol, the 8mm Roth Steyr pistol, the 7.63mm Mauser pistol, the 11mm 1870 Austrian Gasser revolver, the 8mm 1898 Gasser revolver, 7.65 and 9mm German Luger Pistols.

The Serbian army was the military strength behind the unification and had the greatest influence in weapons adoption and standardization policy. The Serbs turned to FN, with whom they had placed several ammunition orders through the years. The approach taken by FN to meeting the Serbs' requirements demonstrates the extent to which the company was willing to go to win military contracts. The available FN handguns of the time did not meet the Kingdom's requirements (in terms of both economics and performance - see development on page 218).

FN's development of the Model 1922 was well received. Orders were placed for 60,000 pistols and six million 9mm Short cartridges. An order for Mauser rifles and 50 million 7.9 mm Mauser cartridges followed on July 14, 1923.

In 1926 the Kingdom approached FN with an offer to purchase manufacturing rights for the Model 1924 Mauser rifle. Additionally, the company was asked to provide the machine tools, expertise and everything else required to create a state arsenal capable of producing 200 rifles and 200,000 cartridges a day. A contract was signed on February 16, 1926 to create the arsenal at Kragujevac called Vojno-Tehnicki Zavod (Army Technical Works). Orders for the Model 1922 pistol continued until the late 1930s.
The pistols were serviced at the Kragujevac arsenal. Many of the pistols were captured by the Germans during World War II. The captured Model 1922 pistols were reissued to German allies including the Bulgarians and Italians. Captured Yugoslavian Model 1922s were designated P641(j) by the Germans. Large quantities remained in hands of the Yugoslav partisans. It became known as the pistol of Tito's partisan army.

(Fig.225-1) A 1928 photograph showing the newly constructed Vojno-Tehnicki Zavod arsenal at Kragujevac. The 1853 date on the façade refers to the old canon foundry. (Photograph courtesy of Carlos Davila)

The Large Yugoslav Orders: Army and Officers' Pistols

The bulk of the pistols ordered by Yugoslavia were army pistols. These were all marked "Army State" in Cyrillic and the majority were ordered with ascending contract numbers. The requirement of a visible contract number marking in lieu of a serial number was new and FN opted to stamp a seperate reference number internally. As such, there is always a 200,300 difference between the external contract number and internal number. This did not work effectively and was largely abandoned by 1925. The Yugoslavs were not consistent in their numbering requirements. Original army and officers' orders required contract numbers. More than 70,000 army and officers' pistols were supplied during the 1920s, all with externally visible contract numbers. Small additional army and officers' orders from the 1930s did not stipulate contract numbers and often show standard FN serial numbers in the 230,000 serial range.

The original officers' contract also stipulated visible contract numbers. These pistols have four digit contract numbers and it is believed that pistols marked in this manner are limited to the first order. Officers pistol orders after 1925 did not require external contract numbers and display standard FN serial numbers. The Yugoslavs used an on-site acceptance commission, and early military contract pistols were most often marked with the commission's acceptance marking (see fig.226-4).

Observed "Army State" pistols: 16, 1038, 3175, 3876, 4928, 5411, 7515, 9273, 11876, 19094, 19826, 24432, 25946, 28532, 31135, 32426, 33893, 37564, 38348, 38602, 41689, 43917, 47079, 58578, 61262, 61767, 66434, 68355, 238902

"Officer" pistols: 5411 (contract n°), 7256 (contract n°), 7306 (contract n°), 213260, 231150, 231260, 238963, 239822, 239875, 243894

(Fig.226-1) The Army State markings on the slide indicate standard military issue. This gun N° 22050 has the contract number on the frame, slide and is also visible on the barrel. FN's internal number is 222350. Like all Yugoslav contract pistols, it features a lanyard ring.

(Fig.226-2) The "Officer" markings on the slide indicate that these were issued to commissioned officers. Pistol N° 238963 has no beveled barrel lug and does not show the serial number through the ejection port. Note the standard FN serial number instead of a contract number.

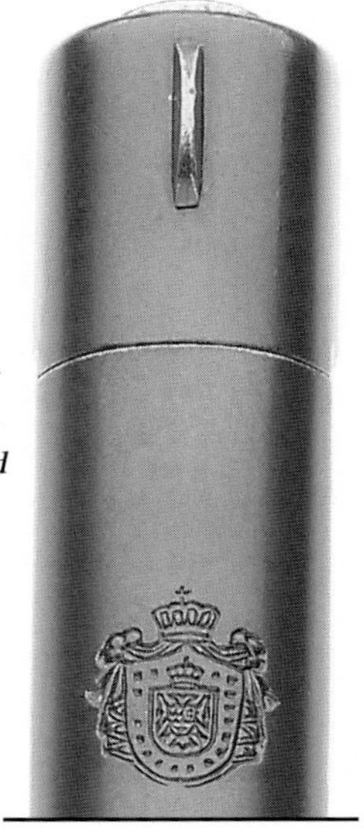

(Fig.226-3) The Yugoslav (Kingdom of Serbs, Croats and Slovenes) crest as applied to all Army State and Officers' pistols. The roll engraved crest was factory applied, several small variants exist between contracts, especially the smaller contracts. Not all of the smaller contracts were marked with the crest.

(Fig.226-4) Yugoslav inspector acceptance markings are usually seen on the first military contracts. The "S" in a circle as seen in fig.226-1 is also believed to be a Yugoslav marking. Its significance is unknown.

The Small Yugoslav Orders: Navy and Law Enforcement Pistols

A myriad of small Yugoslav contracts followed the army's adoption of the Model 1922. The navy as well as numerous law enforcement agencies placed orders for the Model 1922. Most of these small orders had distinct factory contract markings. Contracts were at times so small that samples of some contracts are no longer believed to be existent.

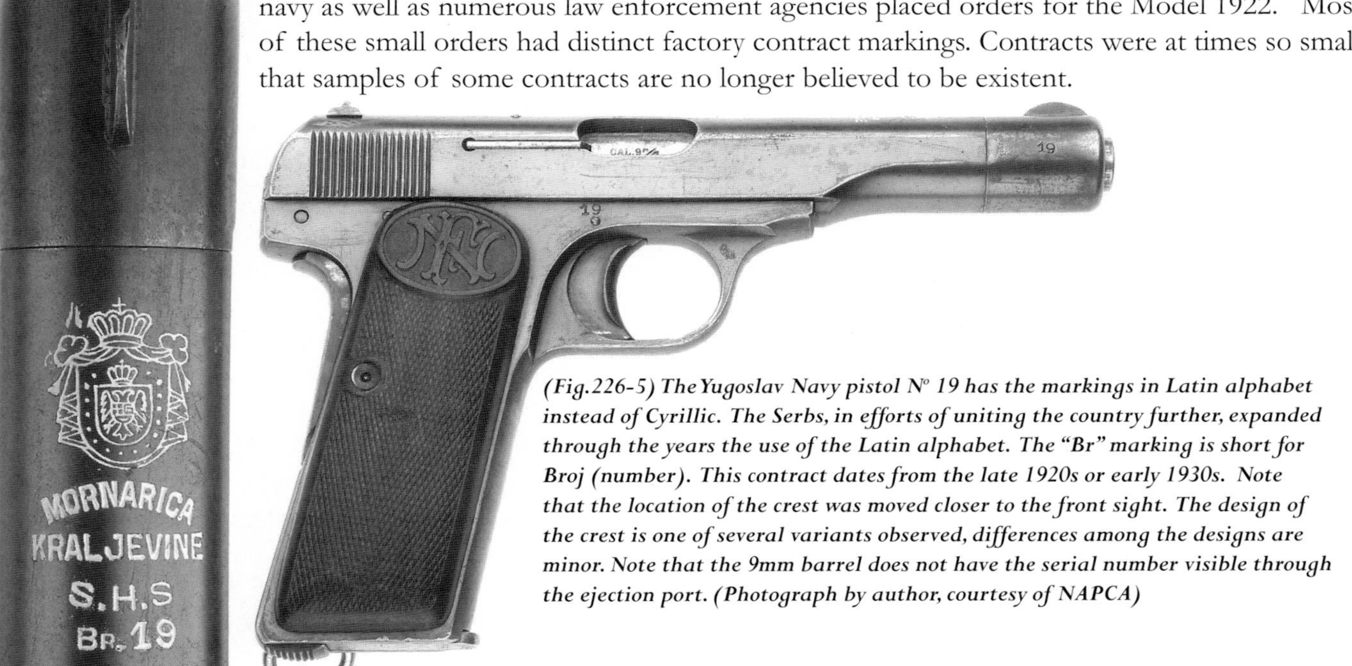

(Fig.226-5) The Yugoslav Navy pistol N° 19 has the markings in Latin alphabet instead of Cyrillic. The Serbs, in efforts of uniting the country further, expanded through the years the use of the Latin alphabet. The "Br" marking is short for Broj (number). This contract dates from the late 1920s or early 1930s. Note that the location of the crest was moved closer to the front sight. The design of the crest is one of several variants observed, differences among the designs are minor. Note that the 9mm barrel does not have the serial number visible through the ejection port. (Photograph by author, courtesy of NAPCA)

(Fig.227-1) (L) Pistol N° 227177 was property marked "Park Authority Varazdin N° 38". The marking was hand engraved. Varazdin is a city in Croatia, it is marked in the Latin alphabet as Croatia did not use the Cyrillic alphabet. The "Br" marking is short for Broj (number). This pistol was shipped circa 1929. This pistol has the optional lanyard ring and is marked with the crest on the slide. The 9mm barrel shows the serial number through the ejection port. The barrel lug is beveled. (R) This early pistol N° 205573 was shipped circa 1925. It was factory marked "Postal Service 88" in Cyrillic. Early pistols are often marked in Cyrillic, even if they were used outside of Serbia. This pistol has the optional lanyard ring and is marked with the crest on the slide. The 9mm barrel shows the serial number through the ejection port. The barrel lug is beveled. (Photographs by author, courtesy of NAPCA)

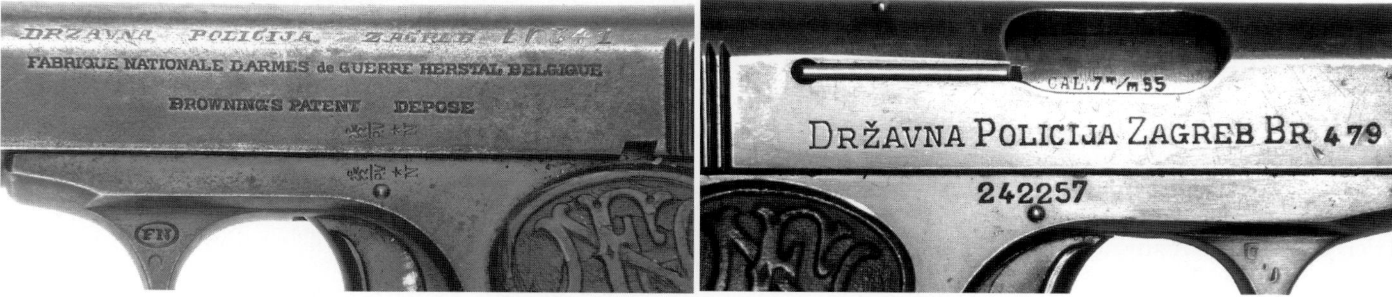

(Fig.227-2) (L) Pistol N° 233057 was property marked "State Police Zagreb N° 741". The marking was hand engraved. Zagreb is a city in Croatia, it is marked in the Latin alphabet as Croatia did not use the Cyrillic alphabet. The "Br" marking is short for Broj (number). This pistol was shipped circa 1929. This pistol has the optional lanyard ring and is marked with the crest on the slide. The 7.65mm barrel does not have the serial number visible through the ejection port. The barrel lug is not beveled. (R) This Zagreb state police pistol N° 242257 is part of a later order circa 1930. The property marking was factory roll marked on the slide, the issue number was hand stamped. This pistol has the optional lanyard ring and is marked with the crest on the slide. The 7.65mm barrel does not have the serial number visible through the ejection port. The barrel lug is not beveled. (Photographs by author, courtesy of NAPCA & Kevin Null)

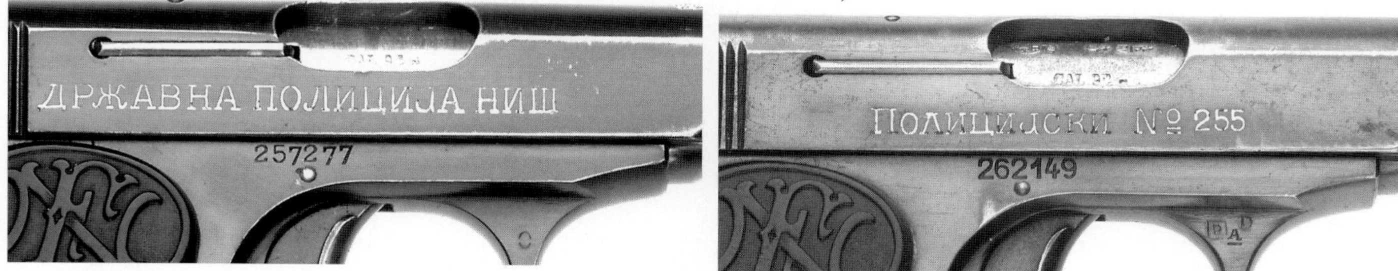

(Fig.227-3) (L) This Nish state police pistol N° 257277 has a factory roll engraved property marking without issue number. Nish is a city in Serbia and the marking is therefore in Cyrillic. This pistol has the optional lanyard ring and is marked with the crest on the slide. The 9mm barrel does not have the serial number visible through the ejection port. The barrel lug is not beveled. (R) This police pistol N° 262149 has a factory roll engraved property marking with issue number. This pistol has the optional lanyard ring and is marked with the crest on the slide. The 9mm barrel does not have the serial number visible through the ejection port. The barrel lug is beveled. (Photographs by author, courtesy of NAPCA & Kevin Null)

(Fig.227-4) Replacement barrels made in Yugoslavia at the arsenal of Kragujevac: Barrels marked "Vojno-Tehnicki Zavod" (Army Technical Works) were made prior to 1941. Barrels made after the war, were typically unmarked or show only the serial number. The arsenal went through several name changes after the war. In the prewar era it manufactured various equipment including military vehicles. The first name reference to Zastava appeared in 1946. During the Soviet years the facilities were known by many names including Zastava Arms Factory. The complex also manufactured Zastava cars for the civilian market, which were based on Italian Fiat models. (Photograph by author, courtesy of Michael Shade)

The Many Dutch Variations

The Dutch began negotiations to acquire the Model 1910 for the "Koninklijke Marechaussee" (Royal Military Constabulary) in January 1914. On April 27, 1914, Dutch trials determined that the 7.65mm cartridge was not powerful enough for use in a service sidearm. The 9mm Short version was considered as a suitable alternative. On May 6, 1914, the Dutch accepted the Model 1910 in 9mm Short and a price for 950 to 1000 pistols was requested. The purchase was delayed while the Dutch developed a suitable holster for the Model 1910. The outbreak of World War I halted the Dutch procurement of the Model 1910. After the war the Model 1910 was no longer considered.

The Dutch government placed its initial order for Model 1922 pistols in October 1924. The original order of 2000 pistols received the Dutch designation "Pistool M25 No.1". This first order, originally all in 7.65mm, was intended for two different law enforcement agencies:

-The "Koninklijke Marechaussee" (Royal Military Constabulary) was established in 1813 with limited duties until 1940. Comprised of about 1200 men, this agency handled police matters in the rural areas of the southern provinces and also handled passport control at border crossings. This agency received 1200 pistols out of this first order. This agency was expanded and restructured after World War II, it was entrusted with guarding the nation's borders. Additional duties included guarding the Royal Palace, and riot control. The Koninklijke Marechaussee continues to perform these duties today.

-The "Politie Troepen" (Police Troops) were managed under the ministry of defense and existed from 1919 to 1940. Their duties were many and included riot control. They received about 800 pistols out of this first order (fig.140-3).

After the purchase of the M25 No.1, the Dutch military decided to arm M20 Lewis machine gun crews with automatic pistols. Since 1922 these crews were only armed with a "stormdolk" (combat dagger). Both the Luger pistol, recommended from trials at the beginning of the century, and the FN Model 1922 were considered, but the more economical FN Model 1922 in 9mm Short, was selected. The army pistol was given the designation "Pistool M25 No.2." This designation was different from the first due to the difference in caliber.

All army pistols were in 9mm Short. Contract numbers for the M25 No.2 started with number 3000. The first army order consisted of 2000 pistols, and was shipped in April 1926. The M25 No.2 was issued to officers, machine-gunners and other specialists, such as barbers and farriers. The Dutch established a "werkplan" or scheduled purchase plan for each year. Army orders continued until the Nazi invasion of 1940. Unlike most foreign contracts, the Dutch purchased pistols on a continuing basis.

Other law enforcement agencies adopted the FN 1922 model. In 1927, 150 M25 No.2 and 10 Model 1905 pistols were purchased by the "Departement van Colonien" (Department of Colonies) for the Curacao police, in the Dutch Antilles. In 1929 the "Rijks Veldwacht" (Rural Guard) purchased 100 M25 No.1 pistols (7.65mm). In 1934 the "Nederlandsche Bank" (Dutch National Bank) exchanged 100 Model 1910 pistols for Model 1922 pistols.

The Dutch used the FN pistols extensively and were meticulous about numbering their pistols and accessories. This proved to be wise considering the length of the contracts and the repeat purchases that were made over the years. Pistols were shipped from FN to Dutch arsenals, most often Hembrug, where the pistols were accepted and stamped with the officer's acceptance marking (see fig.232-3).

The Dutch also purchased special instruction pistols from FN, which were modified and accordingly marked (see fig.142-2).

The Many Dutch Variations: Pistool M25 No.1 (7.65mm)

(Fig.229-1) The Koninklijke Marechaussee firing their M25 pistols, note the lanyard, holster and four-magazine pouch.

All dealings with the Dutch government were handled by FN's agent for Holland, Mr. Allard, whose offices were in Maestricht, a small town close to the Belgian border.

FN marked 1200 pistols "K.Mar" for Koninklijke Marechaussee (Royal Military Constabulary) and 800 pistols "Pol. Tr." for Politie Troepen (Police Troops) with ascending contract numbers. The Marechaussee pistols were numbered 1-1200 and Politie Troepen pistols from 1201 to 2000. In Holland these pistols were designated as M25 No.1 as the pistols were in 7.65mm caliber.

Although both agencies adopted the same pistol, each specified their own requirements for holsters and magazine pouches as well as training and maintenance procedures. Both the Marechausee and the Politie Troepen issued the pistol with a total of six magazines: one in the pistol, one spare in the holster and four in a separate magazine pouch.

On April 28, 1925, the Inspector General of the Marechaussee proposed three courses on the use of the new pistols for the month of May 1925. On May 18, he requested that the first pistols be issued to individuals who had successfully completed the course. Specifically, he requested that the first division of the Marechaussee receive 12 pistols, the second division, nine, the third division, twelve and the fourth division, nine.

At the same time the commander of the Politietroepen conducted two instruction courses during the month of May. Distribution of the M25 No.1 pistols continued through the month of September. Meanwhile, the development of a user's manual went back and forth between the two agencies for several months following the distribution of the pistols.

At that time, all related equipment was purchased from FN including holsters and ammunition. The 7.65mm round was designated as Patroon Scherpe No.19. On December 1928, the Dutch government issued the first report regarding problems with the FN 7.65mm ammunition. The problems were communicated to Mr. Allard in January 1927 and an FN investigation found the primers of the 7.65mm ammunition to be defective. FN consequently offered to replace all of the ammunition supplied. Although the problems with the 7.65mm ammunition were resolved in 1927, they caused the Dutch to change the pistols from 7.65mm caliber to 9mm, and the model designation from M25 No.1 to M25 No.2 in the early 1930s.

The Marechaussee ordered 30 7.65mm pistols on October 24, 1929. This may have been the last Marechaussee order before switching over to the M25 No.2 configuration.

Observed or reported K.Mar. pistols: 25, 32, 348, 1185

Observed or reported Pol.Tr. pistols: 1253, 1620, 1718, 1779, 1814, 2041

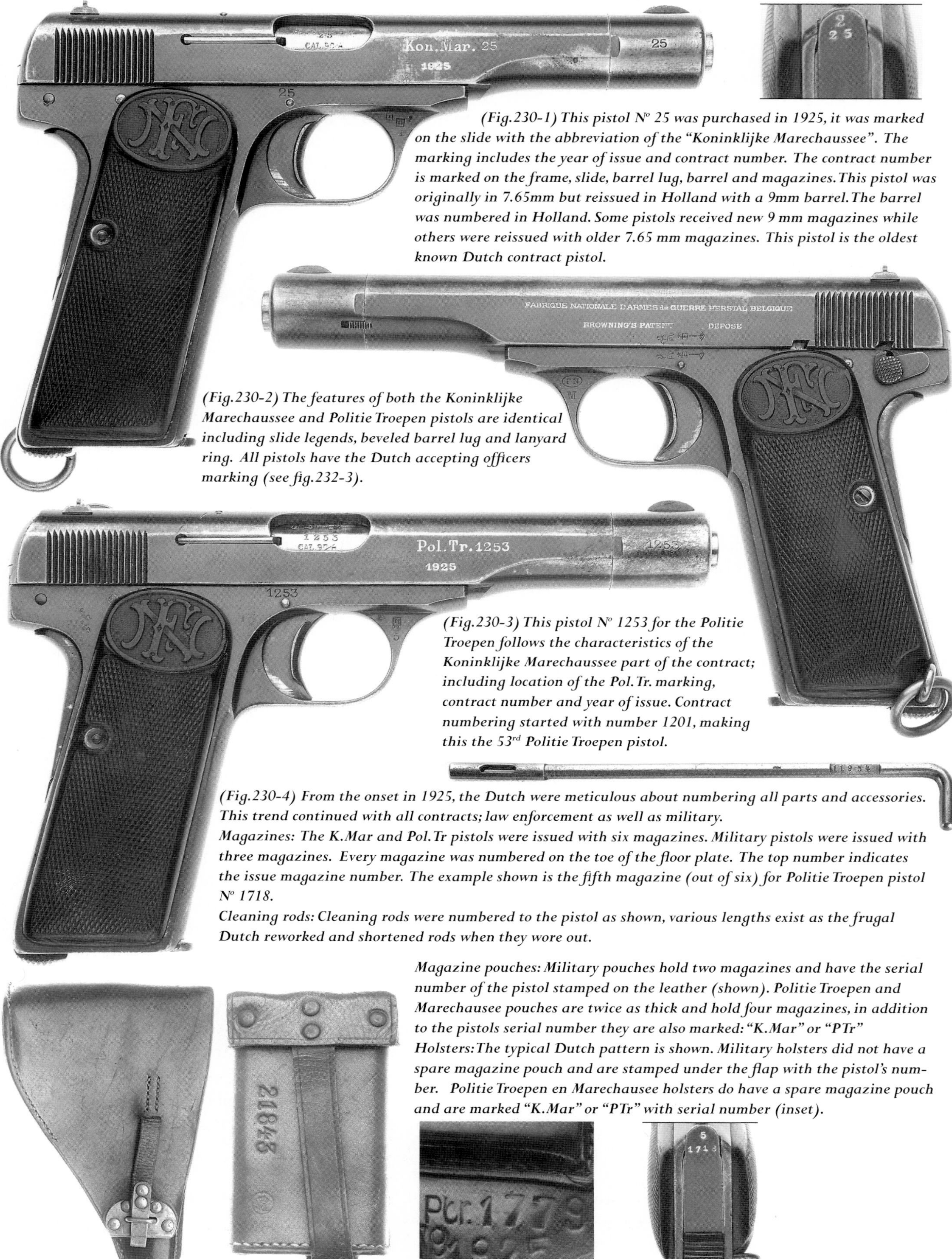

(Fig.230-1) This pistol N° 25 was purchased in 1925, it was marked on the slide with the abbreviation of the "Koninklijke Marechaussee". The marking includes the year of issue and contract number. The contract number is marked on the frame, slide, barrel lug, barrel and magazines. This pistol was originally in 7.65mm but reissued in Holland with a 9mm barrel. The barrel was numbered in Holland. Some pistols received new 9 mm magazines while others were reissued with older 7.65 mm magazines. This pistol is the oldest known Dutch contract pistol.

(Fig.230-2) The features of both the Koninklijke Marechaussee and Politie Troepen pistols are identical including slide legends, beveled barrel lug and lanyard ring. All pistols have the Dutch accepting officers marking (see fig.232-3).

(Fig.230-3) This pistol N° 1253 for the Politie Troepen follows the characteristics of the Koninklijke Marechaussee part of the contract; including location of the Pol.Tr. marking, contract number and year of issue. Contract numbering started with number 1201, making this the 53rd Politie Troepen pistol.

(Fig.230-4) From the onset in 1925, the Dutch were meticulous about numbering all parts and accessories. This trend continued with all contracts; law enforcement as well as military.
Magazines: The K.Mar and Pol.Tr pistols were issued with six magazines. Military pistols were issued with three magazines. Every magazine was numbered on the toe of the floor plate. The top number indicates the issue magazine number. The example shown is the fifth magazine (out of six) for Politie Troepen pistol N° 1718.
Cleaning rods: Cleaning rods were numbered to the pistol as shown, various lengths exist as the frugal Dutch reworked and shortened rods when they wore out.

Magazine pouches: Military pouches hold two magazines and have the serial number of the pistol stamped on the leather (shown). Politie Troepen and Marechausee pouches are twice as thick and hold four magazines, in addition to the pistols serial number they are also marked: "K.Mar" or "PTr"
Holsters: The typical Dutch pattern is shown. Military holsters did not have a spare magazine pouch and are stamped under the flap with the pistol's number. Politie Troepen en Marechausee holsters do have a spare magazine pouch and are marked "K.Mar" or "PTr" with serial number (inset).

The Many Dutch Variations: Pistool M25 No.2 , M25 (9mm Short) and Training Pistols

The Dutch Army's adoption of the Model 1922 resulted from the adoption of the M25 No.1 by the Marechaussee and Politie Troepen. It appears that the army never considered the 7.65mm round and focused on the 9x17mm round.

On June 25, 1925 a request was placed by the army for four Model 1922 pistols. The Dutch government replied on June 27 that the M25 No.2 pistol, the Dutch designation for the Model in 9mm Short, was not yet available. On June 30 and July 1, 1925 the Dutch government indicated that no negotiations had yet taken place with FN for supplying the 2000 M.25 No.2 pistols.

Apparently the Dutch government had already placed 2000 M25 No.2 pistols on their "werkplan" (scheduled purchase plan) although trials had not been completed and no contract had been placed with FN(1).

On October 9, 1925 the military asked the Inspector General of the Marechaussee and the Commander of the Politie Troepen for a brief report regarding experiences with the functioning and firing of the M25 No.1. That same day Mauser was contacted and asked to provide a trials pistol, ammunition and pricing(2). The Mauser pistol was supplied and trials were conducted on April 6, 1926. Trials of the Model 1922 had already been performed on March 19 with pistol N° 200223.

The initial contract for 2000 M25 No.2 pistols(1) was fulfilled on July 2, 1926. Prior to the delivery of the first pistols, the army placed a request for special training pistols on June 2, 1926. On July 7, 1926 the army ordered 41 special training pistols.

The training pistols, called "Exercitie Pistolen," were essential in the distribution of the pistols. Most likely the army anticipated a steep learning curve in the transition from a revolver to a semi-automatic pistol. Issues had arisen resulting from requests for additional dummy cartridges for use in M25 No.1 training., and the training pistols were intended to avoid accidents in educational settings. The training pistols were first made at FN and included a brass identification plate as well as a brass barrel lug. These pistols were not to be fired and were only used for instructional purposes. Holland continued to purchase small quantities of training pistols (e.g., the October 3, 1934 order for 100 training pistols). The Dutch also converted damaged or worn pistols into training pistols.

Issue M25 No.2 pistols were supplied from FN with a Wilhelmina crest roll engraved on the top of the slide, contract numbers on the frame, slide and barrel lug and equipped with a lanyard ring. The Dutch were adamant about numbering the pistols and numbered the barrels in such a way that the numbering was visible through the ejection port. Cleaning rods, magazines(3), holsters and pistol pouches were all numbered to match the pistol. The army issued the pistol with three magazines: one in the pistol and two spares in a separate magazine pouch.

M25 No.2 Contract Numbers:
About 63,000 M25 No.2 pistols were delivered before the German occupation of FN. This chart approximates acquisition years of M25 No.2 pistols. Please note that the M25 No.2 production started with number 3000. This number should be added to the quantities in the chart below for cross-referencing contract numbers. The last order was in production when the Germans invaded and was never delivered.

1926:	**Order of first 2000 pistols, starting with contract N° 3000**
January 1930:	**20,000 M25 No.2 are on hand**
May 1932:	**24,000 M25 No.2 are on hand**
1936:	**M25 No.2 pistols in inventory reached contract number 31499**
1937:	**Unknown**
1938:	**At least 4000 M25 No.2 are ordered and received**
1939:	**At least 15,000 M25 No.2 are ordered and received**
February 1940:	**At least 5000 pistols are received**
May 1940:	**15,000 pistols are ordered (never delivered)**

(Fig.231-1) Portrait of a young Queen Wilhelmina

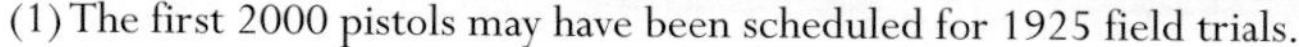

(1) The first 2000 pistols may have been scheduled for 1925 field trials.

(2) No model designation is given, asides from its 9mm caliber

(3) Check matching magazines for originality as numbers are often recently applied

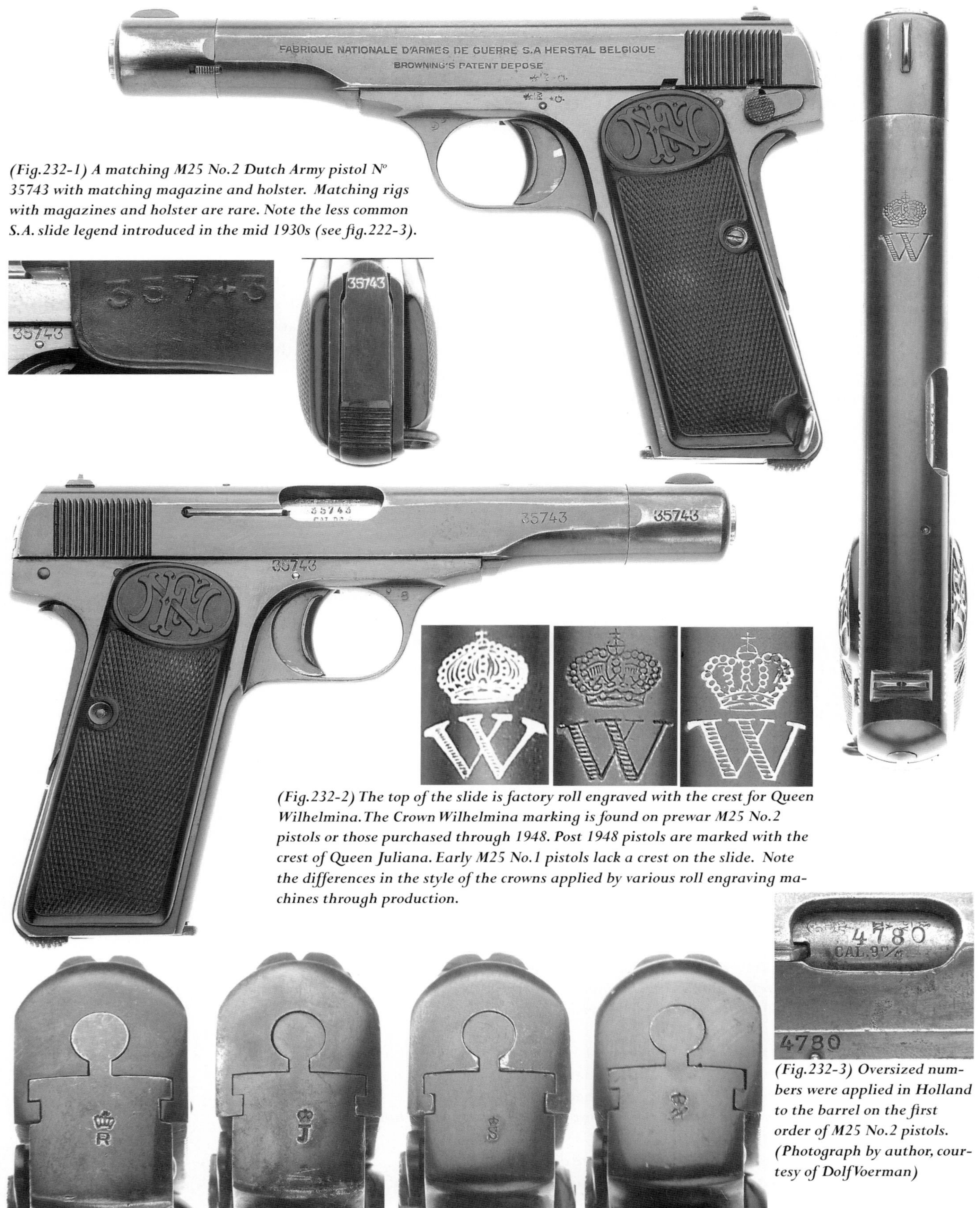

(Fig.232-1) A matching M25 No.2 Dutch Army pistol N° 35743 with matching magazine and holster. Matching rigs with magazines and holster are rare. Note the less common S.A. slide legend introduced in the mid 1930s (see fig.222-3).

(Fig.232-2) The top of the slide is factory roll engraved with the crest for Queen Wilhelmina. The Crown Wilhelmina marking is found on prewar M25 No.2 pistols or those purchased through 1948. Post 1948 pistols are marked with the crest of Queen Juliana. Early M25 No.1 pistols lack a crest on the slide. Note the differences in the style of the crowns applied by various roll engraving machines through production.

(Fig.232-3) Oversized numbers were applied in Holland to the barrel on the first order of M25 No.2 pistols. (Photograph by author, courtesy of Dolf Voerman)

(Fig.232-3) Inspector markings from the Dutch State Arsenal in Hembrug are an easy way to identify Dutch acceptance. The crown over stylized "W" does not refer to Queen Wilhelmina. The letter is the initial of the accepting inspector Mr. Wolf. Other inspector markings are "H" for Captain Holscher, "J" for Lt. Janssen, "Q" for Captain Wu Quesne van Brughem , "R" for Mr. Ringeling and the initial "S' is believed to be for Lt. J.F. Schultink. These inspecting officers accepted the pistols in Holland. This practice became an important clue to identify legitimate early WaA613 wartime pistols (page 244).

Nr. 90j.

VOORSCHRIFT
PISTOOL M. 25.

(Aanschrijving M. v. D. van 3 November 1933, IIe Afd. B Nr. 51).

BREDA.
DE KONINKLIJKE MILITAIRE ACADEMIE.
1933.

(Fig.233-2) The Dutch printed numerous instruction manuals domestically. This 1933 90j manual already refers to the M25 model and no longer to the M25 No.2.

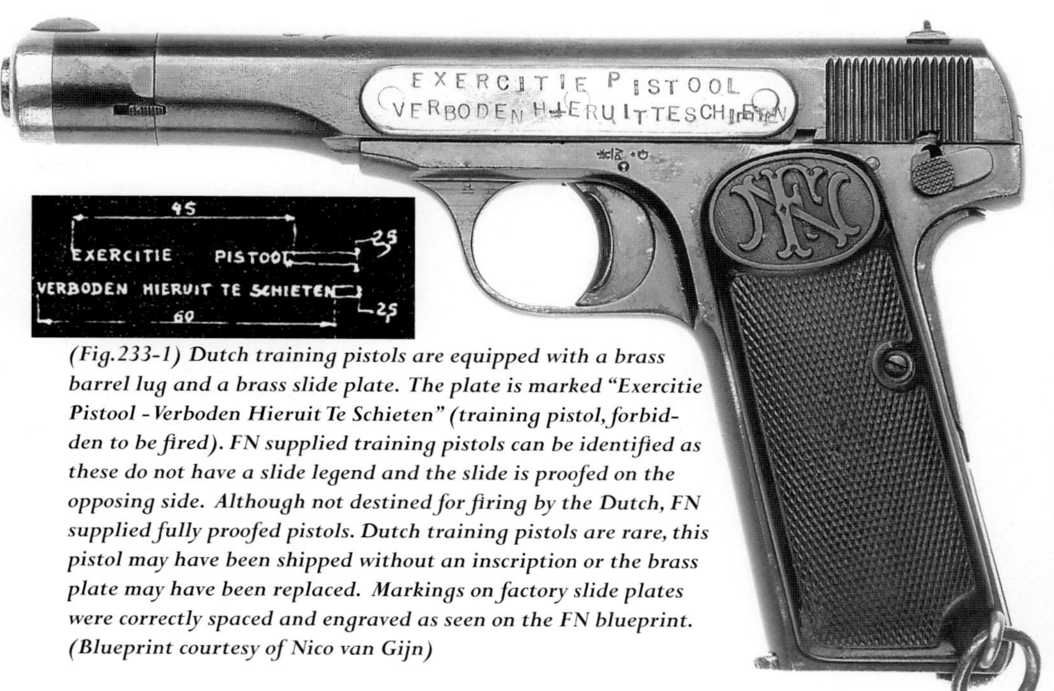

(Fig.233-1) Dutch training pistols are equipped with a brass barrel lug and a brass slide plate. The plate is marked "Exercitie Pistool - Verboden Hieruit Te Schieten" (training pistol, forbidden to be fired). FN supplied training pistols can be identified as these do not have a slide legend and the slide is proofed on the opposing side. Although not destined for firing by the Dutch, FN supplied fully proofed pistols. Dutch training pistols are rare, this pistol may have been shipped without an inscription or the brass plate may have been replaced. Markings on factory slide plates were correctly spaced and engraved as seen on the FN blueprint. (Blueprint courtesy of Nico van Gijn)

The Many Dutch Variations: The R.V. (Rijks Veldwacht) Pistols

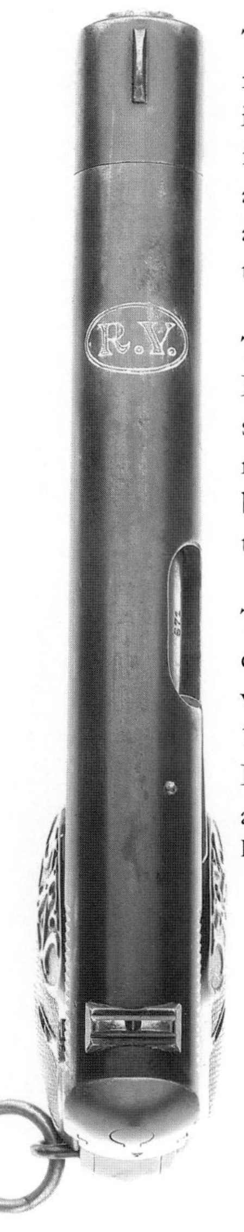

The Veldwacht (field guard) is an old term going back centuries in the Low Countries. In many remote rural areas, veldwachters (field guards) were the only form of law enforcement. Primarily responsible for fish and game enforcement, field guards often took on various law enforcement functions and worked closely with local county administrations. The county field guard (Veldwacht) and royal field guard (Rijks Veldwacht) evolved over time, reflecting the needs of rural and agrarian areas. In many cases field guards worked alone or in small groups of two or three. When needed the field guard relied on the Koninklijke Marechaussee for assistance.

The Rijks Veldwacht was the last of the national law enforcement agencies to be upgraded with Model 1922 pistols. The first order for 100 M.25 No.1 pistols was placed on April 27, 1929, the second, also for 100 pistols, on November 29, 1929. Pistols from the second order bear contract numbers 104 to 203. The bulk of the pistols were ordered in 1931. The last order appears to have been placed in 1939 for 13 pistols. In all, about 1500 pistols were ordered by the Rijks Veldwacht in the prewar era.

The pistols were factory roll marked with the letters R.V. on the top of the slide. All pistols were equipped with a lanyard ring. The 1929 orders were shipped from FN in 7.65mm. These pistols were converted in the 1930s to 9mm caliber (M25 No.2). Contract numbers were ascending; the 1929 orders had no prefix while 1931 orders had a "1931" prefix followed by the contract number. It is not known how later orders were marked. Like all Dutch pistols, the RV pistols were issued with a holster and numbered magazines.

Reported and observed RV contract pistols: 67, 90, 427, 483, 671, 1478

(Fig.233-3) All Rijks Veldwacht pistols were issued with a factory roll engraved "R.V." marking on the slide. The original order of 1929 did not have a contract number prefix as seen here with pistol N°67. The 1931 orders were marked with a "1931-" contract prefix as seen in fig.234-1. (Photograph of N°67 by author, courtesy of Michael Shade)

(Fig.234-1) This Rijks Veldwacht pistol N°671 has the 1931 contract prefix. The pistol features include the FN applied R. V. slide crest and optional lanyard ring. The serial number on the 9mm barrel is visible through the ejection port and the magazine is numbered to the gun.

The Many Dutch Variations: Postwar BZ and DvF Pistols

Postwar supplied Model 1922 pistols usually feature a factory roll marked Queen Wilhelmina or Juliana (post 1948) marking on the top of the slide. The Dutch streamlined the distribution of these pistols, and in most cases it is impossible to identify which department used a pistol as there are no specific markings.

The Binnenlandse Zaken (interior affairs ministry) pistols were not used by a ministry as implied by the name. These pistols were provided by the ministry of interior affairs to small municipalities, which were financially unable to acquire their own pistols. The pistols were loaned to municipalities and property marked BZ or BiZa (Binnenlandse Zaken). These pistols were used by the Gemeentelijke PolitieKorps (Municipal Police Corps). Pistols purchased by the communities directly with tax revenues were not marked other than the crest on top of the slide. .

The Departement van Financien (Department of Finances) switched from its prewar use of the Model 1910 (see page 206) to the Model 1922 immediately after the war. These pistols were all post-liberation pistols made from German wartime parts (see page 206, 250).

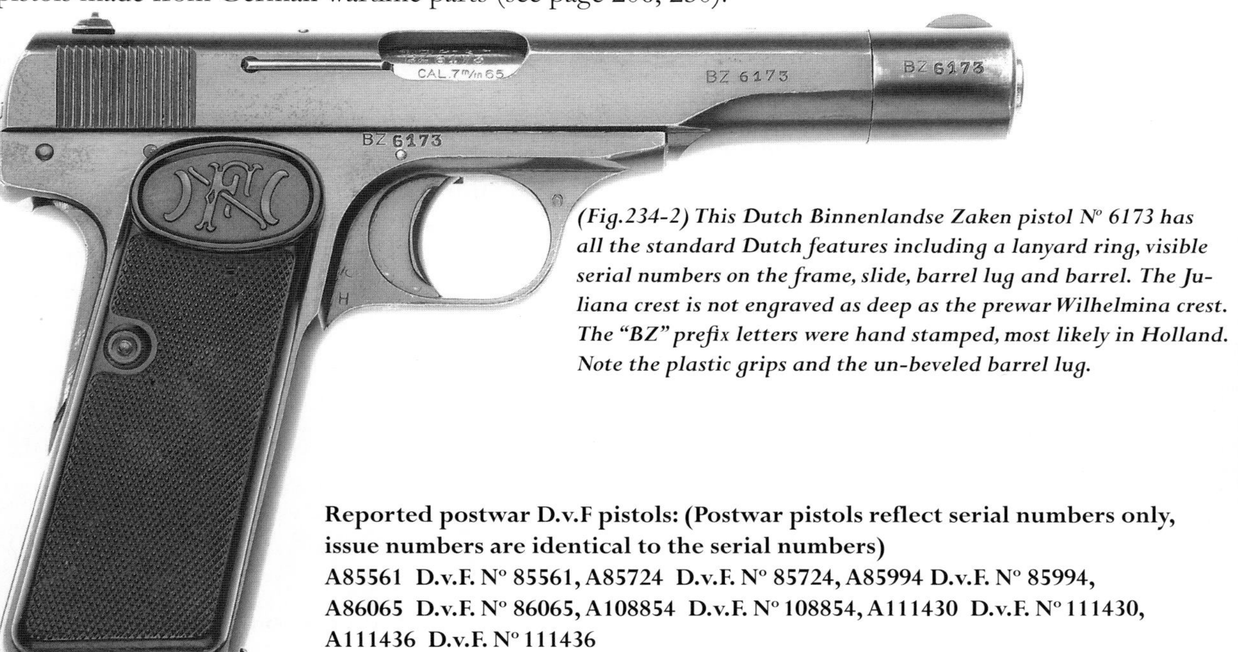

(Fig.234-2) This Dutch Binnenlandse Zaken pistol N° 6173 has all the standard Dutch features including a lanyard ring, visible serial numbers on the frame, slide, barrel lug and barrel. The Juliana crest is not engraved as deep as the prewar Wilhelmina crest. The "BZ" prefix letters were hand stamped, most likely in Holland. Note the plastic grips and the un-beveled barrel lug.

Reported postwar D.v.F pistols: (Postwar pistols reflect serial numbers only, issue numbers are identical to the serial numbers)
A85561 D.v.F. N° 85561, A85724 D.v.F. N° 85724, A85994 D.v.F. N° 85994, A86065 D.v.F. N° 86065, A108854 D.v.F. N° 108854, A111430 D.v.F. N° 111430, A111436 D.v.F. N° 111436

The Mexican Contracts

Mexico became an FN customer in 1924 with the purchase of considerable quantities of FN Mauser rifles and carbines. In 1927 FN's agent in Liège, Schroeder, brokered another contract with Mexico for Model 1922 pistols. The pistols were factory marked on the slide "Gobierno del Distrito Federal" (Federal District Government – Mexico City). Although all shipped from FN in June 1927, variants within the contract have surfaced, including a sample which has an elaborate Mexican crest on the top of the slide and Maritime Police pistols which did not have any factory contract markings. The bulk of the pistols were used by federal law enforcement agencies in the district of Mexico City.

Mexico ordered additional Model 1922 pistols in 1957 and large quantities of spare parts including grips, barrels, frames, slides, barrel lugs and smaller parts. Many Mexican contract pistols are arsenal reworked and refinished, with various degrees of craftsmanship. Postwar replacement parts can be found on prewar pistols and serial numbers are sometimes re-stamped to match the original numbers. The arsenal bluing resembles original FN rust blue. In some cases great care was made to make the pistol match; examples exist on which the Mexicans removed the Liège inspector's marking on a frame or slide and re-stamped it to match the rest of the pistol.

The Maritime or Port Police pistols were stamped in Mexico with the letters P.M. (Policia Maritima) and a small anchor symbol. Mexican Model 1922 contracts were always in 9mm.

Observed or reported serial numbers: 213118, 219741, 219786, 219984, 222495, 222517, 223215, 223244
Observed Maritime Police numbers: 222547 (1927 order), 173256 (1950s order)

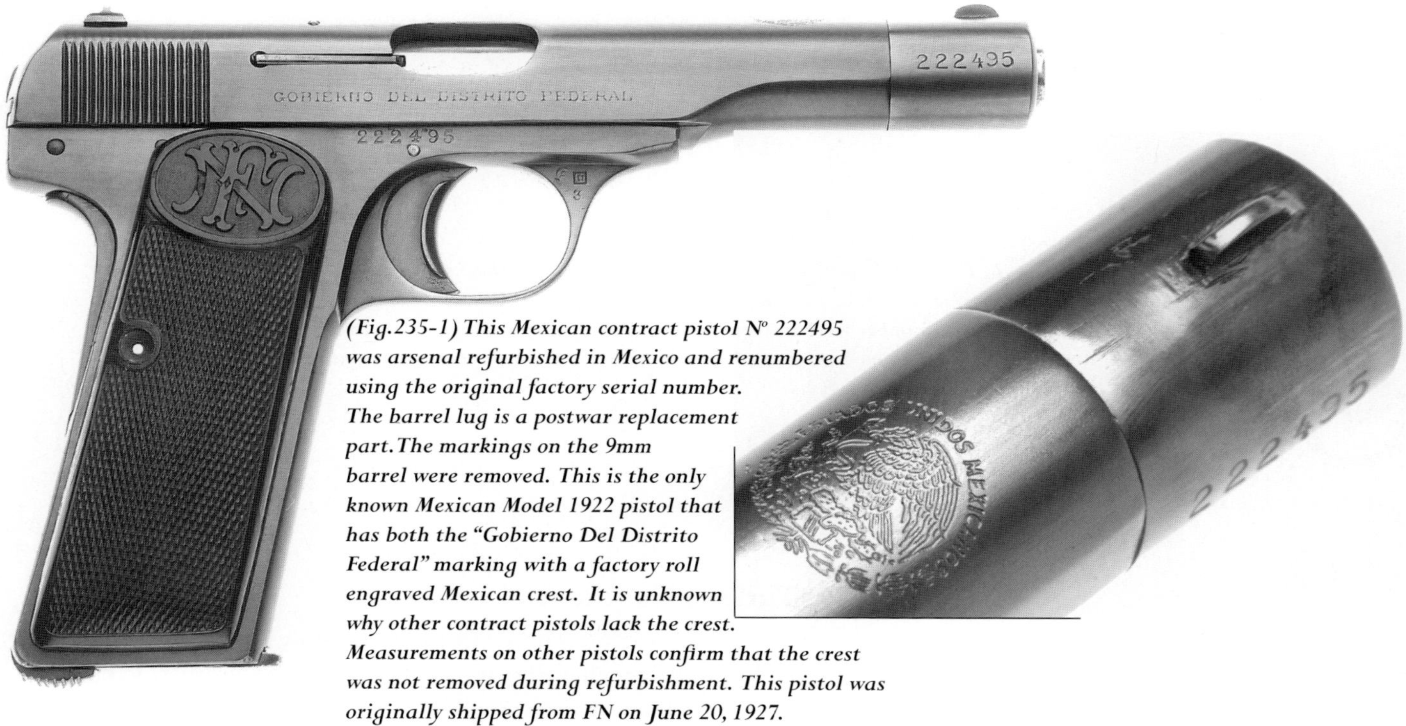

(Fig.235-1) This Mexican contract pistol N° 222495 was arsenal refurbished in Mexico and renumbered using the original factory serial number. The barrel lug is a postwar replacement part. The markings on the 9mm barrel were removed. This is the only known Mexican Model 1922 pistol that has both the "Gobierno Del Distrito Federal" marking with a factory roll engraved Mexican crest. It is unknown why other contract pistols lack the crest. Measurements on other pistols confirm that the crest was not removed during refurbishment. This pistol was originally shipped from FN on June 20, 1927.

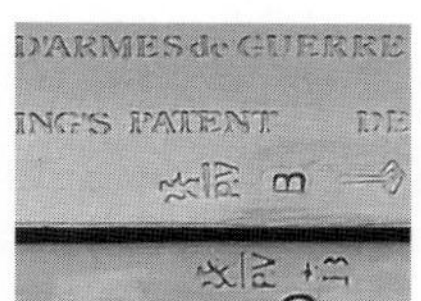

(Fig.235-2) Some of the Mexican arsenal work is surprisingly detailed. Note how the inspector's letter on the slide was removed and re-stamped to match the frame.

(Fig.235-3) The Policia Maritima and anchor markings on pistol N° 222547 were hand stamped. This pistol has no factory applied contract markings and was shipped together with the Gobierno Del Distrito Federal pistols on June 20, 1927. The postwar pistol N° 173256 had identical markings. These pistols, like all Mexican contract pistols, are in 9x17mm.

The FN 1922 Pistol for Greece

The 9x17mm Model 1922 pistol was the official sidearm of the Greek army from 1926 to 1941. 9,980 pistols were purchased by Greece in 1926. The order was shipped from FN on May 1, 1926.

All pistols were marked on the slide with the Greek letters Epsilon Sigma marking for Ellynikis Etrato (Hellenic Army - Greek Army) and their issue number. Unlike the Dutch and Yugoslav pistols, the Greek did not request contract numbers for the pistols. The pistols were numbered in FN's old style; the pistol's serial number with a separate issue number.

The Greek pistols were put to extreme use. In 1940-1941 they were used against the invading Italian and German forces and then by the resistance. After the war, surviving pistols remained in service in various branches including the coast-guard.

Pistols observed or reported: 202966 (issue N° 559), 205492 (issue N° 1577), 211770 (issue N° 2341), 212129 (issue N° 4570), 215100 (issue N° 7916), 215964 (issue N° 8808)

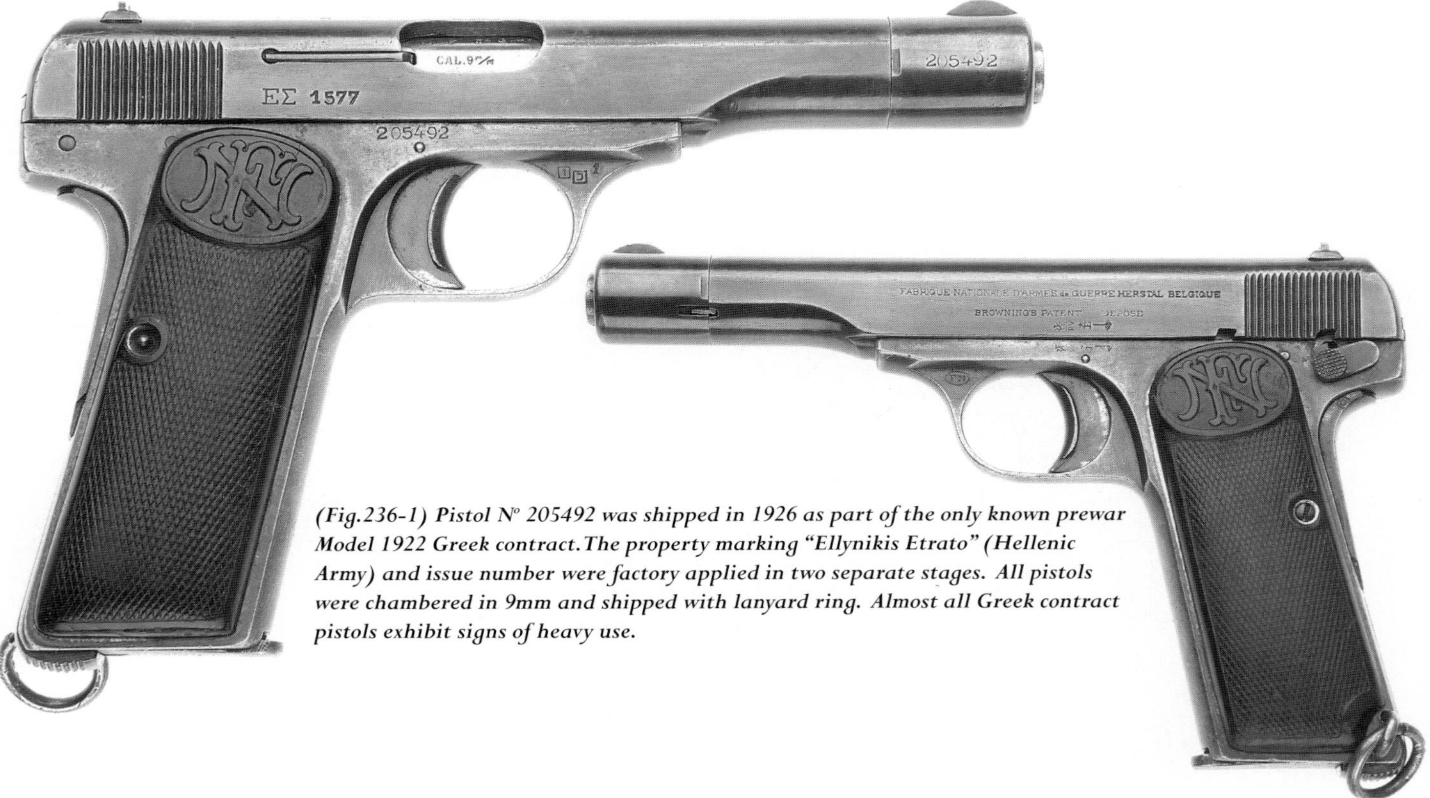

(Fig.236-1) Pistol N° 205492 was shipped in 1926 as part of the only known prewar Model 1922 Greek contract. The property marking "Ellynikis Etrato" (Hellenic Army) and issue number were factory applied in two separate stages. All pistols were chambered in 9mm and shipped with lanyard ring. Almost all Greek contract pistols exhibit signs of heavy use.

The Turkish Contracts

The remnants of the Ottoman Empire were restructured and became Turkey in 1923. Despite strong ties with Germany, both the Ottoman Empire and the Turkish Republic purchased pistols from FN. The Ottoman Empire purchased Model 1903 pistols as police pistols until the model was discontinued in 1927. Turkey purchased Model 1922s for military as well as law-enforcement application after the Model 1903 was discontinued. Turkish Model 1922 contracts were always in 9mm. Several contract variations have surfaced. Contract markings were applied at FN.

-T.C. Subay: (Turkiye Cumhuriyeti Subay) Officer of the Republic of Turkey
contract numbers noted: 774, 1015, 1073, 1080, 1300, 1515, 1569, 1767, 1866, 1996, 2116, 2139, 2229, 2444, 2555, 2829

-T.C. Ordusuna Mahsustur: (Turkiye Cumhuriyeti Mahsustur) Property of the Armed Forces of the Republic of Turkey. Serial numbers noted: 240549 (issue N° 2379), 243,595 (issue N° 4944)

-T.C. Subaylara Mahsustur: (Property of) Officer of the Armed Forces
Serial numbers noted: 256713 (slide only), 256976, 259759

-T.C. Polis: Republic of Turkey, Police
Serial numbers noted: 237602 (issue N° 34), shipped from FN on September 30, 1929

The Turkish Contracts (continued)

(Fig.237-1) This Turkish officer's pistol N° 2829 is part of a contract of about 3000 pistols. Unlike other Turkish contract pistols, these pistols show contract numbers instead of FN serial numbers. Note that all Turkish contract pistols have un-beveled barrel lugs and barrels are chambered in 9mm. (Photograph by author, courtesy of Wendell Patton)

(Fig.237-2) This Turkish Armed Forces pistol N° 240549 has a standard FN serial number. Note the unique method of marking the issue number on the slide. This pistol was shipped from FN in 1930. (Photograph by author, courtesy of Kevin Null)

(Fig.237-3) The slide of this Turkish officer's pistol N° 256713 shows the factory applied roll marking. A large issue number "171" is stamped between the slide serrations and ejection port. These pistols were shipped around 1936. It is not known how their issue differs from the T.C. Subay marked officers' pistols. (Photograph courtesy of Kevin Null)

(Fig.237-4) The Turkish police pistols are the only contract to have the T.C. marking roll engraved on top of the slide. This slide marking is in the typical location between the ejection port and barrel lug. This pistol N° 237602 has the Turkish style issue number on the slide, this pistol was shipped from FN on September 30, 1929. Like all Turkish contract pistols, it is chambered in 9mm. (Photographs courtesy of Timo Martelius, Maanpuolustuskorkeakoulu Sotamuseo / Military Museum of Finland)

The French Orders for the Navy, Police and Shanghai Concession

(Fig.238-1)
See fig.239-1

The relationship between FN and the French government is often overshadowed by the lengthy trials of the Grand Rendement (page 261) and the ultimate rejection of the FN developed 7.65 Long pistols.

While the army did not purchase FN products, the French Air Force purchased Browning machine guns and the French Navy purchased an estimated 5500 Model 1922 pistols in the late 1920s or early 1930s.

Requests from the French Navy for a corrosion resistant finish forced FN to develop an enamel finish. The black enamel finish was applied over a phosphate base (see page 98) and proved to be so good that it became an (optional) finish for decades.

The French Navy contract Model 1922s were the first ones produced without beveled barrel lugs. The contract number on the barrel, visible through the ejection port, resulted from another French Navy specification. The lanyard ring was ordered as well as a specific contract numbering scheme. All guns were roll engraved with an anchor logo on the top of the slide. Most navy Model 1922 pistols were arsenal refinished by the French in the postwar era. A green - gray phosphate finish was applied throughout the gun, including on the barrel and magazine.

French police departments used FN pistols throughout the country. Many of these pistols remained unmarked, except for the Model 1922 contract that was shipped to the Toulouse police in 1937. These were factory marked "Police Municipal de Toulouse". Like the navy pistols, the barrel lug was not beveled and the pistols were equipped with a lanyard ring.

The Shanghai French Concession pistols (see page 191 for the Shanghai police structure) were ordered with the same features as the navy contract; un-beveled barrel lugs and lanyard rings. Like many of the French police orders, no special contract markings were applied, yet these pistols can be identified by the Chinese markings added later in their service lives. The Shanghai French Concession pistols were used extensively, some works report that the French police patrolled the Shanghai streets with loaded pistols in hand. Ultimately these pistols ended up in Chinese arsenals, with some markings being applied after the communist takeover of the country in 1949. The pistols were shipped from FN in August 1932; the contract brokered by Schroeder in Liège. It is possible that more than one order was placed. The various prewar orders were all in 7.65mm caliber, had un-beveled barrel lugs and were equipped with lanyard rings.

France purchased sizeable quantities of post liberation "A" prefix pistols (page 250) in 1945 and placed an order for 30,000 7.65mm Model 1922 pistols in 1946. None of the post liberation pistols had any special characteristics or contract markings. The 1946 pistols can be identified as they are serialized from 1 to 30,000, have wooden grips, un-beveled barrel lugs and all feature the "square 6" stamp for 1946 production on the trigger-guard (see page 86). These pistols were not supplied with lanyard rings, although the French modified many (including wartime pistols) by cutting the grips and adding a large lanyard staple (fig.240-2). Additional orders were placed through the 1950s and 1960s, those pistols reflecting standard postwar serial numbers.

A 1992 letter from the General Administration of Paris indicates that 10,011 Model 1922 pistols were purchased from November 1945 through November 1968. An additional 382 pistols were purchased after November 1968. These large numbers indicate the scope of French purchases. Pistols were purchased for the French Army between 1945 and 1957, French Customs from 1946 to 1983, and for agents of "Les Eaux et Forests" (Forestry Department) from 1950 to the 1980s. France continued to purchase small quantities of FN pistols for the Syrian police, the Model 1910 was replaced in the postwar era by the Model 1922 (see page 207).

French Navy pistols reported: 1009, 1502, 1790, 1825, 1992, 2816, 3799, 4145, 4167, 4208, 4341, 4343, 5121, 5443, 5473
Toulouse police pistols observed or reported: 261814, 263747, 263786, 263788
Shanghai police pistols observed or reported: 245517, 245790, 246251

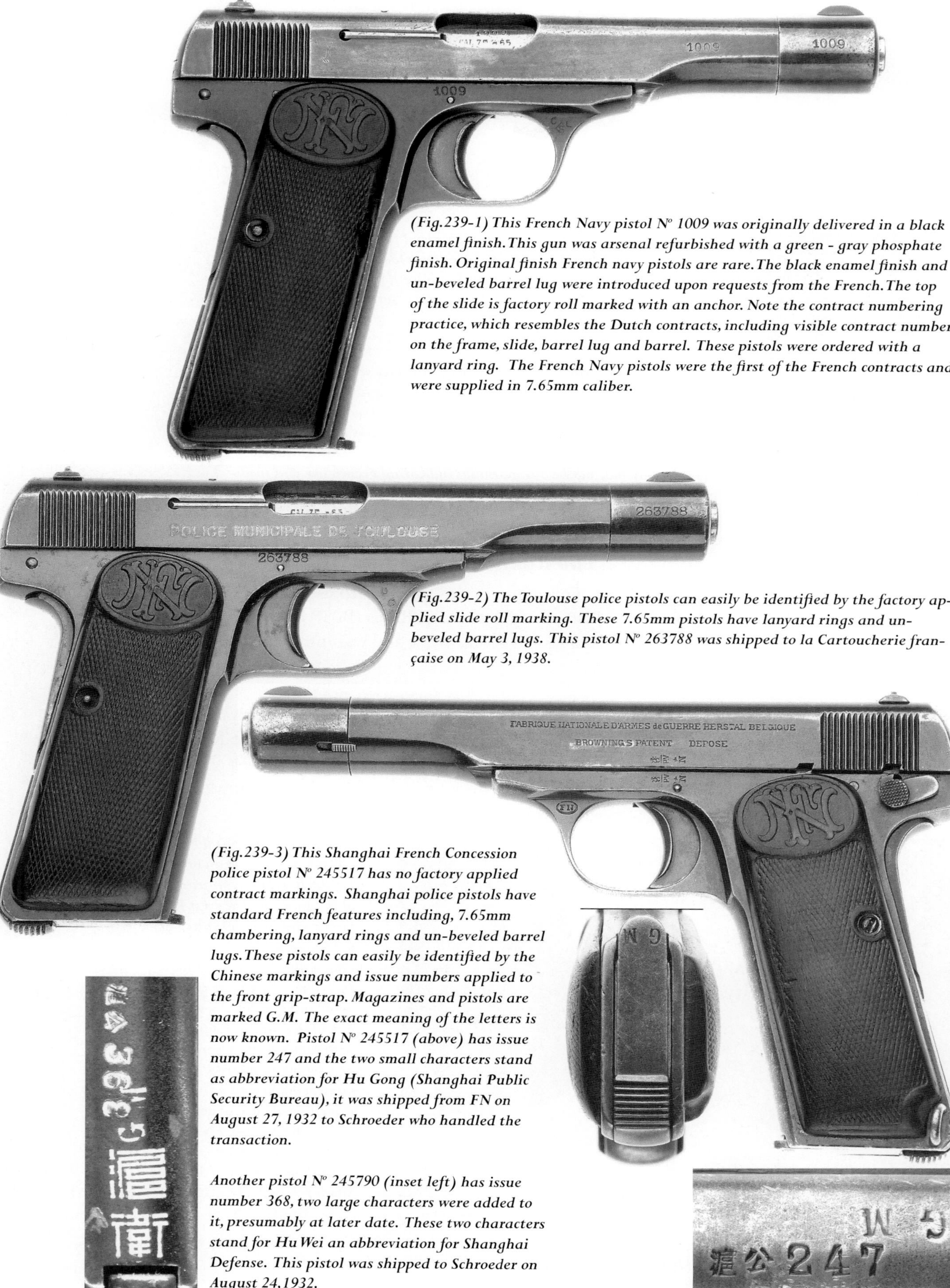

(Fig.239-1) This French Navy pistol N° 1009 was originally delivered in a black enamel finish. This gun was arsenal refurbished with a green - gray phosphate finish. Original finish French navy pistols are rare. The black enamel finish and un-beveled barrel lug were introduced upon requests from the French. The top of the slide is factory roll marked with an anchor. Note the contract numbering practice, which resembles the Dutch contracts, including visible contract numbers on the frame, slide, barrel lug and barrel. These pistols were ordered with a lanyard ring. The French Navy pistols were the first of the French contracts and were supplied in 7.65mm caliber.

(Fig.239-2) The Toulouse police pistols can easily be identified by the factory applied slide roll marking. These 7.65mm pistols have lanyard rings and un-beveled barrel lugs. This pistol N° 263788 was shipped to la Cartoucherie française on May 3, 1938.

(Fig.239-3) This Shanghai French Concession police pistol N° 245517 has no factory applied contract markings. Shanghai police pistols have standard French features including, 7.65mm chambering, lanyard rings and un-beveled barrel lugs. These pistols can easily be identified by the Chinese markings and issue numbers applied to the front grip-strap. Magazines and pistols are marked G.M. The exact meaning of the letters is now known. Pistol N° 245517 (above) has issue number 247 and the two small characters stand as abbreviation for Hu Gong (Shanghai Public Security Bureau), it was shipped from FN on August 27, 1932 to Schroeder who handled the transaction.

Another pistol N° 245790 (inset left) has issue number 368, two large characters were added to it, presumably at later date. These two characters stand for Hu Wei an abbreviation for Shanghai Defense. This pistol was shipped to Schroeder on August 24, 1932.

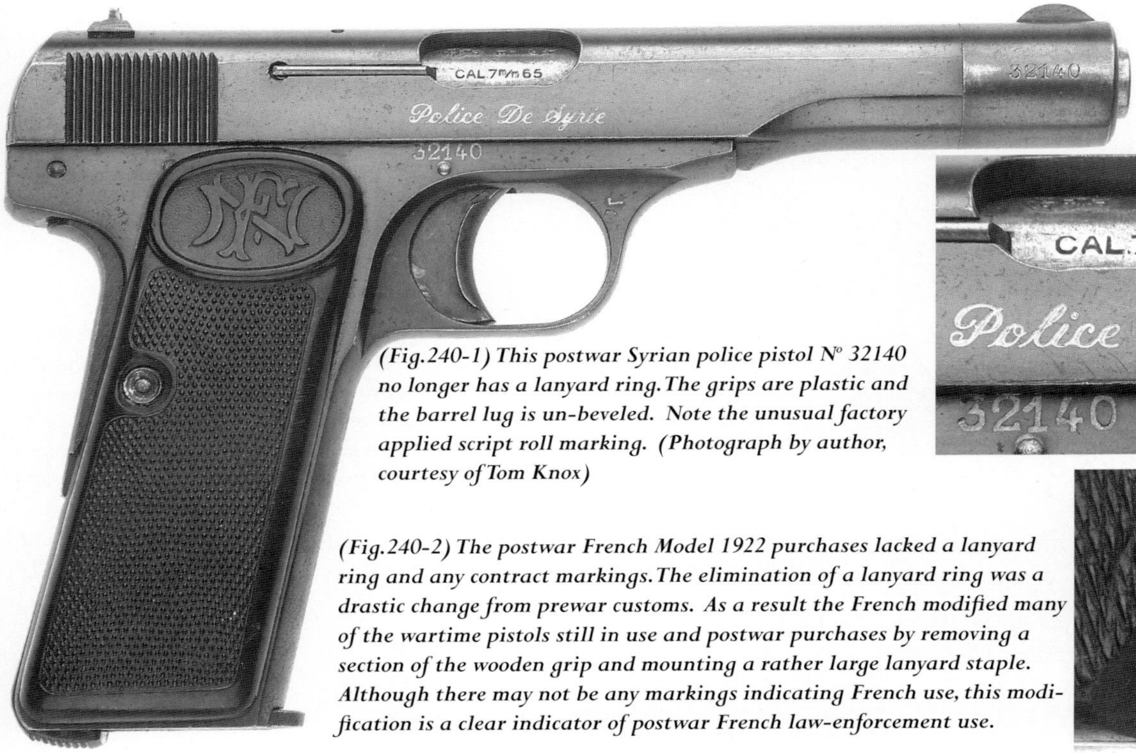

(Fig.240-1) This postwar Syrian police pistol N° 32140 no longer has a lanyard ring. The grips are plastic and the barrel lug is un-beveled. Note the unusual factory applied script roll marking. (Photograph by author, courtesy of Tom Knox)

(Fig.240-2) The postwar French Model 1922 purchases lacked a lanyard ring and any contract markings. The elimination of a lanyard ring was a drastic change from prewar customs. As a result the French modified many of the wartime pistols still in use and postwar purchases by removing a section of the wooden grip and mounting a rather large lanyard staple. Although there may not be any markings indicating French use, this modification is a clear indicator of postwar French law-enforcement use.

The Romanian Contract

Little is known about the Romanian contract. This contract was shipped from FN in September 1935. In 1936 and 1937 Romania purchased Browning Automatic Rifles (BAR) as well as M12 military motorcycles. King Carol II of Romania visited FN in 1938, and was introduced to much of FN's military products and latest innovations.

The crest on the FN 1922 pistols indicates delivery to the Ministry of the Interior, which may in turn indicate that the pistols were used for law enforcement purposes. The pistols for the Romanian government were ordered through the FN dealer and distributor B. D. Zissu in Bucharest. B. D. Zissu was not only the FN distributor, but was also the arms supplier to the Romanian Royal Court.

Observed or reported serial numbers: 209801, 248750

(Fig.240-4) King Carol II of Romania is shown tables filled with FN arms and their options in 1938. Here the king is shown all the Mauser receiver options including finishes and roll engraving options. (Photograph by author, courtesy of Carlos Davila)

(Fig.240-3) This pistol N° 209801 was part of an order for the Romanian Ministry of the Interior. The crest was factory applied and states Romania - Ministerul De Interne (Romania - Ministry of the Interior). Pistols are chambered in 9mm, have beveled barrel lugs and are equipped with lanyard rings. Serial numbers follow standard FN serial numbering practice. This pistol was shipped on September 6, 1935 to B.D. Zissu, FN's agent in Bucharest. (Photograph by author, courtesy of Michael Shade)

The FN 1922 in Scandinavia: The Danish Police & Finnish orders

The Danish Rigspolitiet (Federal Police) was established in 1911. Unlike the municipal police, the federal police was armed with pistols at its inception. The municipal police existed many years prior to the Rigspolitiet but remained unarmed until 1920. The Rigspolitiet was initially armed with a wide range of pistols. Many of the early pistols were transferred to the municipal police after 1920. The Model 1922 (in 7.65mm) was accepted early in the 1920s by the Rigspolitiet and the municipal police. In 1933 border patrols were created and were issued 100 9mm Model 1922 pistols. Denmark placed an order for 3000 7.65mm Model 1922 pistols for the Rigspolitiet late in the 1930s.
This Danish Rigspolitiet order was the first out of four structured orders totaling 5000 pistols. Only the first order was placed with FN (shipped in October 1939). Remaining orders were filled with 7.65mm German Walthers. All the guns were stamped in Denmark with the police marking: "Rplt." and issue number.
It is interesting to note that the issue numbers continued with the transition to the different Walthers.

FN 1922: **Rplt 1-3000**
Walther PP: **Rplt 3001-4200**
Walther PPK: **Rplt 4201-4400**

Denmark centralized all its firearm purchases in 1938. Purchases made prior to 1938 were often conducted by individual police departments, which freely ordered arms and accessories from dealers. The Model 1922 was not only used by the Federal Police but by numerous small departments. Both the Model 1910 and 1922 pistols were common in Danish law-enforcement.

The Model 1922 pistols remained in service for many years. The Danish police acquired M51 Madsen sub-machine guns between 1951 and 1954. Several sub-machine guns were purchased and the police decided to sell many of the older pistols on the commercial market. This was done primarily to finance the acquisition of the Madsen sub-machine guns. Many firearms were sold to the Pasadena Firearms Company and the Western Arms Corporation.
The following arms were sold to these U.S. importers; Colt 1911 pistols, Bergman Bayard pistols, Danish M1910/1921 pistols, various FN pistols, K-98K Mauser rifles and Husqvarna sub-machine guns. Only a fraction of the FN pistols in inventory were sold at that time. In 1989 there were still 20 officers who carried older FN Model 1922 pistols, the officers refusing to trade the guns in for Walther pistols.

Observed or reported "Rplt" pistols: 263935 (issue N° 995), 264150 (issue N° 1160), 267177 (issue N° 2581)

Finland purchased 2500 7.65mm Model 1922 pistols in 1939. The pistols were delivered in February 1940 together with the Model 1910 (page 209) and High Power pistols (page 284). Like all pistols out of the 1940 shipment, these were destined for the military. The Model 1922 was used on the front lines and by the Home Guard.

Known in Finland as the "m22" or "m/10-22", many were transferred to police units in 1950 and remained in service for decades. Pistols exhibiting too much wear after the war were either scrapped or sold on the commercial market.

Finnish pistols can be identified by the military "SA" ("Suomen Armeija" or Finnish Army) marking. The pistols have standard FN serial numbers, un-beveled barrel lugs and are equipped with lanyard rings. No factory contract markings were applied, but Finnish accepting officers' markings may be present (see fig.284-2).

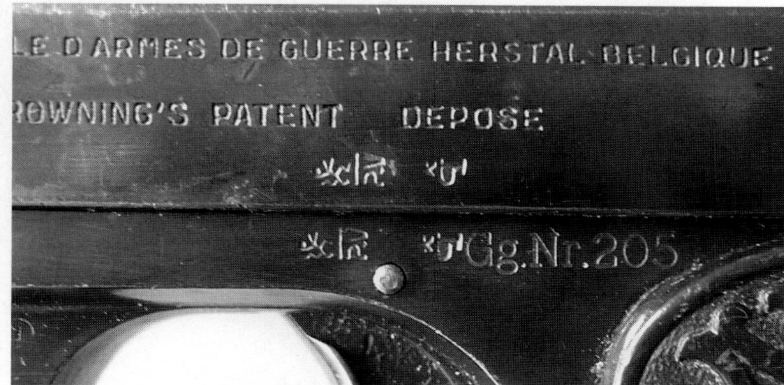

(Fig.241-1) An unknown Danish contract marking: This Model 1922 pistol N° 261545 was shipped on June 29, 1937 to FN's Agent Simonsen & Nielsen in Copenhagen. (Photograph courtesy of Peter Free)

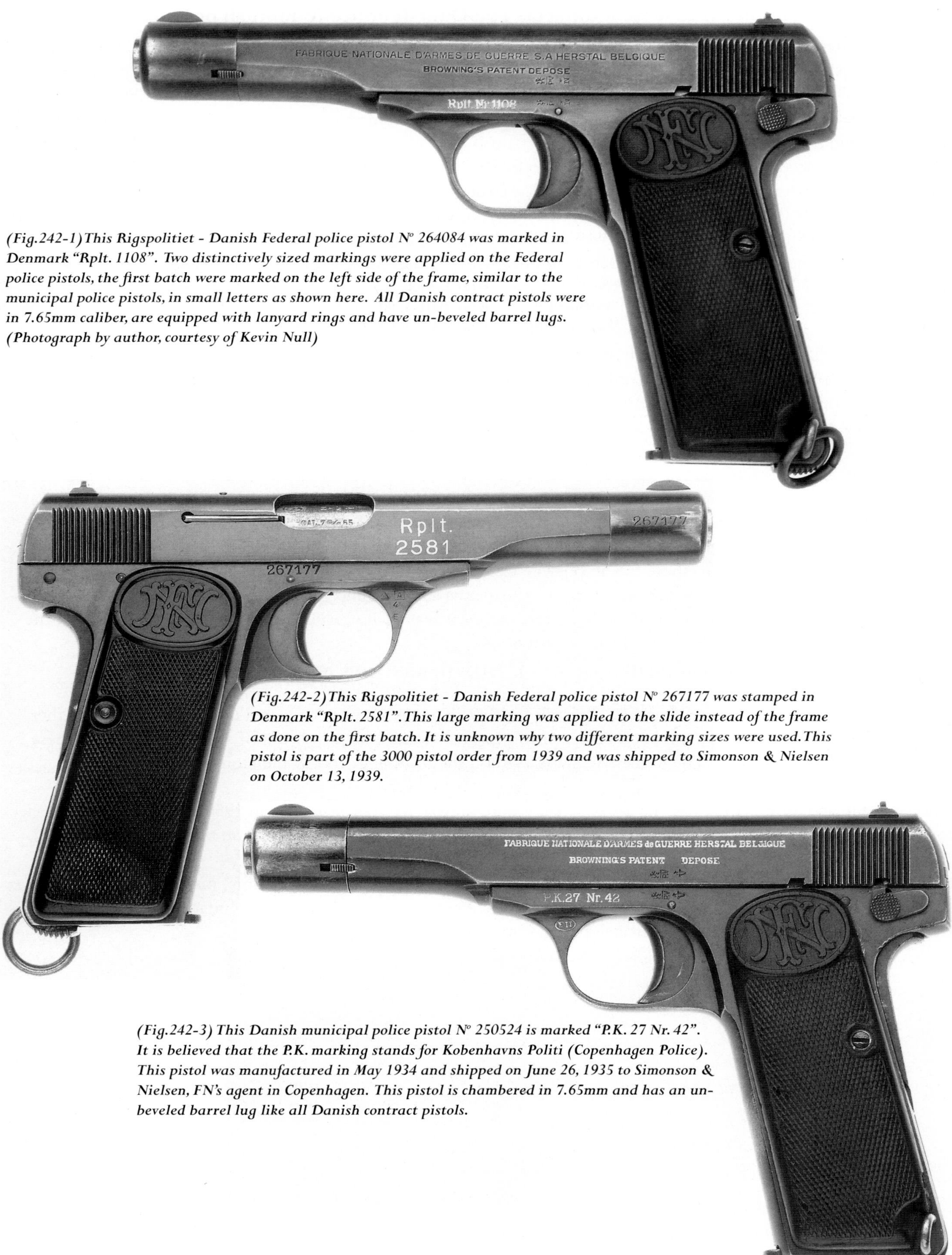

(Fig.242-1) This Rigspolitiet - Danish Federal police pistol N° 264084 was marked in Denmark "Rplt. 1108". Two distinctively sized markings were applied on the Federal police pistols, the first batch were marked on the left side of the frame, similar to the municipal police pistols, in small letters as shown here. All Danish contract pistols were in 7.65mm caliber, are equipped with lanyard rings and have un-beveled barrel lugs. (Photograph by author, courtesy of Kevin Null)

(Fig.242-2) This Rigspolitiet - Danish Federal police pistol N° 267177 was stamped in Denmark "Rplt. 2581". This large marking was applied to the slide instead of the frame as done on the first batch. It is unknown why two different marking sizes were used. This pistol is part of the 3000 pistol order from 1939 and was shipped to Simonson & Nielsen on October 13, 1939.

(Fig.242-3) This Danish municipal police pistol N° 250524 is marked "P.K. 27 Nr. 42". It is believed that the P.K. marking stands for Kobenhavns Politi (Copenhagen Police). This pistol was manufactured in May 1934 and shipped on June 26, 1935 to Simonson & Nielsen, FN's agent in Copenhagen. This pistol is chambered in 7.65mm and has an un-beveled barrel lug like all Danish contract pistols.

German World War II Procured and Produced Model 1922 Pistols

Model 1922 pistols pressed into German service received the designation "Pistole 641b" (9x17mm) or "Pistole 626b" (7.65mm). Captured weapons or weapons produced for German use in occupied countries had this status indicated by the addition of an alphabetical character, indicating country of origin or use. In the case of the Model 1922, the suffix "b" represents the German translation of Belgium; "Belgien". Due to the large number made, wartime Model 1922s, especially those bearing the WaA140 acceptance stamp, are the most commonly encountered Model 1922 pistols. Production estimates during the German occupation vary from 440,000 to 453,000.

Production began slowly. At first only certain parts were manufactured to complete existing prewar parts sets. Prewar Model 1922 parts at the time of the occupation were primarily from the Dutch contract of 1940. Over time, more new parts were produced as prewar stockpiles dwindled and complete pistols were manufactured starting in 1941. Unlike the High Power, Model 1922 production was not targeted by the resistance. Few mechanical problems have been reported resulting from resistance activities. Occupation production ended in early August 1944.

Model 1922 Wartime Production Timeline

May 10, 1940: German invasion
May 12, 1940: Fall of the city of Liège and closing of the Liège proof-house
May 17, 1940: Germans direct FN management to restart production
May 19, 1940: Seizure of the FN plant
May 28, 1940: Capitulation of the Belgian government
May - June 1940: Completed and warehoused FN pistols are moved to the Liège Citadel; unfinished guns and parts remain at the FN factory.

July-August 1940: Pistol assembly starts. Models assembled include the Model 1905, 1910 and High Power. Too many 1940 manufactured Model 1922 pistols have been observed to establish any conclusive trend of the first months of the occupation. These pistols were not entered in FN warehouse logbooks and thus not completed before the invasion, yet no definitive features or data has surfaced that would identify pistols assembled in July- August 1940.

September 1940: Introduction of the WaA613 acceptance marking on guns assembled from prewar parts. Two serial or contract number variants exist; one from the 15,000 unit Dutch military contract (contract numbers 63000 and above) and prewar serial numbers from standard FN production (typically 288,000-289,000 range). A single WaA613 is found on the trigger-guard. The Germans use all of the remaining prewar horn grips. Depending on the stage of completion prior to the invasion, most of these pistols had full or partial Liège proofs.

November-December 1940: Newly produced frames, slides, synthetic grips and barrels are introduced. Serial numbers started at 20,000 (this number was likely selected as FN had produced nearly that number of pistols in 1940). Multiple WaA613 markings are found on the frame and slide. No Liège proofs. Approximate serial number range of WaA613 marked pistols: 20,000-25,000

April 1941: The WaA103 acceptance marking is introduced. Pistols continue to feature prewar levels of fit and finish with synthetic grips. Multiple WaA103 markings are found on the frame and slide. Approximate serial number range of WaA103 marked pistols: 25,000-57,000

November-December 1941: Introduction of the WaA140 acceptance marking. Marked decrease in level of fit and finish. Multiple WaA140 markings are applied on the frame and slide.

January-March 1942: Introduction of commercial production, pistol features are identical as above (or below) but feature Eagle/N markings instead of the WaA140 marking. Wooden grips are introduced as substitutes. Approximate serial number range of WaA140 and Eagle/N marked pistols from November 1941 to May 1943: 57,000-220,000

May 1943: Introduction of the letter suffix serial numbering system. Each letter suffix indicates a block of 100,000 pistols. Numbers ascend from 1a to 99,999a followed by 1b etc.
Approximate serial number range of WaA140 and Eagle/N marked pistols from May 1943 to December 1943: 1a- 79,000b

December 1943-January 1944: Introduction of the three-digit abbreviated letter suffix system. In order to further speed up production, the Germans marked only the slide with the complete serial number and letter suffix, other parts are marked with only the last three digits and letter suffix. Introduction of substitute brown Bakelite grips to complement black synthetic grips and wooden grips.

January 1944: Change from three-digit abbreviated letter suffix system to four-digit abbreviated letter suffix system. Approximate serial number range of WaA140 and Eagle/N marked pistols for 1944: 79,000b-42,000c

WaA613 Accepted Pistols: Dutch Prewar Contract and Prewar Commercial Production (September - October 1940)

Model 1922 pistols bearing the WaA613 acceptance marking are the most desirable and valuable of those produced during the occupation. They are also the most routinely counterfeited, and collectors should take extra care analyzing a prospective purchase in order to avoid costly mistakes. In the course of researching this book, the author examined more than 40 WaA613 marked pistols. More than 30 percent of these were frauds. Only pistols seized inside the plant or unfinished pistols on the manufacturing floor were accepted with the WaA613 marking. Pistols found in the FN warehouses were not marked with any WaA marking as they had been transferred to the Citadel months earlier (page 46, 290).

There are two legitimate WaA613 marked variants:

A) Pistols with standard prewar serial numbers, part of the commercial prewar production. These pistols are rare as FN did not produce many commercial Model 1922 pistols. The serial number range for this variant is between 288,000 and 289,000. These pistols can be either in 7.65mm or 9mm caliber and have one WaA613 marking on the trigger guard. Lack of a WaA613 marking on the trigger-guard can indicate that the pistol was assembled early in the occupation, prior to the use of the WaA613 marking (July -August 1940). These pistols have prewar Liège proofs and have standard prewar features. Observed and reported serial numbers: 288901, 289001, 289757

B) Pistols from the prewar Dutch order with contract numbers, these were on the production floor at the time of the German invasion. Although this contract range spans from 63000 to 77000, large gaps exists and not all numbers were produced.

Two sub-variants can be identified based on stages of completion at the time of the invasion:

A) Pistols with complete Dutch contract features: The most desirable of the WaA613 pistols, these pistols were close to completion at the time of invasion and feature the Wilhelmina crest, lanyard ring and Dutch contract numbers in the 63000 through 64000 range. Characteristically these pistols are usually in 9mm caliber but exceptions in 7.65mm do exist. The pistols have prewar Liège proofs and one WaA613 marking on the trigger-guard. Legitimate pistols will be devoid of any Dutch acceptance marking, which is found on the rear of the pistol (fig.232-3). Any WaA613 marking found on a Dutch contract pistol with a Dutch acceptance marking is a fraud. The Dutch acceptance marking was only applied prior to the invasion. Observed and reported serial numbers: 63123, 63261, 63552, 63699, 64036, 64538

B) Pistols assembled from prewar Dutch contract production but without Wilhelmina crest with, or without lanyard ring: A distinct break in numbers indicates that a large gap exists between those pistols that were near completion and the ones at earlier stages of production. These pistols start at contract number 70,000. Early numbers still feature a lanyard ring and Liège proofs, but these features disappeared as production continued. The pistols still have prewar features and high standards of fit and finish. Most have prewar horn grips; these grips were cut for a lanyard ring and were used on pistols that have no lanyard ring installed. As the supply of horn grips was exhausted (fig.246-2), the same pattern with lanyard cut was made in a black synthetic material. These pistols are usually in their original Dutch contract caliber of 9mm, but exceptions in 7.65mm exist. These pistols have one or multiple WaA613 markings.
Observed and reported serial numbers with lanyard ring: 70133, 70370, 70989
Observed and reported serial numbers without lanyard ring: 72171, 74375, 75073, 76439, 77510

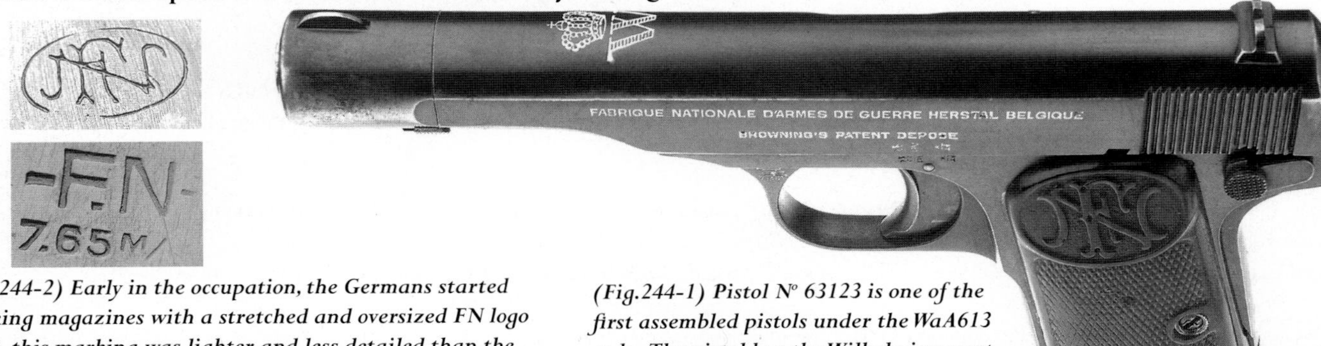

(Fig.244-2) Early in the occupation, the Germans started marking magazines with a stretched and oversized FN logo (top), this marking was lighter and less detailed than the prewar magazine marking (fig.196-3). Later (circa 1941) the FN logo marking was supplemented with the capitalized "-F.N.-" marking, this marking remained in use throughout the war and was adopted as FN's standard postwar magazine marking. Wartime marking variants do not always show the caliber designation.

(Fig.244-1) Pistol N° 63123 is one of the first assembled pistols under the WaA613 code. The pistol has the Wilhelmina crest, lanyard ring, bone grips and WaA613 code on to the trigger-guard. It is in chambered in 9mm and has the serial number visible on the barrel, frame, slide and barrel lug. It correctly does not have the Dutch acceptance marking (see fig.232-3).

(Fig.245-1) Pistol N° 63699 is identical to pistol N° 63123, with the Wilhelmina crest, lanyard ring, bone grips and WaA613 code on to the trigger-guard. It is however chambered in 7.65mm and has the serial number visible on the barrel, frame, slide and barrel lug. It is correctly devoid of the Dutch acceptance marking (see fig.232-3).

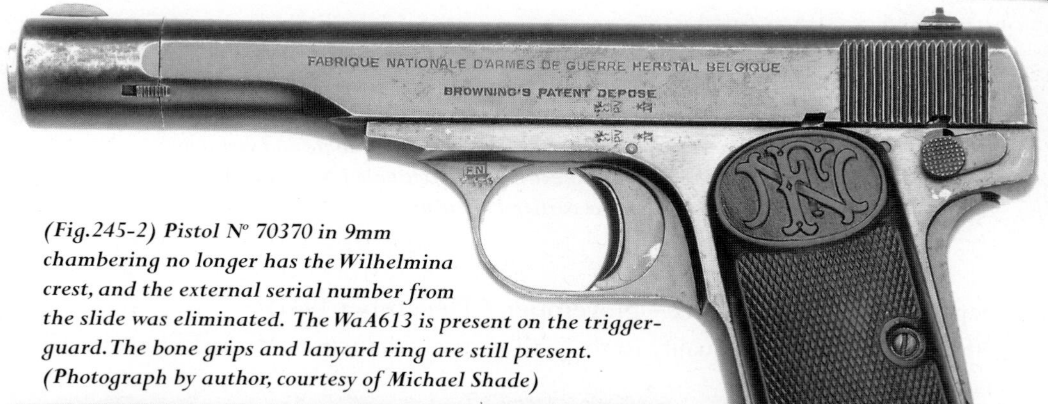

(Fig.245-2) Pistol N° 70370 in 9mm chambering no longer has the Wilhelmina crest, and the external serial number from the slide was eliminated. The WaA613 is present on the trigger-guard. The bone grips and lanyard ring are still present. (Photograph by author, courtesy of Michael Shade)

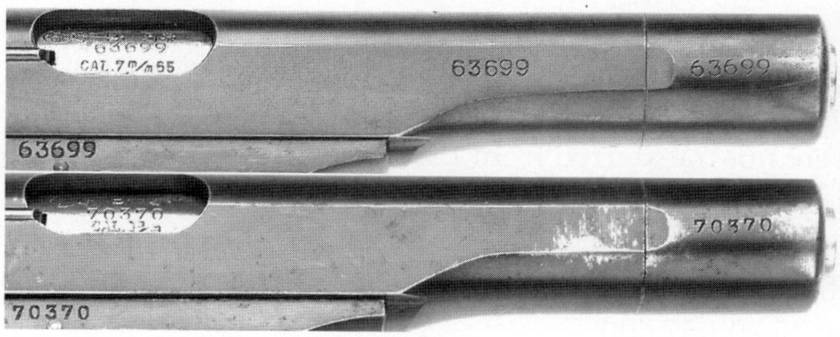

(Fig.245-3) 1942 FN manufactured 9x17mm ammo box. Note that the Germans referred to the 9mm ammo as being "for the Belgian police model". The 9x17mm cartridge was used but not officially accepted as a military round.

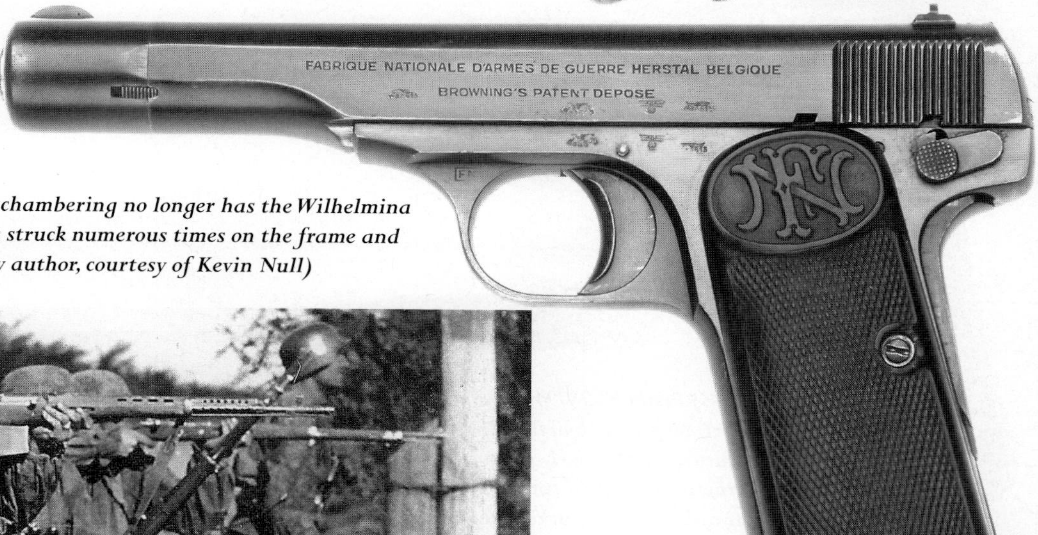

(Fig.245-4) Pistol N° 75073 in 9mm chambering no longer has the Wilhelmina crest or lanyard ring. The WaA613 is struck numerous times on the frame and slide. Grips are bone (Photograph by author, courtesy of Kevin Null)

(Fig.245-5) Waffen SS troops firing at the enemy on the Eastern Front. The soldier in the distance is holding a High Power. Note that the Tokarev shooter has a captured Dutch Model 1922 holster and magazine pouch. (Photograph courtesy of Roger Bender & Collector Grade Publications, Inc.)

WaA613 Accepted Pistols: New Production (November 1940 – April 1941)

German production of the Model 1922 was underway by the end of 1940. German produced Model 1922s begin with serial number 20,000 and continue without serial number gaps. Most parts were of wartime manufacture and the pistols are all in 7.65 mm caliber. WaA markings were now applied to the slide and frame along with the test eagle proof marking. Pistols were of excellent quality and assembled with black synthetic grips, which were molded with a cut for a lanyard ring. Magazines were stamped with a WaA613 marking on the spine. Approximate serial range: 20,000-25,000.

Observed or reported pistols: 20105, 20466, 22566, 23154, 23688

(Fig.246-1) Pistol N° 20466 has all the characteristics of new wartime production, including multiple WaA613 markings (struck upside down), new synthetic black grips cut for lanyard but a frame without lanyard attached (see fig.246-2). There are no Belgian proofs on the barrel, only the test eagle and serial number are marked (fig.246-3). The rectangle FN is marked on the trigger-guard like earlier 1940 pistols.

WaA103 Accepted Pistols: (May 1941 – November / December 1941)

The WaA103 marked pistols are identical in features and quality to the earlier, new production, WaA613 pistols. All WaA103 pistols are in 7.65mm.

Serial numbers of this variant continued the WaA613 serials numbers. The WaA103 marking was introduced around serial number 25,000. Pistol number 25413 is a typical transition piece which has both WaA613 and WaA103 markings. As seen on page 92, the German acceptance officers were not transferred from FN but rather changed job descriptions. Consequently, it is possible to encounter pistols assembled with both WaA613 and WaA103 marked parts.

The Germans continued to use the black synthetics grips with lanyard cut until the supply was exhausted towards the beginning of WaA140 production. Approximate serial range: 25,000-57,000.

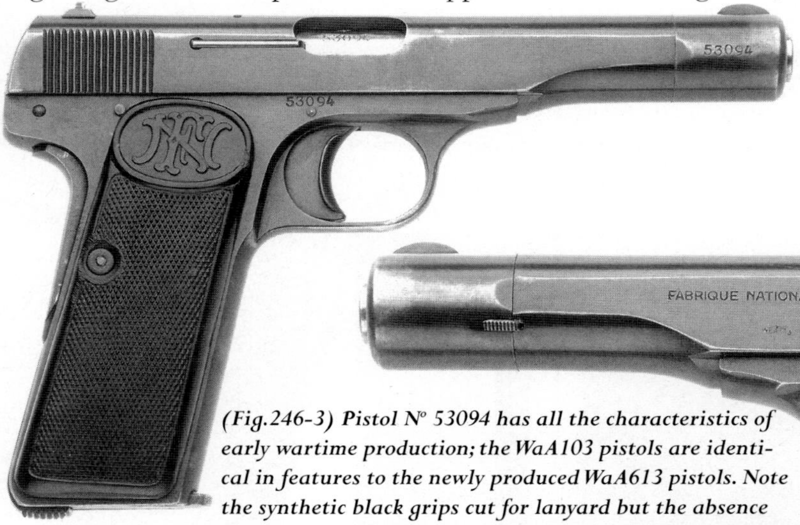

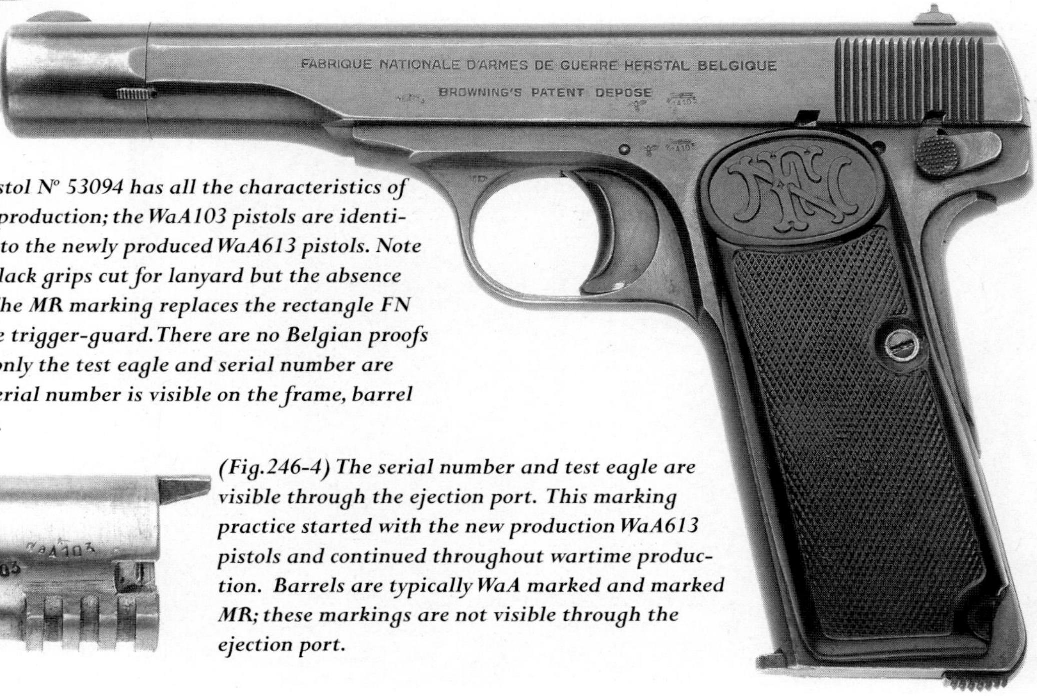

(Fig.246-3) Pistol N° 53094 has all the characteristics of early wartime production; the WaA103 pistols are identical in features to the newly produced WaA613 pistols. Note the synthetic black grips cut for lanyard but the absence of a lanyard. The MR marking replaces the rectangle FN marking on the trigger-guard. There are no Belgian proofs on the barrel, only the test eagle and serial number are marked. The serial number is visible on the frame, barrel and barrel lug.

(Fig.246-4) The serial number and test eagle are visible through the ejection port. This marking practice started with the new production WaA613 pistols and continued throughout wartime production. Barrels are typically WaA marked and marked MR; these markings are not visible through the ejection port.

WaA140 Accepted Pistols: (December 1941 / July 1944)

The WaA140 acceptance marking was introduced at a time when production requirements were raised significantly. Time spent on, and consequently, the quality of fit and finish decreased. Observable differences can be noted on fit and finish, and although some pistols were highly finished, the metal was generally less polished before bluing.

Features of the WaA140 pistols are the same as those of the WaA103 pistols. All WaA140 pistols are in 7.65mm. Early magazines were still marked with a WaA140 stamp until 1942, when magazines were no longer marked.

Early WaA140 marked pistols were assembled with black synthetic grips. These grips did not have a cut for the lanyard ring. In early 1942, the Germans introduced wooden grips as a substitute, on an as needed basis, for the black synthetic grips. Despite the wooden grips' status as a substitute, the majority of pistols were assembled with wooden grips. As the war progressed, the Germans introduced brown Bakelite grips as an alternate substitute. The chocolate brown Bakelite grips were introduced early 1944, but the material was fragile and ill suited for this application. Black synthetic grips were used whenever possible.

Serial numbers of WaA140 marked pistols continued the WaA103 serialization, with numbers starting around 57000 and continued until May 1943, to approximately 220000, when the letter suffix serial number system was introduced. Production demands increased through 1942 and 1943 and standards of fit and finish dropped significantly.

(Fig.247-1) Pistol N° 123510 is featured with early well-finished substitute wooden grips, the pistol still has the early features including serial numbering and trigger flanges. Although this is a commercial pistol, production features are identical to WaA140 accepted pistols. (Photograph by author, courtesy of Tim Hawkins)

First sub variant: "a" and "b" suffix serial numbers from 1a to 79000b
May 1943 – December 1943

As production and demand increased, the Germans looked at feasible ways to speed up production and increase output. By 1943, material shortages had become common at FN and production was frequently halted. Labor remained an issue and resistance activity and sabotage kept increasing. By mid-1943, the Germans began to use the letter suffix serial numbering system and abandoned the earlier ascending system. This system was not unique to FN and was used by many arms makers operating under German control. In this system a letter is assigned to a block of 100,000 pistols (example 1a through 99999a followed by 1b, etc.). At FN this was started with the "a" suffix letter and followed by the "b" and "c" suffix. All 200,000 pistols in the "a" and "b" suffix blocks were produced.

The suffix letter was applied to the parts prior to the serial number in an earlier and separate operation. It is therefore possible to encounter a part or "lunch box special" pistol, which does not have a serial number but does have the suffix letter.

The letter suffix system was one of several steps the Germans undertook to maximize production output. Other production efficiencies included the elimination of the trigger flanges, resulting in a straight flat trigger. This change was introduced at the same time as the letter suffix serial system but appeared a few thousand pistols later, after the existing stockpile of parts was exhausted. Additionally, the Germans abandoned the magazine safety in 1943, midway into the "a" suffix serial block.

Fit and finish degraded considerably under the letter suffix production. Samples inspected indicate that the degradation had more to do with individuals than with policy. Highly polishing a pistol was passive resistance in that it retarded production. Consequently a finely polished pistol and a crudely finished gun can be encountered within a few serial numbers (see page 51-52 for resistance activity).

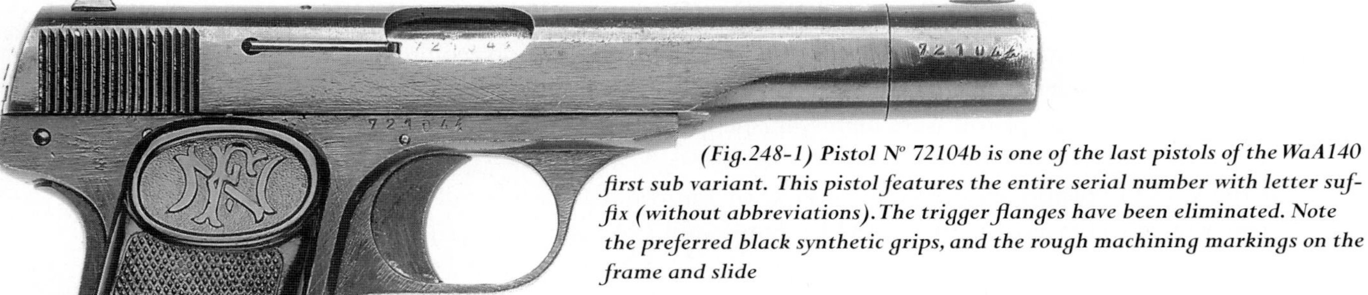

(Fig.248-1) Pistol N° 72104b is one of the last pistols of the WaA140 first sub variant. This pistol features the entire serial number with letter suffix (without abbreviations). The trigger flanges have been eliminated. Note the preferred black synthetic grips, and the rough machining markings on the frame and slide

Second sub variant: "b" and "c" suffix abbreviated serial numbers from approximately 79000b to 42000c
January 1944 – August 1944

Additional production efficiencies were implemented in January 1944, including the use of abbreviated serial numbers on the frame, barrel and muzzle ring. Only the slide retained the pistol's full serial number as the slide is considered the principal part of a firearm in Europe[1]. The new numbering system was applied to external parts, including the frame, slide, barrel and barrel lug. The internal numbering was eliminated and the slide was marked externally, similar to the prewar Dutch contracts.

Initially the serial numbers were abbreviated to three digits, but this caused confusion as thousands of pistols were in production at any given time. The three-digit abbreviation was lengthened to four digits around serial number 90000b.

Production was erratic in 1944 as supply problems forced the factory to remain idle for extended periods of time. Ultimately the wartime management opted to halt production in early August 1944 and prepare for transporting parts, machinery and the factory out of Belgium (see page 56).

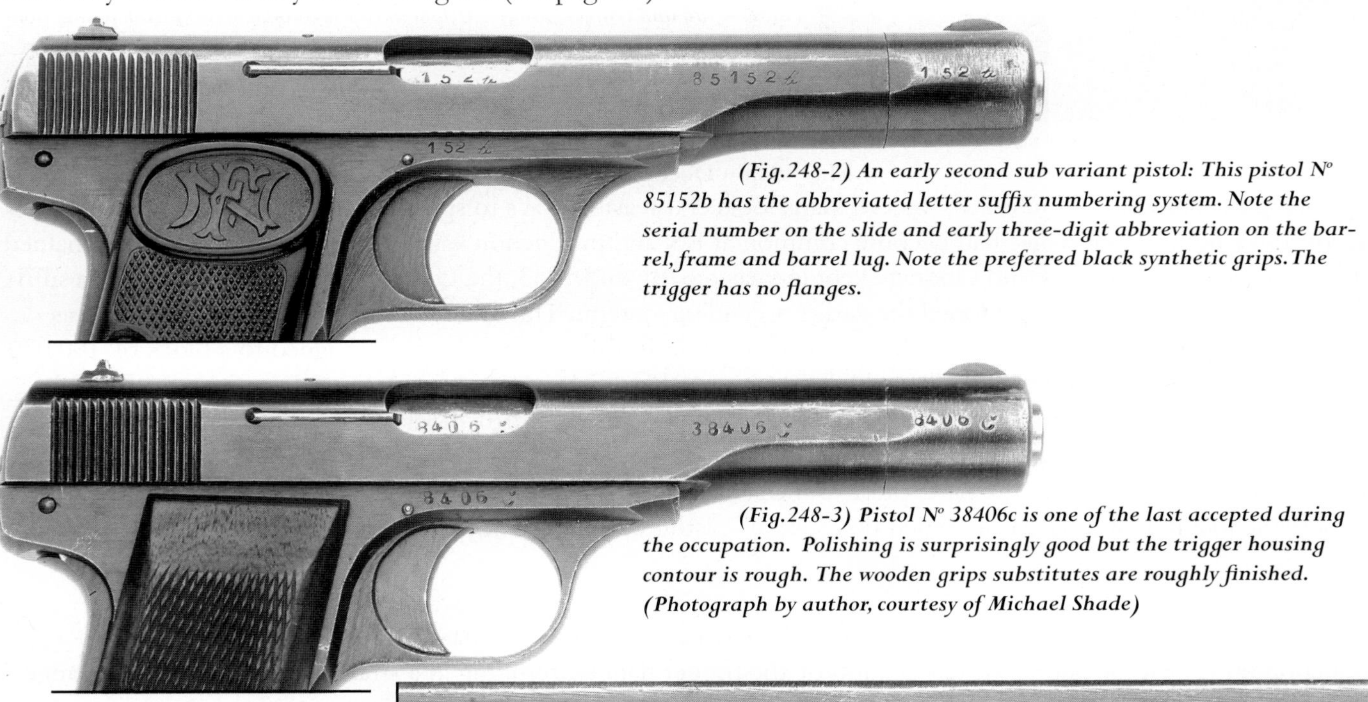

(Fig.248-2) An early second sub variant pistol: This pistol N° 85152b has the abbreviated letter suffix numbering system. Note the serial number on the slide and early three-digit abbreviation on the barrel, frame and barrel lug. Note the preferred black synthetic grips. The trigger has no flanges.

(Fig.248-3) Pistol N° 38406c is one of the last accepted during the occupation. Polishing is surprisingly good but the trigger housing contour is rough. The wooden grips substitutes are roughly finished. (Photograph by author, courtesy of Michael Shade)

(Fig.248-4) The markings on pistol N° 38406c reflect the manufacturing standards at the end of occupation. The slide legend roll engraver is worn out. The MR marking is worn or poorly struck. There are rough machining marks on the metal and the wooden grips are poorly carved. (Photograph by author, courtesy of Michael Shade Shade)

Eagle/N Commercial Pistols (December 1942 - early August 1944)

The Eagle/N pistols are often referred to as commercial pistols. These pistols may have both the Eagle/N acceptance marking and test proof mark or only a test proof mark. The commercial line appeared at approximately the same time as the WaA140 acceptance marking came into use, and the pistols differ only in markings. Features and serial numbering practices are identical to WaA140 pistols (page 247-248).

Research data indicates that commercial pistols account for five to eight percent of pistols made during the WaA140 era. Pistols are random through the WaA140 range and do not fall into any particular serial range or block. Collectors have suggested that Eagle/N pistols were supplied to German law-enforcement agencies while pistols with only test-proofs were true commercial pistols, supplied to company securities as well as select individuals. The author has found no evidence of this. Pistols bearing only test proof marks are more scarce than pistols with Eagle/N markings.

Observed or reported test proof only pistols: 101575,101591, 123510, 137764, 23558a, 43882b, 85152b
Observed or reported Eagle/N pistols: 72609, 100003, 163376, 173522, 177674, 177758, 3887a, 89708a, 90171a, 10760b, 62565b, 62662b, 62789b, 85187b, 87130b, 88164b, 98394b, 1400c, 37113c, 39253c, 41671c

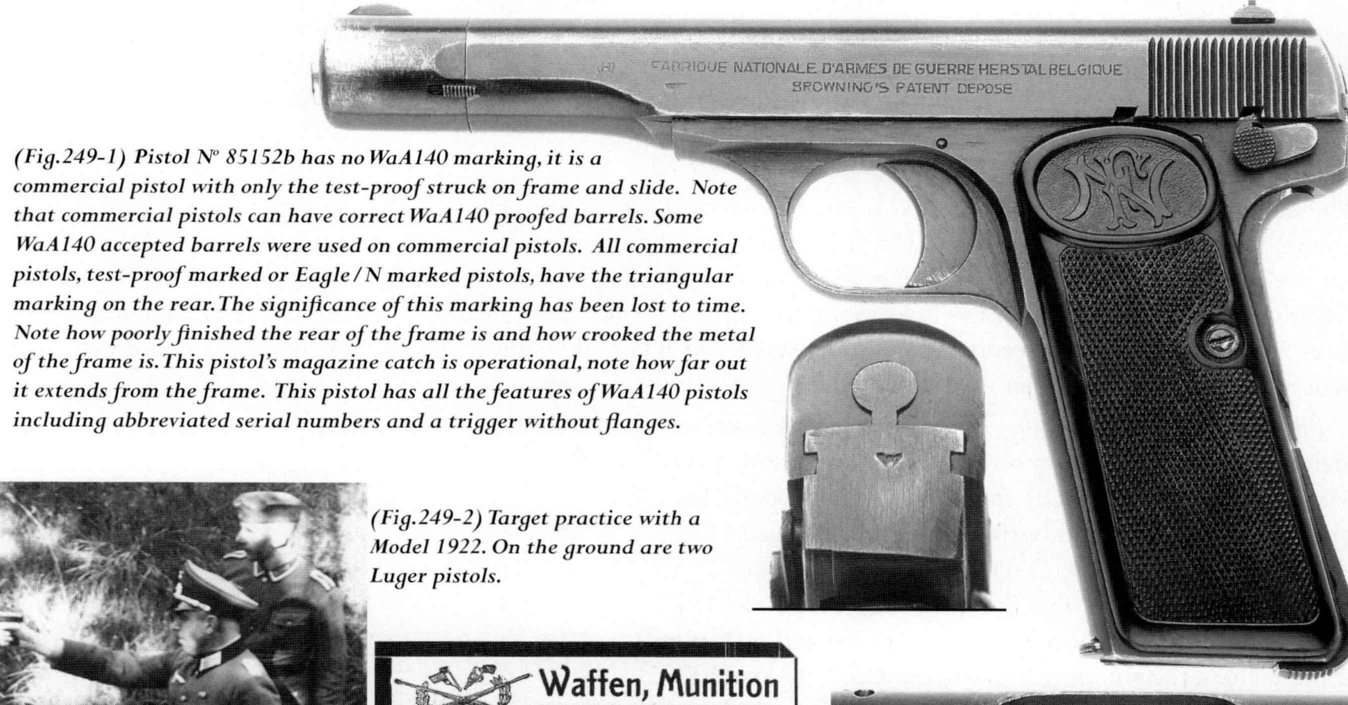

(Fig.249-1) Pistol N° 85152b has no WaA140 marking, it is a commercial pistol with only the test-proof struck on frame and slide. Note that commercial pistols can have correct WaA140 proofed barrels. Some WaA140 accepted barrels were used on commercial pistols. All commercial pistols, test-proof marked or Eagle/N marked pistols, have the triangular marking on the rear. The significance of this marking has been lost to time. Note how poorly finished the rear of the frame is and how crooked the metal of the frame is. This pistol's magazine catch is operational, note how far out it extends from the frame. This pistol has all the features of WaA140 pistols including abbreviated serial numbers and a trigger without flanges.

(Fig.249-2) Target practice with a Model 1922. On the ground are two Luger pistols.

(Fig.249-2) A 1926 Albrecht Kind advertising featuring the shooting policeman logo. (Bottom) Some wartime commercial pistols have been noted with the Kind shooting policeman logo stamped on the slide. The author has not confirmed the authenticity of this marking. (Photographs courtsey of Michael Shade & Kevin Null)

(Fig.249-3) Commercial pistol N° 100003 is property marked "Wachdienst Erkner". The Erkner factory was an important ball-bearing plant near Berlin and commercial pistols were used for factory security. As discussed on page 212 and 290, legitimate special markings and German wartime property markings are roll engraved and not stamped.

(1) In the U.S., the Federal Bureau of Alcohol, Tobacco, Firearms and Explosives (B ATFE) considers the pistol frame the legally regulated component of a firearm.

Post liberation pistols: Late "c" suffix and "A" prefix pistols

The Germans left FN on September 5, 1944, and while they looted much in the way of machinery and machine tools, they did not transplant the factory as planned (see page 56). The Germans did not ignore the stocks of existing pistol parts, as is often reported. These parts were originally destined for assembly in Germany. With the rapid Allied advance time ran out, and the stockpiles were left behind.

FN employees began to assemble guns as soon as the Germans left Liège; even before the liberating U.S. 3rd Armored Division arrived! The first pistols were made in early September 1944, and were pieced together from late occupation parts. These pistols still have wartime serial numbers, but no final German acceptance markings. The Liège proof house had been closed during the war, and the pistols assembled in the first days after liberation were not proofed. Proof house employees abandoned their work in 1940, taking their stamping dies with them. Some returned almost immediately to resume work after the liberation. Some inspectors, like Louis Couchant, were motivated by patriotism and desire to help the war effort.

The first pistols assembled from wartime parts stockpiles were crudely finished and resembled the worst of the late occupation pistols. Pistol assembly at FN began before other services had restarted operation including administration and warehousing. "A" prefix serial numbering started in September 1944. The letter "A" was stamped on the pistols prior to stamping a serial number. Retired FN employees have stated that the letter was used to indicate "Allemand" (German) to identify when the pistols were made.

The numbering system used on the "A" prefix Model 1922 pistols was eclectic. The early pistols (available to GI's and others) were numbered A4000 to A5201. FN started numbering the pistols in September 1944 at A4001 and A90001 for the Belgian government. Beginning in 1945, other serial ranges were used including: A75001-A86100 for Holland. Additional pistols, sold later to the Belgian military, are in A90001-A97700 and A100,000-A104,000 ranges, while those sold to the Dutch government are in the A108,000-A112,000 range. The French government contract range is believed to start with contract number A0001.

FN did not have the capability to produce pistols from raw materials until 1946, relying on stockpiles of wartime pistol parts until that time. Pistols were once again properly finished, being polished and buffed before being blued.

American GIs were the first customers for the Model 1922 pistols. Although the pistols were purchased and picked up at the factory, the shipping logs often include the purchaser's name and rank, becoming a record of the men who passed through FN.

Purchasers were not only American; British, Free Belgian and Luxembourg soldiers also purchased pistols. As the Belgian central government was in disarray, communities ordered pistols directly from FN for law enforcement and civil servants. Towns and cities like Liège, Seraing, Herstal, Jette, Spa, Tienen, Wandre, St. Niklaas and St. Truiden purchased pistols in September 1944.

Fabrique Nationale d'Armes de Guerre
Société Anonyme
Registre du Commerce Liège N° 1184
Compte de Chèques Postaux 15822

Télégr.: "Nationale Liège"
Téléph.: Liège 408.00.

Administration Communale
de et à
THIMISTER
------- Liège

Annexe:
Référence: MM/ND

Herstal lez Liége, le 27 Décembre 1945
(Belgique)

Monsieur le Bourgmestre,

ARMEMENT POLICES COMMUNALES

Nous avons l'honneur d'accuser la bonne réception de votre lettre du 6.10.1945 nous priant de vous fournir pour les besoins de votre police communale :

deux pistolets
100 cartouches

Nous vous remercions sincèrement de votre demande et nous nous empressons de vous faire savoir que nous pourrions vous livrer :

2 pistolets Browning cal 7,65 mm/1922 avec chacun un chargeur de rechange et une baguette de nettoyage au prix unitaire de Frs. 690.- - - - - - - - - - - - - - - - soit Frs. 1.380.00
100 cartouches Browning cal.7,65 mm au prix de Frs. 655,50 le mille - - - - - soit Frs. 65.55
Total: Frs 1.445.55

marchandise,non emballée,prise loco nos usines par vos soins.

Cependant,si vous le désirez,nous pourrions nous charger de l'expédition par chemin de fer,suivant les instructions que vous nous donneriez,mais sous votre unique et entière responsabilité,la marchandise voyageant à vos risques et périls.Nous pourrions éventuellement aussi assurer le transport contre les risques ordinaires c.à.d. exclusion faite des risques de guerre,

(Fig.250-1) The mayor of the small municipality of Thimister wrote FN on October 6, 1945 about purchasing two Model 1922 pistols with cartridges. FN replied on October 10, that the order could not be filled as orders for municipalities from the Belgian Ministry of Defense has already been shipped. FN assumed that Brussels would pay for the order. On December 27, FN acknowledged the order after it was established that the small town would pay for its own purchase. These letters show that the Belgian MDN paid for many law-enforcement pistols in the fall of 1945 but that small communities were left to buy their own equipment.

Resistance groups were settling scores with collaborators throughout the country and there was an urgency to maintain law and order. Local and municipal governments scrambled to control hostilities among the population. Within a month, old time customers like Schroeder and new customers like corporations, banks, coal mines and others ordered pistols. Parts made under German control supplied FN for years. Pistols were readily available to the end of the 1940s. Some remained warehoused for decades. In December 1986, FN pulled several "A" prefix pistols out of the warehouse, where they had been for 42 years, for their internal security force.

Observed post liberation "c" suffix pistols: 44567c, 44830c, 45007c

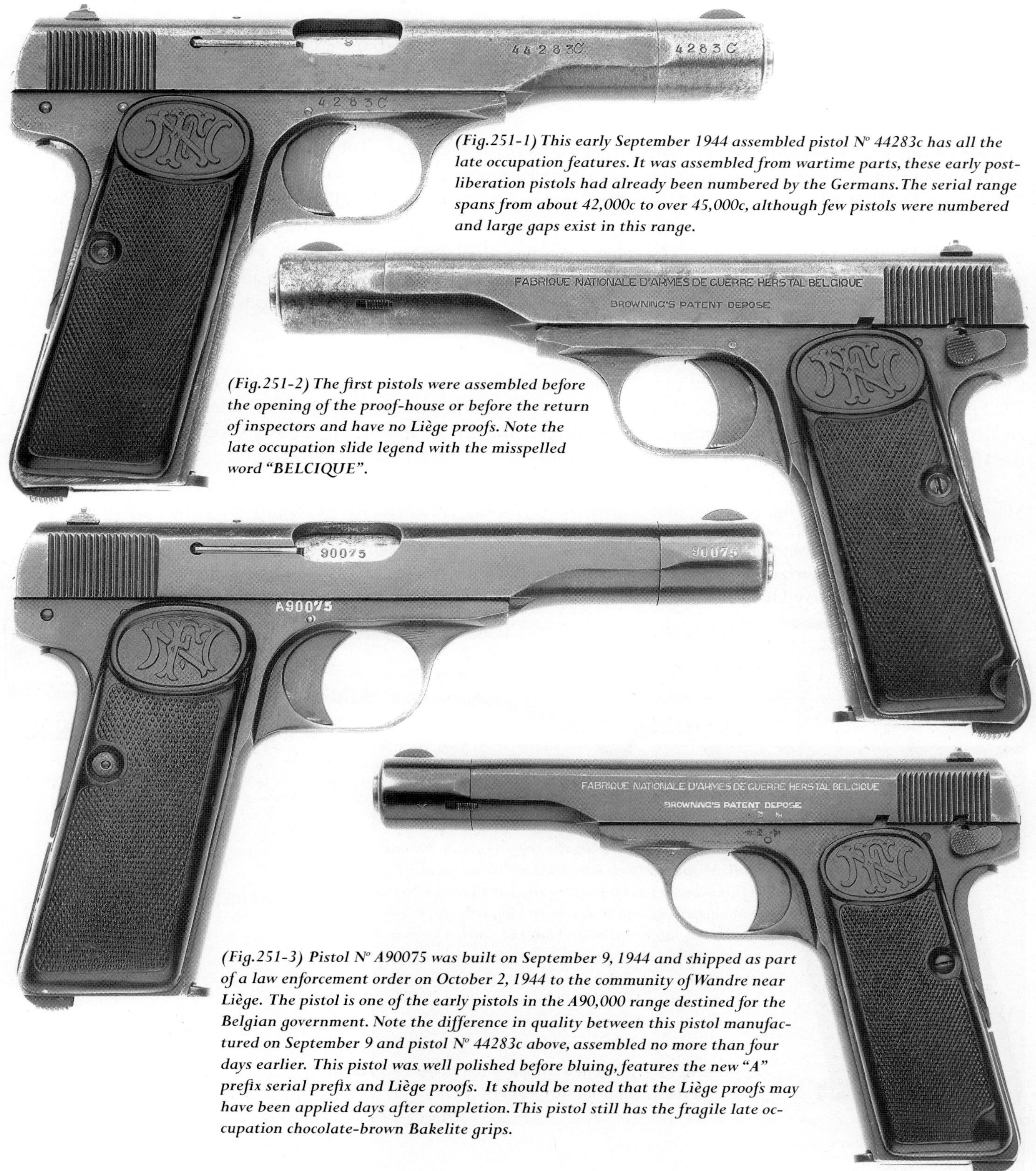

(Fig.251-1) This early September 1944 assembled pistol N° 44283c has all the late occupation features. It was assembled from wartime parts, these early post-liberation pistols had already been numbered by the Germans. The serial range spans from about 42,000c to over 45,000c, although few pistols were numbered and large gaps exist in this range.

(Fig.251-2) The first pistols were assembled before the opening of the proof-house or before the return of inspectors and have no Liège proofs. Note the late occupation slide legend with the misspelled word "BELCIQUE".

(Fig.251-3) Pistol N° A90075 was built on September 9, 1944 and shipped as part of a law enforcement order on October 2, 1944 to the community of Wandre near Liège. The pistol is one of the early pistols in the A90,000 range destined for the Belgian government. Note the difference in quality between this pistol manufactured on September 9 and pistol N° 44283c above, assembled no more than four days earlier. This pistol was well polished before bluing, features the new "A" prefix serial prefix and Liège proofs. It should be noted that the Liège proofs may have been applied days after completion. This pistol still has the fragile late occupation chocolate-brown Bakelite grips.

Postwar Belgian Government Contracts

Official Belgian use of the Model 1922 dates to September 1944. As with the Model 1910 in 1919, the Model 1922 was adopted out of necessity. Communities purchased pistols to arm local law enforcement (see page 250), and the Model 1922 was acquired solely on the basis of its availability. These pistols typically do not bear any contract or acceptance markings.

The first post-liberation military order was placed in 1945, and included both the Model 1922 and the High Power. At that time only "A" prefix pistols were available. FN's initial contract range for the Belgian government Model 1922 pistols was the A90,000-97700 serial range block. The serial range was started on September 25, 1944 for anticipated Belgian government orders. As the Belgian government orders were slow to materialize, many of the early pistols in this range were sold to passing servicemen (page 250-251). Contracts filled in 1946 or later were in the A100,000-A104,000 serial range block.

Military pistols were accepted at the Atelier Central d'Armement (see page 94-95) and marked with a "Crown over AC" stamping on the right side of the trigger guard, similar to markings applied to prewar High Powers (fig.276-1). Features on the 1945 and early 1946 "A" prefix orders were inconsistent, depending largely on available parts. Pistols were shipped with primarily wooden grips; earlier "A" prefix pistols lacked a magazine safety, whereas later pistols were shipped with the magazine safety. These inconsistencies had operational impacts: Having two versions of the same pistol in service, one with a magazine safety and one without, complicated training and made the Model 1922 less desirable than the High Power. Belgian arsenals modified a few of the "A" prefix Model 1922 pistols and turned these into cut-away training pistols.

Over time, the Model 1922 was phased out of military service into a strictly law enforcement role. Military Model 1922 pistols were transferred to the gendarmerie, the Belgian Gendarmerie is under military command but handles civilian law-enforcement. The gendarmerie used both the Model 1922 and the High Power from the 1950s through the 1980s. Starting in the 1950s, the pistols were factory roll marked for the gendarmerie.

Municipal police departments were the first to acquire the Model 1922 after the liberation and continued to use the model for decades.

Observed Belgian police pistols (serial numbers only): A90075 (see fig.251-3)
Reported of observed Belgian military pistols: A93483, A96835, A98028, A101268, A101708
Observed Belgian military training (cut-away) pistols: A98369

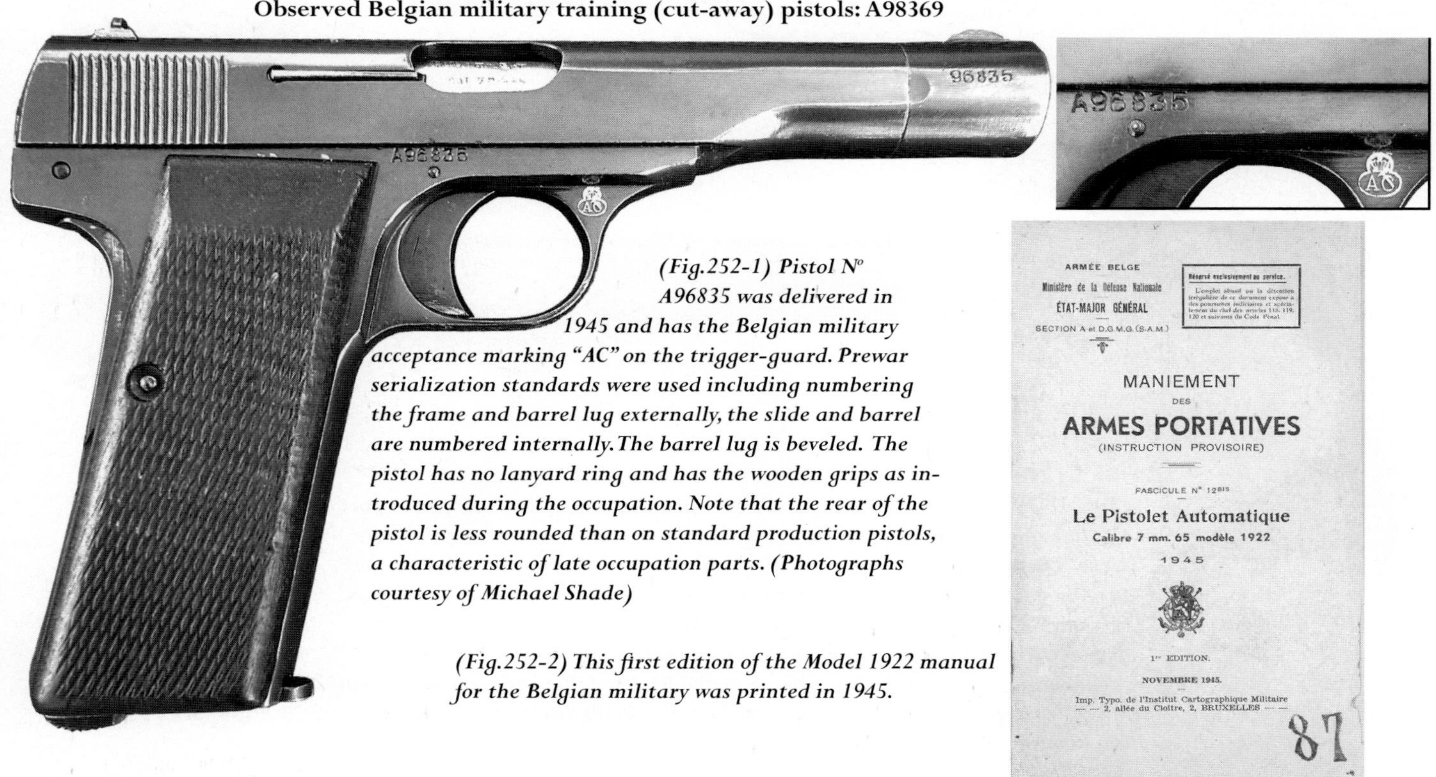

(Fig.252-1) Pistol N° A96835 was delivered in 1945 and has the Belgian military acceptance marking "AC" on the trigger-guard. Prewar serialization standards were used including numbering the frame and barrel lug externally, the slide and barrel are numbered internally. The barrel lug is beveled. The pistol has no lanyard ring and has the wooden grips as introduced during the occupation. Note that the rear of the pistol is less rounded than on standard production pistols, a characteristic of late occupation parts. (Photographs courtesy of Michael Shade)

(Fig.252-2) This first edition of the Model 1922 manual for the Belgian military was printed in 1945.

(Fig.253-1) The 1965 order for the Belgian Gendarmerie was issued with contract numbers and not FN serial numbers. Note the factory applied contract number on the barrel. Pistols were factory roll engraved with the FN logo and the "G.d" marking for Gendarmerie. These pistol were issued with plastic grips and a lanyard ring. Not all grips on the 1965 pistols have the top corner extension (fig.223-1). (Photograph courtesy of Philip Rotmans)

(Fig.253-2) This Belgian medal was widely used for pistol shooting competitions from the 1950s through the 1970s. Several sizes and finishes have been observed, the design was also used on rectangular and square medals.

Postwar German Contracts

After World War II, Germany was prohibited from manufacturing firearms, and the Model 1922 was adopted by German law enforcement. Germans were familiar with the pistol from its wartime usage and many of the wartime Model 1922 pistols still in Germany were reissued to law enforcement, often after Nazi markings were defaced.

Although the use of Model 1922 pistols was widespread, the most common property markings are from the Berlin and Hamburg police departments. Berlin police pistols are identified by the star marking stamped either on the frame or on the front grip-strap. This star marking is often interpreted in the U.S. as a flower with 12 petals. As a result, Berlin police pistols are often misidentified as prewar Japanese contract pistols, many incorrectly interpreting the marking as the Imperial Japanese Chrysanthemum symbol.

Reissued wartime pistols are usually marked on the front grip-strap. In 1946 a directive was issued for all Berlin police pistols to be marked with the sector (known as Kennung Sektor), the administration area (known as Bezirk) and police star symbol.

The directive involved all firearms in use, including the Model 1922 pistol. The following lists the sectors and administration areas according to the directive (This does not imply that Model 1922 pistols were used in all sectors or in all administration areas). Typically the first letter of the sector was marked, followed by a Roman numeral indicating the administration area.

Kennung Sektor (Allied sector)
A: Amerikanischer Sektor (American sector)
B: Britischer Sektor (British sector)
F: Französischer Sektor (French sector)
S: Sowjetischer Sektor (Soviet sector)

Bezirk (Administration area)
I Bezirk: Mitte (Sowjetischer Sektor)
II Bezirk: Tiergarten (Britischer Sektor)
III Bezirk: Wedding (Französischer Sektor)
IV Bezirk: Prenzlauer Berg (Sowjetischer Sektor)
V Bezirk: Friedrichshain (Sowjetischer Sektor)
VI Bezirk: Kreuzberg (Amerikanischer Sektor)
VII Bezirk: Charlottenburg (Britischer Sektor)
VIII Bezirk: Spandau (Britischer Sektor)
IX Bezirk: Wilmersdorf (Britischer Sektor)
X Bezirk: Zehlendorf (Amerikanischer Sektor)

Bezirk (Administration area)
XI Bezirk: Schöneberg (Amerikanischer Sektor)
XII Bezirk: Steglitz (Amerikanischer Sektor)
XIII Bezirk: Tempelhof (Amerikanischer Sektor)
XIV Bezirk: Neukölln (Amerikanischer Sektor)
XV Bezirk: Treptow (Sowjetischer Sektor)
XVI Bezirk: Köpenick (Sowjetischer Sektor)
XVII Bezirk: Lichtenberg (Sowjetischer Sektor)
XVIII Bezirk: Weißensee (Sowjetischer Sektor)
XIX Bezirk: Pankow (Sowjetischer Sektor)
XX Bezirk: Reinickendorf (Französischer Sektor)

Postwar German Contracts (continued)

The 1946 Berlin police marking system was modified in 1948. The early Berlin star had rounded edges, in 1948 the design was slightly modified and featured pointed edges(1). The first pistols purchased from FN after the war were not Model 1922 pistols, but rather 7.65mm Model 1910 pistols. An estimated 2000 pistols were purchased for German police in 1948-1949. The Model 1922 was only acquired during the 1950s. Berlin police Model 1922 pistols acquired in the 1950s were marked with the police star on the right side of the frame instead of the front grip-strap. The Bezirk marking was eliminated.

Hamburg police markings consist of the "HBG" marking and issue number applied to the right side of the frame next to the serial number. Two styles of markings were applied in Germany over time (fig.255-3).

No specific contract numbers were used for any of the German contracts, all pistols had standard postwar FN serial numbers. Other significant users of the Model 1922 during the 1950s were the railroad police in the American sector. Property markings for the railroad police were factory roll engraved, this is in contrast with most of the law enforcement Model 1922 pistols, which were usually stamped in Germany. In 1971 there were 4671 Model 1922s and 202 Model 1910s in use by the German Railway(1). The Model 1922 was used by police units, while the model 1910 was used by detectives. All Model 1910s and 1922s were replaced and sold between 1976 and 1980. Smaller users of the Model 1922 were border-guards and the German Foreign office.

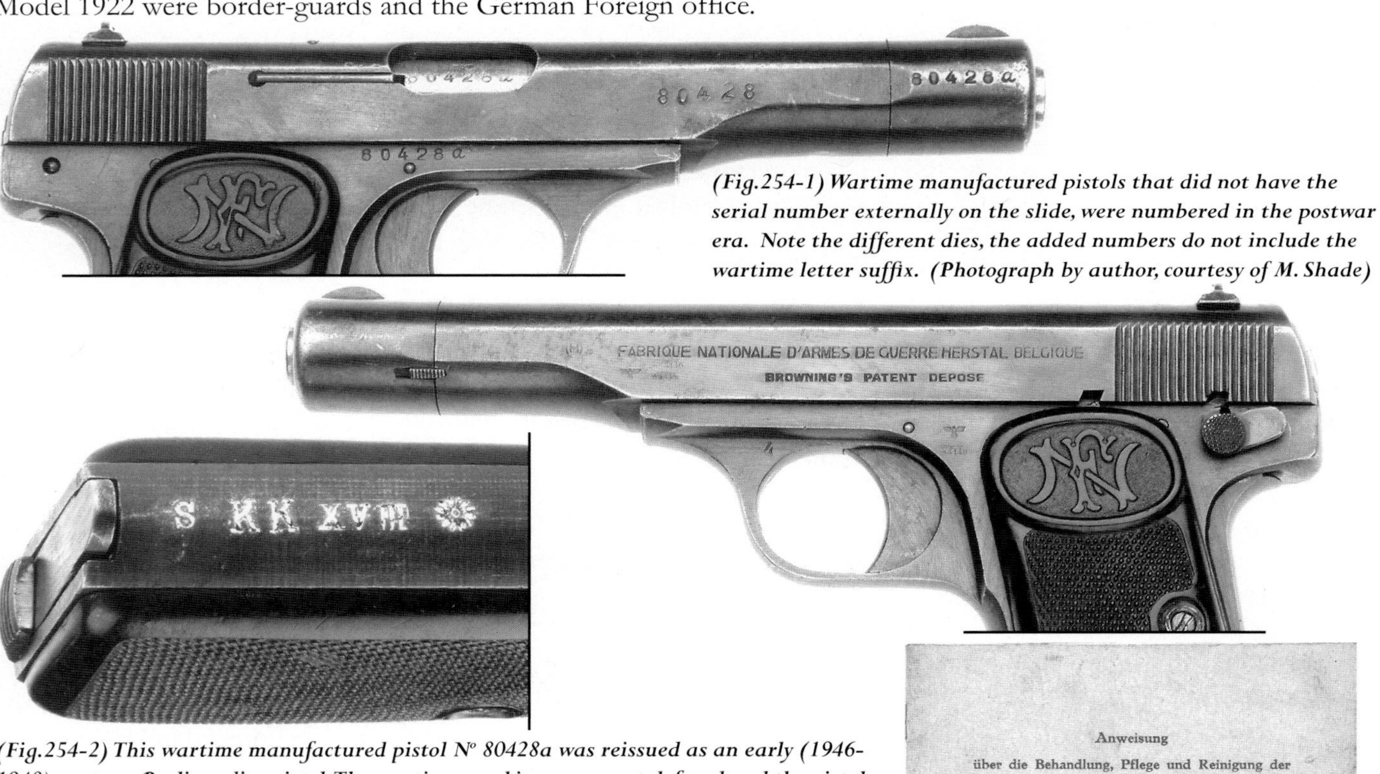

(Fig.254-1) Wartime manufactured pistols that did not have the serial number externally on the slide, were numbered in the postwar era. Note the different dies, the added numbers do not include the wartime letter suffix. (Photograph by author, courtesy of M. Shade)

(Fig.254-2) This wartime manufactured pistol N° 80428a was reissued as an early (1946-1948) postwar Berlin police pistol. The wartime markings were not defaced and the pistol was marked on the grip-strap: "S" for Soviet sector, "KK" for Kriminalkommissariat and "XVIII" for the Bezirk of Weißensee. Most pistols lack the KK marking, these letters were added as the pistol was used by detectives. It is also reported that on occasion the American sector is identified as "BA" for Berlin – American sector and not just "A". Note the early Berlin star with rounded edges. (Photographs by author, courtesy of Michael Shade)

Anweisung
über die Behandlung, Pflege und Reinigung der
Pistole

Herausgegeben vom Bundesminister der Finanzen
Bonn 1962

(Fig.254-3) Several examples of reissued German police pistols with defaced Nazi markings. (Photographs by author, courtesy of M. Shade)
(Fig.254-4) A 1962 German instruction booklet for the Model 1922 and MAB pistol.

(Fig.255-1) Post 1948 Berlin police markings as applied to newly purchased Model 1910 and Model 1922 pistols. Note the revised Berlin star marking with sharp edges. It is believed that the "BA" marking indicates that the pistol was transferred from one sector to another. No Soviet sector markings or French markings have been reported on newly acquired FN pistols. (Photographs by author, courtesy of Michael Shade & Kevin Null)

(Fig.255-2) This 1950s Bremerhaven police pistol N° 492334 was factory marked "Pol.Brh.LS." The LS marking is believed to stand for "Land" and "Stadt"; the city itself and the surrounding communities. Note the matching magazine, the sideways number most likely indicates the magazine number. Another observed Bremerhaven police pistol is N° 487720. (Photographs courtesy of Kevin Null)

(Fig.255-3) Hamburg police property markings were applied in Germany with an issue number. The markings were defaced when the pistols were sold on the commercial market. Note the upper and lower case variants. (Photographs by author, courtesy of Michael Shade & Kevin Null)

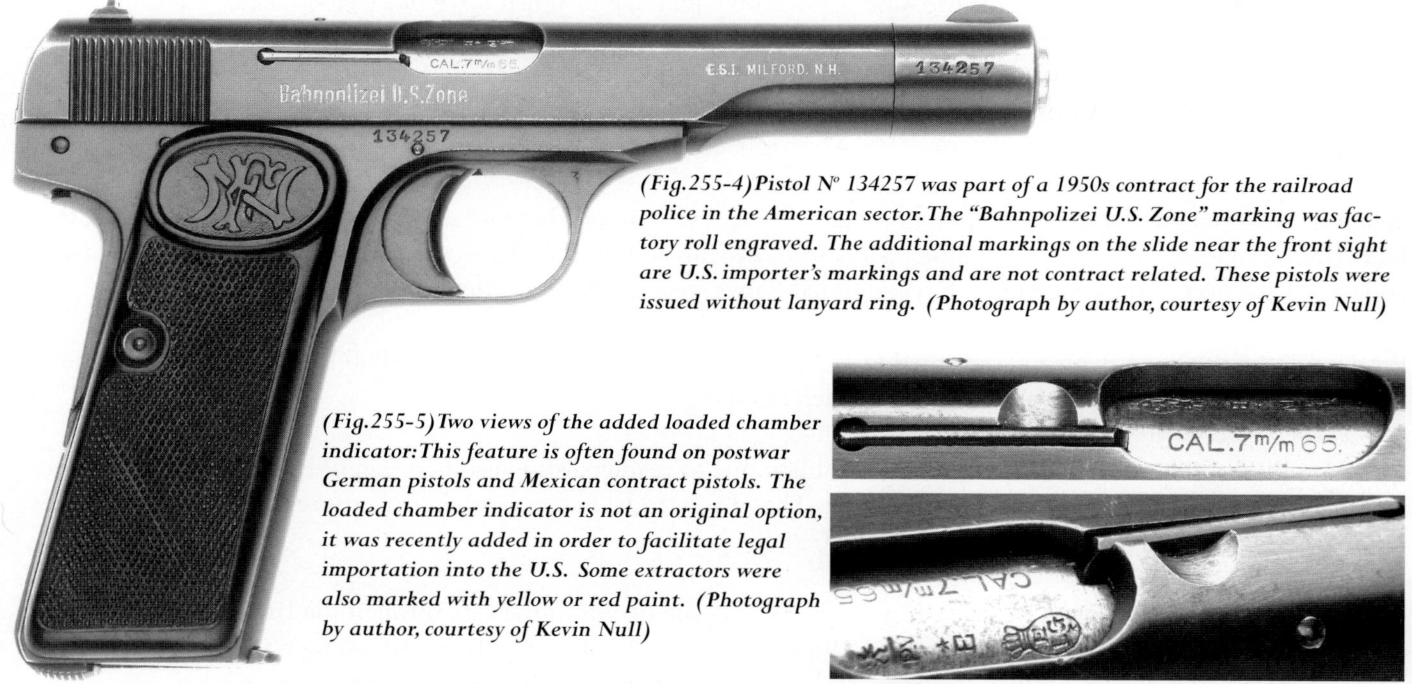

(Fig.255-4) Pistol N° 134257 was part of a 1950s contract for the railroad police in the American sector. The "Bahnpolizei U.S. Zone" marking was factory roll engraved. The additional markings on the slide near the front sight are U.S. importer's markings and are not contract related. These pistols were issued without lanyard ring. (Photograph by author, courtesy of Kevin Null)

(Fig.255-5) Two views of the added loaded chamber indicator: This feature is often found on postwar German pistols and Mexican contract pistols. The loaded chamber indicator is not an original option, it was recently added in order to facilitate legal importation into the U.S. Some extractors were also marked with yellow or red paint. (Photograph by author, courtesy of Kevin Null)

(1) Author's correspondence with Marck Slootweg & Andreas Giersch

The FN Baby Browning

Development History

Contrary to the implications of its name, the Baby Browning had no design roots with John M. Browning or the Browning family. The Baby was both conceived and designed by FN's head engineer, Dieudonné Saive (page 82) with the aim of producing as small a pocket pistol as possible. The Baby's development was entirely at Saive's initiative; there is no evidence to indicate that FN was seeking to develop a new pocket pistol at that time.

(Fig.256-1) A size comparison between the Model 1905 Vest Pocket and FN Baby Browning. This Baby N° 1442 was produced on May 31, 1932 and was shipped to Schroeder on June 6, 1932 who forwarded it on to a retailer.

The new pistol was patented in Belgium on June 10, 1927. While it was likely scheduled for production with the Grand Rendement in 1929, the Great Depression delayed the Baby's production and release until 1931.

The Baby's name derives from an old nickname for the Model 1905 Vest Pocket pistol. The Browning name was included strictly for marketing purposes[1]. Unlike other FN pistols, the Baby Browning's model nomenclature has never been changed or updated and has been used for most markets, regardless of language differences. Internally, FN referred to the pistol as Pistolet Browning 6.35 Allégé (Lightened Browning 6.35mm pistol). As a result, from the time of the Baby's introduction, the two pistols have been confused.

The Model 1905 Vest Pocket displayed strong sales throughout the 1930s. As a result, while FN continued to offer engraving and finish upgrades for the Model 1905, no engraving or finish upgrades were available for the Baby Browning in the 1930s. In fact, even after its introduction in 1931, factory advertising for the Baby was muted. This, coupled with the impact of the Great Depression, resulted in poor initial sales figures. During the 1930s, FN's emphasis was on military products and contracts. New product promotion was left to FN agents and dealers. Consequently, between 1931 and May 1940, only 50,147 pistols were made[2].

When the Germans invaded in May 1940, only a few Babys were in production. Between July and August 1940, the Germans completed 129 pistols[3]. These pistols were assembled before the introduction of the WaA613 acceptance code and have no German markings. No additional Babys were produced during the occupation.

Production of the Baby Browning resumed in 1946 with FN producing more than 10,000 Babys in one year. The Model 1905 remained available until 1950 in limited numbers.

Serial numbers followed the prewar numbers, enabling one to readily distinguish between prewar and postwar manufacture. No contract numbers are known to exist. The pistol model had no known law enforcement or military sales in the prewar era and few in the postwar era (page 260).

In 1953-1954, the decision was made to import and market the pistols in the U.S. through the Browning Arms Company. Production soared from 1,374 pistols in 1953 to 13,313 in 1954[3]. The Baby Browning was an overnight success in the U.S.

(Fig.257-1) Although military and law enforcement contracts were slim, FN did provide classroom instruction posters for the Baby Browning.

Sales gradually increased through the 1960s until the U.S. Gun Control Act of 1968 banned the Baby's importation. Predictably, manufacturing plummeted from 42,588 pistols in 1968 to 1,957 pistols in 1969.

Firearm manufacturing in the 1970s was marked with diversification and internationalization. FN's created new agreements or strengthened ties with companies including Miroku in Japan, Beretta in Italy, and Manufacture d'Armes de Bayonne (MAB) in France. In 1977 FN acquired Browning and became a minority owner of MAB. In 1978, Baby Browning production was moved from FN Herstal to MAB. Machinery, tooling and spare parts were sent in an effort to help the troubled MAB company. MAB Babys have French proofs in place of the Liège proofs found on Belgian made guns. Despite increased production numbers, the MAB plant was closed in 1983, and there was no production of the Baby between 1984 and 1986.

About that time Precision Small Parts acquired the production rights to the Baby Browning. PSP of Ontario, Canada and its subsidiaries were involved in manufacturing parts for the aerospace industry. The pistols were originally intended for production in Ontario, Canada. Legal restrictions prohibited the company from making firearms in Canada. A solution was found by having parts manufactured in Canada while frame production and final assembly would take place in their subsidiary in Charlottesville, Virginia.

The manufacturing machinery and tooling, originating from Bayonne and Herstal were sold together with remaining parts as a package. Much of the manufacturing equipment was outdated and new machinery was acquired for production.

Part of the arrangement allowed PSP to manufacture and sell the Baby model on the American market under its own name. The model was known as the PSP 25 or PSP 25-22. The "22" part of the designation refers to a .22 Short conversion kit that was offered by the company; the pistol could easily be transformed without any modification. As FN retained the Browning trade name, U.S. pistols were not marked with the Browning name. PSP also manufactured the Baby for export to FN. These pistols are marked Fabrique Nationale and have Browning marked grips. PSP production started in 1987 and continued until 1995. No new production took place between 1995 and 1998, pistols were assembled from existing parts inventories until the supply of frames was exhausted. In 1997 the arms company was relocated in Denver, Colorado under the name Precision Small Arms. Only the model designation changed from PSP-25 to PSA-25.

In the early 1990s, U.S. domestic sales totaled about 5,000 pistols per year and FN placed occasional orders for 500 pistols[(4)]. A few FN orders remained unfilled when the company halted assembly in 1998. Production of certain parts was time consuming and new, more efficient ways of production had to be found. Several years were spent in research and in futile attempts to find qualified contractors to produce the parts[(4)].

British engineers were contracted in 2003-2004 to production engineer the Baby for modern machinery and techniques[(4)]. In 2006 these methods were implemented in the Colorado plant[(4)]. Commercial production was restarted in 2008. Plans are in existence to offer the pistol back to FN, which may opt to sell the pistol through Browning International, as it did in the 1990s. Pistols for the domestic market are marked PSA-25 and are available with a wide range of finishes and upgrades.

---

(1) Many collectors through the years have voiced their disapproval of the fact that Mr. Saive always worked in the shadow of John M. Browning and was never publicly credited for his own designs like the Baby Browning and High Power pistol.

(2) Model 1905 production figures were almost ten times those of the Baby Browning in its first nine years of production.

(3) FN data compiled in 1982 by G. Van Belleghem

(4) Author's communication with the president of Precision Small Arms

Luxury Models: Plated and Engraved FN Baby Browning Pistols

There is no indication that FN offered a standardized line of upgrades for the Baby in the prewar era. Custom work was always available, but the emphasis in the 1930s was on military sales. Custom options were available after World War II, but the standardization of upgrades and engraving patters appears to have taken place when FN was working with Browning for U.S. distribution, around 1952.

Traditionally FN has always made an array of guns in various finishes for Browning's evaluation. Only a select few of those were adopted for sales in the U.S.

Browning offered the lightweight and chrome plated Babys, and FN followed Browning's lead. This was strictly a business decision; Browning's sales eclipsed FN's many times over and it made economic sense to maintain a smaller line of upgrades. Even with Browning's overwhelming sales figures, FN's product line was still considerably larger with various upgrades that were never made available in the U.S.

Although nickel plated pistols may have been made as custom work prior to 1955, no examples have been observed by the author. Chrome plated guns were introduced in 1953 with bright or brushed finish.

Sales of the Baby warranted no more than three engraving options. The Type III became known as the Renaissance in the U.S. and was the only one made available for the U.S. market.

The features of the lightweight model were standardized by Browning. Samples submitted to Browning in the early 1950s included alloy frames with bright and brushed nickel slides, blue slides and various gold plated parts options. The production models were made with a Duraluminum frame and steel slide in either blue finish or bright chrome plated finish. Browning took only the chrome version, while FN also offered the blue slide.

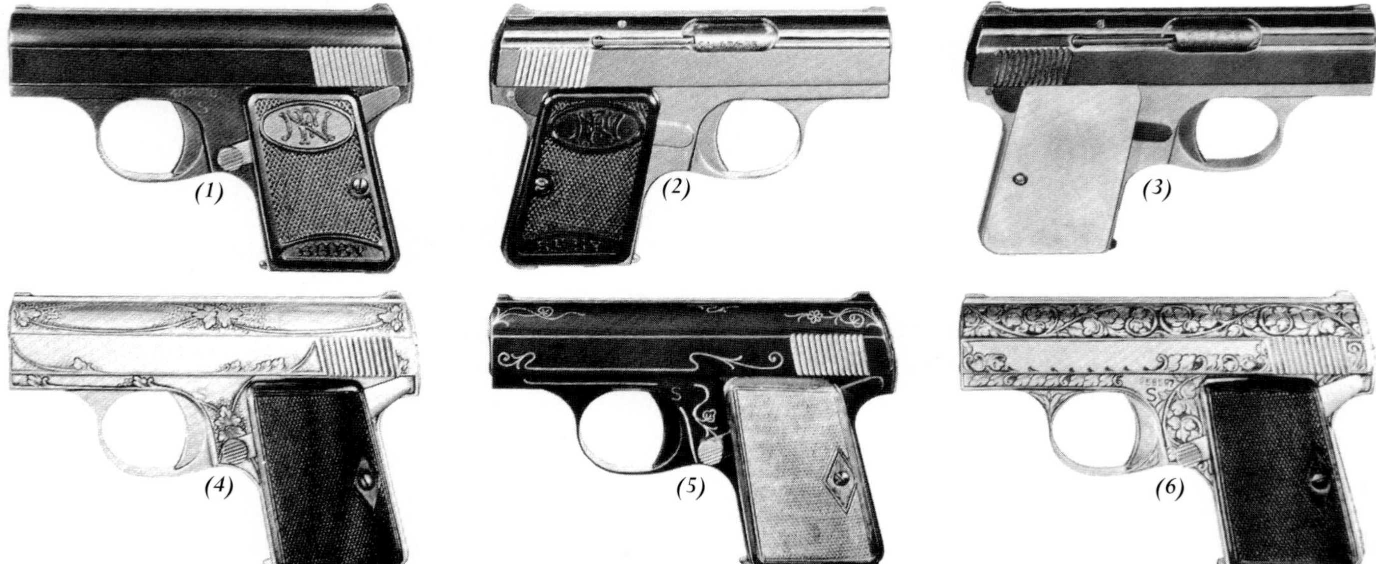

(Fig.258-1) 1973 FN engraving and finish options: (l. to r.) 1- Standard blue finish with black plastic FN Baby grips 2- Chrome finish with black plastic FN Baby grips 3- Lightweight model; Duraluminum frame with blue slide and synthetic Nacrolac grips.
4- Type I engraving on plated pistol with fancy checkered dark wooden grips 5- Type II engraving with gold inlay on blued pistol with fancy checkered light wooden grips 6- Type III engraving on plated pistol with fancy checkered dark wooden grips. Type III engraving was marketed in the U.S. as the Renaissance model.

The current line of the PSA-25 includes more upgrades than were available from Browning including: Traditional (blue finish), Nouveau Satin (brushed nickel), Nouveau Mirror (polished nickel), Stainless Steel, Featherweight (stainless steel slide and aluminum frame), Montreaux (18 or 24-karat gold-plated), Diplomat (Highly polished with gold accents), Renaissance (engraved vine pattern, contracted with former FN engraver, Angelo Bee) and Impériale (Gold line engraving, contracted with former FN engraver, Angelo Bee).

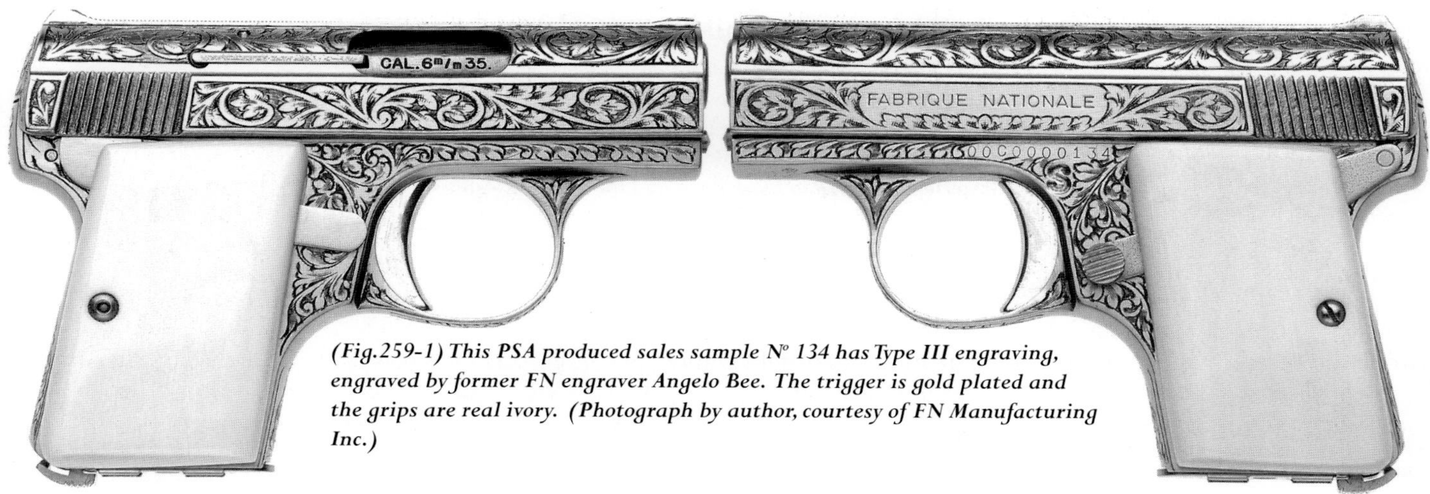

(Fig.259-1) This PSA produced sales sample N° 134 has Type III engraving, engraved by former FN engraver Angelo Bee. The trigger is gold plated and the grips are real ivory. (Photograph by author, courtesy of FN Manufacturing Inc.)

FN Baby Browning: Features & Specifications

Most of the features of the Baby remained unchanged through decades. The slide-legend "FABRIQUE NATIONALE D'ARMES DE GUERRE" was used from 1931 to 1972 when it changed to "FABRIQUE NATIONALE" (see fig 259-1). In the late 1960s FN reduced production costs by replacing the steel trigger and magazine catch with black synthetic parts. The magazine follower was modified from a flat design to a bent model. These changes were transferred over to MAB and later PSP production. Steel parts remained a preferred option for the various manufacturers. Grips were black plastic and illustrated the FN logo and the word "Baby". After 1977, grips feature only the Browning name and are shared among FN and Browning marked guns. The Browning marked pistols remained available through Browning International.

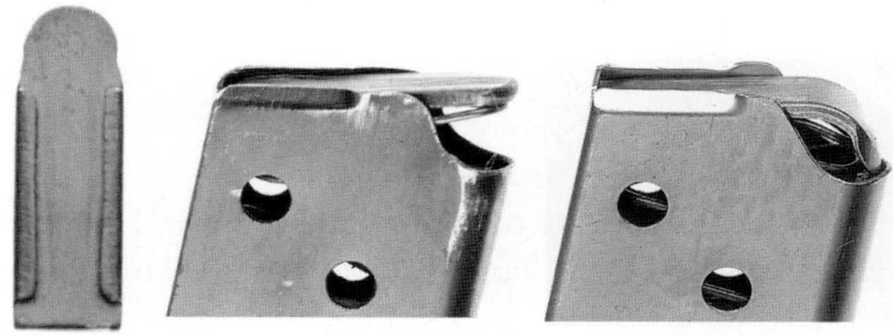

(Fig.259-2) Baby magazines can easily be distinguished by the bend body to secure the floor-plate. Many magazines were "FN" marked, but not all. (Left) Pre-1968 flat magazine follower - (Right) Post-1968 bend magazine follower.

(Fig.259-1) Saive's innovative cocked indicator made the firing pin protrude through the frame, giving both a visual as well as sensory indicator when the pistol was cocked. This system remained standard through the entire Baby production and was introduced on the 100-series pistols decades later.

Specifications Summary

Manufacturer: Fabrique Nationale d'Armes de Guerre, MAB, Precision Small Parts, Precision Small Arms
Belgian patent: 343126 **Filing date:** June 10, 1927
Period offered: 1931-1940 / 1946 – current
Caliber: .25 ACP / 6.35x15.5mm
Operating system: Blowback
Length: 104mm
Barrel length: 54mm
Weight: 230 grams
Grips: Black synthetic "FN Baby" style pre and postwar, "Browning" style post 1977.
Fine checkered wooden grips (postwar upgrade). Nacrolac (postwar upgrade)
Magazine capacity: Six
Sights: Fixed sights incorporated in the slide
Options: Lightweight model (postwar)
Finish offered: Blue, chrome (postwar)
Engraving patterns: Three (postwar)
Production quantity: 505,181 (FN Herstal and MAB production through 1981)

FN Baby Browning: Accessories

(Fig.260-1) Prewar factory presentation cases are rare. This is the same case as used for the Model 1905 (fig.185-3) except it is French fitted for the Baby. A Model 1905 will not fit. The exterior is covered in black linen and the interior has the typical prewar green satin with gold inscription.

(Fig.260-2) This 1950s pink and white instruction booklet was small enough to fit in the shipping box. An oil resistant, glassine paper version was also used.

(Fig.260-3) All cardboard shipping boxes have the traditional embossed FN logo. Prewar shipping boxes are hinged and dark green in color. Postwar cardboard boxes are green or black, with a diamond pattern in the covering (shown).

FN Baby Browning Contracts

There were only a few contracts for the Baby Browning. Several countries used the pistol in small quantities for law enforcement purposes. No prewar contracts have been located, the only prewar official use is pistol N° 13908 for German police, it is marked on the front grip-strap "S.Ko." for Schutzpolizei Koln[1] (see page 152).

The Netherlands purchased less than 200 pistols circa 1950 for police use[2]. The pistols were purchased on the commercial market and have no Dutch acceptance markings. It was found to be too small for official use. The MAB A was found to be more suitable and officially accepted. The Baby Brownings remained in Dutch service until 1968.

Belgium adopted the pistol and purchased small quantities. It was issued NSN 1005-13-107-8122. Belgian air force pilots used the pistols, it is speculated that the pistol was used as part of a survival kit for downed pilots. Some sources state that the Baby Browning was still carried by some officers as late as the mid 1980s.

The largest contract for the Baby was the Peruvian military contract of the 1950s. The pistols were used as officers' pistols together with Model 1910 pistols and were factory marked with the Peruvian crest.

A small quantity was imported into the U.S. after 1968 as back-up pistols for law enforcement.

(Fig.260-4) The 1950s Peruvian contract Baby Browning with Peruvian crest. (Photograph by author, courtesy of Carlos Davila)

(1) Handfeuerwaffen der deutschen Gendarmerie und Polizei des 19 und 20 Jahrhunderts
(2) Author's correspondence with Vincent Cozijn

Le Grand Rendement (The High Efficiency)

Development History

Collectors often believe that the High Power was developed in response to French military specifications for a new pistol in the 1920s. Although the High Power may have its roots in the early years of the French pistol trials, its development represented a distinct and discrete branch. The pistol known as the High Power evolved under the name "Le Grand Rendement" (High Efficiency). "Le Grand Rendement" was the early marketing name for what would become the Grande Puissance (High Power) in 1935.

The Grand Rendement had its birth with a 1921 French request for a military high capacity pistol. Dieudonné Saive developed a 15-round magazine for a modified Model 1903 pistol, and the modified pistol, along with the French specifications were shipped to John M. Browning.

The pair of prototype pistols designed for this effort were to be John Browning's last pistol designs. Browning's son, Val, who lived in Liège, presented several FN pistols derived from these designs at the French trials in 1922. These pistols were known as the Model of 1922. A revival of the pre-World War I Grand Browning was also submitted.

(Fig.261-1) One of the 9x19mm FN produced Model of 1922 pistols for French trials. Note that this pistol is not slotted for shoulder-stock compared to the Model of 1922 in fig.268-2. Although several were manufactured for trials, the pistols were not numbered. Note that the tangent sights are not marked with graduations. (Photographs by author, courtesy of the John M. Browning Firearms Museum - Ogden Union Station)

Overall, the new Browning pistol performed well, but the French trials board indicated that improvements, including an external hammer and a reduction in weight, were required. The new requirements were incorporated into the design by Dieudonné Saive instead of John Browning. While this was done to save the time costs of transatlantic travel, it resulted in Saive's taking ownership of the project. A revised and lighter version of the pistol, including an external hammer whose design was borrowed from the Grand Browning was submitted in 1923[1]. The new, lighter pistol, known as the Model of 1923 (fig.267-2), was entered in the French trials in March 1925.

Again, the French requested a reduction in overall weight. In 1926 the pistol was modified with the elimination of the tangent sights. The board also raised issues regarding the pistol's mechanical complexity and potential difficulties of maintenance in the field.

Until 1926 the trials pistols were equipped with 15-round magazines as stipulated in the early French requirements. Around the time that the tangent sights were eliminated a second version was introduced with a 13-round magazine. The concept of the 16-round pistol was abandoned soon afterward.

(1) A photograph of the first, flat hammer design is shown in The Browning High Power, by Blake Stevens on page 31, caption 26

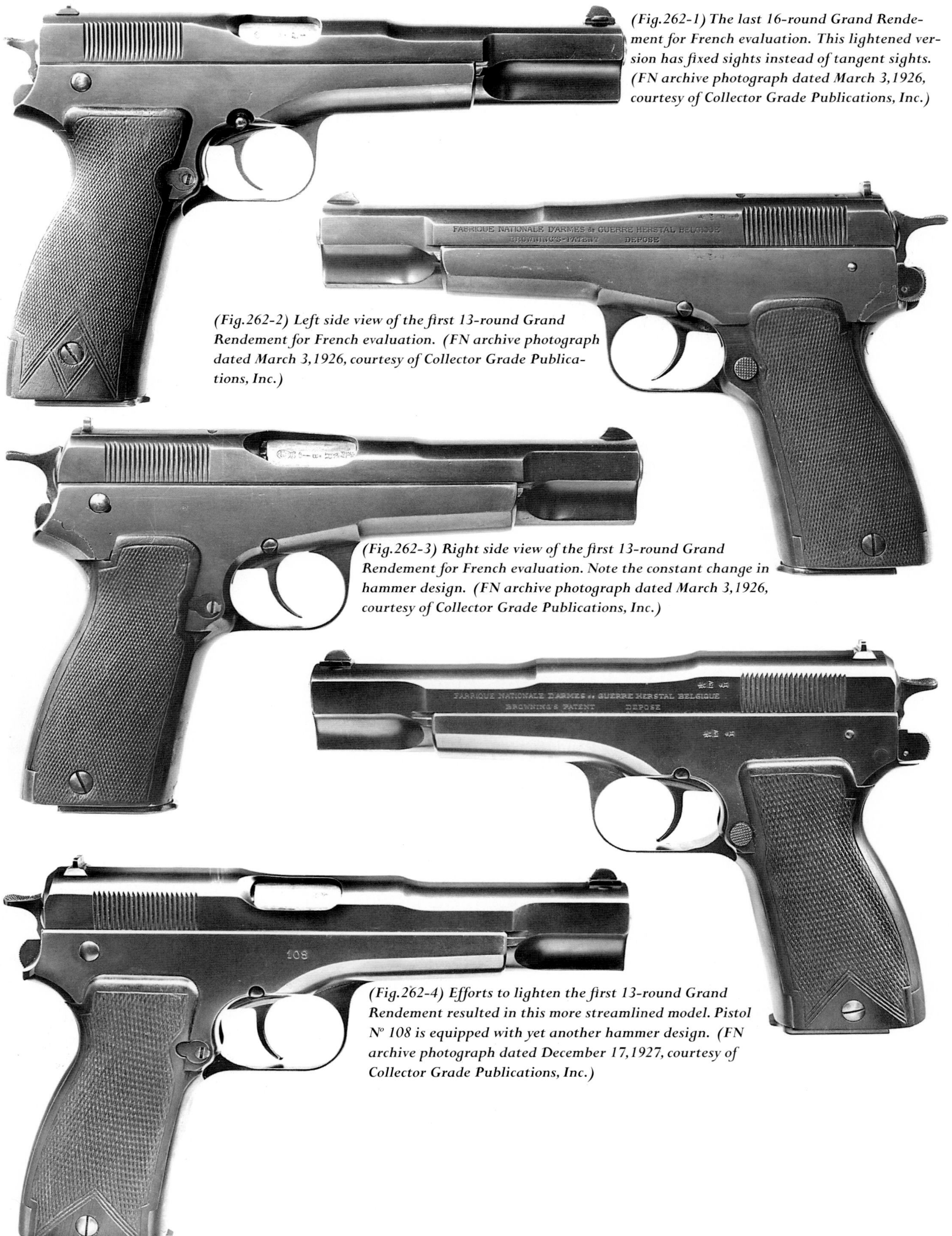

(Fig.262-1) The last 16-round Grand Rendement for French evaluation. This lightened version has fixed sights instead of tangent sights. (FN archive photograph dated March 3,1926, courtesy of Collector Grade Publications, Inc.)

(Fig.262-2) Left side view of the first 13-round Grand Rendement for French evaluation. (FN archive photograph dated March 3,1926, courtesy of Collector Grade Publications, Inc.)

(Fig.262-3) Right side view of the first 13-round Grand Rendement for French evaluation. Note the constant change in hammer design. (FN archive photograph dated March 3,1926, courtesy of Collector Grade Publications, Inc.)

(Fig.262-4) Efforts to lighten the first 13-round Grand Rendement resulted in this more streamlined model. Pistol N° 108 is equipped with yet another hammer design. (FN archive photograph dated December 17,1927, courtesy of Collector Grade Publications, Inc.)

The French trials lasted years. Specifications and requirements were changed continuously during the course of the trials.

Saive continued to refine the design, producing two more models, in 1927 and in 1928. Between 1928 and 1929 FN began to market the Grand Rendement to military customers. At this time, development of the Grand Rendement branched off from the French trials pistols. A contract with France was still the goal, but not the only objective.

Although the Grand Rendement was announced in 1929, FN adopted the same sales plan as it had with the Model 1903 years earlier; specifically production of the pistol would only start after a large contract had been secured. Like the Model 1903 it was only marketed as a military pistol, since the weapon's price and size made it an unlikely candidate for commercial sales.

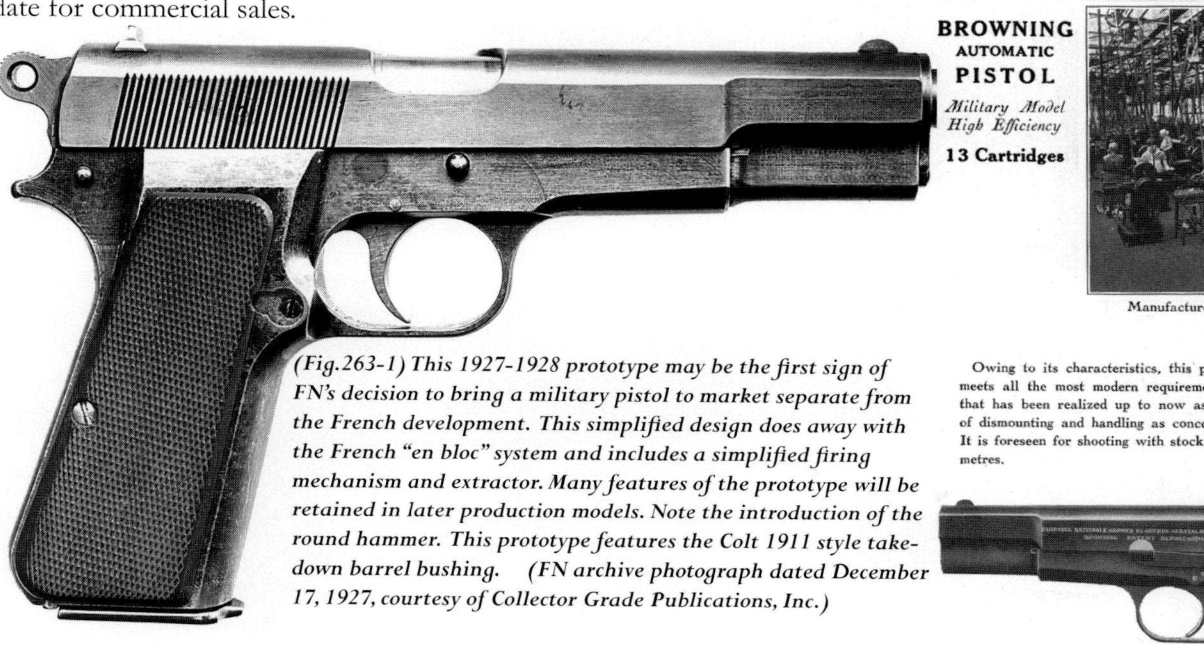

(Fig.263-1) This 1927-1928 prototype may be the first sign of FN's decision to bring a military pistol to market separate from the French development. This simplified design does away with the French "en bloc" system and includes a simplified firing mechanism and extractor. Many features of the prototype will be retained in later production models. Note the introduction of the round hammer. This prototype features the Colt 1911 style take-down barrel bushing. (FN archive photograph dated December 17, 1927, courtesy of Collector Grade Publications, Inc.)

BROWNING
AUTOMATIC
PISTOL
Military Model
High Efficiency
13 Cartridges

Manufacture of parts for arms.

Owing to its characteristics, this pistol is a weapon which meets all the most modern requirements and is to outdo all that has been realized up to now as well regarding easiness of dismounting and handling as concerning shooting efficiency. It is foreseen for shooting with stock and backsight up to 500 metres.

Calibre:	**9 mm**
Number of shot:	**14**
Weight:	**31 1/2 ozs.**
Weight (mag. full) 13 cartridges	**37 ozs.**
Length:	**7 3/4"**
Length of barrel:	**4 5/8"**

(Fig.263-2) The 1928 FN catalog announces that FN will soon release a new military pistol. The 1929 catalog (right) shows for the first time the Grand Rendement or High Efficiency. The 1929 pistol (fig.264-1) is an evolvement from the prototype shown above, most noticeably is the curved grip-strap.

The stock market crash of 1929 and the resulting global depression were of no help to the new model's debut. No military customers were to be found for the Grand Rendement. French pistol development went on a completely different direction after 1929, and the French trials pistols were no longer referred to as Grand Rendements. Saive continued to refine the Grand Rendement between 1930 and 1933. As with the Model 1903, FN's development efforts were carefully economized so as to minimize rework resulting from the unique requirements and specifications from any future military contract. Only a small number of pre-production pistols were manufactured in the early 1930s, these pre-production pieces serving as sales samples as well as trials weapons. The Grand Rendement pre-production guns were not sold but rather lent to specific FN agents for specific demonstrations.

The Belgian government was the first to indicate a strong interest in the new pistol after 1931, ordering 1,000 for field trials in 1933. Just over 1,100 pistols were produced, 1,000 for the Belgian government and a further 100 for use as sales samples for foreign trials. Collectors refer to these last Grand Rendement pistols as "Oval Ports" based on the shape of the ejection port.

Prior to the Belgian Army acceptance of the pistol in 1934-1935, the Belgian purchasing commission requested several changes, including a system that prevented the magazine from dropping to the ground when ejected, and improvements in the hammer design and fired case extraction.

The name of the newly modified pistol was changed to Grande Puissance. It is not known if the name originated with FN or the Belgian military.

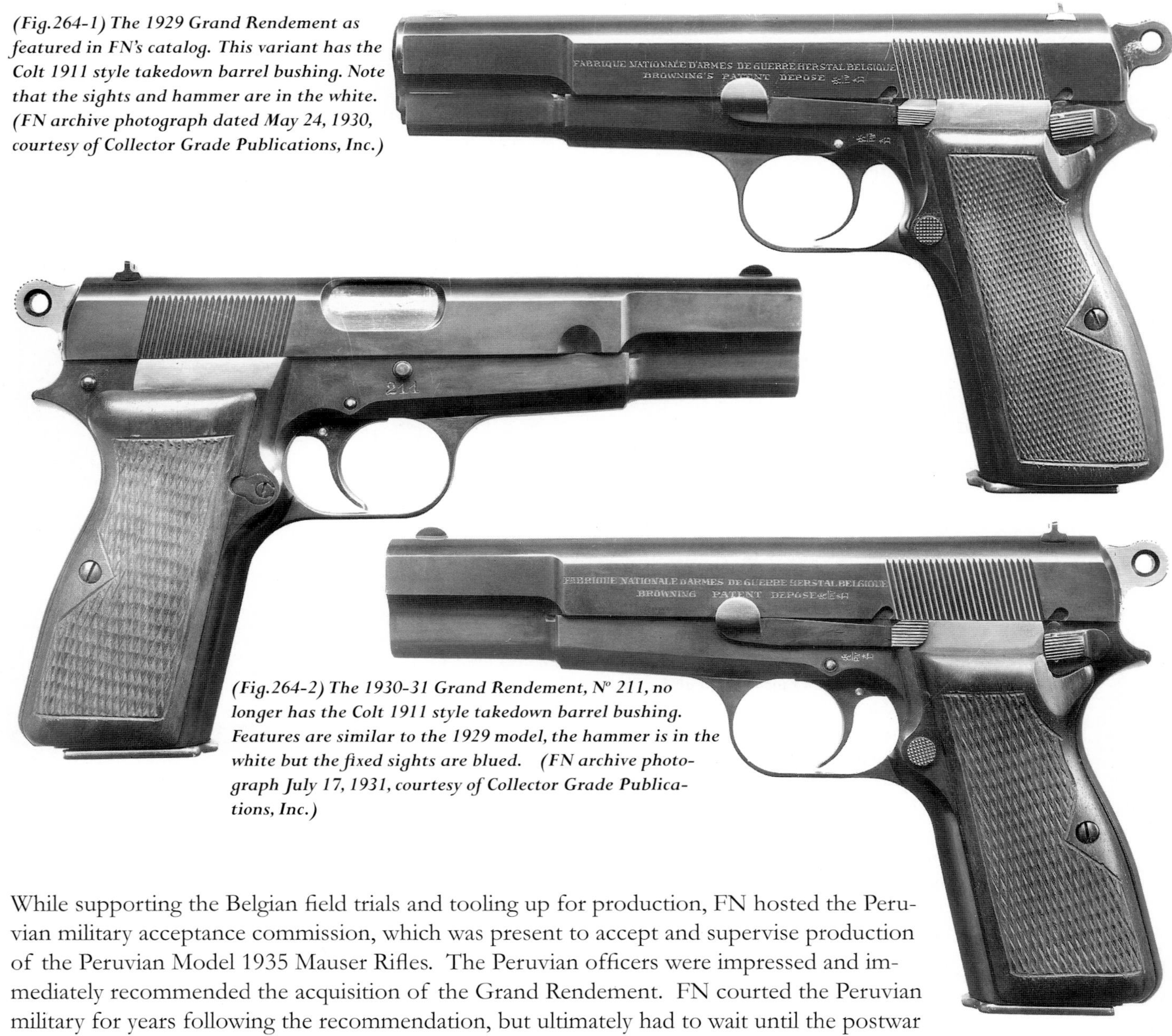

(Fig.264-1) The 1929 Grand Rendement as featured in FN's catalog. This variant has the Colt 1911 style takedown barrel bushing. Note that the sights and hammer are in the white. (FN archive photograph dated May 24, 1930, courtesy of Collector Grade Publications, Inc.)

(Fig.264-2) The 1930-31 Grand Rendement, N° 211, no longer has the Colt 1911 style takedown barrel bushing. Features are similar to the 1929 model, the hammer is in the white but the fixed sights are blued. (FN archive photograph July 17, 1931, courtesy of Collector Grade Publications, Inc.)

While supporting the Belgian field trials and tooling up for production, FN hosted the Peruvian military acceptance commission, which was present to accept and supervise production of the Peruvian Model 1935 Mauser Rifles. The Peruvian officers were impressed and immediately recommended the acquisition of the Grand Rendement. FN courted the Peruvian military for years following the recommendation, but ultimately had to wait until the postwar era to fill the first Peruvian contract.

French trials continued but faced increasing French prejudice against foreign made products. FN tried to solve this problem by marking the pistols supplied for the French trials with the mark of their Paris affiliate, La Manufacture d'Armes de Paris (MAP). MAP had been established in 1915 and FN had acquired majority ownership in the 1920s. Although MAP was known for ammunition manufacturing, it made various other products such as typewriters (see fig.37-2).

Rebadging with a French name proved to be no solution and the French government continued to favor designs from French state arsenals over FN's pistols. The pistols submitted for the 1933, '34 and '35 trials would culminate in the adoption of the French M1935A pistol. In the early 1930s, the caliber for the French trials was changed to the 7.65mm Long cartridge (7.65x20mm) and the firing mechanism was required to be unitary or "en bloc" (encased). This new mechanism facilitated repairs by allowing the firing mechanism to be replaced as a single unit. Ultimately, an amalgam of the French and Swiss Petter designs was adopted in 1937. The French Model 1935A was accepted first and the Model 1935S was adopted later to incorporate production efficiencies. In the event, the French remained short of pistols on the eve of World War II, as they had in World War I.

(Fig.265-1) The 1933 French trials pistols were a complete design departure from the earlier trials pistols and Grand Rendement from 1929-1930. The concept of a double-stack magazine was abandoned, the 9x19mm caliber was replaced with the 7.65mm Long chambering, the locked breech model was replaced with a blowback mechanism. A simpler and easier to use "en bloc" mechanism was incorporated. This pistol N° 1 was submitted for the June 1, 1933 trials. (FN archive photograph, courtesy of Collector Grade Publications, Inc.)

(Fig.265-2) Trials pistol N° 7 was introduced in 1935 and named Model of 1936 by the French. It was the last of the FN French trials pistols before the French adoption of the French-Swiss Petter design. This rare variant varies from the 1933 pistol in the safety and slide-holdopen lever, takedown lever and sinplified "en bloc" takedown mechanism. (Photographs by author, courtesy of Tom Knox)

(Fig.265-3) Although FN was not involved in casting frames in the prewar era, trials pistol N° 7 shows an unusual seam along the center of the bottom of the frame. It is not clear what manufacturing process FN used for the French trials pistols. (Photograph by author, courtesy of Tom Knox)

(Fig.265-4) A detail view of the "Manufacture de Paris" factory roll marking, barrel proofs and serial number. (Photograph by author, courtesy of Tom Knox)

The Last Grand Rendement: The Oval Port

Produced for Belgian military field trials in 1933-1934, just over 1,100 Grand Rendement pistols were manufactured. The Belgian military ordered 1,000 pistols with various shoulder-stock models(1). FN made an additional 100 plus pistols, which were used as sales samples and used in foreign trials and demonstrations. FN used the Belgian military field trials as a way to market the Grand Rendement, especially in South America.

The Belgian military was concerned with the cost of magazines and the ease of which magazines could be discarded when empty. As a result, it was requested that a system be developed whereby the magazine would eject but not drop from the magazine well. Pistol users were instructed to remove the magazine by hand instead of allowing it to drop. Grand Rendement magazines were traditionally blued, but the bluing did not offer any resistance in the magazine well. FN experimented with nickel-plated magazine bodies. The nickel plating offered enough resistance so that the magazine did not drop from the magazine well but also made it difficult to remove. A solution was found by resizing the magazine well and phosphating the body of the magazine, creating just enough friction so that the magazine would not drop from the magazine well.

The concerns of the Belgian military through the trials can be summarized as follows:

The cost of magazines and restricting magazines from dropping to the ground
The function of the magazine safety, where the magazine should be fully inserted before disengaging
The construction of the hammer mechanism and the fact that it should not be removable while field-stripping
The ease of field-stripping and limits as to which parts were removable during field-stripping
Ejection of fired cases

The adoption of the Belgian military shoulder-stock, holsters and magazine pouch were a result from these field-trials.

These last Grand Rendement pistols differ from the later 1935 High Power pistols primarily in the shape of the ejection port. The ejection port is clearly oval in shape, and collectors have often referred to these as "oval port" High Powers. Although no documentation has been found, the oval port may have contributed to the ejection concerns previously listed and the ejection port was reshaped by the time the High Power went in production in 1935. The incorporation of changes based on the Belgian military requirements was patented on March 1, 1935.

Prior to the field trials, the Belgian military had sent a parts inspector to FN to guarantee the quality of the parts made for the trials pistols. As the pistols were going to trials, no additional Belgian military markings were applied. Unlike the later accepted High Power pistols, these guns did not go through the arsenal testing and were not (initially) arsenal marked. They are usually encountered with a circle H marking applied at FN on various parts. Although no documentation exists, it appears that these late Grand Rendement pistols were used as standard service pistols through 1940. It is possible to encounter an oval port Grand Rendement with later applied arsenal markings if it was repaired or overhauled at an arsenal.

The existence of an oval port training pistol (Pistolet de Manipulation) raises questions as to whether the Belgian military purchased any instruction pistols with their field trials pistols (see page 277).

Most of these pistols were captured by the Germans in World War II and some made their way to the U.S. with returning G.I.'s

Reported or observed serial numbers: 33, 35, 52, 97, 128, 349, 354, 444, 521, 882, 1007

(Fig.266-1) A detail view of the distinct oval shaped ejection port of the last Grand Rendement. Note the Belgian military markings on the barrel; circle H and EGB marking (page 95). (Photograph by author, courtesy of Jim Mauloff)

(1) Not all trials pistols were slotted for shoulder-stock. The exact composition and quantities of the accoutrements like shoulder-stocks and holsters is not known. It is however clear that the Belgian military used the field trials to determine the type of shoulder-stock, holster variants and the magazine pouch.

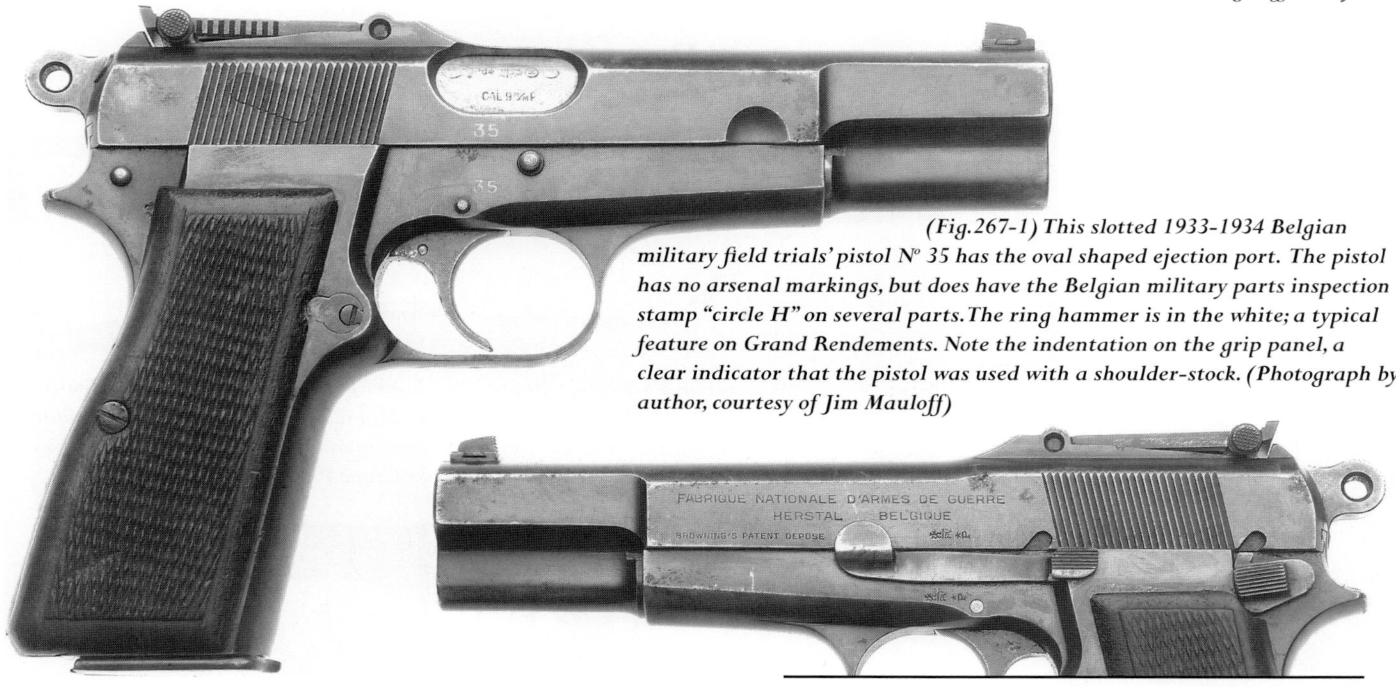

(Fig.267-1) This slotted 1933-1934 Belgian military field trials' pistol N° 35 has the oval shaped ejection port. The pistol has no arsenal markings, but does have the Belgian military parts inspection stamp "circle H" on several parts. The ring hammer is in the white; a typical feature on Grand Rendements. Note the indentation on the grip panel, a clear indicator that the pistol was used with a shoulder-stock. (Photograph by author, courtesy of Jim Mauloff)

The Development of a Suitable Shoulder-Stock

From the early days of the French trials, FN spent a considerable amount of time developing a line of shoulder-stocks. Starting in 1922 steel skeleton and collapsible stocks were made as prototypes, designs were patented and improved upon, and the stocks went through a development process quite similar to that of the Grand Rendement. The accessory was marketed with tangent sighted pistols. When the French eliminated the tangent sights in 1926, FN stopped further development until the Grand Rendement went to market in 1929. A solid metal version was manufactured and used as a sales sample, of which at least two examples are known to exist. The first wooden holster stock was modified from a Model 1903 stock. A simplified wooden slat stock was also manufactured with attached leather holster; the design was first introduced in 1922 and revived in the 1930s. The slat stock, being the most economical, was ultimately adopted as the sole stock for the High Power.

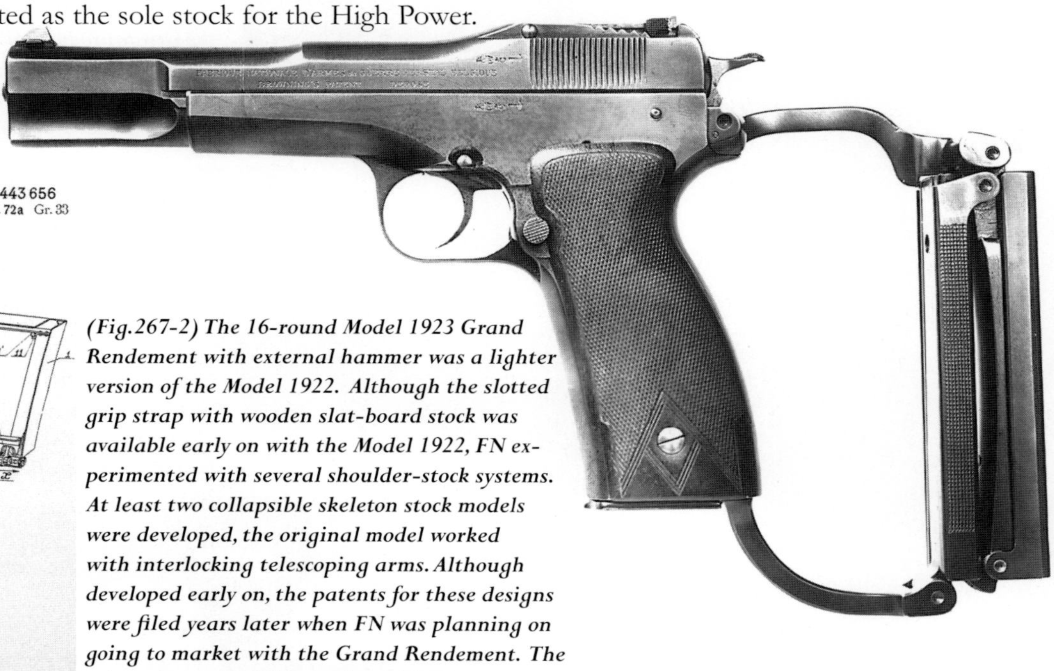

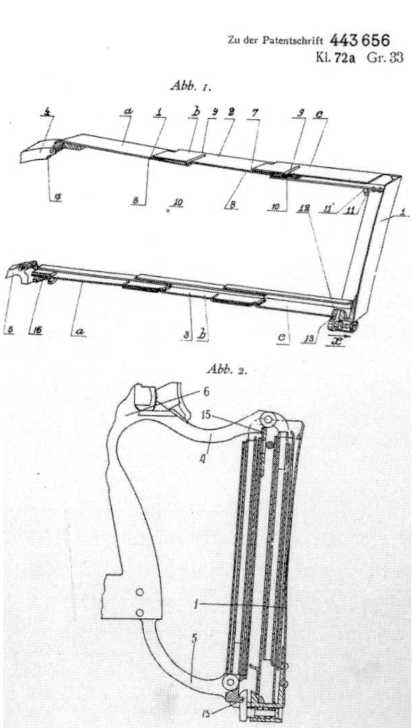

Zu der Patentschrift **443 656**
Kl. **72a** Gr. 33

Abb. 1.

Abb. 2.

(Fig.267-2) The 16-round Model 1923 Grand Rendement with external hammer was a lighter version of the Model 1922. Although the slotted grip strap with wooden slat-board stock was available early on with the Model 1922, FN experimented with several shoulder-stock systems. At least two collapsible skeleton stock models were developed, the original model worked with interlocking telescoping arms. Although developed early on, the patents for these designs were filed years later when FN was planning on going to market with the Grand Rendement. The original patent (left) was issued in Germany on May 4, 1927. The improved design, seen above on the Model 1923, worked with sliding extensions, which locked into place. (Above: FN archive photograph, courtesy of Collector Grade Publications, Inc.)

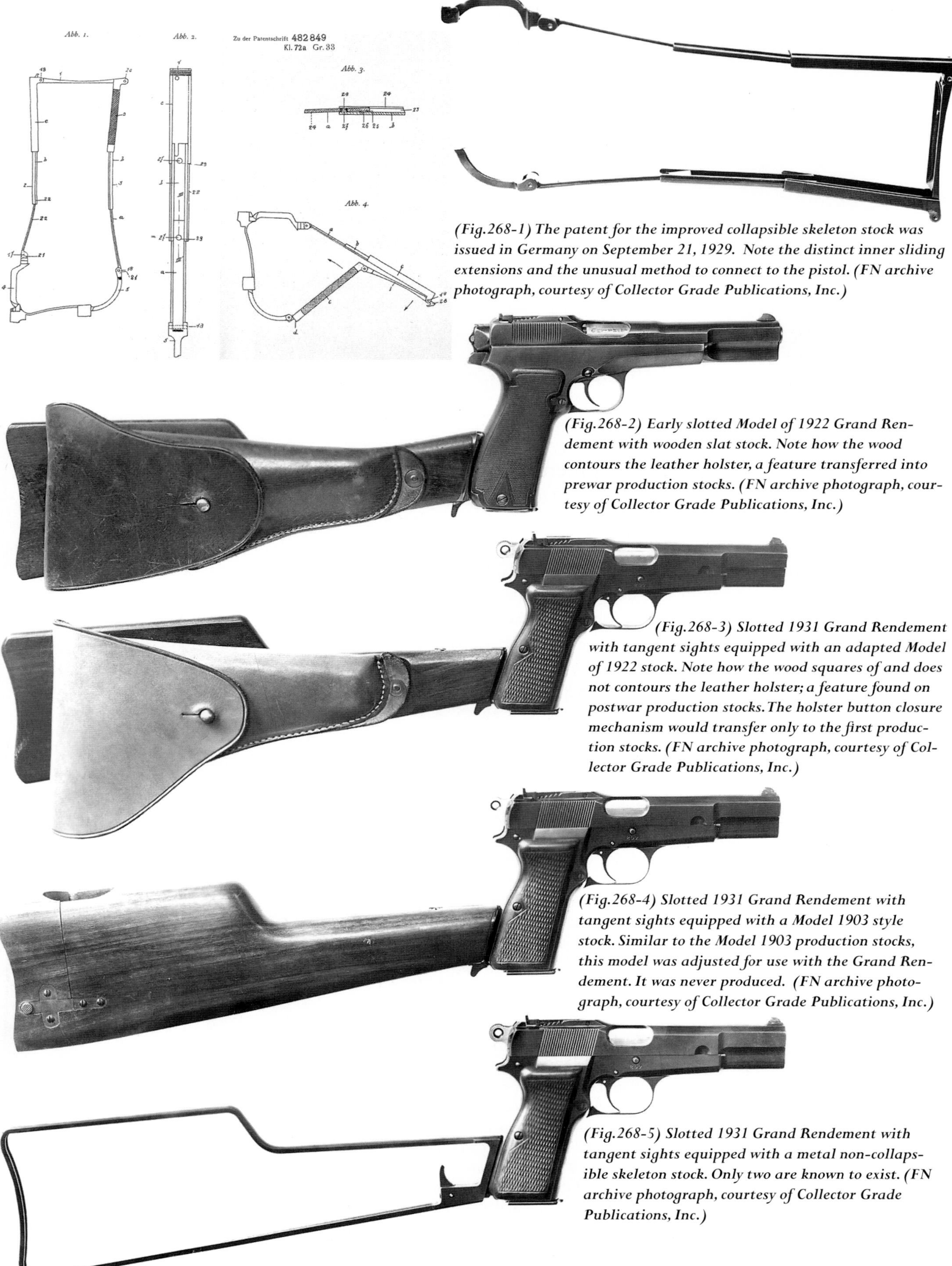

(Fig.268-1) The patent for the improved collapsible skeleton stock was issued in Germany on September 21, 1929. Note the distinct inner sliding extensions and the unusual method to connect to the pistol. (FN archive photograph, courtesy of Collector Grade Publications, Inc.)

(Fig.268-2) Early slotted Model of 1922 Grand Rendement with wooden slat stock. Note how the wood contours the leather holster, a feature transferred into prewar production stocks. (FN archive photograph, courtesy of Collector Grade Publications, Inc.)

(Fig.268-3) Slotted 1931 Grand Rendement with tangent sights equipped with an adapted Model of 1922 stock. Note how the wood squares of and does not contours the leather holster; a feature found on postwar production stocks. The holster button closure mechanism would transfer only to the first production stocks. (FN archive photograph, courtesy of Collector Grade Publications, Inc.)

(Fig.268-4) Slotted 1931 Grand Rendement with tangent sights equipped with a Model 1903 style stock. Similar to the Model 1903 production stocks, this model was adjusted for use with the Grand Rendement. It was never produced. (FN archive photograph, courtesy of Collector Grade Publications, Inc.)

(Fig.268-5) Slotted 1931 Grand Rendement with tangent sights equipped with a metal non-collapsible skeleton stock. Only two are known to exist. (FN archive photograph, courtesy of Collector Grade Publications, Inc.)

The FN Browning Model 1935 GP (Grande Puissance/High Power)

Development History

As with other FN military pistols, the High Power was placed into production only after a sizeable contract was secured. The High Power was built to Belgian military specifications deriving from field trials of the Grand Rendement (page 266) in 1933. FN started producing the High Power in May 1935, the first pistols being assembled on May 15, 1935 and bearing serial numbers 7, 12, 15 and 19. Serial numbers 1 through 5 were never produced. These pistols (among others, including serial numbers 8, 13, 16, 18 and 25) encountered problems during manufacturing and were never completed. Mr. Saive retained more than 50 of the first pistols produced by FN, some of which were marked for Mr. Saive's collection.

The first pistols were marked with FN serial numbers and logged under the heading "Commerce," indicating production for the commercial market. Military production did not begin until FN had tooled up for and perfected the High Power manufacturing processes. Accordingly, the first Belgian military pistols were completed on May 23, 1935. Although prewar Belgian military pistols were normally marked with serial numbers and not contract numbers, the first High Power order was marked with contract numbers from 1 to 10,000 and logged under the heading "Gouvernement Belge" (Belgian government). The practice of logging both commercial guns and Belgian military guns in one shipping log proved cumbersome and was eliminated after the first 1000 pistols. Belgian military pistols shipped after the first order had standard FN serial numbers.

Unlike popular belief the High Power was not manufactured with sequential numbers, the pistol was not warehoused in large numbers. Military orders, even those without special contract markings or numbers, were built to order. This matter has confused collectors with dating pistols and identifying features of the High Power.

Prewar pistols were always finished with a rust blue finish. No contract placed during the prewar period specified a black enamel finish. As the High Power was a military pistol, neither engraving types nor nickel finish was offered. Prewar engraved pistols were custom made as presentation pistols. Postwar military pistols were available in rust blue (salt blue after 1961). Black enamel was available in 1946 and chrome commercial pistols were made starting in the 1950s. A basic phosphate finish was also available starting in the 1970s.

FN Model 1935: Features & Specifications

Sights: Prewar

FN offered two different types of tangent sights for the High Power during the prewar period, differing in both markings on the sight leaf and, correspondingly, the geometry of the elevation ramp. Both were graduated from 50 to 500 meters. On one variant, the numbering fills approximately 60 percent of the sight leaf, while on the other, the numbering fills the entire sight leaf. U.S. collectors have applied an unofficial nomenclature to the sight leaf variants. A "Type 1" leaf is 60 percent marked, while a "Type 2" leaf is fully marked. Based on this naming convention, it is tempting to assume that the Type 1 preceded the Type 2, but this is incorrect as both were introduced in 1935.

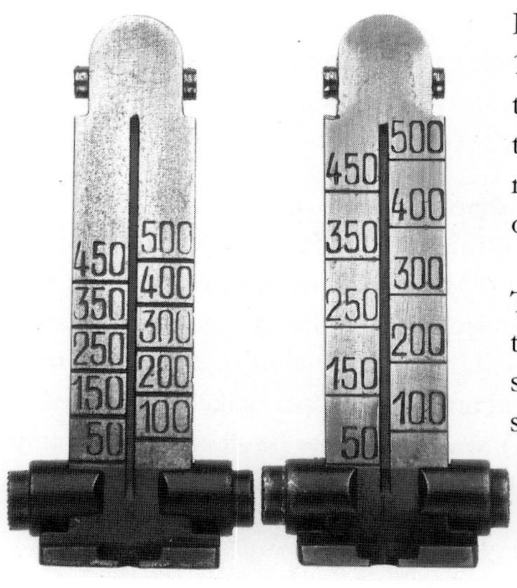

FN offered three types of sights on prewar High Powers. These included Type 1 tangent sights, Type 2 tangent sights and fixed sights. While often assumed to be commercial production, there is no correlation between fixed sights and the pistols provided to the commercial market. As the tangent sights were more common, and thus resulted in production economies of scale, they were offered to agents in far greater quantities than fixed sights.

The determining factor in the type of tangent sights supplied was whether the order included shoulder-stocks. Pistols shipped with numbered shoulder-stocks were supplied with Type 1 sights, pistols shipped without shoulder-stocks were supplied with Type 2 sights, as evidenced by the table below:

(Fig.269-1) The two types of tangent sights introduced in 1935. Type 1 (left) was provided with pistols for use with shoulder-stocks, Type 2 (right) was provided on orders that did not include shoulder-stocks. The sights were blued and the leaf surface was polished, leaving the markings blued and easily visible.

Belgium:	**Orders for NCOs and troops prior to 1939 with shoulder-stocks: Type 1**
Lithuania:	**Order without shoulder-stocks - 1936: Type 2**
Estonia:	**Order without shoulder-stocks - 1936: Type 2**
China:	**First order with shoulder-stocks - 1938: Type 1**
China:	**Second order without shoulder-stocks - 1938: Type 2**
Belgium:	**Officers' replacement pistols without shoulder-stocks - 1939-1940: Type 2**
Finland:	**Order with shoulder-stocks - 1940: Type 1**

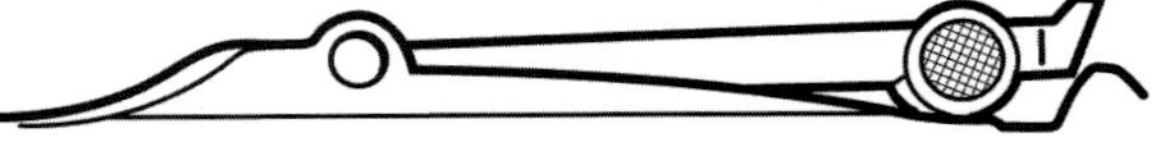

The difference between pistols with the Type 1 and Type 2 sights were not just the graduations on the sight. The slide accommodating the sight was also machined differently, as seen above.

(Fig.270-1) Pistol N° 46 with Type 2 sights is one of the oldest known High Power pistols. Produced on May 19, 1935, it was retained by Mr. Saive on May 20,1935. Notice the round barrel cam. (Photograph by author, courtesy of Freddy Greer)

Sights: Postwar

The concept of tangent sights and shoulder-stocks derived from the tactical notion of a "pistol-carbine" that could fill a niche between pistol and rifle for NCOs and specialty troops. Practicality gradually took over when the Germans produced guns for their war effort and tangent sights were eliminated. Almost all post liberation pistols had fixed sights as these were leftovers from German occupation production. After the war, fixed sights became standard. Tangent sights and shoulder-stocks were available in the postwar era, but rapidly attained novelty status. In the postwar era, FN sold more pistols with tangent sights than shoulder-stocks and the Type 1 sight was never reintroduced. There were no postwar military contracts specifying shoulder-stocks. Postwar tangent sighted pistols were made with Type 2 sights, with either a slotted or un-slotted frame. Postwar stocks were used as sales samples or sold as a novelty accessory for slotted pistols. Adjustable sights were introduced in 1972.

Barrel Cams

Few production changes took place in the prewar era. In 1938 FN changed the shape of the barrel cam from round to square. It has been speculated that the round cam was prone to breakage, but this is unlikely as the round cam was used throughout the development and extensive trials of the Grand Rendement. Most likely the square cam was the request of a customer when placing a contract order, as FN deemed it an improvement, it replaced the earlier round cam in production. FN did not recall the early barrels as is often believed in the U.S. The concept of a product recall is a result of U.S. liability laws and never applied to Belgian industry. Both round and square cam barrels were used from 1938 until stocks of the round cam barrel were depleted. Because of FN's wicker baskets (see page 100), round barrel cams remained in assembly. It is possible to encounter a round barrel cam in either a 1940 Finnish or 1940 Belgian contract pistol. Even a WaA613 early wartime pistol was reported to have been assembled with a round cam barrel.

The year 1938 was the introduction of the square cam, as FN did not produce the High Power in sequential serial numbers, it is not possible to identify the change by serial number.

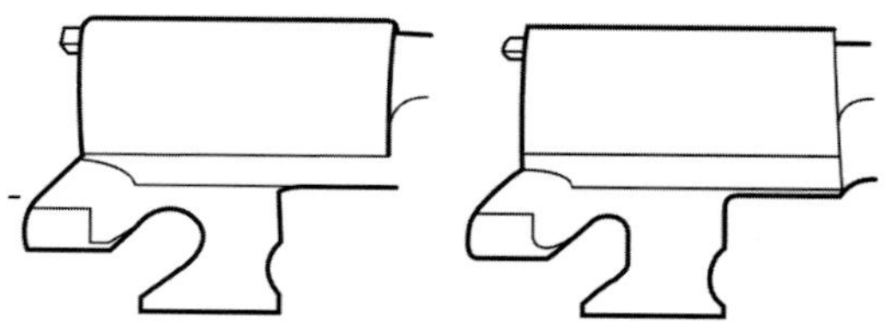

(Fig.271-1) (l.) Round barrel cam - (r.) square barrel cam

Grips and Magazines

(Fig.271-2) Split tail floor-plates (l.) were always blued and made exclusively in the prewar and wartime era. Push-button floor-plates (r.) were introduced in 1946 and replaced the split variant. Push-button floor-plates have been made in a wide variety of finishes.

Prewar grips were always made from French walnut. FN applied a red paint on the back of the grips as a moisture barrier. This paint stopped the wood from retaining moisture and thus prevented rust from building up on the frame.

During World War II, early WaA613 pistols were assembled with red backed grips. As the war progressed and prewar stockpiles dwindled, wooden grips were no longer painted. This transition took place late in the WaA103 assembly.

Brown Bakelite grips were introduced late in the war (page 299). These grips were used as a substitute material when wood was not available. Early post-liberation pistols were also assembled with Bakelite grips, as these were readily available. FN soon discontinued the use of the Bakelite grips as they proved to be brittle and prone to breakage.

Red backed grips were reintroduced in 1946 and were used throughout the 1950s. Black plastic grips appeared during the 1960s. By then, both plastic grips as well as wooden grips were available and FN discontinued the practice of applying the red moisture barrier. The old method of an oil finish on wooden grips was replaced in the 1960s with a sprayed on varnish, later in the 1980s this varnish was replaced with a polyurethane finish.

(Fig.271-3) Aluminum followers were replaced around 1962 with plastic, shortly afterwards FN also introduced the 20-round magazine. Factory 20-round magazines can be identified by the green painted body and protruding metal notch on the spine.

Prewar and wartime magazines can easily be identified by the floor-plate. Starting in 1946 FN changed the floor-plate from the split tail floor-plate type to push-button type. The postwar floor-plates were either black enamel or blued. Black enamel floor-plates were sometimes shipped with blued pistols.

Prewar and early wartime magazine bodies (WaA613, WaA103) have a phosphate finish (see page 266). Most wartime magazines have a blue finish. After the war magazine bodies were blued, some were later painted mat green, resembling the prewar finish in color. Tubes often bear markings indicating pre or postwar manufacture. FN also offered 20-round magazines starting in the 1960s, at the time the aluminum follower was also replaced with a plastic model (circa 1962).

In the 1980s magazine manufacturing was outsourced to Meggar in Italy, early ones were marked "Made in Italy", later models include the Meggar name.

Serial or Contract Numbers

FN offered optional contract numbering to their customers in the prewar era. Only a few customers purchased the option. These included Lithuania, Estonia and Paraguay. The rest of the prewar orders were marked with standard serial numbers. Serial numbers on prewar High Power pistols cannot be used to identify a manufacturing date as pistols were made to order and FN assigned numbers to the orders. FN did manage to fill the number slots, so most numbers were indeed used up through the prewar years. A few examples of manufacturing show the erratic approach to serial numbers: **N° 6666 built in 1935 for Belgium, N° 6644 built in 1938 for China, N° 20395 built in 1939 for China, N° 12779 built in 1940 for Finland, N° 43399 built in 1940 for Belgium**

FN Model 1935: Accessories

The shoulder-stock design was standardized when the High Power went into production. The High Power stock was a variant of the early 1922 wooden slat-board Grand Rendement stock (see fig.268-2), and included an attached leather holster (see fig.285-1 for the standard FN prewar stock). The prewar High Power stock differed from the 1922 Grand Rendement model in that it had a rounded contour on both sides of the stock following the shape of the holster (instead of just one side). Postwar stocks dispensed with the contouring and are squared off. Only Finland and China (first order) purchased the standard FN stock with attached holster. The Belgian military opted for a board stock without attached holster (page 275). Military contract shoulder-stocks were numbered to the gun and collectors should be aware that several dealers have gone into the practice of renumbering stocks. Original matching stocks are rare. No stocks were sold as military contracts in the postwar era.

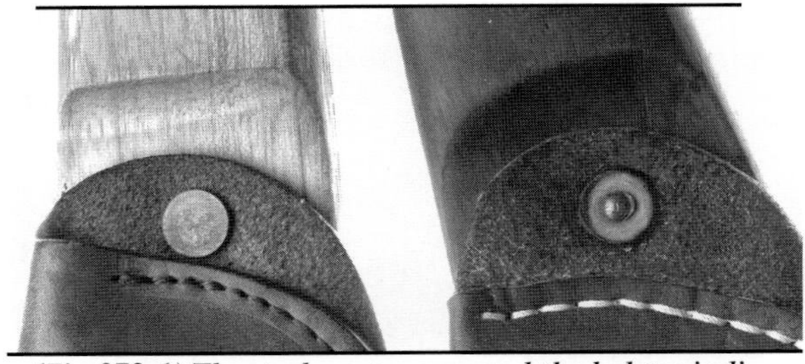

(Fig.272-1) The stock contour around the holster indicates period of manufacture. Round contours (r.) are prewar, while square contours (l.) are postwar.

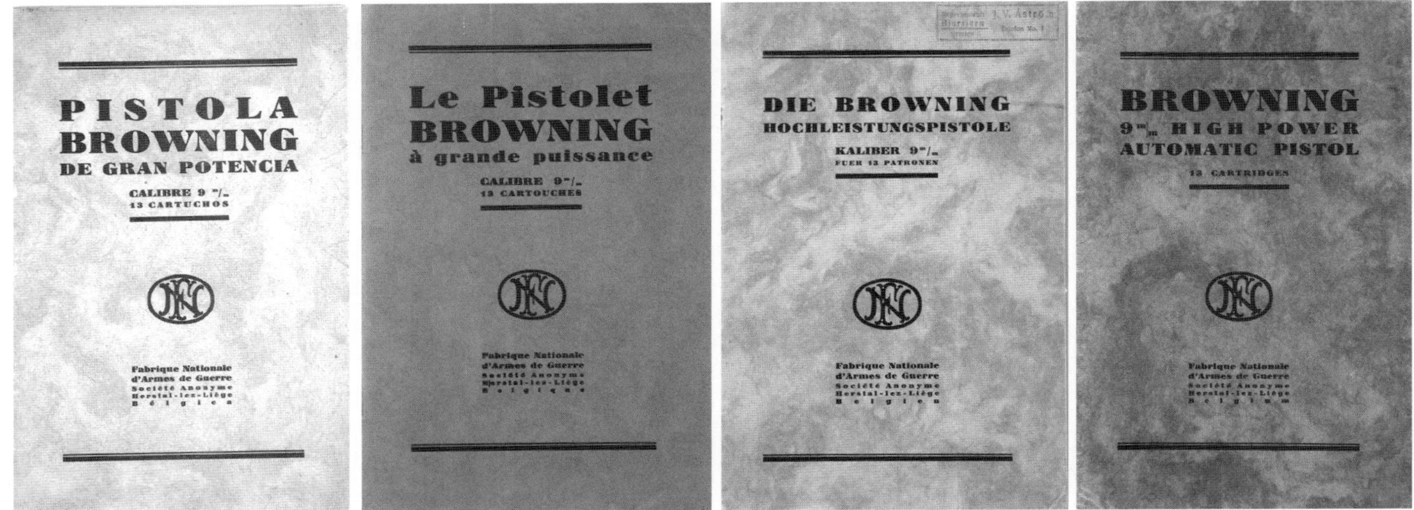

(Fig.272-2) Prewar manuals printed in March 1935 and 1937: (l. to r.) Rare Spanish language with light brown mottled cover, French language with red cover, German language with light gray mottled cover and English language with dark green mottled cover. (below left) Standard postwar manual with blue cover printed in all popular languages.

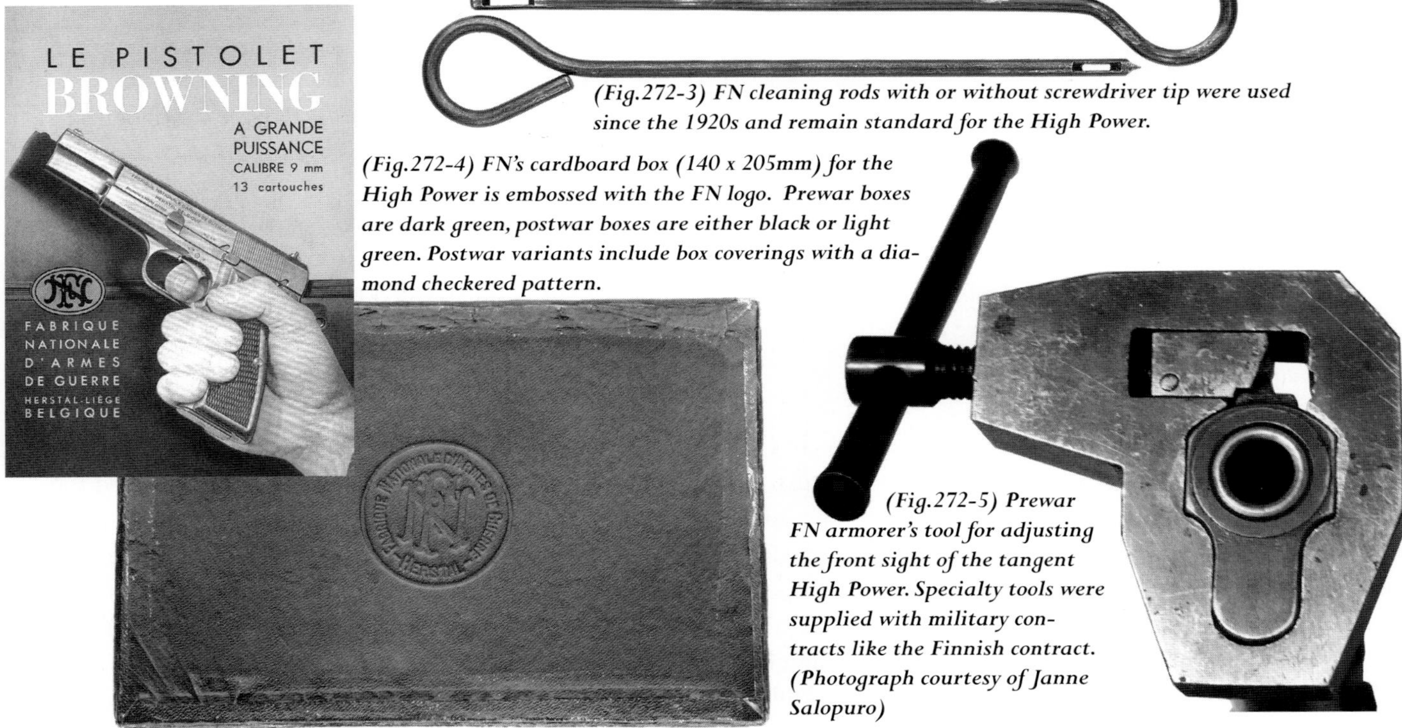

(Fig.272-3) FN cleaning rods with or without screwdriver tip were used since the 1920s and remain standard for the High Power.

(Fig.272-4) FN's cardboard box (140 x 205mm) for the High Power is embossed with the FN logo. Prewar boxes are dark green, postwar boxes are either black or light green. Postwar variants include box coverings with a diamond checkered pattern.

(Fig.272-5) Prewar FN armorer's tool for adjusting the front sight of the tangent High Power. Specialty tools were supplied with military contracts like the Finnish contract. (Photograph courtesy of Janne Salopuro)

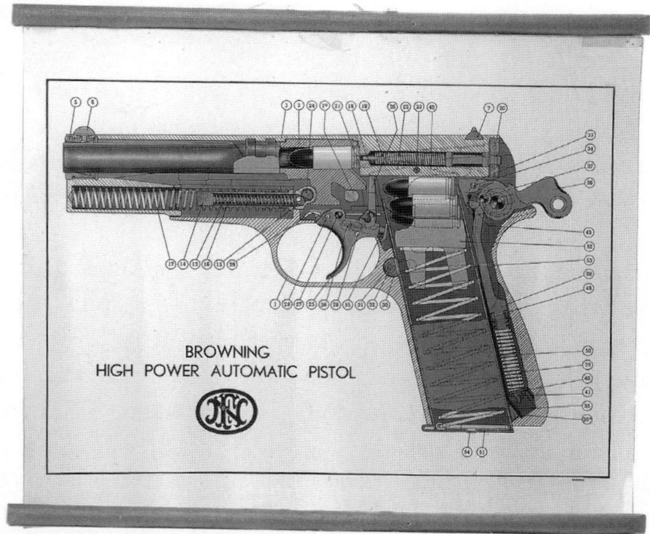

(Fig.273-1) FN offered large classroom instruction posters for military and law-enforcement customers. The posters were made out of linen with wooden slats.The rare prewar variant (l.) illustrates the tangent High power and how it connects to the shoulder-stock.The postwar variant (r.) focuses on the parts of the pistol.

Specifications Summary

Model known as: 1935, Grande Puissance, GP, High Power
Period offered: 1935-1940 / Mass produced during World War II under German occupation / 1944-current
Caliber: 9x19mm
Operating system: Fixed single cam, locked breech barrel
Length: 197mm
Barrel length: 118mm
Weight: 890 grams (fixed sights)
Grips: Wood in prewar years / wood or Bakelite during World War II / wood or plastic after 1945
Magazine capacity: 13-rounds, 20-round magazine option offered after 1962
Sights: Tangent, fixed or adjustable (after 1972)
Options: Prewar: lanyard ring, fixed sights / Postwar: tangent sights, slotted frame, lanyard ring
Finish offered: Prewar: Blue / Postwar: blue, black enamel, phosphate, chrome
Engraving patterns: Special factory presentation pistols only pre-1940 / some patterns introduced after World War II

The Belgian Prewar Contracts

The Belgian military was the largest customer for the High Power, placing orders between 1935 and May of 1940. Belgian procurement was based on a detailed acquisitions plan similar to the Dutch "werkplan" (page 228).

The first order of 10,000 pistols was numbered separately from standard commercial pistols. It should be stressed that these are not real contract numbers and contract numbering was never a requirement from the Belgian military. At the time FN was streamlining production and it was easier to supply a complete series instead of random numbers with gaps of pistols that were never completed or used in factory testing.

Initial Belgian military fielding of the High Power was to select troops and NCO's. Commissioned officers were not a priority as they only wore pistols and holsters on maneuvers or in time of war. Machine-gunners, machine-gun assistants, motorcycle riders, tank crews and others received High Powers, most often with the shoulder-stock, shoulder-stock combination holster and double magazine pouch (fig.275-2). From 1935 through 1937, pistols, holsters, shoulder-stocks and magazine pouches were all marked with matching serial numbers. Pistols were issued with three magazines (one in pistol and two in the separate magazine pouch).

By 1939 the majority of troops and NCO's had been issued High Powers. Replacement of officers' pistols began in 1939. Officers were not issued shoulder-stocks. Officers' pistols all had Type 2 tangent sights. In 1938, the practice of numbering the leather accessories to a specific pistol was abandoned. These were now marked AC38, AC39 or AC40. This military acceptance mark reportedly stands for "Atelier du Cuir" (leather workshop) followed by the two digit acceptance year.

The Belgian Prewar Contracts (continued)

The effort to upgrade officers' pistols was well underway at the time of the German invasion on May 10, 1940. The pistols in final stages of production, as well as those in transit and just delivered to the state arsenal all fell into German hands. The few photographs of officers taken during the May Days[1] show an array of holsters, including High Power holsters, old World War I Colt 1903 holsters and Model 1910 holsters. Although officers did not use the shoulder-stock or combination holster, photographs show the magazine pouch in use by officers.

Belgian contract pistols received their first markings at the factory. A military inspector inspected the parts and marked them with a parts approval marking (circle H, square C or octagonal C), this marking is also found on the magazine body and is the only way of identifying a prewar Belgian contract magazine. Unlike other contracts, serial numbers of Belgian contract guns were also marked on the frame under the grip in addition to the traditional, frame, slide (internal) and barrel markings. After leaving FN, completed pistols were inventoried and further tested at the arsenal and arsenal marked (page 94-95).

(Fig.274-1) Some early pistols produced in 1935 have numbers with a distinct square font. Barrels on early Belgian contract pistols have the serial number in the usual location and some are arsenal marked with issue numbers on the bottom of the barrel lug. The significance of the arsenal number is unknown. Belgian contract pistol N° 9516 (see fig.291-1) was supplied in 1935 and has an arsenal number 5311 stamped on the barrel. Note the square serial number font and Belgian military accepting officer's marking on the barrel.

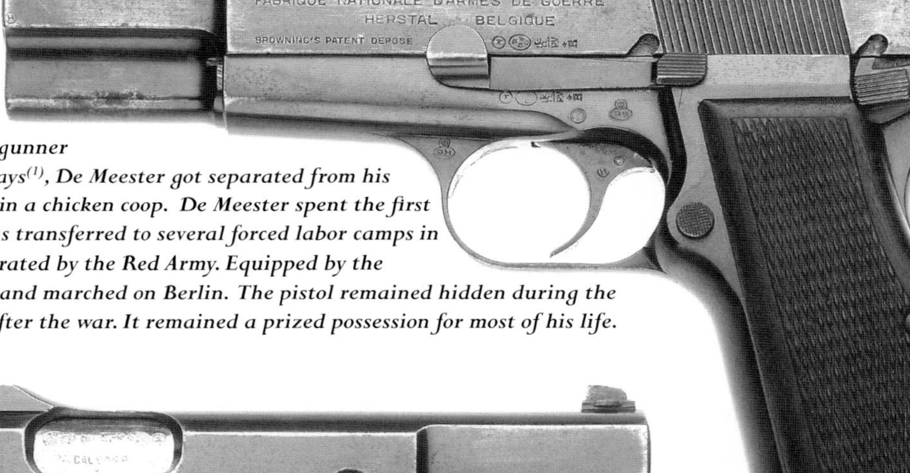

(Fig.274-2) This Belgian Army pistol N° 21631 was manufactured on December 2, 1938 and shipped to the Belgian state arsenal, MAE (p. 94), on December 24, 1938. The pistol was issued with shoulder-stock to machine-gunner Louis De Meester[2]. During the May Days[1], De Meester got separated from his unit. Fearing capture, he hid the pistol in a chicken coop. De Meester spent the first years in POW camps, after which he was transferred to several forced labor camps in Eastern Europe. Eventually he was liberated by the Red Army. Equipped by the Russians, he fought as an independent and marched on Berlin. The pistol remained hidden during the war and was retrieved by De Meester after the war. It remained a prized possession for most of his life.

(Fig.274-3) Pistol N° 21631 has the serial number on the frame, on the barrel and slide. The serial number is also applied under the grip unique to Belgian military contracts. The "H" acceptance marking was applied at FN by the accepting officer (page 95), the marking is found on all major parts and is the only way of identifying a Belgian military magazine. The "H" marking near the muzzle may have been applied as an identifier for pistols in factory crates (see page 296). The magazine and frame (under left grip) have FN's final inspection marking "square A" (page 85). This pistol has Type 1 tangent sights for use with shoulder-stocks by troops and non-commissioned officers.

(Fig.275-1) Belgian army shoulder-stocks have no holster attached. The serial number of the stock is marked on the side near the connecting lug (see fig.285-1). Belgian Army accepted shoulder-stocks have a single acceptance marking stamped into the wood. Original stocks have the holster mounting holes pre-drilled but the wood is flush around the mounting holes (compare with fig.286-3).

(Fig.275-2) The Belgian military used a combination holster that accommodates the flat shoulder-stock and pistol in separate compartments. The combination holsters were issued to troops and NCO's. Early combination holsters and magazine pouches (1936, 1937) were issued with matching numbers, later holsters and pouches (1938, 1939, 1940) were marked only with the acceptance marking AC 38, AC 39 or AC 40.

(Fig.275-3) A rare photograph of tank crews being inspected during the phony war; note the combination holsters and magazine pouches of the crewmembers. (Photograph courtesy of Stefan De Meyer)

---

(1) A Belgian term denoting the military campaign during the German invasion from May 10 through May 28, 1940

(2) No relation to the Belgian composer Louis August Edmond Hendrik De Meester

(Fig.276-1) This officer's pistol N° 43399 with Type 2 sights was shipped from FN to the MAE on April 23, 1940. Note that the "circle H" inspector's marking has been replaced with a "square C" (p.95). The marking is applied on the frame, slide, trigger, barrel, and magazine. FN's final inspection marking "square A" is barely visible under the left grip panel. The arsenal markings "crown AC" and "crown GC" are a clear indication that this pistol was delivered and tested at the state arsenal prior to the invasion. Note that the frame was accepted by Finnish officers (fig.284-2), yet it was assembled for the Belgian military. Commissioned officers' pistols like this one, usually show less wear that pistols used by troops. Most of these officers' pistols were only worn during the May Days. (Photograph by author, courtesy of Ron Pinkenburg)

(Fig.276-2) A rare photograph of a Belgian commissioned officer marching after capture in May 1940. Note the black leather commissioned officers' holster (same as in fig.43-1). Note also the brown double magazine pouch. (Photograph courtesy of Stefan De Meyer)

The Belgian "Pistolet de Manipulation" (Training Pistol)

There is some conjecture as to the date of the first Belgian military training pistol order. Training pistols may have been supplied with either the 1933-1934 Grand Rendement trials pistols or the first High Power production pistols. Two principal variants have been observed, one based on the oval-port Grand Rendement (page 266) and the other on the High Power.

The pistols were painted red and, as they were not suitable for firing, they were never shipped to the Liège proof-house. As a result, the frame and slide bear no Liège proofs. The slide was factory roll engraved "Pistolet de Manipulation" (training pistol). Although the barrels are Liège proofed, there is no indication that these were replaced[1]. The barrels have no caliber designation on them.

Orders were small and most likely placed over a period of time with consecutive contract numbers. The first pistols were painted over a phosphate base, similar to FN's prewar enamel finish (page 98, the phosphate base created a better adhesion for the paint). Later pistols were blued with red paint applied over the bluing. It is not known why the base finish differs on later pistols. An estimated 110 training pistols were delivered prior to 1938.

Most of the training pistols encountered today have very little of the red paint. This has led to speculation that the paint was stripped[1] either by Belgian arsenals or by the Germans during World War II. The answer to this mystery is simple; only select and more expensive paints were oil resistant in the 1930s, and, as these guns were never meant to be fired, FN did not use oil resistant paint. The red paint dissolved over time when these were oiled or cleaned as part of maintenance or training.

Although marked as training pistols and not proofed by the Liège proof-house nor tested and marked at the state arsenals, training pistols are fully functional. The training pistols have the Belgian military parts acceptance marking on various parts (circle H).

Noted or reported contract numbers for oval-port Grand Rendement training pistols: 37

Noted or reported contract numbers for High Power training pistols: 29, 61, 96, 103

(Fig.277-1) The rare oval port Grand Rendement training pistol Nº 37 has a phosphate base finish. Traces of red paint are still visible in protected areas. Note that it does not have any Belgian or arsenal proofs and does only have the military parts acceptance marking "H" on the frame. Note the unusual shape of the front sight and the tangent sight with polished sides.

(Fig.277-2) Training pistol Nº 29 has the early phosphate finish. Note that the barrel has the Lithuanian acceptance marking (page 278) indication 1936 or later assembly. Pistol Nº 37 (above) does not have any Lithuanian markings. (Photograph courtesy of Dr. Bodo von Rhein)

(Fig.277-3) This High Power training pistol Nº 96 has a blued base and traces of red paint are still visible in protected areas. Note that it does not have any Belgian or arsenal proofs and does only have the military parts acceptance marking "H" on the trigger-guard and barrel. Note that the original barrel does not have a caliber designation, an indication that it was not meant to be fired. (Photographs by author, courtesy of Jim Mauloff)

(1) There is an erroneous belief that Belgian arsenals reworked these into service pistols, stripped the paint and installed a renumbered proofed replacement barrel. Close examination of several barrels does not indicate that these were arsenal renumbered. Replacement barrels were caliber marked. There is no basis for the claim of arsenal reworked training pistols.

Lithuanian High Powers

Lieutenant Aleksandras Stauskas is an important figure in the Lithuanian High Power acquisition. Stauskas worked with the chairman of the Lithuanian Pistol Acquisition Commission in January 1937. He was a weapons specialist, a graduate of the Lithuanian War Academy and worked at Lithuanian military headquarters. Early in 1937 he was stationed in Liège and worked in Herstal as a weapons accepting officer for the Lithuanian government. He had dealings with FN, Bofors in Sweden, Schneider in France and Oerlikon and Tararo in Switzerland.

(Fig.278-1) See below

While Stauskas was in Liège, Lithuania purchased High Power pistols, Mauser rifles, Browning machine guns, aviation timers for the machine guns, artillery shells and ammunition from FN.

High Powers, rifles and machine guns were marked with small "Pillars of Gediminas" acceptance stampings during assembly. Lithuanian inspectors accepted many more parts than were used. As a result, Lithuanian acceptance markings appear on many later contract guns, especially Belgian military guns (fig.277-2). The slides were factory roll engraved with the Pillars of Gediminas crest. Lithuanian High Powers were equipped with a unique lanyard staple. Almost 7000 pistols were shipped from FN early in 1937 to the Lithuanian port of Klaipeda. In 1939 Stauskas was given an engraved and personalized High Power pistol as a parting gift. During the war he buried the pistol in Lithuania as he fled the Soviet invasion in 1941.

Noted or reported contract numbers: 72, 194, 299, 414, 1024, 1146, 1344, 2052, 2135, 2164, 2202, 2367, 2486, 2665, 2682, 2802, 2946, 3139, 3280, 3418, 3811, 3829, 3846, 4285, 4874, 4892, 4957, 5595, 5629, 5843, 6079, 6273, 6437

(Fig.278-2) This Lithuanian High Power pistol N° 2802 can easily be identified by the special order contract number, fixed lanyard staple and the Pillars of Gediminas crest roll engraved on the top of the slide. Lithuanian contract pistols were manufactured with Type 2 tangent sights as the order did not include shoulder-stocks. Major parts like barrels, frames, slides, magazines and others were accepted by the Lithuanian accepting commission while being assembled at FN, these parts are marked with small Pillars of Gediminas stampings.

(Fig.278-1) (above) Lieutenant Aleksandras Stauskas before the war. Stauskas was born on June 17, 1908 and graduated with an engineering degree from Kaunas Technical University in 1932. He studied at the Lithuanian war academy and became a weapons specialist. (Photograph courtesy of Henry Gaidis)

The Estonian Contracts

Estonia placed two orders for the High Power pistol. The first order for 120 pistols was placed in 1936 for police forces. In 1937 a second order for 5338 pistols was placed, this time for the Estonian military. The pistols were factory marked with ascending contract numbers. Additionally, the pistols were randomly factory marked "KL" or "EV" on the rear grip strap. The Estonian contracts specified a lighter trigger pull than the standard FN production model.

The army received 3038 pistols marked E.V. for "Eesti Vabarik" (Republic of Estonia) and 2300 marked K.L. for "Kaitseliit" (Home-guard) for issue to the home guard. The border patrol was issued 100 unmarked pistols. The contract for the military and home-guard was filled by December 1937.

All pistols were ordered without shoulder-stocks or holsters. The Tallinn State Arsenal made spare parts for the pistols. In addition they made 3150 shoulder-stocks for the High Power and converted 500 FN 1903 holsters to fit the High Power pistol. This work was performed between 1938 and 1939. The Tallinn Arsenal was successful at making quality replacement parts for the High Power. In 1940 the arsenal planned to produce 500 licensed copies of the High Power. It is not known if any licensing talks took place between the Estonians and FN.

Noted or reported E.V. contract numbers: 586, 727, 1035, 1709, 3019
Noted or reported K.L. contract numbers: 252, 835, 1202, 1274, 1459, 2280

(Fig.279-1) Estonian High Power pistols can easily be identified by the special order contract number, and factory applied E.V. or K.L. marking on the rear grip-strap. Although produced in a contract range, the E.V. and K.L. markings were randomly applied. These pistols were manufactured with Type 2 tangent sights as the FN order did not include shoulder-stocks. Pistol N° 1459 is marked with the less common K.L. marking.

The Paraguayan Order

The little known Paraguayan contract was filled around 1936. The quantity of the order is unknown. Paraguay had fought the costly Chaco war with Bolivia for over two years (1933-1935). Paraguay defeated Bolivia and gained 90,000 square miles in a treaty in July of 1938.

All Paraguayan High Powers have the "Ejercito Paraguayo" (Paraguayan Army) inscription on the slide as well as the last two digits of the contract number. The contract numbers do not reflect standard production serial numbers. All are slotted for shoulder-stocks and have Type 1 tangent sights. Paraguayan contract numbering started with number 1.

The top of the slide is roll engraved with the Paraguayan crest. After World War II, Paraguay placed additional orders for High Power pistols, selecting the fixed sight model with the Paraguayan crest marked on the top of the slide.

Many of the prewar Paraguayan contract pistols were arsenal reworked, and the markings were often buffed before refinishing.

Collectors should use caution when purchasing a pistol that reflects Paraguayan contract markings as more frauds have been observed than originals. Some of the frauds do not have the crest and show only the right slide markings. Others have crudely marked crests. These frauds most often do not have contract numbers and are made out of surplus Chinese or Belgian contract guns. In order to make the style of the markings consistent, the entire slide legend is often removed and re-applied. Central and South American contracts have become favorites for some west-coast outfits. In addition to Paraguayan markings, several markings have been fabricated for prewar contracts that never existed including Mexican, Columbian and Bolivian. These guns are represented as rare originals and are sold at premiums. Carefully reviewing the pistol's bluing, the markings and measuring the width of parts with calipers, especially the slide, will reveal the frauds. Collectors should familiarize themselves with the look and feel of FN roll die markings; the hardness of FN steel makes it difficult for counterfeiters to recreate the look and feel of originals with modern laser engraving machinery.

(Fig.280-1) A side view of the Paraguayan crest as applied to prewar contract pistols

Argentine Contracts

High Powers were ordered by the "Policia de la Capital" in 1937 through a Buenos Aires dealer. 1600 guns were ordered and issued to officers with the rank of inspector and above. The pistols were roll engraved with police markings and were supplied with their own contract numbers. Numbers 1 through 1590 were pistols with fixed sights, numbers 1591 through 1600 were slotted, tangent-sighted pistols with numbered shoulder-stocks. This would be the first of numerous Argentine High Power contracts. A number of Argentine military officers served with the Policia de la Capital in the 1930s, and their experience served to introduce the Argentine military to the High Power. In the postwar era, Argentina purchased thousands of fixed-sighted High Power pistols for the Buenos Aires police department, the bulk were purchased in 1960 and shipped early in 1961. Two different factory markings were applied, the common "Policia Prov. BS. Aires – 61" and less common "Div. Interna Seg." (Division Interna Seguridad) for police detectives. The postwar Argentine contract pistols are common in the U.S. as these were sold as surplus for numerous years. Original pistols feature the typical FN rust blue finish, many surplus pistols were refinished in the U.S. with either a phosphate finish or painted finish, effectively damaging their value as collectibles. The importers also produced a brown cardboard box with a printed description and FN logo. This box is not original and does not enhance the value.

The military used the High Power extensively in the postwar era, manufacturing licenses were purchased from FN and the Argentine High Power and FAL were built in large quantities in Rosario. These are often encountered under the D.G.F.M. or F.M. (Fabrica Militar) name.

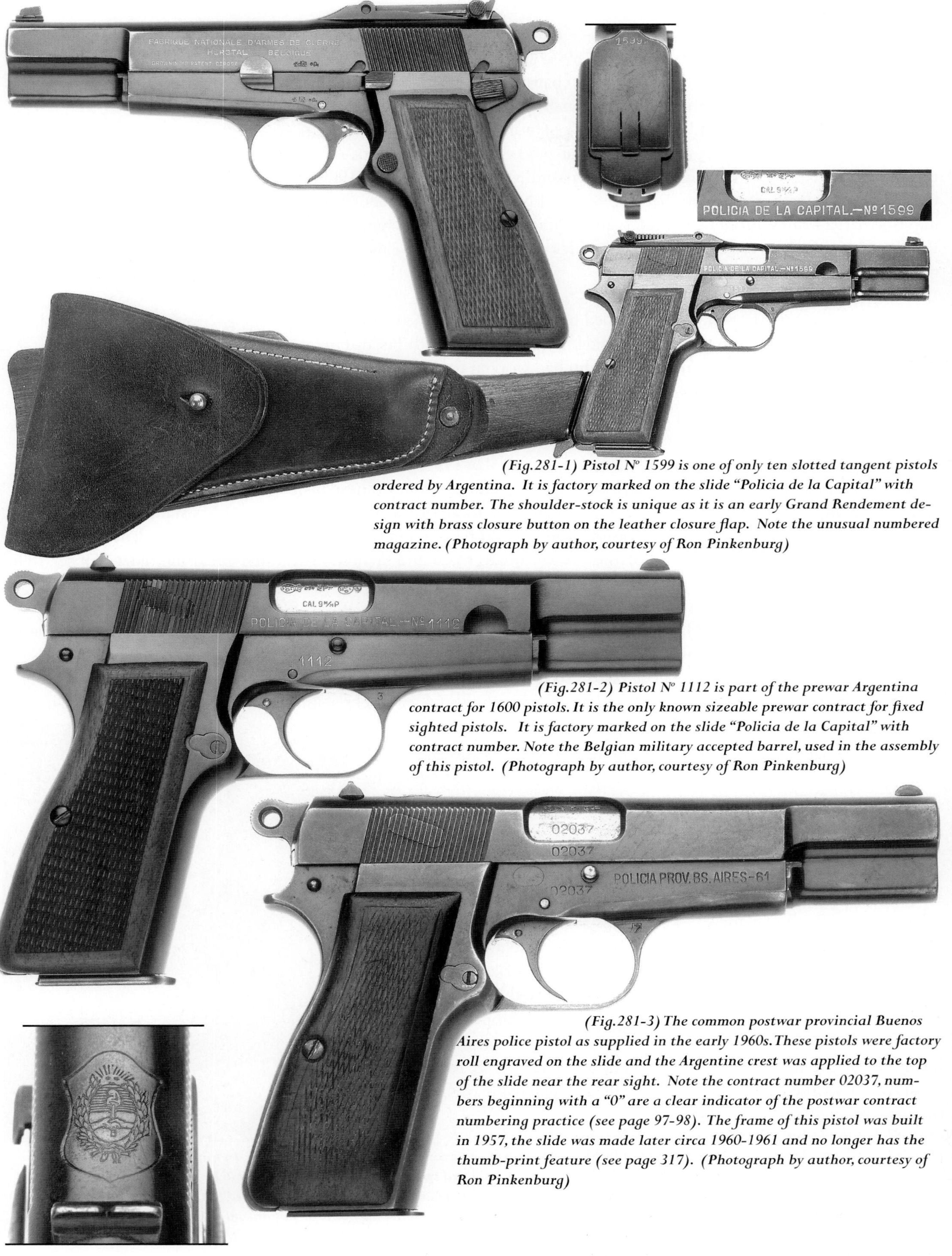

(Fig.281-1) ***Pistol Nº 1599 is one of only ten slotted tangent pistols ordered by Argentina. It is factory marked on the slide "Policia de la Capital" with contract number. The shoulder-stock is unique as it is an early Grand Rendement design with brass closure button on the leather closure flap. Note the unusual numbered magazine. (Photograph by author, courtesy of Ron Pinkenburg)***

(Fig.281-2) ***Pistol Nº 1112 is part of the prewar Argentina contract for 1600 pistols. It is the only known sizeable prewar contract for fixed sighted pistols. It is factory marked on the slide "Policia de la Capital" with contract number. Note the Belgian military accepted barrel, used in the assembly of this pistol. (Photograph by author, courtesy of Ron Pinkenburg)***

(Fig.281-3) ***The common postwar provincial Buenos Aires police pistol as supplied in the early 1960s. These pistols were factory roll engraved on the slide and the Argentine crest was applied to the top of the slide near the rear sight. Note the contract number 02037, numbers beginning with a "0" are a clear indicator of the postwar contract numbering practice (see page 97-98). The frame of this pistol was built in 1957, the slide was made later circa 1960-1961 and no longer has the thumb-print feature (see page 317). (Photograph by author, courtesy of Ron Pinkenburg)***

The Chinese Orders

Chinese relations with FN date back to the 1890s, and FN's business with China boomed with the rise of Chiang Kai-shek. As chairman of the National Military Council and head of the Kuomingtang (Nationalist) party, Chiang Kai-shek campaigned to unify the nation and rid the country of warlord dominance. The Chinese had depended on German military advisors and equipment for years. After the rise of Chiang Kai-shek, the Chinese arms market diversified. Starting in 1929, the Chinese Nationalist Government became one of FN's largest customers, purchasing Model 1924 rifles, Model 1930 rifles, ammunition, Browning machine guns, BAR's, armored motorcycles and large quantities of small and large caliber ammunition.

FN's principal agent, Mr. Schroeder, handled much if not all of the Chinese orders. Schroeder traveled to Berlin where, beginning in 1936, he met with Hsiau-Hua Wang. Hsiau-Hua Wang was an engineer who had worked for Siemens in Shanghai and had experience working with Chinese arsenals. He moved to Berlin with his family in 1936 to work for the commercial trade department at the Chinese embassy, procuring arms and equipment for the Chinese Nationalist Army. He was one of the principal decision makers in the acquisition of the High Power pistol in late 1937. FN started supplying pistols to the Chinese government in May 1938. The pistols left FN in batches in May and July 1938. An additional order was shipped from FN in December 1938. Chinese pistols were manufactured on contract and not pulled out of inventory (page 271). The bulk of these pistols were shipped with FN's standard flat board shoulder-stock and attached holster. Various sources and research into the production of the Canadian Inglis indicates that the Chinese were not fond of the FN flat-board stock and favored instead the enclosing older Mauser 1896 wooden stock system.

Chinese pistols in the May and July 1938 shipments have Type 1 sights. These pistols are in the 6000 to approximately 9500 serial range. During this process, the Chinese added to their original order and requested that FN build additional pistols with Type 2 sights. Those pistols have random numbers between 9500 and approximately 11,000. It is not known if the July 1938 shipment was shipped with any shoulder-stocks as this customer change was mandated in mid-production.

These pistols had a hard service life in the hands of the Nationalists and were primarily used against the communist Chinese forces. Much to the frustration of U.S. and Allied commanders, General Chiang Kai-shek focused primarily on battling the communists rather than the Japanese. His priorities have often been criticized, but history proved him that the communists were indeed the greater threat. Japanese forces were not frequently confronted by Nationalist troops and only few High Powers were captured by the Japanese. The pistols remained in combat after World War II during the Chinese civil war. After the Nationalist defeat the pistols remained in China. Most pistols were reworked and repaired with Inglis High Power parts, few were arsenal marked on the front gripstrap or slide, some were numbered or marked on the grips. Maintenance was not a priority and most pistols show extensive use and wear. Large quantities of the surviving pistols were imported in the U.S. in the 1990s, most were reworked and refinished. Pistols with arsenal markings in good original and unaltered condition are rare.

(Fig.282-1) (above) Portrait of General Chiang Kai-shek

(Fig.282-2) Hsiau-Hua Wang was born in China in 1900 and studied engineering in Darmstadt, Germany. In the 1920s he returned to China and worked as an arsenal engineer from 1927 to 1930 before being employed by Siemens in Shanghai. In 1936 he moved to Berlin and worked at the Chinese embassy acquiring arms and equipment for the Chinese government. In 1939 his family moved to Copenhagen and were guests of Madsen while he remained in Berlin. The German, Italian and Japanese Tripartite pact of 1940 put an end to German-Chinese trade relations. Hsiau-Hua Wang was transferred to Washington D.C. in 1941 and worked in lend-lease until 1944. After 1944 he became a member of the Chinese Nationalist Military mission. He was awarded the United States Legion of Merit for his work in lend-lease. (Photograph courtesy of Claude Tait)

(Fig.283-1) This Chinese contract pistol N° 9073 was shipped from FN on July 5, 1938. It has Type 1 sights and was most likely shipped with shoulder-stock. Note that this pistol was reworked, has a replacement extractor, replacement grips and an Inglis hammer, identified by the Roman numeral "II". (Photograph by author, courtesy of R. Pinkenburg)

(Fig.283-2) This Chinese contract pistol N° 20395 was shipped from FN in December 1938. It has Type 2 sights. It is in original condition and was arsenal marked on the front grip-strap. The marking is interpreted as "Sui" another name for the city of Guangzhou. It is speculated that pistols with city names were used as law enforcement guns after the Nationalist defeat.

The High Power in Finland

Ever since its independence from Russia in 1917, Finland has been a loyal user of FN products. This tiny nation has been threatened by its Russian neighbor throughout history. Finland always remained well armed, often buying guns on a budget and using surplus material. Almost every FN handgun model has been found with Finnish markings. Some Model 1903 pistols have Swedish marks as well as Finish acceptance markings. The pistols made their way into Finland with Swedish volunteers during the Finnish-Russian Winter War (November 1939- March 1940).

Prior to the Winter War, Finland evaluated the High Power. With the outbreak of the Winter War Finland inquired if FN was able to supply 2400 pistols with shoulder-stocks on a short schedule.

The urgency of war made it that FN shipped the guns as soon as these were completed(1). The orders were combined with other orders like those for the Model 1922 (page 241). The first 900 High Power pistols arrived in Finland in February 1940, the remaining 1500 followed in March.

FN did not apply any special contract markings to the pistols. Finnish acceptance officers were sent to FN to accept the parts at the time of manufacture. The Finnish acceptance marking was applied at FN to the right trigger-guard (several variants exist, see fig.284-2). More parts were accepted than were assembled, and as a result, these Finnish markings appear on some Belgian military pistols made in 1940(2).

Finnish pistols are in the 11,000-15,000 serial range. Many pistols were marked in Finland during World War II with the army property mark "SA" (Suomen Armeija - Finnish Army). It is important to note that only 2400 pistols, out of a FN production span of 5000 pistols, went to Finland.

There is a common misconception that High Powers were issued exclusively to the Finnish Air Force. Most of these pistols were in fact issued to the army. The air force was issued the High Power but with less than 150 aircraft, the number of High Powers issued to pilots and crew members remain minimal.

During the war, the army concluded that the shoulder-stocks were impractical. The shoulder-stocks (boards only) were put into storage after the holster was removed and modified for belt or shoulder use.

Many Finnish High Powers were lost in battle. In 1942, an attempt was made to increase the magazine capacity of the High Power pistol. Second Lieutenant Ijas got the idea from the 70-round Suomi machinegun magazine. A project to create a drum - snail magazine for the High Power ensued. Production never took place as the prototypes proved to be too heavy and bulky.

By 1951, only 1378 pistols were still servicable. Seven pistols were sold as surplus to army personnel between January 1, 1965 and June 1, 1971. The Finnish army started selling the pistols to private collectors in January 1986. A total of 1274 pistols were sold, with a few pistols remaining in air force inventory. Starting in 1988, these pistols were sold in auctions at a rate of up to five a year.

Noted or reported Finnish pistols:
11631, 12129, 12438, 12443, 12648, 12702, 12746, 12779, 12941, 13477, 13851, 14202, 14372

Inventory 25th March 1940: SArk T 20209 F-1 sal. (Named as Colt kal 9.0)
Military records T 20209 F-1 secret (…)

I AKE (1.Armeijakunnan esikunta) [Staff of the 1st Army]:	2nd Division	**1** pistol
	Unit " S "	**4** pistols
III AKE(3.Armeijakunnan esikunta) [Staff of the 3rd Army]:	21st Division	**198** pistols
IV AKE(4.Armeijakunnan esikunta) [Staff of the 4th Army]:		**12** pistols
V AKE(5.Armeijakunnan esikunta] [Staff of the 5th Army]:	Unit " W "	**36** pistols
Others:	Cavalry Brigade	**1** pistol
	Lme.P	**1** pistol
	Navy	**7** pistols
	Air force	**77** pistols
Army depots:	1st Army depot	**1675** pistols

Total **2012** pistols

Inventory 12th June 1940: **2224** pistols (Name as: 9.00 pist/Colt) SArk T 18419

Decision of break up 25th October 1943: 7 pistols(PM N.6003/Ase 3/40 G sal, SArk T 20209/F-19 sal)

Break up suggestion 1st January 1946: **1** pistol (TJ 253 9,00 pist/FN) 3rd Army depot
67 pistols (TJ 291 9,00 pist/Colt) 3rd Army depot

Inventory 31st August 1951: **1378** pistols (Named as: 9,00pist/FN) (SArk T 20207/F-16)

(Fig.284-1) A Finnish document showing the inventory of High Power pistols through the branches of the military. It clearly shows the wide-spread use of the High Power. Note that the High Power was first incorrectly identified in the Finnish military as "9,00 Pist/Colt". It was reclassified after the war as "9,00 Pist/FN" (Document courtesy of Janne Salopuro)

(Fig.284-2) Some Finnish inspector markings as applied at FN on High Power trigger-guards

(Fig.285-1) Finnish contract pistol N° 12702 has the Finnish accepting officer's marking on the trigger-guard but is not "SA" marked. Only an estimated 40 percent of the Finnish contract pistols were SA marked. This pistol still has its original numbered shoulder-stock. Matching numbers on pistol and stock are rare. The Finns purchased FN's standard prewar shoulder-stock model with attached holster. (Photograph by author, courtesy of Jim Mauloff)

(Fig.285-2) Finnish contract shoulder-stock N° 13337 still has the holster attached and is "SA" marked on the wood. The Finns removed the majority of holsters from the stocks as the system was deemed too cumbersome. Original complete Finnish contract stocks are rarely encountered.

(Fig.285-3) Finnish pistol N° 14372 is SA (Suomen Armeja / Finnish Army) marked. The location and size of the SA marking varies. Note that this pistol has a replacement front sight. Most Finnish pistols feature a wider and taller Finnish made front sight. The sight modification was done to compensate for perceived loss of accuracy after the absolution of the board stocks. Note the Finnish inspector marking on the trigger-guard. Storing the pistol in the shoulder-stock holster has left a distinct wear pattern on the left grip panel, these wear markings are indicative of the pistol being used with its shoulder-stock.

(Fig.285-4) SA marked cleaning rods are rare. Finnish collectors estimate that only 10 percent of the FN supplied rods were SA marked.

(1) The Finnish contract was manufactured in 1939-1940 and was not pulled from inventory.

(2) This practice was not uncommon and often encountered with Lithuanian, Finnish and Belgian acceptance officers. Belgian military supplied pistols can easily be identified by the Belgian arsenal markings.

(Fig.286-1) *The Finnish SA marking was also applied to magazines, note the two sizes that were used (4mm and 5mm wide). These markings were used on all metal parts including magazines, accessories and pistols.*

(Fig.286-2) *Some pistols and accessories were SA T marked for Suomen Armeja - Taisteluväline" (Finnish Army - Combat Device). (Photograph courtesy of Janne Salopuro)*

(Fig.286-3) *The majority of Finnish shoulder-stocks were modified; the holster was removed and used as a belt holster. The stocks were placed in storage. Modified shoulder-stocks can be identified by the countersink holes in the wood and pressed wood where the rivets were located. Asides from serial numbers, this is an easy method of identifying a Finnish from a Belgian contract stock (fig.275-1). (Photographs by author, courtesy of Jim Mauloff)*

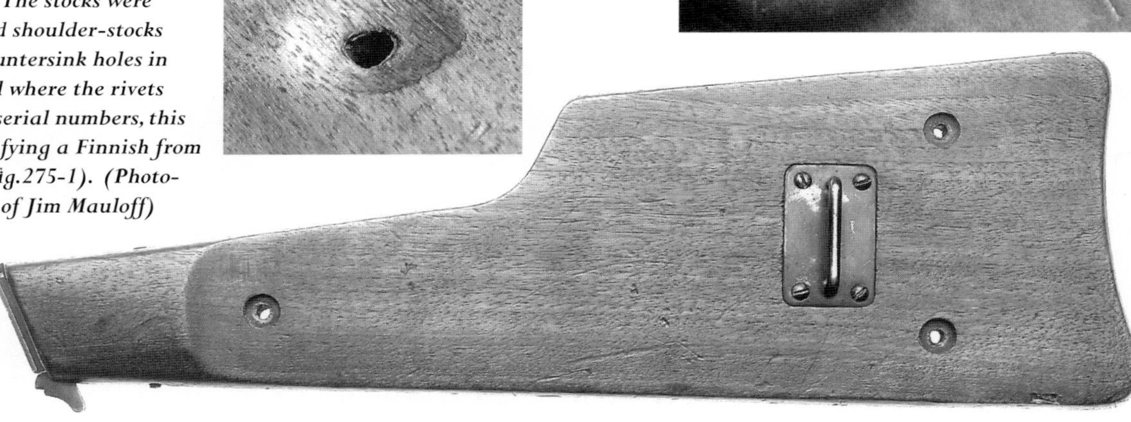

(Fig.286-3) *A Finnish railroad artillery gun in 1942 - 1943. On the right is Lieutenant K. Rissanen who has the High Power shoulder-stock with pistol on his belt. (Photograph courtesy of Janne Salopuro)*

(Fig.286-4) *A Finnish sergeant in World War II, wearing the m/36 uniform with the High Power shoulder-stock with pistol on his belt. (Photograph courtesy of Janne Salopuro)*

(Fig.287-1) A Finnish air force crew during the war, several crew members wear the modified shoulder-stock holster on their belt. (right) A Finnish soldier in the trenches with his High Power and unaltered shoulder-stock. Note that the shoulder-stock is suspended from a shoulder strap. (Photographs courtesy of Janne Salopuro)

Slotted Fixed-Sighted Pistols: The Mysterious French High Power

As tensions rose and rearmament became a priority in the latter part of the 1930s, French attention focused on the slow and delayed procurement of the Model 1935-A pistol. The French initially bolstered the supply of service pistols by accepting the Model 1935-S, produced at the St. Etienne state arsenal, in December 1937. The 1935-S had been beaten in the 1935 trials by the model 1935-A (produced by the Société Alsacienne de Construction Mécanique). Production figures for the second gun, the Model 1935-S (which, despite the misleading nomenclature, does not share any design or development commonalities with the Model 1935-A) were not any better than those of the Model 1935-A. As a result it appears that the French government reconsidered the adoption of the FN Model 1935 pistol.

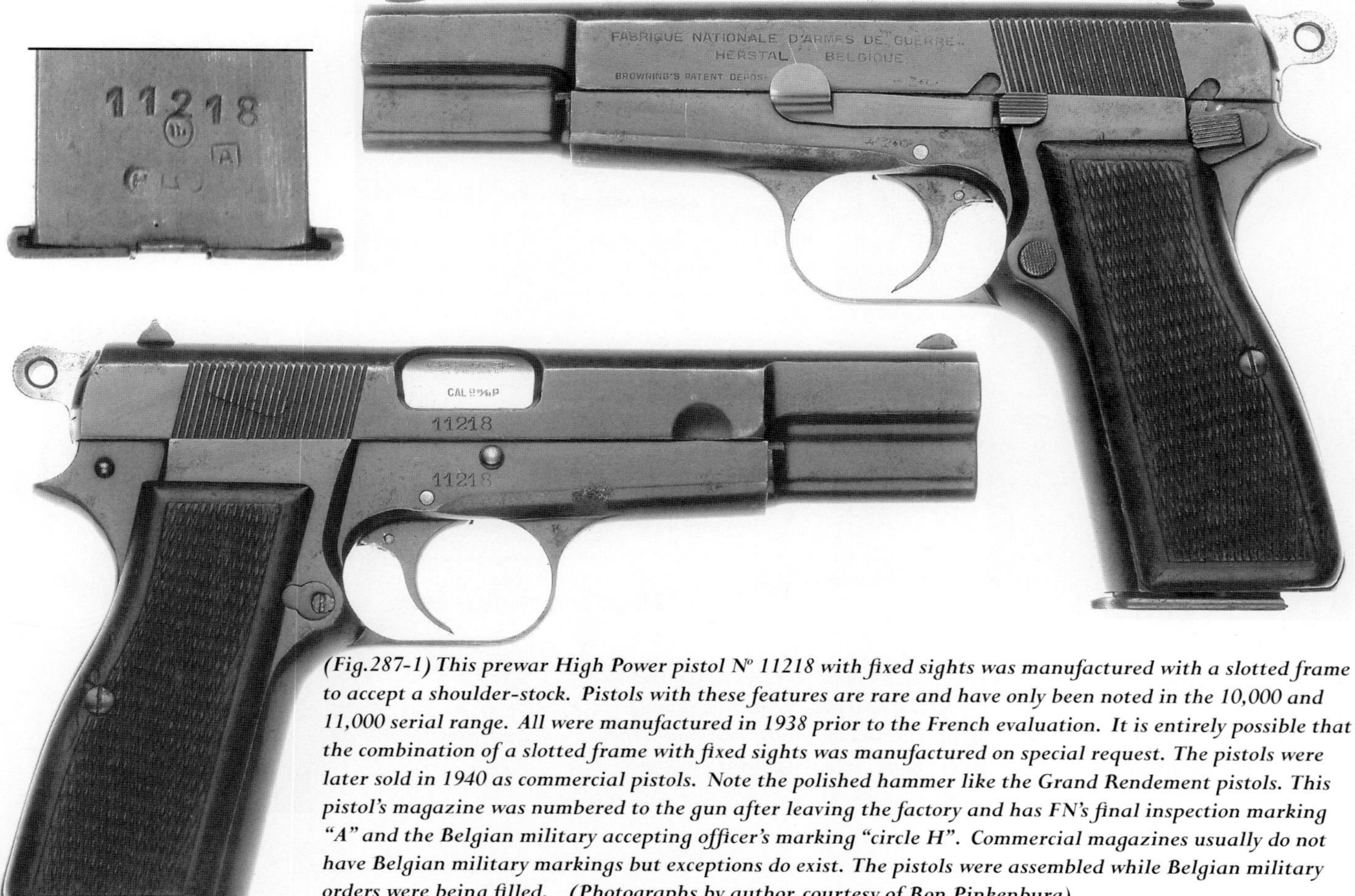

(Fig.287-1) This prewar High Power pistol N° 11218 with fixed sights was manufactured with a slotted frame to accept a shoulder-stock. Pistols with these features are rare and have only been noted in the 10,000 and 11,000 serial range. All were manufactured in 1938 prior to the French evaluation. It is entirely possible that the combination of a slotted frame with fixed sights was manufactured on special request. The pistols were later sold in 1940 as commercial pistols. Note the polished hammer like the Grand Rendement pistols. This pistol's magazine was numbered to the gun after leaving the factory and has FN's final inspection marking "A" and the Belgian military accepting officer's marking "circle H". Commercial magazines usually do not have Belgian military markings but exceptions do exist. The pistols were assembled while Belgian military orders were being filled. (Photographs by author, courtesy of Ron Pinkenburg)

Slotted Fixed-Sighted Pistols: The Mysterious French High Power (continued)

On September 23, 1939, the French military recommended the acquisition of 1000 FN High Power pistols. In the event, the French never tested production High Power pistols. Only two High Power pistols (N° 10933 and 10972) were delivered by an Antwerp dealer "Vogels". These two pistols were rather unique in having fixed sights but slotted frames, and were delivered to Vogels on January 1, 1940, in addition to pistols N° 10969 and 10939.

The two pistols were submitted for trials at "l'Etablissement d'Expériences Techniques de Versailles" between March 19 and 21, 1940. The pistols were tested with modern FN ammunition as well as surplus World War I German ammunition. The trials went flawlessly and the High Power was recommended for adoption on April 5, 1940.

A week after the recommendation, on April 12, 1940, FN shipped pistol N° 10934 to Colonel Loriot, the French military attaché. No additional pistols are known to have been shipped to the French military prior to the German invasion. Several pistols are known to have fixed sights and slotted frames. Some of these pistols were still in warehouse at the time of the invasion or were shipped to Schroeder in Liège for commercial sales.

Pistols shipped to Vogels in Antwerp on January 19, 1940: 10933, 10969, 10939, 10972

Slotted pistols with fixed sights that were Shipped to Schroeder or in warehouse at the time of the invasion: 11202, 11218

(Fig.288-1) This slotted fixed-sighted pistol has the same features as the French evaluation pistols. It is either a lunch box special or a pre-production sample as it is devoid of any serial number, proofs and factory machinist markings. The rear sight is not standard, it is a Model 1922 sight. Note the polished hammer like pistol N° 11218.

German Wartime Procured and Produced High Power Pistols

High Power pistols produced during World War II are among the most sought after variants of this popular pistol. A good working knowledge is essential to avoid both misconception and fraud, and this knowledge includes familiarity with the wartime situation in Belgium in general and FN in particular (see pages 44-59, 92).

High Powers in German service received the designation Pistole 640(b). As with all foreign weapons accepted as a substitute standard by Germans the letter suffix indicates the actual country of production. In the case of the High Power, the letter "b" indicated that the pistol was produced in Belgien (Belgium). High Powers produced under German occupation were first assembled from existing parts in July-August 1940. As existing stockpiles of parts were used up, selected parts were manufactured to complement existing prewar parts. Over time, a greater percentage of the gun's parts were produced until pistols were manufactured entirely of parts made during the occupation. Occupation manufacture ended in early August 1944.

Timeline of the Wartime FN High Power

May 10, 1940: The German invasion
May 12, 1940: Fall of the city of Liège and closing of the Liège proof-house
May 17, 1940: The Germans direct FN management to restart production
May 19, 1940: Seizure of the FN plant
May 28, 1940: Capitulation of the Belgian government

May – June 1940: All completed and warehoused FN pistols are moved to the Liège Citadel. Unfinished guns and parts remain at FN.
July-August 1940: Assembly of pistols starts using existing parts and some minor manufactured parts. These pistols have tangent sights and slotted frames and have Liège (pre-invasion) proof marks. Note that these pistols do not have complete Belgian military acceptance markings or arsenal markings (see page 292)
September 1940: Introduction of the WaA613 acceptance marking (see page 293) on guns assembled primarily from prewar parts. These pistols have tangent sights and slotted frames. As FN was working on filling a Belgian military order at the time of the invasion, two variants are possible:

1- With Liège proofs. Proofed prior to the invasion with partial Belgian military acceptance markings and one WaA613 marking on the trigger guard.
2- No Liège proofs or Belgian military acceptance markings and one WaA613 marking on the trigger guard.

November-December 1940: New production frames, slides and barrels are introduced into the assembly process. Pistols have tangent sights but no slot on the frame. Markings are either a single WaA613 on the trigger-guard or, more commonly, multiple WaA613 markings on the frame and slide (no Belgian proofs or Belgian military acceptance markings).
November-December 1940: Germans modify the prewar barrel lug, changing the thickness and angle. Consequently prewar slide assemblies no longer fit the newly made frames.

April 1941: The WaA103 acceptance stamping is introduced (see page 296). Pistols have tangent sights without the shoulder-stock slot on the frame. Multiple WaA103 markings are found on frame and slide.
November-December 1941: Introduction of the WaA140 acceptance stamping (see page 297). Pistols have tangent sights without the shoulder-stock slot on the frame. Multiple WaA140 markings are applied on the frame and slide.

October 1942: Introduction of fixed sights. Pistols have fixed sights on an unslotted frame. Multiple WaA140 markings on frame and slide. Serial numbers do not have a letter suffix.

1943: Introduction of commercial production, pistols features are identical to post-October 1942 military production, but feature Eagle/N marking(s) instead of the WaA140 marking.
May 1943: Introduction of the "a" letter suffix in the serial number. Pistols have fixed sights, an unslotted frame and multiple WaA140 (or Eagle N) markings on frame and slide.

Early 1944: Introduction of the "b" letter suffix in the serial number. Pistols have fixed sights, an unslotted frame and multiple WaA140 (or Eagle N) markings on frame and slide.
Early 1944: Introduction of brown Bakelite grips as a substitute standard for wood grips.
1944 – Last months of occupation: Introduction of abbreviated serial numbers on High Power production.

Captured and Seized Belgian Military Pistols

Most Belgian military pistols found in the United States arrived with the American soldiers who captured them. The Germans used most of these pistols during World War II.

The Germans recognized the Liège proof system and captured guns do not bear any German proofs or acceptance markings. Most of the Belgian military High Powers used by the Germans were captured in northern France or western Belgium after May 28, 1940. Multiple accounts document the retreat and surrender of the Belgian military. Belgian troops surrendered their guns in either France or western Belgium, but walked to detainment camps wearing all their leather accessories. The Germans were thus faced with a serious shortage of holsters. One early solution was the modification of French Model 1892 revolver holsters for use with the High Power. Belgian Army combination holsters were also modified for use with the High Power.

Interestingly, Belgian military arms captured in France fell under the control of the wartime French administration. Those captured in Belgium became the responsibility of the German military administration in Brussels.

At the time of the invasion in May 1940 High Power pistols were being shipped to the Belgian State Arsenal (Manufacture d'Armes de L'Etat or MAE). Completed guns seized in the FN warehouses or MAE were transferred to the Liège Citadel in an attempt to minimize civilian access to firearms. The Liège Citadel was used by the Germans as a command center, barracks, arms depository, prison and execution site.

(Fig.290-1) The entrance of the Liège Citadel in the 1930s (see also fig.52-2).

Captured or seized firearms were never formally inspected or accepted by the Germans and should not bear any German proofs or acceptance markings. These guns were captured and placed into German service prior to the introduction of the WaA613 code at FN in September of 1940. Numerous Belgian military pistols have been observed with a fraudulent WaA613 marking. WaA613 markings are often added to these guns in an attempt to increase their value. The presence of complete Belgian military acceptance markings indicates that the gun was in circulation prior to the invasion, and the presence of an additional WaA613 marking is a clear indicator of fraud.

Very few special markings have been found to be authentic. These fraudulent markings include SS, SA, totenkopf (death's head) stampings and others. Most of these markings were added to pistols or holsters after the war.

A few rare pistols do exhibit special markings that are original. In every case, the markings were applied to indicate either the specific role in which the firearm was used or the user (rank and last name). These markings are usually (roll) engraved and not stamped. One such example is an early Belgian military pistol that was captured and reissued. It is marked with the user's name and rank: Wachtmeister Daube (see fig.291-1). Wachtmeister Daube was a technical sergeant in the 12th Artillery Regiment[1].

While the Germans did generally not use captured shoulder-stocks, three prewar shoulder-stocks that have had magazine pouches fitted have been noted. Fitting of magazine pouches to shoulder stocks is believed to be a German conversion. The shoulder stocks in question were the standard prewar FN configuration with attached holster and not the standard Belgian military shoulder stock. The following German designations were used[2]:

High Power Pistol: 640 (b) or 640 01(b)
Rig composed of HP pistol with FN shoulder-stock (attached holster): 640 (b) 21 or 640 01 (b) 21
Belgian military shoulder-stock: 640 (b) 25 or 640 01 (b) 25
Belgian military (large combination) holster: 640 (b) 22 or 640 01 (b) 22
Belgian military (double) magazine pouch: 640 (b) 24 or 640 01 (b) 24
Belgian military belt and shoulder strap for carrying holster: 640 (b) 23 or 640 01 (b) 23

(Fig.291-1) Belgian military pistol N° 9516 was manufactured and issued in 1935. It was captured in 1940 and reissued. The name and rank of the German officer was roll engraved on the frame, a wartime German practice found on few FN pistols. Wachtmeister Daube(1) was attached to the 12th Artillery regiment which operated on the Eastern Front. Wachtmeister Daube(1) was killed in action between December 1943 and February 1944.

(Fig.291-2) Belgian military pistol N° 44257 was delivered to the MAE arsenal on Tuesday May 7, 1940, three days before the invasion. This pistol has the correct FN applied military parts acceptance markings but not the final arsenal acceptance marking as applied to the frame and trigger-guard. The Germans seized the arsenal before this pistol could be accepted and issued to a Belgian officer. (Photograph by author, courtesy of James mauloff)

(Fig.291-3) Germans practice with a captured prewar High Power with Type 1 sights. (Photograph courtesy of Janne Salopuro)

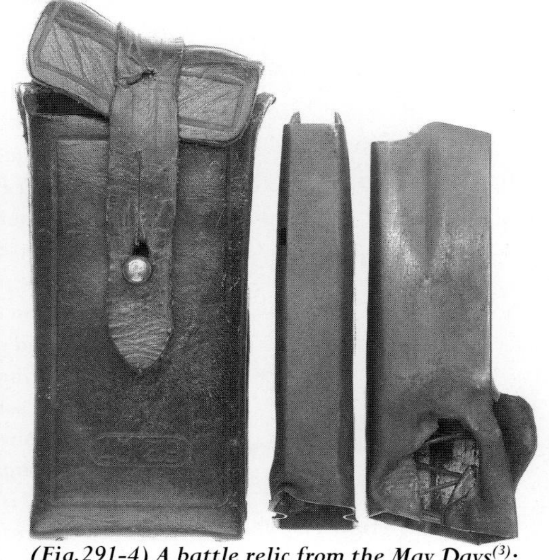

(Fig.291-4) A battle relic from the May Days(3): A Belgian High Power magazine pouch stops a German bullet, both magazines are destroyed.

(1) lexikon-der-wehrmacht.de

(2) Kleine Waffen-Bibliothek, Heft 20 by H.N. Lockhoven

(3) A Belgian term denoting the military campaign during the German invasion from May 10 through May 28, 1940

Pistols Assembled under the Occupation prior to WaA613 (July- August 1940)

This variant of wartime production has never before been documented. Assembly of FN pistols under German auspices began prior to the assignment of a Weapons Office (Waffenamt) inspector to the FN facility. As a result, a small number of High Powers were completed between June and September 1940 before Waffenamt inspector Tennert (Waffenamt inspector code WaA613) arrived at FN (page 50, 92). All observed pistols made during this time have been in the 44,000 serial range, show pre-invasion Liège proofs and have characteristics typical of prewar manufacture, including tangent sights and slotted frames. The pistols do not have Belgian military acceptance markings (page 95). Pistols in this serial range that do have Belgian military acceptance markings were completed prior to the invasion and were not produced under the Occupation. Triggers are the key identifying feature; they do not have the usual safety pin and have not been finished to remove machining marks[1].

FN records fail to show their entry into warehouse logs. This indicates occupation era assembly as FN did not keep High Power warehousing records during the Occupation. Features of pistol N° 44104 are consistent with prewar manufacturing and include FN's prewar internal final proof (Square A) marking on the frame under the grip. These pistols should not be confused with immediate post-liberation or postwar pistols that bear similar serial numbers.

(Fig.292-1) A small inexperienced and newly hired staff assembled some High Power, Model 1905, 1910 and 1922 pistols during the first months of the Occupation. All parts were of prewar manufacture except for the trigger, which was crudely made. This slotted-tangent pistol N° 44104 has features that coincide with early occupation assembly including prewar serial number, prewar frame, slide and grips and a crudely made wartime trigger. Pistols assembled during July and August 1940 have no German markings and their serial numbers are not present in FN warehouse logs as High Power serial numbers were not inventoried during the war. Although this pistol points to early occupation production, the barrel is an enigma, with features usually encountered on early post liberation production pistols. Auguste Jamart, the Liège proof house inspector, who proofed this pistol is known to have been working on High Powers in 1940 but not in the immediate post liberation period. It is also evident that no prewar parts remained after the occupation. (Photographs by author, courtesy of Ron Pinkenburg)

(1) See page 211 for the disposal of triggers at the time of invasion.

WaA613 Tangent Slotted Pistols (September - December 1940)

WaA613 marked pistols with a slotted frame and tangent sights are the most highly valued of all wartime pistols. As a result, this is also the most falsified variant. During the course of researching this volume, more than 40 percent of the WaA613 pistols examined were found to be forgeries.

An authentic WaA613 tangent, slotted pistol will display the following features (only two variants can be considered legitimate. It is considerably difficult to categorize these as manufacturing and completion of prewar pistols was at various stages and features can overlap. Note that serial numbers ranges depend on levels of completion and are therefore just identifying aids. It is impossible to determine or even estimate the quantity of tangent slotted pistols accepted under the WaA613 code, as these were literally assembled from a mixture of available parts without any serial number continuation. The missing serial number block between 45,500 and 50,000 is due to FN's prewar High Power numbering scheme, see page 271):

Sub-Variant 1
***Approximate serial ranges of pistols: 44500-45500**
***The pistol slide and frame has pre-invasion applied Liège proofs**
***The pistol has partial Belgian military acceptance markings:Those markings applied by Belgian accepting officers at FN are present but no arsenal applied markings like AC, GC are present.**
***A single WaA613 marking should be present on the trigger guard**
***The frame, slide and barrel serial numbers should match.**
***The magazine can have prewar markings but this is not required**
***The barrel and magazine can have a WaA613 marking but this is not required**
***Prewar barrel with Belgian proofs and caliber designation visible through ejection port, no serial number visible through the ejection port.**
***Wooden grips typically have the prewar red paint finish on the back (page 271)**

Sub-Variant 2
***Approximate serial ranges of pistols: 50000-52200**
***The pistol slide and frame should not have any Belgian proofs**
***The pistol should not have Belgian military acceptance markings**
***A single WaA613 marking should be present on the trigger guard**
***The frame and slide serial numbers should match**
***The barrel and magazine can have prewar markings but this is not required**
***The barrel and magazine can have a WaA613 marking but this is not required**
***Wooden grips typically have the prewar red paint finish on the back (page 271)**

These pistols were assembled from prewar parts seized on the manufacturing floor. Quality and finish of the WaA613 pistols approaches prewar standards with no visible machining marks. Sights are the Type 2 tangent variant (page 269) as this was in production on the Belgian military order prior to the invasion. Magazines are identical to prewar magazines and feature the phosphate green tube with blue split-tail floor-plate. Early occupation magazines were not WaA613 marked.

Only pistols seized inside the plant or on the manufacturing floor were accepted with the WaA613 marking. High Power pistols found in FN warehouses did not receive a Waffenamt inspection marking as they were transferred to the Citadel prior to Inspector Tennert's arrival. Collectors should be aware that pistols have surfaced where the original markings (slide legend, proofs and Belgian military acceptance markings) were (entirely) removed and new markings were applied with a WaA613 marking.

Reported or observed numbers: 44840, 45331, 45361, 50778, 51161, 51167, 51998, 52028

(Fig.293-1) A German soldier poses with a Type 2 tangent High Power. (Photograph courtesy of Janne Salopuro)

WaA613 Tangent Slotted Pistols (Continued)

(Fig.294-1) Tangent slotted pistol N° 45331 is part of sub-variant 1 of the WaA613 accepted pistols. This pistol was in an advanced stage of completion at the time of the invasion, having Liège proofs as well as the Belgian military parts acceptance markings (applied at FN) on the barrel, frame, slide and trigger. Note that the pistol correctly lacks the final Belgian arsenal acceptance markings on the frame or trigger-guard. The trigger-guard was marked with a single WaA613 stamping. The barrel is a prewar manufactured barrel with complete Liège proofs and Belgian military acceptance markings. (Photographs by author, courtesy of Jim Mauloff)

(Fig.294-2) Tangent slotted pistol N° 51161 is part of sub-variant 2 of the WaA613 accepted pistols. This pistol lacks Liège proofs and only has one Belgian military parts acceptance marking (applied at FN) on the trigger. The latter does not indicate that this pistol was originally destined for the Belgian military as parts were individually stamped before assembly. The trigger-guard was marked with a single WaA613 stamping. The barrel is either a pre-occupation manufactured barrel or new German manufacture. It is marked with a single WaA613 marking visible through the ejection port. This is a transition procedure and was soon replaced for the test eagle and serial number (see fig.295-2). Some green phosphate magazine bodies were stamped with a single WaA613 marking but not all.

WaA613 Tangent Only Pistols (December 1940 – April 1941)

German production became streamlined by the end of 1940. The complex frame slot for the shoulder-stock was abandoned. Serial numbers of this variant were sequential to those on WaA613 marked pistols with slotted frames; pistol number 52028 has tangent sights with a slotted frame whereas pistol 53310 has only the tangent sights.

The Germans also modified the angle and thickness of the barrel lug, the change being implemented with the first run of occupation produced barrels. As a result, the new barrels will not function with prewar slides, and while prewar slide assemblies may fit on a wartime frame, functioning is dubious. This change is difficult to see with the naked eye.

The following features should apply to an original pistol:
***Approximate serial ranges of pistols: 53000-65285 (approximately 12285 accepted – average 3071 a month)**
***Prewar fit and finish, few broken parts due to sabotage have been reported**
***The pistol's slide and frame have the German test proof and two or more WaA613 markings**
***The pistol has no Liège proofs or Belgian military acceptance markings**
***The barrel has the serial number and German test proof visible through the ejection port**
***The magazine has a phosphate body with WaA613 marking**
***Wooden grips usually have the prewar red paint finish on the back (page 271)**

(Fig.295-1) Side view of tangent WaA613 pistol N° 53310. By the time new production started, the Germans standardized the location of markings including multiple Test Eagle and WaA markings on frame and slide, a single WaA marking under the muzzle (see page 296 for details) and one or more WaA markings on the barrel (not visible through the ejection port). The significance of the "LT" marking on the trigger-guard is unknown. (Photographs by author, courtesy of Jim Mauloff)

(Fig.295-2) Angled view of tangent WaA613 pistol N° 60201. Note the standard method of applying the barrel markings, which include both the serial number and Test Eagle visible through the ejection port.

(Fig.295-3) Machinists and assemblers identification markings were not applied to individual parts but were concentrated near the magazine well.

WaA103 Tangent Only Pistols (April 1941 – November / December 1941)

The WaA103 accepted pistols are virtually identical in features and quality to the earlier tangent WaA613 pistols. Serial numbers of this variant followed the WaA613 serials numbers. The WaA103 inspection marking was introduced around serial number 65285. Pistol number 65285 is a typical transition piece which has both the WaA613 markings as well as the WaA103 marking. As seen on page 92, the German inspectors were not transferred from FN but rather changed job functions.

The following features should apply to an original pistol:
***Approximate serial ranges of pistols: 65285-93000 (approximate 27715 accepted – average 3464 a month)**
***Prewar fit and finish; some broken parts reported due to sabotage**
***The pistol slide and frame have German test proofs and three or more WaA103 markings**
***The pistol has no Liège proofs or Belgian military acceptance markings**
***The barrel has the serial number and German test proof, visible through the ejection port**
***The magazine has a green phosphate body with WaA103 marking**
***Wooden grips most often have the prewar red paint finish on the back (page 271)**

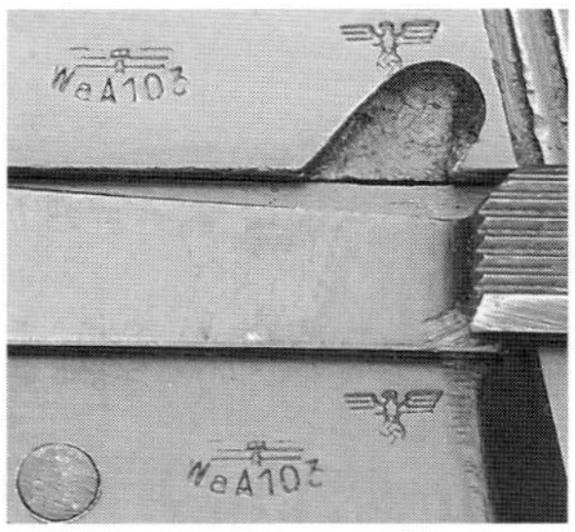

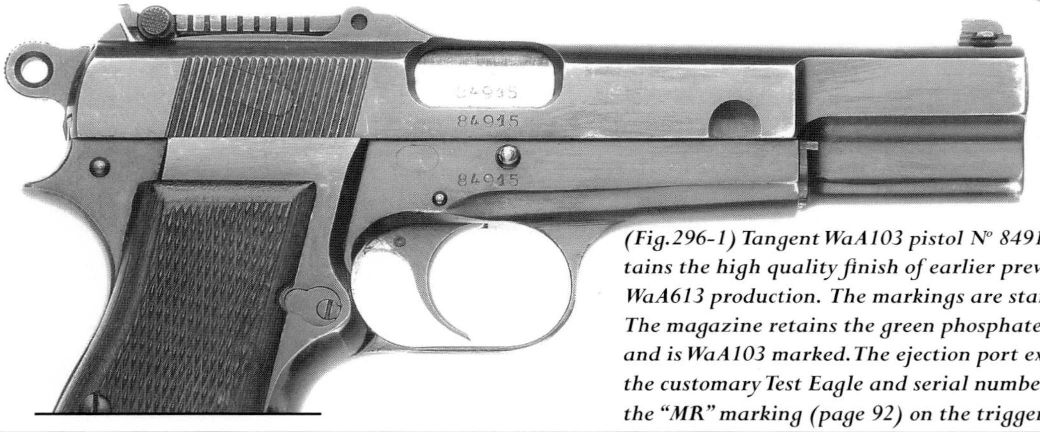

(Fig.296-1) Tangent WaA103 pistol N° 84915 retains the high quality finish of earlier prewar and WaA613 production. The markings are standard. The magazine retains the green phosphate body and is WaA103 marked. The ejection port exhibits the customary Test Eagle and serial number. Note the "MR" marking (page 92) on the trigger-guard.

WaA identification markings near the muzzle

The Germans started marking pistols under the muzzle with the newly manufactured WaA613 pistols, this marking practice remained in effect throughout the war. FN used large wooden crates to house the pistols while being produced and proofed. Only the muzzle area was clearly visible with the pistol seated in a slot of the crate. The Germans marked the muzzle area in order to quickly identify completed and accepted pistols. This eliminated the need to handle each pistol to see if it was accepted. Most likely the practice was carried over from prewar Belgian military assembly. In the prewar years the Belgian military inspector stamped the parts acceptance marking near the muzzle but on the side of the slide (still easily visible when the pistols were crated). Shown are a wooden crate and wartime WaA muzzle markings.

WaA140 Tangent Only Pistols (December 1941 / January 1942 – November 1942)

The WaA140 acceptance was introduced as production quotas were raised. Overall production quality decreased and sabotage increased significantly. Quality differences can be noted on fit and finish, and overall the metal was less polished before bluing.

Serial numbers of this variant followed the WaA103 serial numbers. Features of the tangent WaA140 pistols(1) remain the same as those of the WaA103 pistols. Magazines however were all blue in finish and were marked WaA140. The phosphate magazine body was abandoned making it easier for the magazine to drop free of the frame when ejected. Prewar magazine bodies were phosphated in order to avoid falling free when ejected. Starting with the WaA140 pistols, a large number of parts broke under the stress of repeated firing. This was due to improper heat-treating, which made the parts brittle. Dimensional tolerances were also often out of specification. Some of the most common parts failures:

***Loose or easily broken front sights**
***Broken extractors**
***Broken recoil springs**
***Loose safety pins**

Sabotage increased in direct proportion to the number of forced laborers on the FN factory floor. Steel-hardening and precision tolerancing were prime targets for sabotage as irregularities in these processes could not easily be detected. As a result, many WaA140 marked pistols fail to meet prewar or postwar tolerance standards. The firing of any WaA140 pistol is strongly discouraged.

The following features should apply to an original pistol:
***Approximate serial ranges of pistols: 93000-140000 (approximate 47000 accepted – average 4272 a month)**
***The pistol slide and frame have a German test proof and multiple WaA140 markings**
***The pistol has no Liège proofs or Belgian military acceptance markings**
***The serial number and German test proof are visible through the ejection port**
***The magazine has a WaA140 marking**
***Wooden grips no longer have the prewar red paint finish on the back**

(Fig.297-1) Tangent WaA140 pistol N° 100190 shows the decrease in polishing and overall fit and finish. The markings are standard but are struck with less attention, these often appear lighter and even upside-down. Magazine bodies have a blue finish and are WaA140 marked. The overall magazine finish is inferior to earlier production. (Photographs by author, courtesy of Jim Mauloff)

(1) Several tangent slotted WaA140 forgeries have been observed or reported. In this case the slot was poorly milled out after the war.

WaA140 Fixed Sight Pistols (December 1942 - early August 1944)

First sub-variant: Standard serial numbers (Approximately 140,000 to 210,000)
December 1942 - April 1943

The first fixed sight WaA140 pistols were similar in quality to the earlier WaA140 tangent sight pistols. Serial numbers followed the tangent sight pistols accepted with WaA140 acceptance markings. The fixed sights were introduced as an early attempt to reduce machining operations and increase production. Additionally, there was no rationale for the tangent sight as as the Germans did not use shoulder-stocks. Some pistols were well finished, but the metal was generally less polished in comparison to the WaA613 or WaA103 pistols. Sabotage activities gradually increased as seen above.

Some claim that in this period the aluminum follower was replaced with a Zamak (zinc, aluminum, magnesium and copper alloy) follower. Although this may have happened in other arms factories, the author has found no evidence of such. All wartime magazine followers for the High Power were made out of aluminum. The magazine body was blued and early magazines were still WaA140 marked. The WaA140 marking was abandoned from the magazine during this period.

The following features should apply to an original pistol:
***Approximate serial ranges of pistols: 140000-210000 (approximate 70,000 accepted – approximate average 14,000 a month)**
***The pistol slide and frame have a German test proof and multiple WaA140 markings**
***The pistol has no Liège proofs or Belgian military acceptance markings**
***The serial number and German test proof are visible through the ejection port**
***Certain parts, like extractors, are no longer interchangeable with earlier pistols: they are fitted to the specific pistol**
***The magazine has a WaA140 marking or no WaA marking**
***Magazine tubes are blued**
***Wooden grips no longer have the prewar red paint finish on the back**
***Magazine safety is still present**

(Fig.298-1) The standard location for the WaA marking on all occupation production barrels, except for the early slotted-tangent WaA613 pistols.

Second sub variant: "a" suffix serial numbers from 1a to 99999a
May 1943 – December 1943

As the war progressed, the Germans started to look at ways to increase output. By 1943, material shortages had become common at FN, and production was frequently halted. Labor remained an issue and resistance activity increased.

After changing over to fixed sights, the Germans began using a letter suffix serial number system. This system was not unique to FN and was used by various companies engaged in small arms production for the German military. A letter is assigned to each block of 100,000 pistols. At FN this was started with the "a" suffix letter and followed by the "b" suffix. The "a" suffix block was entirely produced. The suffix letter was pre-stamped or roll engraved in a separate operation, prior to the application of the serial number. It is possible to encounter a part or "lunch box special" pistol, which does not have a serial number but does have the suffix letter.

The Germans also deleted the magazine safety, which had been carried over from prewar production, despite differences in German doctrine.

Standards for fit and finish were lowered considerably under the "a" suffix production. It is a common belief that this happened gradually. Inspected samples indicate that it is more random. The consensus is that this is often due to the individual metal polisher. Wasting time polishing was a passive method to slow down production. A finely polished pistol and a crudely finished gun can be observed within a few numbers. Some of the "a" suffix pistols display extremely crude finishing and are worse than the later "b" suffix pistols.

WaA140 pistols are prone to parts breakage under repeated firing (see page 297).

The following features should apply to an original pistol:
***Serial ranges of pistols: 1a-99999a (99999 accepted – average / approximate 12500 a month)**
***The pistol slide and frame have a German test proof and multiple WaA140 markings**
***The pistol has no Liège proofs or Belgian military acceptance markings**
***The serial number and German test proof are visible through the ejection port**
***The magazine has a crudely finished blued body with no WaA marking**
***Wooden grips no longer have the prewar red paint finish on the back**
***Magazine safety is not present**
***Certain parts, like extractors, are no longer interchangeable with earlier pistols**

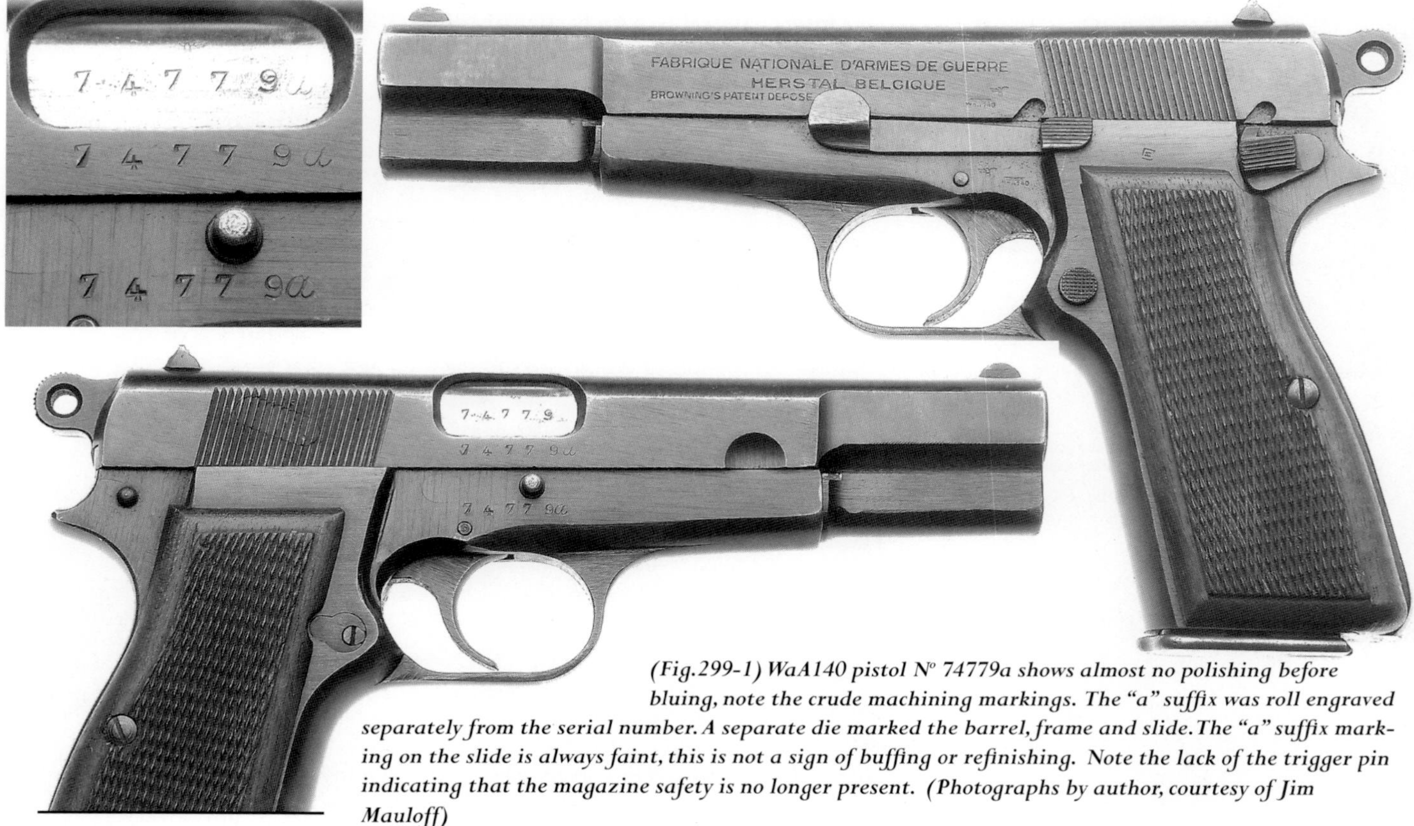

(Fig.299-1) WaA140 pistol N° 74779a shows almost no polishing before bluing, note the crude machining markings. The "a" suffix was roll engraved separately from the serial number. A separate die marked the barrel, frame and slide. The "a" suffix marking on the slide is always faint, this is not a sign of buffing or refinishing. Note the lack of the trigger pin indicating that the magazine safety is no longer present. (Photographs by author, courtesy of Jim Mauloff)

Third sub variant: "b" suffix serial numbers from 1b to approximately 61800b
January 1944 – August 1944

As the war progressed, raw materials, including steel and walnut became scarce. In response, the Germans introduced Bakelite grips as a substitute for the High Power. The Bakelite grips were introduced as supplies of wooden grips grew scarce. Depending on availability at the time, it is possible to encounter a late war "b" suffix pistol with wooden grips. Final attempts at production streamlining included the elimination of most finish polishing and serial number abbreviation. The serial number abbreviation was introduced between number 10000b and 15000b. On guns marked in this manner, the barrel and frame numbers showed only the last three digits followed by the suffix. The full serial number was marked on the slide, the main component in Europe[1].

Although pistol production under the Occupation officially ceased in August 1944, records indicate that little production took place after May 1944.

WaA140 pistols are prone to parts breakage under repeated firing (see page 297).

(1) In the U.S., the Federal Bureau of Alcohol, Tobacco, Firearms and Explosives (B ATFE) considers the pistol frame the legally regulated component of a firearm.

Third sub variant: "b" suffix serial numbers from 1b to approximately 61800b (continued)

The following features should apply to an original pistol:
***Serial ranges of pistols: 1b-61800b (approximately 61800 accepted)**
***The pistol slide and frame have a German test proof and multiple WaA140 markings**
***Abbreviated serial number on barrel and frame after serial number, starting circa number 15,000b**
***The pistol has no Liège proofs or Belgian military acceptance markings**
***The (abbreviated) serial number and German test proof are visible through the ejection port**
***The magazine has a crudely finished blued body with no WaA marking**
***Chocolate brown Bakelite grips are most often encountered, although wooden grips are possible**
***Magazine safety is not present**
***Certain parts like extractors are no longer interchangeable with earlier pistols**

(Fig.300-1) WaA140 pistol N° 59404b is a late occupation production pistol. Pistols produced in 1944 usually have Bakelite grips, fewer have wooden grips. Note the three digit abbreviated serial number; unlike the model 1922 (page 248) the High Power three digit abbreviation was retained and no four-digit abbreviation was ever introduced. Machining markings are clearly visible as little polishing was performed. Note the lack of the trigger pin; this pistol has no magazine safety.

(Fig.300-2) Late war magazines are crudely finished. The welding and grinding was poorly executed, and magazine bodies are known to crack or split open. Overall the blued magazine body shows heavy machining marks and is no longer WaA140 marked. Some small markings identify the builder, although these are not always present.

(Fig.300-3) Degrading finish quality and a lack of production standards are common throughout the WaA140 production span. Quality and parts interchangeability were sacrificed for the sake of increased output. Extractors were no longer interchangeable and required fitting to a specific slide. Where the magazine body locks into the frame varies significantly during this period, affecting proper function and feeding. Seen here are a few examples of the thumbprint size, randomly machined during the WaA140 period.

Eagle N Fixed Sight Pistols (December 1942 - early August 1944)

The Eagle N pistols are commonly referred to as commercial pistols. Pistols have either both the Eagle N acceptance marking and test proof or only the test proof. These pistols were introduced with the fixed sight WaA140 pistols and they coincide with WaA140 production. Features and serial numbering practices are outlined in the WaA140 section.

Eagle N (test proof only) pistols account for between five and eight percent of pistols made during the WaA140 era. Pistols are random through the WaA140 range and do not fall into any particular serial range or block. Test-proof only pistols are more rare than the Eagle N pistols.

Some collectors have suggested that the Eagle N pistols were supplied to German - Nazi law enforcement groups while test proof only pistols were true commercial pistols that were supplied to company securities as well as select individuals. The author has found no proof of this. It is correct however that the Eagle N pistols are more common than those that are only marked with the test proof.

Most commonly encountered are Eagle N pistols with standard frames, while those with factory slotted frames are a rare and original variation. Most likely these frames were leftovers from earlier production. WaA140 and Eagle N pistols are prone to parts breakage under repeated firing (see page 297).

Observed or reported Eagle N pistols with slotted frames:
41512b, 41525b, 41535b, 41577b, 41569b

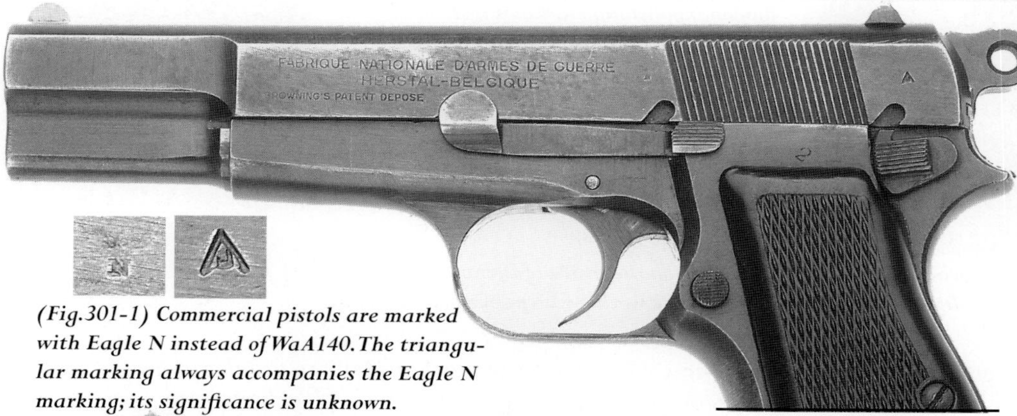

(Fig.301-1) Commercial pistols are marked with Eagle N instead of WaA140. The triangular marking always accompanies the Eagle N marking; its significance is unknown.

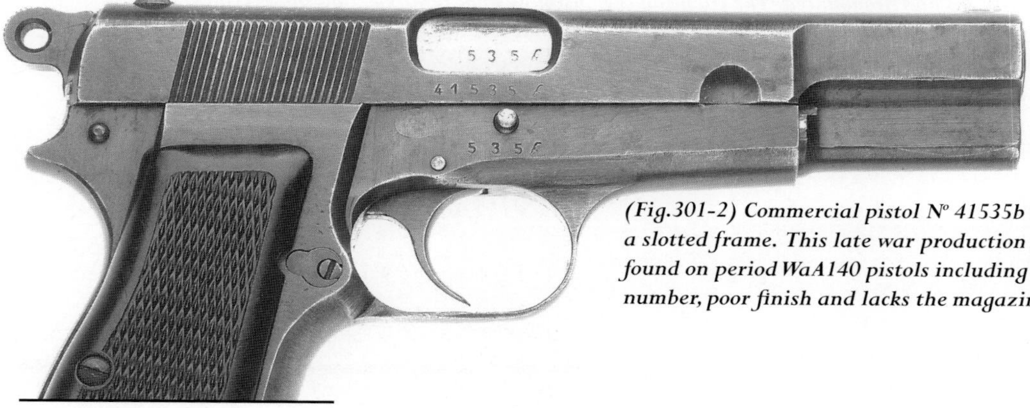

(Fig.301-2) Commercial pistol N° 41535b is one of the few to be assembled with a slotted frame. This late war production pistol has all the typical features found on period WaA140 pistols including Bakelite grips, abbreviated serial number, poor finish and lacks the magazine safety.

Factory reworks: Repaired and refinished pistols

The repair work at FN focused on pistols that had failed factory inspection. The High Power was no exception. Reworked or repaired pistols can be identified by extra machining marks and the obvious plum color bluing of certain parts.

Plum color bluing can be attributed to factors including:
*** A new or too strong solution**
*** Incorrect solution temperature**
*** Bluing over existing bluing**

In the case of the wartime reworks, the pistols were often repaired and re-blued over existing bluing. The plum color is therefor typically visible on certain parts and not the complete pistol.

The Germans marked the pistols that passed quality control before they were submitted for the test proof. While there are no factory records to confirm this practice, the majority of wartime pistols (especially WaA140 / Eagle N) have a letter or digit under or above the left grip. This is roughly the same location as the prewar FN marking "square A" (see page 85). The letter or digit may indicate that the pistol passed internal quality control. Reworked pistols lack this marking, displaying a variety of smaller markings. The author believes these to be codes for the required repair procedures. The significance of these codes is unknown.

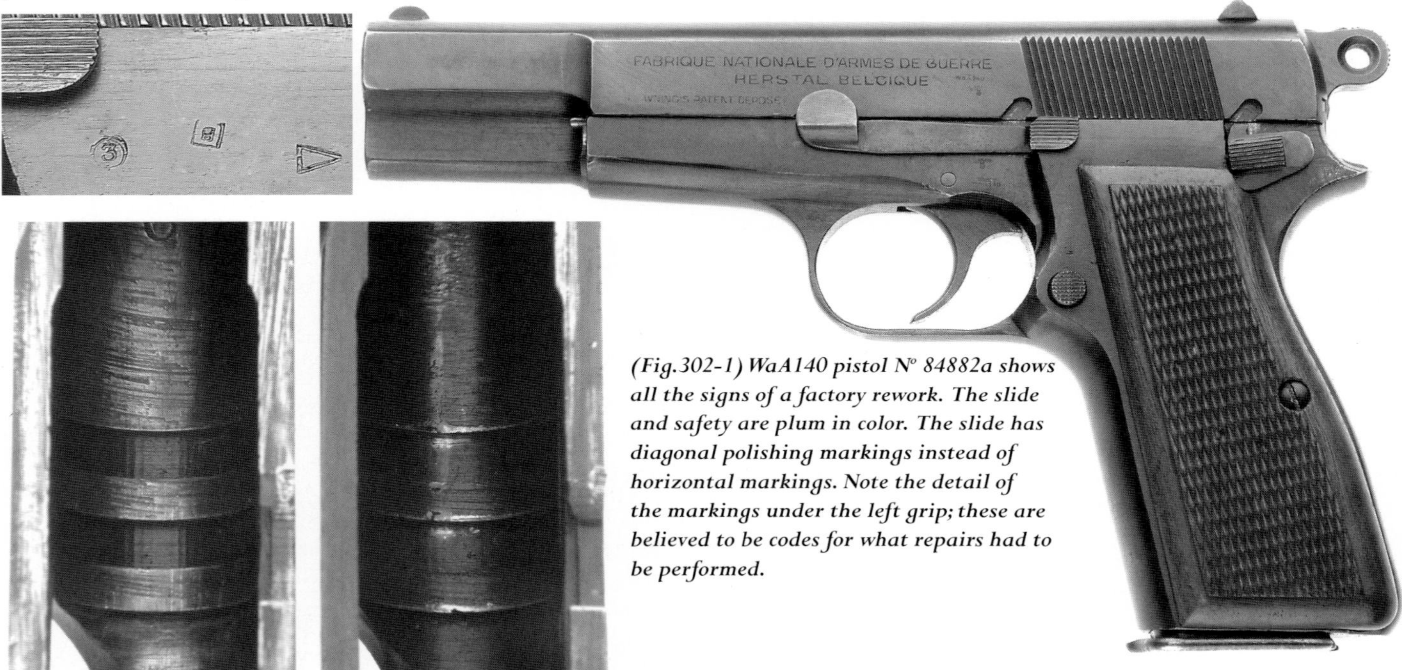

(Fig.302-1) WaA140 pistol N° 84882a shows all the signs of a factory rework. The slide and safety are plum in color. The slide has diagonal polishing markings instead of horizontal markings. Note the detail of the markings under the left grip; these are believed to be codes for what repairs had to be performed.

(Fig.302-2) Deeper and more pronounced machining markings are visible on the inside of the reworked slide (left). These repairs are often also stamped with a letter or digit, most likely identifying the worker who performed the repair.

(Fig.302-3) Compare the fine diagonal polishing slide marks of the rework (left) to the typical horizontal machining marks of a standard slide (right). Such diagonal marks have been observed in different levels of finish, some being fine while others are deep and pronounced. The frame on this pistol was not reworked and shows typical machining mark; horizontal to the right of the serial number and vertical to the left of the serial number.

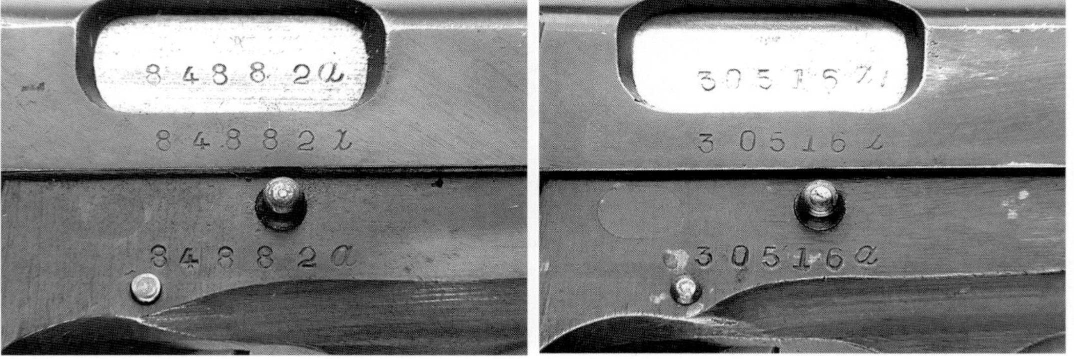

Post liberation pistols: The "A" prefix High Power

The Germans left FN on September 5, 1944, and while they looted much in the way of machinery and machine tools, they did not transplant the factory as planned. The Germans did not ignore the stocks of existing pistol parts, as is often reported. These parts were originally destined for assembly in Germany (see page 56). With the rapid Allied advance, time for the Germans ran out, and parts stockpiles were left behind. FN employees began to assemble guns as soon as the Germans evacuated Liège, prior to the arrival of elements of the U.S. 3rd Armored Division. The first pistols were made in September 1944, and were assembled from parts made late in the Occupation. These pistols have no serial numbers, but were proofed. The Liège proof house was closed during the war. Some proof house employees who had taken their stamping dies with them in 1940 returned almost immediately to resume work after the liberation.

The first pistols assembled in September came from wartime parts stockpiles and were crudely finished and resembled the worst of the late Occupation pistols. Pistols, marked with an "A" prefix serial number, were produced beginning in October 1944. The prefix "A" was stamped on the pistols prior to marking a serial number. Warehousing logs started with pistol A101. The earliest entry in logs was pistol A104, entered on October 20, 1944. Retired FN employees have stated that the letter was used to indicate "Allemand" (German). The "A" prefix pistols were considerably better polished and finished than the September 1944 production. Early features are similar to Occupation production, including the missing magazine safety, Bakelite grips, and altered barrel lug dimensions that often do not interchange with peacetime produced pistols. Bakelite grips were the first to be replaced by walnut grips, the magazine safety was also reintroduced late in 1945.

FN did not have the capability to produce pistols from raw materials until 1946, relying on stocks of wartime pistol parts until that time. At that time pistols were once again properly finished, being polished and buffed before being blued, and polished to prewar standards.

American GIs were the first customers for the High Power. Although the pistols were purchased and picked up at the factory, the shipping logs often include the purchaser's name and rank, becoming a record of the men who passed through FN. Most bought one pistol. Some however purchased many. Gregory Cap bought 12 on October 20, 1944. A Major Bomar purchased 20 High Powers on November 7, 1944.

Purchasers were not only American; British, Free Belgian and Luxembourg soldiers also purchased pistols. The earliest official use for the "A" prefix High Power appears to have been a few pistols sold to a Belgian mine in late 1944 and early 1945. By November 1945 the first substantial orders were placed to rearm the nation's military. High Powers were ordered for the military while the Model 1922 was purchased for the military and law enforcement (page 250).

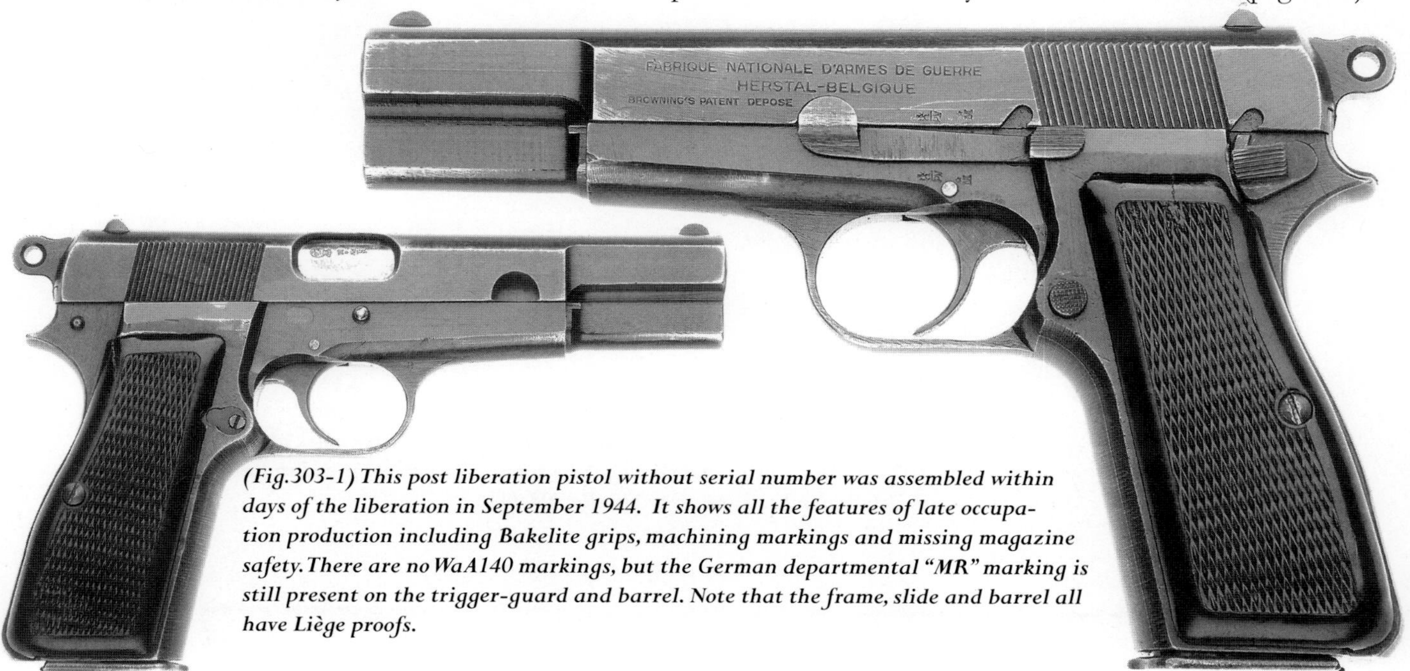

(Fig. 303-1) This post liberation pistol without serial number was assembled within days of the liberation in September 1944. It shows all the features of late occupation production including Bakelite grips, machining markings and missing magazine safety. There are no WaA140 markings, but the German departmental "MR" marking is still present on the trigger-guard and barrel. Note that the frame, slide and barrel all have Liège proofs.

Post liberation pistols: The "A" prefix High Power (continued)

(Fig.304-1) This rare post liberation tangent pistol without serial number was assembled in September 1944. This indicates that wartime produced tangent parts were still present at the factory at the time of the liberation. The pistol has Bakelite grips and lacks the magazine safety. There are no WaA140 markings, but the German departmental "MR" marking is still present on the trigger-guard. The barrel markings are identical to prewar manufacture with the caliber designation visible through the ejection port. Note that the barrel has Liège proofs. (Photographs courtesy of Ron Pinkenburg)

(Fig.304-2) Post liberation pistol N° A466 was purchased by U.S. serviceman N. Fellmann on December 4, 1944. The pistol still has the German letter mark above the left grip. It has Bakelite grips and no magazine safety. Note the high polish finish in comparison with September 1944 assembly (fig.303-1).

The Danish Order; finally delivered

Negotiations for Danish High Power procurement began in 1939-1940. The development of a feature specific to the Danish contract, a rotating lanyard ring, delayed production. The order was placed in 1940, but the German invasion prevented production. The original order specified tangent slotted pistols with a rotating lanyard ring that would not interfere with the use of the shoulder-stock. The Danes had objected to the fixed lanyard staple as supplied to Lithuania. In response, FN developed the rotating ring and mounted it on the underside of the pistol, behind the magazine well. Although this configuration did not interfere with shoulder-stock use, it made ejection and insertion of magazines more difficult.

The original configuration was never built due to World War II, but the contract was filled in 1946. Fixed sight pistols were shipped instead of tangent slotted pistols. The rotating ring was moved to the left grip panel so as not to interfere with magazine changes. The Danish contract was the first to be made completely from raw materials after the war. An estimated 1700 pistols were shipped to Denmark in 1946, these were issued to the military and border guards. Denmark purchased additional pistols between 1958 and 1961. The 1946 purchase can easily be identified by the factory applied contract markings: "M. 1946 H.V." followed by the pistol's issue number (Model of 1946, Haerens Vabenarsenal - Army Weapons Arsenal or The Royal Danish Arsenal). The 'Haerens Vabenarsenal" marking should not to be confused with the Norwegian Home Guard which uses the same abbreviation H.V. (Heim Vernet).

Reported or observed numbers: 0123, 0188, 0311, 0324, 0408, 0452, 1001, 1103, 1244

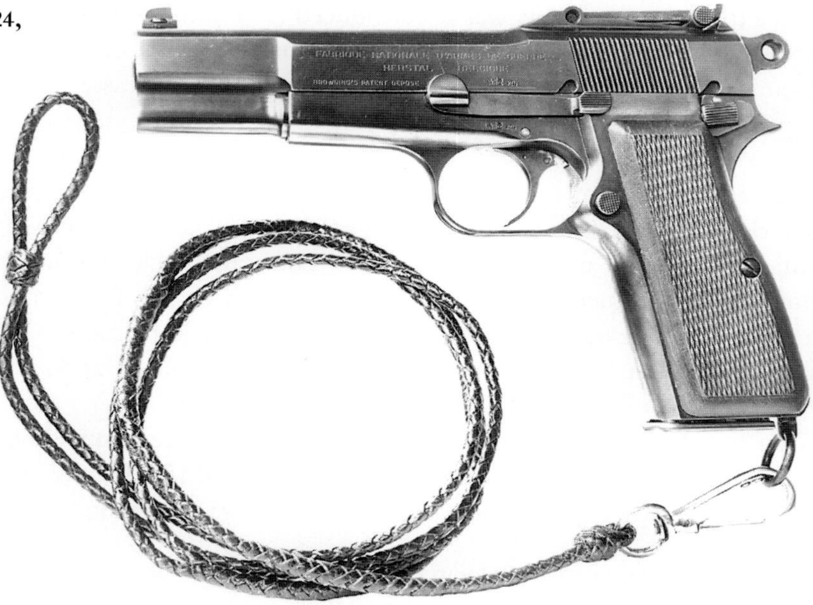

(Fig.305-1) This 1940 pre-production sample illustrates the rotation lanyard design as specified by Denmark. This configuration was not produced due to the German invasion. The braided leather lanyard design remained in Danish service after the war. The metal clasp was not used. (Photograph courtesy of Collector Grade Publications, Inc.)

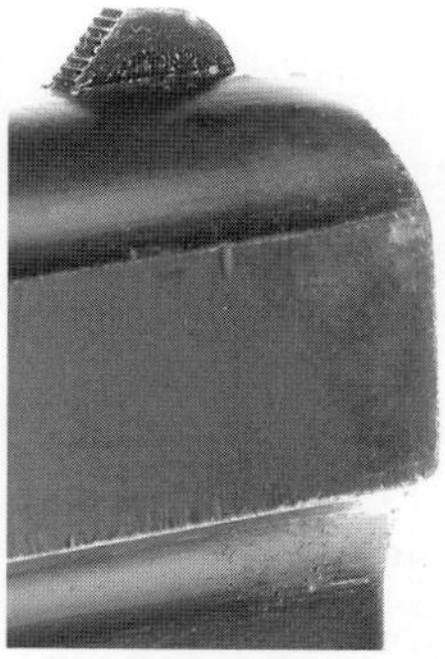

(Fig.305-3) Note the special front sight with serrations on the 1946 contract pistols.

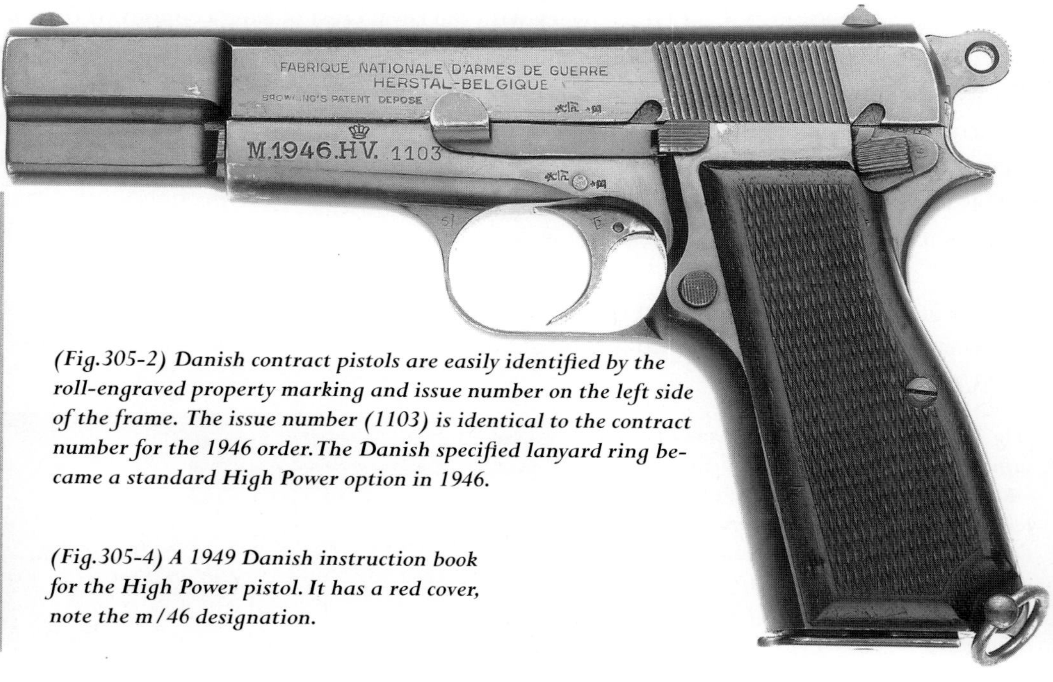

(Fig.305-2) Danish contract pistols are easily identified by the roll-engraved property marking and issue number on the left side of the frame. The issue number (1103) is identical to the contract number for the 1946 order. The Danish specified lanyard ring became a standard High Power option in 1946.

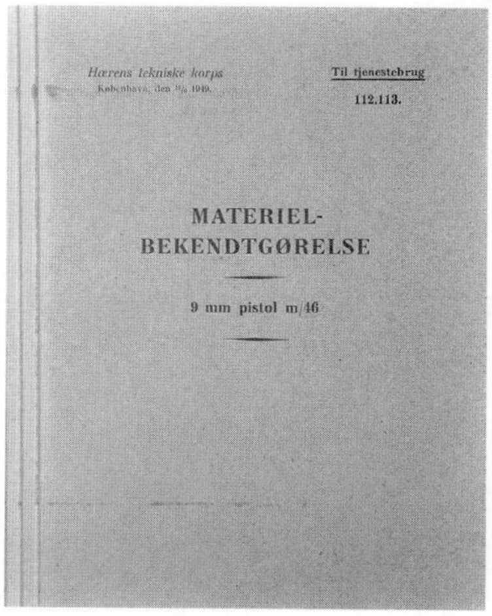

Hærens tekniske korps
København, den 8/6 1949.

Til tjenestebrug

112.113.

MATERIEL-
BEKENDTGØRELSE

9 mm pistol m/46

(Fig.305-4) A 1949 Danish instruction book for the High Power pistol. It has a red cover, note the m/46 designation.

Belgian Contracts: Regent and Royal Markings

The Belgian government was the most significant user of High Power pistols in the prewar era. Short of equipment after the war, the military placed its first order for High Power pistols in 1945. The transition to fixed sights was made out of necessity, as only "A" prefix pistols were available.

The "A" prefix pistols shipped in 1945 and early 1946 were assembled with wooden grips. The first pistols did not have magazine safeties and the Belgian arsenal, Atelier Central d'Armement (Centralized Arms Workshop), did not accept or mark these with acceptance markings. At the time, the facilities of the Manufacture d'Armes de l'Etat were being used by the U.S. military. As a result, proofing and acceptance of small arms occurred in another nearby arsenal operating under the name; Atelier Central d'Armement. These early pistols were never properly accepted, most likely because of the lack of a magazine safety, and were only intended for temporary or emergency use. The arsenal identified these pistols by adding a letter "B" behind the serial number in an effort to mark them with the common prewar abbreviation "A.B." for Armée Belge (Belgian Army). It should be noted that this was primarily an afterthought and that this was not factory applied. The serial number on these pistols was applied in three different operations: First FN roll engraved the frame with the letter "A" for Allemand (page 250). Next, the number was added in a separate FN operation. Finally, the arsenal added the "B" suffix identification letter.

Once the magazine safety was re-introduced (1945), the pistols were arsenal accepted and marked on the trigger-guard with the prewar Crown AC marking (see identical practice on Model 1922 pistols, fig.252-1). State arsenals updated their acceptance markings in 1946. Belgian military pistols assembled from newly manufactured parts were fully accepted and marked by the arsenals on the trigger-guard.

The early concept of the letter prefix and suffix was retained and expanded to create the "ABL" or "AB. B.L" abbreviations. These markings were roll engraved at the factory. The ABL abbreviation accounts for Belgium's two official languages; French and Flemish (Dutch). The marking cleverly amalgamates the acronyms for "Belgian Army" in both French (Armée Belge) and Flemish (Belgisch Leger). Pistols purchased between 1945 and 1949 were devoid of a royal crest, due to the political situation in Belgium at the time. The country was ruled by the Regent Prince Philip while King Leopold III remained in exile due to his collaboration with the Germans during World War II (page 44).

After five years, the Belgian government attempted to reinstate King Leopold. Consequently, pistols supplied in 1951 were factory roll engraved with the crest of Leopold III. Leopold's restoration was met with protests, and he abdicated in favor of his son, Baudouin, on July 16, 1951. Starting in 1952 pistols were marked with the crest of King Baudouin I.

The postwar Belgian military contracts can be categorized in three main variations:
Pre-1951: Regent deliveries without royal crest on slide
1951: Delivery with the royal crest of King Leopold III on top of the slide
Post 1951: Deliveries with the royal crest of King Baudouin I on top of the slide

Pistols marked with the "A.B. B.L." serial number prefix and suffix were used by all branches of the military including the army, air force and navy. Some contracts were specifically ordered for the navy or air force and were marked with service specific prefixes and suffixes (see below). It should be noted however, that these air force and navy marked pistols entered service with the navy or air force but were scattered throughout the military after being repaired or refurbished. No effort was made by the arsenals to return these pistols to the marked branch of the military.

The Belgian Gendarmerie, as part of the military, used standard issue pistols. In the 1970s the gendarmerie ordered lightweight pistols with alloy frames. The gendarmerie was the only organization to use the lightweight High Power in the Belgian military.

(Fig.306-1) Variants of serial number pre- and suffixes: A.B. xxxx B.L. indicating Armée Belge – Belgisch Leger (Belgian army) in French and Flemish. F.A. xxxx L.M. for Force Aérienne – Lucht Macht (Air Force) in French and Flemish. ABL-ZM xxxx for (Belgian Army) in French and Flemish and Zee Macht (Navy) in Flemish. (Photographs courtesy of J. Weckx, B. V. V. W.)

Serial number prefix and suffix variations:
A xxxx B: Arsenal addition of the letter "B" to post liberation "A" prefix High Power pistols in order to create the common prewar abbreviation Armée Belge (Belgian Army). This was only applied to 1945 pistols without magazine safety, which did not comply with set standards and were not officially accepted.

A.B. xxxx B.L.: Factory roll engraved marking indicating Armée Belge – Belgisch Leger (Belgian army) in both French and Flemish. Introduced in the Regent years on newly manufactured pistols after 1946. This prefix / suffix was widely used throughout all the branches of the military and the marking remains in use decades later.

F.A. xxxx L.M.: Factory roll engraved marking indicating Force Aérienne – Lucht Macht (Air Force; in French and Flemish) believed to have been first introduced in 1951 with the royal crested contracts. Although destined for the air force, these pistols ended up in various branches of the military after arsenal repairs.

ABL-ZM xxxx: Factory roll engraved marking indicating Armée Belge – Belgisch Leger (Belgian Army; in both French and Flemish) and Zee Macht (Navy in Flemish). This variation is believed to have first appeared in the 1970s. Although initially used by the navy, these pistols ended up in various branches of the military after arsenal repair.

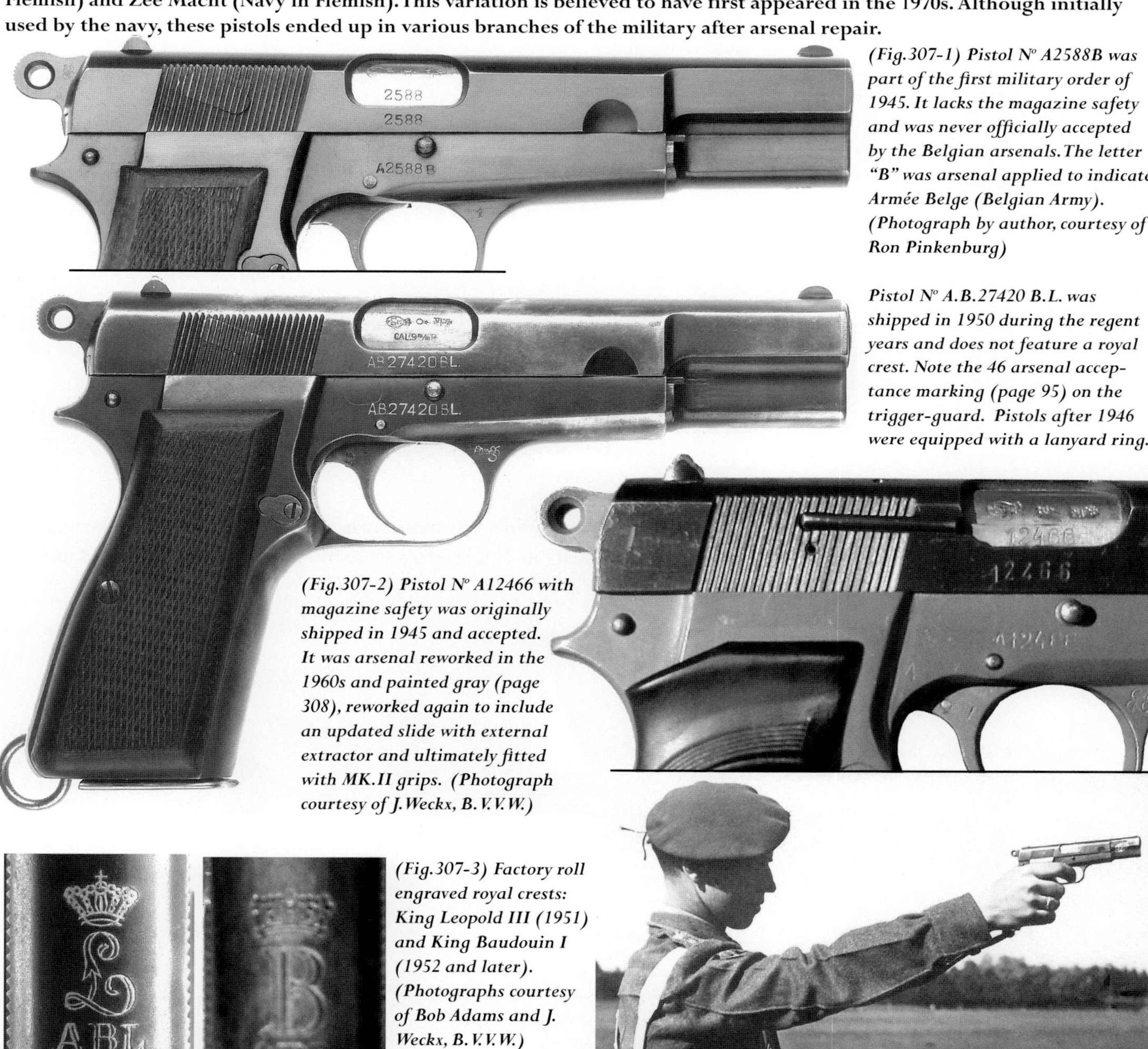

(Fig.307-1) Pistol N° A2588B was part of the first military order of 1945. It lacks the magazine safety and was never officially accepted by the Belgian arsenals. The letter "B" was arsenal applied to indicate Armée Belge (Belgian Army). (Photograph by author, courtesy of Ron Pinkenburg)

Pistol N° A.B.27420 B.L. was shipped in 1950 during the regent years and does not feature a royal crest. Note the 46 arsenal acceptance marking (page 95) on the trigger-guard. Pistols after 1946 were equipped with a lanyard ring.

(Fig.307-2) Pistol N° A12466 with magazine safety was originally shipped in 1945 and accepted. It was arsenal reworked in the 1960s and painted gray (page 308), reworked again to include an updated slide with external extractor and ultimately fitted with MK.II grips. (Photograph courtesy of J. Weckx, B. V. V. W.)

(Fig.307-3) Factory roll engraved royal crests: King Leopold III (1951) and King Baudouin I (1952 and later). (Photographs courtesy of Bob Adams and J. Weckx, B. V. V. W.)

A Belgian soldier aims a postwar High power in the late 1940s, note the British supplied uniform.

Numbered Magazines and Gray Arsenal Paint

Free Belgian troops were equipped throughout the war by England. Britain continued to supply the Belgians after the liberation. British supplied uniforms, kit and Lee Enfield rifles were common in the 1940s. Handguns in use after the liberation included the prewar FN High Power, Colt 1911A1, prewar FN Model 1910, British Webley revolver and "A" prefix post liberation Model 1922 and High Power pistols.

The North Atlantic Treaty Organization (NATO), established in 1949, opened opportunities for NATO members to rearm and acquire new equipment. Under the Defense Appropriation Act of 1950, Canada was able to obtain new U.S. equipment to replace older equipment transferred to NATO members. Canada took advantage of Belgium's use of British equipment and supplied the Belgian War Department in 1950 with equipment for an entire infantry division including artillery, rifles and 1578 Inglis High Power pistols(1).

The pistols were early production guns of the Chinese pattern (slotted with tangent sights). The first production pistols suffered from reliability problems, due to the reverse engineering used to set up production as well as the conversion from metric to English standards. The manufacturer, Inglis in Toronto, addressed the problems with the aid of Belgian engineers (page 82-83) and had implemented the MK.I modification early in 1944. Most of its existing stockpiles at Inglis were retrofitted during the war to MK.I specifications. The pistols shipped to Belgium, however, were not, and were most likely the last unmodified group.

One of the key reliability issues was a failure to consistently feed rounds from the magazine. In response, Belgian armorers selected two working magazines and numbered these to the gun. In order to standardize procedure, the Belgians proceeded by numbering, at first, all High Power magazines and later other pistol magazines. Pistol magazines were not to be interchanged. The Inglis pistols were arsenal retrofitted and ultimately these were withdrawn from active service and stored. Although Belgian use of Inglis pistols was limited, the resulting practice of numbering magazines to specific pistols remained in effect for decades.

In the early 1970s the Belgian arsenal at Rocourt started a large weapons overhaul program that included all small arms, consolidating the work previously done at the Manufacture d'Armes de l'Etat and other small arsenals. Small arms requiring refinishing were painted with a light gray paint. By then, the Belgian military had gradually stepped away from bluing and was using FN's black enamel over a phosphate base. Under normal circumstances, overhauled guns were repainted with black enamel but instead a surplus gray paint was applied. It appears that the Belgian government ordered this paint for use on infrastructure, most notably the painting of steel bridges. The contract was canceled and the Belgian government ended up with large amounts of gray paint.

The feel and color of this paint has led to the erroneous conclusion that it is Teflon paint used exclusively by the Belgian Navy. Dupont did have a manufacturing plant in Belgium but was not known to supply the government, and the Belgian paint company that supplied the government had its own specialized paints. There is no conclusive way of telling if the paint is indeed a Dupont product or an alternative.

There was such an abundance of the surplus paint that it was used to refinish thousands of arms, parts and accessories. Its use was not specific to any branch of the military. Interviews with Navy personnel indicate that the Navy actually got less refurbished equipment than the other branches. Much of this refinished equipment was never used by the Belgian Navy. The following refinished arms and accessories have been noted: FAL (standard, Para and sniper versions), FAL scopes, MAG-58, MAG-58 mounts, 1950s Mauser Rifles, 22 caliber Mauser training rifles, FN-49 (standard and sniper versions), FN-49 scopes, BAR-D, BAR-D mounts, vehicle mounts, and High Power pistols (FN and Inglis manufacture), among others.

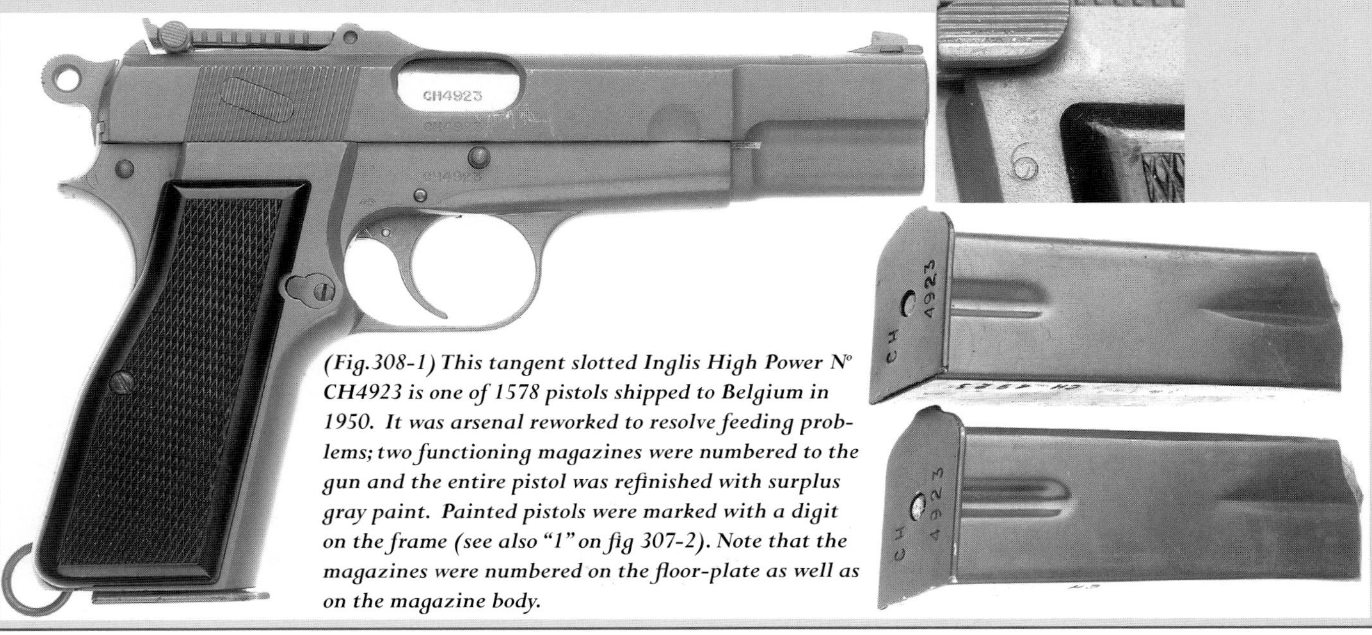

(Fig.308-1) This tangent slotted Inglis High Power N° CH4923 is one of 1578 pistols shipped to Belgium in 1950. It was arsenal reworked to resolve feeding problems; two functioning magazines were numbered to the gun and the entire pistol was refinished with surplus gray paint. Painted pistols were marked with a digit on the frame (see also "1" on fig 307-2). Note that the magazines were numbered on the floor-plate as well as on the magazine body.

Colonial Sales: The Belgian Congo

The Belgian Congo, established in 1908, relied mainly on goods from Belgium. Although the Congo was a colony, it was responsible for its own acquisitions. The Congolese force, known as the Force Publique, was not supplied by the Belgian military. The Ministry of Colonies purchased their armament according to requirements from the Congo and specifications defined in Belgium.

The High Power pistol was widely used by Force Publique officers, and was not available for commercial sale. Three Belgian Congo variations exist: one marked C.B. (Congo Belge – Belgian Congo) with crest, one marked "Etat" (State) with crest and one marked FP (Force Publique – Public Force) with crest.

The Force Publique was composed of Belgian officers and native troops and served in both military and law enforcement capacities, which included border patrols, riot control and plantation security. During World War I, the Force Publique fought with distinction against colonial German troops. During World War II, it fought several battles and was ultimately joined and supplied by British troops.

After the war, the Force Publique supplemented some of its British equipment and adopted the FN Mauser rifle in 1947-1948, a few years before Belgium did. High Powers were also ordered, although quantities were small. Orders increased during the 1950s when unrest was spreading throughout the colonies.

Pistols marked with the Etat (State) or C.B. (Congo Belge) marking were ordered for the ministry of finance including customs, advisors stationed in the Congo as well as administrators and other officials that required a sidearm.

Mutiny in the Force Publique led to the collapse of the colonial system. The Belgian Congo obtained independence on June 30, 1960. Civil unrest and secession plagued the country for many years and foreign forces and UN troops had to intervene to avoid total civil war. The newly independent country maintained strong ties with Belgium. Additional High Power pistols were purchased after 1960. These guns are marked ANC prior to the serial number. ANC stands for Armée Nationale Congolaise (National Army of the Congo). In 1971 the country's name was changed to Zaire, and in 1997, it became the Democratic Republic of Congo.

Most of the Congolese High Powers found on the market today, came from the November 24, 1964 rescue operation to evacuate civilian hostages kept in Stanleyville (now Kinshasa). The operation (Operation Dragon Rouge - Operation Red Dragon) was a joint effort between the U.S. Air Force, Belgian Paratroopers and Congolese regulars. At the same time quantities of captured arms and ammunition including High Power pistols were flown out of the Congo.

Some of the Force Publique orders, all pistols were delivered to the "Ministère des Colonies" (Ministry of Colonies):

- January 8, 1957:	**72 pistols with no special markings**
- May 16, 1957:	**500 pistols. Pistols were marked FP 1958 contract range 1-500**
- 1958-1959:	**Orders are unknown**
- September 3, 1959:	**800 pistols. Pistols were marked FP 1959 contract range 901-1700.**

(Fig.308-1) This 1959 contract pistol N° 011 was marked "Etat" (State). The slide was factory marked with the rampant Belgian lion surrounded by laurel leafs; a logo used in the Belgian Congo. Unlike the Force Publique officer's variant (fig.310-1), it was destined for government officials and administrators. It is not clear how its issue is different from the C.B. (Congo Belge) marked earlier pistols (fig.310-2). This pistol has a blue finish. "Etat" and "C.B." marked pistols are less common than the "F.P." marked variant. (Photograph courtesy of Philip Rotmans)

(1) Inglis Diamond, The Canadian High Power Pistol by Clive M. Law

(Fig.310-1) This 1959 contract pistol N° 322 was ordered for officers of the Force Publique. The slide was factory marked with the rampant Belgian lion surrounded by laurel leafs; a logo used in the Belgian Congo. This pistol has a blue finish. (Photographs by author, courtesy of Charles Bowles)

(Fig.310-2)

(Fig.310-2) This 1953 contract pistol N° 1-0145 was factory marked C.B. (Congo Belge with crest). It was destined for the ministry of finance, customs, advisors stationed in the Congo as well as government administrators. The number 1 preceding 0145 is not part of the contract number but indicates a series, this being the first order or series. This pistol has a black enamel finish. Note the "Crown 52" Belgian military acceptance marking on the trigger-guard.

(Fig.310-3) This contract gun N° T1261 was purchased by the independent state of the Congo. The "ANC" marking stands for Armée Nationale Congolaise (National Army of the Congo) followed by the 1964 issue year. Features are typical of post-1962 production and include the external extractor, black synthetic grips and the optional lanyard ring. No crests or other special markings were applied. (Photograph by author, courtesy of Ron Pinkenburg)

The Netherlands adopts the High Power

The Netherlands placed their first order for the High Power in 1946. The Dutch, like the Danes designated the pistol as M.46. This designation was quite common and was used by the factory, the Belgian military, and others. However it was soon eliminated or replaced in most countries.

The Dutch initial order was for 10,000 pistols(1), marked with the crest of Queen Wilhelmina on the top of the slide. Delivered in batches, the order was completed by the end of 1947. These pistols were destined for the Koninklijke Landmacht (Royal Army). The pistols were extensively used in the Dutch East Indies (Indonesia) between 1946 and 1950. Troops were dispatched from Holland in order to secure the colonies after the Japanese occupation and the proclamation of independence in 1945. The Dutch fought a counterinsurgency until December 1949.

Pistols ordered after 1948 were marked with the crest of Queen Juliana. Additional orders were shipped in 1949 and 1955. An order for 7000 pistols(1) was placed in 1960. A series of 20 special pistols(1) were part of that same order. On these, the location of the Juliana crest was moved forward in order for the pistols to accommodate a special sight. The Dutch supplied FN with adjustable sights and those were mounted at FN to create 20 competition pistols(1) for (international) shooting matches. The special competition pistols were numbered 64427-64446. The 1960 contract number range for standard military pistols started with N° 64447. Additional orders were placed staring in 1967.

Contract variants include navy pistols, which were roll engraved with an anchor instead of the Juliana crest(2). The Dutch Navy designated the High power as "Automatisch Pistool No. 6" (see page 205 for earlier designations). These pistols were originally finished in black enamel over a phosphate base with a phosphated barrel (see prewar Model 1910 fig.205-1). The navy ordered 4,250 FN High Power pistols(1) in the latter part of the 1950s. These pistols were factory marked with the anchor on top of the slide and were ordered with contract numbers from 0001 to 4250.

An additional order for 3000 pistols(1) was placed after 1968, these were contract numbered T4521-T7250. The original navy contract pistols were reworked to feature the external extractor. Reworked pistols were marked with a star symbol next to the contract number(1).

(Fig.311-1) This rare 1950s Dutch Navy contract pistol N° 4185 was arsenal reworked in the 1960s to include a slide with external extractor. Note the added contract number on the slide, followed by the star symbol indicating arsenal rework. Another star symbol was marked on the hammer. The navy crest (right) remained the same for the 1950s and 1960s contracts. Note the phosphate barrel for Navy use. (Photographs courtesy of Philip Rotmans)

(Fig.311-2) Starting in 1946 with the first Wilhelmina marked contract, the crest was always marked on the slide just forward of the rear sight. This location was standard for decades. (Photograph by author, courtesy of Kevin Null)

(Fig.311-3) Asides from the star symbol (see above), this symbol was also used to identify arsenal reworks. (Photographs courtesy of Philip Rotmans)

(1) Correspondence with Vincent Cozijn & Philip Rotmans

(2) Pistols with fake Dutch (navy) crests do circulate in the U.S., observed are 1950s German contract pistols with added crests.

(Fig.312-1) This rare Dutch army target pistol N° KL3443 was made to accommodate the Dutch provided target sights. Note that the Juliana crest was purposely engraved near the ejection port in order not be be obscured by the adjustable rear sights. Compare with the standard Juliana crest location (right). The "KL" marking before the contract number stands for "Koninklijke Landmacht" (Royal Army). (Photographs courtesy of Philip Rotmans)

The High Power in West Germany and Austria

West Germany and Austria were not allowed to manufacture arms after World War II. This led both countries to use and acquire foreign-made small arms both for military and law enforcement purposes.

Germany: High Powers were sold to German police forces starting in 1951 (see page 254 for postwar German police use of the Model 1922). Orders included 7500 High Powers for law enforcement use in North Rhine Westphalia(1). These were delivered in batches over several years. In addition the Munich Police and Bavarian border Guards used postwar FN guns as well as surplus wartime High Power pistols(1). The High Powers were used until 1965 when they were replaced by P-38 pistols. The German High Powers were taken out of service by 1969 and sold on the surplus market. Surplus pistols sold in Germany were usually marked with a retailer marking while those sold in the U.S. did not get any additional markings. Some pistols used by the North Rhine Westphalia departments can have a three or four digit inventory number under or above the wooden grips(1).

German law enforcement pistols cannot easily be identified as they do not have any distinct property markings. Pistols were standard commercial production pistols with standard FN serial numbers. The serial range of these pistols is quite large; between 28,000 and 60,000(1). Some pistols have an "E" prefix serial number which has often incorrectly been attributed to the British L9A1 contract. There is no indication that the "E" serial number prefix had any relation to the British contracts, being instead a FN inventory control method (like the T prefix) to manage large production numbers. German police pistols were issued with numbered black leather (P-38 style) holsters, many of these pistols were sold in the U.S. with their matching holster. The matching holster is an easy indicator of German use.

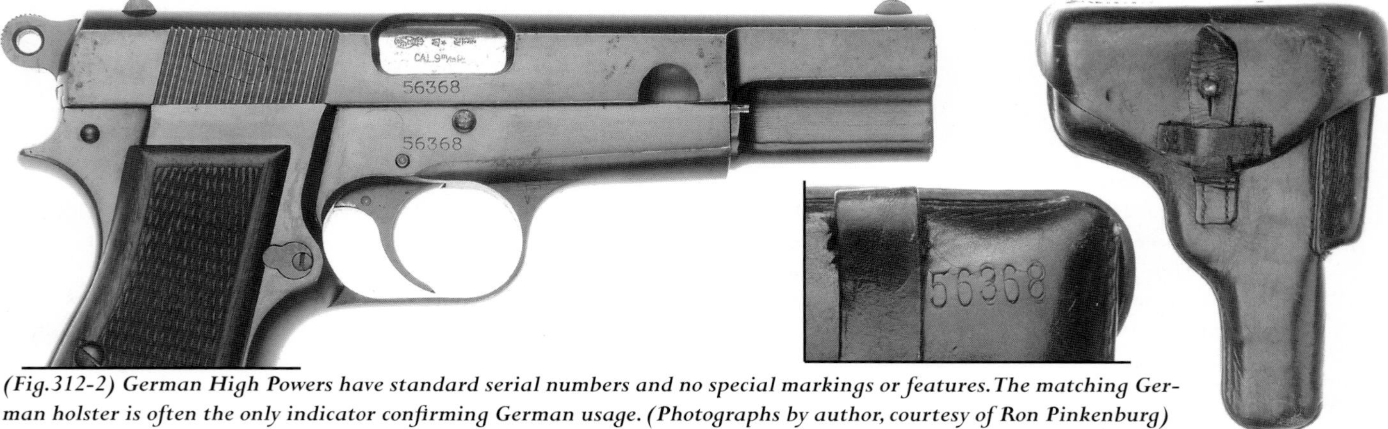

(Fig.312-2) German High Powers have standard serial numbers and no special markings or features. The matching German holster is often the only indicator confirming German usage. (Photographs by author, courtesy of Ron Pinkenburg)

The High Power in West Germany and Austria (continued)

Austria: The Austrian Bundesheer (Army) used approximately 500 High Power pistols between 1955 and 1965[(1)]. These pistols were a mixture of newly acquired FN commercial and wartime surplus High Powers.

The Austrian Federal Gendarmerie started using the High Power in 1949. Like the military, the pistols in use were a mixture of newly acquired commercial guns as well as surplus wartime pistols[(1)]. In 1955 the decision was made to standardize the High Power for the Federal Gendarmerie and a large order for 10,000 pistols was placed. So many pistols were ordered that many remained in arsenals unused in their factory box. Issued pistols as well as those in inventory were marked "LGK" (Landesgendarmeriekommando – State Gendarmerie) followed by a two letter abbreviation for the province in where the pistol was used and the pistol issue number. The markings were applied in Austria to the front grip-strap and to the two magazines issued with the gun. A few pistols were marked "GEK" designating use by the Gendarmerie Einsatz Kommando (Gendarmerie Intervention Unit).

No special markings or contract ranges were ordered from FN, as such most pistols have standard FN serial numbers while some have "E" prefix serial numbers. The Austrian High Powers remained in active service until 1994 when these were replaced by Glocks. Most were sold on the U.S. surplus market, many showed little or no use for being stored un-issued for decades.

Following is a list of provincial identification markings. The list gradually shows the most common (top) to the rarest (bottom) according to their issue quantity.

LGK W :	**Wien (Vienna)**
LGK NO :	**Niederösterreich (Lower Austria)**
LGK OO :	**Oberösterreich (Upper Austria)**
LGK ST :	**Steiermark (Styria)**
LGK T :	**Tirol (Tyrol)**
LGK K :	**Kärnten (Carinthia)**
LGK SB :	**Salzburg Land**
LGK V :	**Vorarlberg**
LGK B :	**Burgenland**

(Fig.313-1) Most Austrian purchases have standard serial numbers, some have "E" prefix numbers. This Austrian Gendarmerie pistol N° E07579 was marked in Austria "LGK K 1068" on the front grip-strap and magazines. The markings indicate gendarmerie use in the province of Carinthia, the pistol has the issue number 1068. Austrian police pistols have no special factory applied markings or options, these have the high quality standards of 1950s manufacture. (Photograph by author, courtesy of Wendell Patton)

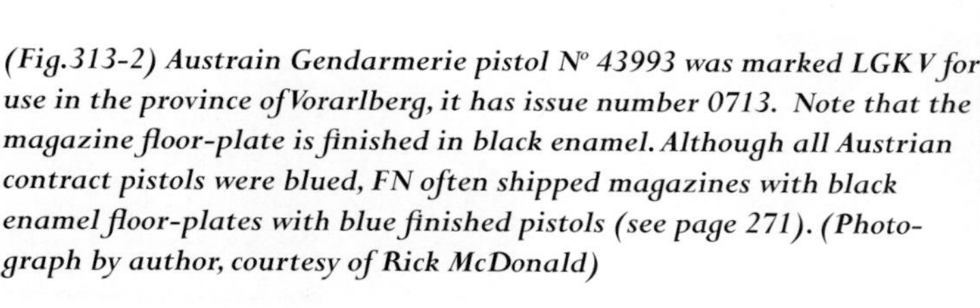

(Fig.313-2) Austrain Gendarmerie pistol N° 43993 was marked LGK V for use in the province of Vorarlberg, it has issue number 0713. Note that the magazine floor-plate is finished in black enamel. Although all Austrian contract pistols were blued, FN often shipped magazines with black enamel floor-plates with blue finished pistols (see page 271). (Photograph by author, courtesy of Rick McDonald)

(1) Hi Powers of Germany by Reinhard J. Henke - Browning Collectors Association Newsletter

The British L9A1

Great Britain had a sufficient amount of Inglis surplus pistols on hand in the immediate postwar era. As the wartime pistols were aging, Canadian Arsenals restarted production in 1952 of the wartime (Inglis) High Power under the nomenclature "No2 Mk2". This move was controversial as the licensing agreements with FN had ended with the war.

By that time the British government had already authorized the appropriation of new FN High Powers from Belgium. It is unclear why Great Britain did not acquire new Canadian pistols, as all parts were interchangeable with their existing inventory. The 1950s British High Powers did not get the L9A1 nomenclature initially. The pistols shipped from FN had an "E" prefix in the serial number. This does not stand for "English" or "Export". Almost all High Power pistols were built for export and the British military did not use the term "English" for identification.

The "E" prefix was initiated by the factory as production numbers were nearing serial number 100,000. This was nothing more than an inventory control method to manage the increasing production quantities and serial numbers. This prefix can be found in many contracts of that era as well as commercial pistols, adding to the confusion. The British contract was most likely the first to be issued with this new prefix.

In 1964 the Ministry of Defense tested the latest High Power variant with an external extractor. The pistol was accepted and designated L9A1. Although all High Powers purchased by NATO members were identified with NATO stock numbers (NSN), only the L9A1 was marked with NATO numbers. British specifications included:

NSN on all major parts like the slide, frame, barrel and magazine
"FN" and the year of manufacture on slide, barrel and magazine
"Pistol Automatic L9A1" incorporated into the slide legend

The marking specifications were relaxed after the initial order, and the "L9A1" designation was not always included in the factory applied slide legend. The NSN number was also omitted from the frame.

The L9A1 became, and remains the standard pistol for the UK. Great Britain purchased extensive amounts of the L9A1. Many of the pistols were sold to the Commonwealth and countries under British influence. Consequently the L9A1 is being used in India, Botswana, Malawi, Malaysia and Nepal. Other countries of the Commonwealth like Canada, Australia and New Zealand also purchased the pistol directly from FN.

(Fig.314-1) This British contract L9A1 pistol N° T125829 includes all the British specifications. The NATO stock number (NSN) is typically found on the barrel, frame, slide and magazines. The NSN number is broken down in the following data: 1005: Ordnance material up to 30mm 13: NCB code for country of manufacturing. 13 is the code for Belgium - 010-0313: serial number dictated by purchaser, insignificant to NATO. (Photographs by author, courtesy of Ron Pinkenburg)

The Alleged U.S. Oman Contract

Confirming the origin of these alleged Omani pistols is challenging as the key individual involved in the contract passed away years ago. The following information was gathered through interviews of individuals involved at the time.

In the late 1960s, Mr. Paul Van Hee was involved with the sale of Cadillac Gage's Commando armored cars to the Omani government. Oman requested FN MAG-58 general purpose machineguns (GPMG) as part of the armament. This request, among others, had established a relationship between Van Hee or Cadillac Gage and FN. During the contract negotiations, Van Hee learned that Oman was interested in acquiring the High Power pistol as a standard military sidearm. Although not an agent or FN representative, Van Hee attempted to secure a contract with Oman for large quantities of High Power pistols.

Several pistols with various features and finishes were shipped from FN to the U.S. in April 1969. These pistols were shipped without any special crests and were sold at standard FN prices. Everything indicates that the pistols were roll engraved with the Omani crest in the U.S. Allegedly 36 pistols with various features and finishes were roll engraved on the slide with a crest. The first nine pistols were roll marked with an error in the crest, the consequent 27 pistols had the corrected crest.

The pistols were shown and demonstrated to an Omani delegation. However there is no indication that these pistols were ever in or used by Oman; these were strictly sales samples for an attempt to secure a contract. FN learned about the dealings, intervened and sold 5000 pistols directly to Oman. It is reported that the 36 pistols were sold for $395 each to a gun dealer after the contract negotiations failed. All were tangent slotted pistols, new in styrofoam boxes. Some had lanyard rings, plastic or wooden grips and there were examples of various finishes including blue and black enamel.

These pistols have been misrepresented as being authentic contract guns. Many of these pistols have been paired with postwar shoulder-stocks in attempts to create the appearance of original rigs. Although it is possible that shoulder-stocks were originally demonstrated, the shoulder-stocks that surface with these pistols today are not all from the proper era. In the past years, a few authentic contract pistols have been reported as coming from the Middle-East.

(Fig.315-1) Pistol Nº T152252 is one of the first nine sales samples with incorrect crest. The scabbard of the dagger points to the right instead of the left. This is one of the various options and finish combinations available; this pistol has a black enamel finish including barrel, lanyard ring and black Cycolac synthetic grips. (Photographs by author, courtesy of Ron Pinkenburg)

(Fig.315-2) Pistol Nº T1177360 is one of the sales samples with correct crest, although the figures above the crest are unknown. This is one of the various options and finish combinations available; this pistol has a blue finish with standard barrel, lanyard ring and black Cycolac synthetic grips. The crest markings are less deep than typical FN applied crests.

U.S. Law Enforcement Imports: Howco

In the 1970s, FN established a separate police and law enforcement sales department. This department sought to market FN products in the USA but opted not to work with Browning. The goal was to separate the FN products from the commercial Browning line. This allowed the marketing of military products that Browning did not distribute, and allowed the marketing of the High Power in finishes and with different features that were not handled by Browning.

Instead of establishing a FN sales office in the U.S., FN entered into agreements with U.S. importers and distributors. These distributors were, in many ways, assuming the role of FN agents. Distribution was limited to firearms that could be sold both to law enforcement and the commercial market. Restricted (select fire) arms were available on special order. FN ensured that the distributors attended trade shows, and provided sales samples and show materials. Promoting the line to law enforcement agencies was a requirement. Three companies were involved with distributing the FN High Power, the FN FAL and FN FNC; these were Howco in Maryland, GunSouth in Alabama and Steyr in New Jersey.

Howco promoted the High power to the FBI. It is not clear if any trials were performed or if this extended only to some demonstrations. No official FBI contract was secured. Howco did market the High Power as the Model 88 and these were factory marked with this designation. It is not clear where this model designation originated. Howco pistols were imported between 1980 and 1984, many were MK.II High Powers in phosphate or black enamel finish with, or without lanyard ring.

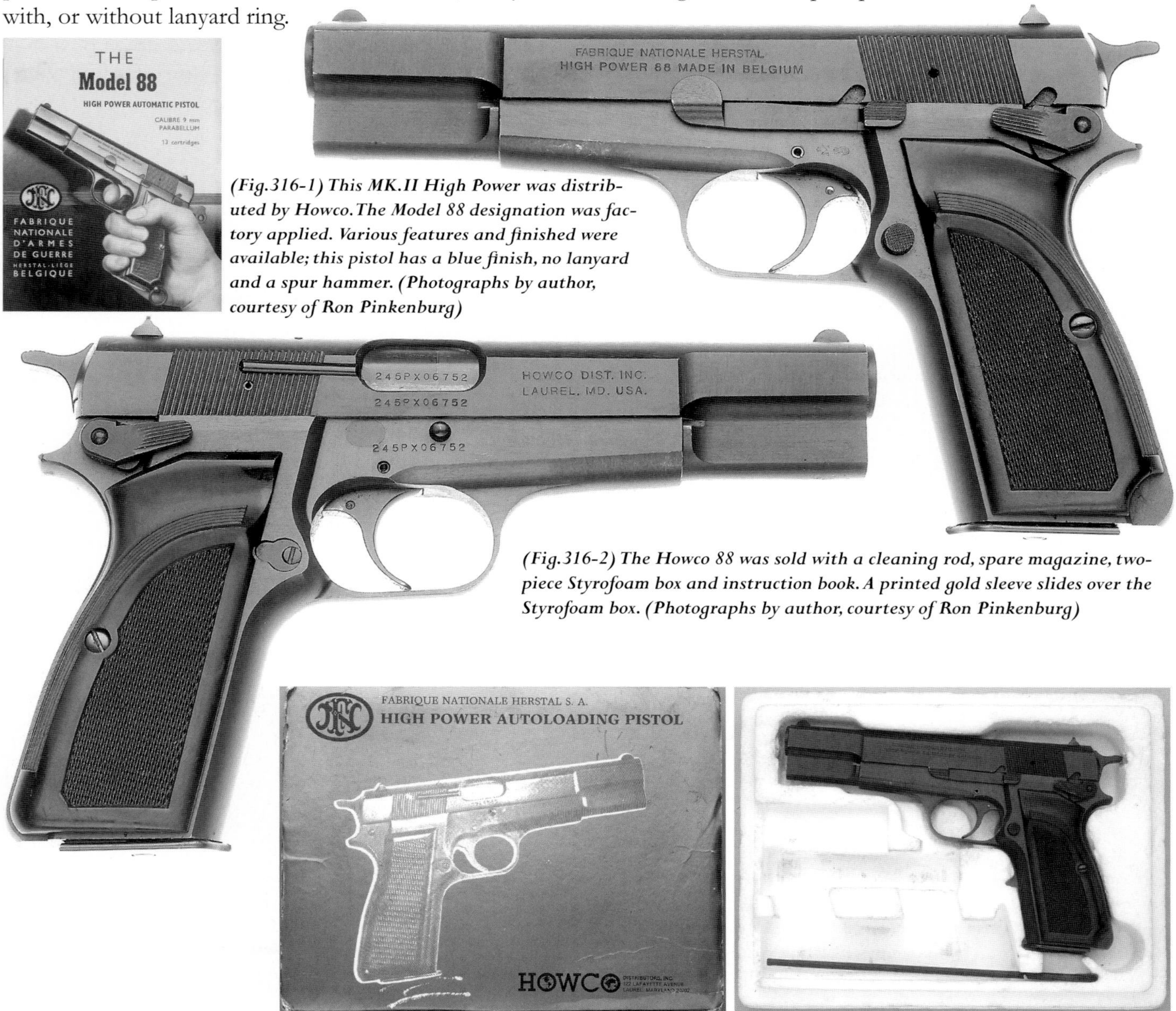

(Fig.316-1) This MK.II High Power was distributed by Howco. The Model 88 designation was factory applied. Various features and finished were available; this pistol has a blue finish, no lanyard and a spur hammer. (Photographs by author, courtesy of Ron Pinkenburg)

(Fig.316-2) The Howco 88 was sold with a cleaning rod, spare magazine, two-piece Styrofoam box and instruction book. A printed gold sleeve slides over the Styrofoam box. (Photographs by author, courtesy of Ron Pinkenburg)

Mass production, Production Simplifications and the Developments of the Classic High Power

When NATO adopted the High Power as a standard sidearm, it became the most prolific handgun in the world. FN was working with an entire line of successful designs and was a one-stop small arms supplier. The High Power, FAL and MAG-58 equipped hundreds of countries. There are more than 250 postwar High Power marking variations. Many countries purchased High Powers over a number of years for various branches of their military and law enforcement, and required a number of different markings. FN standardized the location of roll engraved crests on the top of the slide just forward of the rear sight. Illustrating all these variations is unpractical, many of these pistols are still in use and samples are not available for review.

Increasing labor costs and high demand forced FN to streamline the High Power's production. For the purist, these changes often diminish the collectable value of the later High Powers. Following is a list of changes that were introduced in the postwar era to reduce costs and speed up production:

1960: **Elimination of the Thumb Print depression on the slide. This machined depression was intended to facilitate charging the slide with the left hand, an alternative method to using the rear slide serration and a remnant of a common prewar practice. It also aided in the disassembly of the pistol.**

1962-1963: Replacement of the internal extractor to external model. The external model eliminated extensive machining of the slide and the extractor itself was simpler and less expensive to machine. The external extractor pivots and the resistance is controlled by a spring making it more durable than the older internal model which flexed the steel of the extractor without the use of a spring. Although deemed an improvement, the external extractor deters from the pistol's aesthetics.

1962-1963: FN discontinues the old appealing rust blue finish and replaces it with salt bluing. This process creates a black-blue finish and speeds up the bluing process significantly.

1962-1963: Aluminum magazine followers are replaced by plastic.

1962-1963: High impact strength, chemical resistant, Cycolac ABS synthetic grips are introduced.

1963-1964: The T-series of pistols are introduced. The "T" prefix is nothing more than a production and inventory control aid for FN. The method of managing high production volumes had been introduced in the 1950s with the "E" prefix but unlike the "E" prefix, all production starting in 1963 was marked with the "T" prefix. The "T" prefix series is often regarded by collectors as the last of the highly finished High Power pistols, although these were finished with salt bluing, the amount of polishing and bluing still reflected a great deal of hand fitting and finishing. This level of finish ended with the T-series (1969) and the automation of polishing and bluing in 1970.

1969: **The T-series is replaced by the C-series. The new C-series incorporates the last two digits of the production year prior to the letter "C" which is followed by the serial number. (ex; 69C1550: 1969 Production, C-series, serial number 1550)**

1969-1970: Polishing and bluing are highly automated. FN information refers to the bluing as electrolyte bluing (page 69).

1971: **The location of the serial number is moved from the right side of the frame to the front grip strap. Serial numbers are eliminated from the slide on select export commercial guns like the Browning Arms Company guns.**

1971: **Factory markings like slide markings and serial numbers are applied using faster and modern machinery resulting in obvious lighter (less deeply struck) markings.**

1972: **The spur hammer is introduced and requires less machining. The classic round hammer becomes an option.**

1972: **The adjustable rear sight (with higher front sight) is introduced.**

1975: **The "C" serial number series is replaced with a coded system. The new system reflects use of computer systems available at the time. The first three digits refer to the model number. The model number is determined by the pistol's application and features (like grips, sights, etc). The three digits are followed by two letters designating the production year. These are followed by the pistol's serial number. Following are the early letter codes for identifying production years:**

RV = 1975	**RT = 1976**	**RR = 1977**	**RP = 1978**	**RN = 1979**	**PM = 1980**	**PZ = 1981**
PY = 1982	**PX = 1983**	**PW = 1984**	**PV = 1985**	**PT = 1986**	**PR = 1987**	**PP = 1988**
PN = 1989	**N series 1990s**					

(Fig.317-1) A summery of features of the 1970s High Power: External extractor introduced in 1962, black Cycolac synthetic grips (1962), salt bluing (1962) with automated polishing (1970), "C" series serial number (1969) with serial number visible on front grip-strap (1971) and Liège proof visible on trigger-guard (1970s).

1980: Assembly and finishing of High Power pistols is transferred to Viana, Portugal. Standard commercial guns are assembled in Portugal and so marked. FN does however continue to produce and assemble entire pistols in Herstal for military contracts, special configurations like the competition model as well as special orders for the custom shop.
1981: The MK.II High Power is introduced
1989: The MK.III High Power is introduced, and remains available to this day.

Efforts to modernize the High Power date back to the early 1950s when Dieudonné Saive developed the first double-action High Power. As time passed, it became apparent that more modern versions of the classic single-action were needed. The MK.II configuration was a cosmetic update (with the exception of the ambidextrous safety lever). Efforts to market a double-action High Power model continued and the HP-DA was available outside of the U.S. in the 1980s. It was available in double-action (DA) or double-action only (DAO). Although these pistols resemble the High Power, they are a departure from the original design with only few interchangeable parts. The magazines are not interchangeable.

The .30 caliber model first appeared in the mid 1970s, it was primarily made for the commercial market in Germany and France where military ammunition is restricted. Destined for sale by Browning International, about 1500 were imported into the U.S. by private importers (1986-1989). Sales in the U.S. were mediocre as there was little reason to select a .30 caliber version over the original 9mm pistol. The .30 caliber pistols, as well as the later 1980s Competition model (fig.330-2), were not serviced by Browning.

A .40 S&W caliber single-action High Power was introduced in the 1980s. This was coupled with the introduction of a reinforced cast frame due necessary to cope with the increased pressure and velocities of the .40 caliber. This change was introduced at different times on the different variants. All .40 caliber pistols and Competition pistols have cast frames while MK.II pistols and .30 caliber pistols have either forged (early) or cast frames. The cast frame had no negative impact on performance or finish but was stronger and easier to manufacture.

A slightly updated MK.III version (9mm or .40 cal.) with a passive firing pin safety was introduced in 1989 and remains available to this day. The SFS (Safe-Fast Shooting system; e.g. the hammer is automatically cocked when the safety lever is lowered) variant of the MK.III was launched in 1996. The patented design is not FN's but belongs to the Liège company R.D.I.H. and was a combined venture to bring the MK.III to market with the SFS system. Although the classic High Power is no longer cataloged, it remains available on special order and is available for custom engraving.

(Fig.318-1) This unnumbered and unproofed .30 caliber prototype features a cast frame, wide trigger, spur hammer and adjustable sights. The lanyard was most likely not specified for this prototype but rather already installed on an available frame. (Photograph by author, courtesy of Carlos Davila)

(Fig.318-2) This Fast Action prototype (N° H009) is one of 11 made, the FA concept of the late 1970s was a predecessor of the SFS system. Like the SFS system, the energy to cock the hammer is stored in the hammer spring, the intial travel of the trigger releases the hammer into the cocked position, this differentiates from the SFS system where the hammer is cocked by disengaging the safety. (Photograph by author, courtesy of Rick McDonald)

The Evolution of the Model 1910 & 1922:

The Models 110, 115, 120, 125, 130

The U.S. Gun Control Act of 1968 initiated the development of the model 100-series pistols. Under new regulations Browning could no longer import the Model 1910, which was commonly known in the U.S. as the Model 1955. At Browning's request, FN created the Model 130 in 1969. The Model 130 satisfied the new import requirements and was imported in volume in 1971. The U.S. designation was the Browning Model 10/71. The Model 130 (Browning 10/71) was the only 100-series model to be imported into the U.S.

In the years that followed, FN created a line of pistols based on modernized Model 1910 and 1922 designs. It is likely that this line of pistols was developed on Dutch request. Holland continued to be an important FN customer after World War II. Almost all of the pistols used by the Dutch military and law enforcement agencies were made by FN. Holland was the only country to purchase significant numbers of 100-series pistols. Interestingly, the 100-series pistols seldom appear in any period factory catalogs. The majority are found in Europe, and those are concentrated in the Netherlands.

The Model 110

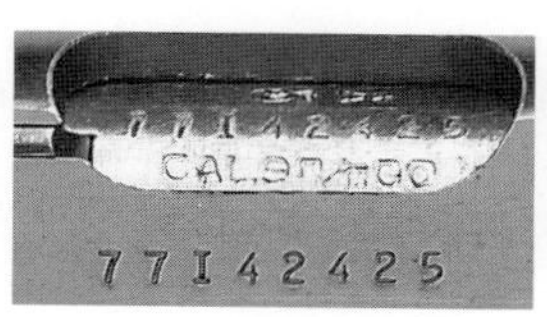

Modernized version of the Model 1910 with similar dimensions
Cocked indicator
Wider grip safety
Raised fixed sights, with a rounded slide top (not matted as the Model 1910)
Standard Model 1910 sized grips
Accepts Model 1910, 110 and 115 magazines
Introduced circa 1975, available until 1983

(Fig.319-1) The Model 110 closely resembles the Model 1910. Note the standard magazine well opening on the frame, compare with fig. 319-2. The serial number is applied on the front grip-strap, the slide and barrel. The grips feature the Browning name and not the FN logo.

It should be noted that there are 110 models in Holland that deviate from the specifications noted above. These are Model 1910s modified to Model 110 specifications. These guns have raised sights but retain remnants of the matted slide top.

The Model 115

(Fig.319-2) The Model 115 differentiates from the Model 110 in the shape of the magazine well opening, note the raised opening for the Model 115 magazine on the front grips-strap. The grips are oversized and feature a thumb-rest. The right grip features the Browning name and not the FN logo. (Photograph by author, courtesy of Dolf Voerman)

Modernized version of the Model 1910 with similar frame and slide dimensions
Raised fixed sights, with a round top of the slide (not matted as the Model 1910)
Cocked indicator
Wider grip safety
Larger grips, featuring a thumb-rest
The Model 115 magazine incorporates a synthetic finger rest, enhancing the grip size and feel. The Model 115 will function with 1910 magazines but inserting and removing 1910 magazines can be cumbersome.
Introduced circa 1975, available until 1983

The Model 120

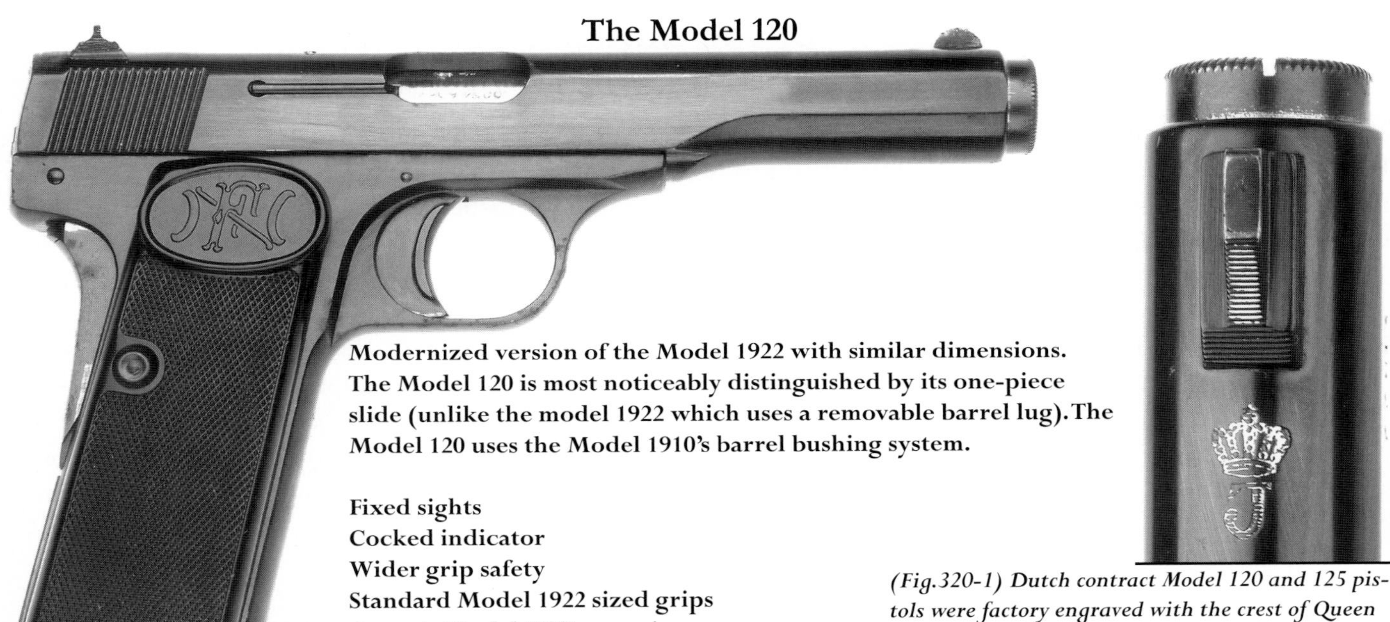

Modernized version of the Model 1922 with similar dimensions. The Model 120 is most noticeably distinguished by its one-piece slide (unlike the model 1922 which uses a removable barrel lug). The Model 120 uses the Model 1910's barrel bushing system.

Fixed sights
Cocked indicator
Wider grip safety
Standard Model 1922 sized grips
Accepts Model 1922 magazines
Introduced circa 1975, available until 1983

(Fig.320-1) Dutch contract Model 120 and 125 pistols were factory engraved with the crest of Queen Juliana near the front sight. Note the long barrel bushing, standard on 100-series pistols. (Photograph by author, courtesy of Michael Shade)

The Model 125

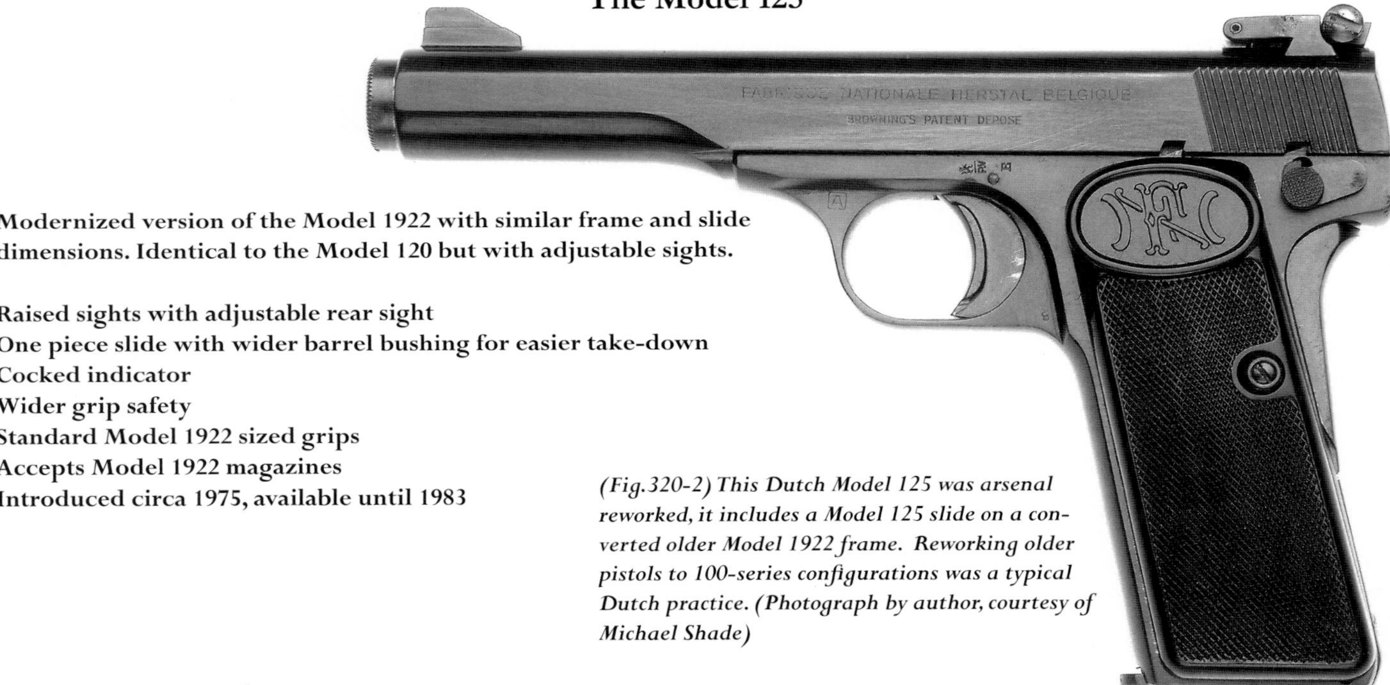

Modernized version of the Model 1922 with similar frame and slide dimensions. Identical to the Model 120 but with adjustable sights.

Raised sights with adjustable rear sight
One piece slide with wider barrel bushing for easier take-down
Cocked indicator
Wider grip safety
Standard Model 1922 sized grips
Accepts Model 1922 magazines
Introduced circa 1975, available until 1983

(Fig.320-2) This Dutch Model 125 was arsenal reworked, it includes a Model 125 slide on a converted older Model 1922 frame. Reworking older pistols to 100-series configurations was a typical Dutch practice. (Photograph by author, courtesy of Michael Shade)

The Model 130 (U.S. Browning 10/71)

The Model 130 combines the frame of the Model 115 with thumb-rest grips and a finger rest magazine together with the slide of the Model 125.

One piece slide with wider barrel bushing for easier take-down
Raised sights with adjustable rear sight
Cocked indicator
Wider grip safety
Larger grips with thumb-rest
The 115 magazine incorporates a synthetic finger rest, enhancing the grip size and feel. The Model 130 will function with 1910 magazines but inserting and removing 1910 magazines can be cumbersome.
Introduced by FN in 1970

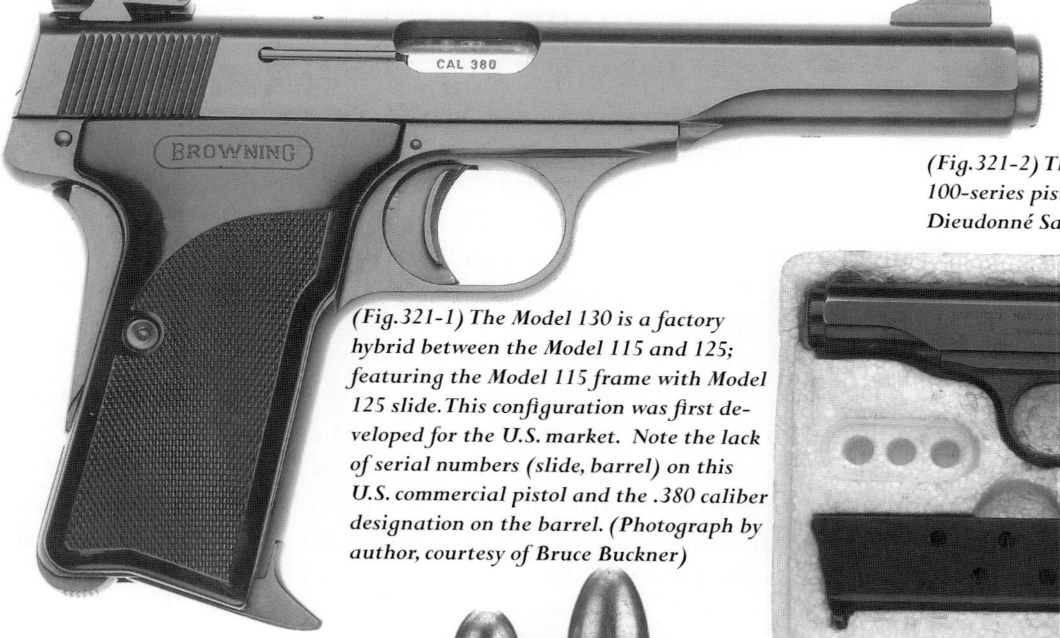

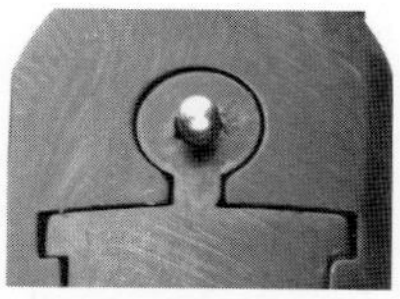

(Fig.321-1) The Model 130 is a factory hybrid between the Model 115 and 125; featuring the Model 115 frame with Model 125 slide. This configuration was first developed for the U.S. market. Note the lack of serial numbers (slide, barrel) on this U.S. commercial pistol and the .380 caliber designation on the barrel. (Photograph by author, courtesy of Bruce Buckner)

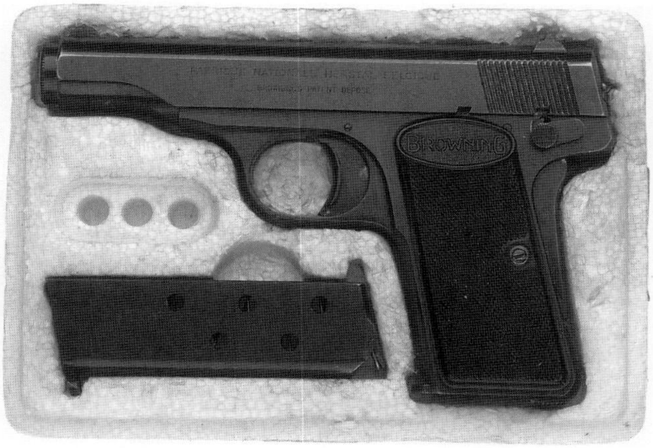

(Fig.321-2) The cocked indicator is standard on 100-series pistols. It was originally developed by Dieudonné Saive in 1927 for the Baby Browning.

(Fig.321-3) Sales of 100-series pistols outside of the U.S. included a two-piece Styrofoam box with cardboard sleeve, spare magazine, three dummy rounds and cleaning rod (fitted under pistol).

(Fig.321-4) It is not clear when FN started including three dummy rounds with each pistol. Dummy rounds were either cross-drilled or lacked a primer. The casing and bullet typically have a nickel appearance. Seen here are 7.65 and 9 mm dummy rounds.

The Model 140 (Browning BDA)

The Model 140 was included in this series, although its design did not evolve from a Browning design. The Model 140 was introduced in 1978, years after FN acquired partial ownership into the Beretta company in 1972. The frame was a Beretta design, the slide was designed by Magi Almara, an Argentine DGFM engineer who was contracted and on loan especially for this project. Mr. Almara worked on the slide design at FN for about a year before returning to Argentina.

The Model 140 was designated as the Browning BDA (Browning Double Action) in the U.S. The Model 140 was sold by FN in both .380 as well as .32 caliber with black synthetic grips (wooden grips were optional). The U.S. market got the .380 caliber version with wooden grips, embellished with a Browning medallion inset standard. A nickel-chrome version was also available, it was marketed as "nickel finish". All pistols were made in Italy by Beretta.

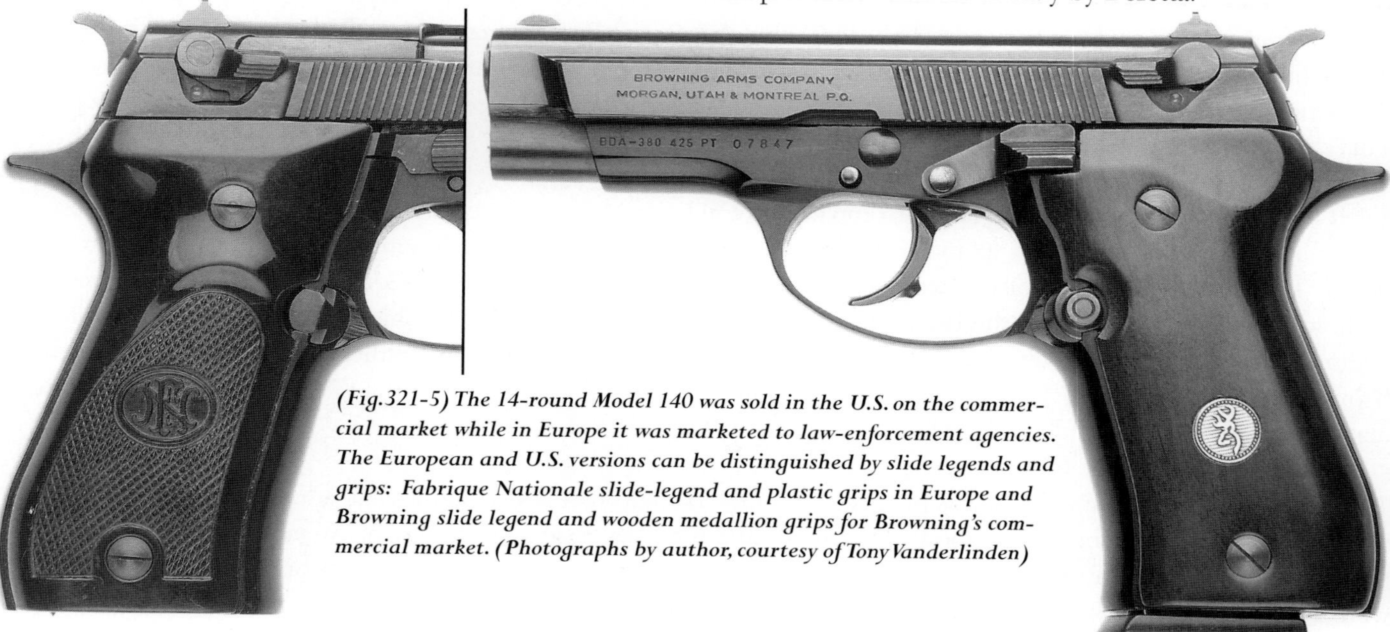

(Fig.321-5) The 14-round Model 140 was sold in the U.S. on the commercial market while in Europe it was marketed to law-enforcement agencies. The European and U.S. versions can be distinguished by slide legends and grips: Fabrique Nationale slide-legend and plastic grips in Europe and Browning slide legend and wooden medallion grips for Browning's commercial market. (Photographs by author, courtesy of Tony Vanderlinden)

Browning Arms Company Pistols

by Bruce Buckner

Browning Arms Company of St. Louis Missouri started importing handguns under its own trademark in 1954. The guns were marked "Browning Arms Company" (BAC) and were produced under contract by Fabrique Nationale (FN) in Belgium. They were identical (except for the markings) to pistols made and sold by FN in many other countries around the world. The models imported included the .25 Caliber Automatic Pistol (sometimes called the "Baby"), the .380 Caliber Automatic Pistol (sometimes called the Model 1955) and the 9mm Parabellum Automatic Pistol (commonly called the "Hi-Power[(1)]") in standard (blue) and Renaissance (engraved) finishes[(2)]. The Renaissance guns were finished in bright nickel[(3)(5)] with full coverage factory engraving.

Examination of 1950s factory catalogs and price lists shows that the full line of center-fire pistols was imported in 1954 with one possible exception. Specifically, the Browning dealer price list for July 1954 does not show the .25 Caliber Lightweight Pistol. The first mention of the .25 Caliber Lightweight is in a price list dated June 1956. However, there exists at least one Lightweight, serial number 133960, which Browning verified as having been shipped in 1955. The blue and Renaissance pistols had steel frames and slides, whereas the Lightweight .25 Caliber Pistol had an aluminum alloy (Duraluminum) frame with a bright nickel finished[(4)] steel slide (see also page 258).

Initially, all the standard pistols and the .25 Caliber Lightweights were imported in appropriately sized black display cases with red interiors. These cases were marked with the Browning name and were usually stamped "Made in Belgium" on the outside bottom. Each case came with a small silver paper insert identifying the caliber of the pistol. The serial number of the pistol was written on a white label, which was applied to the bottom or side of the box. The cases were protected by plain cardboard sleeves, which were sometimes marked with the serial number of the pistol. The Renaissance pistols came in nicer "French fitted" blue velvet presentation cases, which had metal latches and hinges. Again, the cases were marked with the Browning name and were marked on the inside "Made in Belgium". These cases were not marked with the gun's serial number. Renaissance pistols were offered cased singly and as three-gun sets in a special presentation case from the very beginning of importation (1954). Standard finish three-gun sets were also available in 1954.

The .25 Caliber Automatic Pistol was produced with either a blue (standard) finish, Renaissance engraving or as the Lightweight model. The caliber marking, "6m/m35", was stamped on the barrel and the guns had the usual Belgian proof marks. The standard version had black plastic grips with the Browning name molded into the plastic. The Renaissance and Lightweight models were fitted with synthetic mother-of-pearl grips, which Browning called "Nacrolac Pearl". Throughout production, the frame and barrel were marked with the full serial number of the gun and the slide was marked inside with the last four digits. The Renaissance and Lightweight models had gold plated triggers. The magazines were either blued or finished in bright nickel (Renaissance and Lightweight) and marked with the "FN" logo on the side or bottom. The .25 Caliber Automatic Pistol remained essentially unchanged throughout production until the 1968 Gun Control Act (GCA) prohibited further importation. A blue steel trigger was used throughout the BAC production. In 1968 a black plastic trigger was introduced with some standard blue finish pistols. This change appeared at the very end of U.S. importation.

Serial numbering of the Browning Arms Company .25 Caliber pistol is not well documented. FN produced these pistols under its own name prior to and concurrently with the model's introduction into the USA under the Browning name. The Browning marked pistols were numbered within the FN serial number sequence. Some sources incorrectly show the serial numbering of the Browning pistol beginning with "1" in 1954. The .25 Caliber Automatic Pistol is sometimes called the "Pocket Model[(4)]" or "Baby" by U.S. collectors. However, neither of those terms was used in Browning factory literature. In fact, the "Baby" designation should be reserved for the FN pistol whose grips were marked with that name.

The .380 Caliber Automatic Pistol was produced in both standard blue finish and Renaissance engraving. The barrel was marked with the caliber designation, "9m/m00", and the usual Belgian proof marks. The full serial number of the pistol was marked on the frame, barrel and slide throughout production. Magazines were blue or bright nickel and were usually marked "FN 9m/m" on the side (see fig.196-3).

(Fig.323-1) Examples of early Browning Arms Company .25 and .380 Caliber Automatic Pistols with black and red display cases for the standard pistols and French fitted blue velvet presentation cases for the Renaissance models. (Photographs by author, courtesy of Bruce Buckner)

(1) FN's English terminology for the Model 1935 was spelled out as "High Power", the Browning Arms Company used the shorter "Hi-Power" .

(2) "Renaissance engraving" is a marketing term used by the Browning Arms Company, the engraving pattern is FN's postwar Type III.

(3) Although marketed by Browning as a nickel finish from 1955 through 1960, the plating was actually a chrome or nickel-chrome plating. This finish is distinctively different and harder than FN's (prewar) nickel finish. Browning updated the "nickel' description in 1961 to "chrome", even if the plating remained identical. Browning continued to use the word "nickel" to describe various plating looks like "satin nickel".

(4) This term is incorrectly used as the proper Pocket Model or Vest Pocket Model is the FN Model 1905/1906 (see page 182).

(5) Few factory original blue Renaissance pistols were sold in the U.S. by Browning, most were special orders or were shipped to Browning if FN or Browning International had extra inventory. Original blue Renaissance pistols are rare in the U.S. and require provenance documentation to confirm originality.

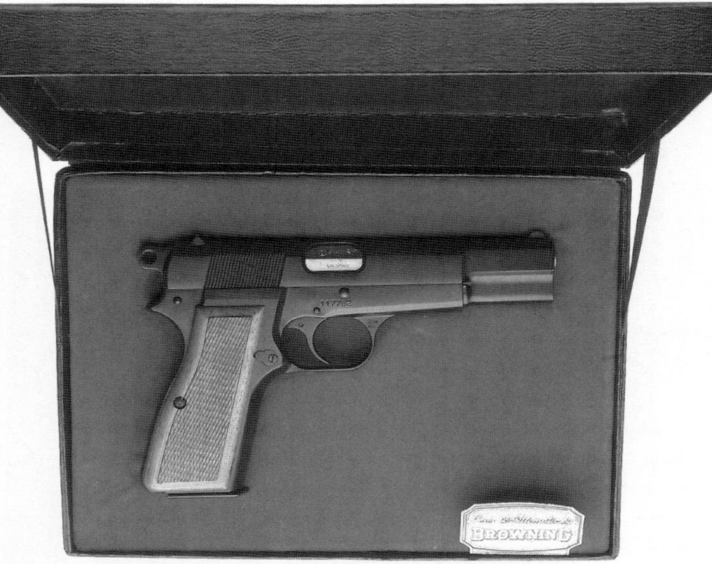

(Fig.324-1) Early Browning Arms Company Hi-Power Pistols with black and red display case for the standard pistol and French fitted blue velvet presentation case for the Renaissance model. (Photographs by author, courtesy of Bruce Buckner)

Grips were either black plastic (with the Browning name) for the standard model or Nacrolac Pearl (Renaissance). The Renaissance model had a gold trigger. Initially, the standard pistol had a blue steel trigger but about 1967 it was changed to black plastic. FN used the synthetic trigger only for known commercial pistols, steel triggers remained in production for pistols destined for military or law-enforcement use. Like the .25 caliber pistol, this gun remained essentially unchanged (except for the trigger) until importation ceased in 1968.

The serial numbering scheme for the .380 caliber pistol is more confusing than that of the .25 caliber pistol. Some sources incorrectly show the numbering to begin with "1" in 1954 and to end in even thousands every year until 1965. FN had been producing the Model 1910 pistol for many years and the Browning Arms Company marked .380 Caliber Automatic Pistol, essentially the same gun, was numbered in FN's standard serial number range.

This model was also produced in .32 caliber (7m/m65) under the Browning name but most such pistols were shipped to Canada until about 1965 when it was added to the American product line. Actual production numbers of the .32 caliber pistol are unknown, but they are quite rare. As FN's serial numbering scheme did not differentiate between calibers, the .32 caliber pistols were numbered in the same sequence as the .380 caliber pistols.

The .380 Caliber Automatic pistol is sometimes known as the "Model 1910" or "Model 1955". The Model 1910 term is a FN designation, the Model 1955 term is a U.S. collectors' designation. Neither designations were used by Browning. In 1971, Browning began importing a modified .380 Caliber Automatic Pistol. This gun was redesigned to comply with the new regulations mandated by the 1968 GCA. Modifications included: a longer barrel and slide, an adjustable rear sight and high blade front sight, a slightly differently shaped grip frame, black plastic grips with the Browning name and a thumb rest on the left panel, a firing pin extended at the rear to act as a cocking indicator and a finger extension on the bottom of the magazine. FN sold the redesigned model outside of the U.S. as the Model 130 (see page 320). The barrel was marked "Cal. .380", and the marking of the serial number on the slide was eliminated. A steel trigger was used in assembly instead of the plastic version. This gun was also offered with Renaissance engraving with satin gray finish and checkered wood grips with thumb rest. This gun was designated the "1971" or "10/71" Model. The serial numbers were the year of manufacture, model code "N" followed by a production serialization (for instance, 73Nxxxxx, a pistol made in 1973). None were offered in the U.S. in .32 caliber. U.S. importation was discontinued about 1974.

(Fig.325-1) Examples of presentation cases for three-gun sets (blue finish or Renaissance): Early cases were made out of walnut while later cases were covered with vinyl. (Photographs by author, courtesy of Bruce Buckner)

(Fig.325-2) Early walnut cases featured hidden hinges, later models were equipped with external hinges. (Photographs by author, courtesy of Bruce Buckner)

The 9mm Automatic Pistol is much better known as the "Hi-Power" and was initially offered in standard (blue) finish or with Renaissance engraving. The standard Hi-Power was fitted with checkered walnut grips. Early pistols had the backs of the grips painted with a red moisture barrier (page 271). The Renaissance guns had Nacrolac Pearl grips. Initially each gun was marked with the serial number on the frame, barrel and slide and with the caliber designation (9m/mP") on the barrel) and the usual Belgian proof marks. Early magazines for the Hi-Power had aluminum followers and were either blued or bright nickel (Renaissance). The pistol had an internal extractor and a semi-circular depression intended to aid disassembly machined into the right side of the slide (colloquially referred to as the "thumbprint", see page 317). It was eliminated about 1960 to reduce production costs. The internal extractor was replaced by an external extractor in the 1963-1964 time frame. The external extractor proved to be less expensive to manufacture and more reliable than the old design. These were the only external modifications to the pistol that were made until the introduction of the spur hammer and adjustable rear sights in 1972.

The first Hi-Powers to enter the USA bearing the Browning Arms Company name were in the 70,000 serial number range (these numbers were in the same sequence as High Power pistols made under the Fabrique Nationale name for sale in countries other than the USA). Numbers continued in sequence until sometime in 1964 when a "T" prefix was added to the number. The series known to collectors as the "T Series Hi-Powers" continued until about 1969, when the numbering was changed to a year prefix and a "C" before the actual sequence number (see page 317).

Chronology of Browning Center Fire Pistols 1954 to 1968

1954 saw the introduction of standard (blue) and Renaissance .25 Caliber Automatic, .380 Caliber Automatic and 9mm Parabellum Automatic (Hi-Power) pistols to the USA under the Browning Arms Company name. Standard guns were shipped in black and red display cases and Renaissance guns were shipped in blue velvet presentation cases. Standard and Renaissance three-gun sets were also offered this year and were shipped in wood cases with blue or red velvet interiors. The Lightweight pistol, introduced in 1955, was shipped in the same black and red display case as the standard pistols.

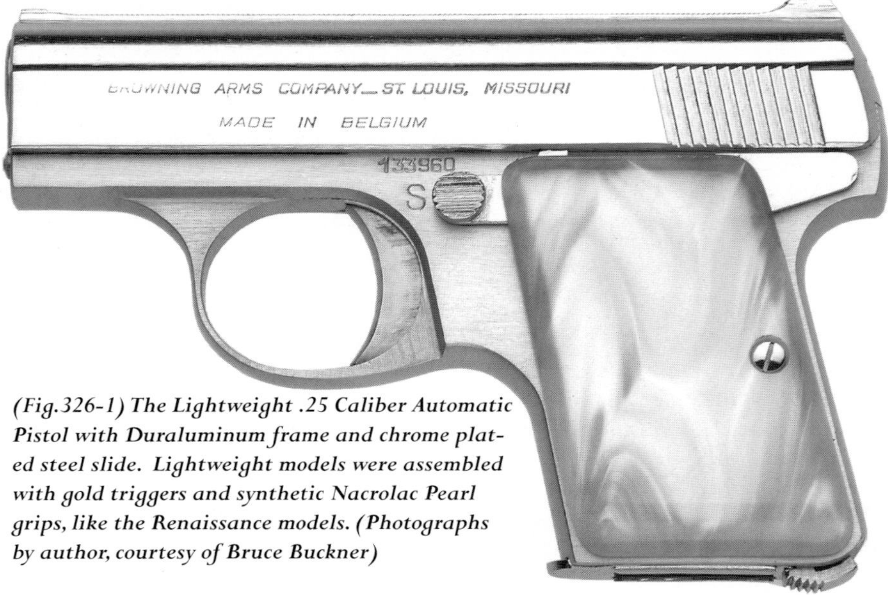

(Fig.326-1) The Lightweight .25 Caliber Automatic Pistol with Duraluminum frame and chrome plated steel slide. Lightweight models were assembled with gold triggers and synthetic Nacrolac Pearl grips, like the Renaissance models. (Photographs by author, courtesy of Bruce Buckner)

About 1962, the black and red presentation cases were discontinued. Browning standard finish and .25 Caliber Lightweight handguns were shipped from Belgium to the USA in small burgundy hinged cardboard boxes that were embossed with the Browning name and marked with the serial number of the gun on the bottom. The bottom of the box was also usually stamped "Made in Belgium". There were different sizes for each type of handgun. Standard grade guns and .25 Caliber Lightweight Pistols were not sold with the FN supplied cardboard boxes but transferred to black & red plastic boxes with the Browning name and marked "Made in USA" with cardboard sleeves. The sleeve was usually marked with the serial number of the gun. The transfer took place at Browning before the guns were shipped to distributors. Renaissance guns continued to be shipped in the blue velvet presentation cases.

The change to an external extractor on the Hi-Power occurred at FN in 1962; however, it did not immediately appear on Browning Arms Company guns (see FN production practices page 100). Browning Hi-Power pistols with serial numbers into 1964 still had internal extractors. Serial number marking of the slide on Hi-Power pistols ceased prior to 1964.

In 1964, the serial numbering of the Hi-Power pistol was changed to include a "T" prefix. At the same time, the Renaissance blue velvet presentation cases were discontinued. All handguns were shipped from Belgium in the burgundy hinged cardboard boxes and transferred to black zippered pouches before being sent to distributors. Black zippered pouches with a red flannel interior were used for the standard pistols; Renaissance guns were provided with pouches with a slightly different shape and a more deluxe white fleece interior. The pouches were made of black vinyl or "leatherette" with heavy brass zippers and the Browning name in gold on one side.

The standard .32 Caliber Automatic Pistol was introduced in the USA under the Browning Arms Company name in 1965. Triggers in the .32 caliber and .380 caliber pistols were changed from blue steel to black plastic about 1967.

After 1968, Browning no longer imported the .25 caliber, .32 caliber and .380 caliber automatic pistols into the USA due to import restrictions contained in the 1968 Gun Control Act. The sole exception was the "1971" .380 caliber pistol which was sold from 1971 to 1979.

(Fig.326-2) Pistols were shipped from FN in burgundy cardboard boxes with embossed Browning logo. Browning did not sell the pistols in these cardboard boxes, instead they were transferred to plastic boxes. The boxes came in several sizes and the bottom was marked with the pistol's serial number, some were stamped "Made in Belgium". These were not mere shipping boxes, FN intended for Browning to sell them with the pistols but the Browning Arms Company decided to substitute these.

(Fig.327-1) Red and black molded pistol boxes were used by Browning after 1962. The box was shipped from Browning with a cardboard sleeve, the sleeve was numbered with the serial number of the pistol. Pictured is the box for the .25 Caliber Pistol (open, closed and with sleeve), the box for the .380 Caliber Pistol (open) and the box for the Hi-Power (open). (Photographs by author, courtesy of Bruce Buckner)

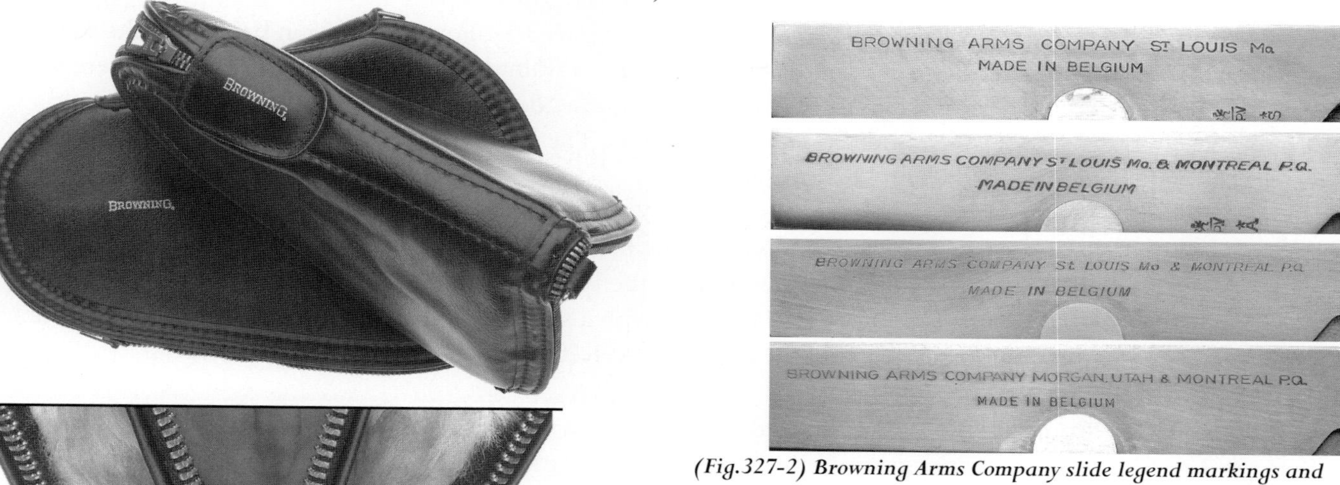

(Fig.327-2) Browning Arms Company slide legend markings and evolvement through time (top is earliest, bottom is latest). Note the lack of Liège proofs on the two Hi-Power slides, these slides were proofed but the proof marks were applied in different locations starting in the 1960s. (Photographs by author, courtesy of Bruce Buckner)

(Fig.327-3) Browning applied commemorative markings for the first anniversary of the Browning Collectors Association. A series of 100 commemorative Hi-Power pistols was made available with walnut presentation cases. (Photographs by author, courtesy of Bruce Buckner)

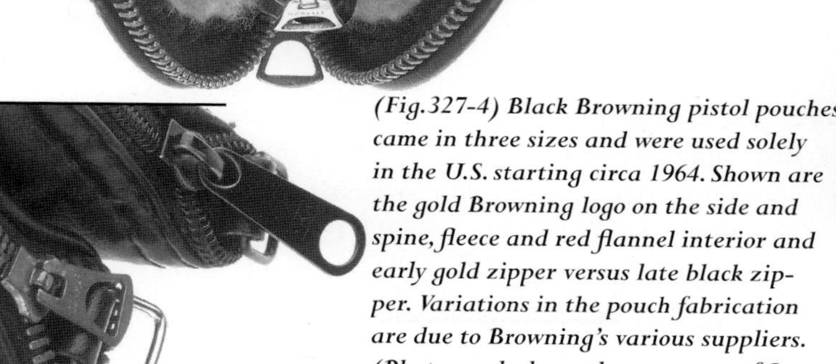

(Fig.327-4) Black Browning pistol pouches came in three sizes and were used solely in the U.S. starting circa 1964. Shown are the gold Browning logo on the side and spine, fleece and red flannel interior and early gold zipper versus late black zipper. Variations in the pouch fabrication are due to Browning's various suppliers. (Photographs by author, courtesy of Bruce Buckner)

Chronology of the Browning Hi-Power Pistol 1969 to 1989

1969 brought the change of serial numbering on Hi-Power pistols from "T" series to xxCyyyyyy format where "xx" was the last two digits of the year "C" was the model code for the Hi-Power and "yyyyyy" was the actual serial number of the pistol.

In 1971 the location of the serial number on the Hi-Power pistol was changed from the right side of the frame to the front grip strap (at various times in later production, serial numbers were sometimes also marked on the slide below the ejection port and on the portion of the barrel which could be seen through the ejection port[(1)]).

The Hi-Power hammer was changed from round profile to a "spur" type in 1972. This change occurred at the same time as the addition of a new model with an adjustable rear sight and a correspondingly higher front sight.

In 1977 a new serial number system was introduced across all models of Browning firearms. Each model was assigned a unique code number. This was "245" for the commercial Hi-Power pistol sold by the Browning Arms Company. The serial number consisted of the code number, an alphabetic date code and another number after the date code. For instance, 245RVxxxxxxx would indicate a Hi-Power pistol made in 1975 (see page 317 for year codes). Renaissance Hi-Power pistols became available with adjustable rear sights.

1978 was the 100th anniversary of the Browning Arms Company and several special firearms were produced to commemorate this event. Among these was the "Centennial" Hi-Power which had a highly polished chrome finish and was fitted with finely checkered walnut grips with a Browning "B" medallion and a gold trigger. Each gun had an inscription on the right side of the slide, which read "Browning Centennial 1878-1978". They also were numbered in a special serial number sequence. These guns were sold in walnut presentation cases with red interiors. A small metal plate was screwed to the lid with an inscription similar to that on the pistol. Production was reported to be 3500 units. The Renaissance Hi-Power was discontinued in 1979.

In 1980, Browning introduced the "Louis XVI" limited edition engraved Hi-Power. This gun had finely checkered walnut grips with a diamond around the grip screw and was sold in a walnut case with red velvet lining. There were separate models with fixed or adjustable sights. In the same year, the Nickel Hi-Power was introduced. This gun had a bright nickel finish[(2)], checkered wood grips and fixed sights. The Louis XVI pistol was also offered with finely checkered walnut grips with the Browning "B" medallion.

A special edition of the Hi-Power pistol was commissioned by the Browning Collector's Association in 1981. These guns commemorated the first anniversary of the founding of the Browning Collector's Association and production was limited to 100 pistols. The gun was a standard Hi-Power with a special inscription on the right side of the frame and slide and was sold with a walnut presentation case with red velvet interior.

Also in 1981, a "silver chrome" pistol was introduced with adjustable rear sight and "wrap-around" black rubber grips. The silver chrome finish was dull silver in appearance and had a gold trigger. Interestingly, the serial numbers of these pistols were marked on the side of the frame because it would not have been visible under the rubber grips. An adjustable sight bright nickel pistol was also offered.

Production of the nickel Hi-Power and the Louis XVI models ceased about 1984. Some pistols were again marked with the serial number on the frame, barrel and slide in this year[(1)].

Production of the "Classic" and "Gold Classic" Hi-Power pistols was announced in 1984 for delivery in 1985. These models commemorated the 50th anniversary of John M. Browning's Model 1935 pistol. These guns were extensively engraved, with a silver gray finish, gold triggers and special walnut grips. The Gold Classic also had several gold inlays and fancier grips. Each gun was signed by the engraver. Browning stated that 5000 of the Classics and 500 of Gold Classics would be made. High price and low demand made the actual production figures quite a bit lower (probably about 2500 and 350, respectively). The guns were serial numbered in a special range and were provided with a velvet lined case.

In 1985, the Hi-Power pistol was offered in a matte blue finish with fixed sights(1). This model was serial numbered on the frame, slide and barrel and was fitted with standard FN black Cycolac synthetic grips (page 317). The grips were changed to MKII grips (incorporated thumb contours. see page 316) in 1986. In 1987, the safety on the matte finished model was replaced with the MKII ambidextrous design.

The Centenaire Model was introduced in 1989. This Hi-Power was produced to celebrate the 100th anniversary of Fabrique Nationale. This gun had a silver finish, hand engraving and was signed by the engraver. Specially checkered walnut grips and a silver trigger were also featured. This model was limited to 100 units and was numbered in a special range.

About 1990, FN began shipping components to Viana, Portugal to be assembled into complete pistols. Our coverage of the Browning Arms Company Hi-Power ends with that development.

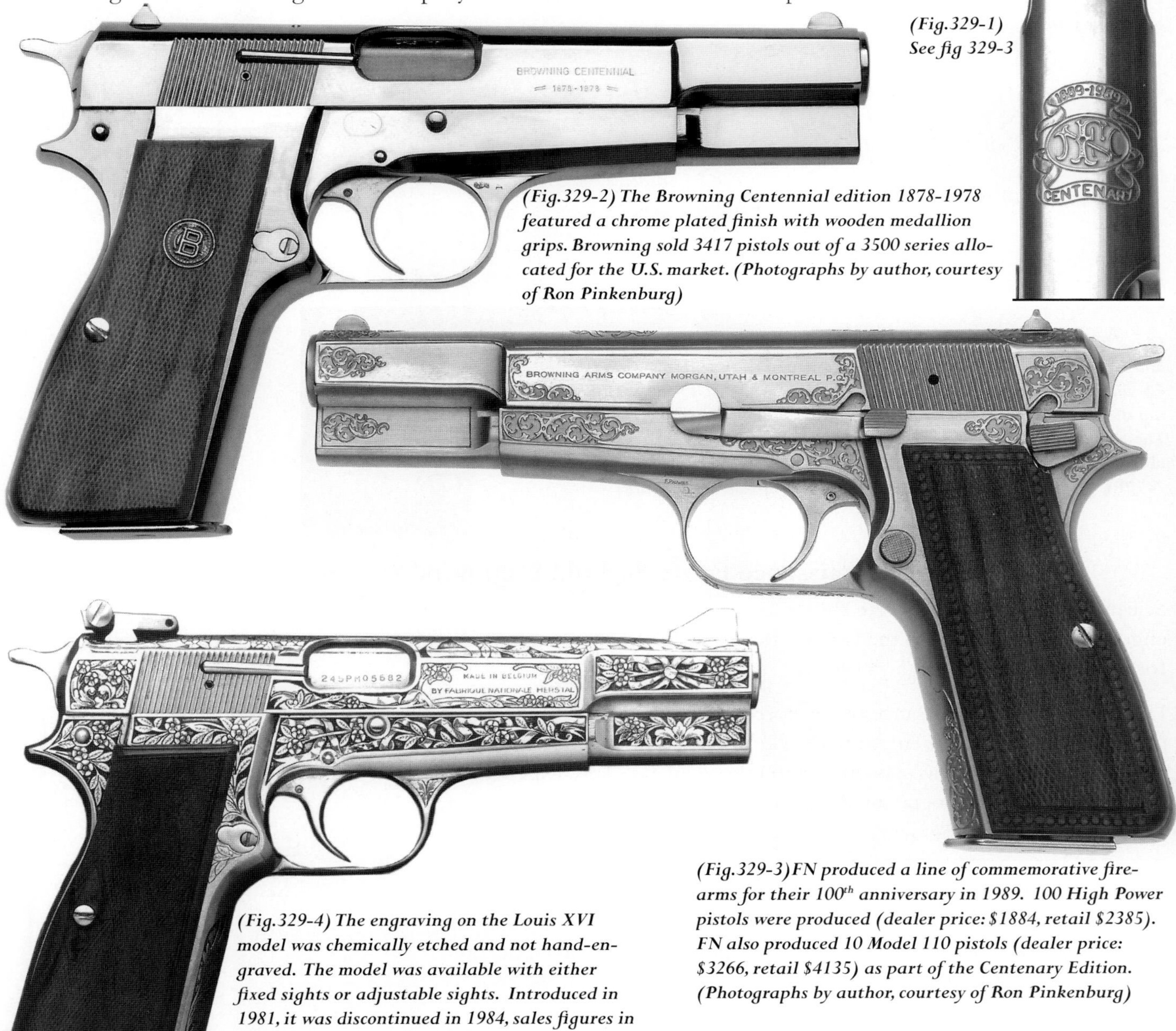

(Fig.329-1) See fig 329-3

(Fig.329-2) The Browning Centennial edition 1878-1978 featured a chrome plated finish with wooden medallion grips. Browning sold 3417 pistols out of a 3500 series allocated for the U.S. market. (Photographs by author, courtesy of Ron Pinkenburg)

(Fig.329-3) FN produced a line of commemorative firearms for their 100th anniversary in 1989. 100 High Power pistols were produced (dealer price: $1884, retail $2385). FN also produced 10 Model 110 pistols (dealer price: $3266, retail $4135) as part of the Centenary Edition. (Photographs by author, courtesy of Ron Pinkenburg)

(Fig.329-4) The engraving on the Louis XVI model was chemically etched and not hand-engraved. The model was available with either fixed sights or adjustable sights. Introduced in 1981, it was discontinued in 1984, sales figures in the U.S. did not exceed 600 (Photograph courtesy of Browning)

(1) This is primarily due to FN production methods. Many military / law-enforcement orders or overruns were redirected to the Browning Arms Company for sale as commercial guns. This was easily accomplished as FN had for long adopted a system of marking the slide late in the production process, as such pistols could easily be marked with either the FN or BAC slide legend.
(2) Although marketed by Browning as a nickel finish, the plating was actually a chrome or nickel-chrome plating. This finish is distinctively different and harder than FN's (prewar) nickel finish.

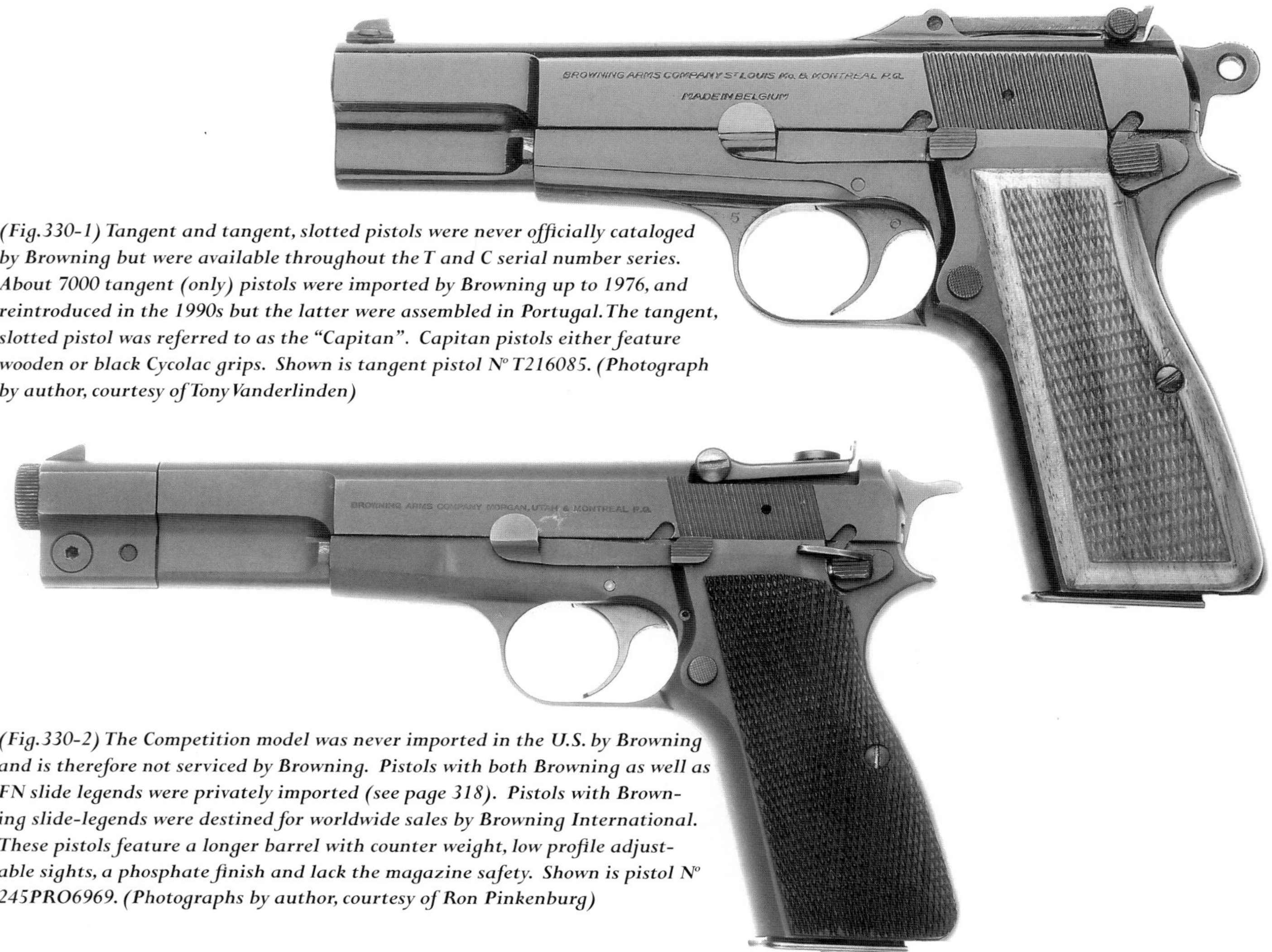

(Fig.330-1) Tangent and tangent, slotted pistols were never officially cataloged by Browning but were available throughout the T and C serial number series. About 7000 tangent (only) pistols were imported by Browning up to 1976, and reintroduced in the 1990s but the latter were assembled in Portugal. The tangent, slotted pistol was referred to as the "Capitan". Capitan pistols either feature wooden or black Cycolac grips. Shown is tangent pistol N° T216085. (Photograph by author, courtesy of Tony Vanderlinden)

(Fig.330-2) The Competition model was never imported in the U.S. by Browning and is therefore not serviced by Browning. Pistols with both Browning as well as FN slide legends were privately imported (see page 318). Pistols with Browning slide-legends were destined for worldwide sales by Browning International. These pistols feature a longer barrel with counter weight, low profile adjustable sights, a phosphate finish and lack the magazine safety. Shown is pistol N° 245PRO6969. (Photographs by author, courtesy of Ron Pinkenburg)

Renaissance Engraving and Engravers' Signatures

Select FN engraving types were chosen by Browning as a cataloged finish. Type III and Type IV (for the Model 1910) engraving was marketed in the U.S. as "Renaissance" finish or engraving and was the only available engraving option for the U.S. market.

High demand for Renaissance pistols forced FN to expand its engraving staff. The meticulous attention to detail, for which the Custom Shop was known, was sometimes compromised to meet demand. Less experienced engravers worked on engraving the Types, resulting in noticeable differences in the quality of the engraving. Engravers were allocated work based on demand. As such, experienced engravers also worked on Type III and IV patterns. Collectors often debate if engravers signed Browning Renaissance pistols or not. Legitimate signed Renaissance pistols do exist. Signing the engraving work had nothing to do with the model or engraving type, only select engravers which had reached a certain skill level were authorized to sign their work and only if they so desired.

(Fig.330-3) A comparative view between the late satin gray finish (left) and earlier highly polished finish of Renaissance pistols. (Photographs by author, courtesy of Bruce Buckner)

Collectors often refer to the high polish finish on Renaissance pistols as "coin finish". This term should not be used as it is a confusing collectors' term that has no roots in any factory terminology. There are noticeably different levels of polishing on Renaissance pistols depending on the amount of time spent finishing a specific pistol. The dull satin gray finish lacked final polishing and was introduced in order to save labor costs.

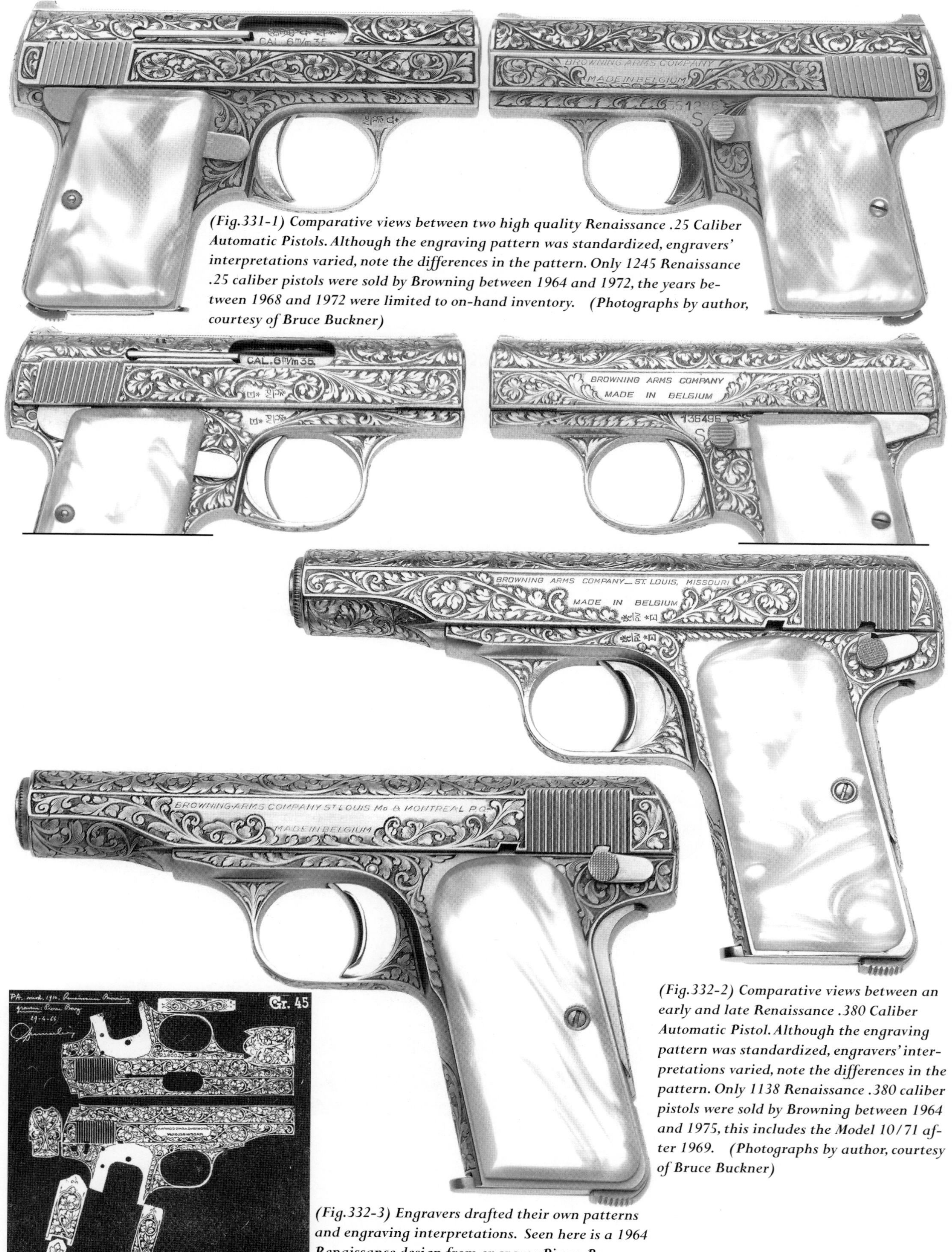

(Fig.331-1) Comparative views between two high quality Renaissance .25 Caliber Automatic Pistols. Although the engraving pattern was standardized, engravers' interpretations varied, note the differences in the pattern. Only 1245 Renaissance .25 caliber pistols were sold by Browning between 1964 and 1972, the years between 1968 and 1972 were limited to on-hand inventory. (Photographs by author, courtesy of Bruce Buckner)

(Fig.332-2) Comparative views between an early and late Renaissance .380 Caliber Automatic Pistol. Although the engraving pattern was standardized, engravers' interpretations varied, note the differences in the pattern. Only 1138 Renaissance .380 caliber pistols were sold by Browning between 1964 and 1975, this includes the Model 10/71 after 1969. (Photographs by author, courtesy of Bruce Buckner)

(Fig.332-3) Engravers drafted their own patterns and engraving interpretations. Seen here is a 1964 Renaissance design from engraver Pierre Bovy.

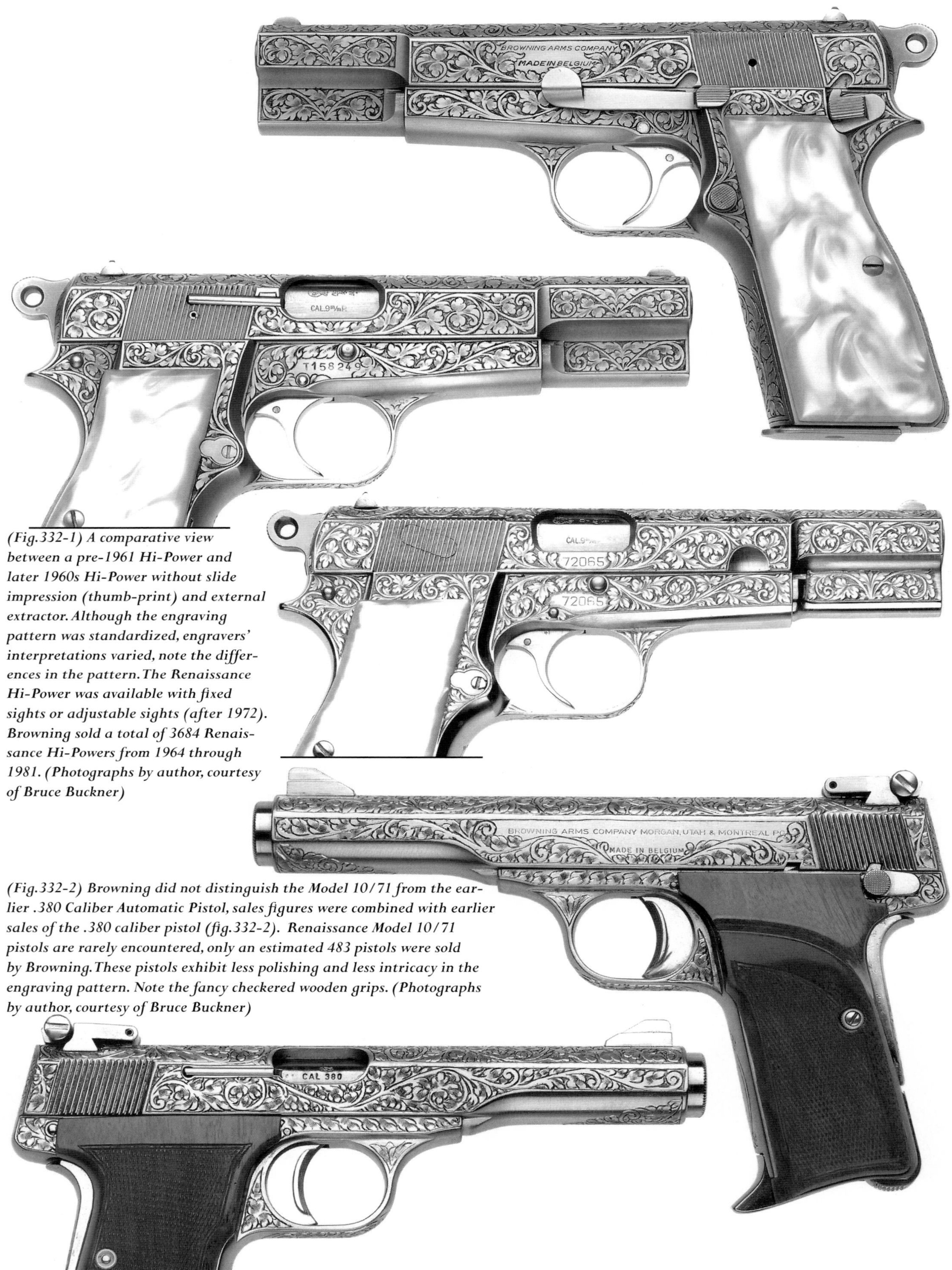

(Fig.332-1) A comparative view between a pre-1961 Hi-Power and later 1960s Hi-Power without slide impression (thumb-print) and external extractor. Although the engraving pattern was standardized, engravers' interpretations varied, note the differences in the pattern. The Renaissance Hi-Power was available with fixed sights or adjustable sights (after 1972). Browning sold a total of 3684 Renaissance Hi-Powers from 1964 through 1981. (Photographs by author, courtesy of Bruce Buckner)

(Fig.332-2) Browning did not distinguish the Model 10/71 from the earlier .380 Caliber Automatic Pistol, sales figures were combined with earlier sales of the .380 caliber pistol (fig.332-2). Renaissance Model 10/71 pistols are rarely encountered, only an estimated 483 pistols were sold by Browning. These pistols exhibit less polishing and less intricacy in the engraving pattern. Note the fancy checkered wooden grips. (Photographs by author, courtesy of Bruce Buckner)

Selected Bibliography

The bibliography reflects works where specific information was deemed original and valuable to the research of this book. Countless other works were reviewed and compared. The author made extensive use of original factory documents such as memos, letters, instruction booklets, and catalogs, but these are not itemized in the bibliography. Additionally the author used his extensive database of more than 6,000 pistols with special features or markings.

Unpublished Documents

Claude Feys, *Guide d'Identification des Poinçons Militaires Belges*

Periodicals & Articles

Colonel W.R. Betz, *John Moses Brownings fruhe Taschen-pistolen*
Jean Clergeau, *Les pistolets Automatiques de l'Armée française,* Gazette des Armes, 125
The German Revolution of 1918, mars.wnec.edu
Gustave Dreze, *La Fabrique Nationale d'Armes de Guerre Herstal,* Bruxelles Exposition, Gustave Dreze, 1908
Handfeuerwaffen der deutschen Gendarmerie und Polizei des 19 und 20 Jahrhunderts
Reinhard Henke, *Hi Powers in Germany,* Browning Collectors Association, 2001
La Meuse, February 2, 1914
Toe Nomn, *Eestin pistoolit ja konepistoolit vuosina 1920-1940,* ASE-lehti, 1995
Philippe Questienne, *Une Usine d'Armement sous l'Occupations Ennemie,* Le Musée d'Armes, 1983
Revue de l'Armée Belge, March-April 1909
Philip Schreier, *A Presidential Model 1900,* American Rifleman, May 2000
Scientific American, April 1, 1893
Arne Thell, *Die Schwedische Ordonnanz Pistole M07*
Dominique Venner, *De "la Bande à Bonnot" a la Grande Guerre, le Browning 1900*
Dominique Venner, *Sarajevo, 28 Juin 1914 Un Coup de Pistolet: 9 Millions de Morts*
Detlef Völkel, *Die geschichtliche Entwicklung der Faustfuerwaffen der deutschen Polizei von 1893 – 1945,* Deutsche Waffen Journal, 1983, 1984

Fabrique Nationale Publications

Les Armes Fines de la Fabrique Nationale Herstal
Fabrique Nationale d'Armes de Guerre 1889-1964
FN Revue, N° 1-204, 1953-1972
FN Sports, N° 1-16, 1929-1931
Auguste Francotte, Claude Gaier, Robert Karlshausen, *Ars Mechanica*, Herstal Group, 2008

Firearms Books

L'Armurerie Liègeoise, Institut d'Etude Economique et Sociale des Classes Moyennes, 1949
Herry Derby III & James Brown, *Japanese Military Cartridge Handguns 1893-1945*, Schiffer Publishing Ltd., 1993
John Brunner, *The Colt Pocket Hammerless Automatic Pistols*, Phillips Publications, 1996
Charles Clawson, *Colt .45 Government Models, Commercial Series*, Charles Clawson, 1996
Edward Ezell, *Handguns of the World*, Barnes & Noble Books, 1981
Edward Ezell, *Small Arms Today*, Stackpole Books, 1988
Auguste Francotte, Claude Gaier, *FN 100 Years*, Didier Hatier, 1989
Claude Gaier, *Five Centuries of Liège Gunmaking*, Editions du Perron
William Goddard, *The Government Models*, Andrew Mowbray Inc. 1998
J.S. Hatcher, *Textbook of Firearms Investigation, Identification and Evidence*, Small Arms Technical Publishing Co., 1935
Ronald Hayes, Ian Skennerton, *The Hayes handgun Omnibus*, Arms & Militaria Press 2007
Wayne Johnson, *The FN-49*, Wet Dog Publications, 2004
Bruno Joos De Ter Beerst, *Trade & Hallmarks on Firearms in Belgium*, Petraco - Pandora
Clive Law, *Canadian Military Handguns*, Museum Restoration Service, 1994
Clive Law, *Inglis Diamond*, Collector Grade Publications, 2001
H.B. Lockhoven, *Kleine Waffeb - bibliothek, Heft 19, 20, 21, 22, 23, 24, 29, 33*, Verlag International Small Arms Publishers
Eugene Medlin & Jean Huon, *Military Handguns of France*, Excalibur Publications, 1993
Eugene Medlin & Jean Huon, *French Service Handguns 1858-2004*, Tommy Gun Publications, 2004
Bernard Meyer, *L'Age d'Or des Armes à Feu*, Editions du Portal, 1994
H.M. Shirley Jr, Anthony Vanderlinden, *Browning Auto-5 Shotguns*, Wet Dog Publications, 2003
R. Blake Stevens, *The Browning High Power Automatic Pistol*, Collector Grade Publications, 1992
Jan Still, *Central Powers Pistols*, Jan Still, 2007
Anthony Vandelinden, *The Belgian Browning Pistols*, Wet Dog Publications, 2001

Firearms Books (continued)

Anthony Vandelinden, *Holsters and Shoulder-Stocks of the World*, Wet Dog Publications, 2005
Gerhard Wirnsberger, *The Standard Directory of Proofmarks*, Jolex
A.B. Zhuk, *The Illustrated Encyclopedia of Handguns*, Greenhill Books, 1995

History Books

Guy De Becker, *Quand la FN Avait Deux Roues*, Guy De Becker
Boghitchevitch, *Le Procès de Salonique*, Delpeuch Paris, 1927
Boudin, De Groote, Gaier, Jaupart, Thieri, *Les Armes à Feu Reglementaires Belges Depuis 1830*, Crédit Communal, 1988
John Browning, Curt Gentry, *John M. Browning American Gunmaker*, Browning, 1994
Viscount Bryce, *Evidence and Documents – Alleged German Outrages*, Macmillan Company
Emile Cammaerts, *Albert of Belgium*, Macmillan Company, 1935
Brian Crozier, *The Man Who Lost China*, Charles Scribner's Sons, 1976
Alain Descy, *Livre Memorial 1803-2003*, Alain Descy, 2003
Marie-Therese Coenen, *La Grève des femmes de la FN en 1966*, Politique et Histoire, 1991
Joachim Fest, *Speer*, Harcourt, 1999
Gilbert Gaspard, *Les Demoiselles de Herstal*, Vaillant-Carmanne, 1975
Jo Gérard, *Chronique de la Régence 1944-1950*, J.M. Collet, 1983
Jos Hakker, *De heldenstrijd der Maquis*, 1945
Robert Halleux, *Cockerill*, Editions du Perron
Ronald Hingley, *The Russian Secret Police*, Simon and Schuster, 1970
Gerald Howson, *Arms for Spain*, St. Martin's Press, 1998
Michael P.E. Hoyt, *Captive in the Congo*, Naval Institute Press, 2000
J. Izart, *La Belgique au Travail*, Pierre Roger et Co., 1921
General E. Janssens, *Histoire de la Force Publique*, Ghesquiere & Partners, 1979
Yvette & Jacques Kupelian, Jacques Sirtaine, *Histoire de l'Automobile Belge*, Paul Legrain
Jean-Louis Lejaxhe, *Liège en Guerres*, Noir Dessin Production, 2004
Livre d'Or de la Resistance Belge, Editions Leclercq
Gilberte Maillard, *Hommage aux Fusillés – Libération de la Citadelle*, Liège a la Belle Epoque
Colonel Naessens, L. Lombard, *Loncin*, G. Leens, 1938
Jacques A.M. Noterman, *Le Roi Tué*, Jourdan le Clerq, 2004
Patricia Parkman, *Nonviolent Insurrection in El Salvador*, The University of Arizona Press, 1988
Richard Pipes, *The Russian Revolution*, Vintage Books, 1991
Technical History and Index - A serial history of technical problems dealt with by Admiralty Departments, Admiralty, 1920
Toivo Raun, *Estonia and the Estonians*, Hoover Institution Press, 1978
Recueil des Arrêtés, Ordonnances et Avis divers Affichés a Liége, (1914-1918)
Rémy, *The Eighteenth Day*, Gateway publishers, 1978
John Reynolds, *André Citroên*, Haynes Publishing, 2006
Peter Robbins, *The Legend of W.E. Fairbairn, Gentleman and Warrior: The Shanghai Years*
Marion Schreiber, *The Twentieth Train*, Grove Press, 2000
Johny – Thierry – Freddy Tacheny, *L'Eopopée Moto, Les Années Jules Tacheny*, Groupe Luc Pire, 2008
Charles Terlinden, *Histoire Militaire des Belges*, La Renaissance Du Livre, 1966
Richard Ullman, *Intervention and the War*, Princeton University Press, 1961
Werner Warmbrunn, *The German Occupation of Belgium 1940-1944*, Peter Lang 1993
Bernard Wasserstein, *Secret War in Shanghai*, Houghton Mifflin Company, 1999

Cover photograph: (Clockwise from top left) 1930s blue motorcycle brochure, prewar Lithuanian contract High Power, Belgian military High Power shoulder-stock, FN automotive 1920s fanion (flag), prewar cleaning rod, Alcock & Pierce commercial Model 1903 pistol, factory High Power brass paperweight, prewar Model 1905 instruction book, prewar "Pastuovic Zagreb" Baby pistol, 9mm FN dummy rounds, early Model 1910 box, 1920s engraved Type II Model 1905 pistol in presentation case, 1910s FN invoice, 1905 Liège World's Fair stamp, 1920s FN MAP typewriter, prewar engraved presentation bayonet, early FN lubrication can, FN Christmas card with envelope, President Martinez' factory engraved Model 1922 presentation pistol, FN Sports Model 1300 automobile booklet, FN automobile Motometer, engraved Type I Model 1900 pistol in presentation case, 1900s Belgian shooting prize pocket watch, 7.65mm FN dummy rounds, 1914 "Un Million" FN gala Model 1905 pistol with suede purse holster, 1914 FN "Un Million" gala menu, commemorative John Browning medal, 1920s FN Grandjean stenograph, 1964 FN 75th Anniversary medal, John Browning's 1920s engraved Type VI Model 1910 with presentation case, 1899 FN bicycle book, Model 1903 shoulder-stock, Model 1899 pistol.

Cover page: The old entrance of "le grand hall": The company name is carved in stone above the entrance in between the coats of arms. The entrance was erected with the first buildings in the 1890s and still stands today. (Photograph courtesy of FN Herstal)

Browning Auto-5 Shotguns

The Belgian FN Production

(Revised, Second Edition)

The Browning Auto-5 Shotguns is the only book devoted to the history, model variations, accessories and production dates of the legendary, FN produced, Browning Auto-5 shotgun.

The authors, H.M. Shirley, Jr. and Anthony Vanderlinden, combined their extensive knowledge on these topics. Shirley brings his expertise to the work through his understanding of the Auto-5 and his meticulous approach in dating the firearms, parts, and accessories. Vanderlinden brings his in-depth knowledge of the history of Fabrique Nationale, its products and production capabilities. For this second edition, the authors have revised and clarified some of the data and added some special edition guns like the Centenary models as well as the Final Tribute model.

The purpose of this book is to introduce the many models and details of the Auto-5's produced by FN, and also gives the collector the only accurate method in dating a specific firearm. The information presented in this work was collected from various reliable sources and was substantiated and confirmed by various company records, documents and photographs.

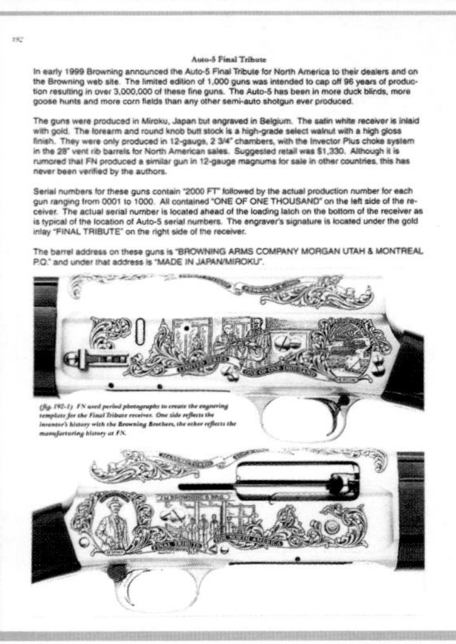

192

Auto-5 Final Tribute

In early 1999 Browning announced the Auto-5 Final Tribute for North America to their dealers and on the Browning web site. The limited edition of 1,000 guns was intended to cap off 96 years of production resulting in over 3,000,000 of these fine guns. The Auto-5 has been in more duck blinds, more goose hunts and more corn fields than any other semi-auto shotgun ever produced.

The guns were produced in Miroku, Japan but engraved in Belgium. The satin white receiver is inlaid with gold. The forearm and round knob butt stock is a high-grade select walnut with a high gloss finish. They were only produced in 12-gauge, 2 3/4" chambers, with the Invector Plus choke system in the 28" vent rib barrels for North American sales. Suggested retail was $1,330. Although it is rumored that FN produced a similar gun in 12-gauge magnums for sale in other countries, this has never been verified by the authors.

Serial numbers for these guns contain "2000 FT" followed by the actual production number for each gun ranging from 0001 to 1000. All contained "ONE OF ONE THOUSAND" on the left side of the receiver. The actual serial number is located ahead of the loading latch on the bottom of the receiver as is typical of the location of Auto-5 serial numbers. The engraver's signature is located under the gold inlay "FINAL TRIBUTE" on the right side of the receiver.

The barrel address on these guns is "BROWNING ARMS COMPANY MORGAN UTAH & MONTREAL P.Q." and under that address is "MADE IN JAPAN/MIROKU".

(fig. 192-1) FN used period photographs to create the engraving template for the Final Tribute receiver. One side reflects the inventor's history with the Browning Brothers, the other reflects the manufacturing history of FN.

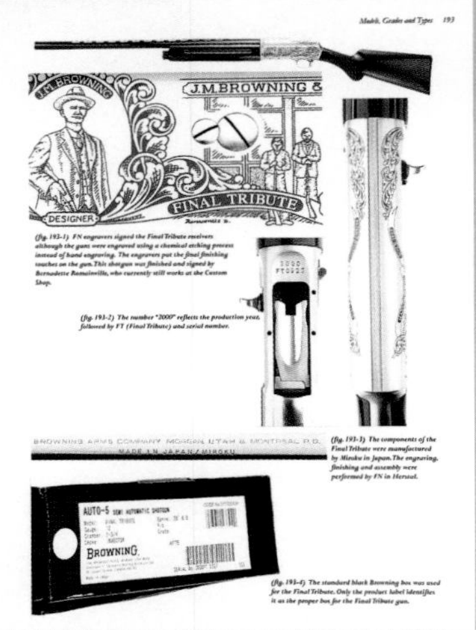

(fig. 193-1) FN engravers signed the Final Tribute receivers although the guns were engraved using a chemical etching process instead of hand engraving. The engravers put the final finishing touches on the gun. This shotgun was finished and signed by Bernadette Romainville, who currently still works at the Custom Shop.

(fig. 193-2) The number "2000" reflects the production year, followed by FT (Final Tribute) and serial number.

(fig. 193-3) The components of the Final Tribute were manufactured by Miroku in Japan. The engraving, finishing and assembly were performed by FN in Herstal.

(fig. 193-4) The standard black Browning box was used for the Final Tribute. Only the product label identifies it as the proper box for the Final Tribute gun.

Title: Browning Auto-5 Shotguns
The Belgian FN Production
Authors: H.M. Shirley, Jr.
Anthony Vanderlinden
Publisher: Wet Dog Publications
ISBN: 0-9707997-6-4
250 pages quality coated paper
Hardbound color cover
Size: 8.75"x 11.25" (22 x 28.5 cm)
Photographs: 400+ color and B/W
Printed and bound in the USA
Retail price: $63.95
Contact us for wholesale pricing

Also available from Wet Dog Publications: (see our site for pricing and availability)

FN Browning Pistols
Side-Arms that Shaped World History

The FN-49
The Last Elegant
Old-World Military Rifle

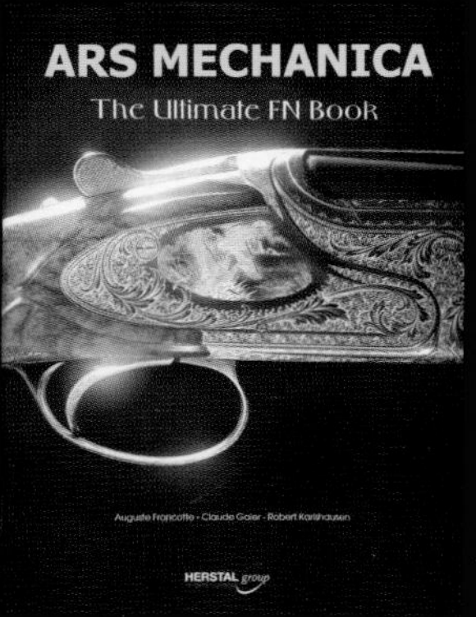

The Ultimate FN Book
Ars Mechanica

Holsters and Shoulder-Stocks of the World

Allied Rifle Contracts in America

Quality Collector Books from

Wet Dog Publications

www.fn-browning.com

Wet Dog Publications
5603-B West Friendly Avenue, Suite 166,
Greensboro, North Carolina 27410
phone: (336) 394-4138
fax: (336) 349-5427

FN Browning Pistols

Side-arms that shaped world history

Title: FN Browning Pistols, Side-Arms that Shaped World History
Author: Anthony Vanderlinden
Publisher: Wet Dog Publications
ISBN: 0-9707997-4-8
334 pages, quality coated paper - Size: 8.75"x 11.25" (22 x 28.5 cm)
Hardbound color cover
Photographs: 1100+ B&W
Printed and bound in the USA
Retail price: $64.95 - Wholesale pricing available

FN Browning Pistols

Side-Arms that Shaped World History

FN Browning Pistols, Side-Arms that Shaped World History reflects the continued work of Anthony Vanderlinden on the topic of FN Browning Pistols. This new book includes information found in the original issue titled *Belgian Browning Pistols* and expands into more variants and details geared toward collector interests.

It includes detailed chapters on FN Browning Models 1899, 1900, 1903, 1905 (06) Vest-Pocket, 1910, 1922, Baby, 1935 High Power, 110, 115, 120, 125, 135 and 140, as well as the Husqvarna Model 1907.

More than 80 contracts and variants are featured. Factory engraving samples as well as special commercial pistols such as extended barrel variants are illustrated. An overview shows the Browning Arms Co. distributed models like the High Power, Baby, Model 1955 and 10/71.

All of John Browning's handmade prototypes are pictured and illustrate the models manufactured by Colt and FN.

This book includes the history of Fabrique Nationale, information on Liège proofs, military acceptance markings as well FN's dealer network and how FN products were distributed worldwide.

Significant historical pistols are featured including those owned by Teddy Roosevelt, King Albert I, General Martinez of El Salvador and John Browning among others. Also included is new information on Gavrilo Princip and the pistol that started World War I.

Much of this information has never been published in English and constitutes the most complete write-up on FN's wartime production, resistance activities, lunch box specials, etc.

Also available from Wet Dog Publications: (see our site for pricing and availability)

Allied Rifle Contracts in America

The FN-49
The Last Elegant Old-World Miltary Rifle

The Ultimate FN Book
Ars Mechanica

Holsters and Shoulder-Stocks of the World

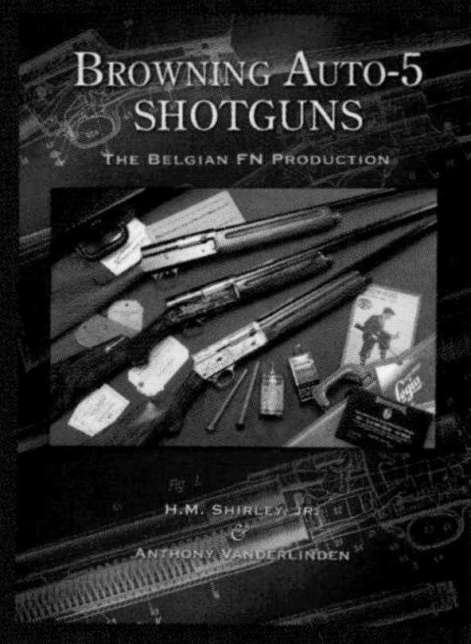

Browning Auto-5 Shotguns
The Belgian FN Production

Quality Collector Books from

Wet Dog Publications

www.fn-browning.com

Wet Dog Publications
5603-B West Friendly Avenue, Suite 166,
Greensboro, North Carolina 27410
phone: (336) 394-4138
fax: (336) 349-5427

Allied Rifle Contracts in America

Mosin-Nagant • Mauser • Enfield • Berthier
Remington • Savage • Winchester

1914-1918

Luke Mercaldo

Allied Rifle Contracts in America

Mosin-Nagant · Mauser · Enfield · Berthier · Remington · Savage · Winchester

Allied Rifle Contracts in America is the first work to fully explore American production of foreign military rifles during the First World War. The demands of the war caused a number of Allied governments to enter into contracts with American industry. These contracts resulted in the production of a number of different rifles. Featured are the histories of the Mosin-Nagant and Winchester Model 1895, which were produced for Imperial Russia, the Model 1889 Mauser, made for Belgium and the Pattern 1914 which was built for the United Kingdom. Additionally the book provides rare insight into lesser known contracts for Berthier and Rolling Block with France, and the Savage Model 1899 with Canada.

The historical circumstances of these contracts are presented for the first time. Primary source materials and original period documentation were used to recreate the timelines of the various contracts, delving into issues including financing, production limitations, labor problems, factory expansions, corruption, and the foreign military personnel who worked in the United States. The work sheds new light on the degree to which American business was involved with the Allied war effort. Readers gain a multifaceted insight into the hurdles that faced the Allied purchasing commissions and American manufacturers.

In addition to the in depth historical perspective, the book offers a detailed description of each rifle intended as a guide for the arms collector. This analysis covers features, specifications, markings and accessories to assist collectors in determining correct period pieces and understanding the history behind the artifacts.

Allied Rifle Contracts in America is a fascinating blend of history, economics, technology and esoterica that is an essential part of any historian's or collector's library.

Title: Allied Rifle Contracts in America
Mosin-Nagant, Mauser, Enfield, Berthier, Remington, Savage, Winchester
Authors: Luke Mercaldo, Adam Firestone, Anthony Vanderlinden
Publisher: Wet Dog Publications
ISBN: 0-9707997-7-2
224 pages, quality coated paper - Size: 8.75"x 11.25" (22 x 28.5 cm)
Hardbound color cover
Photographs: 440+ B/W
Printed and bound in the USA
Retail price: $49.99 - Wholesale pricing available

Also available from Wet Dog Publications: (see our site for pricing and availability)

FN Browning Pistols
Side-Arms that Shaped World History

The FN-49
The Last Elegant
Old-World Miltary Rifle

The Ultimate FN Book
Ars Mechanica

Holsters and Shoulder-Stocks of the World

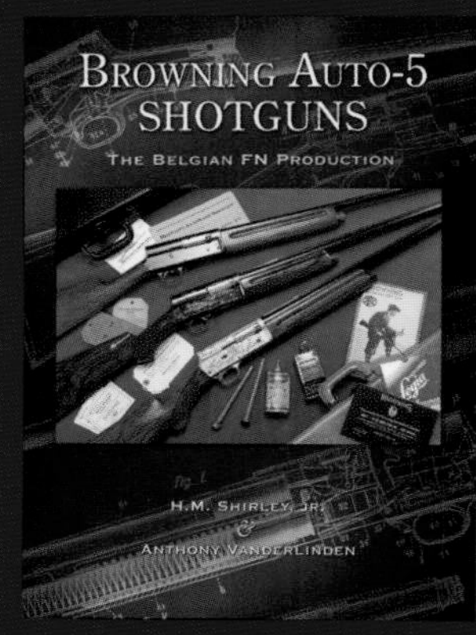

Browning Auto-5 Shotguns
The Belgian FN Production

Quality Collector Books from

Wet Dog Publications

www.fn-browning.com

Wet Dog Publications
5603 - B West Friendly Avenue, Suite 166
Greensboro, North Carolina 27410
phone: (336) 394-4138
fax: (336) 349-5427

Ars Mechanica

The Ultimate FN Book

Ars Mechanica, The Ultimate FN Book took more than five years to research and produce. The authors, Auguste Francotte, Claude Gaier and Robert Karlshausen, have done a magnificent job representing all facets of FN's history from 1889 through 2007, including its factories and affiliates such as Winchester and Browning. Many assumed that Ars Mechanica was to be an update to Auguste Francotte and Claude Gaier's work, FN 100 Years … however, any resemblance to previous history books is at best superficial. Ars Mechanica is by far the most comprehensive work on the subject.

The book recounts FN's rich history like no other. Ars Mechanica is illustrated with over 1500 photographs, many previously unpublished, and is a visual feast for any FN and Browning collector. For many it will introduce FN not only as the ultimate arms maker but reveal its rich history in bicycle, motorcycle and automobile manufacturing and many other successful product lines. These products, like the arms that bear the FN logo, were examples of technical excellence. FN's vehicle models held a number of world speed records, and continue to fuel the passions of motorcycle and automobile collectors. Years of painstaking work are reflected in this massive 576-page all-color volume. Published and funded by FN Herstal, the book was released in two editions, a French and English version. Only a limited printing of the English version is available for the U.S.

Title: Ars Mechanica
The Ultimate FN Book
Authors: Auguste Francotte, Claude Gaier, Robert Karlshausen
Language: English
Publisher: Herstal Group
U.S. distributor: Wet Dog Publications
576 pages quality coated paper
Hardbound cover & color dust-jacket
Size: 10" x 13.75" (25.5x35 cm.)
Photographs: 1500+
Printed and bound in Belgium
Price: Contact us for the best retail and wholesale pricing.

Also available from Wet Dog Publications: (see our site for pricing and availability)

FN Browning Pistols
Side-Arms that Shaped World History

The FN-49
The Last Elegant
Old-World Miltary Rifle

Browning Auto-5 Shotguns
The Belgian FN Production
(Revised Second Edition)

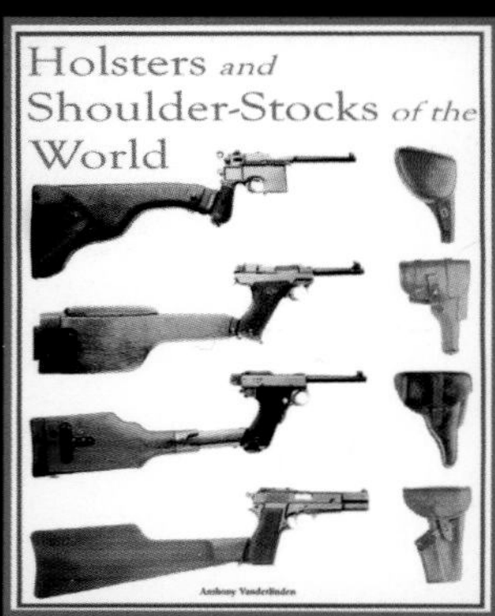

Holsters and Shoulder-Stocks of the World

Allied Rifle Contracts in America